# Learn about poetry online

Visit LITWEB at
http://www.wwnorton.com/introlit

LITWEB is an online companion to
*The Norton Introduction to Literature*
and
*The Norton Introduction to Poetry*

Edited by Ann Woodlief
Virginia Commonwealth University

**User ID: LITWEB**
**Password: WWNLIT7**

## Highlights

- **In-depth workshops on 10 poets and poems**, including biographies, annotated weblinks, and questions/topics for further exploration.
- **Hypertext glossary and "Writing about Literature" sections**, including a guide to MLA citation.
- **Forums and resource pages** for students and instructors.

## Featured Poems and Poets

W. H. Auden, "Musée des Beaux Arts" • William Blake, "London" • Anne Bradstreet, "To My Dear and Loving Husband" • Gwendolyn Brooks, "To the Diaspora" Dickinson, "[Because I could not stop for Death--] Donne, "A Valediction: Forbidding Mourning" • I Lee, "Persimmons" • Edna St. Vincent Millay, "[I, born a woman and distressed]" • Adrienne Rich, " into the Wreck" • Walt Whitman, "[I celebrate my sing myself]"

# The Norton Introduction to Poetry

SEVENTH EDITION

# The Norton Introduction to

# Poetry

SEVENTH EDITION

## J. Paul Hunter

W. W. NORTON & COMPANY

NEW YORK • LONDON

The text of this book is composed in Optima and Stone Serif, with the display set in Optima and Stone Serif. Composition by Binghamton Valley Composition. Manufacturing by R. R. Donnelley & Sons. Book design by Joan Greenfield.

Editor: Peter Simon
Developmental Editor: Carol Flechner
Associate Managing Editor: Marian Johnson
Project Editors: Kurt Wildermuth, Kate Lovelady
Production Manager: Diane O'Connor
Editorial Assistants: Kristin Sheerin, Michelle Lee, Elizabeth Suhay, Katharine Nicholson Ings
Text Design: Joan Greenfield
Cover Design: Debra Morton-Hoyt
Art Research: Neil Ryder Hoos

Library of Congress Cataloging-in-Publication Data

The Norton introducton to poetry / J. Paul Hunter. —7th ed
p.  cm.
Includes bibliographical references and indexes.

**ISBN 0-393-97357-3 (pbk.)**

1. Poetry—Collections.   I. Hunter, J. Paul, 1934–   .
PN6101.N6   1998
808.1—dc21                                      98-23108
                                                     CIP

W. W. Norton & Company, Inc.) 500 Fifth Avenue, New York, NY 10110
http://www.wwnorton.com
W. W. Norton & Company Ltd., 10 Coptic Street, London WC1A 1PU

1 2 3 4 5 6 7 8 9 0

# Contents

## Understanding the Text  33

## Exploring Contexts  316

## Evaluating Poetry  503

## Reading More Poetry  517

# *Appendices*

## Writing about Poetry  A3

## Glossary  A49

# Foreword to the Seventh Edition

Reading is action. Even though it is often done quietly and alone, reading is a profoundly social activity, and a vigorous and demanding one. There is nothing passive about reading; it requires attention, energy, an act of will. Texts have the potential for meaning, implication, response, and result; but the reader must activate them, give them life, and turn them from quiet print into a lively interplay of ideas and feelings. Reading makes things happen, usually in the mind and imagination, but sometimes in the larger world as well, for the process of reading involves not just the consciousness of the self but an awareness of the other—what is beyond the self. Reading doesn't just happen to you; you have to **do** it, and doing it involves decision, reaching out, discovery, awareness. Reading is an act of power, and learning how to get the most out of its possibilities can be an invigorating activity. For all its association with quietness, solitude, and the sedentary life, reading involves—at its deepest level—action and interaction.

Through seven editions, *The Norton Introduction to Poetry* has been committed to helping students learn to read and enjoy poetry. This edition, like those before it, offers many different ways of building and reinforcing the skills of reading; in addition to studying poetry in terms of its elements, this book emphasizes reading works in different contexts—authorial, historical, cultural and critical. I have strengthened the offering of texts in contextual groups in this edition with the addition of a new chapter entitled "Critical Contexts: A Casebook." This chapter includes a primary work, Sylvia Plath's "Daddy," and several critical responses to that poem. As in previous editions, I have provided many new selections.

The Seventh Edition, like its predecessors, offers in a single volume a complete course in reading and writing about poetry. It is both an anthology and a textbook—a teaching anthology—for the indispensable course in which college student and college teacher begin to read poetry, and to write about it, seriously together.

The works are arranged in order to introduce a reader to the study of poetry. *Poetry: Reading, Responding, Writing* treats the purpose and nature of poetry, the reading experience, and the first steps one takes to begin writing about poetry. This is followed by the seven-chapter section called *Understanding the Text,* in which poems are analyzed by questions of craft, the so-called elements of poetry; this section ends with a chapter entitled "The Whole Text," which makes use of all or most of the analytical aids offered in the previous chapters, putting them together to see the work as a whole. The third section, *Exploring Contexts,* suggests some ways of seeing a poem interacting with its temporal and cultural contexts and reaching out beyond the page.

The sections on reading, analyzing, and placing a poem in context are followed by guidance in taking that final and extremely difficult step—evaluation. *Evaluating Poetry* discusses how one would go about assessing the merits of two poems, not to offer definitive judgments, a litmus test, or even a checklist or formula, but to show how one goes about bringing to consciousness, defining, modifying, articulating, and negotiating one's judgments about a poem.

Finally, *Reading More Poetry* is a reservoir of additional examples, for independent study or a different approach. The book's arrangement seeks to facilitate the reader's movement from narrower to broader questions, mirroring the way people read—wanting to learn more as they experience more.

*The Norton Introduction to Poetry* offers a full section on *Writing about Poetry*. In it I deal both with the writing process as applied to literary works—choosing a topic, gathering evidence, developing an argument, and so forth—and with the varieties of a reader's written responses, from copying and paraphrasing to analysis and interpretation: it explores not merely the hows, but the whats and whys as well.

In this section I also offer a discussion of critical approaches, designed to provide the student with a basic overview of contemporary critical theory, as well as an introduction to its terminology.

New to the Seventh Edition is a section on using and citing secondary sources. This section provides a brief but useful first reference for writers of literary research papers.

The Seventh Edition includes 527 poems, 121 of which are new; it has been infused with selections familiar and fresh, with newly included works by Elizabeth Alexander, W.H. Auden, Jimmy Santiago Baca, Aphra Behn, Charles Berstein, Earle Birney, Elizabeth Bishop, Louise Bogan, Robert Browning, Karen Chase, Marilyn Chin, Amy Clampitt, John Clare, John Cleveland, Frances Cornford, Countee Cullen, Greg Delanty, Chitra Banerjee Divakaruni, Hilda Doolittle, Paul Lawrence Dunbar, T. S. Eliot, Martin Espada, Anne Finch, Robert Frost, Allen Ginsberg, Jorie Graham, Eamon Grennan, Marilyn Hacker, Gwen Harwood, Seamus Heaney, Anthony Hecht, Leigh Hunt, Donald Justice, Mary Karr, D.H. Lawrence, Emma Lazarus, Denise Levertov, Dorothy Livesay, Richard Lovelace, Amy Lowell, Andrew Marvell, Richard Michelson, James Masao Mitsui, Pat Mora, Edwin Morgan, Oswald Mbuyiseni Mtshali, Ogden Nash, Dwight Okita, Sharon Olds, Mary Oliver, Simon J. Ortiz, Wilfred Owen, Ezra Pound, Adrienne Rich, Alberto Alvaro Ríos, Theodore Roethke, Isaac Rosenberg, Liz Rosenberg, D.G. Rosetti, Yvonne Sapia, William Shakespeare, Alan Shapiro, Tom Sleigh, Mary Ellen Solt, Cathy Song, Elizabeth Spires, Wallace Stevens, Ruth Stone, Chidioch Tichbourne, Karen Volkman, Diane Wakoski, Alice Walker, Walt Whitman, Richard Wilbur, Miller Williams, and W. B. Yeats.

Certain editorial procedures that proved their usefulness in earlier editions have been retained. First of all, the works are annotated, as is customary in Norton anthologies; the notes are informational and not interpretative, for the aim is to help readers understand and appreciate the work, not to dictate a meaning or a response. In order to avoid giving the impression that all poetry was written at the same time, I have noted at the right margin after each selection the date of first book publication (or, when preceded by a *p*, first periodical publication or, when the date appears at the left margin, the year of composition).

One editorial feature has changed, however. The glossaries that used to appear at the end of each chapter have been replaced by a single, comprehensive glossary in the back of the book. This change was requested by most adopters of the Sixth Edition, and should prove more useful to students.

One exciting new feature of *The Norton Introduction to Poetry* isn't bound into the book itself. *The Norton Introduction to Literature Web Site,* prepared by Annette Woodlief of Virginia Commonwealth University, provides students and teachers with in-depth reading prompts and exercises designed to inspire creative reading and writing about literature, as well as links to useful literary resources. To view a demonstration of this unique ancillary, visit http://www.wwnorton.com/introlit.

In all my work on this edition I have been guided by teachers in other English departments and in my own, by students who wrote to me as the author of the textbook they were using, and by those who were able to approach me after class as their teacher: I hope that with such help I have been able to offer you a solid and stimulating introduction to the experience of poetry.

**Acknowledgments**    I would like to thank my teachers, for their example in the love of poetry and in the art of sharing that love; my students, for their patience as I am learning from them to be a better teacher of literature; my wife and children, for their understanding when the work of preparing this text made me seem less than a perfectly loving husband and father.

I would also like to thank my colleagues, many of whom have taught this book and evaluated my efforts, for their constant encouragement and enlightenment. Of my colleagues at the University of Chicago, I would like especially to thank Jonathan Martin, Robert von Hallberg, Michelle Hawley, Anne Elizabeth Murdy, Janel Mueller, Vicky Olwell, Richard Strier, and John Wright. For their help in selecting papers by student writers, I would like to thank Geneva Ballard, Theresa Budniakiewicz, Rebecca S. Ries, and Avantika Rohatgi, of Indiana University—Purdue University at Indianapolis, and Thomas Miller, Tilly Warnock, Lisa-Anne Culp, Loren Goodman, Brendan McBryde, and Ruthe Thompson, at the University of Arizona. Thanks also to the students whose papers I include: Meaghan E. Parker and Kimberly Smith. For their work on the *Instructor's Guide,* I thank Kelly Mays, New Mexico State University, Nancy Henry, SUNY Binghamton, and Gayla McGlamery and Bryan Crockett, Loyola College in Baltimore.

I would like to thank the many teachers whose comments on the Sixth Edition have helped me plan the Seventh: Professor Frank Acuna, Mt. San Antonio College; Professor Connie Adair, Marshalltown Community College; Professor Howard C. Adams, Frostburg State University; Professor Sandra Adickes, Winona State University; Professor Jan Agard, Muskegon Community College; Professor Alan Ainsworth, Houston Community College; Professor Ken Allen, Modesto Junior College; Professor Mary Ann Ardoline, Northhampton County Community College; Professor Valerie Arms, Drexel University; Professor Herman Asarnow, University of Portland; Professor Earl Bader, Villanova University; Professor Cindy Baer, San Jose State University; Professor Elizabeth Balfour-Boehm, Lakehead University; Professor Mary Baron, University of North Florida; Professor Joseph Bartolomeo, University of Massachusetts, Amherst; Professor John Batty-Sylvan, City College of San Francisco; Professor R. D. Becker, Standing Rock College; Professor Michael Beehler, Montana State University; Professor Franz Blatta, University of Nebraska; Professor John Boening, University of Toledo; Professor Elizabeth Bouchard, Wilbur Wright Junior College; Professor Bridget Boulton, Truckee Meadows Community College; Professor Debra Boyd, Winthrop University; Professor Lawrence Bright, Bakersfield College; Professor Ludiger Brinker, Macomb Community College; Professor Robert Brophy, California State University; Professor V. Brown, Laredo Community College; Professor Jeffrey Brunner, University of Minnesota; Professor David Burton, University of Tennessee–Memphis; Professor Pauline Buss, William Rainey Harper College; Professor Marilyn Button, Lincoln University; Professor Kathleen Carlson, Franklin College; Professor Marilyn A. Carlson, Augustana College; Professor Thomas Carper, University of Southern Maine; Professor Olivia Carr Edenfield, Georgia Southern University; Professor Basil Clark, Saginaw Valley State University; Professor

John Cleman, California State University at Los Angeles; Professor Evelyn Cobley, University of Victoria; Professor Thomas F. Connolly, Suffolk University; Professor C. Gordon Craig, University of Alberta; Professor Bryan Crockett, Loyola College; Professor Kathleen Cronin, Montana State University of Technology; Professor Toni Culjack, LaSalle University; Professor Jackie Cumby, Mercer University; Professor Elizabeth Curtin, Salisbury State University; Professor C. Custer, Plymouth State College; Professor Elizabeth Daeumer, Eastern Michigan University; Professor Frances Davidson, Mercer County College; Professor Frank Day, Clemson University; Professor Nancy Dayton, Taylor University; Professor Isabella Dibari, Diablo Valley College; Professor Wilfred O. Dietrich, Blinn College; Professor Sandy Dimon, Georgia College; Professor Raymond Dolle, Indiana State University; Professor Diana Doswell, Community College at Calvert; Professor Dixie Durham, Chapman University; Professor William Dynes, University of Indianapolis; Professor J. P. Earls, St. John's University; Professor Isaac Elimimian, California Polytechnic–San Luis Obispo; Professor Mary Etter, Davenport College; Dr. LaMona Evans, University of Central Oklahoma; Professor Don Fay, Kennesaw State College; Professor Chris Ferns, Mount Saint Vincent University; Professor James Fetler, Foothill College; Professor Bonnie Flaig, Kalamazoo Valley Community College; Professor Kate Flood, Onondaga Community College; Professor Douglas Fossek, Santa Barbara City College; Professor Craig Foster, Santa Rosa Junior College; Professor Michael Friedlander, Sacramento City College; Professor David Galef, University of Mississippi; Professor Marc Garcia, San Diego State University; Professor Jill Geare, Pasadena City College; Professor Marshall Bruce Gentry, University of Indianapolis; Professor Patricia Genz, Charles County Community College; Professor Jacqueline George, Erie Community College; Professor Karen Gleeman, Normandale Community College; Professor Brad Gooch, William Paterson College; Professor Marcia Goodman, Diablo Valley College; Professor Susan Grady, Greenville Technical College; Professor George L. Grant, San Jose State University; Professor Louis Greiff, Alfred University; Professor Joan Grumman, Santa Barbara City College; Professor Paul Guess, Diablo Valley College; Professor Ellen Haggar, The College of Charleston; Professor Robert Hagstrom, Jamestown Community College; Professor Joan Hall, University of Mississippi; Professor Edward Hancock, Truckee Meadows Community College; Professor F. J. Hartland, St. Francis College; Professor Peter Hawkes, East Stroudsburg University; Professor Margaret Hawks, Glendale College; Professor Tace Hedrick, Penn State at Harrisburg; Professor Lynne Hefferson, University of Vermont; Professor Donna Henrickson, Ball State University; Professor Anne Herzog, West Chester University; Professor Edwin Hetfield, Onondaga Community College; Professor John Hillman, Essex Community College; Professor Eric F. Hoem, Mt. Hood Community College; Professor Peter Hogue, California State University; Professor Elsie Holmes, Trinity Western University; Professor R. C. Hoover, Wenatchee Valley College; Professor Roger Horn, Charles County Community College; Professor Jean Horton, Concordia College; Professor Karen Houck, Bellevue Community College; Professor Douglas Howard, St. John Fisher College; Professor John Hussey, Fairmont State University; Professor Paula Huston, California Polytechnic, San Luis Obispo; Professor Nancy Hynes, College of St. Benedict; Professor Carol Jagielnak, University of Wisconsin, Parkside; Professor Mary Ann Janda, Utica College; Professor Dolores Johnson, Seattle University; Professor Ulrike Kalt, Odessa College; Professor Sukeshi Kamra, Okanagan University College; Dr. M. E. Karim, Rockford College; Professor John Kijinski, Idaho State University; Professor Thomas Kinsella, Richard Stockton College; Professor Lincoln Konkle, Trenton State College; Professor Philip Kowalski, North Shore Community College; Professor Carl Kremer, William Woods University; Professor Jayne Kribbs-Drake, Temple University; Professor Ellen Kruse, Diablo Valley

College; Professor Harold Kugelmass, Onondaga Community College; Professor Paul LaChanc, Frostburg State University; Professor Jane Lasky, Middlesex Community College; Professor David J. Leigh, SJ, Seattle University; Professor Daniel Lowe, Community College of Allegheny County; Professor Mary Anne Lutz, Frostburg State University; Professor Thomas Mack, University of South Carolina at Aiken; Professor Barbara McCarthy, Worcester Polytechnic Institute; Professor Barbara McClain, Contra Costa College; Professor Ken McKay, Brock University; Professor Therese Mackey, West Georgia College; Professor Thomas Madden, Eastern Oregon State College; Professor Rick Madigan, East Stroudsburg University; Professor Nancy Malone, Diablo Valley College; Professor Fort Manno, William Paterson College; Professor Aug Martinez, De Anza College; Professor Charlotte Martinez-Cappellini, Jamestown Community College; Professor J. M. Massi, Washington State University; Professor Tom Miller, University of Arizona; Professor Dorothy Minor, Tulsa Junior College; Professor Susan R. Mondschein, State University of New York at Buffalo; Professor Betty Montgomery, Ittawamba Community College; Professor Renate Muendel, West Chester University; Professor Roxanne Munch, Joliet Junior College; Professor Paul Munn, Saginaw Valley State University; Professor Anne Myles, Richard Stockton College; Professor Joseph Nassar, Rochester Institute of Technology; Professor James Nicosia, Montclair State University; Professor Ervin Nieves, Rutgers University at Newark; Professor Elizabeth Nollen, West Chester University; Professor James Nye, Southwestern Oklahoma State University; Professor Brennan O'Donnell, Loyola College; Professor Maureen O'Leary, Diablo Valley College; Professor Michael O'Neill, Oklahoma State University; Professor Glenn Omans, Temple University; Professor Kofi Owasu, Carleton College; Professor Len Palosaari, Augsberg College; Professor Sharon Papworth, Ricks College; Professor Barbara Patrick, Rowan College; Professor Barbara Pell, Trinity Western University; Professor John Pennington, St. Norbert College; Professor Katrina Perez, Santa Barbara City College; Professor Daniel Peterson, Southern University; Professor Donald Peterson, California State University; Professor Renee Pigeon, California State University, San Bernadino; Professor Gerald Pike, Santa Barbara City College; Professor Linda Plutynski, West Valley College–Saratoga; Professor Fran J. Polek, Gonzaga University; Professor Norman Prinsky, Augusta College; Professor Zelda Provenzano, University of Pennsylvania; Professor Renee Ramsey, Indiana State University; Professor Lyn P. Relph, California State University; Professor Paul Rice, Coastal Carolina University; Professor Michael Riherd, Pasadena City College; Professor Sharon Robinson, Russell Sage College; Professor Allen Rubin, Pace University; Professor John Rudin, Sacramento City College; Professor Helen Ruggieri, Jamestown Community College; Professor Don Russ, Kennesaw State College; Professor Anne Salvatore, Rider University; Professor Peggy Samuels, Drew University; Professor James Saunders, University of Toledo; Professor Nancy Shankle, Abilene Christian University; Professor Marilyn Shapiro, Lawrence Technological University; Professor Michael Sheldon, Indiana State University; Professor Leonard Slade, State University of New York at Albany; Professor Nelson Smith, University of Victoria; Professor Don Smith, Community College of Southern Nevada; Professor Guy Smith, Santa Barbara City College; Professor Betty Solomon, Diablo Valley College; Professor Randy Southard, Moraine Valley Community College; Professor Anne Spurlock, Mississippi State University; Professor Nadine St. Louis, University of Wisconsin–Eau Claire; Professor Rusty Standridge, Greenville Technical College; Professor Stan Stanko, Brescia College; Professor Emily Stauffer, Franklin College; Professor M. H. Strelow, Williamette University; Professor David Strong, Gonzaga University; Professor Jenny Sullivan, Northern Virginia Community College; Professor Phil Sullivan, University of Utah; Professor Timothy Thompson, Pacific University; Professor Dorothy Thompson, Winthrop University;

Professor Lee Tobin, Seton Hill College; Professor Michael Treschow, Okanagan University College; Professor Edna Troiano, Charles County Community College; Professor Jean Troy-Smith, State University of New York at Oswego; Professor John Vacca, University of Wisconsin–Platteville; Professor Kenneth Van Dorn, Lincoln University; Professor John Venne, Ball State University; Professor T. Mike Walker, Cabrillo College; Professor Donna Walsh, Memorial University of Newfoundland; Professor Mason Wang, Saginaw Valley State University; Professor Ruth Warkentin, California State University, Dominguez Hills; Professor Donald Watt, State University of New York, Geneseo; Professor Elizabeth Weber, University of Indianapolis; Professor David Weekes, Eastern Washington University; Professor William West, Onondaga Community College; Professor Terry Whalen, Saint Mary's University; Professor Martha Widmayer, Millersville University of Pennsylvania; Professor Catherine Wilcoxsen, Rowan College; Professor Dale M. Wilkie, University of Alberta; Professor Jack Williams, California State University; Professor Jack Wills, Fairmont State College; Professor Sarah Witte, Eastern Oregon State College; Professor Eric Wolfe, University of Mississippi; Professor Peter Wood, Trenton State College; Professor Regenia Woodberry, University of Central Oklahoma; Professor Kathleen Wright, Westmoreland County Community College; Professor William Yarrow, Joliet Junior College; and Professor Ursula Yates, West Chester University.

Finally, I would like to thank my friends at W. W. Norton & Company: Allen Clawson, Carol Flechner, Roberta Flechner, Lauren Graessle, Steve Hoge, Carol Hollar-Zwick, Neil Hoos, Katharine Nicholson Ings, Marian Johnson, Anna Karvellas, Michelle Lee, Kate Lovelady, Kirsten Miller, Debra Morton-Hoyt, Diane O'Connor, Kristin Sheerin, Peter Simon, and Kurt Wildermuth.

# The Norton Introduction to Poetry

SEVENTH EDITION

# Poetry: Reading, Responding, Writing

If you're already a reader of poetry, you know: poetry reading is not just an intellectual and bookish activity; it is about feeling. Reading poetry well means responding to it: if you respond on a feeling level, you are likely to read more accurately, with deeper understanding, and with greater pleasure. And, conversely, if you read poetry accurately, and with attention to detail, you will almost certainly respond—or learn how to respond—to it on an emotional level. Reading poetry involves conscious articulation through language, and reading and responding come to be, for experienced readers of poetry, very nearly one. But those who teach poetry—and there are a lot of us, almost all enthusiasts about both poetry as a subject and reading as a craft—have discovered something else: writing about poetry helps both the reading and the responding processes. Responding involves remembering and reflecting as well. As you recall your own past and make associations between things in the text and things you already know and feel, you will not only respond more fully to a particular poem, but improve your reading skills more generally. Your knowledge and life experience informs your reading of what is before you, and allows you to connect things within the text—events, images, words, sounds—so that meanings and feelings develop and accumulate. Prior learning creates expectations: of pattern, repetition, association, or causality. Reflecting on the text—and on expectations produced by themes and ideas in the text—re-creates old feelings but directs them in new, often unusual ways. Poems, even when they are about things we have no experience of, connect to things we do know and order our memories, thoughts, and feelings in new and newly challenging ways.

> *Poetry is a way of taking life by the throat.*
>
> —ROBERT FROST

A course in reading poetry can ultimately enrich your life by helping you become more articulate and more sensitive to both ideas and feelings: that's the larger goal. But the more immediate goal—and the route to the larger one—is to make you a better reader of texts and a more precise and careful writer yourself. Close attention to one text makes you appreciate, and understand, textuality and its possibilities more generally. Texts may be complex and even unstable in some ways; they do not affect all readers the same way, and they work through language that has its own volatilities and complexities. But paying attention to how you read—developing specific questions to ask and working on your reading skills systematically—can take a lot of the guesswork out of reading texts and give you a sense of greater satisfaction in your interpretations.

# READING

Poems, perhaps even more than other texts, can sharpen your reading skills because they tend to be so compact, so fully dependent on concise expressions of feeling. In poems, ideas and feelings are packed tightly into just a few lines. The experiences of life are very concentrated here, and meanings emerge quickly, word by word. Poems often show us the very process of putting feelings into a language that can be shared with others—to *say* feelings in a communicable way. Poetry can be intellectual too, explaining and exploring ideas, but its focus is more often on how people feel than how they think. Poems work out a shareable language for feeling, and one of poetry's most insistent virtues involves its attempt to express the inexpressible. How can anyone, for example, put into words what it means to be in love or how it feels to lose someone one cares about? Poetry tries, and it often captures a shade of emotion that feels just right to a reader. No single poem can be said to represent all the things that love or death feels like or means, but one of the joys of experiencing poetry occurs when we read a poem and want to say, "Yes, that is just what it is like; I know exactly what that line means but I've never been able to express it so well." Poetry can be the voice of our feelings even when our minds are speechless with grief or joy. Reading is no substitute for living, but it can make living more abundant and more available.

Here are two poems that talk about the sincerity and depth of love between two people. Each is written as if it were spoken by one person to his or her lover, and each is definite and powerful about the intensity and quality of love; but the poems work in quite different ways—the first one asserting the strength and depth of love, the second implying intense feeling by reminiscing about earlier events in the relationship between the two people.

ELIZABETH BARRETT BROWNING

## *How Do I Love Thee?*

How do I love thee? Let me count the ways.
I love thee to the depth and breadth and height
My soul can reach, when feeling out of sight
For the ends of Being and ideal Grace.
I love thee to the level of every day's     5
Most quiet need, by sun and candlelight.
I love thee freely, as men strive for Right;
I love thee purely, as they turn from Praise;
I love thee with the passion put to use
In my old griefs, and with my childhood's faith.     10
I love thee with a love I seemed to lose
With my lost saints—I love thee with the breath,
Smiles, tears of all my life!—and, if God choose,
I shall but love thee better after death.

                                                   1850

JAROLD RAMSEY

## The Tally Stick

Here from the start, from our first of days, look:
I have carved our lives in secret on this stick
of mountain mahogany the length of your arms
outstretched, the wood clear red, so hard and rare.
5   It is time to touch and handle what we know we share.

Near the butt, this intricate notch where the grains
converge and join: it is our wedding.
I can read it through with a thumb and tell you now
who danced, who made up the songs, who meant us joy.
10   These little arrowheads along the grain,
they are the births of our children. See,
they make a kind of design with these heavy crosses,
the deaths of our parents, the loss of friends.

Over it all as it goes, of course, I
15   have chiseled Events, History—random
hashmarks cut against the swirling grain.
See, here is the Year the World Went Wrong,
we thought, and here the days the Great Men fell.
The lengthening runes of our lives run through it all.

20   See, our tally stick is whittled nearly end to end;
delicate as scrimshaw, it would not bear you up.
egrets have polished it, hand over hand.
Yet let us take it up, and as our fingers
like children leading on a trail cry back
25   our unforgotten wonders, sign after sign,
we will talk softly as of ordinary matters,
and in one another's blameless eyes go blind.

p. 1977

The first poem is direct, but fairly abstract. It lists several ways in which the poet feels love and connects them to some noble ideas of higher obligations—to justice (line 7), for example, and to spiritual aspiration (lines 2–4). It suggests a wide range of things that love can mean and notices a variety of emotions. It is an ardent statement of feeling and asserts a permanence that will extend even beyond death. It contains admirable thoughts and memorable phrases that many lovers would like to hear said to themselves. What it does not do is say very much about what the relationship between the two lovers is like on an everyday basis, what experiences they have had together, what distinguishes their relationship from that of other devoted or ideal lovers. Its appeal is to our general sense of what love is like and how intense feelings can be; it does not offer everyday details. Love may differ from person to person and even from moment to moment, and so can poems about love.

"The Tally Stick" is much more concrete. The whole poem concentrates on a single object that, like "How Do I Love Thee?," "counts" or "tallies" the ways in which this couple love one another. This stick stands for their love and becomes a kind of physical reminder of it: its natural features—the notches and arrowheads and cross marks (lines 6, 10, and 12) along with the marks carved on it (lines 15–16, 20–21)—indicate events in the story of the relationship. (We could say that the stick *symbolizes* their love; later on, we will look at a number of terms like this that can be used to make it easier to talk about some aspects of poems, but for now it is enough to notice that the stick serves the lovers as a reminder and a marker of some specific details of their love.) It is a special kind of reminder to them because its language is "secret" (line 2), something they can share privately (except that we as readers of the poem are sort of looking over their shoulders, not intruding but sharing their secret). The poet interprets the particular features of the stick as standing for particular events—their wedding and the births of their children, for example—and carves marks into it as reminders of other events (lines 15 ff.). The stick itself becomes a very personal object, and in the last stanza of the poem it is as if we watch the lovers touching the stick together and reminiscing over it, gradually dissolving into their emotions and each other as they recall the "unforgotten wonders" (line 25) of their lives together.

Both poems are powerful statements of feelings, each in its own way. Various readers will respond differently to each poem; the effect these poems have on their readers will lead some to prefer one and some the other. Personal preference does not mean that objective standards for poetry cannot be found (some poems are better than others, and later we will look in detail at features that help us to evaluate poems), but we need have no preconceived standard that all poetry must be one thing or another or work in one particular way. Some good poems are quite abstract, others quite specific. Any poem that helps us to articulate and clarify human feelings and ideas has a legitimate claim on us as readers.

Both "How Do I Love Thee?" and "The Tally Stick" are written as if they were addressed to the partner in the love relationship, and both talk directly about the intensity of the love. The poem below talks only indirectly about the quality and intensity of love. It is written as if it were a letter from a woman to her husband who has gone on a long journey on business. It directly expresses how much she misses him and indirectly suggests how much she cares about him.

EZRA POUND

## The River-Merchant's Wife: A Letter

*(after Rihaku[1])*

While my hair was still cut straight across my forehead
I played about the front gate, pulling flowers.
You came by on bamboo stilts, playing horse,
You walked about my seat, playing with blue plums.

---

1. The Japanese name for Li Po, an eighth-century Chinese poet. Pound's poem is a loose paraphrase of Li Po's.

5    And we went on living in the village of Chokan:
     Two small people, without dislike or suspicion.

     At fourteen I married My Lord you.
     I never laughed, being bashful.
     Lowering my head, I looked at the wall.
10   Called to, a thousand times, I never looked back.

     At fifteen I stopped scowling,
     I desired my dust to be mingled with yours
     For ever and for ever and for ever.
     Why should I climb the look out?

15   At sixteen you departed,
     You went into far Ku-to-yen, by the river of swirling eddies,
     And you have been gone five months.
     The monkeys make sorrowful noise overhead.

     You dragged your feet when you went out.
20   By the gate now, the moss is grown, the different mosses,
     Too deep to clear them away!

     The leaves fall early this autumn, in wind.
     The paired butterflies are already yellow with August
     Over the grass in the West garden;
25   They hurt me. I grow older.
     If you are coming down through the narrows of the river Kiang,
     Please let me know beforehand,
     And I will come out to meet you
          As far as Cho-fu-Sa.                                    1915

The "letter" tells us only a few facts about the nameless merchant's wife: that she is about sixteen and a half years old, that she married at fourteen and fell in love with her husband a year later, that she is now very lonely. About their relationship we know only that they were childhood playmates in a small Chinese village, that their marriage originally was not a matter of personal choice, and that the husband unwillingly went away on a long journey five months ago. But the words tell us a great deal about how the young wife feels, and the simplicity of her language suggests her sincere and deep longing. The daily noises she hears seem "sorrowful" (line 18), and she worries about the dangers of the far-away place where her husband is, thinking of it in terms of its perilous "river of swirling eddies" (line 16). She thinks of how moss has grown up over the unused gate, and more time seems to her to have passed than actually has (lines 22–25). Nostalgically she remembers their innocent childhood, when they played together without deeper love or commitment (lines 1–6), and contrasts that with her later satisfaction in their love (lines 11–14) and with her present anxiety, loneliness, and desire. We do not need to know the details of the geography of the river Kiang or how far Cho-fu-Sa is to sense that her wish to see him is very strong, that her desire is powerful enough to make her venture beyond the ordinary geographical bounds of her existence so that their reunion will come sooner. The closest she comes to a direct statement about her love is her statement that she desired that her dust be mingled with his "For ever and for ever and for ever" (lines 12–13). But her single-minded vision of the world, her perception of even the beauty of nature as only a record of her husband's absence and the passage of time, and her plain, apparently uncalculated language about her rejection of other suitors and her shutting out of the rest of the world all show her to be committed, desirous, nearly desperate for his presence. In a different sense, she has also counted the ways that she loves her man.

Here is another poem about marriage that expresses a very different set of attitudes and feelings.

DENISE LEVERTOV

## Wedding-Ring

My wedding-ring lies in a basket
as if at the bottom of a well.
Nothing will come to fish it back up
and onto my finger again.
It lies                               5
among keys to abandoned houses,
nails waiting to be needed and hammered
into some wall,
telephone numbers with no names attached,
idle paperclips.                               10
           It can't be given away
for fear of bringing ill-luck.
           It can't be sold
for the marriage was good in its own
time, though that time is gone.           15
           Could some artificer
beat into it bright stones, transform it
into a dazzling circlet no one could take
for solemn betrothal or to make promises
living will not let them keep? Change it     20
into a simple gift I could give in friendship?          1978

The artifact—the ring—at the center of this poem is out-of-date and abandoned, standing for a worn-out and terminated marriage. Unlike the eager and committed voice in the previous poem, the voice here is tired, resigned, sad; the poem's speaker seems willing to try for a new and better relationship but is also hesitant, cautious, and perhaps somewhat disillusioned by previous experience. This, too, is a poem about love, but the moment of love has long since passed, and the poem focuses on the feelings of aftermath.

Poems can be about the meaning of a relationship or about disappointment just as easily as about emotional fulfillment, and poets are often very good at suggesting the contradictions and uncertainties in relationships. Like other people, poets often find love quaint or downright funny, too, mainly because it involves human beings who, however serious their intentions and concerns, are often inept, uncertain, and self-contradictory—in short, human. Showing us ourselves as others see us is one of the more useful tasks that poems perform, but the poems that result can be just as entertaining and pleasurable as they are educational. Here is a poem that imagines a very strange scene, a kind of fantasy of what happens when we *think* too much about sex or love, and it is likely to leave us laughing, whether or not we take it seriously as a statement of human anxiety and of the tendency to intellectualize too much.

TOM WAYMAN

## Wayman in Love

At last Wayman gets the girl into bed.
He is locked in one of those embraces
so passionate his left arm is asleep
when suddenly he is bumped in the back.
"Excuse me," a voice mutters, thick with German.
Wayman and the girl sit up astounded
as a furry gentleman in boots and a frock coat
climbs in under the covers.

"My name is Doktor Marx," the intruder announces
settling his neck comfortably on the pillow.
"I'm here to consider for you the cost of a kiss."
He pulls out a notepad. "Let's see now,
we have the price of the mattress, this room must be rented,
your time off work, groceries for two,
medical fees in case of accidents . . . "

"Look," Wayman says,
"couldn't we do this later?"
The philosopher sighs, and continues: "You are affected too, Miss.
If you are not working, you are going to resent
your dependent position. This will influence
I assure you, your most intimate moments . . . "

"Doctor, please," Wayman says. "All we want
is to be left alone."
But another beard, more nattily dressed,
is also getting into the bed.
There is a shifting and heaving of bodies
as everyone wriggles out room for themselves.
"I want you to meet a friend from Vienna,"
Marx says. "This is Doktor Freud."

The newcomer straightens his glasses,
peers at Wayman and the girl.
"I can see," he begins,
"that you two have problems . . . "

1973

# RESPONDING

The poems we have looked at so far all describe, though in quite different ways, feelings associated with loving or being attached to someone and the expression—either physical or verbal—of those feelings. Watching how poems work out a language for feeling can help us to work out a language for our own feelings, but the process is also reciprocal: being conscious of feelings we already have can lead us into poems more surely and with more satisfaction. Readers with a strong romantic bent—and with strong yearnings or positive memories of desire—will be likely to find "The Tally Stick" and "The River-Merchant's Wife: A Letter" easy to respond to and like, while those more skeptical of human institutions and male habits may find the disillusionment and resignation of "Wedding-Ring" to be more satisfying.

> *If I feel physically as if the top of my head were taken off, I know that is poetry.*
>
> —EMILY DICKINSON

Poems can be about all kinds of experiences, and not all the things we find in them will replicate (or even relate to) experiences we may have individually had. But sharing through language will often enable us to get in touch with feelings—of love or anger, fear or confidence—we did not know we had. The next few poems involve another, far less pleasant set of feelings than those usually generated by love, but even here, where our experience may be limited, we are able to respond, to feel the tug of emotions within us that we may not be fully aware of. In the following poem, a father struggles to understand and control his grief over the death of a seven-year-old son. We don't have to be a father or to have lost a loved one to be aware of—and even share—the speaker's pain because our own experiences will have given us some idea of what such a loss would feel like. And the words and strategies of the poem may activate expectations created by our previous experiences.

BEN JONSON

## On My First Son

Farewell, thou child of my right hand,[2] and joy;
My sin was too much hope of thee, loved boy:
Seven years thou wert lent to me, and I thee pay,
Exacted by thy fate, on the just[3] day.
O could I lose all father now! for why                                    5
Will man lament the state he should envý,
To have so soon 'scaped world's and flesh's rage,
And, if no other misery, yet age?
Rest in soft peace, and asked, say, "Here doth lie
Ben Jonson his[4] best piece of poetry."                                10

2. A literal translation of the son's name, Benjamin.    3. Exact; the son died on his seventh birthday, in 1603.    4. Ben Jonson's (a common Renaissance form of the possessive).

For whose sake henceforth all his vows be such
As what he loves may never like too much.                    1616


This poem's attempts to rationalize the boy's death are quite conventional. Although the father tries to be comforted by pious thoughts, his feelings keep showing through. The poem's beginning—with its formal "farewell" and the rather distant-sounding address to the dead boy ("child of my right hand")—cannot be sustained for long: both of the first two lines end with bursts of emotion. It is as if the father is trying to explain the death to himself and to keep his emotions under control, but cannot quite manage it. Even the punctuation suggests the way his feelings compete with conventional attempts to put the death into some sort of perspective that will soften the grief, and the comma near the end of each of the first two lines marks a pause that cannot quite hold back the overflowing emotion. But finally the only "idea" that the poem supports is that the father wishes he did not feel so intensely; in the fifth line he fairly blurts that he wishes he could lose his fatherly emotions, and in the final lines he resolves never again to "like" so much that he can be this deeply hurt. Philosophy and religion offer their useful counsels in this poem, but they prove far less powerful than feeling. Rather than drawing some kind of moral about what death means, the poem presents the actuality of feeling as inevitable and nearly all-consuming.

The poem that follows similarly tries to suppress the rawness of feelings about the death of a loved one, but here the survivor is haunted by memories of his wife when he sees a physical object—a vacuum cleaner—that he associates with her.


HOWARD NEMEROV

## The Vacuum

The house is so quiet now
The vacuum cleaner sulks in the corner closet,
Its bag limp as a stopped lung, its mouth
Grinning into the floor, maybe at my
Slovenly life, my dog-dead youth.

I've lived this way long enough,
But when my old woman died her soul
Went into that vacuum cleaner, and I can't bear
To see the bag swell like a belly, eating the dust
And the woolen mice, and begin to howl

Because there is old filth everywhere
She used to crawl, in the corner and under the stair.
I know now how life is cheap as dirt,
And still the hungry, angry heart
Hangs on and howls, biting at air.                    1955

The poem is about a vacuum in the husband's life, but the title refers most obviously to the vacuum cleaner that, like the tally stick we looked at earlier, seems to stand for many of the things that were once important in the life he had together with his wife. The cleaner is a reminder of the dead wife ("my old woman," line 7) because of her devotion to cleanliness. But to the surviving husband buried in the filth of his life it seems as if the machine has become almost human, a kind of ghost of her: it "sulks" (line 2), it has lungs and a mouth (line 3), and it seems to grin, making fun of what has become of him. He "can't bear" (line 8) to see it in action because it then seems too much alive, too much a reminder of her life. The poem records his paralysis, his inability to do more than discover that life is "cheap as dirt" without her ordering and cleansing presence for him. At the end it is *his* angry heart that acts like the haunting machine, howling and biting at air as if he has merged with her spirit and the physical object that memorializes her. This poem puts a strong emphasis on the stillness of death and the way it makes things seem to stop; it captures in words the hurt, the anger, the inability to understand, the vacuum that remains when a loved one dies and leaves a vacant space. But here we do not see the body or hear a direct good-bye to the dead person; rather we encounter the feeling that lingers and won't go away, recalled through memory by an especially significant object, a mere thing but one that has been personalized to the point of becoming nearly human in itself. (The event described here is, by the way, fictional; the poet's wife did not in fact die. Like a dramatist or writer of fiction, the poet may simply *imagine* an event in order to analyze and articulate how such an event might feel in certain circumstances.)

Here is another poem about the death of a loved one:

SHARON OLDS

## The Glass

I think of it with wonder now,
the glass of mucus that stood on the table
next to my father all weekend. The cancer
is growing fast in his throat now,
and as it grows it sends out pus like the                    5
sun sending out flares, those pouring
tongues. So my father has to gargle, hack,
spit a mouth full of thick stuff
into the glass every ten minutes or so,
scraping the rim up his lower lip to                         10
get the last bit off his skin, then he
sets the glass down on the table and it
sits there, like a glass of beer foam,
shiny and faintly golden, he gurgles and
coughs and reaches for it again and                         15
gets the heavy sputum out,
full of bubbles and moving around like yeast—
he is like some god producing food from his own mouth.

He himself can eat nothing anymore,
20    just a swallow of milk sometimes,
cut with water, and even then it
can't always get past the tumor,
and the next time the saliva comes up it's
chalkish and ropey, he has to roll it in his
25    throat to form it and get it up and dis-
gorge the elliptical globule into the cup—
and the wonder to me is that it did not disgust me,
that glass of phlegm that stood there all day and
filled slowly with compound globes and I'd
30    empty it and it would fill again and
shimmer there on the table until the
room seemed to turn around it
in an orderly way, a model of the solar system
turning around the gold sun,
35    my father the dark earth that used to
lie at the center of the universe
now turning with the rest of us
around the bright glass of spit
on the table, these last mouthfuls.                    1990

Like "The Vacuum," "The Glass" reflects on a loved one through unconventional images, material objects that suggest pain and unpleasantness rather than joy and love. The "glass" of the title is not a mirror that reflects a beautiful face, not a crafted objet d'art, but rather a simple tumbler, and it is full of mucus—not a very appealing object. The loved one, the father of the person who is speaking the poem, is dying of cancer, and the indicators of his condition are painfully detailed. The sights and sounds are disgusting rather than pleasant; the body fluids are pus and spit, and the human sounds are gargling, gurgling, and hacking. It is almost as if the poem tries to create a picture as ugly as possible, for the father's physical struggle just to swallow and spit is chronicled moment by painful moment. "[T]he wonder to me," says the daughter who views the daily struggle and records it for us in the poem, "is that it did not disgust me" (line 27), and the poem transforms the central object of disgust ("that glass of phlegm," line 28) into something that stands for the daughter's love and the father's ability to accept it even in his deteriorating condition. The daughter's act of staying and emptying the glass represents not only fortitude and loyalty but the steadying influence of stability and predictability. She begins to see the glass itself—its regular filling and emptying of life and coming death—as a kind of center around which human activity revolves "in an orderly way" (line 33). The father, once the center of the family's universe, now seems to move with the others "around" (line 38) the fact of death as represented by the glass. It is an awful picture—awful in its details, awful in its implications of loss—but it is also beautiful in its own way. The poem shows that life and love can be portrayed, explained, and imprinted on our memories by even the most unattractive events, objects, and words.

Sometimes poems are a way of confronting feelings. Sometimes they explore feelings in detail and try to intellectualize or rationalize them. At other times, poems generate responses by recalling an experience many years in the past. In the following two poems, for example, memories of childhood provide perspective on two very different kinds of events. In the first, written as if the person speaking the poem were in the fifth grade, a child's sense of death is portrayed through her exploration of a photograph that makes her grandfather's earlier presence vivid to her memory—a memory that lingers primarily through smell and touch. In the second poem, another childhood memory—this time of overshoes—takes an adult almost physically back into childhood. As you read the two poems, keep track of (or perhaps even jot down) your responses. How much of your feeling is due to your own past experiences? In which specific places? What family photographs do you remember most vividly? What feelings did they invoke that make them so memorable? How are your memories different from those expressed in "Fifth Grade Autobiography"? in "The Fury of Overshoes"? Which feelings expressed in each poem are similar to your own? Where do your feelings differ most strongly? How would you articulate your responses to memories differently? In what ways does an awareness of your similar—and different—experiences and feelings make you a better reader of the poem?

RITA DOVE

## *Fifth Grade Autobiography*

I was four in this photograph fishing
with my grandparents at a lake in Michigan.
My brother squats in poison ivy.
His Davy Crockett cap
sits squared on his head so the raccoon tail                     5
flounces down the back of his sailor suit.

My grandfather sits to the far right
in a folding chair,
and I know his left hand is on
the tobacco in his pants pocket                                  10
because I used to wrap it for him
every Christmas. Grandmother's hips
bulge from the brush, she's leaning
into the ice chest, sun through the trees
printing her dress with soft                                     15
luminous paws.

I am staring jealously at my brother;
the day before he rode his first horse, alone.
I was strapped in a basket
behind my grandfather.                                           20
He smelled of lemons. He's died—

but I remember his hands.                                  1989

ANNE SEXTON

## *The Fury of Overshoes*

They sit in a row
outside the kindergarten,
black, red, brown, all
with those brass buckles.
Remember when you couldn't
buckle your own
overshoe
or tie your own
shoe
or cut your own meat
and the tears
running down like mud
because you fell off your
tricycle?
Remember, big fish,
when you couldn't swim
and simply slipped under
like a stone frog?
The world wasn't
yours.
It belonged to
the big people.
Under your bed
sat the wolf
and he made a shadow
when cars passed by
at night.
They made you give up
your nightlight
and your teddy
and your thumb.
Oh overshoes,
don't you
remember me,
pushing you up and down
in the winter snow?
Oh thumb,
I want a drink,
it is dark,
where are the big people,
when will I get there,
taking giant steps
all day,
each day

and thinking                                                                45
nothing of it?                                                            1974

There is much more going on in the poems that we have glanced at than we have taken time to consider, but even the quickest look at these poems suggests something of the range of feelings that poems can offer—the depth of feeling, the clarity, the experience that may be articulately and precisely shared. Not all poems are as accessible as those we've looked at so far, and even the ones that are accessible usually yield themselves to us more readily and more fully if we approach them systematically by developing specific reading habits and skills—just as someone learning to play tennis systematically learns the rules, the techniques, the things to watch out for that are distinctive to the pleasures and hazards of that skill or craft. It helps if you develop a sense of what to expect, and the chapters that follow will help you to an understanding of the things that poets can do—and thus of what poems can do for you.

But knowing what to expect isn't everything. As a prospective reader of poetry, you should always be open—to new experiences, new feelings, new ideas. Every poem in the world is a potential new experience, and no matter how sophisticated you become, you can still be surprised (and delighted) by new poems—and by rereading old ones. Good poems bear many, many rereadings, and often one discovers something new with every new reading: there is no such thing as "mastering" a poem, and good poems are not exhausted by repeated readings. Be willing to let poems surprise you when you come to them; let them come on their own terms, let them be themselves. If you are open to poetry, you are also open to much more that the world can offer you.

No one can give you a method that will offer you total experience of all poems. But because many characteristics of an individual poem are characteristics that one poem shares with other poems, there are guidelines that can prompt you to ask the right questions. The chapters that follow will help you in detail with a variety of problems, but meanwhile here is a checklist of some things to remember:

1. *Read the syntax literally.* What the words say literally in normal sentences is only a starting point, but it is the place to start. Not all poems use normal prose syntax, but most of them do, and you can save yourself embarrassment by paraphrasing accurately (that is, rephrasing what the poem literally says, in plain prose) and not simply free-associating from an isolated word or phrase.
2. *Articulate for yourself what the title, subject, and situation make you expect.* Poets often use false leads and try to surprise you by doing shocking things, but defining expectation lets you be conscious of where you are when you begin.
3. *Identify the poem's situation.* What is said is often conditioned by where it is said and by whom. Identifying the speaker and his or her place in the situation puts what he or she says in perspective.
4. *Find out what is implied by the traditions behind the poem.* Verse forms, poetic kinds, and metrical patterns all have a frame of reference, traditions of the way they are usually used and for what. For example, the anapest (two unstressed syllables followed by a stressed one, as in the word *Tennessee*) is usually used for comic poems, and when poets use it "straight" they are aware of their "departure" and are probably making a point by doing it.
5. *Bother the reference librarian.* Look up anything you don't understand: an unfamiliar word (or an ordinary word used in an unfamiliar way), a place, a person, a myth,

an idea—anything the poem uses. When you can't find what you need or don't know where to look, ask for help.

6. *Remember that poems exist in time, and times change.* Not only the meanings of words, but whole ways of looking at the universe vary in different ages. Consciousness of time works two ways: your knowledge of history provides a context for reading the poem, and the poem's use of a word or idea may modify your notion of a particular age.

7. *Take a poem on its own terms.* Adjust to the poem; don't make the poem adjust to you. Be prepared to hear things you do not want to hear. Not all poems are about your ideas, nor will they always present emotions you want to feel. But be tolerant and listen to the poem's ideas, not only to your desire to revise them for yourself.

8. *Be willing to be surprised.* Things often happen in poems that turn them around. A poem may seem to suggest one thing at first, then persuade you of its opposite, or at least of a significant qualification or variation.

9. *Assume there is a reason for everything.* Poets do make mistakes, but in poems that show some degree of verbal control it is usually safest to assume that the poet chose each word carefully; if the choice seems peculiar to us, it is often *we* who are missing something. Try to account for everything in a poem and see what kind of sense you can make of it. Poets make choices; try to figure out a coherent pattern that explains the text as it stands.

10. *Argue.* Discussion usually results in clarification and keeps you from being too dependent on personal biases and preoccupations that sometimes mislead even the best readers. Talking a poem over with someone else (especially someone very different) can expand your perspective.

# WRITING ABOUT POEMS

If you have been keeping notes on your personal responses to the poems you've read, you have already taken an important step toward writing about them. There are many different ways to write about poems, just as there are many different things to say. (The chapter in the back of the book on "Writing about Literature" suggests many different kinds of topics.) But all writing begins from a clear sense of the poem itself and your responses to it, so the first steps (long before formally sitting down to write) are to read the poem over several times and keep notes on the things that strike you and the questions that remain.

Formulating a clear series of questions will usually help lead you to an appropriate approach to the poem and to a good topic. Learning to ask the right questions can save you a lot of time. Some questions—the kinds of questions implied in the ten guidelines for reading listed above—are basic and more or less apply to all poems. But each poem makes demands of its own, too, because of its distinctive way of going about its business, so you will usually want to make a list of what seem to you the crucial questions for that poem. Here are—just to give you an example—some questions that could be useful in leading you to a paper topic on the first of the poems printed at the end of this chapter.

1. How does the title affect your reading of and response to the poem?
2. What is the poem about?
3. What makes the poem interesting to read?
4. Who is the speaker? What role does the speaker have in the poem?
5. What effect does the poem have on you as a reader? Do you think the poet intended to have such an effect?
6. What is distinctive about the poet's use of language? Which words especially contribute to the poem's effect?

What *is* poetry? Let your definition be cumulative as you read more and more poems. No dictionary definition will cover all that you find, and it is better to discover for yourself poetry's many ingredients, its many effects, its many ways of acting. What can it do for you? Wait and see. Begin to add up its effects after you have read carefully— after you have studied and reread—a hundred or so poems; that will be a beginning, and you will be able to add to that total as long as you continue to read new poems or reread old ones.

## PRACTICING READING: SOME POEMS ON LOVE

ANNE BRADSTREET

## *To My Dear and Loving Husband*

If ever two were one, then surely we.
If ever man were loved by wife, then thee;
If ever wife was happy in a man,
Compare with me ye women if you can.
5  I prize thy love more than whole mines of gold,
Or all the riches that the East doth hold.
My love is such that rivers cannot quench,
Nor aught but love from thee give recompense.
Thy love is such I can no way repay;
10  The heavens reward thee manifold, I pray.
Then while we live, in love let's so persever,
That when we live no more we may live ever.                    1678

WILLIAM SHAKESPEARE

## *[Shall I compare thee to a summer's day?]*

Shall I compare thee to a summer's day?
Thou art more lovely and more temperate.
Rough winds do shake the darling buds of May,
And summer's lease hath all too short a date.
5  Sometime too hot the eye of heaven shines,
And often is his gold complexion dimmed;
And every fair from fair sometime declines,
By chance or nature's changing course untrimmed.
But thy eternal summer shall not fade,
10  Nor lose possession of that fair thou ow'st,
Nor shall Death brag thou wand'rest in his shade,
When in eternal lines to time thou grow'st.
    So long as men can breathe or eyes can see,
    So long lives this,[5] and this gives life to thee.              1609

5. This poem.

## LEIGH HUNT

## *Rondeau*

Jenny kissed me when we met,
   Jumping from the chair she sat in;
Time, you thief, who love to get
   Sweets into your list, put that in:
Say I'm weary, say I'm sad,               5
   Say that health and wealth have missed me,
Say I'm growing old, but add,
   Jenny kissed me.              p. 1838

## DENISE LEVERTOV

## *Love Poem*

*'We are good for each other.'*
              —X

What you give me is

the extraordinary sun
splashing its light
              into astonished trees.

A branch               5
of berries, swaying

under the feet of a bird.

I know
other joys—they taste
bitter, distilled as they are          10
from roots, yet I thirst for them.

But you—
you give me

the flash of golden daylight
in the body's              15
midnight,
warmth of the fall noonday
between the sheets in the dark.      1978

W. H. AUDEN

# [*Stop all the clocks, cut off the telephone*]

Stop all the clocks, cut off the telephone,
Prevent the dog from barking with a juicy bone,
Silence the pianos and with muffled drum
Bring out the coffin, let the mourners come.

Let aeroplanes circle moaning overhead
Scribbling on the sky the message He Is Dead,
Put crêpe bows round the white necks of the public doves,
Let the traffic policemen wear black cotton gloves.

He was my North, my South, my East and West,
My working week and my Sunday rest,
My noon, my midnight, my talk, my song;
I thought that love would last for ever: I was wrong.

The stars are not wanted now: put out every one;
Pack up the moon and dismantle the sun;
Pour away the ocean and sweep up the wood;
For nothing now can ever come to any good.

ca. 1936

CAROL JANE BANGS

# *Touching Each Other's Surfaces*

Skin meeting skin, we want to think
we know each other scientifically;
we want to believe
it is objective knowledge
gives this conviction of intimacy,
makes us say it feels so right.
That mole below your shoulder blade,
the soft hair over my thighs—
we examine our bodies with the precision
known only to lovers or surgeons,
all those whose profession is explication,
who have to believe their own words.
And yet, having memorized each turning,
each place where bone strains or bends,
each hollow, each hair, each failure of form,
we still encounter that stubborn wall,

that barrier which hides an infinite vastness
the most sincere gesture can't find.

Nor does emotion take us further
than the shared heat of bodies                                    20
aware of themselves,
the flattery of multiple desires.
We rest in each other's arms unexplained
by these currents of feeling rushing past
like ripples over a pool of water                                 25
whose substance never changes,
reflecting each wave, each ribboned crossing,
without being really moved.
We search each other's eyes so long
beyond our own reflections,                                       30
finding only the black centers,
the immeasurable interior we'll
never reach with candle,
never plumb with love.
Perhaps it is just this ignorance,                                35
this absence of certainty, lack of clear view,
more than anything, brings us together,
draws us into and through each other
to the unknown inside us all,
that gray space from which                                        40
what we know of ourselves
emerges briefly, casts a transient
shadow across the earth
and learns to believe in itself just enough
to believe in some one else.                                      45

                                                    1983


AUDRE LORDE

## *Recreation*

Coming together
it is easier to work
after our bodies
meet
paper and pen                                                      5
neither care nor profit
whether we write or not
but as your body moves
under my hands
charged and waiting                                               10

we cut the leash
you create me against your thighs
hilly with images
moving through our word countries
15    my body
writes into your flesh
the poem
you make of me

Touching you I catch midnight
20    as moon fires set in my throat
I love you flesh into blossom
I made you
and take you made
into me.

1978


MARGE PIERCY

## To Have without Holding

Learning to love differently is hard,
love with the hands wide open, love
with the doors banging on their hinges,
the cupboard unlocked, the wind
5    roaring and whimpering in the rooms
rustling the sheets and snapping the blinds
that thwack like rubber bands
in an open palm.

It hurts to love wide open
10    stretching the muscles that feel
as if they are made of wet plaster,
then of blunt knives, then
of sharp knives.

It hurts to thwart the reflexes
15    of grab, of clutch; to love and let
go again and again. It pesters to remember
the lover who is not in the bed,
to hold back what is owed to the work
that gutters like a candle in a cave
20    without air, to love consciously,
conscientiously, concretely, constructively.

I can't do it, you say it's killing
me, but you thrive, you glow
on the street like a neon raspberry,
25    You float and sail, a helium balloon

bright bachelor's button blue and bobbing
on the cold and hot winds of our breath,
as we make and unmake in passionate
diastole and systole the rhythm
of our unbound bonding, to have                                          30
and not to hold, to love
with minimized malice, hunger
and anger moment by moment balanced.                                    1980


ELIZABETH BISHOP

## *Casabianca*[6]

Love's the boy stood on the burning deck
trying to recite "The boy stood on
the burning deck." Love's the son
   stood stammering elocution
    while the poor ship in flames went down.                5

Love's the obstinate boy, the ship,
even the swimming sailors, who
would like a schoolroom platform, too,
   or an excuse to stay
    on deck. And love's the burning boy.                 10

            1946


LIZ ROSENBERG

## *Married Love*

The trees are uncurling their first
green messages: Spring, and some man
lets his arm brush my arm in a darkened
theatre. Faint-headed, I fight the throb.
Later I dream                                                           5
the gas attendant puts a cool hand
on my breast, asking a question.

---

6. The name of a young boy who remained (during the "Battle of the Nile") at his post on a burning ship because, he believed, his father (an admiral) had not released him from duty. He was celebrated in a popular poem by Felicia Dorothea Hemans (1793–1835) that began "The boy stood on the burning deck" (line 2).

Slowly I rise through the surface of the dream,
brushing his hand and my own heat away.

10 Young, I burned to marry. Married,
the smolder goes on underground,
clutching at weeds, writhing everywhere.
I'm trying to talk to a friend on burning
issues, flaming from the feet up,
15 drinking in his breath, touching his wrist.
I want to grab the pretty woman
on the street, seize the falcon
by its neck, beat my way into whistling steam.

I turn to you in the dark, oh husband,
20 watching your lit breath circle the pillow.
Then you turn to me, throwing first one limb
and then another over me, in the easy brotherly
lust of marriage. I cling to you
as if I were a burning ship and you
25 could save me, as if I won't go sliding down
beneath you soon; as if our lives are made of rise
and fall, and we could ride this out forever,
with longing's thunder rolling heavy in our arms.          1986

JOHN DRYDEN

## [*Why should a foolish marriage vow*][7]

Why should a foolish marriage vow,
    Which long ago was made,
Oblige us to each other now
    When passion is decayed?
5 We loved, and we loved, as long as we could,
    Till our love was loved out in us both;
But our marriage is dead when the pleasure is fled:
    'Twas pleasure first made it an oath.

If I have pleasures for a friend,
10    And farther love in store,
What wrong has he whose joys did end,
    And who could give no more?
'Tis a madness that he should be jealous of me,
    Or that I should bar him of another:
15 For all we can gain is to give ourselves pain,
    When neither can hinder the other.          1671

7. A song, sung by a woman character, in Dryden's play *Marriage à la Mode.*

## MARY, LADY CHUDLEIGH

# *To the Ladies*

Wife and servant are the same,
But only differ in the name:
For when that fatal knot is tied,
Which nothing, nothing can divide,
When she the word *Obey* has said,    5
And man by law supreme has made,
Then all that's kind is laid aside,
And nothing left but state and pride.
Fierce as an eastern prince he grows,
And all his innate rigor shows:    10
Then but to look, to laugh, or speak,
Will the nuptial contract break.
Like mutes, she signs alone must make,
And never any freedom take,
But still be governed by a nod,    15
And fear her husband as her god:
Him still must serve, him still obey,
And nothing act, and nothing say,
But what her haughty lord thinks fit,
Who, with the power, has all the wit.    20
Then shun, oh! shun that wretched state,
And all the fawning flatterers hate.
Value yourselves, and men despise:
You must be proud, if you'll be wise.    1703


## RICHARD LOVELACE

# *To Althea, from Prison*

When love with unconfinèd wings
    Hovers within my gates,
And my divine Althea brings
    To whisper at the grates;
When I lie tangled in her hair,    5
    And fettered to her eye,
The gods that wanton in the air
    Know no such liberty.

When flowing cups run swiftly round,
    With no allaying Thames,[8]    10

8. The river that runs through London.

Our careless heads with roses bound,
   Our hearts with loyal flames;
When thirsty grief in wine we steep,
   When healths and draughts go free,
15  Fishes that tipple in the deep
   Know no such liberty.

When, like committed linnets, I
   With shriller throat shall sing
The sweetness, mercy, majesty
20   And glories of my king;
When I shall voice aloud how good
   He is, how great should be,
Enlargèd winds that curl the flood
   Know no such liberty.

25  Stone walls do not a prison make,
   Nor iron bars a cage;
Minds innocent and quiet take
   That for an hermitage:
If I have freedom in my love,
30   And in my soul am free,
Angels alone that soar above
   Enjoy such liberty.

                                        1649

## CAROLYN FORCHÉ

# *Reunion*

*Just as he changes himself, in the end eternity changes him.*

                              —MALLARMÉ

On the phonograph, the voice
of a woman already dead for three
decades, singing of a man
who could make her do anything.
5  On the table, two fragile
glasses of black wine,
a bottle wrapped in its towel.
It is that room, the one
we took in every city, it is
10  as I remember: the bed, a block
of moonlight and pillows.
My fingernails, pecks of light
on your thighs.
The stink of the fire escape.
15  The wet butts of cigarettes
you crushed one after another.

How I watched the morning come
as you slept, more my son
than a man ten years older.
How my breasts feel, years                                          20
later, the tongues swishing
in my dress, some yours, some
left by other men.
Since then, I have always
wakened first, I have learned                                       25
to leave a bed without being
seen and have stood
at the washbasins, wiping oil
and salt from my skin,
staring at the cupped water                                         30
in my two hands.
I have kept everything
you whispered to me then.
I can remember it now as I see you
again, how much tenderness we could                                 35
wedge between a stairwell
and a police lock, or as it was,
as it still is, in the voice
of a woman singing of a man
who could make her do anything.                                     40

1981

ALAN SHAPIRO

## Ex-Wife: Infatuation

Your voice more bashful the more intimate
it grew on that first night, an indrawn breath
of speech I can't recall beyond the miserly
sweet way it hesitated on the tongue,
chary of giving, chary of taking back,                               5
the same breath doing both at once, it seemed,
to draw me to a closer kind of speech;

yet knowing too, knowing even then
what I—more loved than loving—had the clumsy
luxury not to know, that all too soon                               10
what words we had to say would fail us, each
lingering syllable a syllable less
between the pleasure it held off and invited,

and the bad luck pleasure would become;
a sweet syllable closer to the other nights,                        15

the last nights, nights that would make remembering
that long first night the bitter cost of having
had what we were on the verge of having.                    1996

## EDNA ST. VINCENT MILLAY

# [What lips my lips have kissed, and where, and why]

What lips my lips have kissed, and where, and why,
I have forgotten, and what arms have lain
Under my head till morning; but the rain
Is full of ghosts tonight, that tap and sigh
5    Upon the glass and listen for reply,
And in my heart there stirs a quiet pain
For unremembered lads that not again
Will turn to me at midnight with a cry.
Thus in the winter stands the lonely tree,
10    Nor knows what birds have vanished one by one,
Yet knows its boughs more silent than before:
I cannot say what loves have come and gone;
I only know that summer sang in me
A little while, that in me sings no more.                    1923

## THEODORE ROETHKE

# She

I think the dead are tender. Shall we kiss?—
My lady laughs, delighting in what is.
If she but sighs, a bird puts out its tongue.
She makes space lonely with a lovely song.
5    She lilts a low soft language, and I hear
Down long sea-chambers of the inner ear.

We sing together; we sing mouth to mouth.
The garden is a river flowing south.
She cries out loud the soul's own secret joy;
10    She dances, and the ground bears her away.
She knows the speech of light, and makes it plain
A lively thing can come to life again.

I feel her presence in the common day,
In that slow dark that widens every eye.

She moves as water moves, and comes to me,                    15
Stayed by what was, and pulled by what would be.       1956


W. B. YEATS

## A Last Confession

What lively lad most pleasured me
Of all that with me lay?
I answer that I gave my soul
And loved in misery,
But had great pleasure with a lad                             5
That I loved bodily.

Flinging from his arms I laughed
To think his passion such
He fancied that I gave a soul
Did but our bodies touch,                                     10
And laughed upon his breast to think
Beast gave beast as much.

I gave what other women gave
That stepped out of their clothes,
But when this soul, its body off,                             15
Naked to naked goes,
He it has found shall find therein
What none other knows,

And give his own and take his own
And rule in his own right;                                    20
And though it loved in misery
Close and cling so tight,
There's not a bird of day that dare
Extinguish that delight.                               1933


KAREN CHASE

## Venison

Paul set the bags down, told how they had split
the deer apart, the ease of peeling it
simpler than skinning a fruit, how the buck
lay on the worktable, how they sawed

5  an anklebone off, the smell not rank.
The sun slipped into night.

*Where are you* I wondered as I grubbed
through cupboards for noodles at least.
Then came venison new with blood,
10  stray hair from the animal's fur.
Excited, we cooked the meat.

Later, I dreamt against your human chest,
you cloaked me in your large arms, then
went for me the way you squander food sometimes.
15  By then, I was eating limbs in my sleep, somewhere
in the snow alone, survivor of a downed plane,
picking at the freshly dead. Whistles
of a far-off flute—legs, gristle, juice.
I cracked an elbow against a rock, awoke.
20  Throughout the night, we consumed and consumed.                    p. 1995

APHRA BEHN

## *On Her Loving Two Equally*

I

How strong does my passion flow,
Divided equally twixt⁹ two?
Damon had ne'er subdued my heart
Had not Alexis took his part;
5  Nor could Alexis powerful prove,
Without my Damon's aid, to gain my love.

II

When my Alexis present is,
Then I for Damon sigh and mourn;
But when Alexis I do miss,
10  Damon gains nothing but my scorn.
But if it chance they both are by,
For both alike I languish, sigh, and die.

III

Cure then, thou mighty wingéd god,¹
This restless fever in my blood;

9. Between.    1. Cupid, who, according to myth, shot darts of lead and of gold at the hearts of lovers, corresponding to false love and true love, respectively.

One golden-pointed dart take back:                                    15
But which, O Cupid, wilt thou take?
If Damon's, all my hopes are crossed;
Or that of my Alexis, I am lost.                                    1684


WILLIAM SHAKESPEARE
_____

# [*Let me not to the marriage of true minds*]

Let me not to the marriage of true minds
Admit impediments.[2] Love is not love
Which alters when it alteration finds,
Or bends with the remover to remove:
Oh, no! it is an ever-fixéd mark,                                     5
That looks on tempests and is never shaken;
It is the star to every wandering bark,
Whose worth's unknown, although his height be taken.[3]
Love's not Time's fool, though rosy lips and cheeks
Within his bending sickle's compass come;                            10
Love alters not with his brief hours and weeks,
But bears it out even to the edge of doom.
If this be error and upon me proved,
I never writ, nor no man ever loved.                                 1609


QUESTIONS

1. Which love poem in this chapter seems to you the most effective? the most moving? the most accurate in its representation of human emotions? the most beautiful in its sentiments? Pick out specific things in each poem you have chosen that help to make it work for you. Did you choose the same poem to answer each question? What did you learn about your own tastes and judgments from comparing the answers you gave to each question?
2. In Levertov's "Love Poem," what different "gifts" help to define the quality of affection? Compare the method of summing up ways of loving with that in "How Do I Love Thee?" (Browning) and in "The Tally Stick" (Ramsey).
3. What, exactly, do we know about the person who has just died in Auden's "Stop all the clocks"? What different strategies does the speaker of the poem use to convey the depth of his emotion? In what sense is this a love poem?
4. What does the deer have to do with the speaker's dreams in Chase's "Venison"? with the lovemaking during the night?
5. What is the relationship between burning "to marry" (line 10), "burning issues" (lines 13–

2. The Marriage Service contains this address to the witnesses: "If any of you know cause or just impediments why these persons should not be joined together . . . "    3. That is, measuring the altitude of stars (for purposes of navigation) is not a measurement of value.

14), and the "burning ship" (line 24) in Rosenberg's "Married Love"? What, exactly, is the situation in the poem? In what specific ways does the speaker's attitude change in the course of the poem? How do you interpret the poem's "as ifs" in the final stanza? What is the poem's ultimate attitude toward "married love"?

6. Did you notice that "To the Ladies" was written in 1703? Were you surprised by your response to it when you read it? If not, does the date of publication modify your response? Why?

## WRITING SUGGESTIONS

1. If you were writing a love poem comparing your love to a winter's day, what features of the season would you emphasize? What features of a spring day would you use? Write a paragraph on the virtues of each of these seasons, showing how features associated with them can be made into compliments appropriate to a lover.

2. Of all the love poems in this chapter, which one would you most like to have addressed to you? which least? Write a prose answer to the author of either poem you have chosen, explaining what seemed to you most (or least) complimentary in what the poem said about you.

3. Paraphrase—that is, put into different words line by line and stanza by stanza—Behn's "On Her Loving Two Equally." Summarize the poem's basic statement in one sentence. How accurately do your paraphrase and summary represent the feelings recorded in the poem?

4. Jot down your responses to all of the marriage poems in this chapter. Which one most accurately expresses your ideal of a good marriage? Why do you think so? What does your choice say about you?

# Understanding the Text

TONE

$P$oetry is full of surprises. Poems express anger or outrage just as effectively as love or sadness, and good poems can be written about going to a rock concert or having lunch or cutting the lawn, as well as about making love or smelling flowers or listening to Beethoven. Even poems on "predictable" subjects can surprise us with unpredicted attitudes, unusual events, or a sudden twist. Knowing that a poem is about some particular subject—love, for example, or death—may give us a general idea of what to expect, but it never tells us altogether what we will find in a particular poem. Responding to a poem fully means being open to the poem and its surprises, being willing to let the poem guide us to its own stances, feelings, and ideas—to an explanation of a topic that may be very different from what we expect or what we think. Letting a poem speak to us means being willing to listen to *how* the poem says what it says—hearing the tone of voice implied in the way the words are spoken. *What* a poem says involves its **theme,** a statement about its subject. *How* a poem makes that statement involves its **tone,** the attitude or feelings it expresses about the theme.

The following two poems—one about death and one about love—express different attitudes and feelings from the poems we have read so far.

MARGE PIERCY

## Barbie Doll

This girlchild was born as usual
and presented dolls that did pee-pee
and miniature GE stoves and irons
and wee lipsticks the color of cherry candy.
Then in the magic of puberty, a classmate said:      5
You have a great big nose and fat legs.

She was healthy, tested intelligent,
possessed strong arms and back,

33

abundant sexual drive and manual dexterity.
10    She went to and fro apologizing.
Everyone saw a fat nose on thick legs.

She was advised to play coy,
exhorted to come on hearty,
exercise, diet, smile and wheedle.
15    Her good nature wore out
like a fan belt.
So she cut off her nose and her legs
and offered them up.

In the casket displayed on satin she lay
20    with the undertaker's cosmetics painted on,
a turned-up putty nose,
dressed in a pink and white nightie.
Doesn't she look pretty? everyone said.
Consummation at last.
25    To every woman a happy ending.         1973


W. D. SNODGRASS

## Leaving the Motel

Outside, the last kids holler
Near the pool: they'll stay the night.
Pick up the towels; fold your collar
Out of sight.

5    Check: is the second bed
Unrumpled, as agreed?
Landlords have to think ahead
In case of need,

Too. Keep things straight: don't take
10    The matches, the wrong keyrings—
We've nowhere we could keep a keepsake—
Ashtrays, combs, things

That sooner or later others
Would accidentally find.
15    Check: take nothing of one another's
And leave behind

Your license number only,
Which they won't care to trace;
We've paid. Still, should such things get lonely,
20    Leave in their vase

An aspirin to preserve
Our lilacs, the wayside flowers
We've gathered and must leave to serve
A few more hours;

That's all. We can't tell when                                        25
We'll come back, can't press claims,
We would no doubt have other rooms then,
Or other names.                                                       1968

The first poem, "Barbie Doll," has the strong note of sadness that characterizes many death poems, but its emphasis is not on the girl's death but on the disappointments in her life. The only "scene" in the poem (lines 19–23) portrays the unnamed girl at rest in her casket, but the still body in the casket contrasts not with vitality but with frustration and anxiety: her life since puberty (lines 5–6) had been full of apologies and attempts to change her physical appearance and emotional makeup. The rest she achieves in death is not, however, a triumph, despite what people say (line 23). Although the poem's last two words are "happy ending," this girl without a name has died in embarrassment and without fulfillment, and the final lines are ironic, meaning the opposite of what they say. The cheerful comments at the end lack force and truth because of what we already know; we understand them as ironic because they underline how unhappy the girl was and how false her cosmeticized corpse is to the sad truth of her life.

The poem's concern is to suggest the falsity and destructiveness of those standards of female beauty that have led to the tragedy of the girl's life. In an important sense, the poem is not really *about* death at all in spite of the fact that the girl's death and her repaired corpse are central to it. As the title suggests, the poem dramatizes how standardized, commercialized notions of femininity and prettiness can be painful and destructive to those whose bodies do not precisely fit the conformist models, and the poem attacks vigorously those conventional standards and the widespread, unthinking acceptance of them.

"Leaving the Motel" similarly goes in quite a different direction from many poems on the subject of love. Instead of expressing assurance about how love lasts and endures, or about the sincerity and depth of affection, this poem describes a parting of lovers after a brief, surreptitious sexual encounter. But it does not emphasize sexuality or eroticism in the meeting of the nameless lovers (we see them only as they prepare to leave), nor does it suggest why or how they have found each other, or what either of them is like as a person. Its focus is on how careful they must be not to get caught, how exact and calculating they must be in their planning, how finite and limited their encounter must be, how sealed off this encounter is from the rest of their lives. The poem relates the tiny details the lovers must think of, the agreements they must observe, and the ritual checklist of their duties ("Check . . . Keep things straight . . . Check . . . ," lines 5, 9, 15). Affection and sentiment have their small place in the poem (notice the care for the flowers, lines 19–24, and the thought of "press[ing] claims," line 26), but the emphasis is on temporariness, uncertainty, and limits. The poem is about an illicit, perhaps adulterous, sexual encounter, but there is no sex in the poem, only a kind of archaeological record of lust.

Labeling a poem as a "love poem" or a "death poem" is primarily a matter of convenience; such categories indicate the **subject** of a poem or the event or **topic** it chooses to engage. But as the poems we have been looking at suggest, poems that may be loosely

called love poems or death poems may differ widely from one another, express totally
different attitudes or ideas, and concentrate on very different aspects of the subject. The
main advantages of grouping poems in this way for study is that a reader can become
conscious of individual differences: a reading of two poems side by side may suggest
how each is distinctive in what it has to say and how it says it.

The theme of a poem may be expressed in several different ways, and poems often
have more than one theme. We could say, for example, that the theme of "Leaving the
Motel" is that illicit love is secretive, careful, transitory, and short on emotion and senti-
ment, or that secret sexual encounters tend to be brief, calculated, and characterized by
restrained or hesitant feelings. "Barbie Doll" suggests that commercialized standards
destroy human values; that rigid and idealized notions of normality cripple those who
are different; that people are easily and tragically led to accept evaluations thrust upon
them by others; that American consumers tend to be conformists, easily influenced in
their outlook by advertising and by commercial products; that children who do not
conform to middle-class standards and notions don't have a chance. The poem implies
each of these statements, and all are quite central to it. But none of these statements
individually nor all of them together would fully express or explain the poem itself. To
state the themes in such a brief and abstract way—though it may be helpful in clarifying
what the poem does and does not say—does not do justice to the experience of the
poem, the way it works on us as readers, the way we respond. Poems affect us in all sorts
of ways—emotional and psychological as well as rational—and often a poem's drama-
tization of a story, an event, or a moment bypasses our rational responses and affects us
far more deeply than a clear and logical argument would.

Sometimes poems express feelings directly and quite simply:

LINDA PASTAN

## love poem

I want to write you
a love poem as headlong
as our creek
after thaw
when we stand
on its dangerous
banks and watch it carry
with it every twig
every dry leaf and branch
in its path
every scruple
when we see it
so swollen
with runoff
that even as we watch
we must grab
each other

and step back
we must grab each
other or                                                            20
get our shoes
soaked we must
grab each other                                                    1988

The directness and simplicity of this poem suggest how the art and craft of poems work. The poem expresses the desire to write a love poem even as the love poem itself begins to proceed; the desire and the resultant poem exist side by side, and in reading the poem we seem to watch and hear the poet's creative process at work in developing appropriate metaphors and means of expression. The poem must be "headlong" (line 2), to match the power of a love that needs to be compared to the irresistible forces of nature. The poem should, like the love it expresses and the swollen creek it describes, sweep everything along, and it should represent (and reproduce) the sense of watching that the lovers have when they observe natural processes at work. The poem, like the action it represents, has to suggest to readers the kind of desire that grabbing each other means to the lovers.

The lovers in this poem seem, at least to themselves, to own the world they observe, but in fact they are controlled by it. The creek on whose banks they stand is "our creek" (line 3), but what they observe as they watch its rising currents requires them ("must," lines 16, 19, 22) to "grab each other" over and over again. It is as if their love is part of nature itself, which subjects them to forces larger than themselves. Everything—twigs, leaves, branches, scruples—is carried along by the powerful currents after the "thaw" (line 4), and the poem replicates the repeated action of the lovers as if to power along observant readers just as the lovers are powered along by what they see. But the poem (and their love) admits dangers, too; it is the fact of danger that propels the lovers to each other. The poem suggests that love provides a kind of haven, but the haven hardly involves passivity or peace; instead, it requires the kind of grabbing that means activity and boldness and deep passion. Love here is no quiet or simple matter even if the expression of it in poems can be direct and based on a simple observation of experience. The "love poem" itself—linked as it is with the headlong currents of the creek from which the lovers are protecting themselves—even represents that which is beyond love and that, therefore, both threatens it and at the same time makes it happen. The power of poetry is thus affirmed at the center of the poem, but what poetry is about (love and life) is suggested to be more important. Poetry makes things happen but is not itself a substitute for life, just a means to make it more energetic and meaningful.

Poems, then, differ widely from one another even when they share a common subject. And the subjects of poetry also vary widely. It isn't true that there are certain "poetic" subjects and that there are others that aren't appropriate to poetry. Any human activity, thought, or feeling can be the subject of poetry. Poetry often deals with beauty and the softer, more attractive human emotions, but it can deal with ugliness and unattractive human conduct as well, for poetry seeks to represent human beings and human events, showing us ourselves not only as we would like to be but as we are. Good poetry gets written about all kinds of topics, in all kinds of forms, with all kinds of attitudes. Here, for example, is a poem about a prison inmate—and about the conflict between individual and societal values.

ETHERIDGE KNIGHT

# Hard Rock Returns to Prison from the Hospital for the Criminal Insane

Hard Rock was "known not to take no shit
From nobody," and he had the scars to prove it:
Split purple lips, lumped ears, welts above
His yellow eyes, and one long scar that cut
5   Across his temple and plowed through a thick
Canopy of kinky hair.

The WORD was that Hard Rock wasn't a mean nigger
Anymore, that the doctors had bored a hole in his head,
Cut out part of his brain, and shot electricity
10   Through the rest. When they brought Hard Rock back,
Handcuffed and chained, he was turned loose,
Like a freshly gelded stallion, to try his new status.
And we all waited and watched, like indians at a corral,
To see if the WORD was true.

15   As we waited we wrapped ourselves in the cloak
Of his exploits: "Man, the last time, it took eight
Screws to put him in the Hole."[1] "Yeah, remember when he
Smacked the captain with his dinner tray?" "He set
The record for time in the Hole—67 straight days!"
20   "Ol Hard Rock! man, that's one crazy nigger."
And then the jewel of a myth that Hard Rock had once bit
A screw on the thumb and poisoned him with syphilitic spit.

The testing came, to see if Hard Rock was really tame.
A hillbilly called him a black son of a bitch
25   And didn't lose his teeth, a screw who knew Hard Rock
From before shook him down and barked in his face.
And Hard Rock did *nothing*. Just grinned and looked silly,
His eyes empty like knot holes in a fence.

And even after we discovered that it took Hard Rock
30   Exactly 3 minutes to tell you his first name,
We told ourselves that he had just wised up,
Was being cool; but we could not fool ourselves for long,
And we turned away, our eyes on the ground. Crushed.
He had been our Destroyer, the doer of things
35   We dreamed of doing but could not bring ourselves to do,
The fears of years, like a biting whip,
Had cut grooves too deeply across our backs.          1968

---

1. Solitary confinement. *Screws*: guards.

The picture of Hard Rock as a kind of hero to other prison inmates is established early in the poem through a retelling of the legends circulated about him; the straightforward chronology of the poem sets up the mystery of how he will react after his "treatment" in the hospital. The poem identifies with those who wait; they are hopeful that Hard Rock's spirit has not been broken by surgery or shock treatments, and the lines crawl almost to a stop with disappointment in stanza 4. The *"nothing"* (line 27) of Hard Rock's response to teasing and taunting and the emptiness of his eyes ("like knot holes in a fence," line 28) reduce the heroic hopes and illusions to despair. The final stanza recounts the observers' attempts to reinterpret, to hang onto hope that their symbol of heroism could stand up against the best efforts to tame him, but the spirit has gone out of the hero-worshipers, too, and the poem records them as beaten, conformed, deprived of their spirit as Hard Rock has been of his. The poem records the despair of the hopeless, and it protests against the cruel exercise of power that can curb even as rebellious a figure as Hard Rock.

The following poem is equally full of anger and disappointment, but it expresses its attitudes in a very different way.

WILLIAM BLAKE

## London

I wander through each chartered street,
Near where the chartered Thames does flow,
And mark in every face I meet
Marks of weakness, marks of woe.

In every cry of every man,                                                    5
In every Infant's cry of fear,
In every voice, in every ban,
The mind-forged manacles I hear.

How the Chimney-sweeper's cry
Every black'ning Church appalls;                                              10
And the hapless Soldier's sigh
Runs in blood down Palace walls.

But most through midnight streets I hear
How the youthful Harlot's curse
Blasts the new-born Infant's tear,                                            15
And blights with plagues the Marriage hearse.                    1794

The poem gives a strong sense of how London feels to this particular observer; it is cluttered, constricting, oppressive. The wordplay here articulates and connects the strong emotions he associates with London experiences. The repeated words—"every," for example, or "cry"—intensify the sense of total despair in the city and weld connections between things not necessarily related—the cries of street vendors, for example, with the cries for help. The twice-used word "chartered" implies strong feelings, too. The streets, instead of seeming alive with people or bustling with movement, are rigidly, coldly determined, controlled, cramped. Likewise the river seems as if it were planned, programmed, laid out by an oppressor. In actual fact, the course of the Thames through the city had been altered (slightly) by the government before Blake's time, but most important is the word's emotional force, the sense it projects of constriction and artificiality: the person speaking experiences London as if human artifice had totally altered nature. Moreover, according to the poem, people are victimized, "marked" by their confrontations with urbanness and the power of institutions: the "Soldier's sigh" that "runs in blood down Palace walls" vividly suggests, through a metaphor that visually depicts the speaker's feelings, both the powerlessness of the individual and the callousness of power. The "description" of the city has clearly become, by now, a subjective, highly emotional, and vivid expression of how the speaker feels about London and what it represents to him.

> *Poetry makes nothing happen.*
>
> —W. H. AUDEN

Another thing about "London": at first it looks like an account of a personal experience, as if the speaker is describing and interpreting as he goes along: "I wander through each chartered street." But soon it is clear that he is describing many wanderings, putting together impressions from many walks, re-creating a typical walk—which shows him "every" person in the streets, allows him to generalize about the churches being "appalled" (literally, made white) by the cry of the representative Chimney-sweeper, and leads to his conclusions about soldiers, prostitutes, and infants. What we are given is not a personal record of an event, but a representation of it, as it seems in retrospect—not a story, not a narrative or chronological account of events, but a dramatization of self that compresses many experiences into one.

> *When power leads man toward arrogance, poetry reminds him of his limitations. When power narrows the areas of man's concern, poetry reminds him of the richness and diversity of his existence. When power corrupts, poetry cleanses.*
>
> —JOHN F. KENNEDY

"London" is somber in spite of the poet's playfulness with words. Wordplay may be witty and funny if it calls attention to its own cleverness, but here it involves the discovery of unsuspected (but meaningful) connections between things. The tone of "London" is sad, despairing, and angry; reading "London" aloud, one would try to show in one's voice the strong feelings that the poem expresses, just as one would try to reproduce tenderness and caring and passion in reading aloud "The Tally Stick" or "How Do I Love Thee?"

The following two poems are "about" animals, although both of them place their final emphasis on what human beings are like: the animal in each case is only the means to the end of exploring human nature. The poems share a common assumption that animal behavior may appear to reflect human habits and conduct and may reveal much about ourselves, and in each case the character central to the poem is revealed to be surprisingly unlike the way she thinks of herself. But the poems are very different from one another. Read each poem aloud, and try to imagine what each main character is like. What tones of voice do you use to help express the character of the killer in the first poem? What demands on your voice does the second poem make?

MAXINE KUMIN

## Woodchucks

Gassing the woodchucks didn't turn out right.
The knockout bomb from the Feed and Grain Exchange
was featured as merciful, quick at the bone
and the case we had against them was airtight,
both exits shoehorned shut with puddingstone,[2]    5
but they had a sub-sub-basement out of range.

Next morning they turned up again, no worse
for the cyanide than we for our cigarettes
and state-store Scotch, all of us up to scratch.
They brought down the marigolds as a matter of course    10
and then took over the vegetable patch
nipping the broccoli shoots, beheading the carrots.

The food from our mouths, I said, righteously thrilling
to the feel of the .22, the bullets' neat noses.
I, a lapsed pacifist fallen from grace    15
puffed with Darwinian pieties for killing,
now drew a bead on the littlest woodchuck's face.
He died down in the everbearing roses.

Ten minutes later I dropped the mother. She
flipflopped in the air and fell, her needle teeth    20
still hooked in a leaf of early Swiss chard.
Another baby next. O one-two-three
the murderer inside me rose up hard,
the hawkeye killer came on stage forthwith.

There's one chuck left. Old wily fellow, he keeps    25
me cocked and ready day after day after day.
All night I hunt his humped-up form. I dream
I sight along the barrel in my sleep.
If only they'd all consented to die unseen
gassed underground the quiet Nazi way.    30

1972

ADRIENNE RICH

## Aunt Jennifer's Tigers

Aunt Jennifer's tigers prance across a screen,
Bright topaz denizens of a world of green.

2. A mixture of cement, pebbles, and gravel.

They do not fear the men beneath the tree;
They pace in sleek chivalric certainty.

5    Aunt Jennifer's fingers fluttering through her wool
Find even the ivory needle hard to pull.
The massive weight of Uncle's wedding band
Sits heavily upon Aunt Jennifer's hand.

When Aunt is dead, her terrified hands will lie
10    Still ringed with ordeals she was mastered by.
The tigers in the panel that she made
Will go on prancing, proud and unafraid.                          1951

If you read "Woodchucks" aloud, how would your tone of voice change from begin-
ning to end? What tone would you use to read the ending? How does the hunter feel
about her increasing attraction to violence? Why does the poem begin by calling the
gassing of the woodchucks "merciful" and end by describing it as "the quiet Nazi way"?
What names does the hunter call herself? How does the name-calling affect your feelings
about her? Exactly when does the hunter begin to *enjoy* the feel of the gun and the idea
of killing? How does the poet make that clear?

Why are tigers a particularly appropriate contrast to the quiet and subdued manner
of Aunt Jennifer? What words used to describe the tigers seem particularly significant? In
what ways is the tiger an opposite of Aunt Jennifer? In what ways does it externalize her
secrets? Why are Aunt Jennifer's hands described as "terrified"? What clues does the
poem give about why Aunt Jennifer is so afraid? How does the poem make you feel
about Aunt Jennifer? about her tigers? about her life? How would you describe the tone
of the poem? How does the poet feel about Aunt Jennifer?

Twenty years after writing "Aunt Jennifer's Tigers," Adrienne Rich said this about the
poem:

> In writing this poem, composed and apparently cool as it is, I thought I was creating a
> portrait of an imaginary woman. But this woman suffers from the opposition of her imagi-
> nation, worked out in tapestry, and her life style, "ringed with ordeals she was mastered
> by." It was important to me that Aunt Jennifer was a person as distinct from myself as
> possible—distanced by the formalism of the poem, by its objective, observant tone—even
> by putting the woman in a different generation. In those years formalism was part of the
> strategy—like asbestos gloves, it allowed me to handle materials I couldn't pick up bare-
> handed.[3]

Not often do we have such an explicit comment on a poem by its author, and we
don't actually have to have it to understand and experience the force of the poem
(although such a statement may clarify why the author chose particular modes of pre-
sentation and how the poem fits into the author's own patterns of thinking and growing).
Most poems contain within them what we need to know in order to tap the human and
artistic resources they offer us.

Subject, theme, and tone: each of these categories gives us a way to begin consider-
ing poems and showing how one poem differs from another. Comparing poems on the

---

3. From "When We Dead Awaken: Writing as Re-vision," a talk given in December 1971 at the Women's
Forum of the Modern Language Association.

same subject or with a similar theme or tone can lead to a clearer understanding of each individual poem and can refine our responses to the subtleties of individual differences. The title of a poem ("Leaving the Motel," for example) or the way the poem first introduces its subject often can give us a sense of what to expect, but we need to be open to surprise, too. No two poems are going to be exactly alike in their effect on us; the variety of possible poems multiplies when you think of all the possible themes and tones that can be explored within any single subject. Varieties of feeling often coincide with varieties of thinking, and readers open to the pleasures of the unexpected may find themselves learning, growing, becoming more sensitive to ideas and human issues as well as more articulate about feelings and thoughts they already have.

## MANY TONES: POEMS ABOUT
## FAMILY RELATIONSHIPS

GALWAY KINNELL

### *After Making Love We Hear Footsteps*

For I can snore like a bullhorn
or play loud music
or sit up talking with any reasonably sober Irishman
and Fergus will only sink deeper
5    into his dreamless sleep, which goes by all in one flash,
but let there be that heavy breathing
or a stifled come-cry anywhere in the house
and he will wrench himself awake
and make for it on the run—as now, we lie together,
10    after making love, quiet, touching along the length of our bodies,
familiar touch of the long-married,
and he appears—in his baseball pajamas, it happens,
the neck opening so small
he has to screw them on, which one day may make him wonder
15    about the mental capacity of baseball players—
and says, "Are you loving and snuggling? May I join?"
He flops down between us and hugs us and snuggles himself to sleep,
his face gleaming with satisfaction at being this very child.

In the half darkness we look at each other
20    and smile
and touch arms across his little, startlingly muscled body—
this one whom habit of memory propels to the ground of his making,
sleeper only the mortal sounds can sing awake,
this blessing love gives again into our arms.                    1980

SEAMUS HEANEY

### *Mid-Term Break*

I sat all morning in the college sick bay
Counting bells knelling classes to a close.
At two o'clock our neighbors drove me home.

In the porch I met my father crying—
5    He had always taken funerals in his stride—
And Big Jim Evans saying it was a hard blow.

The baby cooed and laughed and rocked the pram
When I came in, and I was embarrassed
By old men standing up to shake my hand

And tell me they were "sorry for my trouble,"                   10
Whispers informed strangers I was the eldest,
Away at school, as my mother held my hand

In hers and coughed out angry tearless sighs.
At ten o'clock the ambulance arrived
With the corpse, stanched and bandaged by the nurses.          15

Next morning I went up into the room. Snowdrops
And candles soothed the bedside; I saw him
For the first time in six weeks. Paler now,

Wearing a poppy bruise on his left temple,
He lay in the four foot box as in his cot.                     20
No gaudy scars, the bumper knocked him clear.

A four foot box, a foot for every year.                        1966


PAT MORA
_____

## *Elena*

My Spanish isn't enough.
I remember how I'd smile
listening to my little ones,
understanding every word they'd say,
their jokes, their songs, their plots.                         5
　　*Vamos a pedirle dulces a mamá. Vamos.*[4]
But that was in Mexico.
Now my children go to American high schools.
They speak English. At night they sit around
the kitchen table, laugh with one another.                     10
I stand by the stove and feel dumb, alone.
I bought a book to learn English.
My husband frowned, drank more beer.
My oldest said, "*Mama´*, he doesn't want you
to be smarter than he is." I'm forty,                          15
embarrassed at mispronouncing words,
embarrassed at the laughter of my children,
the grocer, the mailman. Sometimes I take
my English book and lock myself in the bathroom,
say the thick words softly,                                     20
for if I stop trying, I will be deaf
when my children need my help.                                 1985

4. "Let's go ask mama for sweets. Let's go."

SUSAN GLICKMAN

## *Beauty*

Maybe there are no easy deaths but Grandpa's
was terrible. The scuttling crab-wise crawl
of the disease eating him
for months, a slow insult.
5   The scotch-and-nicotine smell of him
gone off, festering,
so that even he flinched from his skin,
that strange dank leather
clammy as a wet groundsheet
10  stretched over his bones.
Bones he'd kept modestly hidden
in his patriarch's bulk, his executive jowls,
all naked and poor
in plain view—my fierce private grandfather
15  exposed.

My mother was afraid of him:
his *Sit up straight!* his *Girls
don't go to college.*
My sister, only little when he died, remembers
20  a scowling giant whose moustache spoiled
his kisses.
And he *was* fierce, his longshoreman's fists,
but with me he was always courtly. We discussed things.
And Grandpa, you were right,
25  which I knew even then, about beauty.
*It comes from inside,* you said (But I was only
twelve, desperate for power, afraid I might never
have any) *It has nothing to do
with fashion.*

30  We were sitting in your wood-panelled den, the TV on
to *Bonanza* or *Perry Mason,* your favourites,
and talking. And I knew you were right.
But even now I can feel that hard little knot, that "no,"
stuck in my throat like a candy
35  stolen from your secret cupboard and swallowed guiltily
and whole, that knot of stubbornness which, like the candy,
like everything I took from you, silver dollars, a complete set
of Dickens, your gold pen, was mine
from inside, my true inheritance.

1990

ALBERTO ALVARO RÍOS

## Mi Abuelo[5]

Where my grandfather is is in the ground
where you can hear the future like an
Indian with his ear at the tracks. A
pipe leads down to him so that sometimes
he whispers what will happen to a man                                    5
in town or how he will meet the best-
dressed woman tomorrow and how the best
man at her wedding will chew the ground
next to her. Mi abuelo is the man
who talks through all the mouths in my house. An      10
echo of me hitting the pipe sometimes
to stop him from saying "my hair is a
sieve" is the only other sound. It is a
phrase that among all others is the best,
he says, and "my hair is a sieve" is sometimes        15
repeated for hours out of the ground
when I let him, but mostly I don't. "An
abuelo should be much more than a man
like you!" He stops then, and speaks: "I am a man
who has served ants with the attitude of a            20
waiter, who has made each smile as only an
ant who is fat can, and they liked me best,
but there is nothing left." Yet, I know he ground
green coffee beans as a child, and sometimes
he will talk about his wife, and sometimes            25
about when he was deaf and a man
cured him by mail and he heard ground
hogs talking, or about how he walked with a
cane he chewed on when he got hungry. At best,
mi abuelo is a liar. I see an                          30
old picture of him at nani's with an
off-white yellow center mustache and sometimes
that's all I know for sure. He talks best
about these hills, slowest waves, and where this man
is going, and I'm convinced his hair is a             35
sieve, that his fever is cool now in the ground.
Mi abuelo is an ordinary man.
I look down the pipe, sometimes, and see a
ripple-topped stream in its best suit, in the ground.           1980

5. "My grandfather."

TOM SLEIGH

## Some Larger Motion

After she has pieced together what was done to her,
And he too realized what was done to him,
With reaching hands they feel their fingers
Touch each other's bodies while the bodies
5    Hold inside the touch of hands that each one
Wanted and was shamed by.
                          All evening
They've longed to tell about those hands,
But others they've told shy away somehow;
As if to spare them this, the hands press
10   Hushing fingers to their lips, a touch
Conspiratorial, intimate as trust . . .
                          and so,
With those hands still vividly in mind,
After the small talk they touch each other,
Wreaking on each other what those hands once wreaked,
15   Uncontrollably repeating the cold rage
To be beyond that shame which keeps their bodies
Sealed off as if their flesh were numb:
                          Through her,
Her crippled father touches his body, through him,
His mother's cool, willful fingers touch her;
20   He shivers under the incapable hands
That timidly touch him, she shrinks from
The ravages she senses in those fingers . . .

When they finish, arms and legs motionless on the bed,
As they drift between her fear, his dread,
25   Rousing from this moment comes a rigorous
Balance, each supporting the other,
His body nestled against hers in fragile
Equilibrium as they lie wrapped together,
Her head on his shoulder, his breath fanning
30   Her cheek, their opposed bodies one
In opposition:

                    And in this—especially this,
They begin to feel some larger motion
Lifting them above the bodies tensed
To pull away, while deep inside the other
35   They sense those hands, urgent as a lover's,
Tugging at their fingers locked together.                    1996

SHARON OLDS

## *I Go Back to May 1937*

I see them standing at the formal gates of their colleges,
I see my father strolling out
under the ochre sandstone arch, the
red tiles glinting like bent
plates of blood behind his head, I                                      5
see my mother with a few light books at her hip
standing at the pillar made of tiny bricks with the
wrought-iron gate still open behind her, its
sword-tips black in the May air,
they are about to graduate, they are about to get married,              10
they are kids, they are dumb, all they know is they are
innocent, they would never hurt anybody.
I want to go up to them and say Stop,
don't do it—she's the wrong woman,
he's the wrong man, you are going to do things                          15
you cannot imagine you would ever do,
you are going to do bad things to children,
you are going to suffer in ways you never heard of,
you are going to want to die. I want to go
up to them there in the late May sunlight and say it,                   20
her hungry pretty blank face turning to me,
her pitiful beautiful untouched body,
his arrogant handsome blind face turning to me,
his pitiful beautiful untouched body,
but I don't do it. I want to live. I                                    25
take them up like the male and female
paper dolls and bang them together
at the hips like chips of flint as if to
strike sparks from them, I say
Do what you are going to do, and I will tell about it.                  30

1987

LI-YOUNG LEE

## *Persimmons*

In sixth grade Mrs. Walker
slapped the back of my head
and made me stand in the corner
for not knowing the difference
between *persimmon* and *precision*.                                    5
How to choose

persimmons. This is precision.
Ripe ones are soft and brown-spotted.
Sniff the bottoms. The sweet one
10    will be fragrant. How to eat:
put the knife away, lay down newspaper.
Peel the skin tenderly, not to tear the meat.
Chew the skin, suck it,
and swallow. Now, eat
15    the meat of the fruit,
so sweet,
all of it, to the heart.

Donna undresses, her stomach is white.
In the yard, dewy and shivering
20    with crickets, we lie naked,
face-up, face-down.
I teach her Chinese.
Crickets:   *chiu chiu.* Dew:   I've forgotten.
Naked:   I've forgotten.
25    *Ni, wo:*   you and me.
I part her legs,
remember to tell her
she is beautiful as the moon.

Other words
30    that got me into trouble were
*fight* and *fright, wren* and *yarn.*
Fight was what I did when I was frightened,
fright was what I felt when I was fighting.
Wrens are small, plain birds,
35    yarn is what one knits with.
Wrens are soft as yarn.
My mother made birds out of yarn.
I loved to watch her tie the stuff;
a bird, a rabbit, a wee man.

40    Mrs. Walker brought a persimmon to class
and cut it up
so everyone could taste
a *Chinese apple.* Knowing
it wasn't ripe or sweet, I didn't eat
45    but watched the other faces.

My mother said every persimmon has a sun
inside, something golden, glowing,
warm as my face.

Once, in the cellar, I found two wrapped in newspaper,
50    forgotten and not yet ripe.
I took them and set both on my bedroom windowsill,
where each morning a cardinal
sang, *The sun, the sun.*

Finally understanding
he was going blind,                                                55
my father sat up all one night
waiting for a song, a ghost.
I gave him the persimmons,
swelled, heavy as sadness,
and sweet as love.                                                60

This year, in the muddy lighting
of my parents' cellar, I rummage, looking
for something I lost.
My father sits on the tired, wooden stairs,
black cane between his knees,                                      65
hand over hand, gripping the handle.

He's so happy that I've come home.
I ask how his eyes are, a stupid question.
*All gone,* he answers.

Under some blankets, I find a box.                                 70
Inside the box I find three scrolls.
I sit beside him and untie
three paintings by my father:
Hibiscus leaf and a white flower.
Two cats preening.                                                75
Two persimmons, so full they want to drop from the cloth.

He raises both hands to touch the cloth,
asks, *Which is this?*

*This is persimmons, Father.*

*Oh, the feel of the wolftail on the silk,*                        80
*the strength, the tense*
*precision in the wrist.*
*I painted them hundreds of times*
*eyes closed. These I painted blind.*
*Some things never leave a person:*                               85
*scent of the hair of one you love,*
*the texture of persimmons,*
*in your palm, the ripe weight.*                              1986

RICHARD MICHELSON

## *Undressing Aunt Frieda*

Undressing Aunt Frieda, I think of how,
undressing me, she would tilt back her head
as if listening for footsteps, the faint marching
of the S.S. men whose one great dream

5    was her death. They must have feared
how her young Jewish fingers unbuttoned
and buttoned, as if they had continents
to cross, as if here, in East New York,
I was already tiring, and no one at home
10    to put me to bed.

Undressing Aunt Frieda, I try to imagine her
healthy, undressing herself, slowly at first,
as if for the love of a man, untying
her green checkered apron with the secret pockets,
15    unwrapping the frail "just shy of five foot" body
whose scarred beauty Rubens would surely have missed,
but Rembrandt, in the loneliness of his dying days,
might have immortalized.

My daughter at my side grows restless.
20    She unties her shoes, tugs at each sock.
She has learned, recently, to undress herself,
and pausing occasionally for applause,
does so now. Naked, she shimmies up onto the bed,
curls her thin fingers around Frieda who,
25    as if she wished herself already dead,
doesn't coo or even smile.

"A dream of love," Frieda preached, "is not love,
but a dream." "And bad luck," I'd say, "follows
the bitter heart." But undressing her now,
30    I remember the lightness of her hands
and their strength which somehow lifted me
above the nightmares she had known.
*I'll care for you*, she whispered once,
*as if you were my own*. My daughter yawns.
35    I lift her gently, hoping she'll sleep
the hour drive home.                                          1985


ELIZABETH ALEXANDER

## *West Indian Primer*

*for Clifford L. Alexander, Sr.*
*1898–1989*

"On the road between Spanish Town
and Kingston," my grandfather said,
"I was born." His father a merchant,
Jewish, from Italy or Spain.

5    In the great earthquake the ground split
clean, and great-grandfather fell

in the fault with his goat. I don't know
how I got this tale and do not ask.

His black mother taught my grand-                10
father figures, fixed codfish cakes
and fried plantains, drilled cleanliness,
telling the truth, punctuality.

"There is no man more honest,"
my father says. Years later                      15
I read that Jews passed through my
grandfather's birthplace frequently.

I know more about Toussaint[6]
and Hispaniola[7] than my own
Jamaica and my family tales
I finger the stories like genie                  20

lamps. I write this West Indian primer.          1990


EAMON GRENNAN

## Pause

The weird containing stillness of the neighborhood
just before the school bus brings all the neighborhood kids
home in the middle of the cold afternoon: a moment of pure
waiting, anticipation, before the outbreak of anything,
when everything seems just, seems *justified,* hanging        5
in the wings, about to happen, and in your mind you see
the flashing lights flare amber to scarlet and your daughter
in her blue jacket and white-fringed sapphire hat
stepping gingerly down and out into our world again, to hurry
through silence and snow-grass as the bus door sighs shut      10
and her own front door flies open and she finds you
behind it, father-in-waiting, the stillness in bits
and the common world restored as you bend to touch her,
to take her hat and coat up from the floor
where she's dropped them, hear the live voice of her filling   15
every crack. In the pause before all this happens, you know
something about the shape of the life you've chosen to live
between the silence of almost infinite possibility and that
explosion of things as they are—those vast unanswerable
intrusions of love and disaster, or just the casual scatter    20
of your child's winter clothes on the hall floor.            1993

6. Self-educated, Haitian black soldier and liberator who lived from 1743 to 1803.    7. The first island claimed by Columbus for Spain in 1492. It houses the modern nations of Haiti and the Dominican Republic.

GREG DELANTY

# Leavetaking

After you board the train, you sit & wait,
    to begin your first real journey alone.
You read to avoid the window's awkwardness,
    knowing he's anxious to catch your eye,
            loitering out in never-ending rain,
to wave, a bit shy, another final goodbye;
you are afraid of having to wave too soon.

And for the moment you think it's the train
    next to you has begun, but it is yours,
and your face, pressed to the windowpane,
    is distorted & numbed by the icy glass,
            pinning your eyes upon your father,
as he cranes to defy your disappearing train.
Both of you waving, eternally, to each other.

1992

JIMMY SANTIAGO BACA

# Green Chile

I prefer red chile over my eggs
and potatoes for breakfast.
Red chile *ristras*[8] decorate my door,
dry on my roof, and hang from eaves.
They lend open-air vegetable stands
historical grandeur, and gently swing
with an air of festive welcome.
I can hear them talking in the wind,
haggard, yellowing, crisp, rasping
tongues of old men, licking the breeze.

      But grandmother loves green chile.
When I visit her,
she holds the green chile pepper
in her wrinkled hands.
Ah, voluptuous, masculine,
an air of authority and youth simmers
from its swan-neck stem, tapering to a flowery
collar, fermenting resinous spice.
A well-dressed gentleman at the door

---

8. Braided strings of peppers.

my grandmother takes sensuously in her hand,                                                20
rubbing its firm glossed sides,
caressing the oily rubbery serpent,
with mouth-watering fulfillment,
fondling its curves with gentle fingers.
Its bearing magnificent and taut                                                            25
as flanks of a tiger in mid-leap,
she thrusts her blade into
and cuts it open, with lust
on her hot mouth, sweating over the stove,
bandanna round her forehead,                                                                30
mysterious passion on her face
and she serves me green chile con carne
between soft warm leaves of corn tortillas,
with beans and rice—her sacrifice
to her little prince.                                                                       35
I slurp from my plate
with last bit of tortilla, my mouth burns
and I hiss and drink a tall glass of cold water.

All over New Mexico, sunburned men and women
drive rickety trucks stuffed with gunny-sacks                                               40
of green chile, from Belen, Veguita, Willard, Estancia,
San Antonio y Socorro, from fields
to roadside stands, you see them roasting green chile
in screen-sided homemade barrels, and for a dollar a bag,
we relive this old, beautiful ritual again and again.                                       45

                                                                          1989


ROBERT HAYDEN

## *Those Winter Sundays*

Sundays too my father got up early
and put his clothes on in the blueblack cold,
then with cracked hands that ached
from labor in the weekday weather made
banked fires blaze. No one ever thanked him.                                                5

I'd wake and hear the cold splintering, breaking.
When the rooms were warm, he'd call,
and slowly I would rise and dress,
fearing the chronic angers of that house,

Speaking indifferently to him,                                                              10
who had driven out the cold
and polished my good shoes as well.
What did I know, what did I know
of love's austere and lonely offices?                                 1962

JAMES MASAO MITSUI

## Because of My Father's Job

Spring hailstones would drive us
into the garage. I'd explain away
the smell of my father's tsukemono[9] crock
with its rock-weight,
saying he needed his cabbage
like Popeye's spinach. I'd divert attention
to the moonsnail shell,
carried across the mountains from Puget Sound
by my sister. We'd shake off cobwebs,
listen to the dancing surf.

I still use the smell of cabbage,
like kelp & fishbone, as an anchor
although I have no memories of father
scooping butter clams
out of the gravel at Point-of-Arches
near Shi Shi Beach. Nothing
to connect him to the wind
on the headland at Strawberry Point,
the breakers unfolding a story
of poetry, edges & days
that don't always balance.

I have no memories of father
naming me
after Jimmy Osler of Skykomish,
who worked in the depot
and laughed so easily.
Who didn't change his friendship in '41.

I have copied the moustache
we shaved off my father once
when he was drunk. Last December
I sat at a motel kitchen table,
on the Oregon coast,
writing poems by candlelight.
My shadow fluttered on the walls & ceiling
as white waves
thundered & slid toward the cabin.
Turning to a mirror
I found his thick biceps
flexing themselves.
It doesn't matter now that he drank too much,
embarrassed the moon with his curses & songs.

1986

9. Japanese self-pickled vegetables.

SIMON J. ORTIZ

## My Father's Song

Wanting to say things,
I miss my father tonight.
His voice, the slight catch,
the depth from his thin chest,
the tremble of emotion                                    5
in something he has just said
to his son, his song:

We planted corn one Spring at Acu—
we planted several times
but this one particular time                              10
I remember the soft damp sand
in my hand.

My father had stopped at one point
to show me an overturned furrow;
the plowshare had unearthed                               15
the burrow nest of a mouse
in the soft moist sand.

Very gently, he scooped tiny pink animals
into the palm of his hand
and told me to touch them.                                20
We took them to the edge
of the field and put them in the shade
of a sand moist clod.

I remember the very softness
of cool and warm sand and tiny alive mice                 25
and my father saying things.                          1976

MARTIN ESPADA

## The Sign in My Father's Hands

*for Frank Espada*

The beer company
did not hire Blacks or Puerto Ricans,
so my father joined the picket line
at the Schaefer Beer Pavilion, New York World's Fair,
amid the crowds glaring with canine hostility.           5
But the cops brandished nightsticks
and handcuffs to protect the beer,
and my father disappeared.

In 1964, I had never tasted beer,
and no one told me about the picket signs
torn in two by the cops of brewery.
I knew what dead was: dead was a cat
overrun with parasites and dumped
in the hallway incinerator.
I knew my father was dead.
I went mute and filmy-eyed, the slow boy
who did not hear the question in school.
I sat studying his framed photograph
like a mirror, my darker face.

Days later, he appeared in the doorway
grinning with his gilded tooth.
Not dead, though I would come to learn
that sometimes Puerto Ricans die
in jail, with bruises no one can explain
swelling their eyes shut.
I would learn too that "boycott"
is not a boy's haircut,
that I could sketch a picket line
on the blank side of a leaflet.

That day my father returned
from the netherworld
easily as riding the elevator to apartment 14-F,
and the brewery cops could only watch
in drunken disappointment.
I searched my father's hands
for a sign of the miracle.

1996

SUSAN MUSGRAVE

## *You Didn't Fit*

*for my father*

You wouldn't fit in your coffin
but to me it was no surprise.
All your life you had never fit in
anywhere; you saw no reason to
begin fitting now.

When I was little I remember
a sheriff coming. You were
taken to court because your
false teeth didn't fit and you
wouldn't pay the dentist. It was

your third set, you said none of them
fit properly. I was afraid then
that something would take you from me
as it has done now: death
with a bright face and teeth that                                    15
fit perfectly.

A human smile that shuts me out.
The Court, I remember, returned
your teeth, now marked an exhibit.
You were dismissed with costs—                                       20
I never understood. The teeth were
terrible. We liked you better
without them.

We didn't fit, either, into your
life or your loneliness, though you                                  25
tried, and we did too. Once
I wanted to marry you, and then left;
I'm still the child who won't fit
into the arms of anyone, but is
always reaching.                                                     30

I was awkward for years, my bones
didn't fit in my body but stuck out
like my heart—people used to comment
on it. They said I was very good
at office parties where you took me                                  35
and let others do the talking—the
crude jokes, the corny men—I saw
how they hurt you and I loved you
harder than ever.

Because neither of us fit. Later you                                 40
blamed me, said "You must fit in,"
but I didn't and I still think
it made you secretly happy.

Like I am now: you won't fit in your
coffin. My mother, after a life                                      45
of it, says, "This is the last straw."
And it is. We're all clutching.                                 1985

ALAN DUGAN

## Elegy

I know but will not tell
you, Aunt Irene, why there

are soapsuds in the whiskey:
Uncle Robert had to have
a drink while shaving. May
there be no bloodshed in your house
this morning of my father's death
and no unkept appearance
in the living, since he has
to wear the rouge and lipstick
of your ceremony, mother,
for the first and last time:
father, hello and goodbye.

                                                    1963


REGINA BARRECA

## *Nighttime Fires*

When I was five in Louisville
we drove to see nighttime fires. Piled seven of us,
all pajamas and running noses, into the Olds,
drove fast toward smoke. It was after my father
lost his job, so not getting up in the morning
gave him time: awake past midnight, he read old newspapers
with no news, tried crosswords until he split the pencil
between his teeth, mad. When he heard
the wolf whine of the siren, he woke my mother,
and she pushed and shoved
us all into waking. Once aroused we longed for burnt wood
and a smell of flames high into the pines. My old man liked
driving to rich neighborhoods best, swearing in a good mood
as he followed fire engines that snaked like dragons
and split the silent streets. It was festival, carnival.

If there were a Cadillac or any car
in a curved driveway, my father smiled a smile
from a secret, brittle heart.
His face lit up in the heat given off by destruction
like something was being made, or was being set right.
I bent my head back to see where sparks
ate up the sky. My father who never held us
would take my hand and point to falling cinders that
covered the ground like snow, or, excited, show us
the swollen collapse of a staircase. My mother
watched my father, not the house. She was happy
only when we were ready to go, when it was finally over
and nothing else could burn.
Driving home, she would sleep in the front seat

as we huddled behind. I could see his quiet face in the                                30
rearview mirror, eyes like hallways filled with smoke.                    1986


ERIN MOURÉ

## *Thirteen Years*

I am in a daydream of my uncle,
his shirt out at his daughter's wedding,
white scoop of the shirt-tail bobbing
on the dance floor & him in it, no,
his drunk friend pawing me, it was *his* shirt dangling,                          5
I forgot this
my youngest cousin in his dress pants downing straight whisky,
& me too, tying tin cans to his sister's car.
The sour taste of it. Drink this, he said.

I am wondering how we live at all                                        10
or if we do.
The puppy we grew up with came from the same uncle's farm.
His shirt-tail beneath his suit jacket, dancing.
*The friend of the family* touching my new chest.
They told me not to say so.                                              15
I'll drive you to the motel, he said, his breath close.
No. Be nice to him, they said, & waved me off from the table.
I was so scared.
Everyone had been drinking. Including me. Thirteen years old.
Who the hell did my cousin marry.                                        20
I tell you.                                              1988


QUESTIONS

1. Consider carefully how the tone of Hayden's "Those Winter Sundays" is created. What activities of the father inspire the son's admiration? Which words of the son are especially effective in suggesting his attitude toward his father? Why is the phrase "what did I know" repeated in line 13? What are the connotations of the word "austere" in line 14? How old does the son seem to be at the time the poem is written? How can you tell?

2. What attitude does Dugan's "Elegy" take toward Aunt Irene? toward Uncle Robert? toward the mother? toward the father? How can you tell about the attitudes toward each? What individual words or factual details help to suggest the attitudes? Is "Elegy" an appropriate title for the poem? Why?

3. In Alexander's "West Indian Primer," characterize the speaker's great-grandfather; her great-grandmother. How much specific detail are we given about each? What qualities does the grandfather seem to take from each? How do they fit together? Describe the attitude the poem expresses toward each of these ancestors. Explain the poem's title.

4. In Mora's "Elena," what is the tone of the "smile" in line 2? of the husband's frown and

beer drinking in line 13? (That is, what kind of attitude does each express toward its audience?) In what tone of voice would you read the quotation in lines 14–15?

## WRITING SUGGESTIONS

1. How did you respond to Mouré's "Thirteen Years"? What is the main thing the speaker is trying to say to us? How does she feel about herself and her relatives as she recounts this adolescent experience? How do her attitudes differ from those of other members of her family? Describe the poem's tone. Write a brief narrative paragraph describing as succinctly as possible exactly what happened at the wedding.
2. Compare the tone of voice used in reading Heaney's "Mid-Term Break" aloud to that in Musgrave's "You Didn't Fit." Pick out three or four key words from each poem that seem to help control the tone. Then, concentrating on the words you have isolated, write a short essay—no more than 600 words—in which you compare the tone of the two poems.

# 2

# SPEAKER: WHOSE VOICE DO WE HEAR?

Poems are personal. The thoughts and feelings they express belong to a specific person, and however general or universal their sentiments seem to be, poems come to us as the expression of an individual human voice. That voice is often the voice of the poet. But not always. Poets sometimes create a "character" just as writers of fiction or drama do—people who speak for them only indirectly. A character may, in fact, be very different from the poet, just as a character in a play or story is different from the author, and that person, the **speaker** of the poem, may express ideas or feelings very different from the poet's own. In the following poem, *two* individual voices in fact speak, and it is clear that, rather than himself speaking directly to us, the poet, Thomas Hardy, has chosen to create two speakers, both female, each of whom has a distinctive voice, personality, and character.

THOMAS HARDY

## *The Ruined Maid*

"O 'Melia,[1] my dear, this does everything crown!
Who could have supposed I should meet you in Town?
And whence such fair garments, such prosperi-ty?"—
"O didn't you know I'd been ruined?" said she.

—"You left us in tatters, without shoes or socks,          5
Tired of digging potatoes, and spudding up docks;[2]
And now you've gay bracelets and bright feathers three!"—
"Yes: that's how we dress when we're ruined," said she.

—"At home in the barton[3] you said 'thee' and 'thou,'
And 'thik oon,' and 'theäs oon,' and 't'other'; but now          10

1. Short for Amelia.     2. Spading up weeds.     3. Farmyard.

Your talking quite fits 'ee for high compa-ny!"—
"Some polish is gained with one's ruin," said she.

—"Your hands were like paws then, your face blue and bleak
But now I'm bewitched by your delicate cheek,
15   And your little gloves fit as on any la-dy!"—
"We never do work when we're ruined," said she.

—"You used to call home-life a hag-ridden dream,
And you'd sigh, and you'd sock;[4] but at present you seem
To know not of megrims[5] or melancho-ly!"—
20   "True. One's pretty lively when ruined," said she.

—"I wish I had feathers, a fine sweeping gown,
And a delicate face, and could strut about Town!"—
"My dear—a raw country girl, such as you be,
Cannot quite expect that. You ain't ruined," said she.

1866

The first voice, that of a young woman who has remained back on the farm, is designated typographically (that is, by the way the poem is printed): there are dashes at the beginning and end of each but the first of her speeches. She speaks the first part of each **stanza** (a stanza is a section of a poem designated by spacing), usually the first three lines. The second young woman, a companion and coworker on the farm in years gone by, regularly gets the last line in each stanza (and in the last stanza, two lines), so it is easy to tell who is talking at every point. Also, the two speakers are just as clearly distinguished by what they say, how they say it, and what sort of person each proves to be. The nameless stay-at-home shows little knowledge of the world, and everything surprises her: seeing her former companion at all, but especially seeing her well clothed, cheerful, and polished; and as the poem develops she shows increasing envy of her more worldly friend. She is the "raw country girl" (line 23) that the other speaker says she is, and she still speaks the country dialect ("fits 'ee," line 11, for example) that she notices her friend has lost (lines 9–11). The "ruined" young woman ('Melia), on the other hand, says little except to keep repeating the refrain about having been ruined, but even the slight variations she plays on that theme suggest her sophistication and amusement at her farm friend, although she still uses a rural "ain't" at the end. We are not told the full story of their lives (was the "ruined" young woman thrown out? did she run away from home or work?), but we know enough (that they've been separated for some time, that the stay-at-home did not know where the other had gone) to allow the dialogue to articulate the contrast between them: one is still rural, inexperienced, and innocent; the other is sophisticated, citified, and "ruined." The style of speech of each speaker then does the rest.

It is equally obvious that there is a speaker (or, in this case, actually a singer) in stanzas 2 through 9 of the following poem:

4. Deliver angry blows.   5. Migraine headaches.

X. J. KENNEDY

# In a Prominent Bar in Secaucus One Day

*To the tune of "The Old Orange Flute" or the tune of*
*"Sweet Betsy from Pike"*

In a prominent bar in Secaucus[6] one day
Rose a lady in skunk with a topheavy sway,
Raised a knobby red finger—all turned from their beer—
While with eyes bright as snowcrust she sang high and clear:

"Now who of you'd think from an eyeload of me                      5
That I once was a lady as proud as could be?
Oh I'd never sit down by a tumbledown drunk
If it wasn't, my dears, for the high cost of junk.

"All the gents used to swear that the white of my calf
Beat the down of a swan by a length and a half.                   10
In the kerchief of linen I caught to my nose
Ah, there never fell snot, but a little gold rose.

"I had seven gold teeth and a toothpick of gold.
My Virginia cheroot was a leaf of it rolled
And I'd light it each time with a thousand in cash—               15
Why the bums used to fight if I flicked them an ash.

"Once the toast of the Biltmore,[7] the belle of the Taft,
I would drink bottle beer at the Drake, never draft,
And dine at the Astor on Salisbury steak
With a clean tablecloth for each bite I did take.                 20

"In a car like the Roxy[8] I'd roll to the track,
A steel-guitar trio, a bar in the back,
And the wheels made no noise, they turned over so fast,
Still it took you ten minutes to see me go past.

"When the horses bowed down to me that I might choose,            25
I bet on them all, for I hated to lose.
Now I'm saddled each night for my butter and eggs
And the broken threads race down the backs of my legs.

"Let you hold in mind, girls, that your beauty must pass
Like a lovely white clover that rusts with its grass.            30
Keep your bottoms off barstools and marry you young
Or be left—an old barrel with many a bung.

6. A small town on the Hackensack River in New Jersey, a few miles west of Manhattan.    7. Like the
Taft, Drake, and Astor, a once-fashionable New York hotel.    8. A luxurious old New York theater and
movie house, the site of many "world premieres" in the heyday of Hollywood.

"For when time takes you out for a spin in his car
You'll be hard-pressed to stop him from going too far
35  And be left by the roadside, for all your good deeds,
Two toadstools for tits and a face full of weeds."

All the house raised a cheer, but the man at the bar
Made a phonecall and up pulled a red patrol car
And she blew us a kiss as they copped her away
40  From that prominent bar in Secaucus, N.J.                    1961

Again, we learn about the character primarily through her own words, although we
don't have to believe everything she tells us about her past. From her introduction in the
first stanza we get some general notion of her appearance and condition, but it is she
who tells us that she is a junkie (line 8), a prostitute (line 27), and that her face and figure
have seen better days (lines 32, 36). That information could make her a sad case, and
the poem might lament her state or allow her to lament it, but instead the poem presents
her in a light and friendly way. She is anxious to give advice and sound righteous (line
31, for example), but she's also enormously cheerful about herself, and her spirit repeat-
edly bursts through her song. Her performance gives her a lot of pleasure as she exag-
gerates outrageously about her former luxury and prominence, and even her departure
in a patrol car she chooses to treat as a grand exit, throwing a kiss to her audience. The
comedy is bittersweet, perhaps, but she is allowed to present herself, through her own
words and attitudes, as a likable character—someone who has survived life's disappoint-
ments and retained her dignity and her sense of theatricality. The glorious fiction of her
life, narrated with energy and polish in the manner of a practiced and accomplished liar,
betrays some rather naive notions of good taste and luxurious living (lines 18–26). But
this "lady in skunk" has a picturesque and engaging style, a refreshing sense of humor
about herself, and a flair for drama. Like the cheap fur she wears, her experiences in
what she considers high life satisfy her sense of style and celebration. The self-portrait
accumulates, almost completely through how she talks about herself, and the poet devel-
ops our attitude toward her by allowing her to recount her story herself, in her own
words—or rather in words chosen for her by the author.

The following poem uses the idea of speaker in a very different way and for quite
different tonal purposes:

ADRIENNE RICH

## *Letters in the Family*

I: Catalonia, 1936

Dear Parents:
              I'm the daughter
you didn't bless when she left,

an unmarried woman wearing a khaki knapsack
with a poor mark in Spanish.
                      I'm writing now
from a plaster-dusted desk in a town            5
pocked street by street with hand grenades,
some of them, dear ones, thrown by me.
This is a school: the children are at war.
You don't need honors in schoolroom Spanish here
to be of use and my right arm            10
's as strong as anyone's. I sometimes think
all languages are spoken here,
even mine, which you got zero in.
Don't worry. Don't try to write. I'm happy,
if you could know it.
                    Rochelle.          15

II: Yugoslavia, 1944[9]

Dear Chana,
               where are you now?
Am sending this pocket-to-pocket
(though we both know pockets we'd hate to lie in).
They showed me that poem you gave Reuven,
about the match:            20
Chana, you know, I never was
for martyrdom. I thought we'd try our best,
ragtag mission that we were,
then clear out if the signals looked too bad.
Something in you drives things ahead for me            25
but if I can I mean to stay alive.
We're none of us giants, you know,
just small, frail, inexperienced romantic people.
But there are things we learn.
You know the sudden suck of empty space            30
between the jump and the ripcord pull?
I hate it. I hate it so,
I've hated you for your dropping
ecstatically in free-fall, in the training,
your look, dragged on the ground, of knowing            35
precisely why you were there.
                  My mother's
still in Palestine. And yours

9. "See *Hannah Senesh: Her Life and Diary* (New York: Schocken, 1973). Born in Budapest, 1921, Hannah Senesh became a Zionist and emigrated to Palestine at the age of eighteen; her mother and brother remained in Europe. In 1943, she joined an expedition of Jews who trained under the British to parachute behind Nazi lines in Europe and connect with the partisan underground, to rescue Jews in Hungary, Romania, and Czechoslovakia. She was arrested by the Nazis, imprisoned, tortured, and executed in November 1944. Like the other letter-writers, 'Esther' is an imagined person.

    "See also Ruth Whitman's long poem, *The Testing of Hannah Senesh* (Detroit: Wayne State University Press, 1986)." (AR)

still there in Hungary. Well, there we are.
When this is over—
                        I'm
your earthbound friend to the end, still yours—

40                                                       Esther.

III: Southern Africa, 1986

Dear children:
                        We've been walking nights
a long time over rough terrain,
sometimes through marshes. Days we hide
under what bushes we can find.
45    Our stars steer us. I write
on my knee by a river with a weary hand,
and the weariness will come through
this letter that should tell you
nothing but love. I can't say where we are,
50    what weeds are in bloom, what birds cry at dawn.
The less you know the safer.
But not to know how you are going on—
Matile's earache, Emma's lessons, those tell-tale
eyes and tongues, so quick—are you remembering
55    to be brave and wise and strong?
At the end of this hard road
we'll sit all together at one meal
and I'll tell you everything: the names
of our comrades, how the letters
60    were routed to you, why I left.
And I'll stop and say, "Now you,
grown so big, how was it for you, those times?
Look, I know you in detail, every inch of each
sweet body, haven't I washed and dried you
a thousand times?"
65                        And we'll eat and tell our stories
together. That is my reason.
                        Ma.                                    1989

As in Hardy's "The Ruined Maid," this poem uses different voices, and here they are clearly distinguished as different "historical" characters—Rochelle, Esther, and "Ma," women from three separate places and times who in letter form tell their own stories. In each case, the individual story is part of some larger historical moment, and although all three characters are (as the author's footnote points out) fictional, the three stories together present a kind of history of female heroism in difficult cultural moments.

Try reading the poem aloud so you can hear how different in tone the three voices sound; each woman has distinctive expressions and syntax of her own. All are in part defined by their relationships to families left behind, but all are defined even more fully by their own idealistic determination to resist the larger social and political forces in the cultures where they are at the time they write their letters. Telling stories, the pleasure identified by the third speaker as the ultimate purpose of her actions (lines 56–62), is important to all three speakers as a way of defining themselves in relation to their families; to the poem, the telling of separate stories by the different speakers becomes the collective means to exemplify the power of women in history in action.

Some speakers in poems are not, however, nearly so heroic or attractive, and some poems create a speaker who makes us dislike him or her, also because of what the poet makes him or her say, as the following poem does. Here the speaker, as the title implies, is a monk, but he shows himself to be most unspiritual: mean, self-righteous, and despicable.

# THINKING ABOUT SPEAKER, VOICE, AND PERSPECTIVE: POEMS FOR STUDY

ROBERT BROWNING

## *Soliloquy of the Spanish Cloister*[1]

Gr-r-r—there go, my heart's abhorrence!
　　Water your damned flower-pots, do!
If hate killed men, Brother Lawrence,
　　God's blood, would not mine kill you!
5　What? your myrtle-bush wants trimming?
　　Oh, that rose has prior claims—
Needs its leaden vase filled brimming?
　　Hell dry you up with its flames!

At the meal we sit together:
10　　*Salve tibi!*[2] I must hear
Wish talk of the kind of weather,
　　Sort of season, time of year:
*Not a plenteous cork-crop: scarcely*
　　*Dare we hope oak-galls,*[3] *I doubt:*
15　*What's the Latin name for "parsley"?*
　　What's the Greek name for Swine's Snout?

Whew! We'll have our platter burnished,
　　Laid with care on our own shelf!
With a fire-new spoon we're furnished,
20　　And a goblet for ourself,
Rinsed like something sacrificial
　　Ere 'tis fit to touch our chaps[4]—
Marked with L. for our initial!
　　(He-he! There his lily snaps!)

25　*Saint,* forsooth! While brown Dolores
　　—Squats outside the Convent bank
With Sanchicha, telling stories,
　　Steeping tresses in the tank,
Blue-black, lustrous, thick like horsehairs,
30　　—Can't I see his dead eye glow,
Bright as 'twere a Barbary corsair's?[5]
　　(That is, if he'd let it show!)

---

1. Monastery.    2. "Hail to thee" (Latin). Italics usually indicate the words of Brother Lawrence.    3. Abnormal growth on oak trees, used for tanning.    4. Jaws.    5. African pirate's.

When he finishes refection,[6]
    Knife and fork he never lays
Cross-wise, to my recollection,                                35
    As do I, in Jesu's praise.
I the Trinity illustrate,
    Drinking watered orange-pulp—
In three sips the Arian[7] frustrate;
    —While he drains his at one gulp.                    40

Oh, those melons? If he's able
    We're to have a feast! so nice!
One goes to the Abbot's table,
    All of us get each a slice.
How go on your flowers? None double?                          45
    Not one fruit-sort can you spy?
Strange!—And I, too, at such trouble,
    —Keep them close-nipped on the sly!

There's a great text in Galatians,
    Once you trip on it, entails                           50
Twenty-nine distinct damnations,[8]
    One sure, if another fails:
If I trip him just a-dying,
    Sure of heaven as sure can be,
Spin him round and send him flying                            55
    Off to hell, a Manichee?[9]

Or, my scrofulous French novel
    On gray paper with blunt type!
Simply glance at it, you grovel
    Hand and foot in Belial's gripe:[1]                   60
If I double down its pages
    At the woeful sixteenth print,
When he gathers his greengages,
    Ope a sieve and slip it in't?

Or, there's Satan!—one might venture                          65
    ledge one's soul to him, yet leave
Such a flaw in the indenture
    —As he'd miss till, past retrieve,
Blasted lay that rose-acacia
    We're so proud of! *Hy, Zy, Hine* . . .[2]            70
'St, there's Vespers! *Plena gratiâ*
    *Ave, Virgo.*[3] Gr-r-r—you swine!        1842

---

6. A meal.    7. A heretical sect that denied the Trinity.    8. Galatians 5:15–23 provides a long list of possible offenses, but they do not add up to 29.    9. A heretic. According to the Manichean heresy, the world was divided into the forces of good and evil, equally powerful.    1. In the clutches of Satan.    2. Possibly the beginning of an incantation or curse.    3. The opening words of the *Ave Maria,* here reversed: "Full of grace, Hail, Virgin" (Latin).

Not many poems begin with a growl, and this harsh sound turns out to be fair warning that we are about to get to know a real beast, even though he is in the clothing of a religious man. In line 1, he has already shown himself to hold a most uncharitable attitude toward his fellow monk, Brother Lawrence, and by line 4 he has uttered two profanities and admitted his intense feelings of hatred and vengefulness. His ranting and roaring is full of exclamation points (four in the first stanza!), and he reveals his own personality and character when he imagines curses and unflattering nicknames for Brother Lawrence or plots malicious jokes on him. By the end, we have accumulated no knowledge of Brother Lawrence that makes him seem a fit target for such rage (except that he is pious, dutiful, and pleasant—perhaps enough to make this sort of speaker despise him), but we have discovered the speaker to be lecherous (stanza 4), full of false piety (stanza 5), malicious in trivial matters (stanza 6), ready to use his theological learning to sponsor damnation rather than salvation (stanza 7), a closet reader and viewer of pornography within the monastery (stanza 8)—even willing to risk his own soul in order to torment Brother Lawrence (last stanza).

The speaker is made to characterize himself; the details accrue and accumulate into a fairly full portrait, and here we do not have even an opening and closing "objective" description (as in Kennedy's "In a Prominent Bar") or another speaker (as in Hardy's "The Ruined Maid") to give us perspective. Except for the moments when the speaker mimics or parodies Brother Lawrence (usually in italic type), we have only the speaker's own words and thoughts. But that is enough; the poet has controlled them so carefully that we clearly know what he thinks of the speaker he has created—that he is a mean-spirited, vengeful hypocrite, a thoroughly disreputable and unlikable character. The whole poem has been about him and his attitudes; the point of the poem has been to characterize the speaker and develop in us a dislike of him and what he stands for—total hypocrisy.

In reading a poem like this aloud, we would want our voice to suggest all the unlikable features of a hypocrite. We would also need to suggest, through the tone of voice we used, the author's contemptuous mocking of the rage and hypocrisy, and we would want, like an actor, to create strong disapproval in the hearer. The poem's words (the ones the author has given to the speaker) clearly imply those attitudes, and we would want our voice to express them. Usually there is much more to a poem than the identification and characterization of the speaker, but in many cases it is necessary to identify the speaker and determine his or her character before we can appreciate what else goes on in the poem. And sometimes, as here, in looking for the speaker of the poem, we come near to the center of the poem itself.

Sometimes the effect of a poem depends on our recognizing the temporal position of the speaker as well as her or his identity. The following poem, for example, quickly makes plain that a childhood experience is at the center of the action and that the speaker is female:

TESS GALLAGHER

## Sudden Journey

Maybe I'm seven in the open field—
the straw-grass so high

only the top of my head makes a curve
of brown in the yellow. Rain then.
First a little. A few drops on my                                              5
wrist, the right wrist. More rain.
My shoulders, my chin. Until I'm looking up
to let my eyes take the bliss.
I open my face. Let the teeth show. I
pull my shirt down past the collar-bones.                                     10
I'm still a boy under my breast spots.
I can drink anywhere. The rain. My
skin shattering. Up suddenly, needing
to gulp, turning with my tongue, my arms out
running, running in the hard, cold plenitude                                   15
of all those who reach earth by falling.                            1984

The sense of adventure and wonder here has a lot to do with the childlike sentence structure and choice of words at the beginning of the poem. Sentences are short, observations direct and simple. The rain becomes exciting and blissful and totally absorbing as the child's actions and reactions take over the poem in lines 2–13. But not all of the poem takes place in a child's mind in spite of the precise and impressive re-creation of childish responses and feelings. The opening line makes clear that we are sliding into a supposition of the past; "maybe I'm seven" makes clear that we, as conspiring adults, are pretending ourselves into earlier time. And at the end the word "plenitude"—crucial to interpreting the poem's full effect and meaning—makes clear that we are finding an adult perspective on the incident. Elsewhere, too, the adult world gives the incident meaning. In line 12, for example, the joke about being able to drink anywhere depends on an adult sense of what being a boy might mean. The "journey" of the poem's title is not only the little girl's running in the rain, but also the adult movement into a past re-created and newly understood.

The speaker in the following poem positions herself very differently, but we do not get a full sense of her until the poem is well along. As you read, try to imitate the tone of voice you think this kind of person would use. Exactly when do you begin to feel that you know what she is like?

DOROTHY PARKER

## A Certain Lady

Oh, I can smile for you, and tilt my head,
    And drink your rushing words with eager lips,
And paint my mouth for you a fragrant red,
    And trace your brows with tutored finger-tips.
When you rehearse your list of loves to me,                                    5
    Oh, I can laugh and marvel, rapturous-eyed.
And you laugh back, nor can you ever see

The thousand little deaths my heart has died.
And you believe, so well I know my part,
10      That I am gay as morning, light as snow,
And all the straining things within my heart
        You'll never know.

Oh, I can laugh and listen, when we meet,
        And you bring tales of fresh adventurings—
15  Of ladies delicately indiscreet,
        Of lingering hands, and gently whispered things.
And you are pleased with me, and strive anew
        To sing me sagas of your late delights.
Thus do you want me—marveling, gay, and true—
20      Nor do you see my staring eyes of nights.
And when, in search of novelty, you stray,
        Oh, I can kiss you blithely as you go . . .
And what goes on, my love, while you're away,
        You'll never know.                                    1937

To whom does the speaker seem to be talking? What sort of person is he? How do you feel about him? Which habits and attitudes of his do you like least? How soon can you tell that the speaker is not altogether happy about his conversation and conduct? In what tone of voice would you read the first twenty-two lines aloud? What attitude would you try to express toward the person spoken to? What tone would you use for the last two lines? How would you describe the speaker's personality? What aspects of her behavior are most crucial to the poem's effect?

It is easy to assume that the speaker in a poem is an extension of the poet. Is the speaker in this poem Dorothy Parker? Maybe. A lot of Parker's poems present a similar world-weary posture and a kind of cynicism about romantic love (look, for example, at "Comment" on page 375). But the poem is hardly an example of self-revelation, a giving away of personal secrets. If it were, it would be silly, not to say risky, to address her lover in a way that gives damaging facts about a pose she has been so careful to set up.

In poems such as "The Ruined Maid," "In a Prominent Bar," and "Soliloquy of the Spanish Cloister," we are in no danger of mistaking the speaker for the poet, once we have recognized that poets may create speakers who participate in specific situations much as in fiction or drama. When there is a pointed discrepancy between the speaker and what we know of the poet—when the speaker is a woman, for example, and the poet is a man—we know we have a created speaker to contend with and that the point (or at least *one* point) in the poem is to observe the characterization carefully. In "A Certain Lady" we may be less sure, and in other poems the discrepancy between speaker and poet may be even more uncertain. What are we to make, for example, of the speaker in "Woodchucks" in the previous chapter? Is that speaker the real Maxine Kumin? At best (without knowing something quite specific about the author) we can only say "maybe" to that question. What we can be sure of is the sort of person the speaker is portrayed to be—someone (a man? a woman?) surprised to discover feelings and attitudes that contradict values apparently held confidently. And that is exactly what we need to know for the poem to have its effect.

A similar kind of self-mocking of the speaker is present in the following poem, but here the mockery is put to less revelatory, more comic ends.

A. R. AMMONS

## Needs

I want something suited to my special needs
I want chrome hubcaps, pin-on attachments
and year round use year after year
I want a workhorse with smooth uniform cut,
dozer blade and snow blade & deluxe steering          5
wheel
I want something to mow, throw snow, tow
and sow with
I want precision reel blades
I want a console styled dashboard                      10
I want an easy spintype recoil starter
I want combination bevel and spur gears, 14
gauge stamped steel housing and
washable foam element air cleaner
I want a pivoting front axle and extrawide             15
turf tires
I want an inch of foam rubber inside a vinyl
covering
and especially if it's not too much, if I
can deserve it, even if I can't pay for it             20
I want to mow while riding.                       1970

The poet here may be teasing himself about his desire for comfort and ease—and showing how readily advertisements and catalog descriptions manipulate us. But the speaker doesn't have to be the author for the teasing to work. In fact, the effect is to tease those attitudes no matter who holds them by teasing a speaker who illustrates the attitudes. It doesn't matter to the poem whether the speaker is the poet himself or some totally invented character. If the speaker is a version of the poet himself—perhaps a *side* of his personality that he is exploring—the portrait is still fictional in an important sense. The poem presents not a whole human being (*no* poem could do that) but only a version of him—a mood perhaps, an aspect, an attitude, a part of that person. The poet presents someone with an obsession, in this case a small and not very damaging one, and allows him to spout phrases as if he were reciting from an ad or a sales catalog. The "portrait" is made more comic by a clear sense the poem projects that what we have here is only a part of the person, an interest grown too intense, gone askew, gotten out of proportion, something that happens to most of us from time to time. All we know about the speaker is that he has a one-track mind, that he is obsessed by his own luxurious comfort. He may not even be a "he": there is nothing in the poem that makes us certain that the speaker is male. It is customary to think of the speaker in a poem written by a man as "he" and in a poem written by a woman as "she" (as in Maxine Kumin's "Woodchucks") unless the poem presents contrary evidence; but it is merely a convenience, a habit, nothing more.

Even when poets present themselves as if they were speaking directly to us in their own voices, their poems present only a partial portrait, something considerably less than the full personality and character of the poet. Even when there is not an obviously created character—someone with distinct characteristics that are different from those of the poet—strategies of characterization are used to present the person speaking in one way and not another. Even in a poem like the following one, which contains identifiable autobiographical details, it is still a good idea to talk of the speaker instead of the poet, although here it is probable that the poet is writing about a personal, actual experience, and it is certain that he is making a character of himself—that is, characterizing himself in a certain way, emphasizing some parts of himself and not others.

## WILLIAM WORDSWORTH

## *She Dwelt among the Untrodden Ways*

She dwelt among the untrodden ways
   Beside the springs of Dove,[4]
A Maid whom there were none to praise
   And very few to love:

5   A violet by a mossy stone
     Half hidden from the eye!
—Fair as a star, when only one
   Is shining in the sky.

She lived unknown, and few could know
10    When Lucy ceased to be;
But she is in her grave, and, oh,
   The difference to me!

             1800

It is hard to say whether this poem is more about Lucy or about how the speaker feels about her death. Her simple life, far removed from fame and known only to a few, is said nevertheless to have been beautiful. We know little about her beyond her name and where she lived, in a beautiful but then-isolated section of northern England. We don't know if she was young or old, only that the speaker thinks of her as "fair" and compares her to a "violet by a mossy stone." What we do know is that the speaker is deeply pained by her death, so deeply that he is almost inarticulate with grief, lapsing into simple exclamation ("oh," line 11) and unable to articulate the "difference" that her death makes.

Did Lucy actually live? Was she a friend of the poet? We don't know; the poem doesn't tell us, and even biographers of Wordsworth are unsure. What we do know is that Wordsworth was able to represent grief over the death very powerfully. Whether the speaker is the historical Wordsworth or not, that speaker is a major focus of the poem,

4. A small stream in the Lake District in northern England, near where Wordsworth lived in Dove Cottage at Grasmere.

and it is his feelings that the poem isolates and expresses. We need to recognize some characteristics of the speaker and be sensitive to his feelings for the poem to work.

The following poem similarly seems to draw upon an actual occurrence and to present a speaker who is the poet herself.

### SHARON OLDS

## *The Lifting*

Suddenly my father lifted up his nightie, I
turned my head away but he cried out
*Shar!*, my nickname, so I turned and looked.
He was sitting in the high cranked-up hospital bed with the
gown up, around his neck,                                                       5
to show me the weight he had lost. I looked
where his solid ruddy stomach had been
and I saw the skin fallen into loose
soft hairy rippled folds
lying in a pool of folds                                                        10
down at the base of his abdomen,
the gaunt torso of a big man
who will die soon. Right away
I saw how much his hips are like mine,
the long, white angles, and then                                                15
how much his pelvis is shaped like my daughter's,
a chambered whelk-shell hollowed out,
I saw the folds of skin like something
poured, a thick batter, I saw
his rueful smile, the cast-up eyes as he                                        20
shows me his old body, he knows
I will be interested, he knows I will find him
appealing. If anyone had told me I would sit
by him and he would pull up his nightie and I would look
at him, his naked body, the thick                                               25
bud of his glans, his penis in all that
dark hair, look at him
in affection and uneasy wonder
I would not have believed it. But now I can still
see the tiny snowflakes, white and                                              30
night-blue, on the cotton of the gown as it
rises the way we were promised at death it would rise,
the veils would fall from our eyes, we would know everything.        1990

Other poems by Olds written at about the same time also recount moments in the approaching death of a father—compare, for example, "The Glass" on page 11; and the similar situations may suggest that the poet was herself struggling with such an event; and the nickname in line 3 fits. But even if we were to read enough about the poet's life to be sure that the poem was based on an actual event, we would still have to be careful about assuming that the speaker was, only and simply, the poet herself. It may well be that the "I" in this poem is very close to the historical Sharon Olds in 1990, but we are still well advised as readers to think of the speaker in the poem as the woman characterized specifically in the text and not necessarily as identical to the poet.

The poems we have looked at in this chapter—and the group that follows at the end of the chapter—all suggest the value of beginning the reading of any poem with simple questions: Who is speaking? What do we know about him or her? What kind of person is she or he? Putting together the evidence that the poem presents in answer to such questions can often take us a long way into the poem. For some poems, such questions won't help a great deal because the speaking voice is too indistinct or the character behind the poem too scantily presented. But asking such questions will often lead you toward the central experience the poem offers. At the very least, the question of speaker helps clarify the tone of voice, and it often provides guidance to the larger situation the poem explores.

FRANCES CORNFORD

## The New-Born Baby's Song

When I was twenty inches long,
I could not hear the thrushes' song;
The radiance of morning skies
Was most displeasing to my eyes.

5      For loving looks, caressing words,
I cared no more than sun or birds;
But I could bite my mother's breast,
And that made up for all the rest.

1923

AUDRE LORDE

## Hanging Fire

I am fourteen
and my skin has betrayed me
the boy I cannot live without
still sucks his thumb
5      in secret
how come my knees are
always so ashy
what if I die

before morning
and momma's in the bedroom                                          10
with the door closed.

I have to learn how to dance
in time for the next party
my room is too small for me
suppose I die before graduation                                     15
they will sing sad melodies
but finally
tell the truth about me
There is nothing I want to do
and too much                                                        20
that has to be done
and momma's in the bedroom
with the door closed.

Nobody even stops to think
about my side of it                                                 25
I should have been on Math Team
my marks were better than his
why do I have to be
the one
wearing braces                                                      30
I have nothing to wear tomorrow
will I live long enough
to grow up
and momma's in the bedroom
with the door closed.                                               35

                                                          1978


JOHN BETJEMAN

## *In Westminster Abbey*[5]

Let me take this other glove off
    As the *vox humana*[6] swells,
And the beauteous fields of Eden
    Bask beneath the Abbey bells.
Here, where England's statesmen lie,                                 5
Listen to a lady's cry.

Gracious Lord, oh bomb the Germans.
    Spare their women for Thy Sake,

---

5. Gothic church in London in which English monarchs are crowned and famous Englishmen are buried (see lines 5, 39–40).    6. Organ tones that resemble the human voice.

And if that is not too easy
10      We will pardon Thy Mistake.
But, gracious Lord, whate'er shall be,
Don't let anyone bomb me.

Keep our Empire undismembered
       Guide our Forces by Thy Hand,
15   Gallant blacks from far Jamaica,
       Honduras and Togoland;
Protect them Lord in all their fights,
And, even more, protect the whites.

Think of what our Nation stands for,
20      Books from Boots[7] and country lanes,
Free speech, free passes, class distinction,
       Democracy and proper drains.
Lord, put beneath Thy special care
One-eighty-nine Cadogan Square.[8]

25   Although dear Lord I am a sinner,
       I have done no major crime;
Now I'll come to Evening Service
       Whensoever I have the time.
So, Lord, reserve for me a crown,
30   And do not let my shares go down.

I will labor for Thy Kingdom,
       Help our lads to win the war,
Send white feathers to the cowards[9]
       Join the Women's Army Corps,[1]
35   Then wash the Steps around Thy Throne
In the Eternal Safety Zone.

Now I feel a little better,
       What a treat to hear Thy Word
Where the bones of leading statesmen,
40      Have so often been interred.
And now, dear Lord, I cannot wait
Because I have a luncheon date.                    1940

---

7. A chain of London pharmacies.     8. Presumably where the speaker lives, in a fashionable section of central London.     9. White feathers were sometimes given or sent to men not in uniform to suggest that they were cowards and should join the armed forces.     1. The speaker uses the old World War I name (Women's Army Auxiliary Corps) of the Auxiliary Territorial Service, an organization that performed domestic (and some foreign) defense duties.

HENRY REED

## *Lessons of the War*

Judging Distances

Not only how far away, but the way that you say it
Is very important. Perhaps you may never get
The knack of judging a distance, but at least you know
How to report on a landscape: the central sector,
The right of arc and that, which we had last Tuesday,                    5
    And at least you know

That maps are of time, not place, so far as the army
Happens to be concerned—the reason being,
Is one which need not delay us. Again, you know
There are three kinds of tree, three only, the fir and the poplar,       10
And those which have bushy tops to; and lastly
    That things only seem to be things.

A barn is not called a barn, to put it more plainly,
Or a field in the distance, where sheep may be safely grazing.
You must never be over-sure. You must say, when reporting:               15
At five o'clock in the central sector is a dozen
Of what appear to be animals; whatever you do,
    Don't call the bleeders *sheep.*

I am sure that's quite clear; and suppose, for the sake of example,
The one at the end, asleep, endeavors to tell us                         20
What he sees over there to the west, and how far away,
After first having come to attention. There to the west,
On the fields of summer the sun and the shadows bestow
    Vestments of purple and gold.

The still white dwellings are like a mirage in the heat,                 25
And under the swaying elms a man and a woman
Lie gently together. Which is, perhaps, only to say
That there is a row of houses to the left of arc,
And that under some poplars a pair of what appear to be humans
    Appear to be loving.                                 30

Well that, for an answer, is what we might rightly call
Moderately satisfactory only, the reason being,
Is that two things have been omitted, and those are important.
The human beings, now: in what direction are they,
And how far away, would you say? And do not forget                       35
    There may be dead ground in between.

There may be dead ground in between; and I may not have got
The knack of judging a distance; I will only venture
A guess that perhaps between me and the apparent lovers,
(Who, incidentally, appear by now to have finished,)                     40

At seven o'clock from the houses, is roughly a distance
  Of about one year and a half.                                        1946


GWENDOLYN BROOKS

## We Real Cool

THE POOL PLAYERS,

SEVEN AT THE GOLDEN SHOVEL.

We real cool. We
Left school. We

Lurk late. We
Strike straight. We

5  Sing sin. We
Thin gin. We

Jazz June. We
Die soon.                                                                 1950


SIR THOMAS WYATT

## They Flee from Me

They flee from me, that sometime did me seek,
With naked foot stalking in my chamber.
I have seen them, gentle, tame, and meek,
That now are wild, and do not remember
5  That sometime they put themselves in danger
To take bread at my hand; and now they range,
Busily seeking with a continual change.

Thankéd be Fortune it hath been otherwise,
Twenty times better; but once in special,
10  In thin array, after a pleasant guise,
When her loose gown from her shoulders did fall,
And she me caught in her arms long and small.[2]
And therewith all sweetly did me kiss
And softly said, "Dear heart, how like you this?"

15  It was no dream, I lay broad waking.
But all is turned, thorough[3] my gentleness,

2. Slender.    3. Through.

Into a strange fashion of forsaking;
And I have leave to go, of her goodness,
And she also to use newfangleness.[4]
But since that I so kindely[5] am servéd,                                    20
I fain[6] would know what she hath deservéd.                    1557


AI

## Twenty-year Marriage

You keep me waiting in a truck
with its one good wheel stuck in the ditch,
while you piss against the south side of a tree.
Hurry. I've got nothing on under my skirt tonight.
That still excites you, but this pickup has no windows    5
and the seat, one fake leather thigh,
pressed close to mine is cold.
I'm the same size, shape, make as twenty years ago,
but get inside me, start the engine;
you'll have the strength, the will to move.                  10
I'll pull, you push, we'll tear each other in half.
come on, baby, lay me down on my back.
Pretend you don't owe me a thing
and maybe we'll roll out of here,
leaving the past stacked up behind us;                       15
old newspapers nobody's ever got to read again.     1973


WILLIAM SHAKESPEARE

## [When my love swears that she is made of truth]

When my love swears that she is made of truth,
I do believe her, though I know she lies,
That she might think me some untutored youth,
Unlearnèd in the world's false subtleties.
Thus vainly thinking that she thinks me young,              5
Although she knows my days are past the best,[7]
Simply[8] I credit her false-speaking tongue:
On both sides thus is simple truth suppressed.

---

4. Fondness for novelty.    5. That is, in kind.    6. Eagerly.    7. Shakespeare was thirty-five or younger
when he wrote this sonnet.    8. Like a simpleton.

But wherefore says she not she is unjust?[9]
And wherefore say not I that I am old?
Oh, love's best habit[1] is in seeming trust,
And age in love loves not to have years told.
      Therefore I lie with her and she with me,
      And in our faults by lies we flattered be.

1599

WALT WHITMAN

## [I celebrate myself, and sing myself]

I celebrate myself, and sing myself,
And what I assume you shall assume,
For every atom belonging to me as good belongs to you.

I loafe and invite my soul,
I lean and loafe at my ease observing a spear of summer grass.

My tongue, every atom of my blood, form'd from this soil, this air,
Born here of parents born here from parents the same, and their parents
      the same,
I, now thirty-seven years old in perfect health begin,
Hoping to cease not till death.
Creeds and schools in abeyance,
Retiring back a while sufficed at what they are, but never forgotten,
I harbor for good or bad, I permit to speak at every hazard,
Nature without check with original energy.

1855, 1881

STEPHEN DUNN

## Dancing with God

At first the surprise
of being singled out,
the dance floor crowded
and me not looking my best,
a too-often-worn dress
and the man with me
a budding casualty
of one repetition too much.

9. Unfaithful.    1. Appearance, deportment.

God just touched his shoulder
and he left.                                                    10
Then the confirmation of
an old guess:
God was a wild god,
into the most mindless rock,
but graceful,                                                   15
looking—this excited me—
like no one I could love,
cruel mouth, eyes evocative
of promises unkept.
I never danced better, freer,                                   20
as if dancing were my way
of saying how easily
I could be with him, or apart.
When the music turned slow
God held me close                                               25
and I felt for a moment
I'd mistaken him,
that he was Death
and this the famous embrace
before the lights go out.                                       30
But God kept holding me
and I him
until the band stopped
and I stood looking at a figure
I wanted to slap                                                35
or forgive for something,
I couldn't decide which.
He left then, no thanks,
no sign
that he'd felt anything                                         40
more than an earthly moment
with someone who could've been
anyone on earth.
To this day I don't know why
I thought he was God,                                           45
though it was clear
there was no going back
to the man who brought me,
nice man
with whom I'd slept                                             50
and grown tired,
who danced wrong,
who never again
could do anything right.                        1989

STEVIE SMITH

## *I Remember*

It was my bridal night I remember,
An old man of seventy-three
I lay with my young bride in my arms,
A girl with t.b.
5   It was wartime, and overhead
The Germans were making a particularly heavy raid on Hampstead.
What rendered the confusion worse, perversely
Our bombers had chosen that moment to set out for Germany.
Harry, do they ever collide?
10  I do not think it has ever happened,
Oh my bride, my bride.

                                                                    1957


PAT MORA

## *La Migra*

### I

Let's play *La Migra*[2]
I'll be the Border Patrol.
You be the Mexican maid.
I get the badge and sunglasses.
5   You can hide and run,
but you can't get away
because I have a jeep.
I can take you wherever
I want, but don't ask
10  questions because
I don't speak Spanish.
I can touch you wherever
I want but don't complain
too much because I've got
15  boots and kick—if I have to,
and I have handcuffs.
Oh, and a gun.
Get ready, get set, run.

### II

Let's play *La Migra*
20  You be the Border Patrol.

2. Border patrol agents.

I'll be the Mexican woman.
Your jeep has a flat,
and you have been spotted
by the sun.
All you have is heavy: hat,                                    25
glasses, badge, shoes, gun.
I know this desert,
where to rest,
where to drink.
Oh, I am not alone.                                            30
You hear us singing
and laughing with the wind,
*Agua dulce brota aquí,*
*aquí, aquí,*[3] but since you
can't speak Spanish,                                           35
you do not understand.
Get ready.                                                     1993


SYLVIA PLATH
────────────

# *Mirror*

I am silver and exact. I have no preconceptions.
Whatever I see I swallow immediately
Just as it is, unmisted by love or dislike.
I am not cruel, only truthful—
The eye of a little god, four-cornered.                        5
Most of the time I meditate on the opposite wall.
It is pink, with speckles. I have looked at it so long
I think it is a part of my heart. But it flickers.
Faces and darkness separate us over and over.

Now I am a lake. A woman bends over me,                        10
Searching my reaches for what she really is.
Then she turns to those liars, the candles or the moon.
I see her back, and reflect it faithfully.
She rewards me with tears and an agitation of hands.
I am important to her. She comes and goes.                     15
Each morning it is her face that replaces the darkness.
In me she has drowned a young girl, and in me an old woman
Rises toward her day after day, like a terrible fish.          1961

3. "Sweet water springs here, here, here."

SEAMUS HEANEY

## The Outlaw

Kelly's kept an unlicensed bull, well away
From the road: you risked fine but had to pay

The normal fee if cows were serviced there.
Once I dragged a nervous Friesian on a tether

5   Down a lane of alder, shaggy with catkin,
Down to the shed the bull was kept in.

I gave Old Kelly the clammy silver, though why
I could not guess. He grunted a curt 'Go by

Get up on that gate.' And from my lofty station
10  I watched the business-like conception.

The door, unbolted, whacked back against the wall.
The illegal sire fumbled from his stall

Unhurried as an old steam engine shunting,
He circled, snored and nosed. No hectic panting,

15  Just the unfussy ease of a good tradesman;
Then an awkward, unexpected jump, and

His knobbed forelegs straddling her flank,
He slammed life home, impassive as a tank,

Dropping off like a tipped-up load of sand.
20  'She'll do,' said Kelly and tapped his ash-plant

Across her hindquarters. 'If not, bring her back.'
I walked ahead of her, the rope now slack

While Kelly whooped and prodded his outlaw
Who, in his own time, resumed the dark, the straw.          1969


MARGARET ATWOOD

## Death of a Young Son by Drowning

He, who navigated with success
the dangerous river of his own birth
once more set forth

on a voyage of discovery
5   into the land I floated on
but could not touch to claim.

His feet slid on the bank,
the currents took him;
he swirled with ice and trees in the swollen water

and plunged into distant regions,                                      10
his head a bathysphere;
through his eyes' thin glass bubbles

he looked out, reckless adventurer
on a landscape stranger than Uranus
we have all been to and some remember.                                 15

There was an accident; the air locked,
he was hung in the river like a heart.
They retrieved the swamped body,

cairn of my plans and future charts,
with poles and hooks                                                   20
from among the nudging logs.

It was spring, the sun kept shining, the new grass
leapt to solidity;
my hands glistened with details.

After the long trip I was tired of waves.                              25
My foot hit rock. The dreamed sails
collapsed, ragged.

       I planted him in this country
       like a flag.                                              1970


## SAMUEL TAYLOR COLERIDGE

# *This Lime-Tree Bower My Prison*[4]

Well, they are gone, and here must I remain,
This lime-tree bower my prison! I have lost
Beauties and feelings, such as would have been
Most sweet to my remembrance even when age
Had dimmed mine eyes to blindness! They, meanwhile,          5
Friends, whom I never more may meet again,
On springy[5] heath, along the hilltop edge,
Wander in gladness, and wind down, perchance,
To that still roaring dell, of which I told;
The roaring dell, o'erwooded, narrow, deep,                  10
And only speckled by the midday sun;

4. Coleridge wrote the poem during a visit to his cottage by some friends; an accident on the morning of
their arrival prevented him from accompanying them on walks, during one of which the poem is set.
5. "Elastic, I mean."(STC)

Where its slim trunk the ash from rock to rock
Flings arching like a bridge;—that branchless ash,
Unsunned and damp, whose few poor yellow leaves
15 Ne'er tremble in the gale, yet tremble still,
Fanned by the waterfall! and there my friends
Behold the dark green file of long lank weeds,[6]
That all at once (a most fantastic sight!)
Still nod and drip beneath the dripping edge
Of the blue clay-stone.

20                              Now, my friends emerge
Beneath the wide wide Heaven—and view again
The many-steepled tract magnificent
Of hilly fields and meadows, and the sea,
With some fair bark, perhaps, whose sails light up
25 The slip of smooth clear blue betwixt two Isles
Of purple shadow! Yes! they wander on
In gladness all; but thou, methinks, most glad,
My gentle-hearted Charles![7] for thou hast pined
And hungered after Nature, many a year,
30 In the great City pent,[8] winning thy way
With sad yet patient soul, through evil and pain
And strange calamity! Ah! slowly sink
Behind the western ridge, thou glorious Sun!
Shine in the slant beams of the sinking orb,
35 Ye purple heath-flowers! richlier burn, ye clouds!
Live in the yellow light, ye distant groves!
And kindle, thou blue Ocean! So my friend
Struck with deep joy may stand, as I have stood,
Silent with swimming sense; yea, gazing round
40 On the wide landscape, gaze till all doth seem
Less gross than bodily; and of such hues
As veil the Almighty Spirit, when yet he makes
Spirits perceive his presence.

                         A delight
Comes sudden on my heart, and I am glad
45 As I myself were there! Nor in this bower,
This little lime-tree bower, have I not marked
Much that has soothed me. Pale beneath the blaze
Hung the transparent foliage; and I watched
Some broad and sunny leaf, and loved to see
50 The shadow of the leaf and stem above
Dappling its sunshine! And that walnut-tree
Was richly tinged, and a deep radiance lay
Full on the ancient ivy, which usurps
Those fronting elms, and now, with blackest mass

---

6. Plants usually called adder's tongue or hart's tongue.    7. The poem is addressed to Charles Lamb, one of the visiting friends.    8. Lamb was a clerk at the India House, London.

Makes their dark branches gleam a lighter hue                                      55
Through the late twilight: and though now the bat
Wheels silent by, and not a swallow twitters,
Yet still the solitary humble-bee
Sings in the bean-flower! Henceforth I shall know
That Nature ne'er deserts the wise and pure;                                       60
No plot so narrow, be but Nature there,
No waste so vacant, but may well employ
Each faculty of sense, and keep the heart
Awake to Love and Beauty! and sometimes
'Tis well to be bereft of promised good,                                           65
That we may lift the soul, and contemplate
With lively joy the joys we cannot share.
My gentle-hearted Charles! when the last rook[9]
Beat its straight path along the dusky air
Homewards, I blessed it! deeming its black wing                                    70
(Now a dim speck, now vanishing in light)
Had crossed the mighty orb's dilated glory,
While thou stood'st gazing; or, when all was still,
Flew creeking o'er thy head, and had a charm
For thee, my gentle-hearted Charles, to whom                                       75
No sound is dissonant which tells of Life.                              1797

## QUESTIONS

1. In Reed's "Lessons of the War: Judging Distances," what indicators are there that different voices speak within the poem? Where, exactly, do the changes of speaker take place? How would you characterize each speaker? What words or phrases are especially effective in establishing the different speakers' character and values?
2. What, precisely, do we know about the speaker in Lorde's "Hanging Fire"? How much self-confidence does she have? How can you tell? How does she feel about herself?
3. List all the facts we know about the speaker of Betjeman's "In Westminster Abbey." Which facts are especially important in our view of her? Explain the significance of the poem's setting.
4. Characterize the speaker in Heaney's "The Outlaw." What in particular fascinates him about the breeding operation? What, exactly, does he see? How do the two participants respond to the central event? How do the observers respond? Why does the poem describe the path to Kelly's so fully? Why does the "nervous Friesian" (line 4) have to be dragged? Why is the money paid to Kelly described as "clammy silver" (line 7)? Why does the speaker decide to employ an "unlicensed bull" (line 1)? What or whom does the title of the poem refer to?
5. What kind of journey does the mother make in Atwood's "Death of a Young Son by Drowning"? How are the son's and mother's journeys related? Explain the final image in lines 28–29.

## WRITING SUGGESTIONS

1. In your college library, do some basic research on Westminster Abbey—its location and appearance, its history, its symbolic status in England. Look up some brief summary (an

9. Crow

encyclopedia entry will do) of the effects of World War II on London. Then write a two-page essay on the importance of setting to the tone of "In Westminster Abbey."

2. The speakers in Ammons's "Needs" and Heaney's "The Outlaw" both reveal themselves to have desires and needs that they are not themselves fully conscious of. Analyze carefully just what elements in the poem make clear to us the "secret" aspects of their characters. Compare the character of the speaker (and the strategies used to characterize her) in Maxine Kumin's "Woodchucks" (page 41). Choose either "Needs" or "The Outlaw" to compare in detail with "Woodchucks," and write a short (600- to 700-word) essay in which you characterize the speakers in the two poems, making clear what kind of attitude each poem develops toward its speaker.

3. Analyze carefully the way Plath's "Mirror" is narrated. Evaluate the strategy of using a nonhuman speaker through which to present the words of the poem. Write a brief, two-paragraph account of the poem in which you explain the advantages and disadvantages of its choice of speaker.

# 3

# SITUATION AND SETTING: WHAT HAPPENS? WHERE? WHEN?

Questions about the speaker ("Who" questions) in a poem almost always lead to questions of "Where?" "When?" and "Why?" Identifying the speaker usually is, in fact, part of a larger process of defining the entire imagined **situation** in a poem: What is happening? Where is it happening? Who is the speaker speaking to? Who else is present? Why is this event occurring? In order to understand the dialogue in Hardy's "The Ruined Maid," for example, we need to recognize that the friends are meeting after an extended period of separation, and that they meet in a town setting rather than the rural area in which they grew up together. We infer (from the opening lines) that the meeting is accidental, and that no other friends are present for the conversation. The poem's whole "story" depends on their situation: after leading separate lives for some time they have some catching up to do. We don't know what specific town is involved, or what year, season, or time of day because those details are not important to the poem's effect. But crucial to the poem are the where and when questions that define the situation and relationship of the two speakers, and the answer to the why question—that the meeting is by chance—is important, too. In another poem we looked at in the previous chapter, Parker's "A Certain Lady," the specific moment and place are not important, but we do need to notice that the "lady" is talking to (or having an imaginary conversation with) her lover and that they are talking about a relationship of some duration.

> *It is difficult / to get the news
> from poems / yet men die
> miserably every day / for lack /
> of what is found there.*
>
> —WILLIAM CARLOS WILLIAMS

Sometimes a *specific* time and place (**setting**) may be important. The "lady in skunk" sings her life story "in a prominent bar in Secaucus," a smelly and unfashionable town in New Jersey, but on no particular occasion ("one day"). In "Soliloquy of the Spanish Cloister," the setting (a monastery) adds to the irony because of the gross inappropriateness of such sentiments and attitudes in a supposedly holy place, just as the setting of "In Westminster Abbey" similarly helps us to judge the speaker's ideas, attitudes, and self-conception.

The title of the following poem suggests that place may be important, and it is, although you may be surprised to discover exactly what exists at this address and what uses the speaker makes of it.

JAMES DICKEY

## Cherrylog Road

Off Highway 106
At Cherrylog Road I entered
The '34 Ford without wheels,
Smothered in kudzu,[1]
5    With a seat pulled out to run
Corn whiskey down from the hills,

And then from the other side
Crept into an Essex
With a rumble seat of red leather
10    And then out again, aboard
A blue Chevrolet, releasing
The rust from its other color,

Reared up on three building blocks.
None had the same body heat;
15    I changed with them inward, toward
The weedy heart of the junkyard,
For I knew that Doris Holbrook
Would escape from her father at noon

And would come from the farm
20    To seek parts owned by the sun
Among the abandoned chassis,
Sitting in each in turn
As I did, leaning forward
As in a wild stock-car race

25    In the parking lot of the dead.
Time after time, I climbed in
And out the other side, like
An envoy or movie star
Met at the station by crickets.
30    A radiator cap raised its head,

Become a real toad or a kingsnake
As I neared the hub of the yard,
Passing through many states,
Many lives, to reach
35    Some grandmother's long Pierce-Arrow
Sending platters of blindness forth

From its nickel hubcaps
And spilling its tender upholstery
On sleepy roaches,

---

1. A rapidly growing vine, introduced from Japan to combat erosion but now covering whole fields and groves of trees, especially in the deep South.

The glass panel in between                                      40
Lady and colored driver
Not all the way broken out,

The back-seat phone
Still on its hook.
I got in as though to exclaim,                                   45
"Let us go to the orphan asylum,
John; I have some old toys
For children who say their prayers."

I popped with sweat as I thought
I heard Doris Holbrook scrape                                    50
Like a mouse in the southern-state sun
That was eating the paint in blisters
From a hundred car tops and hoods.
She was tapping like code,

Loosening the screws,                                            55
Carrying off headlights,
Sparkplugs, bumpers,
Cracked mirrors and gear-knobs,
Getting ready, already,
To go back with something to show                                60

Other than her lips' new trembling
I would hold to me soon, soon,
Where I sat in the ripped back seat
Talking over the interphone,
Praying for Doris Holbrook                                       65
To come from her father's farm

And to get back there
With no trace of me on her face
To be seen by her red-haired father
Who would change, in the squalling barn,                        70
Her back's pale skin with a strop,
Then lay for me

In a bootlegger's roasting car
With a string-triggered 12-gauge shotgun
To blast the breath from the air.                                75
Not cut by the jagged windshields,
Through the acres of wrecks she came
With a wrench in her hand,

Through dust where the blacksnake dies
Of boredom, and the beetle knows                                80
The compost has no more life.
Someone outside would have seen
The oldest car's door inexplicably
Close from within:

I held her and held her and held her,                           85
Convoyed at terrific speed

By the stalled, dreaming traffic around us,
So the blacksnake, stiff
With inaction, curved back
90    Into life, and hunted the mouse

With deadly overexcitement,
The beetles reclaimed their field
As we clung, glued together,
With the hooks of the seat springs
95    Working through to catch us red-handed
Amidst the gray breathless batting

That burst from the seat at our backs.
We left by separate doors
Into the changed, other bodies
100    Of cars, she down Cherrylog Road
And I to my motorcycle
Parked like the soul of the junkyard

Restored, a bicycle fleshed
With power, and tore off
105    Up Highway 106, continually
Drunk on the wind in my mouth,
Wringing the handlebar for speed,
Wild to be wreckage forever.                    1964

The *exact* location of the junkyard is not important (there is no Highway 106 near the real Cherrylog Road in North Georgia), but we do need to know that the setting is rural, that the time is summer and that the summer is hot, and that moonshine whiskey is native to the area. Following the story is no problem once we have sorted out these few facts, and we are prepared to meet the cast of characters: Doris Holbrook, her red-haired father, and the speaker. About each we learn just enough to appreciate the sense of vitality, adventure, and power that constitute the major effects of the poem.

The situation of lovemaking in another setting than the junkyard would not produce the same effects, and the exotic sense of a forbidden meeting in this unlikely place helps to re-create the speaker's sense of the episode. For him, it is memorable (notice all the tiny details he remembers), powerful (notice his reaction when he gets back on his motorcycle), dreamlike (notice the sense of time standing still, especially in lines 85–89), and important (notice how the speaker perceives his environment as changed by their lovemaking, lines 88–91 and 98–100). The wealth of details about setting also helps us to raise other, related questions. Why does the speaker fantasize about being shot by the father (lines 72–75)? Why, in a poem so full of details, do we find out so little about what Doris Holbrook looks like? What gives us the sense that this incident is a composite of episodes, an event that was repeated many times? What gives us the impression that the events occurred long ago? What makes the speaker feel so powerful at the end? What does he mean when he talks of himself as being "wild to be wreckage forever"? All of the poem's attention to the speaker's reactions, reflections, and memories is intricately tied up with the particulars of setting. Making love in a junkyard is crucial to the speaker's sense of both power and wreckage, and to him Doris is merely a matter of excitement, adventure, and pale skin, appreciated because she makes the world seem different and because she is willing to take risks and to suffer for meeting him like this. The more we probe the poem with questions about situation, the more likely we are to catch the poem's full effect.

The plot of "Cherrylog Road" is fairly easy to sort out, but its effect is more complex than the simple story suggests. The next poem we will look at is, at first glance, much more difficult to follow. Part of the difficulty is that the poem is from an earlier age and its language and sentence structure may seem a bit unfamiliar, and part is because the action in the poem is so closely connected to what is being said. But its opening lines— addressed to someone who is resisting the speaker's suggestions—disclose the situation, and gradually we can figure out the scene: a man is trying to convince a woman that they should make love. When a flea happens by, the speaker uses it for an unlikely example; it becomes part of his argument. And once we recognize the situation, we can readily follow (and be amused by) the speaker's witty and intricate argument.

## JOHN DONNE

### The Flea

Mark but this flea, and mark in this[2]
How little that which thou deny'st me is;
It sucked me first, and now sucks thee,
And in this flea our two bloods mingled be;
Thou know'st that this cannot be said                     5
A sin, nor shame, nor loss of maidenhead.
   Yet this enjoys before it woo,
   And pampered[3] swells with one blood made of two,
   And this, alas, is more than we would do.[4]

Oh stay, three lives in one flea spare,                    10
Where we almost, yea more than, married are.
This flea is you and I, and this
Our marriage bed, and marriage temple is;
Though parents grudge, and you, we're met
And cloistered in these living walls of jet.               15
   Though use[5] make you apt to kill me,
   Let not to that, self-murder added be,
   And sacrilege, three sins in killing three.

Cruel and sudden, hast thou since
Purpled thy nail in blood of innocence?                    20
Wherein could this flea guilty be,
Except in that drop which it sucked from thee?
Yet thou triumph'st, and say'st that thou

2. Medieval preachers and rhetoricians asked their hearers to "mark" (look at) an object that illustrated a moral or philosophical lesson they wished to emphasize.    3. Fed luxuriously.    4. According to contemporary medical theory, conception involved the literal mingling of the lovers' blood.    5. Habit.

Find'st not thyself, nor me, the weaker now;
'Tis true; then learn how false, fears be;
Just so much honor, when thou yield'st to me,
Will waste, as this flea's death took life from thee.

25

1633

The scene in "The Flea" develops almost as it would in the theater. Action occurs even as the poem is being written. Between stanzas 1 and 2, the woman makes a move to kill the flea (as stanza 2 opens, the speaker is trying to stop her), and between stanzas 2 and 3 she has squashed the flea with her fingernail. Once we make sense of what the speaker says, the action is just as clear from the words as if we had stage directions in the margin. All of the speaker's verbal cleverness and all of his specious arguments follow from the situation, and in this poem (as in Browning's "Soliloquy of the Spanish Cloister" or Betjeman's "In Westminster Abbey") we watch as if we were observing a scene in a play. The speaker is, in effect, giving a dramatic monologue for our benefit.

Neither time nor place is important to "The Flea," except that the speaker and his friend must be assumed to be in the same place and to have the leisure for some playfulness. The situation could occur anywhere a man, a woman, and a flea could be together: indoors, outdoors, morning, evening, city, country, in cottage or palace, on a boat or in a bedroom. We do know, from the date of publication of the poem (1633), that the poet, Donne, was writing about people of almost four centuries ago, but the conduct he describes might equally happen in later ages. Only the habits of language (and perhaps the speaker's religious attitudes) date the poem; the situation could just as easily be set in any age or place.

The two poems that follow have simpler plots, but in each case the heart of the poem is in the basic situation:

RITA DOVE

## Daystar

She wanted a little room for thinking:
but she saw diapers steaming on the line,
a doll slumped behind the door.

So she lugged a chair behind the garage
to sit out the children's naps.

5

Sometimes there were things to watch—
the pinched armor of a vanished cricket,
a floating maple leaf. Other days
she stared until she was assured
when she closed her eyes
she'd see only her own vivid blood.

10

She had an hour, at best, before Liza appeared
pouting from the top of the stairs.

And just *what* was mother doing
out back with the field mice? Why,                                    15

building a palace. Later
that night when Thomas rolled over and
lurched into her, she would open her eyes
and think of the place that was hers
for an hour—where                                                     20
she was nothing,
pure nothing, in the middle of the day.                    1986


LINDA PASTAN

## To a Daughter Leaving Home

When I taught you
at eight to ride
a bicycle, loping along
beside you
as you wobbled away                                                   5
on two round wheels,
my own mouth rounding
in surprise when you pulled
ahead down the curved
path of the park,                                                     10
I kept waiting
for the thud
of your crash as I
sprinted to catch up,
while you grew                                                        15
smaller, more breakable
with distance,
pumping, pumping
for your life, screaming
with laughter,                                                        20
the hair flapping
behind you like a
handkerchief waving
goodbye.                                                     1988


   Both these poems involve motherhood, but they take entirely different stances about it and have very different tones. The mother in Dove's "Daystar" is overwhelmed by the demands of young children and needs a room of her own. All she can manage, however, is a brief hour in a chair behind the garage. The situation is virtually the whole story here. Nothing really happens except that daily events (washing diapers, picking up toys, looking at crickets and leaves, explaining the world to children, having sex) crowd her brief private hour and make it precious. Being "nothing" (lines 21 and 22) takes on great value in these circumstances, and the poem makes much of the setting: an isolated chair behind the garage. Setting in poems often means something much more specific about a particular culture or social history, but here time and place are given value by the circumstances of the situation for one frazzled mother.

The particulars of time and place in Pastan's "To a Daughter Leaving Home" are even less specific, but the incident the poem describes happened a long time ago, and it is important to notice that its vividness in the poem is a function of memory. The mother is the speaker here, and we are told very little about her, at least directly. But she is thinking back nostalgically to a moment long ago when her daughter made an earlier (but briefer) departure from home, and the poem implies the occasion for her doing so. The daughter now is old enough to "leave" home in a full sense; the poem does not tell us why or what the present circumstances are, but the title tells us the situation. We may infer quite a bit about the speaker here—her affection for the daughter, the kind of mother she has been, her anxiety at the new departure that seems to reflect the earlier wobbly ride into the distance—but as in "Daystar" the poem is all situation. There are almost no details of present action, and we have no specific information about place or time for either the remembered event or the present one.

> *A poem . . . begins as a lump*
> *in the throat, a sense of wrong,*
> *a homesickness, a lovesickness.*
> *. . . It finds the thought and the*
> *thought finds the words.*
>
> —ROBERT FROST

Some poems, however, depend heavily on historical specifics and a knowledge of actual places and events. The following poem, for example, depends not only on knowing some facts about a particular event but on the parallels between that event and circumstances surrounding the poet and his immediate readers.

## JOHN MILTON

### *On the Late Massacre in Piedmont*

Avenge, O Lord, thy slaughtered saints, whose bones
   Lie scattered on the Alpine mountains cold;
   Even them who kept thy truth so pure of old
   When all our fathers worshiped stocks and stones,
5 Forget not: in thy book record their groans
   Who were thy sheep and in their ancient fold
   Slain by the bloody Piemontese that rolled
   Mother with infant down the rocks. Their moans
The vales redoubled to the hills, and they
10    To heaven. Their martyred blood and ashes sow
   O'er all th' Italian fields, where still doth sway
The triple tyrant:[6] that from these may grow

6. The Pope's tiara featured three crowns.

A hundredfold, who having learnt thy way
Early may fly the Babylonian woe.[7]

1655

The "slaughtered saints" were members of the Waldensians—a heretical sect that had long been settled in southern France and northern Italy (the Piedmont). Though a minority, the Waldensians were allowed freedom of worship until 1655, when their protection under the law was taken away and locals attacked them, killing large numbers. This poem, then, is not a private meditation, but rather a public statement about a well-known "news" event. The reader, to fully understand the poem and respond to it meaningfully, must therefore be acquainted with its historical context, including the massacre itself and the significance it had for Milton and his English audience.

Milton wrote the poem shortly after the Piedmont massacre of 1655 became known in England, and implicit in its "meaning" is a parallel Milton's readers would have felt between the events in the Piedmont and current English politics. Milton signals the analogy early on by calling the dead Piedmontese "saints," the term then regularly used by English Protestants of the Puritan stamp to describe themselves and to thereby assert their belief that every individual Christian—not just those few "special" religious heroes singled out in the Catholic tradition—lived a heroic life. By identifying the Waldensians with the English Puritans—their beliefs were in some ways quite similar, and both were minorities in a larger political and cultural context—Milton was warning his fellow Puritans that, if the Stuart monarchy were reestablished, what had just happened to the Waldensians could happen to them as well. Following the Restoration in 1660, tight restrictions were in fact placed on the Puritan "sects" under the new monarchy. In lines 12 and 14, the poem alludes to dangers of religious rule by dominant groups by invoking standard images of Catholic power and persecution; the heir to the English throne (who succeeded to the throne as Charles II in 1660) was spending his exile in Catholic Europe and was, because of his sympathetic treatment of Catholic associates and friends, thought perhaps to be himself a Catholic. Chauvinistic Englishmen, who promoted rivalries with Catholic powers like France, considered him a traitor.

Many poems, like this one, make use of historical occurrences and situations to create a widely evocative set of angers, sympathies, and conclusions. Sometimes a poet's intention in recording a particular moment or event is to commemorate it or comment upon it. A poem written about a specific occasion is usually called an **occasional poem,** and such a poem is **referential;** that is, it *refers* to a certain historical time or event. Sometimes, it is hard to place ourselves fully enough in another time or place to imagine sympathetically what a particular historical moment would have been like, and even the best poetic efforts do not necessarily transport us there. For such poems we need, at the least, specific historical information—plus a willingness on our part as readers to be transported, by a name, a date, or a dramatic situation.

Time or place may, of course, be used much less specifically and still be important to a poem; frequently a poem's setting draws upon common notions of a particular time or place. Setting a poem in a garden, for example, or writing about apples almost inevitably reminds many readers of the Garden of Eden because it is part of the Western heritage

---

7. In Milton's day, Protestants often likened the Roman Church to Babylonian decadence, called the church "the whore of Babylon," and read Revelation 17 and 18 as an allegory of its coming destruction.

of belief or knowledge. Even people who don't read at all or who lack Judeo-Christian religious commitments are likely to know about Eden, and a poet writing in our culture can count on that. An **allusion** is a reference to something outside the poem that carries a history of meaning and strong emotional associations. (There's a longer account of allusion in Chapter 23.) For example, gardens may carry suggestions of innocence and order, or temptation and the Fall, or both, depending on how the poem handles the allusion. Well-known places from history or myth may be popularly associated with particular ideas or values or ways of life.

The place involved in a poem is its **spatial setting,** and the time is its **temporal setting.** The temporal setting may involve a specific date or an era, a season of the year or a time of day. We tend, for example, to think of spring as a time of discovery and growth, and poems set in spring are likely to make use of that association; morning usually suggests discovery as well—beginnings, vitality, the world fresh and new—even to those of us who in reality take our waking slow. Temporal or spatial setting is often used to influence our expectation of theme and tone, although the poet may then go on to surprise us by making something very different of our expectation. Setting is often an important factor in creating the mood in poems just as in stories, plays, or films. Often the details of setting have a lot to do with the way we ultimately respond to the poem's subject or theme, as in this poem:

SYLVIA PLATH

## Point Shirley

From Water-Tower Hill to the brick prison
The shingle booms, bickering under
The sea's collapse.
Snowcakes break and welter. This year
5    The gritted wave leaps
The seawall and drops onto a bier
Of quahog chips,[8]
Leaving a salty mash of ice to whiten

In my grandmother's sand yard. She is dead,
10    Whose laundry snapped and froze here, who
Kept house against
What the sluttish, rutted sea could do.
Squall waves once danced
Ship timbers in through the cellar window;
15    A thresh-tailed, lanced
Shark littered in the geranium bed—

Such collusion of mulish elements
She wore her broom straws to the nub.
Twenty years out

8. Chips from quahog clam shells, common on the New England coast.

Of her hand; the house still hugs in each drab        20
Stucco socket
The purple egg-stones: from Great Head's knob
To the filled-in Gut
The sea in its cold gizzard ground those rounds.

Nobody wintering now behind        25
The planked-up windows where she set
Her wheat loaves
And apple cakes to cool. What is it
Survives, grieves
So, over this battered, obstinate spit        30
Of gravel? The waves'
Spewed relics clicker masses in the wind,

Gray waves the stub-necked eiders ride.
A labor of love, and that labor lost.
Steadily the sea        35
Eats at Point Shirley. She died blessed,
And I come by
Bones, bones only, pawed and tossed,
A dog-faced sea.
The sun sinks under Boston, bloody red.        40

I would get from these dry-papped stones
The milk your love instilled in them.
The black ducks dive.
And though your graciousness might stream,
And I contrive,        45
Grandmother, stones are nothing of home
To that spumiest dove.
Against both bar and tower the black sea runs.        1960

One does not have to know the New England coast by personal experience to find it vividly re-created in Plath's poem. A reader who knows that coast or another like it may have an advantage in being able to respond more quickly to the poem's precision of description, but the poem does not depend on the reader's having such knowledge. The exact location of Point Shirley, near Boston, is not especially important, but visualization of the setting is. Crucial to the poem's tone and mood is the sense of the sea as aggressor, a force powerful enough to change the contours of the coast and invade the privacy of yards and homes. The energy, relentlessness, and impersonality of the sea met their match, though only temporarily, in the speaker's grandmother, who "[k]ept house against/ What the sluttish, rutted sea could do" (lines 11–12). The grandmother *belonged* in this setting, and it seemed hers, but twenty years of her absence (since her death) now begin to show. Still, the marks of her obstinacy and love are there, although ultimately doomed by the sea's more enduring power.

Details—and how they are amassed—are important here rather than historic particulars of time and place. The grays and whites and drab colors of the sea and its leavings provide both a visual sense of the scene and the mood for the poem. The stubbornness that the speaker admired in the grandmother comes to seem a part of that tenacious grayness. Nothing happens rapidly here; things wear down. Even the "bloody red" (line 40) of the sun's setting—an ominous sign that adds a vivid fright to the dullness rather than brightening it—makes promises that seem slow and long-term. The toughness of the boarded-up house is a monument to the grandmother's loving care and becomes a way for the speaker to touch her human spirit, but the poem's final emphasis is on the relentless black sea, which continues to run against the landmarks and fortresses that had been identified with the setting in the very first line.

Queries about situation and setting begin as simple questions of identification but frequently become more complex when we sort out all the implications. Often it takes only a moment to determine a poem's situation, but it may take much longer to discover all of the things that time and place imply, for their meanings may depend upon visual details, or upon actual historical occurrences, or upon habitual ways of thinking about certain times and places—or all three at once. As you read the following poem, notice how the setting—another shore—prepares us for the speaker's moods and ideas, and then watch how the movement of his mind is affected by what he sees.

MATTHEW ARNOLD

## Dover Beach[9]

The sea is calm tonight.
The tide is full, the moon lies fair
Upon the straits; on the French coast the light
Gleams and is gone; the cliffs of England stand,
5    Glimmering and vast, out in the tranquil bay.
Come to the window, sweet is the night-air!
Only, from the long line of spray
Where the sea meets the moon-blanched land,
Listen! you hear the grating roar
10   Of pebbles which the waves draw back, and fling,
At their return, up the high strand,
Begin, and cease, and then again begin,
With tremulous cadence slow, and bring
The eternal note of sadness in.

15   Sophocles long ago
Heard it on the Aegean, and it brought
Into his mind the turbid ebb and flow
Of human misery;[1] we
Find also in the sound a thought,
20   Hearing it by this distant northern sea.

The Sea of Faith
Was once, too, at the full, and round earth's shore

9. At the narrowest point on the English Channel. The light on the French coast (lines 3–4) would be about twenty miles away.   1. In *Antigone*, lines 637–46, the chorus compares the fate of the house of Oedipus to the waves of the sea.

Lay like the folds of a bright girdle furled.
But now I only hear
Its melancholy, long, withdrawing roar,    *onomatopoeia*           25
Retreating, to the breath
Of the night-wind, down the vast edges drear
And naked shingles[2] of the world.

Ah, love, let us be true
To one another! for the world, which seems                   30
To lie before us like a land of dreams,
So various, so beautiful, so new,
Hath really neither joy, nor love, nor light,
Nor certitude, nor peace, nor help for pain;
And we are here as on a darkling plain                      35
Swept with confused alarms of struggle and flight,
Where ignorant armies clash by night.

ca. 1851

Exactly what is the dramatic situation in "Dover Beach"? How soon are you aware that someone is being spoken to? How much are we told about the person spoken to? How would you describe the speaker's mood? What does the speaker's mood have to do with time and place? Do any details of present place and time help to account for his tendency to talk repeatedly of the past and the future? How important is it to the poem's total effect that the beach here involves an international border? What particulars of the Dover Beach seem especially important to the poem's themes? to its emotional effects?

Not all poems have an identifiable situation or setting, just as not all poems have a speaker who is entirely distinct from the author. Poems that simply present a series of thoughts and feelings directly, in a contemplative, meditative, or reflective way, may not set up any kind of action, plot, or situation at all, preferring to speak directly without the intermediary of a dramatic device. But most poems depend crucially upon a sense of place, a sense of time, and an understanding of human interaction in scenes that resemble the strategies of drama or film. And questions about these matters will often lead you to define not only the "facts," but also the feelings central to the design a poem has upon us.

2. Pebble-strewn beaches.

## SITUATIONS

JAROLD RAMSEY

### *Hunting Arrowheads*

Under the throbbing power lines, whose steel towers
stalk the ridge like servile dinosaurs in traces,
I find a perfect arrowhead—obsidian,
a deadly leaf, whose shaping branch was a human hand.
5   They say in many tribes the blind were specialists
at knapping tools, and as I lick the stone and taste
the mineral centuries beyond its single flight
I picture a man, led out to a boulder by a child,
a man with the milky eyes of trachoma, who turns with the sun
10   all day as his hands, busy with deerhorn flaker and rawhide,
empower the brittle stone to fly true and kill.
He sings, endlessly, *ya-ta-ta*
                    *ya-ta-ta*
                          *ya-ta-ta*
and the ring of subtracted flakes around him grows, as he dreams
of the hunt to which his flawless weapons go.

15   I sometimes think my true calling is finding arrowheads—
like Thoreau, I seem to have a knack, the mind aimless
and alert, the cricket heart easy in the harmlessness
of the search—like poetry, perhaps. *We are injurious*
*to no one, doing our things,* I hear New America
20   singing its anthem—but neither do we help, do we?
Do I? What's incumbent on me way up here?
Without a memory, cicadas sing all day.
Brother, were you there when they crucified
our neighbor? Was I there when they took him from the street?
25   Because we die we must be sorry for each other;
we must help each other; by throngs our human hearts are tried.

Shattered glass gleams on the sidewalks, on the streets.
Is the pattern of our lives to be read there, then,
where we live, a great desultory flaking
30   from some ultimate crystal? In the city, the senses
jangle, they turn away, grudge us the physical world.
It is a terrible price to pay. Once, after a summer
in these hills, I found my children in a parking lot,
under a web of power lines, searching for arrowheads in the gravel.

1989

MARGARET ATWOOD

## *Siren Song*

This is the one song everyone
would like to learn: the song
that is irresistible:

the song that forces men
to leap overboard in squadrons                    5
even though they see the beached skulls

the song nobody knows
because anyone who has heard it
is dead, and the others can't remember.

Shall I tell you the secret                        10
and if I do, will you get me
out of this bird suit?

I don't enjoy it here
squatting on this island
looking picturesque and mythical                   15

with these two feathery maniacs,
I don't enjoy singing
this trio, fatal and valuable.

I will tell the secret to you,
to you, only to you.                               20
Come closer. This song

is a cry for help: Help me!
Only you, only you can,
you are unique

at last. Alas                                      25
it is a boring song
but it works every time.                    1974


ANDREW MARVELL

## *To His Coy Mistress*

   Had we but world enough, and time,
This coyness,[3] lady, were no crime.
We would sit down, and think which way

---

3. Hesitancy, modesty (not necessarily suggesting calculation).

To walk, and pass our long love's day.
Thou by the Indian Ganges' side
Shouldst rubies[4] find; I by the tide
Of Humber[5] would complain. I would
Love you ten years before the Flood,
And you should if you please refuse
Till the conversion of the Jews.[6]
My vegetable love[7] should grow
Vaster than empires, and more slow;
An hundred years should go to praise
Thine eyes, and on thy forehead gaze;
Two hundred to adore each breast,
But thirty thousand to the rest.
An age at least to every part,
And the last age should show your heart.
For, lady, you deserve this state;[8]
Nor would I love at lower rate.
    But at my back I always hear
Time's wingéd chariot hurrying near;
And yonder all before us lie
Deserts of vast eternity.
Thy beauty shall no more be found,
Nor, in thy marble vault, shall sound
My echoing song; then worms shall try
That long preserved virginity,
And your quaint honor turn to dust,
And into ashes all my lust:
The grave's a fine and private place,
But none, I think, do there embrace.
    Now therefore, while the youthful hue
Sits on thy skin like morning dew,[9]
And while thy willing soul transpires[1]
At every pore with instant fires,
Now let us sport us while we may,
And now, like am'rous birds of prey,
Rather at once our time devour
Than languish in his slow-chapped[2] pow'r.
Let us roll all our strength and all
Our sweetness up into one ball,
And tear our pleasures with rough strife
Thorough[3] the iron gates of life.

---

4. Talismans that are supposed to preserve virginity.    5. A small river that flows through Marvell's hometown of Hull. *Complain*: write love complaints, conventional songs lamenting the cruelty of love.    6. Which, according to popular Christian belief, will occur just before the end of the world.    7. Which is capable only of passive growth, not of consciousness. The "vegetable soul" is lower than the other two divisions of the soul, "animal" and "rational."    8. Dignity.    9. The text reads "glew." "Lew" (warmth) has also been suggested as an emendation.    1. Breathes forth.    2. Slow-jawed. Chronos (Time), ruler of the world in early Greek myth, devoured all of his children except Zeus, who was hidden. Later, Zeus seized power (see line 46 and note).    3. Through.

Thus, though we cannot make our sun  ⌐|
Stand still,[4] yet we will make him run.[5]  ⌐⌐ ›                                45

1681

MARY OLIVER

## *Singapore*

In Singapore, in the airport,
a darkness was ripped from my eyes.
In the women's restroom, one compartment stood open.
A woman knelt there, washing something
    in the white bowl.                                                        5

Disgust argued in my stomach
and I felt, in my pocket, for my ticket.

A poem should always have birds in it.
Kingfishers, say, with their bold eyes and gaudy wings.
Rivers are pleasant, and of course trees.                                    10
A waterfall, or if that's not possible, a fountain
    rising and falling.
A person wants to stand in a happy place, in a poem.

When the woman turned I could not answer her face.
Her beauty and her embarrassment struggled together, and        15
    neither could win.
She smiled and I smiled. What kind of nonsense is this?
Everybody needs a job.

Yes, a person wants to stand in a happy place, in a poem.
But first we must watch her as she stares down at her labor,         20
    which is dull enough.
She is washing the tops of the airport ashtrays, as big as
    hubcaps, with a blue rag.
Her small hands turn the metal, scrubbing and rinsing.
She does not work slowly, nor quickly, but like a river.                25
Her dark hair is like the wing of a bird.

I don't doubt for a moment that she loves her life.
And I want her to rise up from the crust and the slop
    and fly down to the river.
This probably won't happen.                                                  30
But maybe it will.
If the world were only pain and logic, who would want it?

Of course, it isn't.
Neither do I mean anything miraculous, but only

4. To lengthen his night of love with Alcmene, Zeus made the sun stand still.     5. Each sex act was
believed to shorten life by one day.

35   the light that can shine out of a life. I mean
the way she unfolded and refolded the blue cloth,
the way her smile was only for my sake; I mean
the way this poem is filled with trees, and birds.                    1990


## LOUISE GLÜCK

### Labor Day

Requiring something lovely on his arm
Took me to Stamford, Connecticut, a quasi-farm,
His family's; later picking up the mammoth
Girlfriend of Charlie, meanwhile trying to pawn me off
5   On some third guy also up for the weekend.
But Saturday we still were paired; spent
It sprawled across that sprawling acreage
Until the grass grew limp
With damp. Like me. Johnston-baby, I can still see
10   The pelted clover, burrs' prickle fur and gorged
Pastures spewing infinite tiny bells. You pimp.                       1969


## RICHARD SNYDER

### A Mongoloid Child Handling Shells on the Beach

She turns them over in her slow hands,
as did the sea sending them to her;
broken bits from the mazarine maze,
they are the calmest things on this sand.
5   The unbroken children splash and shout,
rough as surf, gay as their nesting towels.
But she plays soberly with the sea's
small change and hums back to it its slow vowels.                     1971


## MARY KARR

### Hubris

The man in the next office
was born a dwarf.

Mornings, when we wait
for the elevator, he quotes Whitman,
while I shamelessly covet                                                    5
his gray baseball jacket.
Maybe he doesn't mean
to be a figure of courage
with his cane and his corkscrew knee,
this smart man who can't reach                                              10
some sinks. No doubt he'd like
to take the stairs like me,
two at a pop. Instead,
as the elevator numbers fail
to fall to us fast enough,                                                  15
he waves me on—*It'll come
eventually,* he says with cheer.
He grows ever smaller
in the stairwell. I ascend.                                    p. 1996

JOHN DONNE

## *The Sun Rising*

Busy old fool, unruly sun,
Why dost thou thus,
Through windows, and through curtains, call on us?
Must to thy motions lovers' seasons run?
Saucy pedantic wretch, go chide                               5
Late schoolboys, and sour prentices,[6]
Go tell court-huntsmen that the king will ride,
Call country ants[7] to harvest offices;
Love, all alike, no season knows, nor clime,
Nor hours, days, months, which are the rags of time.         10

Thy beams, so reverend and strong
Why shouldst thou think?
I could eclipse and cloud them with a wink,
But that I would not lose her sight so long:
If her eyes have not blinded thine,                          15
Look, and tomorrow late, tell me
Whether both the Indias[8] of spice and mine
Be where thou left'st them, or lie here with me.
Ask for those kings whom thou saw'st yesterday,
And thou shalt hear, all here in one bed lay.               20

6. Apprentices.    7. Farmworkers.    8. The East and West Indies, commercial sources of spices and gold.

She is all states, and all princes I,
        Nothing else is.
Princes do but play us; compared to this,
All honor's mimic, all wealth alchemy.[9]
25              Thou, sun, art half as happy as we,
            In that the world's contracted thus;
        Thine age asks[1] ease, and since thy duties be
        To warm the world, that's done in warming us.
Shine here to us, and thou art every where;
30  This bed thy center[2] is, these walls thy sphere.                    1633


HART CRANE

## *Episode of Hands*

The unexpected interest made him flush.
Suddenly he seemed to forget the pain,—
Consented,—and held out
One finger from the others.

5   The gash was bleeding, and a shaft of sun
That glittered in and out among the wheels,
Fell lightly, warmly, down into the wound.

And as the fingers of the factory owner's son,
That knew a grip for books and tennis
10  As well as one for iron and leather,—
As his taut, spare fingers wound the gauze
Around the thick bed of the wound,
His own hands seemed to him
Like wings of butterflies
15  Flickering in sunlight over summer fields.

The knots and notches,—many in the wide
Deep hand that lay in his,—seemed beautiful.
They were like the marks of wild ponies' play,—
Bunches of new green breaking a hard turf.

20  And factory sounds and factory thoughts
Were banished from him by that larger, quieter hand
That lay in his with the sun upon it.
And as the bandage knot was tightened
The two men smiled into each other's eyes.

1920

9. Imposture, like the "scientific" procedures for turning base metals into gold. *Mimic:* hypocritical.
1. Requires.    2. Of orbit.

DOROTHY LIVESAY

## Green Rain

I remember long veils of green rain
Feathered like the shawl of my grandmother—
Green from the half-green of the spring trees
Waving in the valley.

I remember the road                                                    5
Like the one which leads to my grandmother's house,
A warm house, with green carpets,
Geraniums, a trilling canary
And shining horse-hair chairs;
And the silence, full of the rain's falling                            10
Was like my grandmother's parlor
Alive with herself and her voice, rising and falling—
Rain and wind intermingled.

I remember on that day
I was thinking only of my love                                         15
And of my love's house.
But now I remember the day
As I remember my grandmother.
I remember the rain as the feathery fringe of her shawl.        p. 1929


EMILY BRONTË

## The Night-Wind

In summer's mellow midnight,
A cloudless moon shone through
Our open parlor window
And rosetrees wet with dew.

I sat in silent musing,                                                5
The soft wind waved my hair:
It told me Heaven was glorious,
And sleeping Earth was fair.

I needed not its breathing
To bring such thoughts to me,                                          10
But still it whispered lowly,
"How dark the woods will be!

"The thick leaves in my murmur
Are rustling like a dream,

15      And all their myriad voices
        Instinct³ with spirit seem."

        I said, "Go, gentle singer,
        Thy wooing voice is kind,
        But do not think its music
20      Has power to reach my mind.

        "Play with the scented flower,
        The young tree's supple bough,
        And leave my human feelings
        In their own course to flow."

25      The wanderer would not leave me;
        Its kiss grew warmer still—
        "O come," it sighed so sweetly,
        "I'll win thee 'gainst thy will.

        "Have we not been from childhood friends?
30      Have I not loved thee long?
        As long as thou hast loved the night
        Whose silence wakes my song.

        "And when thy heart is laid at rest
        Beneath the church-yard stone
35      I shall have time enough to mourn
        And thou to be alone."

    September 11, 1840

3. Infused.

# TIMES

WILLIAM SHAKESPEARE

## [*Full many a glorious morning have I seen*]

Full many a glorious morning have I seen
Flatter the mountain-tops with sovereign eye,
Kissing with golden face the meadows green,
Gilding pale streams with heavenly alchymy;
Anon permit the basest clouds to ride                        5
With ugly rack[4] on his celestial face,
And from the forlorn world his visage hide,
Stealing unseen to west with this disgrace:
Even so my sun one early morn did shine,
With all-triumphant splendor on my brow;                    10
But, out! alack! he was but one hour mine,
The region cloud hath mask'd him from me now.
   Yet him for this my love no whit disdaineth;
   Suns of the world may stain when heaven's sun staineth.    1609

JOHN DONNE

## The Good-Morrow

I wonder, by my troth, what thou and I
   Did, till we loved? were we not weaned till then?
But sucked on country pleasures, childishly?
   Or snorted we in the Seven Sleepers' den?[5]
'Twas so; but[6] this, all pleasures fancies be.               5
If ever any beauty I did see,
Which I desired, and got,[7] twas but a dream of thee.

And now good-morrow to our waking souls,
   Which watch not one another out of fear;
For love, all love of other sights controls,                  10
   And makes one little room an everywhere.
Let sea-discoverers to new worlds have gone,

---

4. Moss.    5. According to tradition, seven Christian youths escaped Roman persecution by sleeping in a cave for 187 years. *Snorted*: snored.    6. Except for.    7. Sexually possessed. *Beauty*: beautiful woman.

Let maps to other,[8] worlds on worlds have shown,
Let us possess one world, each hath one, and is one.

15      My face in thine eye, thine in mine appears,[9]
            And true plain hearts do in the faces rest;
        Where can we find two better hemispheres,
            Without sharp north, without declining west?
        Whatever dies was not mixed equally,[1]
20          If our two loves be one, or, thou and I
        Love so alike that none do slacken, none can die.                    1633


SYLVIA PLATH

## Morning Song

Love set you going like a fat gold watch.
The midwife slapped your footsoles, and your bald cry
Took its place among the elements.

Our voices echo, magnifying your arrival. New statue.
5    In a drafty museum, your nakedness
Shadows our safety. We stand round blankly as walls.

I'm no more your mother
Than the cloud that distils a mirror to reflect its own slow
Effacement at the wind's hand.

10   All night your moth-breath
Flickers among the flat pink roses. I wake to listen:
A far sea moves in my ear.

One cry, and I stumble from bed, cow-heavy and floral
In my Victorian nightgown.
15   Your mouth opens clean as a cat's. The window square

Whitens and swallows its dull stars. And now you try
Your handful of notes;
The clear vowels rise like balloons.                    1961

8. Other people.     9. That is, each is reflected in the other's eyes.     1. Perfectly mixed elements,
according to scholastic philosophy, were stable and immortal.

## T. S. ELIOT

# *Morning at the Window*

They are rattling breakfast plates in basement kitchens,
And along the trampled edges of the street
I am aware of the damp souls of housemaids
Sprouting despondently at area gates.

The brown waves of fog toss up to me                                            5
Twisted faces from the bottom of the street,
And tear from a passer-by with muddy skirts
An aimless smile that hovers in the air
And vanishes along the level of the roofs.                                      1917

## JONATHAN SWIFT

# *A Description of the Morning*

Now hardly here and there a hackney-coach[2]
Appearing, showed the ruddy morn's approach.
Now Betty[3] from her master's bed had flown,
And softly stole to discompose her own.
The slip shod 'prentice from his master's door                                  5
Had pared the dirt, and sprinkled round the floor.
Now Moll had whirled her mop with dext'rous airs,
Prepared to scrub the entry and the stairs.
The youth with broomy stumps began to trace
The kennel-edge[4] where wheels had worn the place.                             10
The small-coal man[5] was heard with cadence deep,
Till drowned in shriller notes of chimney-sweep:
Duns[6] at his lordship's gate began to meet;
And brick-dust Moll had screamed through half the street.[7]
The turnkey now his flock returning sees,                                       15
Duly let out a-nights to steal for fees.[8]
The watchful bailiffs take their silent stands,[9]
And schoolboys lag with satchels in their hands.                                p. 1709

2. Hired coach. *Hardly*: scarcely; that is, they are just beginning to appear.    3. A stock name for a servant girl. Moll (lines 7, 14) is a frequent lower-class nickname.    4. Edge of the gutter that ran down the middle of the street. *Trace*: "To find old Nails." (JS)    5. A seller of coal and charcoal.    6. Bill collectors.    7. Selling powdered brick that was used to clean knives.    8. Jailers collected fees from prisoners for their keep and often let them out at night so they could steal to pay expenses.    9. Looking for those on their "wanted" lists.

AMY CLAMPITT

# Meridian

First daylight on the bittersweet-hung
sleeping porch at high summer  :  dew
all over the lawn, sowing diamond-
point-highlighted shadows  :
5   the hired man's shadow revolving
along the walk, a flash of milkpails
passing  :  no threat in sight, no hint
anywhere in the universe, of that

apathy at the meridian, the noon
10   of absolute boredom  :  flies
crooning black lullabies in the kitchen,
milk-soured crocks, cream separator
still unwashed  :  what is there to life
but chores and more chores, dishwater,
15   fatigue, unwanted children  :  nothing
to stir the longueur of afternoon

except possibly thunderheads  :
climbing, livid, turreted alabaster
lit up from within by splendor and terror
20   —forked lightning's
                    split-second disaster.                    1985

KAREN VOLKMAN

# Evening

The child calling and calling
his lost dog home on the long
suburban block, doesn't know he is part
of a peculiar orchestration,
5   along with traffic, and the predictable
humming of my fridge, and the tick
of the clock still not set back
from daylight savings—a music
specific to a private
10   kitchen view, in the unfolding
dimensions of a sepia twilight
from which comes, again
and again, the high far note
of the child in his chanting,

so natural and knowing that it                                    15
    might happen every dusk,
as if loss were an inevitable
    condition of nightfall,
spread from streets and houses
to an open, barren hill, and to                                   20
the hulking, enigmatic water-
tower, bulbous, beneath which
a frail white dog must be asleep.                    1996


W. H. AUDEN

## As I Walked Out One Evening

As I walked out one evening,
    Walking down Bristol Street,
The crowds upon the pavement
    Were fields of harvest wheat.

And down by the brimming river                                    5
    I heard a lover sing
Under an arch of the railway:
    'Love has no ending.

'I'll love you, dear, I'll love you
    Till China and Africa meet,                                   10
And the river jumps over the mountain
    And the salmon sing in the street,

'I'll love you till the ocean
    Is folded and hung up to dry
And the seven stars go squawking                                  15
    Like geese about the sky.

'The years shall run like rabbits,
    For in my arms I hold
The Flower of the Ages,
    And the first love of the world.'                             20

But all the clocks in the city
    Began to whirr and chime:
'O let not Time deceive you,
    You cannot conquer Time.

'In the burrows of the Nightmare                                  25
    Where Justice naked is,
Time watches from the shadow
    And coughs when you would kiss.

'In headaches and in worry
    Vaguely life leaks away,                                      30

And Time will have his fancy
    To-morrow or to-day.

'Into many a green valley
    Drifts the appalling snow;
35   Time breaks the threaded dances
    And the diver's brilliant bow.

'O plunge your hands in water,
    Plunge them in up to the wrist;
Stare, stare in the basin
40   And wonder what you've missed.

'The glacier knocks in the cupboard,
    The desert sighs in the bed,
And the crack in the tea-cup opens
    A lane to the land of the dead.

45   'Where the beggars raffle the banknotes
    And the Giant is enchanting to Jack,
And the Lily-white Boy is a Roarer,
    And Jill goes down on her back.

'O look, look in the mirror,
50   O look in your distress;
Life remains a blessing
    Although you cannot bless.

'O stand, stand at the window
    As the tears scald and start;
55   You shall love your crooked neighbour
    With your crooked heart.'

It was late, late in the evening,
    The lovers they were gone;
The clocks had ceased their chiming,
60   And the deep river ran on.

November 1937

## WILLIAM SHAKESPEARE

## *Spring*[1]

When daisies pied and violets blue
    And ladysmocks all silver-white
And cuckoobuds of yellow hue
    Do paint the meadows with delight,
5   The cuckoo then, on every tree,

---

1. Song from *Love's Labour's Lost* V.ii.

Mocks married men;[2] for thus sings he,
                    Cuckoo;
Cuckoo, cuckoo: Oh word of fear,
Unpleasing to a married ear!

When shepherds pipe on oaten straws,                    10
    And merry larks are plowmen's clocks,
When turtles tread,[3] and rooks, and daws,
    And maidens bleach their summer smocks,
The cuckoo then, on every tree,
Mocks married men; for thus sings he,                    15
                    Cuckoo;
Cuckoo, cuckoo: Oh word of fear,
Unpleasing to a married ear!

ca. 1595


## ARCHIBALD LAMPMAN

# *In November*

The hills and leafless forests slowly yield
    To the thick-driving snow. A little while
    And night shall darken down. In shouting file
The woodmen's carts go by me homeward-wheeled,
Past the thin fading stubbles, half concealed,                    5
    Now golden-gray, sowed softly through with snow,
    Where the last ploughman follows still his row,
Turning black furrows through the whitening field.
Far off the village lamps begin to gleam,
    Fast drives the snow, and no man comes this way;                    10
        The hills grow wintry white, and bleak winds moan
        About the naked uplands. I alone
    Am neither sad, nor shelterless, nor gray,
Wrapped round with thought, content to watch and dream.                    1888


## WILLIAM SHAKESPEARE

# *Winter*[4]

When icicles hang by the wall
    And Dick the shepherd blows[5] his nail,

---

2. By the resemblance of its call to the word "cuckold."    3. Copulate. *Turtles*: turtledoves.    4. From *Love's Labour's Lost* v.ii.    5. Breathes on for warmth. *Nail*: fingernail; that is, hands.

And Tom bears logs into the hall,
   And milk comes frozen home in pail.
5  When blood is nipped and ways be fowl,
Then nightly sings the staring owl,
              Tu-who;
Tu-whit, tu-who: a merry note,
While greasy Joan doth keel[6] the pot.

10  When all aloud the wind doth blow,
   And coughing drowns the parson's saw,[7]
And birds sit brooding in the snow,
   And Marian's nose looks red and raw,
When roasted crabs[8] hiss in the bowl,
15  Then nightly sings the staring owl,
              Tu-who;
Tu-whit, tu-who: a merry note
While greasy Joan doth keel the pot.

ca. 1595

---

6. Cool: stir to keep it from boiling over.    7. Maxim, proverb.    8. Crabapples.

# PLACES

JOHN ASHBERY

## City Afternoon

A veil of haze protects this
Long-ago afternoon forgotten by everybody
In this photograph, most of them now
Sucked screaming through old age and death.

If one could seize America                                    5
Or at least a fine forgetfulness
That seeps into our outline
Defining our volumes with a stain
That is fleeting too

But commemorates                                              10
Because it does define, after all:
Gray garlands, that threesome
Waiting for the light to change,
Air lifting the hair of one
Upside down in the reflecting pool.                           15

                                                    1975

APRIL BERNARD

## Praise Psalm of the City-Dweller

              *for C. B.*

Lift your heads, all you peoples, to the wet heat rising in the airshaft,
to the pigeon feathers scattered on the sills, to the grey
triangle of sky that drifts like a soft, wet shawl

For this is the day of the heat, when yellow sedans herd like goats,
when the smell of the body contains its own joyful death        5

See how the young men of the city weep and fall upon one another's
shoulders, see how they turn their shining faces away from us who
     stand
encumbered by the changing sky

There was a place made, a clearing in the wilderness of bricks,
where they gathered to sing—the microphone warbled,              10
the hot smell of tar and hope fanned in wings of smoke

Shout singing in your praises, all you peoples, for there will be more
days like this, when the mouths of all the dogs fall open, pink
and quivering, and the cats lie down like lambs and close their eyes

15   While the hot grey heat rises like tissue from the skin, accumulating
in clouds of tears, there will be more days

Break the stick across your knee, O my brother, begin again
in the heat of further days                                        1993


ANTHONY HECHT

## A Hill

In Italy, where this sort of thing can occur,
I had a vision once—though you understand
It was nothing at all like Dante's, or the visions of saints,
And perhaps not a vision at all. I was with some friends,
5   Picking my way through a warm sunlit piazza
In the early morning. A clear fretwork of shadows
From huge umbrellas littered the pavement and made
A sort of lucent shallows in which was moored
A small navy of carts. Books, coins, old maps,
10   Cheap landscapes and ugly religious prints
Were all on sale. The colors and noise
Like the flying hands were gestures of exultation,
So that even the bargaining
Rose to the ear like a voluble godliness.
15   And then, when it happened, the noises suddenly stopped,
And it got darker; pushcarts and people dissolved
And even the great Farnese Palace itself
Was gone, for all its marble; in its place
Was a hill, mole-colored and bare. It was very cold,
20   Close to freezing, with a promise of snow.
The trees were like old ironwork gathered for scrap
Outside a factory wall. There was no wind,
And the only sound for a while was the little click
Of ice as it broke in the mud under my feet.
25   I saw a piece of ribbon snagged on a hedge,
But no other sign of life. And then I heard
What seemed the crack of a rifle. A hunter, I guessed;
At least I was not alone. But just after that
Came the soft and papery crash
30   Of a great branch somewhere unseen falling to earth.

And that was all, except for the cold and silence
That promised to last forever, like the hill.

Then prices came through, and fingers, and I was restored
To the sunlight and my friends. But for more than a week

I was scared by the plain bitterness of what I had seen.                    35
All this happened about ten years ago,
And it hasn't troubled me since, but at last, today,
I remembered that hill; it lies just to the left
Of the road north of Poughkeepsie; and as a boy
I stood before it for hours in wintertime.                                   40

1967

## SUSAN MUSGRAVE

# I Am Not a Conspiracy
# Everything Is Not Paranoid
# The Drug Enforcement Administration
# Is Not Everywhere

Paul comes from Toronto on Sunday
to photograph me here in my
new image. We drive to a cornfield
where I stand looking uncomfortable.
The corn-god has an Irish accent—                                           5
I can hear him whispering, "Whiskey!"

And the cows. They, too, are in the
corn, entranced like figures in effigy.
Last summer in Mexico I saw purses at the
market made from unborn calfskin—                                           10
I've been wondering where they came from
ever since, the soft skins I ran my hands
down over, that made me feel like shuddering.

I was wrong. The corn-god is whispering
"Cocaine!" He is not Irish, after all,                                       15
but D.E.A. wanting to do business. He
demands to know the names of all my friends,
wants me to tell him who's dealing.

I confess I'm growing restless as the
camera goes on clicking, standing naked in the                              20
high-heel shoes I bought last summer in Mexico.
"We want names," say the cows, who suddenly
look malevolent. They are tearing the ears
off the innocent corn. They call it an
investigation.                                                              25

Paul calls to them, "Come here, cows!"
though I don't even want them in the picture.
What Paul sees is something different from

me; my skin feels like shuddering when those
30    cows run their eyes down over me.

"But didn't you smuggle this poem into Canada?"
asks the cow with the mirrored sunglasses.
"As far as we can tell, this is not a
Canadian poem. Didn't you write it
35    in Mexico?"                                                    1985

THOMAS GRAY

## Elegy Written in a Country Churchyard

The curfew tolls the knell of parting day,
    The lowing herd wind slowly o'er the lea,
The plowman homeward plods his weary way,
    And leaves the world to darkness and to me.

5    Now fades the glimmering landscape on the sight,
    And all the air a solemn stillness holds,
Save where the beetle wheels his droning flight,
    And drowsy tinklings lull the distant folds;

Save that from yonder ivy-mantled tower
10    The moping owl does to the moon complain
Of such, as wandering near her secret bower,
    Molest her ancient solitary reign.

Beneath those rugged elms, that yew tree's shade,
    Where heaves the turf in many a moldering heap,
15    Each in his narrow cell forever laid,
    The rude[9] forefathers of the hamlet sleep.

The breezy call of incense-breathing Morn,
    The swallow twittering from the straw-built shed,
The cock's shrill clarion, or the echoing horn.[1]
20    No more shall rouse them from their lowly bed.

For them no more the blazing hearth shall burn,
    Or busy housewife ply her evening care;
No children run to lisp their sire's return,
    Or climb his knees the envied kiss to share.

25    Oft did the harvest to their sickle yield,
    Their furrow oft the stubborn glebe[2] has broke;
How jocund did they drive their team afield!
    How bowed the woods beneath their sturdy stroke!

9. Unlearned.    1. The hunter's horn.    2. Soil.

Let not Ambition mock their useful toil,
   Their homely joys, and destiny obscure;                           30
Nor Grandeur hear with a disdainful smile
   The short and simple annals of the poor.

The boast of heraldry,[3] the pomp of power,
   And all that beauty, all that wealth e'er gave,
Awaits alike the inevitable hour.                                    35
   The paths of glory lead but to the grave.

Nor you, ye proud, impute to these the fault,
   If Memory o'er their tomb no trophies[4] raise,
Where through the long-drawn aisle and fretted[5] vault
   The pealing anthem swells the note of praise             40

Can storied urn or animated[6] bust
   Back to its mansion call the fleeting breath?
Can Honor's voice provoke the silent dust,
   Or Flattery soothe the dull cold ear of Death?

Perhaps in this neglected spot is laid                        45
   Some heart once pregnant with celestial fire;
Hands that the rod of empire might have swayed,
   Or waked to ecstasy the living lyre.

But Knowledge to their eyes her ample page
   Rich with the spoils of time did ne'er unroll;             50
Chill Penury repressed their noble rage,
   And froze the genial current of the soul.

Full many a gem of purest ray serene,
   The dark unfathomed caves of ocean bear:
Full many a flower is born to blush unseen,             55
   And waste its sweetness on the desert air.

Some village Hampden,[7] that with dauntless breast
   The little tyrant of his fields withstood;
Some mute inglorious Milton here may rest,
   Some Cromwell guiltless of his country's blood.        60

The applause of listening senates to command,
   The threats of pain and ruin to despise,
To scatter plenty o'er a smiling land,
   And read their history in a nation's eyes,

Their lot forbade: nor circumscribed alone                65
   Their growing virtues, but their crimes confined;
Forbade to wade through slaughter to a throne,
   And shut the gates of mercy on mankind,

---

3. Noble birth.    4. An ornamental or symbolic group of figures depicting the achievements of the deceased.    5. Decorated with intersecting lines in relief.    6. Lifelike. *Storied urn:* a funeral urn with an epitaph or pictured story inscribed on it.    7. John Hampden (1594–1643), who, both as a private citizen and as a member of Parliament, zealously defended the rights of the people against the autocratic policies of Charles I.

The struggling pangs of conscious truth to hide,
    To quench the blushes of ingenuous shame,
Or heap the shrine of Luxury and Pride
    With incense kindled at the Muse's flame.

Far from the madding crowd's ignoble strife,
    Their sober wishes never learned to stray;
Along the cool sequestered vale of life
    They kept the noiseless tenor of their way.

Yet even these bones from insult to protect
    Some frail memorial still erected nigh,
With uncouth rhymes and shapeless sculpture decked,[8]
    Implores the passing tribute of a sigh.

Their name, their years, spelt by the unlettered Muse,
    The place of fame and elegy supply:
And many a holy text around she strews,
    That teach the rustic moralist to die.

For who to dumb Forgetfulness a prey,
    This pleasing anxious being e'er resigned,
Left the warm precincts of the cheerful day,
    Nor cast one longing lingering look behind?

On some fond breast the parting soul relies,
    Some pious drops the closing eye requires;
Even from the tomb the voice of Nature cries,
    Even in our ashes live their wonted fires.

For thee, who mindful of the unhonored dead
    Dost in these lines their artless tale relate;
If chance, by lonely contemplation led,
    Some kindred spirit shall inquire thy fate,

Haply some hoary-headed swain may say,
    "Oft have we seen him at the peep of dawn
Brushing with hasty steps the dews away
    To meet the sun upon the upland lawn.

"There at the foot of yonder nodding beech
    That wreathes its old fantastic roots so high,
His listless length at noontide would he stretch,
    And pore upon the brook that babbles by.

"Hard by yon wood, now smiling as in scorn,
    Muttering his wayward fancies he would rove,
Now drooping, woeful wan, like one forlorn,
    Or crazed with care, or crossed in hopeless love.

"One morn I missed him on the customed hill,
    Along the heath and near his favorite tree;

---

8. Cf. the "storied urn or animated bust" (line 41) dedicated inside the church to the "proud" (line 37).

Another came; nor yet beside the rill,
   Nor up the lawn, nor at the wood was he;

"The next with dirges due in sad array
   Slow through the churchway path we saw him borne.
Approach and read (for thou canst read) the lay,                    115
   Graved on the stone beneath yon aged thorn."

### The Epitaph

*Here rests his head upon the lap of Earth*
   *A youth to Fortune and to Fame unknown.*
*Fair Science⁹ frowned not on his humble birth,*
   *And Melancholy marked him for her own.*                          120

*Large was his bounty, and his soul sincere,*
   *Heaven did a recompense as largely send:*
*He gave to Misery all he had, a tear,*
   *He gained from Heaven ('twas all he wished) a friend.*

*No farther seek his merits to disclose,*                            125
   *Or draw his frailties from their dread abode*
*(There they alike in trembling hope repose),*
   *The bosom of his Father and his God.*                            1751

9. Learning.

## COMPARING PLACES AND TIMES: THE SENSE OF CULTURAL OTHERNESS

YVONNE SAPIA

### *Grandmother, a Caribbean Indian, Described by My Father*

Nearly a hundred when she died,
mi viejita[1]
was an open boat,
and I had no map
5   to show her the safe places.
There was much to grieve.
Her shoulders were stooped.
Her hands were never young.
They broke jars
10   at the watering holes,
like bones, like hearts.

When she was a girl,
she was given the island
but no wings.
15   She wanted wings,
though she bruised
like a persimmon.
She was not ruined
before her marriage.
20   But after the first baby died,
she disappeared in the middle
of days to worship
her black saint,
after the second,
25   to sleep with a hand towel
across her eyes.

I had to take care
not to exhume
from the mound of memory
30   these myths, these lost ones.
Born sleek as swans
on her river, my brother,
the man you have met

1. My little old woman or mother. (YS)

who has one arm,
and I glided into the sun.                              35
Other children poured forth,
and by the time I was sixteen
I lost my place
in her thatched house.

She let me go,                                          40
and she did not come to the pier
the day the banana boat
pushed away from her shore
towards Nueva York
where I had heard                                       45
there would be room for me.                    1987


SIMON J. ORTIZ

## Speaking

I take him outside
under the trees,
have him stand on the ground.
We listen to the crickets,
cicadas, million years old sound.                       5
Ants come by us.
I tell them,
"This is he, my son.
This boy is looking at you.
I am speaking for him."                                 10

The crickets, cicadas,
the ants, the millions of years
are watching us,
hearing us.
My son murmurs infant words,                            15
speaking, small laughter
bubbles from him.
Tree leaves tremble.
They listen to this boy
speaking for me.                                        20

1977

AGHA SHAHID ALI

# Postcard from Kashmir

*(for Pavan Sahgal)*

Kashmir shrinks into my mailbox,
my home a neat four by six inches.

I always loved neatness. Now I hold
the half-inch Himalayas in my hand.

5   This is home. And this the closest
I'll ever be to home. When I return,
the colors won't be so brilliant,
the Jhelum's waters[2] so clean,
so ultramarine. My love
10  so overexposed.

And my memory will be a little
out of focus, in it
a giant negative, black
and white, still undeveloped.

1987

CATHY SONG

# Heaven

He thinks when we die we'll go to China.
Think of it—a Chinese heaven
where, except for his blond hair,
the part that belongs to his father,
5   everyone will look like him.
China, that blue flower on the map,
bluer than the sea
his hand must span like a bridge
to reach it.
10  An octave away.

I've never seen it.
It's as if I can't sing that far.
But look—
on the map, this black dot.
15  Here is where we live,
on the pancake plains

---

2. The river Jhelum runs through Kashmir and Pakistan.

just east of the Rockies,
on the other side of the clouds.
A mile above the sea,
the air is so thin, you can starve on it.                                20
No bamboo trees
But the alpine equivalent,
reedy aspen with light, fluttering leaves.
Did a boy in Guangzhou[3] dream of this
as his last stop?                                                        25

I've heard the trains at night
whistling past our yards,
what we've come to own,
the broken fences, the whiny dog, the rattletrap cars.
It's still the wild west,                                                 30
mean and grubby,
the shootouts and fistfights in the back alley.
With my son the dreamer
and my daughter, who is too young to walk,
I've sat in this spot                                                     35
and wondered why here?
Why in this short life,
this town, this creek they call a river?

He had never planned to stay,
the boy who helped to build                                              40
the railroads for a dollar a day.[4]
He had always meant to go back.
When did he finally know
that each mile of track led him further away,
that he would die in his sleep,                                          45
dispossessed,
having seen Gold Mountain,
the icy wind tunneling through it,
these landlocked, makeshift ghost towns?

It must be in the blood,                                                 50
this notion of returning.
It skipped two generations, lay fallow,
the garden an unmarked grave.
On a spring sweater day
it's as if we remember him.                                             55
I call to the children.
We can see the mountains
shimmering blue above the air.
If you look really hard
says my son the dreamer,                                                60
leaning out from the laundry's rigging,

3. Usually called Canton, a seaport city in southeastern China.    4. The railroads used immigrant day
labor (most of it Chinese) to lay the tracks in the nineteenth century.

the work shirts fluttering like sails,
you can see all the way to heaven.

1988


MARILYN CHIN

## We Are Americans Now,
## We Live in the Tundra

Today in hazy San Francisco, I face seaward
Toward China, a giant begonia—

Pink, fragrant, bitten
By verdigris and insects. I sing her

5   A blues song; even a Chinese girl gets the blues,
Her reticence is black and blue.

Let's sing about the extinct
Bengal tigers, about giant Pandas—

"Ling Ling loves Xing Xing . . . yet,
10   We will not mate. We are

Not impotent, we are important.
We blame the environment, we blame the zoo!"

What shall we plant for the future?
Bamboo, sassafras, coconut palms? No!

15   Legumes, wheat, maize, old swine
To milk the new.

We are Americans now, we live in the tundra
Of the logical, a sea of cities, a wood of cars.

Farewell my ancestors:
20   Hirsute Taoists, failed scholars, farewell

My wetnurse who feared and loathed the Catholics,
Who called out:

Now that the half-men have occupied Canton
Hide your daughters, lock your doors!

1987


CHITRA BANERJEE DIVAKARUNI

## Indian Movie, New Jersey

Not like the white filmstars, all rib
and gaunt cheekbone, the Indian sex-goddess

smiles plumply from behind a flowery
branch. Below her brief red skirt, her thighs
are satisfying-solid, redeeming                                     5
as tree trunks. She swings her hips
and the men-viewers whistle. The lover-hero
dances in to a song, his lip-sync
a little off, but no matter, we
know the words already and sing along.                             10
It is safe here, the day
golden and cool so no one sweats,
roses on every bush and the Dal Lake
clean again.
            The sex-goddess switches                15
to thickened English to emphasize
a joke. We laugh and clap. Here
we need not be embarrassed by words
dropping like lead pellets into foreign ears.
The flickering movie-light                                          20
wipes from our faces years of America, sons
who want mohawks and refuse to run
the family store, daughters who date
on the sly.
            When at the end the hero              25
dies for his friend who also
loves the sex-goddess and now can marry her,
we weep, understanding. Even the men
clear their throats to say, "What *qurbani!*[5]
What *dosti!*"[6] After, we mill around                             30
unwilling to leave, exchange greetings
and good news: a new gold chain, a trip
to India. We do not speak
of motel raids, canceled permits, stones
thrown through glass windows, daughters and sons                    35
raped by Dotbusters.[7]
            In this dim foyer
we can pull around us the faint, comforting smell
of incense and *pakoras,*[8] can arrange
our children's marriages with hometown boys and girls,             40
open a franchise, win a million
in the mail. We can retire
in India, a yellow two-storied house
with wrought-iron gates, our own
Ambassador car. Or at least                                         45
move to a rich white suburb, Summerfield
or Fort Lee, with neighbors that will
talk to us. Here while the film-songs still echo
in the corridors and restrooms, we can trust

---

5. Sacrifice.    6. Friendship.    7. Anti-Indian gangs in New Jersey.    8. Fried appetizers.

50          in movie truths: sacrifice, success, love and luck,
            the America that was supposed to be.                                    1990

## QUESTIONS

1. How much do we know about the child in Snyder's "A Mongoloid Child Handling Shells on the Beach"? What do each of the following words contribute to the portrait of her: "slow" (lines 1, 8), "unbroken" (line 5), "soberly" (line 7), "hums" (line 8)? How does the boisterousness of the other children help to characterize the main character? What does the seaside setting contribute to the poem? What is the poem's tone?
2. What is the plot of Glück's "Labor Day"? How long ago did the central events occur? How can you tell? In what ways has the speaker's attitudes toward the events changed?
3. In Karr's "Hubris," explain exactly how the narrative sequence works. How (and why) does the speaker's perspective on the "dwarf" change? What does the title mean?
4. Compare the tone of the two Donne poems, "The Sun Rising" and "The Good-Morrow."
5. In Ortiz's "Speaking," each stanza of the short poem contains ten lines. The first three lines of the first stanza and the final three lines of the second make up a "frame." Inside that frame are two seven-line sections, each made up of two or three sentences. Compare the first sentences of each section (lines 4–6 and 11–14). What is the function of the opening frame (lines 1–3)? of the closing frame (lines 18–20)?
6. In Agha Shahid Ali's "Postcard from Kashmir," how far away from "home" does the speaker seem to be when he receives the postcard? Would the poem be more effective if we knew more specifics about place and how long he had been away from Kashmir? Why or why not?

## WRITING SUGGESTIONS

1. Choose one of the poems you've read in this chapter, and try to connect it to an experience in your own life that has helped you to appreciate the poem. Write a page or two explaining how the poem speaks to your particular situation.
2. What, exactly, happens in Donne's "The Good-Morrow"? How does the speaker feel about his lover? about the night of love? about himself? What is the evidence for his feelings about each of these things? What does the dawn have to do with the speaker's state of mind? with the tone of the poem? Write a brief two-page paper about the significance of the time setting.
3. Consult at least three handbooks of literary terms, and compare their definitions of *aubade* and *aube*. Consider the morning poems by Shakespeare, Donne, Swift, and Plath. Choose *one* of these poems, and analyze how closely it relates to the tradition of morning poems described in the handbooks. Write a short essay (no more than two pages long) in which you explain how the poem achieves its effects by employing and modifying or rejecting the standard expectations of how mornings are to be described in poetry.
4. Consult a handbook of classical literature, and find out how Roman poets represented sunrises mythologically. (Hint: look up Phoebus, then—guided by the handbook or a reference librarian—look at several poems in which Phoebus or his fiery car is described in detail.) Consider carefully the opening lines of Swift's "A Description of the Morning." Write a short account (no more than three paragraphs) of how Swift's first two lines work: in what ways do they use and modify the standard mythological expectations? What do you make of the comparison of modern ordinary life to mythic patterns? What kind of evaluation of modern life (or of mythology) seems to be implied?

# STUDENT WRITING

Below is an excerpt from one student's first response to Linda Pastan's "To a Daughter Leaving Home." The student's assignment was similar to Writing Suggestion 1. Note how she asks Pastan questions about meaning as a way of articulating her own response to and questions about the poem.

---

A Letter to an Author

Kimberly Smith

Dear Linda,

I read your poem "To a Daughter Leaving Home" and it really grabbed my attention. I felt as if I were in your head knowing exactly how you felt when you wrote it. It was a feeling that a father, mother or even a child could understand. I also understand that you were born in New York, as I was. After reading the poem and finding out that we were born in the same place, I felt a connection to you. I came to Tucson from New Jersey and it was a very big culture shock. Knowing you are from the east gave me an easy feeling, a feeling of home.

I can remember back when I learned how to ride a bike. My father gave me the incentive that if I could ride to him without falling, then he would take me out for a lobster dinner. So, I did. I was ten and I got on that bike and peddled away until I could catch my balance and my Dad could let me go. I know now that learning to ride my bike meant more than my father watching me ride down the road. It was a symbol of freedom and growing up. It was time for my parents to let go a little

more. I saw that same feeling in your poem also. Is that what you
meant? Did you intend the bike image to portray a feeling of growing up
and moving along in life?

It seemed to me that you wrote the poem to represent stages of a
child's life. The first stage is from the beginning to the line "on two
round wheels" (line 6). This stage, I believe, is when a baby is
learning to walk and he or she wobbles around until getting the hang of
it. The second stage is until the line "sprinted to catch up" (line
14). These are the elementary years and maybe junior high, when the
child is trying to be on her own and do things for herself. I can
remember this stage very well. I thought that I was at an age where I
did not need my parents' help anymore. I used to say, "Mom, I am eleven
years old and I am old enough to stay alone. I don't need a baby-
sitter." The next stage, which I believe is one of the biggest changes
in a child's life, ends at the line "with laughter" (line 20). This
stage, to me, is very clearly marked high school. The idea about
growing more distant I related to very well. That is because I
definitely grew up a lot and learned a lot during high school. I got a
car and finally felt like an individual, with her own mind. I was able
to make my own decisions which was very important to me.

The language you have chosen is very simple, just like the stages of
a child's life. Your sentences are short and to the point. I believe
that you arranged the poem in the way you did to show a balance. The
arrangement of the poem on paper is straight, just like a bike ride and
just as parents want their child's life to be. I believe that you chose
your words very carefully. For example, "thud" (line 12) has a deep and
powerful meaning. It coincides with the last word of the poem,
"goodbye" (line 24). Thud is a very final word as if you fell and you
heard a big thud. "Goodbye" (line 24) has that same meaning here. You
get a feeling of the end instead of just a new beginning. That is what
I felt when I read those words. Did you intend to show that same
connection between the words "thud" (line 12) and "goodbye" (line 24)
that I saw?

There is one impression that I am getting from you in your poem that
I do not agree with. I am not sure if you are intending this, but I got
the feeling that you have the idea that as children go farther away

that they become more fragile. That may be true in some cases, but if children are brought up in an environment that they are held in a glass box all of their life, then, in that case, it is definitely about time that they moved out on their own. Everyone is going to make mistakes but they only mean something if you can fix them yourself. I always tell my father that I appreciate his advice but sometimes I need to figure things out on my own and that making mistakes is all about growing up.

   I learned a lot from your poem. I hope you enjoy my comments and feelings.

                                        Yours truly,
                                        Kimberly Smith

# 4

## LANGUAGE

Fiction and drama depend upon language just as poetry does, but in a poem almost everything comes down to the particular meanings and implications of individual words. In stories and plays, we are likely to keep our attention primarily on character and plot— what is happening in front of us or in the action as we imagine it in our minds—and although words are crucial to how we imagine the characters and how we respond to what happens to them, we are not as likely to pause over any one word as we may need to in a poem. Because poems often are short and use only a few words, a lot depends on every single one. Poetry sometimes feels like prose that is distilled: only the most essential words are there. Just barely enough is said to communicate in the most basic way, using the most elemental signs of meaning and feeling—and each chosen for exactly the right shade of meaning. But elemental does not necessarily mean simple, and these signs may be very rich in their meanings and complex in their effects.

### PRECISION AND AMBIGUITY

Let's look first at poems that create some of their most important effects by examining— or playing with—a single word. Often multiple meanings of a word or its shiftiness and uncertainty are at issue. Here, for example, is a short poem that depends almost entirely on the way we think about the word *play*. It was written by a writer traveling through the American South early in the twentieth century when she saw a textile mill, which then employed quite young children, right next to a golf course.

SARAH CLEGHORN

## *[The golf links lie so near the mill]*

The golf links lie so near the mill
That almost every day

The laboring children can look out
And see the men at play.                                      p. 1915


The poem doesn't *say* that we expect men to work and children to play; it just assumes our expectation and builds an effect of **dramatic irony**—an incongruity between what we expect and what actually occurs—out of the observation. Almost all of the poem's devastating effect is saved for the final word, after the situation has been carefully described and the irony set up.

The following two poems depend on the ambiguity of a word used over and over to illustrate its refusal to be pinned down to a single meaning.


## ANNE FINCH, COUNTESS OF WINCHELSEA

# *There's No To-Morrow*

## A Fable imitated from Sir Roger L'Estrange

Two long had Lov'd, and now the Nymph desir'd,
The Cloak of Wedlock, as the Case requir'd;
Urg'd that, the Day he wrought her to this Sorrow,
He Vow'd, that he wou'd marry her To-Morrow.
Agen he Swears, to shun the present Storm,                                5
That he, To-Morrow, will that Vow perform.
The Morrows in their due Successions came;
Impatient still on Each, the pregnant Dame
Urg'd him to keep his Word, and still he swore the same.
When tir'd at length, and meaning no Redress,                            10
But yet the Lye not caring to confess,
He for his Oath this Salvo chose to borrow,
That he was Free, since there was no To-Morrow;
For when it comes in Place to be employ'd,
'Tis then To-Day; To-Morrow's ne'er enjoy'd.                             15
The Tale's a Jest, the Moral is a Truth;
To-Morrow and To-Morrow, cheat our Youth:
In riper Age, To-Morrow still we cry,
Not thinking, that the present Day we Dye;
Unpractis'd all the Good we had Design'd;                                20
There's No To-Morrow to a Willing Mind.                        1713

CHARLES BERNSTEIN

## *Of Time and the Line*

George Burns[1] likes to insist that he always
takes the straight lines; the cigar in his mouth
is a way of leaving space between the
lines for a laugh. He weaves lines together
5    by means of a picaresque narrative;
not so Hennie Youngman,[2] whose lines are strict-
ly paratactic. My father pushed a
line of ladies' dresses—not down the street
in a pushcart but upstairs in a fact'ry
10   office. My mother has been more concerned
with her hemline. Chairman Mao[3] put forward
Maoist lines, but that's been abandoned (most-
ly) for the East-West line of malarkey
so popular in these parts. The prestige
15   of the iambic line has recently
suffered decline, since it's no longer so
clear who "I" am, much less who *you* are. When
making a line, better be double sure
what you're lining in & what you're lining
20   out & which side of the line you're on; the
world is made up so (Adam didn't so much
name as delineate). Every poem's got
a prosodic lining, some of which will
unzip for summer wear. The lines of an
25   imaginary are inscribed on the
social flesh by the knifepoint of history.
Nowadays, you can often spot a work
of poetry by whether it's in lines
or no; if it's in prose, there's a good chance
30   it's a poem. While there is no lesson in
the line more useful than that of the pick-
et line, the line that has caused the most ad-
versity is the bloodline. In Russia
everyone is worried about long lines;
35   back in the USA, it's strictly soup-
lines. "Take a chisel to write," but for an
actor a line's got to be cued. Or, as
they say in math, it takes two lines to make
an angle but only one lime to make
40   a Margarita.                          1991

1. American comedian (1896–1996), who played straight man to his wife, Gracie Allen.   2. American comedian (1906–1998).   3. Mao Zedong (1893–1976), leader of the revolution that established China as a communist nation.

The Finch poem repeatedly explores the shifting sands of the word "to-morrow," first noting how different people may think of its meanings differently, then showing how its ambiguity is anchored in time and the whole process of meaning. The Bernstein poem finds a great variety of completely different meanings of the word "line." How many different meanings can you distinguish in the poem? What does "Time" (in the title) have to do with the poem?

Here is a far more personal and emotional poem that uses a single word, "terminal," to explore the changing relationship between two people—a father (who speaks the poem) and daughter.

YVOR WINTERS

## At the San Francisco Airport

*to my daughter, 1954*

This is the terminal: the light
Gives perfect vision, false and hard;
The metal glitters, deep and bright.
Great planes are waiting in the yard—
They are already in the night.                           5

And you are here beside me, small,
Contained and fragile, and intent
On things that I but half recall—
Yet going whither you are bent.
I am the past, and that is all.                          10

But you and I in part are one:
The frightened brain, the nervous will,
The knowledge of what must be done,
The passion to acquire the skill
To face that which you dare not shun.                    15

The rain of matter upon sense
Destroys me momently. The score:
There comes what will come. The expense
Is what one thought, and something more—
One's being and intelligence.                            20

This is the terminal, the break.
Beyond this point, on lines of air,
You take the way that you must take;
And I remain in light and stare—
In light, and nothing else, awake.                       25

1954

The key word here is chosen because it can mean more than one thing; in this case, the importance of the word involves its **ambiguity** (an ability to mean more than one thing) rather than its **precision** (exactness).

The several possible meanings of a single word are probed soberly and thoughtfully. What does it *mean* to be in a place called a "terminal"? the poem asks. As the parting of father and daughter is explored carefully, the place of parting and the means of transportation begin to take on meanings larger than their simple referential ones. The poem is full of contrasts—young and old, light and dark, past and present, security and adventure. The father ("I am the past," line 10) remains in the light, among known objects and experience familiar to his many years; the daughter is about to depart into the night, the unknown, the uncertain future. But they both share a sense of the necessity of the parting, of the need for the daughter to mature, gain knowledge, acquire experience. Is she going off to school? to college? to her first job? We don't know, but her plane ride clearly means a new departure and a clean break with childhood, dependency, the past.

So much depends upon the word "terminal." It refers to the airport building, of course, but it also implies a boundary, an extremity, a terminus, something that is limited, a junction, a place where a connection may be broken. Important as well is the unambiguous meaning of certain words, that is, what these other words **denote.** The final stanza is articulated flatly, as if the speaker has recovered from the momentary confusion of stanza 4, when "being and intelligence" are lost in the emotion of the parting itself. The words "break," "point," "way," and "remain" are almost unemotional and colorless; they do not make value judgments or offer personal views, but rather define and describe. The sharp articulation of the last stanza stresses the **denotations** of the words employed. It is as if the speaker is trying to disengage himself from the emotion of the situation and just give the facts.

Words, however, are more than hard blocks of meaning on whose sense everyone agrees. They also have a more personal side, and they carry emotional force and shades of suggestion. The words we use indicate not only what we mean but how we feel about it, and we choose words that we hope will engage others emotionally and persuasively, in conversation and daily usage as well as in poems. A person who holds office is, quite literally (and unemotionally), an "officeholder," a word that clearly denotes what he or she does. But if we want to convince someone that an officeholder is wise, trustworthy, and deserving of political support we may call that person a "civil servant," a "political leader," or an "elected official," whereas if we want to promote distrust or contempt of officeholders we might call them "politicians" or "bureaucrats" or "political hacks." These latter words have clear **connotations**—suggestions of emotional coloration that imply our attitude and invite a similar one on the part of our hearers. What words **connote** can be just as important to a poem as what they denote, although some poems depend primarily on denotation and some more on connotation.

*A poet is, before anything else, a person who is passionately in love with language.*

—W. H. AUDEN

"At the San Francisco Airport" seems to depend primarily on denotation; the speaker tries to *specify* the meanings and implications of the parting with his daughter, and his tendency to split categories neatly for the two of them at first contributes to the sense of clarity and certainty which the speaker wants to project. He is the past (line 10) and what remains (line 24); he has age and experience, his life is the known quantity, he stands in the light. She, on the other hand, is committed to the adventure of going into the night; she seems small, fragile, and her identity exists in the uncertain future. Yet the connotations of some words carry strong emotional force as well as clear definition: that the daughter seems "small" and "fragile" to the speaker suggests his fear for her, something quite different from her sense of adventure. The neat, clean categories keep breaking down, and the speaker's feelings keep showing through. In stanza 1, the speaker tells us that the light in the terminal gives "perfect vision," but he also notices, indirectly, its artificial quality: it is "false" and "hard," suggesting the limits of the rationalism he tries to maintain. That artificial light shines over most of the poem and honors the speaker's effort, but the whole poem represents his struggle, and in stanza 4 the signals of disturbance are very strong as, despite an insistence on a vocabulary of calculation, his rational facade collapses completely. If we have observed his verbal strategies carefully, we should not be surprised to find him at the end just *staring* in the artificial light, merely awake, although the poem has shown him to be unconsciously awake to much more than he will candidly admit.

"At the San Francisco Airport" is an unusually intricate and complicated poem, and it offers us, if we are willing to examine precisely its carefully crafted fabric, rich insight into how complex it is to be human and to have human feelings and foibles when we think we must be rational machines. But connotations can work more simply. The following epitaph, for example, even though it describes the mixed feelings one person has about another, depends heavily on the common connotations of fairly common words.

WALTER DE LA MARE

## Slim Cunning Hands

Slim cunning hands at rest, and cozening eyes—
Under this stone one loved too wildly lies;
How false she was, no granite could declare;
   Nor all earth's flowers, how fair.                    1950

*What* the speaker in "Slim Cunning Hands" remembers about the dead woman—her hands, her eyes—tells part of the story; her physical presence was clearly important to him, and the poem's other nouns—stone, granite, flowers—all remind us of her death and its finality. All these words denote objects having to do with rituals that memorialize a departed life. Granite and stone connote finality as well, and flowers connote fragility and suggest the shortness of life (which is why they have become the symbolic language of funerals). The way the speaker talks about the woman expresses, in just a few words, the complexity of his love for her. She was loved, he says, too "wildly"—by him perhaps, and apparently by others. The excitement she offered is suggested by the word, and also the lack of control. The words "cunning" and "cozening" help us interpret both her wildness and falsity; they suggest her calculation, cleverness, and untrustworthiness as well as her skill, persuasiveness, and ability to please. And the word "fair," a simple yet very inclusive word, suggests how totally attractive the speaker finds her: her beauty is just as incapable of being expressed by flowers as her fickleness is of being expressed in something as permanent as stone. But the word "fair," in the emphatic position as the final word, also implies two other meanings that seem to resonate, ironically with what we have already learned about her from the speaker: "impartial" and "just." "Impartial" she may be in her preferences (as the word "false" suggests), but to the speaker she is hardly "just," and the final defining word speaks both to her appearance and (ironically) to her character. Simple words here tell us perhaps all we need to know of a long story— or at least the speaker's version of it.

Words like "fair" and "cozening" are clearly loaded; they imply more emotionally than they literally mean. They have strong, clear connotations and tell us what to think, what evaluation to make, and they suggest the basis for the evaluation. Both words in the title of the following poem similarly turn out to be key ones in its meaning and effect:

PAT MORA

## Gentle Communion

Even the long-dead are willing to move.
Without a word, she came with me from the desert.
Mornings she wanders through my rooms
making beds, folding socks.

5   Since she can't hear me anymore,
Mamande[4] ignores the questions I never knew
to ask, about her younger days, her red
hair, the time she fell and broke her nose
in the snow. I will never know.

10  When I try to make her laugh,
to disprove her sad album face, she leaves
the room, resists me as she resisted
grinning for cameras, make-up, English.

While I write, she sits and prays,
15  feet apart, legs never crossed,
the blue housecoat buttoned high
as her hair dries white, girlish
around her head and shoulders.

She closes her eyes, bows her head,
20  and like a child presses her hands together,
her patient flesh steeple, the skin
worn, like the pages of her prayer book.

Sometimes I sit in her wide-armed
chair as I once sat in her lap.
25  Alone, we played a quiet I Spy.
She peeled grapes I still taste.

She removes the thin skin, places
the luminous coolness on my tongue.

4. A child's conflation of *mama grande* (Spanish for "grandmother").

I know not to bite or chew. I wait
for the thick melt,                                                    30
our private green honey.                                             1991

Neither of the words in the title appears in the text itself, but both resonate throughout the poem. "Communion" is the more powerful of the words; here, it comes to imply the close ritualized relationship between the speaker and "Mamande." Mamande has long been dead but now returns, recalling to the speaker a host of memories and providing a sense of history and family identity. To the speaker, the reunion has a powerful value, reminding her of rituals, habits, and beliefs that "place" her and affirm her heritage. The past is strong in the speaker's mind and in the poem. Many details are recalled from album photographs—the blue housecoat (line 16), the sad face (line 11), the white hair that was once red (lines 7–8 and 17), the posture at prayer (lines 19–22), the big chair (lines 23–24), the plain old-fashioned style (line 13)—and the speaker's childhood memories fade into them as she recalls a specific intimate moment.

The full effect of the word "communion"—which describes an intimate moment of union and a ritual—comes only in the final lines when the speaker remembers the secret of the grapes and recalls their sensuous feel and taste. The moment brings together the experience of different generations and cultures and represents a sacred sharing: the Spanish grandmother had resisted English, modernity, and show (line 13), and the speaker is a poet, writing (and publishing) in English, but the two have a common "private" (line 31) moment ritually shared and forever memorable. At the end, too, the full sense of "gentle" becomes evident—a word that sums up the softness, quietness, and understatedness of the experience, the personal qualities of "Mamande," and the unpretentious but dignified social level of the family heritage. Throughout the text, other words—ordinary, simple, and precise—are chosen with equal care to suggest the sense of personal dignity, revealed identity, and verbal power that the speaker comes to accept as her own. Look especially at the words "move" (line 1), "steeple" (line 21), and "luminous" (line 28).

In the two poems that follow we can readily see why the specific words are chosen because, although both poems express a male preference for the same sort of feminine appearance, the grounds of appeal are vastly different.

### BEN JONSON

## *Still to Be Neat*[5]

Still[6] to be neat, still to be dressed,
As you were going to a feast;
Still to be powdered, still perfumed;
Lady, it is to be presumed,

---

5. A song from Jonson's play *The Silent Woman* (1609–1610).    6. Continually.

5

Though art's hid causes are not found,
All is not sweet, all is not sound.

Give me a look, give me a face
That makes simplicity a grace;
Robes loosely flowing, hair as free;
Such sweet neglect more taketh me
Than all th' adulteries of art.
They strike mine eyes, but not my heart.                1609

ROBERT HERRICK

## *Delight in Disorder*

A sweet disorder in the dress
Kindles in clothes a wantonness.
A lawn[7] about the shoulders thrown
Into a fine distraction;
An erring lace, which here and there
Enthralls the crimson stomacher,[8]
A cuff neglectful, and thereby
Ribbands[9] to flow confusedly;
A winning wave, deserving note,
In the tempestuous petticoat;
A careless shoestring, in whose tie
I see a wild civility;
Do more bewitch me than when art
Is too precise[1] in every part.                1648

The poem "Still to Be Neat" begins by describing a woman who looks too neat and orderly; she seems too perfect to be believed, the speaker says, and he has to assume that there is a reason for such overly fastidious grooming, that she is covering up something. He worries that something is wrong underneath—that not all is "sweet" and "sound." "Sweet" could mean several things; its meaning becomes clearer when it is repeated in the next stanza in a more specific context. "Sound" begins to suggest the speaker's moral earnestness: it is a strong word, implying a suspicion that something is deeply wrong.

When "sweet" is repeated in line 10, it has taken on specific attributes from what the speaker has said about things he likes in a less calculated physical appearance. Now it appears to mean easy, attractive, unpremeditated. And when the speaker springs "adulteries" on us in the next line as a description of the woman's cosmeticizing, it is clear what he fears—that the appearance of the too neat, too made-up woman covers moral

7. Scarf of fine linen.    8. Ornamental covering for the breasts.    9. Ribbons.    1. In the sixteenth and seventeenth centuries, Puritans were often called Precisians because of their fastidiousness.

flaws, that she is trying to appear as someone she is not. "Adulteries" suggests the addition of something foreign, something unlike her own nature, and it is a strong, disapproving word. The "soundness" he had worried about involves her integrity; his objection is certainly moral, probably sexual. He wants a woman to be simple and chaste; he wants women to be just what they seem to be.

The speaker in "Delight in Disorder" wants his women easy and simple too, but for different reasons. He finds disorder "sweet" (line 1), and seems almost to be answering the first speaker, providing a different rationale for artless appearance. His grounds of preference are clear early: his support of "wantonness" (line 2) is close to the opposite in its moral suppositions of the first speaker's disapproval of "adulteries." This speaker wants a careless look because he thinks it's sexy, and many of the words he chooses suggest sensuality and availability: "distraction" (line 4), "erring" (line 5), "tempestuous" (line 10), "wild" (line 12). The speakers in the two poems read informality of dress very differently and have very different expectations of the person who dresses in a particular way. We find out quite a lot about each speaker. Their common subject allows us to see clearly how different they are, and how what one sees is in the eye of the beholder, how values and assumptions are built into the words one chooses even for description. Jonson has created a speaker who wants an informally clad woman who has a natural grace and ease of manner because she is confident of herself, dependable, and chaste. Herrick has created a speaker who finds informality of dress fetching and sexy and indicative of sensuality and availability.

Words are the starting point for all poetry, and almost every word is likely to be significant, either denotatively, connotatively, or both. Poets who know their craft pick each word with care to express exactly what needs to be expressed and to suggest every emotional shade that the poem is calculated to evoke in us. Often individual words qualify and amplify one another—suggestions clarify other suggestions, and meanings grow upon meanings—and thus the way the words are put together can be important, too. Notice, for example, that in "Slim Cunning Hands" the final emphasis is on how *fair* in appearance the woman was; the speaker's last word describes the quality he can't forget in spite of her lack of a different kind of fairness and his distrust of her, the quality that, even though it doesn't justify everything else, mitigates all the disappointment and hurt.

That word does not stand all by itself, however, any more than any other word in a poem can be considered all alone. Every word exists within larger units of meaning— sentences, patterns of comparisons and contrasts, the whole poem—and where the word is and how it is used are often important. The final word or words may be especially emphatic (as in "Slim Cunning Hands"), and words that are repeated take on a special intensity, as "terminal" does in "At the San Francisco Airport" or as "chartered" and "cry" do in "London" (p. 39). Certain words often stand out, because they are used in an unusual way (like "chartered" in "London" or "adulteries" in "Still to Be Neat") or because they are given an artificial prominence—through unusual sentence structure, for example, or because the title calls special attention to them.

Sometimes word choice in poems is less dramatic and less obviously "significant" but equally important. Simple appropriateness is often, in fact, what makes the words in a poem work, and when words do not call special attention to themselves they are sometimes the most effective. Precision of denotation may be just as impressive and productive of specific effects as the resonance or ambiguous suggestiveness of connotation. Often poems achieve their power by a combination of verbal effects, setting off elaborate figures of speech (which we will discuss shortly) or other complicated strategies with simple words chosen to mark exact actions, moments, or states of mind.

Notice, for example, how carefully the following poem produces its complex description of emotional patterns by delineating precise stages (which are then elaborated) of feeling.

EMILY DICKINSON

## [*After great pain, a formal feeling comes—*]

After great pain, a formal feeling comes—
The Nerves sit ceremonious, like Tombs—
The stiff Heart questions was it He, that bore,
And Yesterday, or Centuries before?

5    The Feet, mechanical, go round—
Of Ground, or Air, or Ought—
A Wooden way
Regardless grown,
A Quartz contentment, like a stone—

10    This is the Hour of Lead—
Remembered, if outlived,
As Freezing Persons recollect the Snow—
First—Chill—then Stupor—then the letting go—

ca. 1862

In the following poem, notice how the title calls upon us to wonder, from the beginning, how playful and how patterned the boy's bedtime romp with his father is. As you read it, try to be conscious of the emotional effects created by the choice of words that seem to be key ones. Which words establish the bond between the two males?

THEODORE ROETHKE

## *My Papa's Waltz*

The whiskey on your breath
Could make a small boy dizzy;
But I hung on like death:
Such waltzing was not easy.

5    We romped until the pans
Slid from the kitchen shelf;

My mother's countenance
Could not unfrown itself.

The hand that held my wrist                                              10
Was battered on one knuckle;
At every step you missed
My right ear scraped a buckle.

You beat time on my head
With a palm caked hard by dirt,                                          15
Then waltzed me off to bed
Still clinging to your shirt.                                1948

Exactly what is the situation in "My Papa's Waltz"? What are the economic circum-
stances in the family? How can you tell? What indications are there of the family's social
class? of the father's line of work? How would you characterize the speaker? How does
the poem indicate his pleasure in the bedtime ritual? Which words suggest the boy's
excitement? Which suggest his anxiety? How can you tell how the speaker feels about
his father? What clues are there about what the mother is like? How can you tell that the
experience is remembered at some years' distance? What clues are there in the word
choice that an adult is remembering a childhood experience? How scared was the boy
at the time? How does the grown adult now evaluate his emotions when he was a boy?
In what sense is the poem a tribute to memories of the father? How would you describe
the poem's tone?

The subtlety and force of word choice is sometimes very much affected by **word
order,** the way the sentences are put together. Sometimes poems are driven to unusual
word order because of the demands of rhyme and meter, but ordinarily poets use word
order very much as prose writers do, to create a particular emphasis. When an unusual
word order is used, you can be pretty sure that something there merits special attention.
Notice the odd constructions in the second and third stanzas of "My Papa's Waltz"—the
way the speaker talks about the abrasion of buckle on ear in line 12, for example. He
does not say that the buckle scraped his ear, but rather puts it the other way round—a
big difference in the kind of effect created, for it avoids placing blame and refuses to
specify any unpleasant effect. Had he said that the buckle scraped his ear—the normal
way of putting it—we would have to worry about the fragile ear. The **syntax** (sentence
structure) of the poem channels our feeling and helps to control what we think of the
"waltz."

The most curious part of the poem is the second stanza, for it is there that the silent
mother appears, and the syntax there is peculiar in two places. In lines 5–6, the connec-
tion between the romping and the pans falling is stated oddly: "We romped *until* the
pans/ Slid from the kitchen shelf." The speaker does not say that they knocked down the
pans or imply that there was awkwardness, but he does suggest energetic activity and
duration. He implies intensity, almost design—as though the romping would not be
complete until the pans fell. And the sentence about the mother—odd but effective—
makes her position clear. She is a silent bystander in this male ritual, and her frown
seems molded on her face. It is not as if she is frightened or angry, but as if she, too, is
performing a ritual, holding a frown on her face as if it is part of her role in the ritual, as
well as perhaps a facet of her stern character. The syntax implies that she *has to* maintain

the frown, and the falling of the pans almost seems to be for her benefit. She disapproves, but she is still their audience.

Sometimes poems create, as well, a powerful sense of the way minds and emotions work by varying normal syntactical order in special ways. Listen, for example, in the following poem to the speaker's sudden loss of vocal control in the midst of what seems to be a calm analysis of her feelings about sexual behavior.

SHARON OLDS

## Sex without Love

How do they do it, the ones who make love
without love? Beautiful as dancers,
gliding over each other like ice-skaters
over the ice, fingers hooked
inside each other's bodies, faces                                    5
red as steak, wine, wet as the
children at birth whose mothers are going to
give them away. How do they come to the
come to the   come to the   God   come to the
still waters, and not love                                          10
the one who came there with them, light
rising slowly as steam off their joined
skin? These are the true religious,
the purists, the pros, the ones who will not
accept a false Messiah, love the                                    15
priest instead of the God. They do not
mistake the lover for their own pleasure,
they are like great runners: they know they are alone
with the road surface, the cold, the wind,
the fit of their shoes, their over-all cardio-                      20
vascular health—just factors, like the partner
in the bed, and not the truth, which is the
single body alone in the universe
against its own best time.

                                                                    1984

The poem starts calmly enough, with a simple rhetorical question implying that the speaker just cannot understand sex without love. The second through fourth lines compare such sexual activity with some distant aesthetic, with two carefully delineated examples, and the speaker—although plainly disapproving—seems coolly, almost chillingly, in control of the analysis and evaluation. But by the end of the fourth line, something begins to seem odd: "hooked" seems too ugly and extreme a way to characterize the lovers' fingers, however much the speaker may disapprove, and by line 6, the syntax seems to break down. How does "wine" fit the syntax of the line? Is it parallel with "steak," another example of redness? or is it somehow related to the last part of the sentence, parallel with "faces"? But neither of these possibilities quite works. At best, the punctuation is faulty; at worst the speaker's mind is working too fast for the language it can generate, scrambling its images. We can't yet be quite sure what is going on, but by the ninth line the lack of control is manifest with the compulsive repeating (three times) of "come to the" and the interjected "God."

Such verbal behavior—here concretized by the way the poem orders its words—invites us to reevaluate the speaker's moralism relative to her emotional involvement with the issues and with her representation of sexuality itself. The speaker's values, as well as those who have sex without love, become a subject for evaluation.

Words are the basic building materials of poetry. They are of many kinds and are used in many different ways and in different—sometimes surprising—combinations. Words are seldom simple or transparent, even when we know their meanings and recognize their syntax as ordinary and conventional. The careful examination of them individually and collectively is a crucial part of the process of reading poems, and learning exactly what kinds of questions to ask about the words that poems use and how poems use them is one of the most basic—and rewarding—skills a reader of poetry can develop.

Here is a group of poems illustrating varieties of word usages and word orders. The discussion of language continues later in this chapter with an explanation of figures of speech.

## GERARD MANLEY HOPKINS

### Pied Beauty[2]

Glory be to God for dappled things—
    For skies of couple-color as a brinded[3] cow;
        For rose-moles all in stipple[4] upon trout that swim;
Fresh-firecoal chestnut-falls;[5] finches' wings;
    Landscape plotted and pieced—fold, fallow, and plow;       5
        And all trades, their gear and tackle and trim.
All things counter, original, spare, strange;
    Whatever is fickle, freckled (who knows how?)
        With swift, slow; sweet, sour; adazzle, dim;
He fathers-forth whose beauty is past change:       10
        Praise him.       1877

---

2. Particolored beauty: having patches or sections of more than one color.    3. Streaked or spotted.
4. Rose-colored dots or flecks.    5. Fallen chestnuts as red as burning coals.

ROBERT GRAVES

## The Naked and the Nude

For me, the naked and the nude
(By lexicographers construed
As synonyms that should express
The same deficiency of dress
Or shelter) stand as wide apart
As love from lies, or truth from art.

Lovers without reproach will gaze
On bodies naked and ablaze;
The Hippocratic[6] eye will see
In nakedness, anatomy;
And naked shines the Goddess when
She mounts her lion among men.[7]

The nude are bold, the nude are sly
To hold each treasonable eye.
While draping by a showman's trick
Their dishabille in rhetoric,
They grin a mock-religious grin
Of scorn at those of naked skin.

The naked, therefore, who compete
Against the nude may know defeat;
Yet when they both together tread
The briary pastures of the dead,
By Gorgons[8] with long whips pursued,
How naked go the sometime nude!

1958

MARY OLIVER

## Morning

Salt shining behind its glass cylinder.
Milk in a blue bowl. The yellow linoleum.
The cat stretching her black body from the pillow.
The way she makes her curvaceous response to the small, kind gesture.
Then laps the bowl clean.

---

6. Hippocrates (c. 460–375 B.C.) is traditionally considered the father of medicine.    7. In *The White Goddess,* Graves glosses the title figure as "Muse, the Mother of all living." Riding a lion symbolizes, according to Graves, the sexual dominance of the goddess.    8. In Greek mythology, female monsters who had snakes on their heads instead of hair and whose glance could turn mortals to stone.

Then wants to go out into the world
where she leaps lightly and for no apparent reason across the lawn,
then sits, perfectly still, in the grass.
I watch her a little while, thinking:
what more could I do with wild words?                                          10
I stand in the cold kitchen, bowing down to her.
I stand in the cold kitchen, everything wonderful around me.          1992


WILLIAM CARLOS WILLIAMS

## The Red Wheelbarrow

*Childhood?*
*memories?*
*A moment? encapsulated*
*epiphany? power of image*

so much depends
upon

a red wheel
barrow

glazed with rain                                                                       5
water

beside the white
chickens.                                                                                  1923


CAROLYN KIZER

## Bitch

Now, when he and I meet, after all these years,
I say to the bitch inside me, don't start growling.
He isn't a trespasser anymore,
Just an old acquaintance tipping his hat.
My voice says, "Nice to see you,"                                                5
As the bitch starts to bark hysterically.
He isn't an enemy now,
Where are your manners, I say, as I say,
"How are the children? They must be growing up."
At a kind word from him, a look like the old days,                          10
The bitch changes her tone: she begins to whimper.
She wants to snuggle up to him, to cringe.
Down, girl! Keep your distance
Or I'll give you a taste of the choke-chain.
"Fine, I'm just fine," I tell him.                                                    15
She slobbers and grovels.
After all, I am her mistress. She is basically loyal.

It's just that she remembers how she came running
Each evening, when she heard his step;
20   How she lay at his feet and looked up adoringly
Though he was absorbed in his paper;
Or, bored with her devotion, ordered her to the kitchen
Until he was ready to play.
But the small careless kindnesses
25   When he'd had a good day, or a couple of drinks,
Come back to her now, seem more important
Than the casual cruelties, the ultimate dismissal.
"It's nice to know you are doing so well," I say.
He couldn't have taken you with him;
30   You were too demonstrative, too clumsy,
Not like the well-groomed pets of his new friends.
"Give my regards to your wife," I say. You gag
As I drag you off by the scruff,
Saying, "Goodbye! Goodbye! Nice to have seen you again."          1984

---

### E. E. CUMMINGS

## [in Just-][9]

in Just-
spring      when the world is mud-
luscious the little
lame balloonman

5   whistles      far      and wee

and eddieandbill come
running from marbles and
piracies and it's
spring

10   when the world is puddle-wonderful

the queer
old balloonman whistles
far      and      wee
and bettyandisbel come dancing

15   from hop-scotch and jump-rope and
it's
spring
and
            the
20              goat-footed

9. The first poem in the series *Chansons innocentes*.

```
balloonMan      whistles
far
and
wee¹                                                    1923
```

RITA DOVE

## *Parsley*²

### 1. THE CANE FIELDS

There is a parrot imitating spring
in the palace, its feathers parsley green.
Out of the swamp the cane appears

to haunt us, and we cut it down. El General
searches for a word; he is all the world          5
there is. Like a parrot imitating spring,

we lie down screaming as rain punches through
and we come up green. We cannot speak an R—
out of the swamp, the cane appears

and then the mountain we call in whispers *Katalina*.³    10
The children gnaw their teeth to arrowheads.
There is a parrot imitating spring.

El General has found his word: *perejil*.
Who says it, lives. He laughs, teeth shining
out of the swamp. The cane appears          15

in our dreams, lashed by wind and streaming.
And we lie down. For every drop of blood
there is a parrot imitating spring.
Out of the swamp the cane appears.

### 2. THE PALACE

The word the general's chosen is parsley.          20
It is fall, when thoughts turn
to love and death; the general thinks
of his mother, how she died in the fall
and he planted her walking cane at the grave
and it flowered, each spring stolidly forming          25
four-star blossoms. The general

1. Pan, whose Greek name means "everything," is traditionally represented with a syrinx (or the pipes of Pan). The upper half of his body is human, the lower half goat, and as the father of Silenus he is associated with the spring rites of Dionysus.    2. "On October 2, 1937, Rafael Trujillo (1891–1961), dictator of the Dominican Republic, ordered 20,000 blacks killed because they could not pronounce the letter 'r' in *perejil*, the Spanish word for parsley." (RD)    3. That is, "Katarina."

pulls on his boots, he stomps to
her room in the palace, the one without
curtains, the one with a parrot
30    in a brass ring. As he paces he wonders
*Who can I kill today.* And for a moment
the little knot of screams
is still. The parrot, who has traveled

all the way from Australia in an ivory
35    cage, is, coy as a widow, practising
spring. Ever since the morning
his mother collapsed in the kitchen
while baking skull-shaped candies
for the Day of the Dead,[4] the general
40    has hated sweets. He orders pastries
brought up for the bird; they arrive

dusted with sugar on a bed of lace.
The knot in his throat starts to twitch;
he sees his boots the first day in battle
45    splashed with mud and urine
as a soldier falls at his feet amazed—
how stupid he looked—at the sound
of artillery. *I never thought it would sing*
the soldier said, and died. Now

50    the general sees the fields of sugar
cane, lashed by rain and streaming.
He sees his mother's smile, the teeth
gnawed to arrowheads. He hears
the Haitians sing without R's
55    as they swing the great machetes:
*Katalina*, they sing, *Katalina,*

*mi madle, mi amol en muelte.*[5] God knows
his mother was no stupid woman; she
could roll an R like a queen. Even
60    a parrot can roll an R! In the bare room
the bright feathers arch in a parody
of greenery, as the last pale crumbs
disappear under the blackened tongue. Someone

calls out his name in a voice
65    so like his mother's, a startled tear
splashes the tip of his right boot.
*My mother, my love in death.*
The general remembers the tiny green sprigs
men of his village wore in their capes
70    to honor the birth of a son. He will
order many, this time, to be killed

for a single, beautiful word.                    1983

---

4. All Souls' Day, November 1.    5. Line 67 translates this phrase.

SUSAN MUSGRAVE

## Hidden Meaning

Imagine hailing a taxi
and the driver is a poet.
You could say, "Tell me a poem
and take me to Costa Rica."
As you drive away.                                                          5

Imagine getting into a taxi
where the driver is a *real* poet.
You could quote Robert Penn Warren
without feeling ridiculous: "Driver,
do you truly, truly know what flesh is?"                                    10

Imagine getting into a taxi
and it's snowy Saskatchewan
and the poet has not made a dollar.
The snow goes on falling
and now you're both stuck in it; poetry                                     15
gets you nowhere faster than anything.

Imagine breaking into a taxi
and finding two poets frozen together.
You'd look at one another as if the world
had meaning for the first time, hidden                                      20
meaning, and wouldn't it be a kind
of terrible occasion.                                                     1991


RICHARD ARMOUR

## Hiding Place

*A speaker at a meeting of the New York State Frozen Food Locker*
*Association declared that the best hiding place in event of an*
*atomic explosion is a frozen-food locker, where "radiation will not*
*penetrate."*[6]

—NEWS ITEM

Move over, ham
    And quartered cow,
My Geiger says
    The time is now.

---

6. Before home freezers became popular, many Americans rented lockers in specially equipped commercial buildings.

5     Yes, now I lay me
       Down to sleep,
    And if I die,
       At least I'll keep.

1954

## OGDEN NASH

## *Reflections on Ice-Breaking*

Candy
Is dandy
But liquor
Is quicker.[7]

1929

## *Here Usually Comes the Bride*

June means weddings in everyone's lexicon,
Weddings in Swedish, weddings in Mexican.
Breezes play Mendelssohn, treeses play Youmans,
Birds wed birds, and humans wed humans.
5  All year long the gentlemen woo,
But the ladies dream of a June "I do."
Ladies grow loony, and gentlemen loonier;
This year's June is next year's Junior.

1949

## HEATHER McHUGH

## *Two St. Petersburgs*

I. RUSSIA

The statue turned
upon a chain; beneath its broken knees
were thirty feet of air. Under its sway
of handwide eye stood, ludicrous,
5  a pedestal with only
feet on top. And under that

---

7. Nash later is said to have proposed two more lines: "Pot / Is not."

ranged real but little people, tiny
uprightnesses, all
abruptly free. Freely they milled,
collectively buzzed. They                                              10
feuded over food, they fell
in love anew, had words anew, had different
differences than heretofore. The differences were free

to spread; an air of half-lights made
for deep misgivings in the minds                                       15
of brand-new sunshade salesmen . . .


                II. FLORIDA

The desk clerk's disposition is
professionally sunny. In the waterbed room I can ask
to be tied up, but nicely; you know
nooses that release.                                                   20

Detachment has apartments and
attachment has departments. We can order
long and cool, or quick and hot. Or quick
and cool or long and hot. But can we

pull ourselves together? Keep the living daylights ever-               25
loving? Kill the cough?
For broken is a place
where something gave; a joint's

a place where something moved.
And eloquent is just                                                   30
a mess of hinge and sign: a MO where the TEL
is not yet fallen off . . .                               1993


_____
EMILY DICKINSON

# [*I dwell in Possibility*—]

I dwell in Possibility—
A fairer House than Prose—
More numerous of Windows—
Superior—for Doors—

Of Chambers as the Cedars—                                             5
Impregnable of Eye—
And for an Everlasting Roof
The Gambrels[8] of the Sky—

_____
8. Roofs with double slopes.

Of Visitors—the fairest—
For Occupation—This—
The spreading wide my narrow Hands
To gather Paradise—

ca. 1862

JOHN MILTON

## *from* Paradise Lost[9]

I

Of man's first disobedience, and the fruit[1]
Of that forbidden tree whose mortal taste
Brought death into the world, and all our woe,
With loss of Eden, till one greater Man
Restore us, and regain the blissful seat,
Sing, Heav'nly Muse,[2] that, on the secret top
Of Oreb, or of Sinai, didst inspire
That shepherd who first taught the chosen seed
In the beginning how the Heav'ns and Earth
Rose out of Chaos: or, if Sion hill
Delight thee more, and Siloa's brook that flowed
Fast[3] by the oracle of God, I thence
Invoke thy aid to my adventurous song,
That with no middle flight intends to soar
Above th' Aonian mount,[4] while it pursues
Things unattempted yet in prose or rhyme.
And chiefly thou, O Spirit,[5] that dost prefer
Before all temples th' upright heart and pure,
Instruct me, for thou know'st; thou from the first
Wast present, and, with mighty wings outspread,

9. The opening lines of Books I and II and a short passage from Book III. The first passage states the poem's subject, and the second describes Satan's beginning address to the council of fallen angels meeting to discuss strategy; in the third, God is looking down from Heaven at his new human creation and watching Satan approach the Earth.    1. The apple, but also the consequences.    2. Addressing one of the muses and asking for aid is a convention for the opening lines of an epic; Milton complicates the standard procedure here by describing sources and circumstances of Judeo-Christian revelation rather than specifically invoking one of the nine classical muses. Sinai is the spur of Mount Oreb, where Moses ("That shepherd," line 8, who was traditionally regarded as author of the first five books of the Bible) received the Law; Sion hill and Siloa (lines 10–11), near Jerusalem, correspond to the traditional mountain (Helicon) and springs of classical tradition. Later, in Book VII, Milton calls upon Urania, the muse of astronomy, but he does not mention by name the muse of epic poetry, Calliope.    3. Close.    4. Mount Helicon, home of the classical muses.    5. The divine voice that inspired the Hebrew prophets. Genesis 1:2 says that "the Spirit of God moved upon the face of the waters" as part of the process of Creation; Milton follows tradition in making the inspirational and communicative function of God present in Creation itself. The passage echoes and merges many biblical references to Creation and divine revelation.

Dovelike sat'st brooding on the vast abyss,
And mad'st it pregnant: what in me is dark
Illumine; what is low, raise and support;
That, to the height of this great argument,[6]
I may assert Eternal Providence,                                    25
And justify the ways of God to men.
    Say first (for Heav'n hides nothing from thy view,
Nor the deep tract of Hell), say first what cause
Moved our grand parents, in that happy state,
Favored of Heav'n so highly, to fall off                           30
From their Creator, and transgress his will
For one restraint, lords of the world besides?[7]
Who first seduced them to that foul revolt?
Th' infernal serpent; he it was, whose guile,
Stirred up with envy and revenge, deceived                         35
The mother of mankind, what time[8] his pride
Had cast him out from Heav'n, with all his host
Of rebel angels, by whose aid, aspiring
To set himself in glory above his peers,
He trusted to have equaled the Most High,                          40
If he opposed; and with ambitious aim
Against the throne and monarchy of God,
Raised impious war in Heav'n and battle proud,
With vain attempt. Him the Almighty Power
Hurled headlong flaming from th' ethereal sky,                     45
With hideous ruin and combustion down
To bottomless perdition, there to dwell
In adamantine chains and penal fire,
Who durst defy th' Omnipotent to arms.[9]

* * *

        II

High on a throne of royal state, which far
Outshone the wealth of Ormus and of Ind,[1]
Or where the gorgeous East with richest hand
Show'rs on her kings barbaric pearl and gold,
Satan exalted sat, by merit raised                                  5
To that bad eminence; and, from despair
Thus high uplifted beyond hope, aspires
Beyond thus high, insatiate to pursue
Vain war with Heav'n, and by success[2] untaught,
His proud imaginations thus displayed:                             10
    "Powers and Dominions, Deities of Heav'n,
For since no deep within her gulf can hold

---

6. Subject.    7. In all other respects. *For*: because of.    8. When.    9. After invoking the muse and
giving a brief summary of the poem's subject, an epic regularly begins *in medias res* ("in the midst of
things").    1. India. *Ormus*: Hormuz, an island in the Persian Gulf, famous for pearls.    2. Outcome,
either good or bad.

Immortal vigor, though oppressed and fall'n,
I give not Heav'n for lost. From this descent
15 Celestial virtues rising will appear
More glorious and more dread than from no fall,
And trust themselves to fear no second fate.
Me though just right and the fixed laws of Heav'n
Did first create your leader, next, free choice,
20 With what besides, in council or in fight,
Hath been achieved of merit, yet this loss,
Thus far at least recovered, hath much more
Established in a safe unenvied throne
Yielded with full consent. The happier state
25 In Heav'n, which follows dignity, might draw
Envy from each inferior; but who here
Will envy whom the highest place exposes
Foremost to stand against the Thunderer's aim
Your bulwark, and condemns to greatest share
30 Of endless pain? Where there is then no good
For which to strive, no strife can grow up there
From faction; for none sure will claim in hell
Precédence, none, whose portion is so small
Of present pain, that with ambitious mind
35 Will covet more. With this advantage then
To union, and firm faith, and firm accord,
More than can be in Heav'n, we now return
To claim our just inheritance of old,
Surer to prosper than prosperity
40 Could have assured us; and by what best way,
Whether of open war or covert guile,
We now debate; who can advise, may speak."

\* \* \*

III

\* \* \*

56     Now had th' Almighty Father from above,
From the pure empyrean where he sits
High throned above all height, bent down his eye,
His own works and their works at once to view:
60 About him all the sanctities of Heav'n[3]
Stood thick as stars, and from his sight received
Beatitude past utterance; on his right
The radiant image of his glory sat,
His only Son. On earth he first beheld
65 Our two first parents, yet the only two
Of mankind, in the happy garden placed,
Reaping immortal fruits of joy and love,
Uninterrupted joy, unrivaled love,

3. The hierarchies of angels.

In blissful solitude. He then surveyed
Hell and the gulf between, and Satan there                          70
Coasting the wall of Heav'n on this side Night
In the dun air sublime,[4] and ready now
To stoop[5] with wearied wings and willing feet
On the bare outside of this world, that seemed
Firm land embosomed without firmament,                             75
Uncertain which, in ocean or in air.                        1667

4. Aloft in the twilight atmosphere.    5. Swoop down, like a bird of prey.

## METAPHOR AND SIMILE

The language of poetry is almost always visual and pictorial. Rather than depending primarily on abstract ideas and elaborate reasoning, poems depend mainly upon concrete and specific words that create images in our minds. Poems thus help us to see things fresh and new, or to feel them suggestively through our other physical senses, such as hearing or touch. But, most often, poetry uses the sense of sight in that it helps us form, in our minds, visual impressions, images that communicate more directly than concepts. We "see" yellow leaves on a branch, a father and son waltzing precariously, or two lovers sitting together on the bank of a stream, so that our response begins from a vivid impression of exactly what is happening. Some people think that those media and arts that challenge the imagination of a hearer or reader—radio drama, for example, or poetry—allow us to respond more fully than those (such as television or theater) that actually show things more fully to our physical senses. Certainly they leave more to our imagination, to our mind's eye.

But being visual does not just mean describing, telling us facts, indicating shapes, colors, and specific details and giving us precise discriminations through exacting verbs, nouns, adverbs, and adjectives. Often the vividness of the picture in our minds depends upon comparisons. What we are trying to imagine is pictured in terms of something else familiar to us, and we are asked to think of one thing as if it were something else. Many such comparisons, or **figures of speech,** in which something is pictured or figured forth in terms of something already familiar to us, are taken for granted in daily life. Things we can't see or that aren't familiar to us are imaged as things we already know; for example, God is said to be like a father, Italy is said to be shaped like a boot, life is compared to a forest, a journey, or a sea. When the comparison is explicit—that is, when one thing is directly compared to something else—the figure is called a **simile.** When the comparison is implicit, with something described as if it were something else, it is called a **metaphor.**

Poems use **figurative language** much of the time. A poem may insist that death is like a sunset or sex like an earthquake or that the way to imagine how it feels to be spiritually secure is to think of the way a shepherd takes care of his sheep. The pictorialness of our imagination may *clarify* things for us—scenes, states of mind, ideas—but at the same time it stimulates us to think of how those pictures make us *feel*. Pictures, even when they are mental pictures or imagined visions, may be both denotative and connotative, just as individual words are: they may clarify and make precise, and they may channel our feelings.

In the poem that follows, the poet helps us to visualize the old age and approaching death of the speaker by making comparisons with familiar things—the coming of winter, the approach of sunset, and the dying embers of a fire.

WILLIAM SHAKESPEARE

# [That time of year thou mayst in me behold]

That time of year thou mayst in me behold
When yellow leaves, or none, or few, do hang

Upon those boughs which shake against the cold,
Bare ruined choirs, where late the sweet birds sang.
In me thou see'st the twilight of such day 5
As after sunset fadeth in the west;
Which by and by[6] black night doth take away,
Death's second self,[7] that seals up all in rest.
In me thou see'st the glowing of such fire,
That on the ashes of his youth doth lie, 10
As the deathbed whereon it must expire,
Consumed with that which it was nourished by.
This thou perceiv'st, which makes thy love more strong,
To love that well which thou must leave ere long. 1609

The first four lines of "That time of year" evoke images of the late autumn; but notice that the poet does not have the speaker say directly that his physical condition and age make him resemble autumn. He draws the comparison without stating that it is a comparison: you can see, he says, my own state in the coming of winter, when the leaves are almost all off the trees. The speaker portrays himself *indirectly* by talking about the passing of the year. The poem uses metaphor; that is, one thing is pictured *as if* it were something else. "That time of year" goes on to another metaphor in lines 5–8 and still another in lines 9–12, and each of the metaphors contributes to our understanding of the speaker's sense of his old age and approaching death. More important, however, is the way the metaphors give us feelings, an emotional sense of the speaker's age and of his own attitude toward aging. Through the metaphors we come to understand, appreciate, and to some extent share the increasing sense of anxiety and urgency that the poem expresses. Our emotional sense of the poem is largely influenced by the way each metaphor is developed and by the way each metaphor leads, with its own kind of internal logic, to another.

The images of late autumn in the first four lines all suggest loneliness, loss, and nostalgia for earlier times. As in the rest of the poem, our eyes are imagined to be the main vehicle for noticing the speaker's age and condition; the phrase "thou mayst in me behold" (line 1) introduces what we are asked to see, and in both lines 5 and 9 we are similarly told "In me thou see'st. . . ." The picture of the trees shedding their leaves suggests that autumn is nearly over, and we can imagine trees either with yellow leaves, or without leaves, or with just a trace of foliage remaining—the latter perhaps most feelingly suggesting the bleakness and loneliness that characterize the change of seasons, the ending of the life cycle. But other senses are invoked, too. The boughs shaking against the cold represent an appeal to our tactile sense, and the next line appeals to our sense of hearing, although only as a reminder that the birds no longer sing. (Notice how exact the visual representation is of the bare, or nearly bare, limbs, even as the cold and the lack of birds are noted; birds lined up like a choir on risers would have made a striking visual image on the barren limbs one above the other, but now there is only the *reminder* of what used to be. The present is quiet, bleak, trembly, and lonely; it is the absence of color, song, and life that creates the strong visual impression, a reminder of what formerly was.)

6. Shortly.    7. Sleep.

The next four lines are slightly different in tone, and the color changes. From a black-and-white landscape with a few yellow leaves, we come upon a rich and almost warm reminder of a faded sunset. But a somber note does enter the poem in these lines through another figure of speech, **personification,** which involves treating an abstraction, such as death or justice or beauty, as if it were a person. The poem is talking about the coming of night and of sleep, and Sleep is personified and identified as the "second self" of Death (that is, as a kind of "double" for death). The main emphasis is on how night and sleep close in on our sense of twilight, and only secondarily does a reminder of death enter the poem. But it does enter.

The third metaphor—that of the dying embers of a fire—begins in line 9 and continues to color and warm the bleak cold that the poem began with, but it also sharpens the reminder of death. The three main metaphors in the poem work in a way to make our sense of old age and approaching death more familiar, but also more immediate: moving from barren trees, to fading twilight, to dying embers suggests a sensuous increase of color and warmth, but also an increasing urgency. The first metaphor involves a whole season, or at least a segment of one, a matter of days or possibly weeks; the second involves the passing of a single day, reducing the time scale to a matter of minutes, and the third draws our attention to that split second when a glowing ember fades into a gray ash. The final part of the fire metaphor introduces the most explicit sense of death so far, as the metaphor of embers shifts into a direct reminder of death. Embers, which had been a metaphor of the speaker's aging body, now themselves become, metaphorically, a deathbed; the vitality that nourishes youth is used up just as a log in a fire is. The urgency of the reminder of coming death has now peaked. It is friendlier but now seems immediate and inevitable, a natural part of the life process, and the final two lines then make an explicit plea to make good and intense use of the remaining moments of human relationship.

"That time of year" represents an unusually intricate use of images to organize a poem and focus its emotional impact. Not all poems are so skillfully made, and not all depend on such a full and varied use of metaphor. But most poems use metaphors for at least part of their effect, and often a poem is based on a single metaphor that is fully developed as the major way of making the poem's statement and impact, as in the following poem about the role of a mother and wife.

LINDA PASTAN

## Marks

My husband gives me an A
for last night's supper,
an incomplete for my ironing,
a B plus in bed.
My son says I am average,
an average mother, but if
I put my mind to it
I could improve.
My daughter believes

in Pass/Fail and tells me                                        10
I pass. Wait 'til they learn
I'm dropping out.                                              1978

The speaker in "Marks" is obviously not thrilled with the idea of continually being judged, and the metaphor of marks (or grades) as a way of talking about her performance of roles in the family suggests her irritation. The list of the roles implies the many things expected of her, and the three different systems of marking (letter grades, categories to be checked off on a chart, and pass/fail) detail the difficulties of multiple standards. The poem retains the language of schooldays all the way to the end ("learn," line 11; "dropping out," line 12), and the major effect of the poem depends on the irony of the speaker's surrendering to the metaphor the family has thrust upon her; if she is to be judged as if she were a student, she retains the right to leave the system. Ironically, she joins the system (adopts the metaphor for herself) in order to defeat it.

The following poem depends from the beginning—even from its title—on a single metaphor and the values associated with it.

DAVID WAGONER

## My Father's Garden

On his way to the open hearth where white-hot steel
Boiled against furnace walls in wait for his lance
To pierce the fireclay and set loose demons
And dragons in molten tons, blazing
Down to the huge satanic caldrons,                               5
Each day he would pass the scrapyard, his kind of garden.

In rusty rockeries of stoves and brake drums,
In grottoes of sewing machines and refrigerators,
He would pick flowers for us: small gears and cogwheels
With teeth like petals, with holes for anthers,                  10
Long stalks of lead to be poured into toy soldiers,
Ball bearings as big as grapes to knock them down.

He was called a melter. He tried to keep his brain
From melting in those tyger-mouthed mills
Where the same steel reappeared over and over                    15
To be reborn in the fire as something better
Or worse: cannons or cars, needles or girders,
Flagpoles, swords, or plowshares.

But it melted. His classical learning ran
Down and away from him, not burning bright.                      20
His fingers culled a few cold scraps of Latin

And Greek, *magna sine laude*,[8] for crosswords
And brought home lumps of tin and sewer grills
As if they were his ripe prize vegetables.                                    1987

The poem is a tribute to the speaker's father and the things he understands and values in his ordinary, workingman's life. The father is a "melter" (line 13) in the steel mills (lines 14–15), and what he values are the things made from what he helps to produce. His avocation has developed from his vocation: he collects metal objects from the scrapyard and brings them home just as some other men would pick flowers for their families. The scrapyard is, says the speaker, "his kind of garden" (line 6). The life led by the father has been a hard one, but he shows love for his children in the only way he knows how—by bringing home things that mean something to him and that can be made into toys his children will come to value. Describing these scraps as the products of his garden—"As if they were his ripe prize vegetables" (line 24)—has the effect of making them seem home-grown, carefully tended, nurtured by the father into a useful beauty. Instead of crude and ugly pieces of scrap, they become—through the metaphor of the poem— examples of value and beauty corresponding to the warm feelings the speaker has for a father who did what he could with what he knew and what he had.

Poets often are self-conscious and explicit about the ways they use language metaphorically, and sometimes (as in the following poem) they celebrate the richness of language that makes their art possible:

### ROBERT FRANCIS

## *Hogwash*

The tongue that mothered such a metaphor
Only the purest purist could despair of.

Nobody ever called swill sweet but isn't
Hogwash a daisy in a field of daisies?

5      What beside sports and flowers could you find
To praise better than the American language?

Bruised by American foreign policy.
What shall I soothe me, what defend me with

But a handful of clean unmistakable words—
10     Daisies, daisies, in a field of daisies?                                    1965

The poet here claims little for his own invention and not much for the art of poetry, insisting that the American language itself is responsible for miraculous conceptions.

---

8. Without great distinction; a reversal of the usual *magna cum laude.*

The poet plays cheerfully here with what words offer—the pun on "purest" and "purist" (line 2), for example, and the taunting (but misleading) similarity of the beginnings of "swill" and "sweet" (line 3)—but insists that poems and poets only articulate things already realized in common speech, where metaphors are "mothered" (line 1). "Hogwash," although never explicitly glossed or discussed in the poem, is the primary example: What *does* "hogwash" mean? How do hogs wash themselves and in what? to what purpose and effect? How did the term get invented as a metaphor, and what are its visual implications? And what is it doing as an example of beauty in a poem about "clean unmistakable words" (line 9)? But then the poem plays even more fully with "daisy" (lines 4 and 10) as metaphor and idiomatic expression. A "daisy" is a great success, a breakthrough, a beaut, a perfect example, and the word "hogwash" is such a daisy, an instance of such a success: a "daisy in a field of daisies," a success of successes, a wonder in a language full of wonders.

Not everything American, according to this poem, is as praiseworthy as its language, and the word "hogwash" ultimately has its context established in the poem's fourth stanza when the speaker finally tells us why the word is so soothing and so pertinent. Poets, the poem says, need words and metaphors that are not always images of beauty because the world is full of things that are not altogether beautiful, and metaphors of ugliness can be "daisies," too.

Not all poets feel as positive as Francis claims to be here about the raw materials they have to work with in language. Ultimately, of course, the modesty of the poet's claims here about his own inventiveness becomes as comic as the metaphor of "hogwash" itself and the poem's characterization of foreign policy, for it is the poem that makes this particular use of the metaphor, no matter where or when it was invented: the wit belongs to the poem, not the language. Poets make use of whatever idioms, expressions, inherited metaphors, and traditions of language come their way, and they turn them to their own uses, sometimes quite surprisingly.

The difficulty of conveying what some experiences are like and how we feel about them sometimes leads poets to startling comparisons and figures of speech that may at first seem far-fetched but that, in one way or another, do in fact suggest the quality of the experience or the feelings associated with it. Sometimes they use a series of metaphors, as if no single act of visualization will serve but several together may suggest the full complexity of the experience or cumulatively define the feeling precisely. Metaphors open up virtually endless possibilities of comparison, giving words a chance to be more than words, offering our mind's eye a challenge to keep up with the fertile and articulate imagination of writers who make it their business to see things that ordinary people miss, noticing the most surprising likenesses and conveying feelings more powerfully than politicians usually do.

Sometimes, in poetry as in prose, comparisons are made explicitly, as in the following poem.

ROBERT BURNS

## A Red, Red Rose

O, my luve's like a red, red rose
That's newly sprung in June.

O, my luve is like the melodie
That's sweetly played in tune.

5   As fair art thou, my bonnie lass,
So deep in luve am I;
And I will luve thee still, my dear,
Till a' the seas gang[9] dry.

Till a' the seas gang dry, my dear,
10   And the rocks melt wi' the sun;
And I will luve thee still, my dear,
While the sands o' life shall run.

And fare thee weel, my only luve,
And fare thee weel a while!
15   And I will come again, my luve,
Though it were ten thousand mile.                    1796

The first four lines make two explicit comparisons: the speaker says that his love is "like a . . . rose" and "like [a] melodie." Such *explicit* comparison is called a simile, and usually (as here) the comparison involves the words "like" or "as." Similes work much as do metaphors, except that they usually are used more passingly, more incidentally; they make a quick comparison and usually do not elaborate, whereas metaphors often extend over a long section of a poem (in which case they are called **extended metaphors**) or even over the whole poem, as in "Marks" (in which case they are called **controlling metaphors**).

The two similes in "A Red, Red Rose" assume that we already have a favorable opinion of roses and of melodies. Here the poet does not develop the comparison or even remind us of attractive details about roses or tunes. He pays the quick compliment and moves on. Similes sometimes develop more elaborate comparisons than this and occasionally even control long sections of a poem (in which case they are called **analogies**), but usually a simile is briefer and relies more fully on something we already know. The speaker in "My Papa's Waltz" says that he hung on "like death"; he doesn't have to explain or elaborate the comparison: we know the anxiety he refers to.

Like metaphors, similes may imply both meaning and feeling; they may both explain something and invoke feelings about it. All figurative language involves an attempt to clarify something *and* to help readers feel a certain way about it. Saying that one's love is like a rose implies a delicate and fragile beauty and invites our senses into play so that we can share sensuously a response to fragrant appeal and soft touch, just as the shivering boughs and dying embers in "That time of year" explain separation and loss at the same time that they invite us to share the cold sense of loneliness and the warmth of old friendship.

Once you are alerted to look for them, you will find figures of speech in poem after poem; they are among the most common devices through which poets share their vision with us.

The following poem uses a variety of metaphors to describe sexual experiences.

9. Go.

ADRIENNE RICH

## *Two Songs*

### 1

Sex, as they harshly call it,
I fell into this morning
at ten o'clock, a drizzling hour
of traffic and wet newspapers.
I thought of him who yesterday                                    5
clearly didn't
turn me to a hot field
ready for plowing,
and longing for that young man
piercéd me to the roots                                          10
bathing every vein, etc.[1]
All day he appears to me
touchingly desirable,
a prize one could wreck one's peace for.
I'd call it love if love                                         15
didn't take so many years
but lust too is a jewel
a sweet flower and what
pure happiness to know
all our high-toned questions                                     20
breed in a lively animal.

### 2

That "old last act"!
And yet sometimes
all seems post coitum triste[2]
and I a mere bystander.                                          25
Somebody else is going off,
getting shot to the moon.
Or, a moon-race!
Split seconds after
my opposite number lands                                         30
I make it—
we lie fainting together
at a crater-edge
heavy as mercury in our moonsuits
till he speaks                                                   35
in a different language
yet one I've picked up
through cultural exchanges . . .

1. See the opening lines of the Prologue to Chaucer's *Canterbury Tales*.   2. Sadness after sexual union.

we murmur the first moonwords:
    *Spasibo*.[3] Thanks. O.K.                                        1964

40

    The first "song" begins straightforwardly as narration ("Sex . . . I fell into this morn-ing/at ten o'clock"), but the vividness of sex and desire is communicated mostly by figure. The speaker describes her body as "a hot field/ready for plowing" (lines 7–8)— quite unlike her resistant body yesterday—and her longing is also described by meta-phor, in this case an elaborate one borrowed from another poem. After so sensual and urgent a beginning, the song turns more thoughtful and philosophical, but even the intellectual sorting between love and lust comes to depend on figures: lust is a "jewel" (line 17) and a "flower" (line 18). After the opening pace and excitement, those later metaphors seem calm and tame, moving the poem from the lust of its beginning to a contemplative reflection on the value and beauty of momentary physical pleasures.

    The second song depends on two closely related metaphors, and here the metaphors for sex are highly self-conscious and a little comic. The song begins on a plaintive note, considering the classic melancholic feeling after sex; the speaker pictures herself as isolated, left out, "a bystander" (line 25), while someone else is having sexual pleasure. This pleasure of others is described through two colloquial expressions (both metaphors) for sexual climax: "going off" (line 26) and "getting shot to the moon" (line 27). Suddenly the narrator pretends to take sex as space travel seriously and creates a metaphor of her own: sexual partners running a "moon-race" (line 28). The rest of the poem enacts the metaphor in the context of the space race between the United States and Russia in the early 1960s. The race, not exactly even but close enough, is described in detail, and the speaker tells her story in a self-conscious, comic way. These are international relations, foreign affairs, and the lovers appropriately say their thank-yous separately in Russian and English, then communicate an international *"O.K."*

RANDALL JARRELL

## *The Death of the Ball Turret Gunner*[4]

From my mother's sleep I fell into the State,
And I hunched in its belly till my wet fur froze.
Six miles from earth, loosed from its dream of life,
I woke to black flak and the nightmare fighters.
When I died they washed me out of the turret with a hose.                    1945

5

3. Russian for "thanks."     4. "A ball turret a plexiglass sphere set into the belly of a B-17 or B-24 and inhabited by two .50 caliber machine-guns and one man, a short, small man. When this gunner tracked with his machine-guns a fighter attacking his bomber from below, he revolved with the turret; hunched upside-down in his little sphere, he looked like the foetus in the womb. The fighters which attacked him were armed with cannon firing explosive shells. The hose was a steam hose." (RJ)

LINDA PASTAN

## *Erosion*

We are slowly
undermined. Grain
by grain . . .
inch by inch . . .
slippage.                                                    5
It happens as we watch.
The waves move their long row
of scythes over the beach.

It happens as we sleep,
the way the clock's hands                                    10
move continuously
just out of sight,
but more like an hourglass
than a clock,
for here sand                                                15
is running out.

We wake to water.
Implacably lovely
is this view
though it will swallow                                       20
us whole, soon
there will be
nothing left
but view.

We have tried a seawall.                                     25
We have tried prayer.
We have planted grasses
on the bank, small tentacles
hooks of green that catch
on nothing. For the wind                                     30
does its work, the water
does its sure work.

One day the sea will simply
take us. The children
press their faces to the glass                               35
as if the windows were portholes,
and the house fills
with animals: two dogs,
a bird, cats—we are becoming
an ark already.                                              40

The gulls will follow
our wake.

We are made of water anyway,
I can feel it in the yielding
of your flesh, though sometimes
I think that you are sand,
moving slowly, slowly
from under me.                                    1988

DOROTHY LIVESAY

## *Other*

### 1

Men prefer an island
With its beginning ended:
Undertone of waves
Trees overbended.

Men prefer a road
Circling, shell-like
Convex and fossiled
Forever winding inward.

Men prefer a woman
Limpid in sunlight
Held as a shell
On a sheltering island . . .

Men prefer an island.

### 2

But I am mainland
O I range
From upper country to the inner core:
From sageland, brushland, marshland
To the sea's floor.

Show me an orchard where I have not slept,
A hollow where I have not wrapped
The sage about me, and above, the still
Stars clustering
Over the ponderosa pine, the cactus hill.

Tell me a time
I have not loved,
A mountain left unclimbed:
A prairie field
Where I have not furrowed my tongue,
Nourished it out of the mind's dark places;

Planted with tears unwept                                              30
And harvested as friends, as faces.

O find me a dead-end road
I have not trodden
A logging road that leads the heart away
Into the secret evergreen of cedar roots                               35
Beyond sun's farthest ray—
Then, in a clearing's sudden dazzle,
There is no road; no end; no puzzle.

But do not show me! For I know
The country I caress:                                                  40
A place where none shall trespass
None possess:
A mainland mastered
From its inaccess.

 ——

Men prefer an island.                                                  45

                                                                  1955


HART CRANE

## Forgetfulness

Forgetfulness is like a song
That, freed from beat and measure, wanders.
Forgetfulness is like a bird whose wings are reconciled,
Outspread and motionless,—
A bird that coasts the wind unwearyingly.                              5

Forgetfulness is rain at night,
Or an old house in a forest,—or a child.
Forgetfulness is white,—white as a blasted tree,
And it may stun the sybil into prophecy,
Or bury the Gods.                                                      10

I can remember much forgetfulness.                           p. 1918


CAROLYN FORCHÉ

## Taking Off My Clothes

I take off my shirt, I show you.
I shaved the hair out under my arms.

I roll up my pants, I scraped off the hair
on my legs with a knife, getting white.

My hair is the color of chopped maples
My eyes dark as beans cooked in the south.
(Coal fields in the moon on torn-up hills)

Skin polished as a Ming bowl
showing its blood cracks, its age, I have hundreds
of names for the snow, for this, all of them quiet.

In the night I come to you and it seems a shame.
to waste my deepest shudders on a wall of a man.

You recognize strangers,
think you lived through destruction.
You can't explain this night, my face, your memory.

You want to know what I know?
Your own hands are lying.                                    1976


EMILY DICKINSON

# [*Wild Nights—Wild Nights!*]

Wild Nights—Wild Nights!
Were I with thee
Wild Nights should be
Our luxury!

Futile—the Winds—
To a Heart in port—
Done with the Compass—
Done with the Chart!

Rowing in Eden—
Ah, the Sea!
Might I but moor—Tonight—
In Thee!

ca. 1861

AGHA SHAHID ALI

## The Dacca Gauzes

*. . . for a whole year he sought*
*to accumulate the most exquisite*
*Dacca gauzes.*
      —OSCAR WILDE / *The Picture*
            *of Dorian Gray*

Those transparent Dacca gauzes
known as woven air, running
water, evening dew:

a dead art now, dead over
a hundred years. "No one                                        5
now knows," my grandmother says,

"what it was to wear
or touch that cloth." She wore
it once, an heirloom sari from

her mother's dowry, proved                                      10
genuine when it was pulled, all
six yards, through a ring.

Years later when it tore,
many handkerchiefs embroidered
with gold-thread paisleys                                       15

were distributed among
the nieces and daughters-in-law.
Those too now lost.

In history we learned: the hands
of weavers were amputated,                                      20
the looms of Bengal silenced,

and the cotton shipped raw
by the British to England.
History of little use to her,

my grandmother just says                                        25
how the muslins of today
seem so coarse and that only

in autumn, should one wake up
at dawn to pray, can one
feel that same texture again.                                   30

One morning, she says, the air
was dew-starched: she pulled
it absently through her ring.                        1987

AMY LOWELL

## Aubade

As I would free the white almond from the green husk
So would I strip your trappings off,
Beloved.
And fingering the smooth and polished kernel
5    I should see that in my hands glittered a gem beyond counting.        1917


JOHN DONNE

## [*Batter my heart, three-personed God; for You*][5]

Batter my heart, three-personed God; for You
As yet but knock, breathe, shine, and seek to mend;
That I may rise and stand, o'erthrow me, and bend
Your force, to break, blow, burn, and make me new.
5    I, like an usurped town, to another due,
Labor to admit You, but Oh, to no end!
Reason, Your viceroy[6] in me, me should defend,
But is captived, and proves weak or untrue.
Yet dearly I love You, and would be loved fain,[7]
10   But am betrothed unto Your enemy:
Divorce me, untie or break that knot again,
Take me to You, imprison me, for I,
Except You enthrall me, never shall be free,
Nor ever chaste, except You ravish me.                              1633


ANONYMOUS[8]

## The Twenty-third Psalm

The Lord is my shepherd; I shall not want.
He maketh me to lie down in green pastures: he leadeth me beside
        the still waters.
He restoreth my soul: he leadeth me in the paths of righteousness
        for his name's sake.

---

5. *Holy Sonnets*, 14.      6. One who rules as the representative of a higher power.      7. Gladly.
8. Traditionally attributed to King David. The English translation printed here is from the King James
Version.

Yea, though I walk through the valley of the shadow of death,
    I will fear no evil: for thou art with me;
    thy rod and thy staff they comfort me.
Thou preparest a table before me in the presence of mine enemies:
    thou anointest my head with oil; my cup runneth over.      5
Surely goodness and mercy shall follow me all the days of my life:
    and I will dwell in the house of the Lord for ever.

## SYMBOL

The word *symbol* is often used sloppily and sometimes pretentiously, but properly used the term suggests one of the most basic things about poems—their ability to get beyond what words signify and make larger claims about meanings in the verbal world. All words go beyond themselves. They are not simply a collection of sounds: they signify something beyond their sounds, often things or actions or ideas. Words describe not only a verbal universe but a world in which actions occur, acts have implications, and events mean. Sometimes words not only signify something beyond themselves—a rock or a tree or a cloud—but symbolize something as well—solidity or life or dreams. Words can—when their implications are agreed on by tradition, convention, or habit—stand for things beyond their most immediate meanings or significations and become symbols, and even simple words that have accumulated no special power from previous use may be given special significance in special circumstances—either in poetry or in life itself.

A **symbol** is, put simply, something that stands for something else. The everyday world is full of common examples; a flag, a logo, a trademark, or a skull and crossbones all suggest things beyond themselves, and everyone is likely to understand what their display is meant to indicate, whether or not the viewer shares a commitment to what the object represents. In common usage a prison is a symbol of confinement, constriction, and loss of freedom, and in specialized traditional usage a cross may symbolize oppression, cruelty, suffering, death, resurrection, triumph, or the intersection of two separate things, traditions, or ideas (as in crossroads and crosscurrents, for example). The specific symbolic significance is controlled by the context; a reader may often decide what it is by looking at contiguous details in the poem and by examining the poem's attitude toward a particular tradition or body of beliefs. A star means one kind of thing to a Jewish poet and something else to a Christian poet, still something else to a sailor or actor. In a very literal sense, words themselves are all symbols (they stand for an object, action, or quality, not just for letters or sounds), but symbols in poetry are said to be those words and groups of words that have a range of reference beyond their literal signification or denotation.

Poems sometimes create a symbol out of a thing, action, or event that has no previously agreed upon symbolic significance. In the following poem, for example, a random gesture is given symbolic significance.

SHARON OLDS

## *Leningrad Cemetery, Winter of 1941*[9]

That winter, the dead could not be buried.
The ground was frozen, the gravediggers weak from hunger,
the coffin wood used for fuel. So they were covered with something
and taken on a child's sled to the cemetery
5    in the sub-zero air. They lay on the soil,
some of them wrapped in dark cloth

---

9. The 900-day siege of Leningrad during World War II began in September 1941.

bound with rope like the tree's ball of roots
when it waits to be planted; others wound in sheets,
their pale, gauze, tapered shapes
stiff as cocoons that will split down the center                              10
when the new life inside is prepared;
but most lay like corpses, their coverings
coming undone, naked calves
hard as corded wood spilling
from under a cloak, a hand reaching out                                       15
with no sign of peace, wanting to come back
even to the bread made of glue and sawdust,
even to the icy winter, and the siege.                              p. 1979

All of the corpses—frozen, neglected, beginning to be in disarray—vividly stamp upon our minds a sense of the horrors of war, and the detailed picture of the random, uncounted clutter of bodies is likely to stay in our minds long after we have finished reading the poem. Several of the details are striking, and the poem's language heightens our sense of them. The corpses wound in sheets, for example, are described in "their pale, gauze, tapered shapes" (line 9), and they are compared to cocoons that one day will split and emit new life; and the limbs that dangle loose when the coverings come undone are said to be "hard as corded wood spilling" (line 14). But clearly the most memorable sight is the hand dangling from one corpse that is coming unwrapped, for the poet invests that hand with special significance, giving its gesture *meaning.* The hand is described as "reaching out . . . wanting to come back" (lines 15–16): it is as if the dead can still gesture even if they cannot speak, and the gesture seems to signify the desire of the dead to come back at any price. They would be glad to be alive, even under the grim conditions that attend the living in Leningrad during this grim war. Suddenly the grimness that we—living—have been witnessing pales by comparison with what the dead have lost simply by being dead. The hand has been made to *symbolize* the desire of the dead to return, to be alive, to be still among us, anywhere. The hand reaches out in the poem as a gesture that means; the poet has made it a symbol of desire.

The whole array of dead bodies in the poem might be said to be symbolic as well. As a group, they stand for the human waste that the war has produced, and their dramatic visual presence provides the poem with a dramatic visualization of how war and its requirements have no time for decency, not even the decency of burial. The bodies are a symbol in the sense that they stand for what the poem as a whole asserts.

The poem that follows also arises out of a historical moment, but this time the event is a personal one that the poet gives a significance by the interpretation he puts upon it.

JAMES DICKEY

## The Leap

The only thing I have of Jane MacNaughton
Is one instant of a dancing-class dance.
She was the fastest runner in the seventh grade,

My scrapbook says, even when boys were beginning
To be as big as the girls,
But I do not have her running in my mind,
Though Frances Lane is there, Agnes Fraser,
Fat Betty Lou Black in the boys-against-girls
Relays we ran at recess: she must have run

Like the other girls, with her skirts tucked up
So they would be like bloomers,
But I cannot tell; that part of her is gone.
What I do have is when she came,
With the hem of her skirt where it should be
For a young lady, into the annual dance
Of the dancing class we all hated, and with a light
Grave leap, jumped up and touched the end
Of one of the paper-ring decorations

To see if she could reach it. She could,
And reached me now as well, hanging in my mind
From a brown chain of brittle paper, thin
And muscular, wide-mouthed, eager to prove
Whatever it proves when you leap
In a new dress, a new womanhood, among the boys
Whom you easily left in the dust
Of the passionless playground. If I said I saw
In the paper where Jane MacNaughton Hill,

Mother of four, leapt to her death from a window
Of a downtown hotel, and that her body crushed-in
The top of a parked taxi, and that I held
Without trembling a picture of her lying cradled
In that papery steel as though lying in the grass,
One shoe idly off, arms folded across her breast,
I would not believe myself. I would say
The convenient thing, that it was a bad dream
Of maturity, to see that eternal process

Most obsessively wrong with the world
Come out of her light, earth-spurning feet
Grown heavy: would say that in the dusty heels
Of the playground some boy who did not depend
On speed of foot, caught and betrayed her.
Jane, stay where you are in my first mind:
It was odd in that school, at that dance.
I and the other slow-footed yokels sat in corners
Cutting rings out of drawing paper

Before you leapt in your new dress
And touched the end of something I began,
Above the couples struggling on the floor,
New men and women clutching at each other
And prancing foolishly as bears: hold on

To that ring I made for you, Jane—
My feet are nailed to the ground
By dust I swallowed thirty years ago—
While I examine my hands.                                    1967

Memory is crucial to "The Leap." The fact that Jane MacNaughton's graceful leap in dancing class has stuck in the speaker's mind for all these years means that this leap was important to him, meant something to him, stood for something in his mind. For the speaker, the leap is an "instant" and the "only thing" he has of Jane. Its grace and ease are what he remembers, and he struggles at several points to articulate its meaning (lines 15–26, 44–50), but even without articulation or explanation it is there in his head as a visual memory, a symbol for him of something beyond himself, something he cannot do, something he wanted to be. What that leap had stood for, or symbolized, was boldness, confidence, accomplishment, maturity, the ability to go beyond her fellow students in dancing class—the transcending of childhood by someone beginning to be a woman. Her feet now seem "earth-spurning" (line 38) in that original leap, and they separate her from everyone else. Jane MacNaughton was beyond the speaker's abilities and any attempt he could make to articulate his hopes, but not beyond his dreams. And even before articulation, she symbolized that dream.

The leap to her death seems cruelly inappropriate and ironic in the context of her earlier leap. In memory she is suspended in air, as if there were no gravity, no coming back to earth, as if life could exist as dream. And so the photograph, re-created in precise detail, is a cruel dashing of the speaker's dream—a detailed record of the ending of a leap, a denial of the suspension in which his memory had held her. His dream is grounded; her mortality is insistent. But what the speaker wants to hang on to (line 42) is still that symbolic moment which, although now confronted in more mature implications, will never be altogether replaced or surrendered.

The leap is ultimately symbolic in the *poem*, too, not just in the speaker's mind. In the poem (and for us as readers) the symbolism of the leap is double: the first leap is aspiration, and the second is the frustration and grounding of high hopes; the two are complementary, one unable to be imagined without the other. The poem is horrifying in some ways, a dramatic reminder that human beings don't ultimately transcend their mortality, their limits, no matter how heroic or unencumbered by gravity they may seem to an observer. But it is not altogether sad and despairing either, partly because it notices and affirms the validity of the original leap and partly because another symbol is created and elaborated in the poem. That symbol is the paper chain.

The chain connects Jane to the speaker both literally and figuratively. It is, in part, *his* paper chain which she had leaped to touch in dancing class (lines 18–19), and he thinks of her first leap as "touch[ing] the end of something I began" (line 47). He and the other "slow-footed," earthbound "yokels" (line 44) were the makers of the chain, and thus they are connected to her original leap, just as a photograph glimpsed in the paper connects the speaker to her second leap. The paper in the chain is "brittle" (line 21), and its creators seem dull artisans compared to the artistic performer that Jane was. They are heavy and "left in the dust" (lines 25, 52–53), and she is "light" (line 16) and able to transcend them but even in transcendence touching their lives and what they are able to do. And so the paper chain becomes the poem's symbol of linkage, connecting lower accomplishment to higher possibility, the artisan to the artist, material substance to the act of imagination. And the speaker at the end examines the hands that made the chain because those hands certify his connection to her and the imaginative leap she had made for him. The chain thus symbolizes not only the lower capabilities of those who cannot leap like the budding Jane could, but (later) the connection with her leap as both transcendence and mortality. Like the leap itself, the chain has been elevated to special meaning, given symbolic significance, by the poet's treatment of it. A leap and a chain have no necessary significance in themselves to most of us—at least no significance that we have all agreed upon together—but they may be given significance in specific circumstances or a specific text.

But some objects and acts do have a significance built in because of past usage in literature, or tradition, or the stories a culture develops to explain itself and its values. Over the years some things have acquired an agreed-upon significance, an accepted value in our minds. They already stand for something before the poet cites them; they are **traditional symbols.** Their uses in poetry have to do with the fact that poets can count on a recognition of their traditional suggestions and meanings outside the poem, and the poem does not have to propose or argue a particular symbolic value. Birds, for example, traditionally symbolize flight, freedom from confinement, detachment from earthbound limits, the ability to soar beyond rationality and transcend mortal limits. Traditionally, birds have also been linked with imagination, especially poetic imagination, and poets often identify with them as pure and ideal singers of songs, as in Keats's "Ode to a Nightingale." One of the most traditional symbols is the rose. It may be a simple and fairly plentiful flower in its season, but it has been allowed to stand for particular qualities for so long that to name it raises predictable expectations. Its beauty, delicacy, fragility, shortness of life, and depth of color have made it a symbol of the transitoriness of beauty, and countless poets have counted on its accepted symbolism—sometimes to compliment a friend (as Burns does in "A Red, Red Rose") or sometimes to make a point about the nature of symbolism. The following poem draws on, in a quite traditional way, the traditional meanings.

### JOHN CLARE

## *Love's Emblem*

Go, rose, my Chloe's[1] bosom grace:
   How happy should I prove,
Could I supply that envied place
   With never-fading love.

5    Accept, dear maid, now summer glows,
   This pure, unsullied gem,
Love's emblem in a full-blown rose,
   Just broken from the stem.

Accept it as a favorite flower
10    For thy soft breast to wear;

---

1. A standard "poetic" name for a woman in traditional love poetry.

'Twill blossom there its transient hour,
   A favorite of the fair.

Upon thy cheek its blossom glows,
   As from a mirror clear,
Making thyself a living rose,                    15
   In blossom all the year.

It is a sweet and favorite flower
   To grace a maiden's brow,
Emblem of love without its power—
   A sweeter rose art thou.          20

The rose, like hues of insect wing,
   May perish in an hour;
'Tis but at best a fading thing,
   But thou'rt a living flower.

The roses steeped in morning dews                25
   Would every eye enthrall,
But woman, she alone subdues;
   Her beauty conquers all.              1873

The speaker in "Love's Emblem" sends the rose to Chloe to decorate her bosom (lines 1, 10) and reflect the blush of her cheek and brow (lines 13, 18), and he goes on to mention some of the standard meanings: the rose is pure (line 6), transitory (line 11), fragrant, beautiful, and always appreciated (line 17). The poet here does not elaborate or argue these things; he counts on the tradition, habits of mind built on familiarity and repetition (though, of course, readers unfamiliar with the tradition will not respond in the same way—that is one reason it is difficult to read with full appreciation texts from another linguistic or cultural tradition). To say that the rose is an emblem of love is to say that it traditionally symbolizes love, and the speaker expects Chloe to accept his gift readily; she will understand it as a compliment, a pledge, and a bond. She will understand, too, that her admirer is being conventional and complimentary in going on to call her (and women in general) a rose (line 20), except that her qualities are said to be more lasting than those of a momentary flower.

Poems often use traditional symbols to invoke predictable responses—in effect using shortcuts to meaning and power by repeating acts of signification and symbolization sanctioned by time and cultural habit. But often poets examine the tradition even as they employ it, and sometimes they revise or reverse meanings built into the tradition. Some of the poems at the end of this chapter question the usual meanings of roses in poetry and evaluate as they go. Symbols do not necessarily stay the same over time, and poets often turn even the most traditional of symbols to their own original uses. Knowing the traditions of poetry—reading a lot of poems and observing how they tend to use certain words, metaphors, and symbols—can be very useful in reading new poems, but traditions modify and individual poems do highly individual things. Knowing the past never means being able to predict new texts with confidence. Symbolism makes things happen, but individual poets and texts determine what will happen and how.

Sometimes symbols—traditional or not—become so insistent in the world of a poem that the larger referential world is left almost totally behind. In such cases the symbol is everything, and the poem does not just *use* symbols but becomes a **symbolic poem,** usually a highly individualized one dependent on an internal system introduced by the individual poet.

Here is an example of such a poem:

WILLIAM BLAKE

## The Sick Rose[2]

O rose, thou art sick.
The invisible worm
That flies in the night
In the howling storm

5   Has found out thy bed
Of crimson joy,
And his dark secret love
Does thy life destroy.

1794

The poem does not seem to be about a rose, but about what the rose represents—not in this case something altogether understandable through the traditional meanings of rose.

We know that the rose is usually associated with beauty and love, often with sex; and here several key terms have sexual connotations: "bed," "worm," and "crimson joy." The violation of the rose by the worm is the poem's main concern; the violation seems to have involved secrecy, deceit, and "dark" motives, and the result is sickness rather than the joy of love. The poem is sad; it involves a sense of hurt and tragedy, nearly of despair. The poem cries out against the misuse of the rose, against its desecration, implying that instead of a healthy joy in sensuality and sexuality, there has been in this case destruction and hurt because of misunderstanding and repression and lack of sensitivity.

But to say so much about this poem I have had to extrapolate from other poems by this poet, and have introduced information from outside the poem. Fully symbolic poems often require that, and thus they ask us to go beyond the formal procedures of reading that we have discussed so far. As presented in this poem, the rose is not part of the normal world that we ordinarily see, and it is symbolic in a special sense. The poet does not simply take an object from that everyday world and give it special significance, making it a symbol in the same sense that the leap or the corpse's hand is a symbol. Here the rose seems to belong to its own world, a world made entirely inside the poem or the poet's head. The rose is not referential, or not primarily so. The whole poem is symbolic; it is not paraphrasable; it lives in its own world. But what is the rose here a symbol of? In general terms, we can say from what the poem tells us; but we may not be

---

2. In Renaissance emblem books, the scarab beetle, worm, and rose are closely associated: the beetle feeds on dung, and the smell of the rose is fatal to it.

as confident as we can be in the more nearly everyday world of "The Leap" or "Leningrad Cemetery, Winter of 1941," poems that contain actions we recognize from the world of probabilities in which we live. In "The Sick Rose," it seems inappropriate to ask the standard questions: What rose? Where? Which worm? What are the particulars here? In the world of this poem worms can fly and may be invisible. We are altogether in a world of meanings that have been formulated according to a particular system of knowledge and code of belief. We will only feel comfortable and confident in that world if we read many poems written by the poet (in this case William Blake) within the same symbolic system.

Negotiation of meanings in symbolic poems can be very difficult indeed. The skill of reading symbolic poems is an advanced skill that depends on special knowledge of authors and of the special traditions they work from. But usually the symbols you will find in poems *are* referential, and these meanings are readily discoverable from the careful study of the poems themselves, as in poems like "The Leap" and "Love's Emblem."

EDMUND WALLER

## *Song*

Go, lovely rose!
Tell her that wastes her time and me
   That now she knows,
When I resemble[3] her to thee,
How sweet and fair she seems to be.              5

Tell her that's young,
And shuns to have her graces spied,
   That hadst thou sprung
In deserts, where no men abide,
Thou must have uncommended died.        10

Small is the worth
Of beauty from the light retired;
   Bid her come forth,
Suffer herself to be desired,
And not blush so to be admired.         15

Then die! that she
The common fate of all things rare
   May read in thee;
How small a part of time they share
That are so wondrous sweet and fair!      20

1645

3. Compare.

JOHN GAY

## [*Virgins are like the fair flower in its luster*][4]

Virgins are like the fair flower in its luster,
Which in the garden enamels the ground;
Near it the bees in play flutter and cluster,
And gaudy butterflies frolic around.
But, when once pluck'd, 'tis no longer alluring,
To Covent-Garden[5] 'tis sent, (as yet sweet),
There fades, and shrinks, and grows past all enduring,
Rots, stinks, and dies, and is trod under feet.

1728

EMILY DICKINSON

## [*Go not too near a House of Rose—*]

Go not too near a House of Rose—
The depredation of a Breeze
Or inundation of a Dew
Alarms its walls away—

Nor try to tie the Butterfly,
Nor climb the Bars of Ecstasy,
In insecurity to lie
Is Joy's insuring quality.

ca. 1878

WILLIAM CARLOS WILLIAMS

## *Poem*

The rose fades
and is renewed again
by its seed, naturally
but where

save in the poem
shall it go
to suffer no diminution
of its splendor

1962

4. From *The Beggar's Opera*.    5. A fruit and vegetable market in London (but also a haven for prostitutes).

MARY OLIVER

_____

## Roses, Late Summer

What happens
to the leaves after
they turn red and golden and fall
away? What happens

to the singing birds                                                     5
when they can't sing
any longer? What happens
to their quick wings?

Do you think there is any
personal heaven                                                         10
for any of us?
Do you think anyone,

the other side of that darkness,
will call to us, meaning us?
Beyond the trees                                                        15
the foxes keep teaching their children

to live in the valley.
So they never seem to vanish, they are always there
in the blossom of light
that stands up every morning                                            20

in the dark sky.
And over one more set of hills,
along the sea,
the last roses have opened their factories of sweetness

and are giving it back to the world.                                    25
If I had another life
I would want to spend it all on some
unstinting happiness.

I would be a fox, or a tree
full of waving branches.                                                30
I wouldn't mind being a rose
in a field full of roses.

Fear has not yet occurred to them, nor ambition.
Reason they have not yet thought of.
Neither do they ask how long they must be roses, and then what.        35
Or any other foolish question.

                                                            1990

ALFRED, LORD TENNYSON

## *Now Sleeps the Crimson Petal*[6]

Now sleeps the crimson petal, now the white;
Nor waves the cypress in the palace walk;
Nor winks the gold fin in the porphyry font;[7]
The firefly wakens; waken thou with me.

5   Now droops the milk-white peacock like a ghost,
And like a ghost she glimmers on to me.

Now lies the Earth all Danaë[8] to the stars,
And all thy heart lies open unto me.

Now slides the silent meteor on, and leaves
10  A shining furrow, as thy thoughts in me.

Now folds the lily all her sweetness up,
And slips into the bosom of the lake;
So fold thyself, my dearest, thou, and slip
Into my bosom and be lost in me.                              1847

ROBERT FROST

## *The Rose Family*[9]

The rose is a rose,
And was always a rose.
But the theory now goes
That the apple's a rose,
5   And the pear is, and so's
The plum, I suppose.
The dear only knows
What will next prove a rose.
You, of course, are a rose—
10  But were always a rose.                                  1928

6. A song from *The Princess*.     7. Stone fishbowl. *Porphyry*: a red stone containing fine white crystals.
8. A princess, confined in a tower, seduced by Zeus after he became a shower of gold in order to gain
access to her.     9. A response to Gertrude Stein's famous line, "Rose is a rose is a rose is a rose."

DOROTHY PARKER

## One Perfect Rose

A single flow'r he sent me, since we met.
   All tenderly his messenger he chose;
Deep-hearted, pure, with scented dew still wet—
   One perfect rose.

I knew the language of the floweret;              5
   "My fragile leaves," it said, "his heart enclose."
Love long has taken for his amulet
   One perfect rose.

Why is it no one ever sent me yet
   One perfect limousine, do you suppose?         10
Ah no, it's always just my luck to get
   One perfect rose.                      1937

KATHA POLLITT

## Two Fish

Those speckled trout we glimpsed in a pool last year
you'd take for an image of love: it too should be
graceful, elusive, tacit, moving surely
among half-lights of mingled dim and clear,
forced to no course, of no fixed residence,        5
its only end its own swift elegance.
What would you say
if you saw what I saw the other day:
that pool heat-choked and fevered where sick blue
bubbled green scum and blistered water lily?       10
A white like a rolled-back eye or fish's belly
I thought I saw far out—but doubtless you
prefer to think our trout had left together
to seek a place with less inclement weather.      1981

JORIE GRAHAM

## The Geese

Today as I hang out the wash I see them again, a code
as urgent as elegant,

tapering with goals.
For days they have been crossing. We live beneath these geese

5    as if beneath the passage of time, or a most perfect heading.
Sometimes I fear their relevance.
Closest at hand,
between the lines,

the spiders imitate the paths the geese won't stray from,
10    imitate them endlessly to no avail:
things will not remain connected,
will not heal,

and the world thickens with texture instead of history,
texture instead of place.
15    Yet the small fear of the spiders
binds and binds

the pins to the lines, the lines to the eaves, to the pincushion bush,
as if, at any time, things could fall further apart
and nothing could help them
20    recover their meaning. And if these spiders had their way,

chainlink over the visible world,
would we be in or out? I turn to go back in.
There is a feeling the body gives the mind
of having missed something, a bedrock poverty, like falling

25    without the sense that you are passing through one world,
that you could reach another
anytime. Instead the real
is crossing you,

your body an arrival
30    you know is false but can't outrun. And somewhere in between
these geese forever entering and
these spiders turning back,

this astonishing delay, the everyday, takes place.        1980

ROO BORSON

# *After a Death*

Seeing that there's no other way,
I turn his absence into a chair.
I can sit in it,
gaze out through the window.
5    I can do what I do best
and then go out into the world.
And I can return then with my useless love,

to rest,
because the chair is there.                                    1989


HOWARD NEMEROV

## *The Town Dump*

*"The art of our necessities is strange,
That can make vile things precious."*[1]

A mile out in the marshes, under a sky
Which seems to be always going away
In a hurry, on that Venetian land threaded
With hidden canals, you will find the city
Which seconds ours (so cemeteries, too,                          5
Reflect a town from hillsides out of town),
Where Being most Becomingly[2] ends up
Becoming some more. From cardboard tenements,
Windowed with cellophane, or simply tenting
In paper bags, the angry mackerel eyes                          10
Glare at you out of stove-in, sunken heads
Far from the sea; the lobster, also, lifts
An empty claw in his most minatory
Of gestures; oyster, crab, and mussel shells
Lie here in heaps, savage as money hurled                       15
Away at the gate of hell. If you want results,
These are results.
                            Objects of value or virtue,
However, are also to be picked up here,
Though rarely, lying with bones and rotten meat,
Eggshells and mouldy bread, banana peels                        20
No one will skid on, apple cores that caused
Neither the fall of man nor a theory
Of gravitation.[3] People do throw out
The family pearls by accident, sometimes,
Not often; I've known dealers in antiques                       25
To prowl this place by night, with flashlights, on
The off-chance of somebody's having left
Derelict chairs which will turn out to be
By Hepplewhite,[4] a perfect set of six

---

1. *King Lear* III.ii.70–71.    2. "Being" and "Becoming" have been, since Heraclitus, the standard antin-omies in Western philosophy, standing for (respectively) the eternal and that which changes. 3. According to legend, Sir Isaac Newton's discovery of the principle of gravitation followed his being hit on the head by a falling apple.    4. A late-eighteenth-century cabinetmaker and furniture designer, famed for his simplification of neoclassic lines. No pieces known to have been actually made by Hepple-white survive.

30   Going to show, I guess, that in any sty
     Someone's heaven may open and shower down
     Riches responsive to the right dream; though
     It is a small chance, certainly, that sends
     The ghostly dealer, heavy with fly-netting
35   Over his head, across these hills in darkness,
     Stumbling in cut-glass goblets, lacquered cups,
     And other products of his dreamy midden[5]
     Penciled with light and guarded by the flies.

     For there are flies, of course. A dynamo
40   Composed, by thousands, of our ancient black
     Retainers, hums here day and night, steady
     As someone telling[6] beads, the hum becoming
     A high whine at any disturbance; then,
     Settled again, they shine under the sun
45   Like oil-drops, or are invisible as night,
     By night.
               All this continually smoulders,
     Crackles, and smokes with mostly invisible fires
     Which, working deep, rarely flash out and flare,
     And never finish. Nothing finishes;
50   The flies, feeling the heat, keep on the move.
     Among the flies, the purefying fires,
     The hunters by night, acquainted with the art
     Of our necessities, and the new deposits
     That each day wastes with treasure, you may say
55   There should be ratios. You may sum up
     The results if you want results. But I will add
     That wild birds, drawn to the carrion and flies,
     Assemble in some numbers here, their wings
     Shining with light, their flight enviably free,
60   Their music marvelous, though sad, and strange.                    1958

## QUESTIONS

1. List all of the neologisms and other unusual words in Hopkins's "Pied Beauty." Find the most precise synonym you can for each. How can you tell exactly what these words contribute to the poem? Explain the effects of the repeated consonant sounds (alliteration) and repeated vowel sounds (assonance) in the poem. What are the advantages of making up original words to describe highly individualized effects? What are the disadvantages?

2. Compare Dickinson's "I dwell in Possibility—" with two of her other poems, "A narrow Fellow in the Grass" (page 221) and "After great pain, a formal feeling comes—." What patterns of word use do you see in the three poems? What kinds of vocabulary do they have in common? what patterns of syntax? what strategies of organization?

3. Read aloud the passages from Milton's *Paradise Lost.* Then ask a friend to read the pas-

5. Refuse heap. (The term is usually used to describe those primitive refuse heaps that have been untouched for centuries and in which archaeologists dig for shards and artifacts of older cultures.)
6. Counting.

sages aloud as well. As the friend reads, note which words—and which choices of word order—provide especially useful guides for reading aloud. Make a list of all the lines in which the "normal" word order would be different if the poem were not written in a metrical form designed for reading aloud. In each case in which the poem uses unusual word order, try to figure out exactly what effect is produced by the variation.

4. Characterize as fully as you can the speaker in Donne's "Batter my heart, three-personed God." Explain how the metaphor of invasion and resistance works in the poem. What effect does this central metaphor have on our conception of the speaker? Explain the terms "imprison" (line 12) and "enthrall" (line 13). Explain "chaste" and "ravish" (line 14). How do these two sets of terms relate to the poem's central metaphor?

5. List every term in "The Twenty-third Psalm" that relates to the central metaphor of shepherding. Explain the metaphors of anointing and the overfull cup in line 5. (If you have trouble with this metaphor and do not understand the historical/cultural reference, ask a reference librarian to guide you to biblical commentaries that explain the practices referred to here.) What is the "house of the Lord" (line 6), and how does it relate to the basic metaphor of the psalm? (Again, if you are not sure of the historical/cultural reference, consult biblical commentaries or other historical sources on social and economic structures of the ancient Middle East.)

6. Compare the symbolism of the fish and seafood in Nemerov's "The Town Dump" with that of the two trout in Pollitt's "Two Fish."

## WRITING SUGGESTIONS

1. Read back through the poems you have read so far in the course, and pick out one in which a single word seems to you crucial to that poem's total effect. Write a short essay in which you work out carefully how the poem's meaning and tone depend upon that one word.

2. With the help of a reference librarian, find several pictures of B-17 bombers, and study carefully the design and appearance of the ball turret. Try to find a picture of the gunner at work in the turret, and note carefully his body position. Explain, in a paragraph, how Jarrell's poem "The Death of the Ball Turret Gunner" uses the visual details of the ball turret to create the fetal and birth metaphors in the poem.

3. Consider carefully the symbolism of the trout in Pollitt's "Two Fish." Exactly how do the fish become symbolic to the lovers? How do they become invested with meaning? What do this year's trout look like? Is the difference between last year's trout and this year's in the fish themselves or in their settings? What power does the weather have over the fish? What is the implied moral for the lovers? What does each lover believe about what the trout represent? What are the temperamental differences between the two lovers? What does the poem conclude about the "meaning" of the fish? Write an essay of about three pages in which you show how the poem opens and develops the question of what "symbols" mean.

4. With the help of a reference librarian, find at least half a dozen more poems that are about roses. Read them all carefully, and make a list of all the things that the rose seems to stand for in the poems. Write a paragraph about each poem showing how a specific symbolism for rose is established.

# 5

---

## THE SOUNDS OF POETRY

A lot of what happens in a poem happens in your mind's eye, but some of it happens in your voice. Poems are full of sounds and silences as well as words and sentences that are meaningful. Besides choosing words for their meanings, poets sometimes choose words because words involve certain sounds, and poems use sound effects to create a mood or establish a tone, just as films do. Sometimes the sounds of words are crucial to what is happening in the text of the poem.

The following poem explores the sounds of a particular word, tries them on, and analyzes them in relation to the word itself.

HELEN CHASIN

### *The Word* Plum

The word *plum* is delicious

pout and push, luxury of
self-love, and savoring murmur

full in the mouth and falling
like fruit

taut skin
pierced, bitten, provoked into
juice, and tart flesh

question
and reply, lip and tongue
of pleasure.                                              1968

The poem savors the sounds of the word as well as the taste and feel of the fruit itself. It is almost as if the poem is tasting the sounds and rolling them carefully on the tongue.

The second and third lines even replicate the *p, l, uh,* and *m* sounds of the word while at the same time imitating the squishy sounds of eating the fruit. Words like "delicious" and "luxury" sound juicy, and other words imitate sounds of satisfaction and pleasure— "murmur," for example. Even the process of eating is in part re-created aurally. The tight, clipped sounds of "taut skin/pierced" suggest the way teeth sharply break the skin and slice quickly into the solid flesh of a plum, and as the tartness is described, the words ("provoked," "question") force the lips to pucker and the tongue and palate to meet and hold, as if the mouth were savoring a tart fruit. The poet is having fun here re-creating the various sense appeals

> *Poetry is a comforting piece of fiction set to more or less lascivious music.*
>
> —H. L. MENCKEN

of a plum, teasing the sounds and meanings out of available words. The words must mean something appropriate and describe something accurately first of all, of course, but when they can also imitate the sounds and feel of the process, they can do double duty. Not many poems manipulate sound as intensely or as fully as "The Word *Plum*," but many poems at least contain passages in which the sounds of life are reproduced by the human voice reading the poem. To get the full effect of this poem—and of many others— reading aloud is essential; that way, you can pay attention to the vocal rhythms and artic- ulate the sounds as the poem calls for them to be reproduced by the human voice.

Almost always a poem's effect will be helped by reading it aloud, using your voice to pronounce the words so that the poem becomes a spoken communication. Historically, poetry began as an oral phenomenon, and often poems that seem very difficult when looked at silently come alive when they are turned into sound. Early bards chanted their verses, and the music of poetry—its cadences and rhythms—developed from this kind of performance. Often performances of primitive poetry (and sometimes in later ages) were accompanied by some kind of musical instrument. The rhythms of any poem become clearer when you say or hear them.

Poetry is almost always a vocal art, dependent on the human voice to become its full self (for some exceptions look at the shaped verse in Chapter 7). In a sense, it begins to exist as a real phenomenon when a reader reads and actualizes it. Poems don't really achieve their full meaning when they merely exist on a page; a poem on a page is more a score or set of stage directions for a poem than a poem itself. Sometimes, in fact, it is hard to expe- rience the poem at all unless you hear it; the actual experience of saying the words aloud or hearing them spoken is very good practice for learning to hear in your mind's ear when you read silently. A good poetry reading might easily convince you of the importance of a good voice sensitive to the poem's requirements, but you can also persuade yourself by reading poems aloud in the privacy of your own room. An audience is even better, how- ever, because then there is someone to share the pleasure in the sounds themselves and consider what they imply. At its oral best, much poetry is communal.

MONA VAN DUYN

## *What the Motorcycle Said*

Br-r-r-am-m-m, rackety-am-m, OM, *Am:*
*All*—r-r-room, r-r-ram, ala-bas-ter—
*Am,* the world's my oyster.

I hate plastic, wear it black and slick,
hate hardhats, wear one on my head,
that's what the motorcycle said.

Passed phonies in Fords, knocked down billboards, landed
on the other side of The Gap, and Whee,
bypassed history.

When I was born (The Past), baby knew best.
They shook when I bawled, took Freud's path,
threw away their wrath.

R-r-rackety-am-m. *Am.* War, rhyme,
soap, meat, marriage, the Phantom Jet
are shit, and like that.

Hate pompousness, punishment, patience, am into Love,
hate middle-class moneymakers, live on Dad,
that's what the motorcycle said.

Br-r-r-am-m-m. It's Nowsville, man. Passed Oldies, Uglies,
Straighties, Honkies. I'll never be
mean, tired or unsexy.

Passed cigarette suckers, souses, mother-fuckers,
losers, went back to Nature and found
how to get VD, stoned.

Passed a cow, too fast to hear her moo, "*I* rolled
our leaves of grass into one ball.
*I* am the grassy All."

Br-r-r-am-m-m, rackety-am-m, OM, *Am:*
*All*—gr-r-rin, oooohgah, gl-l-utton—
*Am,* the world's my smilebutton.                    1973

Saying this poem as if you were a motorcycle with the power of speech (sort of) is part of the poem's fun, and the rich, loud sounds of a motorcycle revving up concentrate and intensify the effect and enrich the pleasure. It's a shame not to hear a poem like this aloud; a lot of it is missed if you don't try to imitate the sounds or to pick up the motor's rhythms in the poem. A performance here is clearly worth it: a human being as motorcycle, motorcycle as human being.

And it's a good poem, too. It does something interesting, important, and maybe a bit subversive. The speaking motorcycle seems to take on the values of some of its riders, the noisy and obtrusive ones that readers are most likely to associate with motorcycles. The riders made fun of here are themselves sort of mindless and mechanical; they are the sort who have cult feelings about their group, who travel in packs, and who live no life beyond their machines. The speaking motorcycle, like such riders, grooves on power and speed, lives for the moment, and has little respect for people, the past, institutions, or anything beyond its own small world. It is self-centered, modish, ignorant, and inarticulate; but it is proud as well, mighty proud, and feels important in its own sounds. That's what the motorcycle says.

The following poem uses sound effects efficiently, too.

KENNETH FEARING

# *Dirge*

1-2-3 was the number he played but today the number came 3-2-1;
Bought his Carbide at 30, and it went to 29; had the favorite at Bowie[1]
   but the track was slow—

O executive type, would you like to drive a floating-power, knee-action,
   silk-upholstered six? Wed a Hollywood star? Shoot the course in 58?
   Draw to the ace, king, jack?
O fellow with a will who won't take no, watch out for three cigarettes on
   the same, single match; O democratic voter born in August under
   Mars, beware of liquidated rails—

Denouement to denouement, he took a personal pride in the certain,
   certain way he lived his own, private life,                    5
But nevertheless, they shut off his gas; nevertheless, the bank foreclosed;
   nevertheless, the landlord called; nevertheless, the radio broke,

And twelve o'clock arrived just once too often,
Just the same he wore one gray tweed suit, bought one straw hat, drank
   one straight Scotch, walked one short step, took one long look, drew
   one deep breath,
Just one too many,

And wow he died as wow he lived,                            10
Going whop to the office and blooie home to sleep and biff got married
   and bam had children and oof got fired,
Zowie did he live and zowie did he die,

With who the hell are you at the corner of his casket, and where the
   hell're we going on the right-hand silver knob, and who the hell cares
   walking second from the end with an American Beauty[2] wreath from
   why the hell not,

Very much missed by the circulation staff of the New York Evening Post;
   deeply, deeply mourned by the B.M.T.[3]
Wham, Mr. Roosevelt; pow, Sears Roebuck; awk, big dipper; bop, sum-
   mer rain; Bong, Mr., bong, Mr., bong, Mr., bong.            15

1935

    As the title implies, "Dirge" is a kind of musical lament, in this case for a certain sort of businessman who took a lot of chances and saw his investments and life go down the drain in the depression of the early 1930s. Reading this poem aloud is a big help partly because it contains expressive cartoon words that echo the action, words like "oof" and "blooie" (which primarily carry their meaning in their sounds, for they have practically no literal or referential meaning). Reading aloud also helps us notice that the poem

1. A racetrack in Maryland. *Carbide*: the Union Carbide Corporation.    2. A variety of rose.    3. A New
York City subway line.

employs rhythms much as a song would and that it frequently shifts its pace and mood. Notice how carefully the first two lines are balanced, and then how quickly the rhythm shifts as the "executive type" begins to be addressed directly in line 3. (Line 2 is long and dribbles over in the narrow pages of a book like this; a lot of the lines here are especially long, and the irregularity of the line lengths is one aspect of the special sound effects the poem creates.) In the direct address, the poem first picks up a series of advertising features, which it recites in rapid-fire order rather like the advertising phrases in "Needs" (page 75). In stanza 3 here, the rhythm shifts again, but the poem gives us helpful clues about how to read. Line 5 sounds like prose and is long, drawn out, and rather dull (rather like its subject), but line 6 sets up a regular (and monotonous) rhythm with its repeated "nevertheless," which punctuates the rhythm like a drumbeat: "But nevertheless, *tuh-tuh-tuh-tuh-tuh;* nevertheless, *tuh-tuh-tuh-tuh;* nevertheless, *tuh-tuh-tuh-tuh;* nevertheless, *tuh-tuh-tuh-tuh-tuh.*" In the next stanza, the repetitive phrasing comes again, this time guided by the word "one" in cooperation with other words of one syllable: "wore *one* gray tweed suit, bought *one* straw hat, *tuh* one *tuh-tuh, tuh* one *tuh-tuh, tuh* one *tuh-tuh, tuh* one *tuh-tuh.*" And then a new rhythm and a new technique in stanza 5 as the language of comic books is imitated to describe in violent, exaggerated terms the routine of his life. You have to say words like "whop" and "zowie" aloud and in the rhythm of the whole sentence to get the full effect of how boring his life is, no matter how he tries to jazz it up with exciting words. And so it goes—repeated words, shifting rhythms, emphasis on routine and averageness—until the final bell ("Bong . . . bong . . . bong . . . bong") tolls rhythmically for the dead man in the final clanging line.

> *There are only three things . . . that a poem must reach: the eye, the ear, and what we may call the heart or the mind. It is the most important of all to reach the heart of the reader. And the surest way to reach the heart is through the ear.*
>
> —ROBERT FROST

Sometimes sounds in poems just provide special effects, rather like a musical score behind a film, setting mood and getting us into an appropriate frame of mind. But often sound and meaning go hand in hand, and the poet finds words that in their sounds echo the action. A word that captures or approximates the sound of what it describes, such as "splash" or "squish" or "murmur" is called an **onomatopoeic** word, and the device itself is called **onomatopoeia.** And similar things can be done poetically with pacing and rhythm, sounds and pauses. The punctuation, the length of vowels, and the combination of consonant sounds help to control the way we read so that we can use our voice to imitate what is being described. The poems at the end of this discussion (pages 208–23) suggest several ways that such imitations of pace and pause may occur: by echoing the lapping of waves on a shore, for example ("Like as the waves"), or reproducing the rhythms of a musical style ("Dear John, Dear Coltrane").

Here is a classic passage in which a skillful poet talks about the virtues of making the sound echo the sense—and shows at the same time how to do it:

ALEXANDER POPE

## *Sound and Sense*[4]

But most by numbers[5] judge a poet's song,                                337
And smooth or rough, with them, is right or wrong;
In the bright muse though thousand charms conspire,[6]
Her voice is all these tuneful fools admire,                               340
Who haunt Parnassus[7] but to please their ear,
Not mend their minds; as some to church repair,
Not for the doctrine, but the music there.
These, equal syllables[8] alone require,
Though oft the ear the open vowels tire,                                   345
While expletives[9] their feeble aid do join,
And ten low words oft creep in one dull line,
While they ring round the same unvaried chimes,
With sure returns of still expected rhymes.
Where'er you find "the cooling western breeze,"                            350
In the next line, it "whispers through the trees";
If crystal streams "with pleasing murmurs creep,"
The reader's threatened (not in vain) with "sleep."
Then, at the last and only couplet fraught
With some unmeaning thing they call a thought,                             355
A needless Alexandrine[1] ends the song,
That, like a wounded snake, drags its slow length along.
Leave such to tune their own dull rhymes, and know
What's roundly smooth, or languishingly slow;
And praise the easy vigor of a line,                                       360
Where Denham's strength and Waller's[2] sweetness join.
True ease in writing comes from art, not chance,
As those move easiest who have learned to dance.
'Tis not enough no harshness gives offense,
The sound must seem an echo to the sense:                                  365
Soft is the strain when Zephyr[3] gently blows,
And the smooth stream in smoother numbers flows;
But when loud surges lash the sounding shore,
The hoarse, rough verse should like the torrent roar.
When Ajax[4] strives, some rock's vast weight to throw,                    370
The line too labors, and the words move slow;

---

4. From *An Essay on Criticism,* Pope's poem on the art of poetry and the problems of literary criticism. The passage excerpted here follows a discussion of several common weaknesses of critics—failure to regard an author's intention, for example, or overemphasis on clever metaphors and ornate style.    5. Meter, rhythm, sound.    6. Unite.    7. A mountain in Greece, traditionally associated with the muses and considered the seat of poetry and music.    8. Regular accents.    9. Filler words, such as "do."    1. A six-foot line, sometimes used in pentameter poems to vary the pace mechanically. Line 357 is an alexandrine.    2. Sir John Denham and Edmund Waller, seventeenth-century poets credited with perfecting the heroic couplet.    3. The west wind.    4. A Greek hero of the Trojan War, noted for his strength.

Not so, when swift Camilla[5] scours the plain,
Flies o'er th' unbending corn, and skims along the main.
Hear how Timotheus'[6] varied lays surprise,
375    And bid alternate passions fall and rise!
While, at each change, the son of Libyan Jove[7]
Now burns with glory, and then melts with love;
Now his fierce eyes with sparkling fury glow,
Now sighs steal out, and tears begin to flow:
380    Persians and Greeks like turns of nature[8] found,
And the world's victor stood subdued by sound!
The pow'r of music all our hearts allow,
And what Timotheus was, is DRYDEN now.                    1711

A lot of things are going on here simultaneously. The poem uses a number of echoic or onomatopoeic words, and pleasant and unpleasant consonant sounds are used in some lines to underline a particular point or add some mood music. When the poet talks about a particular weakness in poetry, he illustrates it at the same time—by using open vowels (line 345), expletives (line 346), monosyllabic words (line 347), predictable rhymes (lines 350–53), or long, slow lines (line 357). And the good qualities of poetry he talks about and illustrates as well (line 360, for example). But the main effects of the passage come from an interaction of several strategies at once. The effects are fairly simple and easy to spot, but their causes involve a lot of poetic ingenuity. In line 340, for example, a careful cacophonous effect is achieved by the repetition of the oo vowel sound and the repetition of the *l* consonant sound together with the interruption (twice) of the rough *f* sound in the middle; no one wants to be caught admiring that music when the poet gets through with us, but the careful harmony of the preceding sounds has set us up beautifully. And the pace of lines 347, 357, and 359 is carefully controlled by clashing consonant sounds as well as by the use of long vowels. Line 347 moves incredibly slowly and seems much longer than it is because almost all the one-syllable words end in a consonant that refuses to blend with the beginning of the next word, making the words hard to say without distinct, awkward pauses between them. In lines 357 and 359, long vowels such as those in "wounded," "snake," "slow," "along," "roundly," and "smooth" help to slow down the pace, and the trick of juxtaposing awkward, unpronounceable consonants is again employed. The commas also provide nearly a full stop in the midst of these lines to slow us down still more. Similarly, the harsh lashing of the shore in lines 368–69 is partly accomplished by onomatopoeia, partly by a shift in the pattern of stress, which creates irregular waves in line 368, and partly by the dominance of rough consonants in line 369. (In Pope's time, the English *r* was still trilled gruffly so that it could be made to sound extremely rrrough and harrrsh.) Almost every line in this passage demonstrates how to make sound echo sense.

As "Sound and Sense" and "Dirge" suggest, sound is most effectively manipulated in

5. A woman warrior in *The Aeneid.*    6. The court musician of Alexander the Great, celebrated in a famous poem by Dryden (see line 383) for the power of his music over Alexander's emotions.    7. In Greek tradition, the chief god of any people was often given the name Zeus (Jove), and the chief god of Libya (the Greek name for all of Africa) was called Zeus Ammon. Alexander visited his oracle and was proclaimed son of the god.    8. Similar alternations of emotion.

poetry when the rhythm of the voice is carefully controlled so that not only are the proper sounds heard, but they are heard at precisely the right moment. Pace and rhythm are nearly as important to a good poem as they are to a good piece of music. The human voice naturally develops certain rhythms in speech; some syllables and some words receive more stress than others. Just as multisyllabic words put more stress on some syllables than others (dictionaries always indicate which syllables are stressed), words in the context of a sentence receive more or less stress, depending on meaning. One-syllable words are thus sometimes stressed and sometimes not. A careful poet controls the flow of stresses so that, in many poems, a certain basic rhythm (or **meter**) develops almost like a quiet percussion instrument in the background. Not all poems are metered, and not all metered poems follow a single dominant rhythm, but many poems are written in one pervasive pattern, and it is useful to look for patterns of stress.

Here is a poem that names and illustrates many of the meters. If you hear someone reading it aloud and chart the unstressed (˘) and stressed (¯) syllables, you should have a chart similar to that done by the poet himself in the text.

SAMUEL TAYLOR COLERIDGE

## Metrical Feet

Lesson for a Boy

Trōchĕe trĭps frŏm lōng tŏ shōrt;[9]
From long to long in solemn sort
Slōw Spōndēe stālks; strōng fōot! yet ill able
Evĕr tŏ cōme ŭp wĭth Dāctўl trĭsўllăblĕ.
Ĭambĭcs mārch frŏm shōrt tŏ lōng—                              5
Wĭth ă lēap ănd ă bōund thĕ swĭft Ānăpĕsts thrōng;
One syllable long, with one short at each side,
Ămphībrăchўs hāstes wĭth ă stātelў stride—
Fīrst ănd lāst bēĭng lōng, mīddlĕ shōrt, Ămphĭmācer
Strīkes hĭs thūndērĭng hōofs līke ă prōud hīgh-brĕd Rācer.    10
If Derwent[1] be innocent, steady, and wise,
And delight in the things of earth, water, and skies;
Tender warmth at his heart, with these meters to show it,
With sound sense in his brains, may make Derwent a poet—
May crown him with fame, and must win him the love        15
Of his father on earth and his Father above.
                    My dear, dear child!
Could you stand upon Skiddaw,[2] you would not from its whole ridge
See a man who so loves you as your fond s. t. COLERIDGE.

1806

9. The long and short marks over syllables are Coleridge's.      1. Written originally for Coleridge's son Hartley, the poem was later adapted for his younger son, Derwent.      2. A mountain in the lake country of northern England (where Coleridge lived in his early years), near the town of Derwent.

The following poem exemplifies **dactylic** rhythm (-˘˘, or a stressed syllable followed by two unstressed ones).

WENDY COPE

## Emily Dickinson

Higgledy-piggledy
Emily Dickinson
Liked to use dashes
Instead of full stops.

5    Nowadays, faced with such
Idiosyncrasy,
Critics and editors
Send for the cops.                                    1986

Limericks rely on **anapestic** meter (˘˘-, or two unstressed syllables followed by a stressed one), although usually the first two syllables are in iambic meter (see below).

ANONYMOUS

## [There was a young lady of Riga]

There was a young lady of Riga
Who went for a ride on a tiger;
    They returned from the ride
    With the lady inside,
5    And a smile on the face of the tiger.

The following poem is composed in the more common **trochaic** meter (-˘, a stressed syllable followed by an unstressed one).

SIR JOHN SUCKLING

## Song

Why so pale and wan, fond Lover?
    Prithee why so pale?

Will, when looking well can't move her,
  Looking ill prevail?
  Prithee why so pale?                                        5

Why so dull and mute, young Sinner?
  Prithee why so mute?
Will, when speaking well can't win her,
  Saying nothing do 't?
  Prithee why so mute?                                      10

Quit, quit, for shame, this will not move,
  This cannot take her;
If of her self she will not love,
  Nothing can make her,
  The Devil take her.                                      15

                                                1646

The basic meter in the following poem, as in "Sound and Sense," is the most common one in English, **iambic** ( ˘ ¯, an unstressed syllable followed by a stressed one).

JOHN DRYDEN

## *To the Memory of Mr. Oldham*[3]

Farewell, too little, and too lately known,
Whom I began to think and call my own;
For sure our souls were near allied, and thine
Cast in the same poetic mold with mine.
One common note on either lyre did strike,                 5
And knaves and fools we both abhorred alike.
To the same goal did both our studies drive;
The last set out the soonest did arrive.
Thus Nisus fell upon the slippery place,
While his young friend performed and won the race.[4]       10
O early ripe! to thy abundant store
What could advancing age have added more?
It might (what nature never gives the young)
Have taught the numbers[5] of thy native tongue.
But satire needs not those, and wit will shine           15
Through the harsh cadence of a rugged line.[6]

---

3. John Oldham (1653–1683), who like Dryden (see lines 3–6) wrote satiric poetry.     4. In Virgil's *Aeneid* (Book V), Nisus (who is leading the race) falls and then trips the second runner so that his friend Euryalus can win.     5. Rhythms.     6. In Dryden's time, the English *r* was pronounced with a harsh, trilling sound.

A noble error, and but seldom made,
When poets are by too much force betrayed.
Thy generous fruits, though gathered ere their prime,
20   Still showed a quickness; and maturing time
But mellows what we write to the dull sweets of rhyme.
Once more, hail and farewell; farewell, thou young,
But ah too short, Marcellus[7] of our tongue;
Thy brows with ivy, and with laurels bound;
25   But fate and gloomy night encompass thee around.                    1684


Once you have figured out the basic meter or rhythm of a poem, you can often find some interesting things by looking carefully at the departures from the pattern. Departures from the basic iambic meter of "To the Memory of Mr. Oldham," for example, suggest some of the imaginative things that poets can do within the apparently very restrictive requirements of traditional meter. Try marking the stressed and unstressed syllables in "To the Memory of Mr. Oldham" and then look carefully at each place that varies from the basic iambic pattern. Which of these variations call special attention to a particular sound or action being talked about in the poem? Which ones specifically mimic or echo the sense? Which variations seem to exist primarily for emphasis? Which ones seem primarily intended to mark structural breaks in the poem?


MICHAEL HARPER

## Dear John, Dear Coltrane

*a love supreme, a love supreme*[8]
a love supreme, a love supreme


Sex fingers toes
in the marketplace
near your father's church
in Hamlet, North Carolina—[9]
5   witness to this love
in this calm fallow
of these minds,
there is no substitute for pain:
genitals gone or going,
10   seed burned out,

7. The nephew of the Roman emperor Augustus; he died at twenty, and Virgil celebrated him in *The Aeneid*, Book VI.    8. Coltrane wrote "A Love Supreme" in response to a spiritual experience in 1957, which led to his quitting heroin and alcohol. The record was released in 1965.    9. Coltrane's birthplace. His family shared a house with Coltrane's grandfather, who was the minister of St. Stephen's AME Zion Church there.

you tuck the roots in the earth,
turn back, and move
by river through the swamps,
singing: *a love supreme, a love supreme;*
what does it all mean?                                                    15
Loss, so great each black
woman expects your failure
in mute change, the seed gone.
You plod up into the electric city—
your song now crystal and                                                 20
the blues. You pick up the horn
with some will and blow
into the freezing night:
*a love supreme, a love supreme—*

Dawn comes and you cook                                                   25
up the thick sin 'tween
impotence and death, fuel
the tenor sax cannibal
heart, genitals and sweat
that makes you clean—                                                     30
*a love supreme, a love supreme—*

*Why you so black?*
*cause I am*
*why you so funky?*
*cause I am*                                                              35
*why you so black*
*cause I am*
*why you so sweet?*
*cause I am*
*why you so black?*                                                       40
*cause I am*
*a love supreme, a love supreme:*

So sick
you couldn't play *Naima,*[1]
so flat we ached                                                          45
for song you'd concealed
with your own blood,
your diseased liver gave
out its purity,
the inflated heart                                                        50
pumps out, the tenor kiss,
tenor love:
*a love supreme, a love supreme—*
*a love supreme, a love supreme—*                              1970

---

1. A song Coltrane wrote for and named after his first wife, recorded in 1959.

STEPHEN SPENDER

## *The Express*

After the first powerful, plain manifesto
The black statement of pistons, without more fuss
But gliding like a queen, she leaves the station.
Without bowing and with restrained unconcern
5    She passes the houses which humbly crowd outside,
The gasworks, and at last the heavy page
Of death, printed by gravestones in the cemetery.
Beyond the town, there lies the open country
Where, gathering speed, she acquires mystery,
10   The luminous self-possession of ships on ocean.
It is now she begins to sing—at first quite low
Then loud, and at last with a jazzy madness—
The song of her whistle screaming at curves,
Of deafening tunnels, brakes, innumerable bolts.
15   And always light, aerial, underneath,
Retreats the elate meter of her wheels.
Streaming through metal landscape on her lines,
She plunges new eras of white happiness,
Where speed throws up strange shapes, broad curves
20   And parallels clean like trajectories from guns.
At last, further than Edinburgh or Rome,
Beyond the crest of the world, she reaches night
Where only a low stream-line brightness
Of phosphorus on the tossing hills is light.
25   Ah, like a comet through flame, she moves entranced,
Wrapt in her music no bird song, no, nor bough
Breaking with honey buds, shall ever equal.                    1933

JUDITH WRIGHT

## *"Dove-Love"*

The dove purrs—over and over the dove
purrs its declaration. The wind's tone
changes from tree to tree, the creek on stone
alters its sob and fall, but still the dove
5    goes insistently on, telling its love
        "I could eat you."

And in captivity, they say, doves do.
Gentle, methodical, starting with the feet
(the ham-pink succulent toes

on their thin stems of rose),                                    10
baring feather by feather the wincing meat:
    "I could eat you."

That neat suburban head, that suit of grey,
watchful conventional eye and manicured claw—
these also rhyme with us. The doves play            15
on one repetitive note that plucks the raw
helpless nerve, their soft "I do. I do.
    I could eat you."                          1962

CYNTHIA ZARIN

## Song

My heart, my dove, my snail, my sail, my
   milktooth, shadow, sparrow, fingernail,
     flower-cat and blossom-hedge, mandrake

root now put to bed, moonshell, sea-swell,
   manatee, emerald shining back at me,            5
     nutmeg, quince, tea leaf and bone, zither,

cymbal, xylophone; paper, scissors, then
   there's stone—Who doesn't come through the door
     to get home?                                1993

WILLIAM SHAKESPEARE

## [Like as the waves make towards the pebbled shore]

Like as the waves make towards the pebbled shore,
So do our minutes hasten to their end,
Each changing place with that which goes before,
In sequent toil all forwards do contend.[2]
Nativity, once in the main[3] of light,                      5
Crawls to maturity, wherewith being crowned,
Crooked[4] eclipses 'gainst his glory fight,
And Time that gave doth now his gift confound.[5]

2. Struggle. *Sequent:* successive.   3. High seas. *Nativity:* newborn life.   4. Perverse.   5. Bring to
nothing.

Time doth transfix[6] the flourish set on youth
10    And delves the parallels[7] in beauty's brow,
Feeds on the rarities of nature's truth,
And nothing stands but for his scythe to mow.
And yet to times in hope[8] my verse shall stand,
Praising thy worth, despite his cruel hand.

1609

JAMES MERRILL

## *Watching the Dance*

### 1. BALANCHINE'S[9]

Poor savage, doubting that a river flows
But for the myriad eddies made
By unseen powers twirling on their toes,

Here in this darkness it would seem
5    You had already died, and were afraid.
Be still. Observe the powers. Infer the stream.

### 2. DISCOTHÈQUE

Having survived entirely your own youth,
Last of your generation, purple gloom
Investing you, sit, Jonah,[1] beyond speech,

10    And let towards the brute volume VOOM whale mouth
VAM pounding viscera VAM VOOM
A teenage plankton luminously twitch.

1967

ALFRED, LORD TENNYSON

## *Break, Break, Break*

Break, break, break,
    On thy cold gray stones, O Sea!
And I would that my tongue could utter
    The thoughts that arise in me.

5    O, well for the fisherman's boy,
    That he shouts with his sister at play!

6. Pierce.    7. Lines, wrinkles.    8. In the future.    9. George Balanchine, Russian-born (1894) ballet choreographer and teacher.    1. According to Jonah 4, Jonah sat in gloom near Nineveh after its residents repented and God decided to spare the city from destruction.

O, well for the sailor lad,
   That he sings in his boat on the bay!

And the stately ships go on
   To their haven under the hill;                                     10
But O for the touch of a vanished hand,
   And the sound of a voice that is still!

Break, break, break,
   At the foot of thy crags, O Sea!
But the tender grace of a day that is dead                           15
   Will never come back to me.

ca. 1834


### BEN JONSON

## Slow, Slow, Fresh Fount [2]

Slow, slow, fresh fount, keep time with my salt tears;
Yet slower, yet, O faintly, gentle springs!
List to the heavy part the music bears.
Woe weeps out her division,[3] when she sings.
   Droop herbs and flowers;                                       5
   Fall grief in showers;
   Our beauties are not ours.
     O, I could still,
Like melting snow upon some craggy hill,
   Drop, drop, drop, drop,                                        10
Since nature's pride is now a withered daffodil.          1600


### THOMAS NASHE

## A Litany in Time of Plague

Adieu, farewell, earth's bliss;
This world uncertain is;
Fond[4] are life's lustful joys;
Death proves them all but toys;[5]
None from his darts can fly;                                          5

2. This lyric, from Jonson's play *Cynthia's Revels,* is a lament sung by Echo for Narcissus, who was entranced by his own reflection and ultimately transformed into a flower.   3. Grief at parting, but also a rapid melodic passage of music.   4. Foolish.   5. Trifles.

I am sick, I must die.
    Lord, have mercy on us!

Rich men, trust not in wealth,
Gold cannot buy you health;
Physic himself must fade.
All things to end are made,
The plague full swift goes by;
I am sick, I must die.
    Lord, have mercy on us!

Beauty is but a flower
Which wrinkles will devour;
Brightness falls from the air;
Queens have died young and fair;
Dust hath closed Helen's eye.
I am sick, I must die.
    Lord, have mercy on us!

Strength stoops unto the grave,
Worms feed on Hector brave;
Swords may not fight with fate,
Earth still holds ope her gate.
"Come, come!" the bells do cry.
I am sick, I must die.
    Lord, have mercy on us.

Wit with his wantonness
Tasteth death's bitterness;
Hell's executioner
Hath no ears for to hear
What vain art can reply.
I am sick, I must die.
    Lord, have mercy on us.

Haste, therefore, each degree,
To welcome destiny;
Heaven is our heritage,
Earth but a player's stage;
Mount we unto the sky.
I am sick, I must die.
    Lord, have mercy on us.

1600

## STEVIE SMITH

# *Our Bog Is Dood*

Our Bog is dood, our Bog is dood,
They lisped in accents mild,
But when I asked them to explain

They grew a little wild.
How do you know your Bog is dood                                    5
My darling little child?

We know because we wish it so
That is enough, they cried,
And straight within each infant eye
Stood up the flame of pride,                                        10
And if you do not think it so
You shall be crucified.

Then tell me, darling little ones,
What's dood, suppose Bog is?
Just what we think, the answer came,                                15
Just what we think it is.
They bowed their heads. Our Bog is ours
And we are wholly his.

But when they raised them up again
They had forgotten me                                               20
Each one upon each other glared
In pride and misery
For what was dood, and what their Bog
They never could agree.

Oh sweet it was to leave them then,                                 25
And sweeter not to see,
And sweetest of all to walk alone
Beside the encroaching sea,
The sea that soon should drown them all,
That never yet drowned me.                                          30

1950

## LEWIS CARROLL

# *Jabberwocky*[6]

'Twas brillig, and the slithy toves
    Did gyre and gimble in the wabe;
All mimsy were the borogoves,
        And the mome raths outgrabe.

"Beware the Jabberwock, my son!                                     5
    The jaws that bite, the claws that catch!

6. Of the "hard words" in this poem, Carroll wrote: "Humpty-Dumpty's theory, of two meanings packed into one word like a portmanteau, seems to me the right explanation for all. For instance, take the two words 'fuming' and 'furious.' Make up your mind that you will say both words, but leave it unsettled which you will say first. . . . If you have that rarest of gifts, a perfectly balanced mind, you will say "frumious.' "

Beware the Jubjub bird, and shun
    The frumious Bandersnatch!"

He took his vorpal sword in hand:
    Long time the manxome foe he sought—
So rested he by the Tumtum tree,
    And stood awhile in thought.

And as in uffish thought he stood,
    The Jabberwock, with eyes of flame,
Came whiffling through the tulgey wood,
    And burbled as it came!

One, two! One, two! And through and through
    The vorpal blade went snicker-snack!
He left it dead, and with its head
    He went galumphing back.

"And hast thou slain the Jabberwock?
    Come to my arms, my beamish boy!
O frabjous day! Callooh! Callay!"
    He chortled in his joy.

'Twas brillig, and the slithy toves
    Did gyre and gimble in the wabe;
All mimsy were the borogoves,
    And the mome raths outgrabe.

1871

## DONALD JUSTICE

## *Counting the Mad*

This one was put in a jacket,
This one was sent home,
This one was given bread and meat
But would eat none,
And this one cried No No No No
All day long.

This one looked at the window
As though it were a wall,
This one saw things that were not there,
This one things that were,
And this one cried No No No No
All day long.

This one thought himself a bird,
This one a dog,
And this one thought himself a man,
An ordinary man,

And cried and cried No No No No
All day long.                                                    1960


## EARLE BIRNEY

### *Irapuato* [7]

For reasons any
                    brigadier
                                        could tell
this is a favorite nook for
                    massacre                                        5

Toltex by Mixtex Mixtex by Aztex
Aztex by Spanishtex Spanishtex by
Mexitex by Mexitex by Mexitex by Texaco
So any farmer can see how the strawberries
are the biggest and reddest                                         10
    in the whole damn continent

but why
            when arranged under
                            the market flies

do they look like small clotting hearts?                           15

                                                            1962


## EDGAR ALLAN POE

### *The Raven*

Once upon a midnight dreary, while I pondered, weak and weary,
Over many a quaint and curious volume of forgotten lore,
While I nodded, nearly napping, suddenly there came a tapping,
As of some one gently rapping, rapping at my chamber door.
" 'Tis some visitor," I muttered, "tapping at my chamber door—     5
                    Only this, and nothing more."

Ah, distinctly I remember it was in the bleak December,
And each separate dying ember wrought its ghost upon the floor.
Eagerly I wished the morrow;—vainly I had sought to borrow
From my books surcease of sorrow—sorrow for the lost Lenore—       10

---

7. A city in central Mexico, northwest of Mexico City.

For the rare and radiant maiden whom the angels name Lenore—
           Nameless here for evermore.

And the silken sad uncertain rustling of each purple curtain
Thrilled me—filled me with fantastic terrors never felt before;
15   So that now, to still the beating of my heart, I stood repeating
" 'Tis some visitor entreating entrance at my chamber door;—
Some late visitor entreating entrance at my chamber door;
           This it is, and nothing more."

Presently my soul grew stronger; hesitating then no longer,
20   "Sir," said I, "or Madam, truly your forgiveness I implore;
But the fact is I was napping, and so gently you came rapping,
And so faintly you came tapping, tapping at my chamber door,
That I scarce was sure I heard you"—here I opened wide the door;—
           Darkness there, and nothing more.

25   Deep into that darkness peering, long I stood there wondering, fearing,
Doubting, dreaming dreams no mortal ever dared to dream before;
But the silence was unbroken, and the darkness gave no token,
And the only word there spoken was the whispered word, "Lenore!"
This I whispered, and an echo murmured back the word, "Lenore!"—
30           Merely this, and nothing more.

Back into the chamber turning, all my soul within me burning,
Soon I heard again a tapping somewhat louder than before.
"Surely," said I, "surely that is something at my window lattice;
Let me see, then, what thereat is, and this mystery explore—
35   Let my heart be still a moment and this mystery explore;—
           'Tis the wind and nothing more!"

Open here I flung the shutter, when, with many a flirt and flutter,
In there stepped a stately raven of the saintly days of yore;
Not the least obeisance made he; not an instant stopped or stayed he;
40   But, with mien of lord or lady, perched above my chamber door—
Perched upon a bust of Pallas[8] just above my chamber door—
           Perched, and sat, and nothing more.

Then this ebony bird beguiling my sad fancy into smiling,
By the grave and stern decorum of the countenance it wore,
"Though thy crest be shorn and shaven, thou," I said, "art sure no
45     craven,
Ghastly grim and ancient raven wandering from the Nightly shore—
Tell me what thy lordly name is on the Night's Plutonian shore!"
           Quoth the raven, "Nevermore."

Much I marvelled this ungainly fowl to hear discourse so plainly,
50   Though its answer little meaning—little relevancy bore,
For we cannot help agreeing that no living human being
Ever yet was blessed with seeing bird above his chamber door—

8. Athena, the Greek goddess of wisdom.

Bird or beast upon the sculptured bust above his chamber door,
  With such name as "Nevermore."

But the raven, sitting lonely on the placid bust, spoke only                                55
That one word, as if his soul in that one word he did outpour.
Nothing farther then he uttered—not a feather then he fluttered—
Till I scarcely more than muttered "Other friends have flown before—
On the morrow *he* will leave me, as my hopes have flown before."
  Then the bird said "Nevermore."                                                           60

Startled at the stillness broken by reply so aptly spoken,
"Doubtless," said I, "what it utters is its only stock and store
Caught from some unhappy master whom unmerciful Disaster
Followed fast and followed faster till his songs one burden bore—
Till the dirges of his Hope that melancholy burden bore                                      65
  Of 'Never—nevermore.' "


But the raven still beguiling all my sad soul into smiling,
Straight I wheeled a cushioned seat in front of bird and bust and door;
Then, upon the velvet sinking, I betook myself to linking
Fancy unto fancy, thinking what this ominous bird of yore—                                   70
What this grim, ungainly, ghastly, gaunt, and ominous bird of yore
  Meant in croaking "Nevermore."

This I sat engaged in guessing, but no syllable expressing
To the fowl whose fiery eyes now burned into my bosom's core;
This and more I sat divining, with my head at ease reclining                                 75
On the cushion's velvet lining that the lamplight gloated o'er,
But whose velvet violet lining with the lamplight gloating o'er,
  *She* shall press, ah, nevermore!

Then, methought, the air grew denser, perfumed from an unseen censer
Swung by angels whose faint foot-falls tinkled on the tufted floor.                           80
"Wretch," I cried, "thy God hath lent thee—by these angels he hath
  sent thee
Respite—respite and nepenthe[9] from thy memories of Lenore!
Quaff, oh quaff this kind nepenthe and forget this lost Lenore!"
  Quoth the raven, "Nevermore."

"Prophet!" said I, "thing of evil!—prophet still, if bird or devil!—                          85
Whether Tempter sent, or whether tempest tossed thee here ashore,
Desolate, yet all undaunted, on this desert land enchanted—
On this home by Horror haunted—tell me truly, I implore—
Is there—*is* there balm in Gilead?[1]—tell me—tell me, I implore!"
  Quoth the raven, "Nevermore."                                                               90

"Prophet!" said I, "thing of evil—prophet still, if bird or devil!
by that Heaven that bends above us—by that God we both adore—
Tell this soul with sorrow laden if, within the distant Aidenn,
It shall clasp a sainted maiden whom the angels name Lenore—

9. A drug reputed by the Greeks to cause forgetfulness or sorrow.    1. Cf. Jeremiah 8:22.

95   Clasp a rare and radiant maiden whom the angels name Lenore."
        Quoth the raven, "Nevermore."

"Be that word our sign of parting, bird or fiend!" I shrieked upstarting—
"Get thee back into the tempest and the Night's Plutonian shore!
Leave no black plume as a token of that lie thy soul hath spoken!
100   Leave my loneliness unbroken!—quit the bust above my door!
Take thy beak from out my heart, and take thy form from off my door!"
        Quoth the raven, "Nevermore."

And the raven, never flitting, still is sitting, still is sitting
On the pallid bust of Pallas just above my chamber door;
105   And his eyes have all the seeming of a demon's that is dreaming,
And the lamp-light o'er him streaming throws his shadow on the floor;
And my soul from out that shadow that lies floating on the floor
        Shall be lifted—nevermore!

                                                                    1844


GERARD MANLEY HOPKINS

## *Spring and Fall:*

### *to a young child*

Márgarét áre you gríeving
Over Goldengrove unleaving?
Leáves, like the things of man, you
With your fresh thoughts care for, can you?
5   Áh! ás the heart grows older
It will come to such sights colder
By and by, nor spare a sigh
Though worlds of wanwood leafmeal² lie;
And yet you wíll weep and know why.
10   Now no matter, child, the name:
Sórrow's spríngs áre the same.
Nor mouth had, no nor mind, expressed
What heart heard of, ghost³ guessed:
It ís the blight man was born for,
15   It is Margaret you mourn for.

    1880

---

2. Broken up, leaf by leaf (analogous to "piecemeal"). *Wanwood:* pale, gloomy woods.    3. Soul.

IRVING LAYTON

# The Way the World Ends

Before me on the dancestand
A god's vomit or damned by his decrees
The excited twitching couples shook and
Wriggled like giant parentheses.

A pallid Canadienne                                                    5
Raised a finger and wetted her lip,
And echoing the nickelodeon
'Chip,' she breathed drowsily, 'Chip, chip.'

Aroused, her slavish partner
Smiled, showed his dentures through sodapop gas,          10
and 'chip' he said right back to her
And 'chip, chip' she said and shook her ass.

Denture to denture, 'Pas mal'[4]
They whispered and were glad, jerked to and fro:
Their distorted bodies like bits of steel                          15
Controlled by that throbbing dynamo.

They stomped, flung out their arms, groaned;
And in a flash I saw the cosmos end
And last of all the black night cover this:
*'Chip, chip' and a shake of the ass.*                             20

1956

EMILY DICKINSON

# [A narrow Fellow in the Grass]

A narrow Fellow in the Grass
Occasionally rides—
You may have met Him—did you not
His notice sudden is—

The Grass divides as with a Comb—                                  5
A spotted shaft is seen—
And then it closes at your feet
And opens further on—

He likes a Boggy Acre
A Floor too cool for Corn—                                         10

4. "Not bad" (French).

Yet when a Boy, and Barefoot—
I more than once at Noon

Have passed, I thought, a Whip lash
Unbraiding in the Sun
When stooping to secure it
It wrinkled, and was gone—

Several of Nature's People
I know, and they know me—
I feel for them a transport
Of cordiality—

But never met this Fellow
Attended, or alone
Without a tighter breathing
And Zero at the Bone—                                     1866


ROBERT HERRICK
_____

## *To the Virgins, to Make Much of Time*

Gather ye rosebuds while ye may,
    Old time is still a-flying;
And this same flower that smiles today
    Tomorrow will be dying.

The glorious lamp of heaven, the sun,
    The higher he's a-getting,
The sooner will his race be run,
    And nearer he's to setting.

That age is best which is the first,
    When youth and blood are warmer;
But being spent, the worse, and worst
    Times still succeed the former.

Then be not coy, but use your time,
    And, while ye may, go marry;
For, having lost but once your prime,
    You may forever tarry.                                  1648

JEAN TOOMER

## *Reapers*

Black reapers with the sound of steel on stones
Are sharpening scythes. I see them place the hones[5]
In their hip-pockets as a thing that's done,
And start their silent swinging, one by one.
Black horses drive a mower through the weeds          5
And there, a field rat, startled, squealing bleeds.
His belly close to ground. I see the blade,
Blood-stained, continue cutting weeds and shade.                    1923

## QUESTIONS

1. Read Lee's "Persimmons" (page 49) and Kinnell's "Blackberry Eating" (page 511), and compare their sound effects with those in Chasin's "The Word *Plum*." How visual an image does each poem create? To what purposes does Lee put the visual qualities of the persimmon? Which other of the five senses are evoked in each poem? to what specific purpose?
2. Read the following poems aloud: "Break, Break, Break," "A Litany in Time of Plague," and "The Raven." As you read each, try to be especially conscious of the way punctuation and spacing guide your pauses and of the pace you develop as you become accustomed to the prevailing rhythms of the poem. What function does repetition have in the reading aloud of each poem?
3. Scan—that is, mark all of the stressed syllables and chart their pattern in—Shakespeare's "Like as the waves make towards the pebbled shore." What variations do you find on the basic iambic pentameter pattern? What functions do the variations perform in each case?
4. Read Herrick's "To the Virgins, to Make Much of Time" aloud. Then have someone else read it aloud to you. Compare the *pace* of the readings. Compare the stress on particular words and syllables. To what extent does the basic metrical pattern in the poem come to control the voice? Do you notice more similarities in the two readings as you and the other reader progress through the poem? why?

## WRITING SUGGESTIONS

1. Read Pope's "Sound and Sense" over carefully twice—once silently and once aloud—and then mark the stressed and unstressed syllables. Draw up a chart indicating, line by line, exactly what the patterns of stress are, and then single out all the lines that have major variations from the basic iambic pentameter pattern. Pick out half a dozen lines with variations that seem to you worthy of comment, and write a paragraph on each in which you show how the varied metrical pattern contributes to the specific effects achieved in that line. (You will probably notice that in most of the lines other strategies also contribute to the sound effects, but confine your discussion to the achievement through metrical pattern.)
2. Try your hand at writing limericks in imitation of "There was a young lady of Riga" (study the rhythmic patterns and line lengths carefully, and imitate them exactly in your poem).

---

5. Instruments for sharpening blades.

Begin your limerick with "There once was a ——— from ———" (use a place for which you think you can find a comic rhyme).

3. Scan line by line Suckling's "Song." In an essay of no more than 500 words, show in detail how the varied metrical pattern in the final stanza abruptly changes the tone of the poem and reverses the poem's direction.

4. Read Birney's "Anglosaxon Street" (page 283) aloud. Then go through the poem line by line and pick out half a dozen words and patterns of sound that seem to you especially effective in creating vocal effects. Analyze carefully the effects created by each of these words or word groups, and try to account for exactly how the passage works. Then, using these examples as the primary (though not necessarily the exclusive) basis, write a three-page paper on the uses of sound in the poem.

6

# INTERNAL STRUCTURE

Proper words in proper places": that is the way one great writer of English prose (Jonathan Swift) described good writing. Finding appropriate words is not the easiest of tasks for a poet, and already we have looked at some of the implications for readers of the verbal choices a poet makes. But a poet's decision about where to put those words—how to arrange them for maximum effect—is also difficult, for individual words, metaphors, and symbols not only exist as part of a phrase or sentence or rhythmic pattern but also as part of the larger whole of the poem itself. How are the words to be ordered and the poem organized? What will come first and what last? What will be its "plot"? How will it be conceived as a whole? How is some sort of structure to be created? What principle or idea of organization will inform the poem? How are words, sentences, images, ideas, and feelings to be combined into something that holds together, seems complete, and will have an effect upon us as readers?

Looking at these questions from the point of view of the poet (What shall I plan? Where shall I begin?) can help the reader notice the effect of structural decisions. Every poem is different from every other one, and independent, individual decisions must, therefore, be made about how to organize. But there are also patterns of organization that poems fall into, sometimes because of the subject matter, sometimes because of the effect intended, sometimes for other reasons. Often poets consciously decide on a particular organizational strategy; sometimes they may reach instinctively for one or happen into a structure that suits the needs of the moment, one onto which a creator can hang the words and sentences one by one and group by group.

When there is a story to be told, the organization of a poem may be fairly simple. Here, for example, is a poem that tells a rather simple story, largely in chronological fashion (first . . . and then . . . ):

EDWIN ARLINGTON ROBINSON

## *Mr. Flood's Party*

Old Eben Flood, climbing alone one night
Over the hill between the town below

225

And the forsaken upland hermitage
That held as much as he should ever know
5   On earth again of home, paused warily.
The road was his and not a native near;
And Eben, having leisure, said aloud,
For no man else in Tilbury Town to hear:

"Well, Mr. Flood, we have the harvest moon
10   Again, and we may not have many more;
The bird is on the wing, the poet says,[1]
And you and I have said it here before.
Drink to the bird." He raised up to the light
The jug that he had gone so far to fill,
15   And answered huskily: "Well, Mr. Flood,
Since you propose it, I believe I will."

Alone, as if enduring to the end
A valiant armor of scarred hopes outworn
He stood there in the middle of the road
20   Like Roland's ghost winding a silent horn.[2]
Below him, in the town among the trees,
Where friends of other days had honored him,
A phantom salutation of the dead
Rang thinly till old Eben's eyes were dim

25   Then, as a mother lays her sleeping child
Down tenderly, fearing it may awake
He set the jug down slowly at his feet
With trembling care, knowing that most things break;
And only when assured that on firm earth
30   It stood, as the uncertain lives of men
Assuredly did not, he paced away,
And with his hand extended paused again:

"Well, Mr. Flood, we have not met like this
In a long time; and many a change has come
35   To both of us, I fear, since last it was
We had a drop together. Welcome home!"
Convivially returning with himself,
Again he raised the jug up to the light;
And with an acquiescent quaver said:
40   "Well, Mr. Flood, if you insist, I might.

"Only a very little, Mr. Flood—
For auld lang syne. No more, sir; that will do."
So, for the time, apparently it did,
And Eben evidently thought so too;
45   For soon amid the silver loneliness

1. Edward Fitzgerald, in "The Rubáiyat of Omar Khayyám" (more or less a translation of an Arab original), so describes the "Bird of Time."    2. In French legend Roland's powerful ivory horn was used to warn his allies of impending attack.

Of night he lifted up his voice and sang,
Secure, with only two moons listening,
Until the whole harmonious landscape rang—

"For auld lang syne." The weary throat gave out,
The last word wavered, and the song was done.                    50
He raised again the jug regretfully
And shook his head, and was again alone.
There was not much that was ahead of him,
And there was nothing in the town below—
Where strangers would have shut the many doors              55
That many friends had opened long ago.                    1921

The fairly simple **narrative structure** here is based on the gradual unfolding of the story. Old Eben is introduced and "placed" in relation to the town and his home, and then the "plot" unfolds: he sits down in the road, reviews his life, reflects on the present, and has a drink. Several drinks, in fact, as he thinks about passing time and growing old; and he sings and considers going "home." Not much happens, really: what we get is a vignette of Mr. Flood between two places and two times, but there *is* action, and the poem's movement—its organization and structure—depends on it: Mr. Flood in motion, in stasis, and then, again, contemplating motion. Here is story, and chronological movement, such as it is. You could say that a narrative of sort takes place (rather like that in Dickey's "Cherrylog Road" [page 94]), though sparely. The poem's organization—its structural principle—involves the passing of time, action moving forward, a larger story being revealed by the few moments depicted here.

"Mr. Flood's Party" presents about as much story as a short poem ever does, but as with most poems the emphasis is not really on the developing action—which all seems fairly predictable once we "get" who Eben is, how old he is, and what "position" he occupies in the communal memory of Tilbury Town and vice versa. Rather, the movement forward in time dictates the shape of the poem, determines the way it presents its images, ideas, themes. There's an easy-to-follow chronology here, and nearly everything takes place within it: you could say that a story is told—with a beginning, middle, and end—and that time structures how the revelation of facts takes place.

But even here, in one of the most simple of narrative structures, there are complications to be noted. One complication is in the use of time itself, for "old" time and "present" time seem posed against each other as a structural principle, too, one in tension with the chronological movement: Eben's past, as contrasted with his present and limited future, focuses the poem's attention, and in some ways the contrast between what was and what is seems even more important than the brief movement through present time that gets the most obvious attention in the poem. Then, too, "character"— Eben's character and that of the townspeople of later generations—gets a lot of the poem's attention, even as the chronology moves forward. More than one structural principle is at work here. We may identify the main movement of the poem as chronological and its principal structure as narrative, but to be fair and full in our discussion we have to note several other competing organizational forces at work—principles of comparison and contrast, for example, and of descriptive elaboration.

Most poems work with this kind of complexity, and identifying a single structure behind any poem involves a sense of what kind of organizational principle makes it work, while at the same time recognizing that other principles repeatedly, perhaps continually, compete for our attention. A poem's *structure* involves its conceptual framework—what principle best explains its organization and movement—and it is often useful to identify one dominating kind of structure, such as narrative structure, that gives the poem its shape. But it is well to recognize from the start that most poems follow paradigmatic models loosely. As with other "elements" of a poem, finding an appropriate label to describe the structure of a particular poem can help in analyzing the poem's other aspects, but there is nothing magic in the label itself.

> *Back of the idea of organic form is the concept that there is a form in all things (and in our experience) which the poet can discover and reveal.*
>
> —DENISE LEVERTOV

Purely narrative poems are often very long, much longer than can be included in a book like this, and often there are many features that are not, strictly speaking, closely connected to the narrative or linked to a strict chronology. Very often a poem moves on from a narrative of an event to some sort of commentary or reflection upon it, as in Karl Shapiro's "Auto Wreck" (page 239). Reflection can be included along the way or may be implicit in the way the story is narrated, as in Kumin's "Woodchucks" (page 41), where our major attention is more on the narrator and her responses than on the events in the story as such.

Just as poems sometimes take on a structure like that of a story, they sometimes borrow the structures of plays. The following poem has a **dramatic structure;** it consists of a series of scenes, each of which is presented vividly and in detail:

HOWARD NEMEROV

## The Goose Fish

On the long shore, lit by the moon
To show them properly alone,
Two lovers suddenly embraced
So that their shadows were as one.
5   The ordinary night was graced
For them by the swift tide of blood
That silently they took at flood.
And for a little time they prized
  Themselves emparadised.

10  Then, as if shaken by stage-fright
Beneath the hard moon's bony light,
They stood together on the sand
Embarrassed in each other's sight
But still conspiring hand in hand,
15  Until they saw, there underfoot,
As though the world had found them out,
The goose fish turning up, though dead,
  His hugely grinning head.

There in the china light he lay,
20  Most ancient and corrupt and gray.

They hesitated at his smile,
Wondering what it seemed to say
To lovers who a little while
Before had thought to understand,
By violence upon the sand,                                    25
The only way that could be known
        To make a world their own.

It was a wide and moony grin
Together peaceful and obscene;
They knew not what he would express,                          30
So finished a comedian
He might mean failure or success,
But took it for an emblem of
Their sudden, new and guilty love
To be observed by, when they kissed,                          35
        That rigid optimist.

So he became their patriarch,
Dreadfully mild in the half-dark.
His throat that the sand seemed to choke,
His picket teeth, these left their mark                       40
But never did explain the joke
That so amused him, lying there
While the moon went down to disappear
Along the still and tilted track
        That bears the zodiac.                                45

                                                    1955

The first stanza sets the scene—a sandy shore in moonlight—and presents, in fact, the major action of the poem. The rest of the poem dramatizes the lovers' reactions: their initial embarrassment and feelings of guilt (stanza 2), their attempt to interpret the goose fish's smile (stanza 3), their decision to make him, whatever his meaning, the "emblem" of their love (stanza 4), and their acceptance of the fish's ambiguity and of their own relationship (stanza 5). The five stanzas do not exactly present five different scenes, but they do present separate dramatic moments, even if only a few minutes apart. Almost like a play of five very short acts, the poem traces the drama of the lovers' discovery of themselves, of their coming to terms with the meaning of their action. As in many plays, the central event (their lovemaking) is not the central focus of the drama, although the drama is based upon that event and could not take place without it. Here, that event is depicted only briefly but very vividly through figurative language: "they took at flood" the "swift tide of blood," and the immediate effect is to make them briefly feel "emparadised." But the poem concentrates on their later reactions, not on the act of love itself.

Their sudden discovery of the fish is a rude shock and injects a grotesque, almost macabre, note into the poem. From a vision of paradise, the poem seems for a moment to turn toward gothic horror when the lovers discover that they have, after all, been seen—and by such a ghoulish spectator. The last three stanzas gradually re-create the intruder in their minds, as they are forced to admit that their act of love does not exist in isolation as they had at first hoped, and they begin to see it as part of a continuum, as part of their relationship to the larger world, even (at the end) putting it into the context of the rotating world and its seasons as the moon disappears into its zodiac. In retrospect, we can see that even at the moment of passion they were in touch with larger processes controlled by the presiding mood ("the swift tide of blood"), but neither the lovers nor we had understood their act as such then, and the poem is about their gradual recognition of their "place" in time and space.

Stages of feeling and knowing rather than specific visual scenes are responsible for the poem's progress, and its dramatic structure depends upon internal perceptions and internal states of mind rather than dialogue and events. Visualization and images help to organize the poem, too. Notice in particular how the two most striking visual features of the poem—the fish and the moon—are presented stanza by stanza. In stanza 1, the fish is not yet noticed, and the moon exists plain; it is only mentioned, not described, and its light serves as a stage spotlight to assure not center-stage attention, but rather total privacy: it is a kind of lookout for the lovers. The stage imagery, barely suggested by the light in stanza 1, is articulated in stanza 2, and there the moon is said to be "hard" and its light "bony"; its features have characteristics that seem more appropriate to the fish, which has now become visible. In stanza 3, the moon's light has come to seem fragile ("china") as it is said to expose the fish directly; the role of the moon as lookout and protector seems abandoned, or at least endangered. No moon appears in stanza 4, but the fish's grin is described as "wide and moony," almost as if the two onlookers, one earthly and dead, the other heavenly and eternal, had become merged in the poem, as they nearly had been by the imagery in stanza 2. And by stanza 5, the fish has become a friend—by now he is a comedian, optimist, emblem, and a patriarch of their love— and his new position in collaboration with the lovers is presided over by the moon going about its eternal business. The moon has provided the stage light for the poem and the means by which not only the fish but the meaning of the lovers' act has been discovered. The moon has also helped to organize the poem, partly as a dramatic accessory, partly as imagery.

The following poem is also dramatic, but it seems to represent a composite of several similar experiences (compare Blake's "London" [page 39] and Dickey's "Cherrylog Road" [page 94]) rather than a single event—a fairly common pattern in dramatic poems:

PHILIP LARKIN

## Church Going

Once I am sure there's nothing going on
I step inside, letting the door thud shut.
Another church: matting, seats, and stone,
And little books; sprawlings of flowers, cut
5    For Sunday, brownish now; some brass and stuff
Up at the holy end; the small neat organ;
And a tense, musty, unignorable silence,
Brewed God knows how long. Hatless, I take off
My cycle-clips in awkward reverence,

10    Move forward, run my hand around the font.
From where I stand, the roof looks almost new—

Cleaned, or restored? Someone would know: I don't.
Mounting the lectern, I peruse a few
Hectoring large-scale verses, and pronounce
"Here endeth" much more loudly than I'd meant.
The echoes snigger briefly. Back at the door
I sign the book, donate an Irish sixpence,
Reflect the place was not worth stopping for.

Yet stop I did: in fact I often do,
And always end much at a loss like this,
Wondering what to look for; wondering, too,
When churches fall completely out of use
What we shall turn them into, if we shall keep
A few cathedrals chronically on show,
Their parchment, plate and pyx in locked cases,
And let the rest rent-free to rain and sheep.
Shall we avoid them as unlucky places?

Or, after dark, will dubious women come
To make their children touch a particular stone;
Pick simples³ for a cancer; or on some
Advised night see walking a dead one?
Power of some sort or other will go on
In games, in riddles, seemingly at random;
But superstition, like belief, must die,
And what remains when disbelief has gone?
Grass, weedy pavement, brambles, buttress, sky,

A shape less recognizable each week,
A purpose more obscure. I wonder who
Will be the last, the very last, to seek
This place for what it was; one of the crew
That tap and jot and know what rood-lofts⁴ were?
Some ruin-bibber,⁵ randy for antique,
Or Christmas-addict, counting on a whiff
Of gown-and-bands and organ-pipes and myrrh?
Or will he be my representative,

Bored, uninformed, knowing the ghostly silt
Dispersed, yet tending to this cross of ground
Through suburb scrub because it held unspilt
So long and equably what since is found
Only in separation—marriage, and birth,
And death, and thoughts of these—for whom was built
This special shell? For, though I've no idea
What this accoutered frowsty barn is worth,
It pleases me to stand in silence here;

15
20
25
30
35
40
45
50

3. Medicinal herbs.    4. Galleries atop the screens (on which crosses are mounted) that divide the naves or main bodies of churches from the choirs or chancels.    5. Literally, ruin-drinker: someone extremely attracted to antiquarian objects.

55    A serious house on serious earth it is,
      In whose blent air all our compulsions meet,
      Are recognized, and robed as destinies.
      And that much never can be obsolete,
      Since someone will forever be surprising
60    A hunger in himself to be more serious,
      And gravitating with it to this ground,
      Which, he once heard, was proper to grow wise in,
      If only that so many dead lie round.                          1955


Ultimately, the poem's emphasis is upon what it means to visit churches, what sort of phenomenon church buildings represent, and what is to be made of the fact that "church going" (in the usual sense of the word) has declined so much. The poem uses a *different* sort of church going (visitation by tourists) to consider larger philosophical questions about the relationship of religion to culture and history. The poem is, finally, a rather philosophical one about the directions of English culture, and through an enumeration of religious objects and rituals it reviews the history of how we got to our present historical circumstance. It tells a kind of story first, through one lengthy dramatized scene, in order to comment later on what the place and the experience may mean, and the larger conclusion derives from the particulars of what the speaker does and touches. The action is really over by the end of stanza 2, and that action, we are told, stands for many such visits to similar churches; after that, all is reflection and discussion, five stanzas' worth.

"Church Going" is a curious poem in many ways. It goes to a lot of trouble to characterize its speaker, who seems a rather odd choice as a commentator on the state of religion. His informal attire (he takes off his cycle-clips at the end of stanza 1) and his not exactly worshipful behavior do not at first make us expect him to be a serious philosopher about what all this means. He is not disrespectful or sacrilegious, and before the end of stanza 1 he has tried to describe the "awkward reverence" he feels; but his overly somber imitation of part of the service stamps him as playful, a little satirical, and as a tourist here, not someone who regularly drops in for prayer or meditation in the usual sense. And yet those early details do give him credentials, in a way; he knows the names of religious objects and has some of the history of churches in his grasp. Clearly he does this sort of church going often ("Yet stop I did: in fact I often do," line 19) because he wonders seriously what it all means—now—in comparison to what it meant to religious worshipers in times past. Ultimately, he takes the church itself seriously and its cultural meaning and function just as seriously (lines 55 ff.), and understands the importance of the church in the history of his culture. In this poem, the drama is, relatively speaking, brief, but it gives a context for the more digressive and rambling free-floating reflections that grow out of the dramatic experience.

Sometimes poems are organized by contrasts, setting one thing up conveniently against another that is quite different. Look, for example, at the two worlds in the following poem, and notice how carefully the contrasts are developed.

PAT MORA

## Sonrisas

I live in a doorway
between two rooms, I hear
quiet clicks, cups of black
coffee, *click, click* like facts
   budgets, tenure, curriculum,            5
from careful women in crisp beige
suits, quick beige smiles
that seldom sneak into their eyes.

I peek
in the other room señoras            10
in faded dresses stir sweet
milk coffee, laughter whirls
with steam from fresh *tamales*
   *sh, sh, mucho ruido,*[6]
they scold one another,           15
press their lips, trap smiles
in their dark, Mexican eyes.         1986

Here different words, habits, and values characterize the different worlds of the two sets of characters, and the poem is largely organized on the basis of the contrasts between them. The meaning of the poem (the difference between the two worlds) is very nearly the same as the structure itself.

Poems often have **discursive structures,** too; that is, they are sometimes organized like a treatise, an argument, or an essay. "First," they say, "and second . . . and third. . . ." This sort of 1-2-3 structure takes a variety of forms depending on what one is enumerating or arguing. Here, for example, is a poem that is about three people who have died. The poem honors all three, but makes clear and sharp distinctions among them. Most of the differences are, in fact, articulated by the way comparisons and contrasts are suggested by the structure itself: the earth is "sweet," "bright," or "dark," depending on the person about to be described. As you read the poem, try to articulate just what sort of person each of the three is represented to be.

JAMES WRIGHT

## Arrangements with Earth for Three Dead Friends

Sweet earth, he ran and changed his shoes to go
Outside with other children through the fields.

---

6. A lot of noise.

He panted up the hills and swung from trees
Wild as a beast but for the human laughter
That tumbled like a cider down his cheeks.
Sweet earth, the summer has been gone for weeks,
And weary fish already sleeping under water
Below the banks where early acorns freeze.
Receive his flesh and keep it cured of colds.
Button his coat and scarf his throat from snow.

And now, bright earth, this other is out of place
In what, awake, we speak about as tombs.
He sang in houses when the birds were still
And friends of his were huddled round till dawn
After the many nights to hear him sing.
Bright earth, his friends remember how he sang
Voices of night away when wind was one.
Lonely the neighborhood beneath your hill
Where he is waved away through silent rooms.
Listen for music, earth, and human ways.

Dark earth, there is another gone away,
But she was not inclined to beg of you
Relief from water falling or the storm.
She was aware of scavengers in holes
Of stone, she knew the loosened stones that fell
Indifferently as pebbles plunging down a well
And broke for the sake of nothing human souls.
Earth, hide your face from her where dark is warm.
She does not beg for anything, who knew
The change of tone, the human hope gone gray.                    1957

Why, in stanza 1, is the earth represented as a parent? What does addressing the earth here as "sweet" seem to mean? How does the address to earth as "bright" fit the dead person described in stanza 2? In what different senses is the person described in stanza 3 "dark"? Why is the earth asked to give attention secretly to this person? Exactly what kind of person was she? How does the poem make you feel about her? Is there any cumulative point in describing three such different people in the same poem? What is accomplished by having the poem's three stanzas addressed to various aspects of earth? Similar discursive structures help to organize poems such as Shelley's "Ode to the West Wind" (page 246), where the wind is shown driving a leaf in Part I, a cloud in Part II, a wave in Part III, and then, after a summary and statement of the speaker's ambitious hope in Part IV, is asked to make the speaker a lyre in Part V.

Poems may borrow their organizational strategies from many places, imitating chronological, visual, or discursive shapes in reality or in other works of art. Sometimes poems strive to be almost purely descriptive of someone or something (using **descriptive structures**), in which case organizational decisions have to be made much as a painter or photographer would make them, deciding first how the whole scene should look, then putting the parts into proper place for the whole. But there are differences demanded by the poetic medium: a poem has to present the details sequentially, not all at once as an actual picture more or less can, so the poet must decide where the description starts (at the left? center? top?) and what sort of movement to use (linear across the scene? clockwise?). But if having words instead of paint or film has some disadvantages, it also has particular assets: figurative language can be a part of description, or an adjunct to it. A poet can insert a comparison at any point without necessarily disturbing the unity of what he or she describes.

Some poems use **imitative structures,** mirroring as exactly as possible the structure of something that already exists as an object and can be seen—another poem perhaps, as in Koch's "Variations on a Theme by William Carlos Williams" (page 391). Or a poem may use **reflective** (or **meditative) structures,** pondering a subject, theme, or event, and letting the mind play with it, skipping (sometimes illogically but still usefully) from one sound to another, or to related thoughts or objects as the mind receives them.

Here is a poem that involves several different organizational principles but ultimately takes its structure from an important emotional shift in the speaker's attitude as her mind reviews, ponders, and rethinks events of long ago.

SHARON OLDS

## *The Victims*

When Mother divorced you, we were glad. She took it and
took it, in silence, all those years and then
kicked you out, suddenly, and her
kids loved it. Then you were fired, and we
grinned inside, the way people grinned when     5
Nixon's helicopter lifted off the South
Lawn for the last time.[7] We were tickled
to think of your office taken away,
your secretaries taken away,
your lunches with three double bourbons,     10
your pencils, your reams of paper. Would they take your
suits back, too, those dark
carcasses hung in your closet, and the black
noses of your shoes with their large pores?
She had taught us to take it, to hate you and take it     15
until we pricked with her for your
annihilation, Father. Now I
pass the bums in doorways, the white
slugs of their bodies gleaming through slits in their
suits of compressed silt, the stained     20
flippers of their hands, the underwater
fire of their eyes, ships gone down with the
lanterns lit, and I wonder who took it and

7. When Richard Nixon resigned the U.S. presidency on August 8, 1974, his exit from the White House (by helicopter from the lawn) was televised live.

took it from them in silence until they had
25    given it all away and had nothing
left but this.                                                          1984


"The Victims" divides basically into two parts. In the first two-thirds of the poem (from line 1 to the middle of line 17), the speaker evokes her father (the "you" of lines 1, 3, and so forth), who had been guilty of terrible habits and behavior when the speaker was young and was kicked out suddenly and divorced by the speaker's mother (lines 1–3). He was then fired from his job (line 4) and lost his whole way of life (lines 8–12), and the speaker (taught by the mother, lines 15–17) recalls celebrating every defeat and every loss ("we pricked with her for your annihilation," lines 16–17). The mother is regarded as a victim ("She took it and took it, in silence, all those years" [lines 1–2]), and the speaker forms an indivisible unit with her and the other children ("her kids," lines 3–4). They are the "we" of the first part of the poem. They were "glad" (line 1) at the divorce; they "loved it" (line 4) when the mother kicked out the father; they "grinned" (line 5) when the father was fired; they were "tickled" (line 7) when he lost his job, his secretaries, and his daily life. Only at the end of the first section does the speaker (now older but remembering what it was like to be a child) recognize that the mother was responsible for the easy, childish vision of the father's guilt ("She had taught us to take it, to hate you and take it" [line 15]); nevertheless, all sympathy in this part of the poem is with the mother and her children, while all of the imagery is entirely unfavorable to the father. The family reacted to the father's misfortunes the way observers responded to the retreat in disgrace of Richard Nixon from the U.S. presidency. The father seems to have led a luxurious and insensitive life, with lots of support in his office (lines 8–11), fancy clothes (lines 12–14), and decadent lunches (line 10); his artificial identity seemed haunting and daunting (lines 11–14) to the speaker as child.

But in line 17, the poem shifts focus and shifts gears. The "you" in the poem is now, suddenly, "Father." A bit of sympathy begins to surface for "bums in doorways" (line 18), who begin to seem like victims, too; their bodies are "slugs" (line 19), their suits are made of residual waste pressed into regimented usefulness (lines 19–20), and their hands are constricted into mechanical "flippers" (line 21). Their eyes contain fire (line 22), but it is as if they retain only a spark of life in their submerged and dying state. The speaker has not forgotten the cruelty and insensitivity remembered in the first part of the poem, but the blame seems to have shifted somewhat and the father is not the only villain, nor are the mother and children the only victims. Look carefully at how the existence of street people recalls earlier details about the father, how sympathy for his plight is elicited from us, and how the definition of victim shifts.

Imagery, words, attitudes, and narrative are different in the two parts of the poem, and the second half carefully qualifies the first, as if to illustrate the more mature and considered attitudes of the speaker in her older years—a qualification of the easy imitation of the earlier years when the mother's views were thoroughly dominant and seemed sensible and adequate. Change has governed the poem's structure here; differences in age, attitude, and tone are supported by entirely different sets of terms, attitudes, and versions of causality.

The paradigms (or models) for organizing poems are, finally, not all that different from those of prose. It may be easier to organize something short rather than something long, but the question of intensity becomes comparatively more important in shorter works. Basically, the problem of how to organize one's material is, for the writer, first of all a matter of deciding what kind of thing one wants to create, of having its purposes and effects clearly in mind. That means that every poem will differ somewhat from every other, but it also means that patterns of purpose—narrative, dramatic, discursive, descriptive, imitative, or reflective—may help writers organize and formulate their ideas. A consciousness of purpose and effect can help the reader see *how* a poem proceeds toward its goal. Seeing how a poem is organized is, in turn, often a good way of seeing where it is going and what its real concerns and purposes may be. Often a poem's organization helps to make clear the particular effects that the poet wishes to generate. In a good poem, means and end are closely related, and a reader who is a good observer of one will be able to discover the other.

## ANONYMOUS

## *Sir Patrick Spens*

The king sits in Dumferling toune,[8]
   Drinking the blude-reid[9] wine:
"O whar will I get guid sailor,
   To sail this ship of mine?"

Up and spake an eldern knicht,            5
   Sat at the king's richt knee:
"Sir Patrick Spens is the best sailor
   That sails upon the sea."

The king has written a braid[1] letter
   And signed it wi' his hand,          10
And sent it to Sir Patrick Spens,
   Was walking on the sand.

The first line that Sir Patrick read,
   A loud lauch[2] lauched he;
The next line that Sir Patrick read,      15
   The tear blinded his ee.[3]

"O wha is this has done this deed,
   This il deed done to me,
To send me out this time o' the year,
   To sail upon the sea?          20

"Make haste, make haste, my merry men all,
   Our guid ship sails the morn."
"O say na sae,[4] my master dear,
   For I fear a deadly storm.

"Late, late yestre'en I saw the new moon    25
   Wi' the auld moon in her arm,

8. Town.    9. Blood-red.    1. Broad: explicit.    2. Laugh.    3. Eye.    4. Not so.

And I fear, I fear, my dear mastér,
    That we will come to harm."

O our Scots nobles were richt laith[5]
30    To weet their cork-heeled shoon,[6]
But lang owre a'[7] the play were played
    Their hats they swam aboon.[8]

O lang, lang, may their ladies sit,
    Wi' their fans into their hand,
35 Or ere they see Sir Patrick Spens
    Come sailing to the land.

O lang, lang, may the ladies stand
    Wi' their gold kems[9] in their hair,
Waiting for their ain[1] dear lords,
40    For they'll see them na mair.

Half o'er, half o'er to Aberdour
    It's fifty fadom deep,
And there lies guid Sir Patrick Spens
    Wi' the Scots lords at his feet.

probably thirteenth century

T. S. ELIOT

## *Journey of the Magi*[2]

"A cold coming we had of it,
Just the worst time of the year
For a journey, and such a long journey:
The ways deep and the weather sharp,
5 The very dead of winter."[3]
And the camels galled, sore-footed, refractory,
Lying down in the melting snow.
There were times we regretted
The summer palaces on slopes, the terraces,
10 And the silken girls bringing sherbet.
Then the camel men cursing and grumbling
And running away, and wanting their liquor and women,
And the night-fires going out, and the lack of shelters,
And the cities hostile and the towns unfriendly
15 And the villages dirty and charging high prices:

5. Right loath: very reluctant.    6. To wet their cork-heeled shoes. Cork was expensive, and, therefore, such shoes were a mark of wealth and status.    7. Before all.    8. Their hats swam above them. 9. Combs.    1. Own.    2. The wise men who followed the star of Bethlehem. See Matthew 2:1–12. 3. An adaptation of a passage from a 1622 sermon by Lancelot Andrews.

A hard time we had of it.
At the end we preferred to travel all night,
Sleeping in snatches,
With the voices singing in our ears, saying
That this was all folly.                                            20

    Then at dawn we came down to a temperate valley,
Wet, below the snow line, smelling of vegetation;
With a running stream and a water-mill beating the darkness,
And three trees on the low sky,[4]
And an old white horse galloped away in the meadow.                 25
Then we came to a tavern with vine-leaves over the lintel,
Six hands at an open door dicing for pieces of silver,
And feet kicking the empty wine-skins.
But there was no information, and so we continued
And arrived at evening, not a moment too soon                       30
Finding the place; it was (you may say) satisfactory.

    All this was a long time ago, I remember,
And I would do it again, but set down
This set down
This: were we led all that way for                                  35
Birth or Death? There was a Birth, certainly,
We had evidence and no doubt. I had seen birth and death,
But had thought they were different; this Birth was
Hard and bitter agony for us, like Death, our death.
We returned to our places, these Kingdoms,[5]                       40
But no longer at ease here, in the old dispensation,
With an alien people clutching their gods.
I should be glad of another death.                          1927


## KARL SHAPIRO

## *Auto Wreck*

Its quick soft silver bell beating, beating,
And down the dark one ruby flare
Pulsing out red light like an artery,
The ambulance at top speed floating down
Past beacons and illuminated clocks                                 5
Wings in a heavy curve, dips down,

4. Suggestive of the three crosses of the Crucifixion (Luke 23:32–33). The Magi see several objects that suggest later events in Christ's life: pieces of silver (see Matthew 26:14–16), the dicing (see Matthew 27: 35), the white horse (see Revelation 6:2 and 19:11–16), and the empty wine-skins (see Matthew 9:17, possibly relevant also to lines 41–42).    5. The Bible only identifies the wise men as "from the east," and subsequent tradition has made them kings. In Persia, magi were members of an ancient priestly caste.

And brakes speed, entering the crowd.
The doors leap open, emptying light;
Stretchers are laid out, the mangled lifted
10 And stowed into the little hospital.
Then the bell, breaking the hush, tolls once,
And the ambulance with its terrible cargo
Rocking, slightly rocking, moves away,
As the doors, an afterthought, are closed.

15 We are deranged, walking among the cops
Who sweep glass and are large and composed.
One is still making notes under the light.
One with a bucket douches ponds of blood
Into the street and gutter.
20 One hangs lanterns on the wrecks that cling,
Empty husks of locusts, to iron poles.

Our throats were tight as tourniquets,
Our feet were bound with splints, but now,
Like convalescents intimate and gauche,
25 We speak through sickly smiles and warn
With the stubborn saw of common sense,
The grim joke and the banal resolution.
The traffic moves around with care,
But we remain, touching a wound
30 That opens to our richest horror.
Already old, the question Who shall die?
Becomes unspoken Who is innocent?

For death in war is done by hands;
Suicide has cause and stillbirth, logic;
35 And cancer, simple as a flower, blooms.
But this invites the occult mind,
Cancels our physics with a sneer,
And spatters all we knew of denouement
Across the expedient and wicked stones.                    1942


W. S. MERWIN

## Burning the Cat

In the spring, by the big shuck-pile
Between the bramble-choked brook where the copperheads
Curled in the first sun, and the mud road,
All at once it could no longer be ignored.
5 The season steamed with an odor for which
There has never been a name, but it shouted above all.
When I went near, the wood-lice were in its eyes

And a nest of beetles in the white fur of its armpit.
I built a fire there by the shuck-pile
But it did no more than pop the beetles 10
And singe the damp fur, raising a stench
Of burning hair that bit through the sweet day-smell.
Then thinking how time leches after indecency,
Since both grief is indecent and the lack of it,
I went away and fetched newspaper, 15
And wrapped it in kerosene and put it in
With the garbage on a heaped nest of sticks:
It was harder to burn than the peels of oranges,
Bubbling and spitting, and the reek was like
Rank cooking that drifted with the smoke out 20
Through the budding woods and clouded the shining dogwood.
But I became stubborn: I would consume it
Though the pyre should take me a day to build
And the flames rise over the house. And hours I fed
That burning, till I was black and streaked with sweat; 25
And poked it out then, with charred meat still clustering
Thick around the bones. And buried it so
As I should have done in the first place, for
The earth is slow, but deep, and good for hiding;
I would have used it if I had understood 30
How nine lives can vanish in one flash of a dog's jaws,
A car or a copperhead, and yet how one small
Death, however reckoned, is hard to dispose of. 1955


RICHARD WILBUR

## *The Pardon*


My dog lay dead five days without a grave
In the thick of summer, hid in a clump of pine
And a jungle of grass and honeysuckle-vine.
I who had loved him while he kept alive

Went only close enough to where he was 5
To sniff the heavy honeysuckle-smell
Twined with another odor heavier still
And hear the flies' intolerable buzz.

Well, I was ten and very much afraid.
In my kind world the dead were out of range 10
And I could not forgive the sad or strange
In beast or man. My father took the spade

And buried him. Last night I saw the grass
Slowly divide (it was the same scene

15  But now it glowed a fierce and mortal green)
And saw the dog emerging. I confess

I felt afraid again, but still he came
In the carnal sun, clothed in a hymn of flies,
And death was breeding in his lively eyes.
20  I started in to cry and call his name,

Asking forgiveness of his tongueless head.
. . . I dreamt the past was never past redeeming:
But whether this was false or honest dreaming
I beg death's pardon now. And mourn the dead.          1950


JOHN CLARE

## Badger

When midnight comes a host of dogs and men
Go out and track the badger to his den,
And put a sack within the hole, and lie
Till the old grunting badger passes by.
5   He comes and hears—they let the strongest loose.
The old fox hears the noise and drops the goose.
The poacher shoots and hurries from the cry,
And the old hare half wounded buzzes by.
They get a forkéd stick to bear him down
10  And clap the dogs and take him to the town,
And bait him all the day with many dogs,
And laugh and shout and fright the scampering hogs.
He runs along and bites at all he meets:
They shout and hollo down the noisy streets.

15  He turns about to face the loud uproar
And drives the rebels to their very door.
The frequent stone is hurled where'er they go;
When badgers fight, then everyone's a foe.
The dogs are clapped and urged to join the fray;
20  The badger turns and drives them all away.
Though scarcely half as big, demure and small,
He fights with dogs for hours and beats them all.
The heavy mastiff, savage in the fray,
Lies down and licks his feet and turns away.
25  The bulldog knows his match and waxes cold,
The badger grins and never leaves his hold.
He drives the crowd and follows at their heels
And bites them through—the drunkard swears and reels.

The frighted women take the boys away,
30  The blackguard laughs and hurries on the fray.
He tries to reach the woods, an awkward race,

But sticks and cudgels quickly stop the chase.
He turns again and drives the noisy crowd
And beats the many dogs in noises loud.
He drives away and beats them every one,                    35
And then they loose them all and set them on.
He falls as dead and kicked by boys and men,
Then starts and grins and drives the crowd again;
Till kicked and torn and beaten out he lies
And leaves his hold and crackles, groans, and dies.         40

1835–37                                                   1920


EMILY DICKINSON

## [The Wind begun to knead the Grass—]

The Wind begun to knead the Grass—
As Women do a Dough—
He flung a Hand full at the Plain—
A Hand full at the Sky—
The Leaves unhooked themselves from Trees—                  5
And started all abroad—
The Dust did scoop itself like Hands—
And throw away the Road—
The Wagons quickened on the Street—
The Thunders gossiped low—                                  10
The Lightning showed a Yellow Head—
And then a livid Toe—
The Birds put up the Bars to Nests—
The Cattle flung to Barns—
Then came one drop of Giant Rain—                           15
And then, as if the Hands
That held the Dams—had parted hold—
The Waters Wrecked the Sky—
But overlooked my Father's House—
Just Quartering a Tree—                                     20

1864


ROO BORSON

## Save Us From

Save us from night,
from bleak open highways

without end, and the fluorescent
oases of gas stations,
from the gunning of immortal
engines past midnight,
when time has no meaning,
from all-night cafés,
their ghoulish slices of pie,
and the orange ruffle on the
apron of the waitress,
the matching plastic chairs,
from orange and brown and
all unearthly colors,
banish them back to the test tube,
save us from them,
from those bathrooms with a
moonscape of skin in the mirror,
from fatigue, its merciless brightness,
when each cell of the body stands on end,
and the sensation of teeth,
and the mind's eternal sentry,
and the unmapped city
with its cold bed.
Save us from insomnia,
its treadmill,
its school bells and factory bells,
from living-rooms like the tomb,
their plaid chesterfields
and galaxies of dust,
from chairs without arms,
from any matched set of furniture,
from floor-length drapes which
close out the world,
from padded bras and rented suits,
from any object in which horror is concealed.
Save us from waking after nightmares,
save us from nightmares,
from other worlds,
from the mute, immobile contours
of dressers and shoes,
from another measureless day, save us.                1989

DENISE LEVERTOV

## What Were They Like?

1)  Did the people of Viet Nam
    use lanterns of stone?

2)  Did they hold ceremonies
    to reverence the opening of buds?
3)  Were they inclined to rippling laughter?                              5
4)  Did they use bone and ivory,
    jade and silver, for ornament?
5)  Had they an epic poem?
6)  Did they distinguish between speech and singing?

1)  Sir, their light hearts turned to stone.                            10
    It is not remembered whether in gardens
    stone lanterns illumined pleasant ways.
2)  Perhaps they gathered once to delight in blossom,
    but after the children were killed
    there were no more buds.                                            15
3)  Sir, laughter is bitter to the burned mouth.
4)  A dream ago, perhaps. Ornament is for joy.
    All the bones were charred.
5)  It is not remembered. Remember,
    most were peasants; their life                                      20
    was in rice and bamboo.
    When peaceful clouds were reflected in the paddies
    and the water buffalo stepped surely along terraces,
    maybe fathers told their sons old tales.
    When bombs smashed the mirrors                                      25
    there was time only to scream.
6)  There is an echo yet, it is said,
    of their speech which was like a song.
    It is reported their singing resembled
    the flight of moths in moonlight.                                   30
    Who can say? It is silent now.                          1966

## WILLIAM CARLOS WILLIAMS

## *The Dance*

In Brueghel's great picture, The Kermess,[6]
the dancers go round, they go round and
around, the squeal and the blare and the
tweedle of bagpipes, a bugle and fiddles
tipping their bellies (round as the thick-                               5
sided glasses whose wash they impound)
their hips and their bellies off balance
to turn them. Kicking and rolling about
the Fair Grounds, swinging their butts, those

6. A painting by Pieter Brueghel the Elder (1525?–1569).

10    shanks must be sound to bear up under such
     rollicking measures, prance as they dance
     in Brueghel's great picture, The Kermess.           1944

PERCY BYSSHE SHELLEY

## *Ode to the West Wind*

### I

O wild West Wind, thou breath of Autumn's being,
Thou, from whose unseen presence the leaves dead
Are driven, like ghosts from an enchanter fleeing,

Yellow, and black, and pale, and hectic red,
5   Pestilence-stricken multitudes: O thou,
Who chariotest to their dark wintry bed

The wingéd seeds, where they lie cold and low,
Each like a corpse within its grave, until
Thine azure sister of the Spring shall blow

10  Her clarion[7] o'er the dreaming earth, and fill
(Driving sweet buds like flocks to feed in air)
With living hues and odors plain and hill:

Wild Spirit, which art moving everywhere;
Destroyer and preserver; hear, oh, hear!

### II

15  Thou on whose stream, mid the steep sky's commotion,
Loose clouds like earth's decaying leaves are shed,
Shook from the tangled boughs of Heaven and Ocean,

Angels[8] of rain and lightning: there are spread
On the blue surface of thine aëry surge,
20  Like the bright hair uplifted from the head

Of some fierce Maenad,[9] even from the dim verge
Of the horizon to the zenith's height,
The locks of the approaching storm. Thou dirge

Of the dying year, to which this closing night
25  Will be the dome of a vast sepulcher,
Vaulted with all thy congregated might

7. Trumpet call.    8. Messengers.    9. A frenzied female votary of Dionysus, the Greek god of vegetation and fertility who was supposed to die in the fall and rise again each spring.

Of vapors, from whose solid atmosphere
Black rain, and fire, and hail will burst: oh, hear!

### III

Thou who didst waken from his summer dreams
The blue Mediterranean, where he lay,                                    30
Lulled by the coil of his crystálline streams,

Beside a pumice isle in Baiae's bay,[1]
And saw in sleep old palaces and towers
Quivering within the wave's intenser day,

All overgrown with azure moss and flowers                                 35
So sweet, the sense faints picturing them! Thou
For whose path the Atlantic's level powers

Cleave themselves into chasms, while far below
The sea-blooms and the oozy woods which wear
The sapless foliage of the ocean, know                                    40

Thy voice, and suddenly grow gray with fear,
And tremble and despoil themselves:[2] oh, hear!

### IV

If I were a dead leaf thou mightest bear;
If I were a swift cloud to fly with thee;
A wave to pant beneath thy power, and share                               45

The impulse of thy strength, only less free
Than thou, O uncontrollable! If even
I were as in my boyhood, and could be

The comrade of thy wanderings over Heaven,
As then, when to outstrip thy skyey speed                                 50
Scarce seemed a vision; I would ne'er have striven

As thus with thee in prayer in my sore need.
Oh, lift me as a wave, a leaf, a cloud!
I fall upon the thorns of life! I bleed!

A heavy weight of hours has chained and bowed                             55
One too like thee: tameless, and swift, and proud.

### V

Make me thy lyre, even as the forest is:
What if my leaves are falling like its own!
The tumult of thy mighty harmonies

1. Where Roman emperors had erected villas, west of Naples.    2. "The vegetation at the bottom of the sea . . . sympathizes with that of the land in the change of seasons." (PBS)

60     Will take from both a deep, autumnal tone,
       Sweet though in sadness. Be thou, Spirit fierce,
       My spirit! Be thou me, impetuous one!

       Drive my dead thoughts over the universe
       Like withered leaves to quicken a new birth!
65     And, by the incantation of this verse,

       Scatter, as from an unextinguished hearth
       Ashes and sparks, my words among mankind!
       Be through my lips to unawakened earth

       The trumpet of a prophecy! O Wind,
70     If Winter comes, can Spring be far behind?                    1820


LOUISE BOGAN

## *Evening in the Sanitarium*[3]

       The free evening fades, outside the windows fastened with decorative
           iron grilles.
       The lamps are lighted; the shades drawn; the nurses are watching a
           little.
       It is the hour of the complicated knitting on the safe bone needles; of
           the games of anagrams and bridge;
       The deadly game of chess; the book held up like a mask.

5      The period of the wildest weeping, the fiercest delusion, is over.
       The women rest their tired half-healed hearts; they are almost well.
       Some of them will stay almost well always: the blunt-faced woman
           whose thinking dissolved
       Under academic discipline; the manic-depressive girl
       Now leveling off; one paranoiac afflicted with jealousy.
10     Another with persecution. Some alleviation has been possible.

       O fortunate bride, who never again will become elated after childbirth!
       O lucky older wife, who has been cured of feeling unwanted!
       To the suburban railway station you will return, return,
       To meet forever Jim home on the 5:35.
15     You will be again as normal and selfish and heartless as anybody else.

       There is life left: the piano says it with its octave smile.
       The soft carpets pad the thump and splinter of the suicide to be.
       Everything will be splendid: the grandmother will not drink habitually.
       The fruit salad will bloom on the plate like a bouquet
20     And the garden produce the blue-ribbon aquilegia.

3. "Originally published with the subtitle 'Imitated from Auden.' " (LB)

The cats will be glad; the fathers feel justified; the mothers relieved.
The sons and husbands will no longer need to pay the bills.
Childhoods will be put away, the obscene nightmare abated.

At the ends of the corridors the baths are running.
Mrs. C. again feels the shadow of the obsessive idea.                    25
Miss R. looks at the mantel-piece, which must mean something.

                                                                    1941

## QUESTIONS

1. How many different "scenes" can you identify in "Sir Patrick Spens"? Where does each scene begin and end? How are the transitions made from scene to scene? How is the "fading" effect between scenes accomplished?
2. Why does the last line of Williams's "The Dance" repeat the first line? How do the line breaks early in the poem help to control the poem's rhythm and pace? What differences do you notice in the choice of words early in the poem and then later? How is the poem organized?
3. What words and patterns are repeated in the different stanzas of Shelley's "Ode to the West Wind"? What differences are there from stanza to stanza? What "progress" does the poem make? In what sense is the poem "revolutionary" or "cyclical"? What contribution to the structure of the poem do the sound patterns make? How do the rhymes and repeated stanza patterns contribute to the tone of the poem? to its meaning?
4. Look back over the poems you have read earlier in the course, and pick out one of them that seems to you particularly effective in the way it is put together. Read it over several times and consider carefully how it is organized, that is, what principles of structure it uses. What does the choice of speaker, situation, and setting have to do with its structure? What other artistic decisions seem to you crucial in creating the poem's structure?

## WRITING SUGGESTIONS

1. After doing the reading and analysis suggested in question 4 above, write a detailed essay in which you consider fully the structural principles at work in the poem. The length of your essay will depend on the length of the poem you choose—but also on the complexity of its structure.
2. Look back at Dickey's "Cherrylog Road" (page 94) and reread it carefully. Then look for another poem in which memory of a much earlier event plays an important structural function. Compare the poems in detail, noting how (in each case) memory influences the way the event is reconstructed. What details of the event are in each case omitted in the retelling? What parts are lengthened or dwelt upon? What, in each case, is the point of having the event recalled later rather than from an immediate recollection?

    Write a three- or four-page essay comparing the structuring function of memory in the two poems, noting in each case exactly how the structural principles at work in the poem help to create the poem's final tone.

# STUDENT WRITING

Below is one student's response to the first Writing Suggestion. The student focuses primarily on the phrases in "The Victims" that involve "taking" as he describes the structure of the poem.

---

Structure and Language in "The Victims"

by Sharon Olds

In Sharon Olds' poem "The Victims" we hear a son or daughter, already grown, speaking to a father whom he/she lost as a result of divorce. It reads like part accusation and part confession. As the poem progresses attitudes such as bitterness and spite toward the father soften, and at the end the reader is left with the same ambivalent feelings as the speaker herself[1] feels.

The poem is divided into two parts, from line 1 to line 17 and from there to the end. The first portion is in many ways a narration, the story line. The speaker relives the experience. Both the language ("her kids loved it," "we grinned inside," "We were tickled") and symbolism (the comparison of suits to carcasses and shoe tips to noses) used here suggest that this is a child's perspective on the situation. This portion is also spoken in the past tense. In the second portion we hear a more reflective and contemplative adult. It is spoken in the present tense ("Now I . . ." [line 17]), and combines both the speaker's bitterness (which dominates the first portion) as well as her pity and sense of guilt toward her father.

The two portions are framed by similar phrases: "She took it and took it, in silence . . ." (line 1), "She had taught us to take it, to hate you and take it . . ." (line 15), "I wonder who took it and took it from them in silence . . ." (lines 23–24). In the final lines of the poem these words take on a deep meaning and enable the reader to read the poem in a completely different manner.

When we first read the words "took it and took it in silence" we assume the mother took some sort of abuse in silence. She taught her children to take the abuse in silence and to hate their father. The final repetition of that phrase: "I wonder who took it and took it from them in silence until they had given it all away and had nothing left but this" (lines 23–26), reminds us of the meaning of the word "take." "Taking it" can mean taking abuse, but it can also mean taking in the ordinary sense as in taking money or a gift or love. One is active and one is passive. If we adopt the active form, the poem is still meaningful, only this time it is the father who is the victim. He is the one who gave all he had. The mother took and took (money, love, attention) and taught her children to take and to hate. One hint to support this interpretation might be the first line of the poem, which suggests that the mother was something more than a passive victim ("When mother divorced you . . . ," ". . . kicked you out . . ."). Again the ambiguity of the phrase strengthens the sense of ambivalence which a child must feel when her parents divorce. It is never clear who "the Victims" are in the poem, perhaps all of them.

Silence is another strong theme in the poem. Note the following examples: "took it, in silence" (line 2), "we grinned inside . . ." (line 5), "I wonder . . ." (line 23), "took it from them in silence . . ." (line 24). The strongest example of the silence, the lack of communication, and the alienation comes in the last section and the metaphor of the bums in doorways. The speaker compares her father to the drunken bums she sees and describes them in such a way that the image of fish or sunken ships becomes vivid ("white slugs of their bodies," "slits in their suits of compressed silt," "stained flippers," "underwater fire of their eyes"). The father is in some other, "underwater" world where sounds from the outside are inaudible. The only sound we hear in this poem is the speaker's voice. Silence and alienation predominated in her childhood, and now as an adult she is still unable to reach her father.

While on the surface this poem seems to be one of anger and accusation, a closer reading indicates a deeper, more complex view of human experience. Things are seldom as clearly defined and one-sided as they appear to a child.

Note

[1] It is not apparent whether the speaker is male or female. I chose to refer to her as a female simply because the poet is a female. It seems that the experience and feelings related are not exclusive to one sex or the other.

# 7

## EXTERNAL FORM

Most poems of more than a few lines are divided into stanzas, groups of lines divided from other groups by white space on the page. Putting some space between groupings of lines has the effect of sectioning the poem, giving its physical appearance a series of divisions that often mark breaks in thought, changes of scenery or imagery, or other shifts in structure or direction. In Donne's "The Flea" (page 97), for example, the stanza divisions mark distinctive stages in the action: between the first and second stanzas, the speaker stops his companion from killing the flea; between the second and third stanzas, the companion follows through on her intention and kills the flea. In Nemerov's "The Goose Fish" (page 228), the stanzas mark stages in the self-perception of the lovers; each of the stanzas is a more or less distinct scene, and the scenes unfold almost like a series of slides. Not all stanzas are quite so neatly patterned as are the ones in these two poems, but any formal division of a poem into stanzas is important to consider: what appear to be gaps or silences may be structural indicators.

Historically, stanzas have most often been organized by patterns of rhyme, and thus stanza divisions have been a visual indicator of patterns in sound. In most traditional stanza forms, the pattern of rhyme is repeated in stanza after stanza throughout the poem, until voice and ear become familiar with the pattern and come to expect it and, in a sense, to depend on it. The accumulation of pattern allows us to "hear" variations as well, just as we do in music. The rhyme thus becomes an organizational device in the poem—a formal, external determiner of organization, as distinguished from the internal, structural determiners we considered in Chapter 6—and ordinarily the metrical patterns stay constant from stanza to stanza. In Shelley's "Ode to the West Wind," for example, the first and third lines in each stanza rhyme, and the middle line then rhymes with the first and third lines of the next stanza. (In indicating rhyme, a different letter of the alphabet is conventionally used to represent each sound; in the following example, if we begin with "being" as *a* and "dead" as *b*, then "fleeing" is also *a*, and "red" and "bed" are *b*.)

| | |
|---|---|
| O wild West Wind, thou breath of Autumn's being, | *a* |
| Thou, from whose unseen presence the leaves dead | *b* |
| Are driven, like ghosts from an enchanter fleeing, | *a* |
| | |
| Yellow, and black, and pale, and hectic red, | *b* |
| Pestilence-stricken multitudes: O thou, | *c* |
| Who chariotest to their dark wintry bed | *b* |

> The wingéd seeds, where they lie cold and low,    *c*
> Each like a corpse within its grave, until    *d*
> Thine azure sister of the Spring shall blow    *c*

In this stanza form, known as **terza rima,** the stanzas are linked to each other by a common sound: one rhyme sound from each stanza is picked up in the next stanza, and so on to the end of the poem (though sometimes poems have sections that use varied rhyme schemes). This stanza form was used by Dante in *The Divine Comedy,* written in Italian in the early 1300s. Terza rima is not all that common in English because it is a rhyme-rich stanza form—that is, it requires many rhymes, and thus many different rhyme words—and English is, relatively speaking, a rhyme-poor language (not as rich in rhyme possibilities as Italian or French). One reason for this is that English derives from so many different language families that it has fewer similar word endings than languages that have remained more "pure"—that is, more dependent for vocabulary on the roots and patterns found in a single language family.

Contemporary poets seldom use rhyme, finding it neither necessary nor appealing, but until the twentieth century the music of rhyme was central to both the sound and the formal conception of most poems. Because poetry was originally an oral art (and its texts not always written down) various kinds of **memory devices** (sometimes called **mnemonic devices**) were built into poems to help reciters remember them. Rhyme was one such device, and most people still find it easier to memorize poetry that rhymes. The simple pleasure of hearing familiar sounds repeated at regular intervals may also help to account for the traditional popularity of rhyme, and perhaps plain habit (for both poets and hearers) had a lot to do with why rhyme flourished for so many centuries as a standard expectation. Rhyme also helps to give poetry a special aural quality that distinguishes it from prose, a significant advantage in ages that worry about decorum and propriety and are anxious to preserve a strong sense of poetic tradition. Some ages have been very concerned that poetry should not in any way be mistaken for prose or made to serve prosaic functions, and the literary critics and theorists in those ages made extraordinary efforts to emphasize the distinctions between poetry, which was thought to be artistically superior, and prose, which was thought to be primarily utilitarian. A pride in elitism and a fear that an expanded reading public could ultimately dilute the possibilities of traditional art forms have been powerful cultural forces in Western civilization, and if such forces were not themselves responsible for creating rhyme in poetry, they at least helped to preserve a sense of its necessity. But rhyme and other patterns of repeated sounds are also important, for various historical and cultural reasons, to non-Western languages and poetic traditions as well.

There are at least two other reasons for rhyme. One is complex and hard to state justly without long explanations. It involves traditional ideas about the symmetrical relationship of different aspects of the world and the function of poetry to reflect the universe as human learning has understood it. Many cultures (especially in earlier centuries) have assumed that rhyme was proper to verse, perhaps even essential. Poets in these ages and cultures would have felt themselves eccentric to compose poems any other way. Some English poets (especially in the Renaissance) did experiment—very successfully—with **blank verse** (that is, verse that did not rhyme but that nevertheless had strict metrical requirements), but the cultural pressure for rhyme was almost constant. Why? As noted above, custom or habit may account for part of the assumption that rhyme was necessary, but probably not all of it. Rather, the poets' sense that poetry was an imitation of larger relationships in the universe made it seem natural to use rhyme to represent or re-create a sense of harmony, correspondence, symmetry, and order. The sounds of poetry were thus (they thought) reminders of the harmonious cosmos, of the music of the spheres that animated the planets, the processes of nature, the interrelationship of all created things and beings. Probably poets never said to themselves, "I shall now tunefully emulate the harmony of God's carefully ordered universe," but the tendency to use rhyme and other repetitions or re-echoings of sound (such as **alliteration** or **assonance**) nevertheless stemmed ultimately from basic assumptions about how the universe worked. In a modern world increasingly perceived as fragmented, rambling, and unrelated, there is of course less of a tendency to testify to a sense of harmony and symmetry. It would be too easy and too mechanical to think that rhyme in a poem specifically means that the poet has a firm sense of cosmic order, and that an unrhymed poem testifies to chaos, but cultural assumptions do affect the expectations of both poets and readers, and cultural tendencies create a kind of pressure upon the individual creator. If you take a survey course (or a series of related "period" courses in English or American literature), you will readily notice the diminishing sense of the need for—or relevance of—rhyme. And other linguistic and national traditions similarly vary usages in different times, depending on the philosophical and cultural assumptions of the time and place.

One other reason for using rhyme is that it provides a kind of discipline for the poet, a way of harnessing poetic talents and keeping a rein on the imagination, so that the results are ordered, controlled, put into some kind of meaningful and recognizable form. Robert Frost used to be fond of saying that writing poems without rhyme was like playing tennis without a net. Writing good poetry does require a lot of discipline, and Frost speaks for many (perhaps most) traditional poets in suggesting that rhyme can be a major source of that discipline. But it is not the only possible source, and more recent poets have usually felt they would rather play by new rules or invent their own as they go along; they have, therefore, sought their sources of discipline elsewhere, preferring the sparer tones that unrhymed poetry provides. It is not that contemporary poets cannot think of rhyme words or that they do not care about the sounds of their poetry; rather, recent poets have consciously decided not to work with rhyme and to use instead other aural and metrical devices and other strategies-

*Concentration is the very essence of poetry.*

—AMY LOWELL

for organizing stanzas, just as they have chosen to work with experimental and variable rhythms instead of writing necessarily in the traditional English meters. Some modern poets, though, have protested the abandonment of rhyme and have continued to write rhymed verse successfully in a more or less traditional way.

The amount and density of rhyme vary widely in stanza and verse forms, from elaborate and intricate patterns of rhyme to more casual or spare sound repetitions. The **Spenserian stanza,** for example, is even more rhyme-rich than terza rima, using only three rhyme sounds in nine rhymed lines, as in Keats's *The Eve of St. Agnes:*

| | |
|---|---|
| Her falt'ring hand upon the balustrade, | *a* |
| Old Angela was feeling for the stair, | *b* |
| When Madeline, St. Agnes' charméd maid, | *a* |
| Rose, like a missioned spirit, unaware: | *b* |
| With silver taper's light, and pious care, | *b* |
| She turned, and down the agéd gossip led | *c* |
| To a safe level matting. Now prepare, | *b* |
|    Young Porphyro, for gazing on that bed; | *c* |
| She comes, she comes again, like ring dove frayed and fled | *c* |

On the other hand, the **ballad stanza** has only one set of rhymes in four lines; lines 1 and 3 in each stanza do not rhyme at all (from "Sir Patrick Spens"):

> The king sits in Dumferling toune,    *a*
> Drinking the blude-reid wine:    *b*
> "O whar will I get guid sailor,    *c*
> To sail this ship of mine?"    *b*

Most stanza forms use a metrical pattern as well as a rhyme scheme. Terza rima, for example, involves iambic meter (unstressed and stressed syllables alternating regularly) and each line has five beats (pentameter). Most of the Spenserian stanza (the first eight lines) is also in iambic pentameter, but the ninth line in each stanza has one extra foot (thus, the last line is in iambic hexameter). The ballad stanza, also iambic, as are most English stanza and verse forms, alternates three-beat and four-beat lines; lines 1 and 3 are unrhymed iambic tetrameter (four beats), and lines 2 and 4 are rhymed iambic trimeter (three beats).

# THE SONNET

The **sonnet** is one of the most persistent verse forms. From its origins in the Middle Ages as a prominent form in Italian and French poetry, it dominated English poetry in the late sixteenth and early seventeenth centuries and then was revived several times from the early nineteenth century onward. A sonnet, except for some early experiments with length, is always fourteen lines long and is usually written in iambic pentameter. It is most often printed as if it were a *single* stanza, although in reality it has several formal divisions that represent its rhyme schemes and formal breaks. As a popular and traditional verse form in English for more than four centuries, the sonnet has been surprisingly resilient even in ages that largely reject rhyme. It continues to attract a variety of poets, including (curiously) radical and even revolutionary poets who find its formal demands, discipline, and set outcome very appealing. Its uses, although quite varied, can be illustrated fairly precisely. As a verse form, the sonnet is contained, compact, demanding; whatever it does, it must do concisely and quickly. To be effective, it must take advantage of the possibilities inherent in its shortness and its relative rigidity. It is best suited to intensity of feeling and concentration of expression. Not too surprisingly, one subject it frequently discusses is confinement itself.

## WILLIAM WORDSWORTH

### *Nuns Fret Not*

Nuns fret not at their convent's narrow room;
And hermits are contented with their cells;
And students with their pensive citadels;
Maids at the wheel, the weaver at his loom,
Sit blithe and happy; bees that soar for bloom,                    5
High as the highest Peak of Furness-fells,[1]
Will murmur by the hour in foxglove bells:[2]
In truth the prison, unto which we doom
Ourselves, no prison is: and hence for me,
In sundry moods, 'twas pastime to be bound                        10
Within the sonnet's scanty plot of ground;
Pleased if some souls (for such there needs must be)
Who have felt the weight of too much liberty,
Should find brief solace there, as I have found.                  1807

Most sonnets are structured according to one of two principles of division. On one principle, the sonnet divides into three units of four lines each and a final unit of two lines, and sometimes the line spacing reflects this division. On the other, the fundamen-

---

1. Mountains in England's Lake District, where Wordsworth lived.   2. Flowers from which digitalis (a heart medicine) began to be made in 1799.

tal break is between the first eight lines (called an octave) and the last six (called a sestet). The 4-4-4-2 sonnet is usually called the **English** or **Shakespearean sonnet,** and ordinarily its rhyme scheme reflects the structure: the scheme of *abab cdcd efef gg* is the classic one, but many variations from that pattern still reflect the basic 4-4-4-2 division. The 8-6 sonnet is usually called the **Italian** or **Petrarchan sonnet** (the Italian poet Petrarch was an early master of this structure), and its "typical" rhyme scheme is *abbaabba cdecde,* although it too produces many variations that still reflect the basic division into two parts.

The two kinds of sonnet structures are useful for two different sorts of argument. The 4-4-4-2 structure works very well for constructing a poem that wants to make a three-step argument (with a quick summary at the end), or for setting up brief, cumulative images. "That time of year thou mayst in me behold" (page 166), for example, uses the 4-4-4-2 structure to mark the progressive steps toward death and the parting of friends by using three distinct images, then summarizing. "Let me not to the marriage of true minds" (page 31) works very similarly, following the kind of organization that in Chapter 6 was referred to as the 1-2-3 structure—and doing it compactly and economically.

Here, on the other hand, is a poem that uses the 8-6 pattern:

HENRY CONSTABLE

# [My lady's presence makes the roses red]

My lady's presence makes the roses red,
Because to see her lips they blush for shame.
The lily's leaves, for envy, pale became,
And her white hands in them this envy bred.
5  The marigold the leaves abroad doth spread,
Because the sun's and her power is the same.
The violet of purple colour came,
Dyed in the blood she made my heart to shed.
In brief: all flowers from her their virtue take;
10  From her sweet breath their sweet smells do proceed;
The living heat which her eyebeams doth make
Warmeth the ground and quickeneth the seed.
The rain, wherewith she watereth the flowers,
Falls from mine eyes, which she dissolves in showers.          1594

The first eight lines argue that the lady's presence is responsible for the color of all of nature's flowers, and the final six lines summarize and extend that argument to smells and heat—and finally to the rain that the lady draws from the speaker's eyes. That kind of two-part structure, in which the octave states a proposition or generalization and the sestet provides a particularization or application of it, has a variety of uses. The final lines may, for example, reverse the first eight and achieve a paradox or irony in the poem, or the poem may nearly balance two comparable arguments. Basically, the 8-6 structure lends itself to poems with two points to make, or to those that wish to make one point and then illustrate it.

Sometimes the neat and precise structure is altered—either slightly, as in Wordsworth's "Nuns Fret Not," above (where the 8-6 structure is more of an 8½-5½ structure), or more radically as particular needs or effects may demand. And the two basic structures certainly do not define all the structural possibilities within a fourteen-line poem, even if they do suggest the most traditional ways of taking advantage of the sonnet's compact and well-kept container.

The sonnets in this chapter by Sidney, Shakespeare, and Constable survive from a golden age of English sonnet writing in the late sixteenth century, an age that set the pattern for expectations in the English tradition of form, subject matter, and tone. The sonnet came to England from Italy via France, and imitations of Petrarch's famous sonnet sequence to Laura became the rage. Thousands upon thousands of sonnets were written in those years, often in sequences of a hundred or more sonnets each; the sequences explored the many moods of love and usually had a light thread of narrative that purported to recount a love affair between the male poet and a female lover who was almost always golden-haired, beautiful, disdainful, and inaccessible. Her beauty was described in a series of exaggerated comparisons: her eyes were like the sun ("When Nature made her chief work, Stella's eyes"), her teeth like pearls, her cheeks like roses, her skin like ivory, and so on, but the adherence to these conventions was always playful, and it became a game of wit to play variations upon expectations ("My lady's presence makes the roses red" and "My mistress' eyes are nothing like the sun"). Sometimes the female lover was unreceptive, unavailable, or rejecting, and sometimes male friendship or homosexual love rivaled the usual male/female relationship. Almost always teasing and witty, these poems were not necessarily as true to life as they pretended, but they provided historically an expectation of what sonnets were to be.

Many modern sonnets continue to be about love or private life, and many continue to use a personal, apparently open and sincere tone. But poets often find the sonnet's compact form and rigid demands equally useful for many varieties of subject, theme, and tone. Besides love, sonnets often treat other subjects: politics, philosophy, discovery of a new world. And tones vary widely too, from the anger and remorse of "Th' expense of spirit in a waste of shame" (page 506) and righteous outrage of "On the Late Massacre in Piedmont" (page 100) to the tender awe of "How Do I Love Thee?" (page 3). Many poets seem to take the kind of comfort Wordsworth describes in the careful limits of the form, finding in its two basic variations (the English sonnet such as "My mistress' eyes" [page 269] and the Italian sonnet such as "On First Looking into Chapman's Homer" [page 318]) a sufficiency of convenient ways to organize their materials into coherent structures.

_____
JOHN KEATS

## On the Sonnet

If by dull rhymes our English must be chained,   *a*
And like Andromeda,[3] the sonnet sweet   *b*
Fettered, in spite of painéd loveliness,   *c*

_____
3. Who, according to Greek myth, was chained to a rock so that she would be devoured by a sea monster. She was rescued by Perseus, who married her. When she died she was placed among the stars.

Let us find, if we must be constrained, A
Sandals more interwoven and complete B
To fit the naked foot of Poesy:[4] D
Let us inspect the lyre, and weigh the stress E
Of every chord,[5] and see what may be gained A
By ear industrious, and attention meet; B
Misers of sound and syllable, no less C.
Than Midas[6] of his coinage, let us be D
Jealous of dead leaves in the bay-wreath crown;[7] E
So, if we may not let the Muse be free, D
She will be bound with garlands of her own. E

1819

---

LOUISE BOGAN

## Single Sonnet

Now, you great stanza, you heroic mould,
Bend to my will, for I must give you love:
The weight in the heart that breathes, but cannot move,
Which to endure flesh only makes so bold.

Take up, take up, as it were lead or gold
The burden; test the dreadful mass thereof.
No stone, slate, metal under or above
Earth, is so ponderous, so dull, so cold.

Too long as ocean bed bears up the ocean,
As earth's core bears the earth, have I borne this;
Too long have lovers, bending for their kiss,
Felt bitter force cohering without motion.

Staunch meter, great song, it is yours, at length,
To prove how stronger you are than my strength.

1937

---

4. In a letter that contained this sonnet, Keats expressed impatience with the traditional Petrarchan and Shakespearean sonnet forms: "I have been endeavoring to discover a better sonnet stanza than we have."   5. Lyre string.   6. The legendary king of Phrygia who asked, and got, the power to turn all he touched to gold.   7. The bay tree sacred to Apollo, god of poetry, and bay wreaths came to symbolize true poetic achievement. The withering of the bay tree is sometimes considered an omen of death. *Jealous*: suspiciously watchful.

## DANTE GABRIEL ROSSETTI

# A Sonnet Is a Moment's Monument

A Sonnet is a moment's monument—
   Memorial from the Soul's eternity
   To one dead deathless hour. Look that it be,
Whether for lustral[8] rite or dire portent,
Of its own arduous fullness reverent.                          5
   Carve it in ivory or in ebony,
   As Day or Night may rule; and let Time see
Its flowering crest impearled and orient.[9]

A Sonnet is a coin: its face reveals
   The soul—its converse, to what Power 'tis due—              10
Whether for tribute to the august appeals
   Of Life or dower in Love's high retinue,

It serve; or 'mid the dark wharf's cavernous breath,
In Charon's[1] palm it pay the toll to Death.                  1881


## GWEN HARWOOD

# In the Park

She sits in the park. Her clothes are out of date.
Two children whine and bicker, tug her skirt.
A third draws aimless patterns in the dirt.
Someone she loved once passes by—too late

to feign indifference to that casual nod.                      5
"How nice," et cetera. "Time holds great surprises."
From his neat head unquestionably rises
a small balloon . . . "but for the grace of God . . . "

They stand a while in flickering light, rehearsing
the children's names and birthdays. "It's so sweet            10
to hear their chatter, watch them grow and thrive,"
she says to his departing smile. Then, nursing
the youngest child, sits staring at her feet.
To the wind she says, "They have eaten me alive."             1963

---

8. Purificatory.    9. Sparkling.    1. The boatman who, in classical myth, rowed souls of the dead
across the river Styx. Ancient Greeks put a small coin in the hand of the dead to pay his fee.

EMMA LAZARUS

## The New Colossus

Not like the brazen giant of Greek fame,
With conquering limbs astride from land to land;
Here at our sea-washed, sunset gates shall stand
A mighty woman with a torch, whose flame
5  Is the imprisoned lightning, and her name
Mother of Exiles.[2] From her beacon-hand
Glows world-wide welcome; her mild eyes command
The air-bridged harbor that twin cities frame.
"Keep ancient lands, your storied pomp!" cries she
10  With silent lips. "Give me your tired, your poor,
Your huddled masses yearning to breathe free,
The wretched refuse of your teeming shore.
Send these, the homeless, tempest-tost to me,
I lift my lamp beside the golden door!"

November 1883

HELEN CHASIN

## Joy Sonnet in a Random Universe

Sometimes I'm happy: la la la la la la la
la la la la la la la la la la la la la la la la la
la la la la. Tum tum ti tum. La la la la la la
la la la la la la la la la la la la la la la la la.
5  Hey nonny nonny. La la la la la la la la la
la la la la la la la la la la la. Vo do di o do.
Poo poo pi doo. La la la la la la la la la la
la la la la la la la la la la la la la la la la la
la la. Whack a doo. La la la la la la la. Sh-
10  boom, sh-boom. La la la la la la la la la la
la la la la la la la la la la la la la la la la la
la la. Dum di dum. La la la la la la la la la
la la la la la la la la la. Tra la la. Tra la la
la la la la la la la la la la. Yeah yeah yeah.

1968

---

2. The Statue of Liberty, in New York harbor.

EDWIN MORGAN

## Opening the Cage

14 variations on 14 words

*I have nothing to say and I am saying it and that is poetry.*
                                        —*John Cage*[3]

I have to say poetry and is that nothing and am I saying it
I am and I have poetry to say and is that nothing saying it
I am nothing and I have poetry to say and that is saying it
I that am saying poetry have nothing and it is I and to say
And I say that I am to have poetry and saying it is nothing         5
I am poetry and nothing and saying it is to say that I have
To have nothing is poetry and I am saying that and I say it
Poetry is saying I have nothing and I am to say that and it
Saying nothing I am poetry and I have to say that and it is
It is and I am and I have poetry saying say that to nothing        10
It is saying poetry to nothing and I say I have and am that
Poetry is saying I have it and I am nothing and to say that
And that nothing is poetry I am saying and I have to say it
Saying poetry is nothing and to that I say I am and have it         1968

JOHN MILTON

## [*When I consider how my light is spent*]

When I consider how my light is spent,
    Ere half my days, in this dark world and wide,
    And that one talent which is death to hide[4]
    Lodged with me useless, though my soul more bent
To serve therewith my Maker, and present                            5
    My true account, lest he returning chide;
    "Doth God exact day-labor, light denied?"
    I fondly ask; but Patience to prevent[5]
That murmur, soon replies, "God doth not need
    Either man's work or his own gifts; who best                    10
    Bear his mild yoke, they serve him best. His state

3. Twentieth-century American artist and composer, noted for his startling experiments in sound and silence.    4. In the parable of the talents (Matthew 25), the servants who earned interest on their master's money (his talents) while he was away were called "good and faithful"; the one who hid the money and simply returned it was condemned and sent away. Usury, a deadly sin under Catholicism, was regarded by Puritans as a metaphor for attaining salvation.    5. Forestall. *Fondly:* foolishly.

Is kingly. Thousands at his bidding speed
  And post o'er land and ocean without rest:
  They also serve who only stand and wait."

1652?

CLAUDE McKAY

## The Harlem Dancer

Applauding youths laughed with young prostitutes
And watched her perfect, half-clothed body sway;
Her voice was like the sound of blended flutes
Blown by black players upon a picnic day.
She sang and danced on gracefully and calm,
The light gauze hanging loose about her form;
To me she seemed a proudly-swaying palm
Grown lovelier for passing through a storm.
Upon her swarthy neck black shiny curls
Luxuriant fell; and tossing coins in praise,
The wine-flushed, bold-eyed boys, and even the girls,
Devoured her shape with eager, passionate gaze;
But looking at her falsely-smiling face,
I knew her self was not in that strange place.

1922

HELENE JOHNSON

## Sonnet to a Negro in Harlem

You are disdainful and magnificent—
Your perfect body and your pompous gait,
Your dark eyes flashing solemnly with hate,
Small wonder that you are incompetent
To imitate those whom you so despise—
Your shoulders towering high above the throng,
Your head thrown back in rich, barbaric song,
Palm trees and mangoes stretched before your eyes.
Let others toil and sweat for labor's sake
And wring from grasping hands their meed of gold.
Why urge ahead your supercilious feet?
Scorn will efface each footprint that you make.
I love your laughter arrogant and bold.
You are too splendid for this city street.

p. 1927

WILLIAM WORDSWORTH

## [*The world is too much with us*]

The world is too much with us; late and soon,
Getting and spending, we lay waste our powers:
Little we see in Nature that is ours;
We have given our hearts away, a sordid boon![6]
This Sea that bares her bosom to the moon;                    5
The winds that will be howling at all hours,
And are up-gathered now like sleeping flowers;
For this, for every thing, we are out of tune;
It moves us not.—Great God! I'd rather be
A Pagan suckled in a creed outworn;                          10
So might I, standing on this pleasant lea,
Have glimpses that would make me less forlorn;
Have sight of Proteus rising from the sea;
Or hear old Triton[7] blow his wreathed horn.

1802–1804                                                  1807

PERCY BYSSHE SHELLEY

## *Ozymandias*[8]

I met a traveler from an antique land
Who said: Two vast and trunkless legs of stone
Stand in the desert. . . . Near them, on the sand,
Half sunk, a shattered visage lies, whose frown,
And wrinkled lip, and sneer of cold command,                 5
Tell that its sculptor well those passions read
Which yet survive, stamped on these lifeless things,
The hand that mocked them, and the heart that fed:
And on the pedestal these words appear:
"My name is Ozymandias, King of Kings:                       10
Look on my works, ye Mighty, and despair!"
Nothing beside remains. Round the decay
Of that colossal wreck, boundless and bare
The lone and level sands stretch far away.                   1818

6. Gift.    7. A sea deity, usually represented as blowing on a conch shell. *Proteus:* an old man of the sea who (in *The Odyssey*) could assume a variety of shapes.    8. The Greek name for Rameses II, thirteenth-century-B.C. pharaoh of Egypt. According to a first-century-B.C. Greek historian, Diodorus Siculus, the largest statue in Egypt was inscribed: "I am Ozymandias, king of kings; if anyone wishes to know what I am and where I lie, let him surpass me in some of my exploits."

ARCHIBALD LAMPMAN

## Winter Evening

To-night the very horses springing by
Toss gold from whitened nostrils. In a dream
The streets that narrow to the westward gleam
Like rows of golden palaces; and high
5    From all the crowded chimneys tower and die
A thousand aureoles. Down in the west
The brimming plains beneath the sunset rest,
One burning sea of gold. Soon, soon shall fly
The glorious vision, and the hours shall feel
10   A mightier master; soon from height to height,
With silence and the sharp unpitying stars,
Stern creeping frosts, and winds that touch like steel,
Out of the depth beyond the eastern bars,
Glittering and still shall come the awful night.                    1899

SIR CHARLES G. D. ROBERTS

## The Potato Harvest

A high bare field, brown from the plough, and borne
    Aslant from sunset; amber wastes of sky
    Washing the ridge; a clamor of crows that fly
In from the wide flats where the spent tides mourn
5    To yon their rocking roosts in pines wind-torn;
    A line of grey snake-fence that zigzags by
    A pond and cattle; from the homestead nigh
The long deep summonings of the supper horn.
Black on the ridge, against that lonely flush,
10   A cart, and stoop-necked oxen; ranged beside
    Some barrels; and the day-worn harvest-folk,
Here emptying their baskets, jar the hush
    With hollow thunders. Down the dusk hillside
    Lumbers the wain; and day fades out like smoke.          1886

ROBERT FROST

## Once by the Pacific

The shattered water made a misty din.
Great waves looked over others coming in,

And thought of doing something to the shore
That water never did to land before.
The clouds were low and hairy in the skies,                        5
Like locks blown forward in the gleam of eyes.
You could not tell, and yet it looked as if
The shore was lucky in being backed by cliff,
The cliff in being backed by continent;
It looked as if a night of dark intent                            10
Was coming, and not only a night, an age.
Someone had better be prepared for rage.
There would be more than ocean-water broken
Before God's last *Put out the Light* was spoken.                 1928


GWENDOLYN BROOKS

## First Fight. Then Fiddle.

First fight. Then fiddle. Ply the slipping string
With feathery sorcery; muzzle the note
With hurting love; the music that they wrote
Bewitch, bewilder. Qualify to sing
Threadwise. Devise no salt, no hempen thing                       5
For the dear instrument to bear. Devote
The bow to silks and honey. Be remote
A while from malice and from murdering.
But first to arms, to armor. Carry hate
In front of you and harmony behind.                               10
Be deaf to music and to beauty blind.
Win war. Rise bloody, maybe not too late
For having first to civilize a space
Wherein to play your violin with grace.                           1949


LOUIS MacNEICE

## Sunday Morning

Down the road someone is practicing scales,
The notes like little fishes vanish with a wink of tails,
Man's heart expands to tinker with his car
For this is Sunday morning, Fate's great bazaar;
Regard these means as ends, concentrate on this Now,             5
And you may grow to music or drive beyond Hindhead⁹ anyhow,

9. In Surrey; the direction of a typical Sunday outing from London.

Take corners on two wheels until you go so fast
That you can clutch a fringe or two of the windy past,
That you can abstract this day and make it to the week of time
10    A small eternity, a sonnet self-contained in rhyme.
But listen, up the road, something gulps, the church spire
Opens its eight bells out, skulls' mouths which will not tire
To tell how there is no music or movement which secures
Escape from the weekday time. Which deadens and endures.                1935

WILLIAM WORDSWORTH

## London, 1802

Milton! thou should'st be living at this hour:
England hath need of thee: she is a fen
Of stagnant waters: altar, sword, and pen,
Fireside, the heroic wealth of hall and bower,
5    Have forfeited their ancient English dower
Of inward happiness. We are selfish men;
Oh! raise us up, return to us again;
And give us manners, virtue, freedom, power.
Thy soul was like a star, and dwelt apart:
10    Thou hadst a voice whose sound was like the sea:
Pure as the naked heavens, majestic, free,
So didst thou travel on life's common way,
In cheerful godliness; and yet thy heart
The lowliest duties on herself did lay.

1802

CLAUDE McKAY

## The White House

Your door is shut against my tightened face,
And I am sharp as steel with discontent;
But I possess the courage and the grace
To bear my anger proudly and unbent.
5    The pavement slabs burn loose beneath my feet,
And passion rends my vitals as I pass,
A chafing savage, down the decent street,
Where boldly shines your shuttered door of glass.
Oh, I must search for wisdom every hour,
10    Deep in my wrathful bosom sore and raw,

And find in it the superhuman power
To hold me to the letter of your law!
Oh, I must keep my heart inviolate
Against the poison of your deadly hate.                    1937


SIR PHILIP SIDNEY

# [*When Nature made her chief work, Stella's eyes*][1]

When Nature made her chief work, Stella's eyes,
In color black[2] why wrapped she beams so bright?
Would she in beamy black, like painter wise,
Frame daintiest luster mixed of shades and light?
Or did she else that sober hue devise,                              5
In object best to knit and strength our sight,
Lest if no veil those brave gleams did disguise,
They sunlike should more dazzle than delight?
Or would she her miraculous power show,
That, whereas black seems Beauty's contrary,                       10
She even in black doth make all beauties flow?
Both so and thus: she, minding[3] Love should be
Placed ever there, gave him this mourning weed
To honor all their deaths who for her bleed.

1582


WILLIAM SHAKESPEARE

# [*My mistress' eyes are nothing like the sun*]

My mistress' eyes are nothing like the sun;
Coral is far more red than her lips' red;
If snow be white, why then her breasts are dun;[4]
If hairs be wires, black wires grow on her head.
I have seen roses damasked[5] red and white,                        5
But no such roses see I in her cheeks;
And in some perfumes is there more delight

---

1. From Sidney's sonnet sequence *Astrophel and Stella,* usually credited with having started the vogue of sonnet sequences in Elizabethan England.      2. Black was frequently used in the Renaissance to mean absence of light, and ugly or foul (see line 10).      3. Remembering that.      4. Mouse-colored.
5. Variegated.

Than in the breath that from my mistress reeks.
I love to hear her speak, yet well I know
That music hath a far more pleasing sound;
I grant I never saw a goddess go;[6]
My mistress, when she walks, treads on the ground.
And yet, by heaven, I think my love as rare
As any she belied with false compare.

1609

DIANE ACKERMAN

## Sweep Me through Your Many-Chambered Heart

Sweep me through your many-chambered heart
if you like, or leave me here, flushed
amid the sap-ooze and blossom: one more dish
in the banquet called April, or think me hard-
won all your days full of women. Weeks
later, till I felt your arms around
me like a shackle, heard all the sundown
wizardries the fired body speaks.
Tell me why, if it was no more than this,
the unmuddled tumble, the renegade kiss,
today, rapt in a still life and unaware,
my paintbrush dropped like an amber hawk;
thinking I'd heard your footfall on the stair,
I listened, heartwise, for the knock.

1978

6. Walk.

# STANZA FORMS

Many stanza forms are represented in this book. Some have names because they have been used over and over by different poets. Others were invented for a particular use in a particular poem and may never be repeated again. Most traditional stanzas are based on rhyme schemes, but some use other kinds of predictable sound patterns; early English poetry, for example, used alliteration to construct a balance between the first and second half of each line (see Earle Birney's "Anglosaxon Street" [page 283] for a modern imitation of this principle). Sometimes, especially when poets interact with each other within a strong community, highly elaborate *verse forms* have been developed that set up stanzas as part of a scheme for the whole poem. The poets of medieval Provence were especially inventive, subtle, and elaborate in their construction of complex verse forms, some of which have been copied by poets ever since. The **sestina,** for example, depends on the measured repetition of words (rather than just sounds) in particular places; see, for example, Bishop's "Sestina" (page 273, and try to decipher the pattern. (There are also double and even triple sestinas, tough tests of a poet's ingenuity.) And the **villanelle,** another Provençal form, depends on the patterned repetition of whole lines (see Dylan Thomas's "Do Not Go Gentle into That Good Night" [page 272]). Different cultures and different languages develop their own patterns and measures—not all poetries are parallel to English poetry—and they vary from age to age as well as nation to nation.

You can probably deduce the principles involved in each of the following stanza or verse forms by looking carefully at a poem that uses it; if you have trouble, look at the definitions in the glossary on page A49.

| | | |
|---|---|---|
| **heroic couplet** | "Sound and Sense" | page 203 |
| **tetrameter couplet** | "To His Coy Mistress" | page 107 |
| **limerick** | "There was a young lady of Riga" | page 206 |
| **free verse** | "Dirge" | page 201 |
| **blank verse** | from *Paradise Lost* | page 162 |

What are stanza forms good for? What use is it to recognize them? Why do poets bother? Matters discussed in this chapter so far have suggested two reasons: (1) Breaks between stanzas provide convenient pauses for reader and writer, something roughly equivalent to paragraphs in prose. The eye thus picks up the places where some kind of pause or break or change of focus occurs. (2) Poets sometimes use stanza forms, as they do rhyme itself, as a discipline: writing in a certain kind of stanza form imposes a shape on their act of imagination. But visual spaces and unexpected print divisions also mean that poems sometimes *look* unusual and require special visual attention, attention that does not always follow the logic of sound patterns or syntax. After the following poems illustrating some common stanza forms, you will find a section on poems that employ special configurations and shapes to establish their meanings and effects.

DYLAN THOMAS

## *Do Not Go Gentle into That Good Night*[7]

Do not go gentle into that good night,
Old age should burn and rave at close of day;
Rage, rage against the dying of the light.

Though wise men at their end know dark is right,
5   Because their words had forked no lightning they
Do not go gentle into that good night.

Good men, the last wave by, crying how bright
Their frail deeds might have danced in a green bay,
Rage, rage against the dying of the light.

10   Wild men who caught and sang the sun in flight,
And learn, too late, they grieved it on its way,
Do not go gentle into that good night.

Grave men, near death, who see with blinding sight
Blind eyes could blaze like meteors and be gay,
15   Rage, rage against the dying of the light.

And you, my father, there on the sad height,
Curse, bless, me now with your fierce tears, I pray.
Do not go gentle into that good night.
Rage, rage against the dying of the light.                    1952

MARIANNE MOORE

## *Poetry*

I, too, dislike it: there are things that are important beyond all this
                                                              fiddle.
    Reading it, however, with a perfect contempt for it, one discovers in
    it after all, a place for the genuine.
        Hands that can grasp, eyes
5        that can dilate, hair that can rise
            if it must, these things are important not because a

high-sounding interpretation can be put upon them but because they
                                                              are
    useful. When they become so derivative as to become unintelligible,
    the same thing may be said for all of us, that we
10        do not admire what

---

7. Written during the final illness of the poet's father.

we cannot understand: the bat
   holding on upside down or in quest of something to

eat, elephants pushing, a wild horse taking a roll, a tireless wolf under
  a tree, the immovable critic twitching his skin like a horse that feels a
         flea, the base-
ball fan, the statistician—                                                  15
   nor is it valid
     to discriminate against "business documents and

school-books"[8]; all these phenomena are important. One must make a
         distinction
  however: when dragged into prominence by half poets, the result is
         not poetry,
nor till the poets among us can be                                           20
   "literalists of
   the imagination"[9]—above
    insolence and triviality and can present

for inspection, "imaginary gardens with real toads in them," shall we
         have
it. In the meantime, if you demand on the one hand,                          25
the raw material of poetry in
  all its rawness and
  that which is on the other hand
    genuine, you are interested in poetry.                       1921

---

ELIZABETH BISHOP

## *Sestina*

September rain falls on the house.
In the failing light, the old grandmother
sits in the kitchen with the child
beside the Little Marvel Stove,
reading the jokes from the almanac,                                          5
laughing and talking to hide her tears.

She thinks that her equinoctial tears
and the rain that beats on the roof of the house

8. "*Diary of Tolstoy*, p. 84: 'Where the boundary between prose and poetry lies, I shall never be able to understand. The question is raised in manuals of style, yet the answer to it lies beyond me. Poetry is verse: Prose is not verse. Or else poetry is everything with the exception of business documents and school books.' " (MM)     9. " 'Literalists of the imagination.' Yeats, *Ideas of Good and Evil* (A. H. Bullen, 1903), p. 182. The limitation of his view was from the very intensity of his vision; he was a too literal realist of imagination, as others are of nature; and because he believed that the figures seen by the mind's eye, when exalted by inspiration, were "eternal existences," symbols of divine essences, he hated every grace of style that might obscure their lineaments.' "(MM)

were both foretold by the almanac,
but only known to a grandmother.
The iron kettle sings on the stove.
She cuts some bread and says to the child,

*It's time for tea now;* but the child
is watching the teakettle's small hard tears
dance like mad on the hot black stove,
the way the rain must dance on the house.
Tidying up, the old grandmother
hangs up the clever almanac

on its string. Birdlike, the almanac
hovers half open above the child,
hovers above the old grandmother
and her teacup full of dark brown tears.
She shivers and says she thinks the house
feels chilly, and puts more wood in the stove.

*It was to be,* says the Marvel Stove.
*I know what I know,* says the almanac.
With crayons the child draws a rigid house
and a winding pathway. Then the child
puts in a man with buttons like tears
and shows it proudly to the grandmother.

But secretly, while the grandmother
busies herself about the stove,
the little moons fall down like tears
from between the pages of the almanac
into the flower bed the child
has carefully placed in the front of the house.

*Time to plant tears,* says the almanac.
The grandmother sings to the marvellous stove
and the child draws another inscrutable house.                    1965

---

ISHMAEL REED

## *beware  :  do not read this poem*

tonite  ,  thriller was
abt an ol woman   , so vain she
surrounded herself w /
    many mirrors

it got so bad that finally she
locked herself indoors & her
whole life became the
    mirrors

one day the villagers broke
into her house   ,   but she was too
swift for them   .   she disappeared
   into a mirror

each tenant who bought the house
after that   ,   lost a loved one to
   the ol woman in the mirror :
   first a little girl
   then a young woman
   then the young woman/s husband

the hunger of this poem is legendary
it has taken in many victims
back off from this poem
it has drawn in yr feet
back off from this poem
it has drawn in yr legs

back off from this poem
it is a greedy mirror
you are into this poem   .   from
   the waist down
nobody can hear you can they   ?
this poem has had you up to here
   belch
this poem aint got no manners
you cant call out frm this poem
relax now & go w/ this poem
move & roll on to this poem
do not resist this poem
this poem has yr eyes
this poem has his head
this poem has his arms
this poem has his fingers
this poem has his fingertips
this poem is the reader & the
reader this poem

statistic   :   the us bureau of missing persons reports
          that in 1968 over 100,000 people disappeared
          leaving no solid clues
             nor trace       only
     a space       in the lives of their friends

10

15

20

25

30

35

40

45

1970

## ARCHIBALD MacLEISH

### *Ars Poetica*[1]

A poem should be palpable and mute
As a globed fruit,

Dumb
As old medallions to the thumb,

5   Silent as the sleeve-worn stone
Of casement ledges where the moss has grown—

A poem should be wordless
As the flight of birds.

A poem should be motionless in time
10   As the moon climbs.

Leaving, as the moon releases
Twig by twig the night-entangled trees,

Leaving, as the moon behind the winter leaves,
Memory by memory the mind—

15   A poem should be motionless in time
As the moon climbs.

A poem should be equal to:
Not true.

For all the history of grief
20   An empty doorway and a maple leaf.

For love
The leaning grasses and two lights above the sea—

A poem should not mean
But be.                                              1926

---

1. "The Art of Poetry," title of a poetical treatise by the Roman poet Horace (65–8 B.C.).

# THE WAY A POEM LOOKS

Stanza breaks and other kinds of print spaces are important, primarily to guide the voice and mind to a clearer sense of sound and meaning. But there are exceptions. A few poems are written to be seen rather than heard, and their appearance on the page is crucial to their effect. Cummings's poem "l(a," for example, tries to visualize typographically what the poet asks you to see in your mind's eye. Occasionally, too, poems are composed in a specific shape so that the poem looks like a physical object. The poems that follow in this chapter—some old, some new—illustrate ways in which visual effects may be created. Even though poetry has traditionally been thought of as oral—words to be said, sung, or performed rather than looked at—the idea that poems can also be related to painting and the visual arts is an old one. Theodoric in ancient Greece is credited with inventing **technopaegnia**—that is, the construction of poems with visual appeal. Once, the shaping of words to resemble an object was thought to have mystical power, but more recent attempts at **concrete poetry** or **shaped verse** are usually playful exercises (such as Hollander's "You Too? Me Too—Why Not? Soda Pop") that attempt to supplement (or replace) verbal meanings with devices from painting and sculpture.

Reading a poem like Herbert's "Easter Wings" aloud wouldn't make much sense. Our eyes are everything for a poem like that. A more frequent poetic device involves asking the eyes to become a guide for the voice. The following poem depends upon recognition of some standard typographical symbols and knowledge of their names. We have to say those names to read the poem.

FRANKLIN P. ADAMS

## *Composed in the Composing Room*

At stated .ic times
I love to sit and—off rhymes
Till ,tose at last I fall
Exclaiming "I don't ∧ all."

Though I'm an * objection                                              5
By running this in this here §
This ☞ of the Fleeting Hour,
This lofty -ician Tower—

A ¶er's hope dispels
All fear of deadly ‖.                                                        10
You think these [ ] are a pipe?
Well, not on your †eotype.

                                                                     1914

We create the right term here when we verbalize, putting the visual signs together with the words or letters printed in the poem, for example making the word "periodic" out of ".ic" or "high Phoenician" out of "-ician." Like "Easter Wings," "Composed in the

Composing Room" uses typography in an extreme way; here the eyes (and mind) are drawn into a punlike game that offers more puzzle-solving pleasure than emotional effect. More often poets give us—by the visual placement of sounds—a guide to reading, inviting us to regulate the pace of our reading, notice pauses or silences, pay attention both to the syntax of the poem and to the rhetoric of the voice, thus providing us a kind of musical score for reading.

### E. E. CUMMINGS

## [*Buffalo Bill 's*]²

Buffalo Bill 's
defunct
     who used to
     ride a watersmooth-silver
5
                stallion
and break onetwothreefourfive pigeonsjustlikethat
                     Jesus

     he was a handsome man
              and what i want to know is
10
how do you like your blueeyed boy
Mister Death

                           1923

The unusual spacing of words here, with some run together and others widely separated, provides a guide to reading, regulating both speed and sense, so that the poem can capture aloud some of the excitement and wonder of a boy's enthusiasm for a theatrical act as spectacular as that of Buffalo Bill. A good reader-aloud, with only this typographical guidance, can capture some of the wide-eyed boy's responses, remembered now in retrospect from a later perspective.

In prose, syntax and punctuation are the main guides to the voice of a reader, providing indicators of emphasis, pace, and speed; in poetry as well they are more conventional and more common guides than extreme forms of typography, such as in "Buffalo Bill 's." Reading a poem sensitively is in some ways a lot like reading a piece of prose sensitively: one has to pay close attention to the way the sentences are put together and how they are punctuated. A good reader makes use of appropriate pauses as well as thundering emphasis; silence as well as sound is part of any poem, and reading punctuation is as important as knowing how to say the words.

Beyond punctuation, the placement and spacing of lines on the page may be helpful to a reader even when that placement is not as radical as it is in "Buffalo Bill 's." The fact that poetry looks different from prose is not an accident; decisions to make lines one length instead of another have as much to do with vocal breaks and phrasing as with functions of syntax or meaning. In a good poem, there are few accidents, not even in the

2. Portraits XXI.

way the poem meets the eye, for as readers our eyes are the most direct route to our voices; they are our scanner and director, our prompter and guide.

The eye also may help the ear in poetry in another way—guiding us to notice repeated sounds by repeated visual patterns in letters. The most common rhymes in poems occur at the ends of lines, and the arrangement of lines (the typography of the poem) often calls attention to the pattern of sounds because of the similar appearance of line-ending words, as in sonnets and other traditional verse forms and sometimes in radically unconventional patterns. Not all words that rhyme have similar spellings, of course, but similarities of word appearance seem to imply a relationship of sound, too, and many poems hint at their stanza patterns and verse forms by their spatial arrangement and repeated patterns at ends of lines. The following poem takes advantage of such expectations and plays with them by forcing a letter into arbitrary line relationships, forcing words ("stew," line 2) in order to create rhymes, setting up rhyme patterns and then breaking them (lines 9–11), using false or near rhymes (lines 10–11), and creating long lines with multisyllabic rhymes that seem silly (the final two lines).

STEVIE SMITH

## *The Jungle Husband*

Dearest Evelyn, I often think of you
Out with the guns in the jungle stew
Yesterday I hittapotamus
I put the measurements down for you but they got lost in the fuss
It's not a good thing to drink out here                                  5
You know, I've practically given it up dear.
Tomorrow I am going alone a long way
Into the jungle. It is all grey
But green on top
Only sometimes when a tree has fallen                                    10
The sun comes down plop, it is quite appalling.
You never want to go in a jungle pool
In the hot sun, it would be the act of a fool
Because it's always full of anacondas, Evelyn, not looking ill-fed
I'll say. So no more now, from your loving husband, Wilfred.            15

                                                                    1957

Visual devices are often entertainments to amuse, puzzle, or tease readers of poetry whose chief expectations are about sound, but sometimes poets achieve surprising (and lasting) original effects by manipulations of print space. Stanzas—visual breaks in poems that indicate some kind of unit of meaning or measurement—ultimately are more than visual devices, for they point to structural questions and ultimately frame and formalize the content of poems. But they involve—as do the similar visual patterns of words that rhyme—part of the "score" of poems, and suggest one more way that sight becomes a guide to sound in many poems.

## GEORGE HERBERT

# *Easter Wings*

Lord, who createdst man in wealth and store,[3]
Though foolishly he lost the same,
Decaying more and more,
Till he became
Most poor:
With thee
O let me rise
As larks,[4] harmoniously,
And sing this day thy victories:
Then shall the fall further the flight in me.

My tender age in sorrow did begin;
And still with sicknesses and shame
Thou didst so punish sin,
That I became
Most thin.
With thee
Let me combine,
And feel this day thy victory;
For, if I imp[5] my wing on thine,
Affliction shall advance the flight in me.

1633

## ROBERT HERRICK

# *The Pillar of Fame*

Fame's pillar here, at last, we set,
Out-during *Marble, Brass,* or *Jet,*[6]
Charmed and enchanted so,
As to withstand the blow
Of          overthrow:
Nor shall the seas,
Or          OUTRAGES
Of storms o'erbear
What we up-rear;
Tho Kingdoms fall,
This    pillar    never    shall
Decline   or   waste   at   all;
But stand for ever by his own
Firm and well fixed foundation.

1648

5

10

3. In plenty.    4. Which herald the morning.    5. Engraft. In falconry, to engraft feathers in a damaged wing, so as to restore the powers of flight (*OED*).    6. Black lignite or black marble. *Out-during:* outlasting.

MARY OLIVER

## *Goldenrod*

On roadsides,
  in fall fields,
    in rumpy bunches,
      saffron and orange and pale gold,

in little towers,                      5
  soft as mash,
    sneeze-bringers and seed-bearers,
      full of bees and yellow beads and perfect flowerlets

and orange butterflies.
  I don't suppose                   10
    much notice comes of it, except for honey,
      and how it heartens the heart with its

blank blaze.
  I don't suppose anything loves it except, perhaps,
    the rocky voids                15
      filled by its dumb dazzle.

For myself,
  I was just passing by, when the wind flared
    and the blossoms rustled,
      and the glittering pandemonium      20

leaned on me.
  I was just minding my own business
    when I found myself on their straw hillsides,
      citron and butter-colored,

and was happy, and why not?          25
  Are not the difficult labors of our lives
    full of dark hours?
      And what has consciousness come to anyway, so far,

that is better than these light-filled bodies?
  All day                   30
    on their airy backbones
    they toss in the wind,

they bend as though it was natural and godly to bend,
  they rise in a stiff sweetness,
    in the pure peace of giving     35
      one's gold away.        1992

## E. E. CUMMINGS

# [*l(a*]

l(a

le
af
fa

ll

s)
one
l

iness

1958

## MARY ELLEN SOLT

# *Lilac*

1968

JOHN HOLLANDER

## A State of Nature

                              Some broken
                           Iroquois adze
                        prounded southward
                        and resembled this
                     outlined once But now          5
                      boundaries foul-lines
                  and even sea-coasts are
                    naturally involved with
                  mappers and followers of
                  borders So that we who grew        10
                 up here might think That steak is
       shaped too much like New York to be real And like
      the shattered flinty implement whose ghost lives
       inside our sense of what this rough chunk should
      by right of history recall the language spoken by    15
      its shapers now inhabits only streams and lakes and
      hills The natural names are only a chattering and mean
    only the land they label How shall we live in a forest of
                         such murmurs with
                        no ideas but in          20
                       forms a state
                      whose name
                       passes
                        for
                       a city        25

                         1969


EARLE BIRNEY

## Anglosaxon Street

Dawn drizzle ended      dampness steams from
blotching brick and      blank plasterwaste
Faded housepatterns      hoary and finicky
unfold stuttering      stick like a phonograph

Here is a ghetto      gotten for goyim          5
O with care denuded      of nigger and kike
No coonsmell rankles      reeks only cellarrot
Ottar[7] of carexhaust      catcorpse and cookinggrease

7. Roselike fragrance.

Imperial hearts    heave in this haven
10    Cracks across windows    are welded with slogans
There'll Always Be An England    enhances geraniums
and V's for Victory    vanquish the housefly

Ho! with climbing sun    march the bleached beldames
festooned with shopping bags    farded[8] flatarched
15    bigthewed Saxonwives    stepping over buttrivers
waddling back wienerladen    to suckle smallfry

Hoy! with sunslope    shrieking over hydrants
flood from learninghall    the lean fingerlings
Nordic nobblecheeked[9]    not all clean of nose
20    leaping Commandowise    into leprous lanes

What! after whistleblow!    spewed from wheelboat
after daylight doughtiness    dire handplay
in sewertrench or sandpit    come Saxonthegns
Junebrown Jutekings[1]    jawslack for meat

25    Sit after supper    on smeared doorsteps
not humbly swearing    hatedeeds on Huns
profiteers politicians    pacifists Jews

Then by twobit magic    to muse in movie
unlock picturehoard    or lope to alehall
30    soaking bleakly    in beer skittleless

Home again to hotbox    and humid husbandhood
in slumbertrough adding    sleepily to Anglekin
Alongside in lanenooks    carling and leman[2]
caterwaul and clip[3]    careless of Saxonry
35    with moonglow and haste    and a higher heartbeat

Slumbers now slumtrack    unstinks cooling
waiting brief for milkmaid    mornstar and worldrise

Toronto 1942, revised 1966

EDWIN MORGAN

## Message Clear

    am          i
                        if
  i am             he

8. Rouged.    9. Pimpled.    1. The Jutes were the German tribe that invaded England in the fifth century and spearheaded the Anglo-Saxon conquest. *Saxonthegns*: freemen who provided military services for the Saxon lords.    2. Lover. *Carling*: old woman.    3. Embrace.

```
   he r        o
   h    ur   t                                            5
   the re          and
   he     re     and
   he re
a                n   d
   th  e   r              e                               10
i am    r                      ife
              i n
        s     ion and
i                 d      i e
   am   e re    ct                                        15
   am   e re    ction
                  o         f
   the                    life
              o         f
   m   e          n                                       20
         sur e
      the            d     i e
i        s
         s   e t    and
i am the  sur        d                                    25
   a   t   res    t
                  o         life
i am  he r                    e
i a           ct
i      r  u      n                                        30
i  m   e e    t
i          t              i e
i      s    t    and
i am th          o    th
i am   r          a                                       35
i am the  su    n
i am the  s       on
i am the  e   rect on      e if
i am    re       n    t
i am       s       a      fe                              40
i am      s  e   n    t
i    he e            d
i    t e  s    t
i      re        a d
   a   th re       a d                                    45
   a      s    t on          e
   a   t  re        a d
   a   th r      on          e
i         resurrect
                   a     life                             50
i am            i n     life
i am    resurrection
i am the resurrection and
```

                    i am
55          i am the resurrection and the life[4]                                    1968


## QUESTIONS

1. Chart the rhyme scheme of Keats's "On the Sonnet," and then, after a careful reading aloud of the poem, mark the major structural breaks in the poem. At what points do the structural breaks and the breaks in rhyme pattern coincide? At what points do they conflict? Can you account for the variations in terms of the poem's meaning?
2. Describe the structure of Shelley's "Ozymandias." In what sense is it an Italian sonnet? Describe the rhyme scheme of this sonnet, and justify (if you can) its unusual pattern.
3. Is Chasin's "Joy Sonnet in a Random Universe" a sonnet? What about Morgan's "Opening the Cage"? On what grounds can you justify calling them sonnets?
4. What conventions of description is Shakespeare's "My mistress' eyes are nothing like the sun" working against? How can you tell? Describe the tone of the poem. What strategies, beyond the basic one of inverting conventions, help to create the poem's special tone?
5. Characterize the "you" in Johnson's "Sonnet to a Negro in Harlem." Describe the speaker's tone toward him. Describe the function of setting in the poem.
6. What principles seem to determine the form of Birney's "Anglosaxon Street"? How do sound patterns in the poem relate to its form?


## WRITING SUGGESTIONS

1. Consider the structure of McKay's "The White House" and the poem's themes of confinement and exclusion. In what specific ways does the poem use the tight restrictions of the sonnet form? Write an essay of about two pages on the way content and form interact in the poem.
2. Compare "The Harlem Dancer" (also by McKay) with "The White House," considering the very different uses the sonnet form accommodates. Write a parallel essay to that above in which you show how "The Harlem Dancer" uses the sonnet form to further its themes and tones.
3. Consider carefully the structure and sequencing in Brooks's "First Fight. Then Fiddle." Notice how various uses of sound in the poem (rhyme, onomatopoeia, and alliteration, for example) help to enforce its themes and tones. In an essay of about 600 words, show the relationship between "sound and sense" in the poem.
4. In an essay of no more than 500 words, explain how the choice of the sonnet form furthers the sense of limitation and confinement in Harwood's "In the Park."


4. John 11.25.

# 8

# THE WHOLE TEXT

In the previous seven chapters, we have been thinking about one thing at a time—setting, word choice, symbolism, meter, stanza form, and so on—and we have discussed each poem primarily in terms of a single issue. Learning to deal with one problem at a time is good educational practice and in the long run will make you a more careful and more effective reader of poems. Still, the elements of poems do not work individually but in combination, and in considering even the simplest elements (speaker, for example, or setting) we have noticed how categories overlap—how, for example, the question of setting in Dickey's "Cherrylog Road" quickly merges into questions about the speaker, his state of mind, his personality, his distance from the central events in the poem. Thinking about a single issue never fully does justice to an individual poem; no poem depends for all its effects on just one device or one element of craft. Poems are complex wholes that demand varieties of attention, and ultimately *all* the questions you have been learning to ask need to be applied to any poem you read. Reading any poem fully and well involves all the questions about craft, form, and tradition that you can think to ask, all the ones we've asked so far, and many others you may learn to ask on the basis of more experience in reading poems. Not all questions are equally relevant to all poems, of course, but moving systematically through your whole list of questions will ultimately enable you to get beyond the fragmentation of particular issues and approach the whole poem and its multiple ways of creating effects. In this chapter we will consider how the various elements of poems work together.

> *All good poetry . . . is forged slowly and patiently, and link by link with sweat and blood and tears.*
>
> —LORD ALFRED DOUGLAS

Here is a short poem in which several of the issues we have considered come up almost simultaneously:

ELIZABETH JENNINGS

## *Delay*

The radiance of that star that leans on me
Was shining years ago. The light that now

Glitters up there my eye may never see
And so the time lag teases me with how

5    Love that loves now may not reach me until
Its first desire is spent. The star's impulse
Must wait for eyes to claim it beautiful
And love arrived may find us somewhere else.                    1953

In most poems, several issues come up more or less at once, and the analytic practice of separating issues is a convenience rather than an assertion of priority or order. In "Delay," a lot of the basic questions (about speaker, situation, and setting, for example) seem to be put on hold in the beginning, but if we proceed systematically the poem begins to open itself to us. The first line identifies the "I" (or rather, in this case, "me") of the poem as an observer of the bright star that is the main object in the poem and the principal source of its imagery, its "plot," and its analogical argument. But we learn little detail about the speaker. She surfaces again in lines 4 and 5 and with someone else ("us") in line 8, but she is always in the objective case—acted on rather than acting. All that is certain about her is that she has some knowledge of the time it takes light from the stars to reach her and that she contemplates deeply and at length about the meaning and effect of such time lags. We are given even less detail about setting and situation; somewhere the speaker is watching a bright star and meditating on the fact that she is seeing it long, long after its actual light was sent forth. Her location is not specified, and the time, though probably night, could be any night (we do know that the speaker lives in the age of modern astronomy, that is, that the speed of light and the distance of the stars from Earth are understood); the only other explicit clues we have about situation involves the "us" of the final line and the fact that the speaker's concern with time seems oddly personal, something that matters to her emotional life—not merely a matter of stellar knowledge.

The poem's language helps us understand much more about the speaker and her situation, as does the poem's structure and stanza form. The most crucial word in the first stanza is probably the verb "leans" (line 1); certainly it is the most unusual and surprising word. Because a star cannot literally *lean* on its observer, the word seems to suggest the speaker's perception of her relationship to the star. Perhaps she feels that the star impinges on her, that she is somehow *subject* to its influence, though not in the popular, astrological sense. Here the star influences the speaker because she understands something about the way the universe works and can apply her knowledge of light and light years in an analogical way to her own life: it "leans" because it tells her something about how observers are affected by their relationships to what they observe. And it is worth noticing how fully the speaker thinks of herself as object rather than actor. Here, as throughout the poem, she is acted upon; things happen *to* her—the star leans on her, the time lag teases her (line 4), love may not reach her (line 5), and she (along with someone else) is the object sought in the final line.

Other crucial words also help clarify the speaker and her situation. The words "radiance" (line 1) and "[g]litters" (line 3) are fairly standard ones to describe stars, but here their standard meanings are carefully qualified by their position in time. The radiance is from years ago and seems to be unavailable to the speaker, who now sees only glitter, something far less warm and resonant. And the word "impulse" in line 6 invokes technical knowledge about light. Here a star is not impulsive or quickly spent but must "wait" for its reception in the eye of the beholder, where it becomes "beautiful"; in physics, an impulse combines force and duration. Hence, the receiver of light—the beholder, the acted-upon—becomes important, and we begin to see why the speaker always appears as object: she is the receiver and interpreter, and the light is not complete—its duration not established—until she receives and interprets it. The star does, after all, "lean" on (depend on) her in some objective sense as well as the subjective one in which she first seems to report it.

The stanza form suggests that the poem may have stages and that its meaning may emerge in two parts, a suggestion that is in fact confirmed by the poem's form and structure. The first stanza is entirely about stars and star-gazing, but the second stanza establishes the analogy with love that becomes the poem's central metaphor. Now, too, more becomes clear about the speaker and her situation. Her concern is about delay, "time lag" (line 4), and the fact that "Love that loves now may not reach me until/Its first desire is spent" (lines 5–6), a strong indication that her initial observation of the star is driven by feeling and her emotional context. Her attempt to put the remoteness of feeling into a perspective that will enable understanding and patience becomes the "plot" of the poem, and her final calm recognition about "us"—that "love arrived may find us some-where else"—is, if not comforting, nevertheless a recognition that patience is important and that some things do last. Even the sounds of the poem—in this case the way rhyme is used—help support the meaning of the poem and the tone it achieves. The rhymes in the first part of the poem reflect perfectly the stable sense of ancient stars, while in the second stanza the sounds involve near-rhyme: there is harmony here, but in human life and emotion nothing is quite perfect.

Here is another short poem that deserves similar detailed attention to its several elements:

ANONYMOUS

## Western Wind

Western wind, when wilt thou blow,
　The small rain down can rain?
Christ, if my love were in my arms
　And I in my bed again!                                   fifteenth century

Perhaps the most obvious thing here is the poem's structure: its first two lines seem to have little to do with the last two. How are we to account for these two distinct and apparently unrelated directions, the calm concern with natural processes in the first part and the emotional outburst about loneliness and lovelessness in the second? The best route to the whole poem is still to begin with the most simple of questions—who? when? where? what is happening?—and proceed to more difficult and complex ones.

As in Jennings's "Delay," the speaker here offers little explicit autobiography. In the first two lines, there is no personal information. The question these lines ask could be delivered quite impersonally; they could be part of a philosophical meditation. The abbreviated syntax at the end of line 1 (the question of causality is not fully stated, and we have to supply the "so that" implied at the end of the line) may suggest strong feeling and emotional upset, but it tells us nothing intimate and offers little information except that the time is spring (that's when the western wind blows). No place is indicated, no year, no particulars of situation. But the next two lines, while remaining inexplicit about exact details, make the speaker's situation clear enough: his love is no longer in his arms, and he wishes she were. (We don't really know genders here, and our guess is based on what we think of as typical practice in fifteenth-century England.)

The poem's language is a study in contrast, and it guides us to see the two-part structure clearly. The question asked of the wind in the first two lines involves straight-forward, steady language, but the third line bursts with agony and personal despair. The power of the first word of the third line—especially in an age of belief—suggests a speaker ready to state his loss in the strongest possible terms, and the parallel statements of loss in lines 3 and 4 suggest not only the speaker's physical relationship to his love but also his displacement from home: he is deprived of both place and love, human contact and contact with his past. His longing for a world ordered according to his past experience is structured to parallel his longing for the spring wind that brings the world back to life. The two parts of the poem both express a desire for return—to life, to order, to causal relationships within the world. Setting has in fact become a central theme in the poem, and what the poem expresses tonally involves a powerful desire for stability and belonging—an effect that grows out of our sense of the speaker's situation and character. Speaker, setting, language, and structure here intertwine to create the intense focus of the poem.

Here is another short poem in which the several elements noticeably interrelate:

## ROBERT HERRICK

### *Upon Julia's Clothes*

Whenas in silks my Julia goes
Then, then, methinks, how sweetly flows
That liquefaction of her clothes.

Next, when I cast mine eyes, and see
That brave[1] vibration, each way free,
O, how that glittering taketh me!

1648

5

---

The poem is unabashed in its admiration of the way Julia looks, and nearly everything in its six short lines contributes to its celebratory tone. Perhaps the most striking thing about the poem involves its unusual, highly suggestive use of words. "[G]oes" at the end of line 1 may be the first word to call special attention to itself, though we will return in a minute to the very first word of the poem. "Walks" or "moves" would seem to be more obvious choices; "goes" is more neutral and less specific and in most circumstances would seem an inferior choice, but here the point seems to be to describe Julia in a kind

1. Handsome, showy.

of seamless and unspecified motion and from a specific angle, because the poem is anxious to record the effect of Julia's movement on the speaker (already a second element becomes crucial) rather than the specifics of Julia herself. Another word that seems especially important is "liquefaction" (line 3), also an unusual and suggestive word about motion. Again it implies no specific kind of motion, just smoothness and seamlessness, and it is applied not to Julia but to her clothes—the kind of indirection that doesn't really fool anybody. Other words that might repay a close look include "vibration" in line 5 (the speaker is finally willing to be a little more direct), "brave" and "free" (also in line 5), and "glittering" and "taketh" in line 6.

Had we begun conventionally by thinking about speaker, situation, and setting, we would have quickly noticed the precise way that the speaker chose to clothe Julia: "in silks," which move almost as one with her body. And we would have noticed that the speaker positions himself almost as voyeur (standing for us as observers, of course, but also for himself as the central figure in the poem). Not much detail about situation or setting is given (and the speaker is characterized only as a viewer and appreciator), but one thing about the scene is crucial. It takes us back to the first word of the poem, "whenas." The slightly quaint quality of the word may at first obscure, to a modern reader, just what it tells us about the situation, that it is a *kind* of scene rather than a single event. "Whenas" is very close to "whenever"; the speaker's claim seems to be that he responds this way *whenever* Julia dons her silks—apparently fairly often, at least in his memory or imagination.

Most of the speaker's language is sensual and rather provocative (he is anxious to share his responses with others so that *everyone* will know just how "taking" Julia is), but there is one rather elaborate (though somewhat disguised) metaphor that suggests his awareness of his own calculation and its consequences. In the beginning of the second stanza he describes how he "cast" his eyes: it is a metaphor from fishing, a frequent one in love poetry about luring, chasing, and catching. Julia is the object. The metaphor continues two lines later, but the angler is himself caught: he is taken by the "glittering" lure. This turning of the tables, drawing as it does on a traditional, common image that is then modified to help characterize the speaker, gives a little depth to the show: whatever the slither and glitter, there is not just showing off and sensuality but a catch in this angling.

Many other elements in the poem are worth comment, especially because they quickly relate to each other. Consider the way the poet uses sounds, first of all in picking words like "liquefaction" that are themselves almost onomatopoeic, but then also using rhyme very cleverly. There are only two rhyme sounds in the poem, one in the first stanza, the other in the second. The long *ee* of the second becomes almost exclamatory, and the three words of the first seem to become linked in a kind of separate grammar of their own, as if "goes," "flows," and "clothes" were all part of a single action—pretty much what the poem claims on a thematic level. A lot is going on in this short and simple poem, and although a reader can get at it step by step by thinking about element after element, the interlocking of the elements is finally what is most impressive. It's easy to see that the plot here reenacts the familiar stances of woman as object and man as gazer, but we need to be flexible enough in our analysis and reading to consider not only all the analytical categories, but also the ways in which they work together.

Going back to poems read earlier in the book—with the methods and approaches you have learned since then—can be useful in seeing how different elements of poems interrelate. Look, for example, at the stanza divisions in Dickey's "Cherrylog Road" (page 94) and consider how the neatly spaced, apparently discrete units work against the sometimes frantic pacing of the poem. Or consider the character of the speaker, or the fundamental metaphor of "wreckage" that sponsors the poem, relative to the idea of the speaker. Go back and read Kumin's "Woodchucks" (page 41) while thinking about structural questions; or consider how the effaced speaker works in Rich's "Aunt Jennifer's Tigers" (page 41); or think about metaphor in Nemerov's "The Vacuum" (page 10).

Here are several new poems to analyze. As you read them, think about the elements discussed in the first seven chapters—but rather than thinking about a single element at a time, try to consider relationships, how the different elements combine to make you respond not to a single device but to a complex set of strategies and effects.

W. H. AUDEN

## *Musée des Beaux Arts*[2]

About suffering they were never wrong,
The Old Masters: how well they understood
Its human position; how it takes place
While someone else is eating or opening a window or just walking dully
    along;
5  How, when the aged are reverently, passionately waiting
For the miraculous birth, there always must be
Children who did not specially want it to happen, skating
On a pond at the edge of the wood:
They never forgot
10  That even the dreadful martyrdom must run its course
Anyhow in a corner, some untidy spot
Where the dogs go on with their doggy life and the torturer's horse
Scratches its innocent behind on a tree.
In Brueghel's *Icarus*,[3] for instance: how everything turns away
15  Quite leisurely from the disaster; the plowman may
Have heard the splash, the forsaken cry,
But for him it was not an important failure; the sun shone
As it had to on the white legs disappearing into the green
Water; and the expensive delicate ship that must have seen
20  Something amazing, a boy falling out of the sky,
Had somewhere to get to and sailed calmly on.

1938

2. The Museum of the Fine Arts, in Brussels.    3. *Landscape with the Fall of Icarus*, by Pieter Brueghel the Elder (1525?–1569), located in the Brussels Museum. According to Greek myth, Daedalus and his son Icarus escaped from imprisonment by using homemade wings of feathers and wax; but Icarus flew too near the sun, the wax melted, and he fell into the sea and drowned. In the Brueghel painting the central figure is a peasant plowing, and several other figures are more immediately noticeable than Icarus, who, disappearing into the sea, is easy to miss in the lower right-hand corner. Equally ignored by the figures is a dead body in the woods.

GEORGE HERBERT

## The Collar

I struck the board[4] and cried, "No more;
        I will abroad!
What? shall I ever sigh and pine?
My lines[5] and life are free, free as the road,
    Loose as the wind, as large as store.[6]          5
           Shall I be still in suit?[7]
Have I no harvest but a thorn
To let me blood, and not restore
What I have lost with cordial[8] fruit?
          Sure there was wine          10
Before my sighs did dry it; there was corn
    Before my tears did drown it.
    Is the year only lost to me?
      Have I no bays[9] to crown it,
No flowers, no garlands gay? All blasted?          15
          All wasted?
    Not so, my heart; but there is fruit,
        And thou hast hands.
    Recover all thy sigh-blown age
On double pleasures: leave thy cold dispute          20
Of what is fit, and not. Forsake thy cage,
        Thy rope of sands,[1]
Which petty thoughts have made, and made to thee
    Good cable, to enforce and draw,
        And be thy law,          25
    While thou didst wink[2] and wouldst not see.
        Away! take heed;
        I will abroad.
Call in thy death's-head[3] there; tie up thy fears.
        He that forbears          30
    To suit and serve his need,
      Deserves his load."
But as I raved and grew more fierce and wild
        At every word,
Methought I heard one calling, *Child!*          35
        And I replied, *My Lord.*          1633

---

4. Table.    5. Lot.    6. A storehouse; that is, in abundance.    7. In service to another.    8. Reviving, restorative.    9. Laurel wreaths of triumph.    1. Moral restrictions.    2. That is, close your eyes to the weaknesses of such restrictions.    3. *Memento mori*, a skull intended to remind people of their mortality.

EMILY DICKINSON

## [My Life had stood—a Loaded Gun—]

My Life had stood—a Loaded Gun—
In Corners—till a Day
The Owner passed—identified—
And carried Me away—

5   And now We roam in Sovereign Woods—
And now We hunt the Doe—
And every time I speak for Him—
The Mountains straight reply—

And do I smile, such cordial light
10   Upon the Valley glow—
It is as a Vesuvian face
Had let its pleasure through—

And when at Night—Our good Day done—
I guard My Master's Head—
15   'Tis better than the Eider-Duck's
Deep Pillow—to have shared—

To foe of His—I'm deadly foe—
None stir the second time—
On whom I lay a Yellow Eye—
20   Or an emphatic Thumb—

Though I than He—may longer live
He longer must—than I—
For I have but the power to kill,
Without—the power to die—

ca. 1863

ROBERT FROST

## Design

I found a dimpled spider, fat and white,
On a white heal-all,[4] holding up a moth
Like a white piece of rigid satin cloth—
Assorted characters of death and blight
5   Mixed ready to begin the morning right,
Like the ingredients of a witches' broth—

---

4. A plant, also called the "all-heal" and "self-heal," with tightly clustered violet-blue flowers.

A snow-drop spider, a flower like a froth,
And dead wings carried like a paper kite.

What had that flower to do with being white,
The wayside blue and innocent heal-all?                              10
What brought the kindred spider to that height,
Then steered the white moth thither in the night?
What but design of darkness to appall?—
If design govern in a thing so small.                                1936


D. H. LAWRENCE

## Piano

Softly, in the dusk, a woman is singing to me;
Taking me back down the vista of years, till I see
A child sitting under the piano, in the boom of the tingling strings
And pressing the small, poised feet of a mother who smiles as she sings.

In spite of myself, the insidious mastery of song                    5
Betrays me back, till the heart of me weeps to belong
To the old Sunday evenings at home, with winter outside
And hymns in the cozy parlor, the tinkling piano our guide.

So now it is vain for the singer to burst into clamor
With the great black piano appassionato. The glamour                 10
Of childish days is upon me, my manhood is cast
Down in the flood of remembrance, I weep like a child for the past.
                                                                     1918


LIZ ROSENBERG

## A Lesson in Anatomy

"Breathe light into the page," he said—
as if it really could be done.
As if the painting were a great, illuminated book.
And while he stood there talking
with his calm face uplifted, his cup of coffee               5
perched before him on the lectern like a dove,
something foreign flew through the room
and burned her breast, weakened her legs
She had always been bewildered by the body—
his wood dowel pointing at the fibula,                       10

the cage of ribs she'd never known
went all the way around from front to back.

So when he came and stood behind her,
and they gazed down together at that heap of lines
she'd drawn to trace the human form,
which did not understand how one hand folds another,
or how the penis rises from the center, like Venus on the foam,
she wanted to reach out and touch something,
and when he leaned on the desk, say, Lean on me.

1994

JONATHAN SWIFT

## A Description of a City Shower

Careful observers may foretell the hour
(By sure prognostics) when to dread a shower:
While rain depends,[5] the pensive cat gives o'er
Her frolics, and pursues her tail no more
Returning home at night, you'll find the sink[6]
Strike your offended sense with double stink.
If you be wise, then go not far to dine;
You'll spend in coach hire more than save in wine.
A coming shower your shooting corns presage,
Old achés throb, your hollow tooth will rage.
Sauntering in coffeehouse is Dulman[7] seen;
He damns the climate and complains of spleen.
   Meanwhile the South, rising with dabbled wings,
A sable cloud athwart the welkin flings,
That swilled more liquor than it could contain,
And, like a drunkard, gives it up again.
Brisk Susan whips her linen from the rope,
While the first drizzling shower is borne aslope:
Such is that sprinkling which some careless quean[8]
Flirts on you from her mop, but not so clean:
You fly, invoke the gods; then turning, stop
To rail; she singing, still whirls on her mop.
Not yet the dust had shunned the unequal strife,
But, aided by the wind, fought still for life,
And wafted with its foe by violent gust,
'Twas doubtful which was rain and which was dust.
Ah! where must needy poet seek for aid,
When dust and rain at once his coat invade?
Sole coat, where dust cemented by the rain
Erects the nap, and leaves a mingled stain.

5. Impends, is imminent.    6. Sewer.    7. A type name (from "dull man").    8. Wench, slut.

Now in contiguous drops the flood comes down,
Threatening with deluge this devoted town.
To shops in crowds the daggled females fly,
Pretend to cheapen[9] goods, but nothing buy.
The Templar spruce, while every spout's abroach,[1]     35
Stays till 'tis fair, yet seems to call a coach.
The tucked-up sempstress walks with hasty strides,
While streams run down her oiled umbrella's sides.
Here various kinds, by various fortunes led,
Commence acquaintance underneath a shed.     40
Triumphant Tories and desponding Whigs
Forget their feuds, and join to save their wigs.
Boxed in a chair the beau impatient sits,
While spouts run clattering o'er the roof by fits,
And ever and anon with frightful din     45
The leather sounds; he trembles from within.
So when Troy chairmen bore the wooden steed,
Pregnant with Greeks impatient to be freed
(Those bully Greeks, who, as the moderns do,
Instead of paying chairmen, run them through),[2]     50
Laocoön struck the outside with his spear,
And each imprisoned hero quaked for fear[3]
    Now from all parts the swelling kennels[4] flow,
And bear their trophies with them as they go:
Filth of all hues and odors seem to tell     55
What street they sailed from, by their sight and smell.
They, as each torrent drives with rapid force,
From Smithfield or St. Pulchre's shape their course,
And in huge confluence joined at Snow Hill ridge,
Fall from the conduit prone to Holborn Bridge.[5]     60
Sweepings from butchers' stalls, dung, guts, and blood,
Drowned puppies, stinking sprats[6] all drenched in mud,
Dead cats, and turnip tops, come tumbling down the flood.     1710

## RICHARD EBERHART

## *The Groundhog*

In June, amid the golden fields,
I saw a groundhog lying dead.
Dead lay he; my senses shook,
And mind outshot our naked frailty.

---

9. Bargain for. *Daggled* (line 33): spattered with mud.     1. Pouring out water. *The Templar*: a young man studying law.     2. Run them through with swords.     3. *The Aeneid* II.40–53.     4. Open gutters in the middle of the street.     5. *Smithfield*: site of cattle and sheep markets at the foot of Snow Hill. *St. Pulchre's*: church of St. Sepulchre. Holborn Conduit drained into a foul-smelling sewer at Holborn Bridge.
6. Small herrings.

5

There lowly in the vigorous summer
His form began its senseless change,
And made my senses waver dim
Seeing nature ferocious in him.
Inspecting close his maggots' might
And seething cauldron of his being,
Half with loathing, half with a strange love,
I poked him with an angry stick.
The fever rose, became a flame
And Vigour circumscribed the skies,
Immense energy in the sun,
And through my frame a sunless trembling.
My stick had done nor good nor harm.
Then stood I silent in the day
Watching the object, as before;
And kept my reverence for knowledge
Trying for control, to be still,
To quell the passion of the blood;
Until I had bent down on my knees
Praying for joy in the sight of decay.
And so I left; and I returned
In Autumn strict of eye, to see
The sap gone out of the groundhog,
But the bony sodden hulk remained.
But the year had lost its meaning,
And in intellectual chains
I lost both love and loathing,
Mured up[7] in the wall of wisdom.
Another summer took the fields again
Massive and burning, full of life,
But when I chanced upon the spot
There was only a little hair left,
And bones bleaching in the sunlight
Beautiful as architecture;
I watched them like a geometer,[8]
And cut a walking stick from a birch.
It has been three years, now.
There is no sign of the groundhog.
I stood there in the whirling summer,
My hand capped a withered heart,
And thought of China and of Greece,
Of Alexander in his tent;
Of Montaigne in his tower,
Of Saint Theresa[9] in her wild lament.

1936

---

7. Confined.   8. Geometrician, one skilled in measuring properties and arrangement.   9. Alexander
the Great, ancient king of Macedonia and conqueror of the East; Michel de Montaigne, the Renaissance
French essayist who used a tower near his house for a study; and St. Theresa of Spain, famous for intense
trances and visions.

SIR WALTER RALEGH

## The Author's Epitaph, Made by Himself

Even such is time, which takes in trust
Our youth, our joys, and all we have,
And pays us but with age and dust,
Who in the dark and silent grave
When we have wandered all our ways                    5
Shuts up the story of our days,
And from which earth, and grave, and dust
The Lord shall raise me up, I trust.                          1628

ANNE SEXTON

## With Mercy for the Greedy

*for my friend, Ruth, who urges me to make an appointment for The*
*Sacrament of Confession*

Concerning your letter in which you ask
me to call a priest and in which you ask
me to wear The Cross that you enclose;
your own cross,
your dog bitten cross,                                          5
no larger than a thumb,
small and wooden, no thorns, this rose.

I pray to its shadow,
that gray place
where it lies on your letter . . . deep, deep.               10
I detest my sins and I try to believe
in The Cross. I touch its tender hips, its dark jawed face,
its solid neck, its brown sleep.

True. There is
a beautiful Jesus.                                              15
He is frozen to his bones like a chunk of beef.
How desperately he wanted to pull his arms in!
How desperately I touch his vertical and horizontal axes!
But I can't. Need is not quite belief.

All morning long                                               20
I have worn
your cross, hung with package string around my throat.
It tapped me lightly as a child's heart might,

tapping second hand, softly waiting to be born.
25   Ruth, I cherish the letter you wrote.

My friend, my friend, I was born
doing reference work in sin, and born
confessing it. This is what poems are:
with mercy
30   for the greedy;
they are the tongue's wrangle,
the world's pottage, the rat's star.                    1962

---

OLIVER GOLDSMITH

## The Deserted Village

   Sweet Auburn! loveliest village of the plain,
Where health and plenty cheered the laboring swain,
Where smiling spring its earliest visit paid,
And parting summer's lingering blooms delayed:
5   Dear lovely bowers of innocence and ease,
Seats of my youth, when every sport could please,
How often have I loitered o'er thy green,
Where humble happiness endeared each scene;
How often have I paused on every charm,
10   The sheltered cot, the cultivated farm,
The never-failing brook, the busy mill,
The decent church that topped the neighboring hill,
The hawthorn bush, with seats beneath the shade,
For talking age and whispering lovers made;
15   How often have I blessed the coming day,[1]
When toil remitting lent its turn to play,
And all the village train, from labor free,
Led up their sports beneath the spreading tree,
While many a pastime circled in the shade,
20   The young contending as the old surveyed;
And many a gambol frolicked o'er the ground,
And sleights of art and feats of strength went round;
And still as each repeated pleasure tired,
Succeeding sports the mirthful band inspired;
25   The dancing pair that simply sought renown,
By holding out to tire each other down;
The swain mistrustless of his smutted face,
While secret laughter tittered round the place;
The bashful virgin's sidelong looks of love,
30   The matron's glance that would those looks reprove:

---

1. Holiday.

These were thy charms, sweet village! sports like these,
With sweet succession, taught even toil to please;
These round thy bowers their cheerful influence shed,
These were thy charms—But all these charms are fled.

Sweet smiling village, loveliest of the lawn,                                    35
Thy sports are fled, and all thy charms withdrawn;
Amidst thy bowers the tyrant's hand is seen,
And desolation saddens all thy green:
One only master grasps the whole domain,
And half a tillage stints thy smiling plain;                                     40
No more thy glassy brook reflects the day,
But choked with sedges, works its weedy way;
Along thy glades, a solitary guest,
The hollow-sounding bittern guards its nest;
Amidst thy desert walks the lapwing flies,                                       45
And tires their echoes with unvaried cries.
Sunk are thy bowers, in shapeless ruin all,
And the long grass o'ertops the moldering wall,
And, trembling, shrinking from the spoiler's hand,
Far, far away thy children leave the land.                                       50

Ill fares the land, to hastening ills a prey,
Where wealth accumulates, and men decay;
Princes and lords may flourish, or may fade;
A breath can make them, as a breath has made;
But a bold peasantry, their country's pride,                                     55
When once destroyed, can never be supplied.

A time there was, ere England's griefs began,
When every rood of ground maintained its man;
For him light labor spread her wholesome store,
Just gave what life required, but gave no more:                                  60
His best companions, innocence and health;
And his best riches, ignorance of wealth.

But times are altered; Trade's unfeeling train
Usurp the land and dispossess the swain;
Along the lawn, where scattered hamlets rose,                                    65
Unwieldy wealth, and cumbrous pomp repose;
And every want to opulence allied,
And every pang that folly pays to pride.
These gentle hours that plenty bade to bloom,
Those calm desires that asked but little room,                                   70
Those healthful sports that graced the peaceful scene,
Lived in each look, and brightened all the green;
These far departing seek a kinder shore,
And rural mirth and manners are no more.

Sweet Auburn! parent of the blissful hour,                                       75
Thy glades forlorn confess the tyrant's power.
Here, as I take my solitary rounds,
Amidst thy tangling walks, and ruined grounds,
And, many a year elapsed, return to view
Where once the cottage stood, the hawthorn grew,                                 80

Remembrance wakes with all her busy train,
Swells at my breast, and turns the past to pain.
    In all my wanderings round this world of care,
    In all my griefs—and God has given my share—
85    I still had hopes my latest hours to crown,
    Amidst these humble bowers to lay me down;
    To husband out life's taper at the close,
    And keep the flame from wasting by repose.
    I still had hopes, for pride attends us still,
90    Amidst the swains to show my book-learned skill,
    Around my fire an evening group to draw,
    And tell of all I felt, and all I saw;
    And, as an hare whom hounds and horns pursue,
    Pants to the place from whence at first she flew,
95    I still had hopes, my long vexations past,
    Here to return—and die at home at last.
        O blest retirement, friend to life's decline,
    Retreats from care that never must be mine,
    How happy he who crowns in shades like these
100    A youth of labor with an age of ease;
    Who quits a world where strong temptations try,
    And, since 'tis hard to combat, learns to fly!
    For him no wretches, born to work and weep,
    Explore the mine, or tempt the dangerous deep;
105    No surly porter stands in guilty state
    To spurn imploring famine from the gate;
    But on he moves to meet his latter end,
    Angels around befriending virtue's friend;
    Bends to the grave with unperceived decay,
110    While Resignation gently slopes the way;
    And, all his prospects brightening to the last,
    His Heaven commences ere the world be passed!
        Sweet was the sound when oft at evening's close,
    Up yonder hill the village murmur rose;
115    There, as I passed with careless steps and slow,
    The mingling notes came softened from below;
    The swain responsive as the milkmaid sung,
    The sober herd that lowed to meet their young,
    The noisy geese that gabbled o'er the pool,
120    The playful children just let loose from school;
    The watchdog's voice that bayed the whispering wind,
    And the loud laugh that spoke the vacant[2] mind;
    These all in sweet confusion sought the shade,
    And filled each pause the nightingale had made.
125    But now the sounds of population fail,
    No cheerful murmurs fluctuate in the gale,
    No busy steps the grass-grown footway tread,

2. Carefree.

For all the bloomy flush of life is fled.
All but yon widowed, solitary thing
That feebly bends beside the plashy³ spring;                                     130
She, wretched matron, forced, in age, for bread,
To strip the brook with mantling cresses spread,
To pick her wintry faggot⁴ from the thorn,
To seek her nightly shed, and weep till morn;
She only left of all the harmless train,                                          135
The sad historian of the pensive plain.
    Near yonder copse,⁵ where once the garden smiled,
And still where many a garden flower grows wild,
There, where a few torn shrubs the place disclose,
The village preacher's modest mansion rose.                                       140
A man he was, to all the country dear,
And passing rich with forty pounds a year;
Remote from towns he ran his godly race,
Nor e'er had changed, nor wished to change his place;
Unpracticed he to fawn, or seek for power,                                        145
By doctrines fashioned to the varying hour;
Far other aims his heart had learned to prize,
More skilled to raise the wretched than to rise.
His house was known to all the vagrant train,
He chid their wanderings, but relieved their pain;                               150
The long-remembered beggar was his guest,
Whose beard descending swept his aged breast;
The ruined spendthrift, now no longer proud,
Claimed kindred there, and had his claims allowed;
The broken soldier, kindly bade to stay,                                          155
Sate by his fire, and talked the night away;
Wept o'er his wounds, or tales of sorrow done,
Shouldered his crutch, and showed how fields were won.
Pleased with his guests, the good man learned to glow,
And quite forgot their vices in their woe;                                        160
Careless their merits, or their faults to scan,
His pity gave ere charity began.
    Thus to relieve the wretched was his pride,
And even his failings leaned to Virtue's side;
But in his duty prompt at every call,                                             165
He watched and wept, he prayed and felt, for all.
And, as a bird each fond endearment tries,
To tempt its new-fledged offspring to the skies,
He tried each art, reproved each dull delay,
Allured to brighter worlds, and led the way.                                      170
    Beside the bed where parting life was laid,
And sorrow, guilt, and pain, by turns dismayed,
The reverend champion stood. At his control,
Despair and anguish fled the struggling soul;

3. Marshy.    4. Firewood.    5. Grove.

175 Comfort came down the trembling wretch to raise,
And his last faltering accents whispered praise.
   At church, with meek and unaffected grace,
His looks adorned the venerable place;
Truth from his lips prevailed with double sway,
180 And fools, who came to scoff, remained to pray.
The service past, around the pious man,
With steady zeal each honest rustic ran;
Even children followed with endearing wile,
And plucked his gown, to share the good man's smile.
185 His ready smile a parent's warmth expressed.
Their welfare pleased him, and their cares distressed;
To them his heart, his love, his griefs were given,
But all his serious thoughts had rest in Heaven.
As some tall cliff that lifts its awful form,
190 Swells from the vale, and midway leaves the storm,
Though round its breast the rolling clouds are spread,
Eternal sunshine settles on its head.
   Beside yon straggling fence that skirts the way,
With blossomed furze unprofitably gay,
195 There, in his noisy mansion, skilled to rule,
The village master taught his little school;
A man severe he was, and stern to view,
I knew him well, and every truant knew;
Well had the boding[6] tremblers learned to trace
200 The day's disasters in his morning face;
Full well they laughed with counterfeited glee,
At all his jokes, for many a joke had he;
Full well the busy whisper circling round,
Conveyed the dismal tidings when he frowned;
205 Yet he was kind, or if severe in aught,
The love he bore to learning was in fault;
The village all declared how much he knew;
'Twas certain he could write, and cipher too;
Lands he could measure, terms and tides presage,
210 And even the story ran that he could gauge.
In arguing too, the parson owned his skill,
For even though vanquished, he could argue still;
While words of learned length, and thundering sound,
Amazed the gazing rustics ranged around;
215 And still they gazed, and still the wonder grew,
That one small head could carry all he knew.
   But past is all his fame. The very spot
Where many a time he triumphed, is forgot.
Near yonder thorn, that lifts its head on high,
220 Where once the signpost caught the passing eye,
Low lies that house where nut-brown draughts inspired,

6. Anxious.

Where graybeard Mirth and smiling Toil retired,
Where village statesmen talked with looks profound,
And news much older than their ale went round.
Imagination fondly stoops to trace                              225
The parlor splendors of that festive place:
The whitewashed wall, the nicely sanded floor,
The varnished clock that clicked behind the door;
The chest contrived a double debt to pay,
A bed by night, a chest of drawers by day;                     230
The pictures placed for ornament and use,
The twelve good rules, the royal game of goose;
The hearth, except when winter chilled the day,
With aspen boughs, and flowers, and fennel gay,
While broken teacups, wisely kept for show,                    235
Ranged o'er the chimney, glistened in a row.
    Vain transitory splendors! Could not all
Reprieve the tottering mansion from its fall!
Obscure it sinks, nor shall it more impart
An hour's importance to the poor man's heart;                  240
Thither no more the peasant shall repair
To sweet oblivion of his daily care;
No more the farmer's news, the barber's tale,
No more the woodman's ballad shall prevail;
No more the smith his dusky brow shall clear,                  245
Relax his ponderous strength, and lean to hear;
The host himself no longer shall be found
Careful to see the mantling bliss go round;
Nor the coy maid, half willing to be pressed,
Shall kiss the cup to pass it to the rest.                     250
    Yes! let the rich deride, the proud disdain,
These simple blessings of the lowly train,
To me more dear, congenial to my heart,
One native charm, than all the gloss of art;
Spontaneous joys, where nature has its play,                   255
The soul adopts, and owns their first-born sway;
Lightly they frolic o'er the vacant mind,
Unenvied, unmolested, unconfined.
But the long pomp, the midnight masquerade,
With all the freaks of wanton wealth arrayed,                  260
In these, ere[7] triflers half their wish obtain,
The toiling pleasure sickens into pain;
And, even while fashion's brightest arts decoy,
The heart distrusting asks if this be joy.
    Ye friends to truth, ye statesmen, who survey              265
The rich man's joys increase, the poor's decay,
'Tis yours to judge how wide the limits stand
Between a splendid and an happy land.

7. Before.

Proud swells the tide with loads of freighted ore,
270    And shouting Folly hails them from her shore;
Hoards, even beyond the miser's wish abound,
And rich men flock from all the world around.
Yet count our gains. This wealth is but a name
That leaves our useful products still the same.
275    Not so the loss. The man of wealth and pride,
Takes up a space that many poor supplied;
Space for his lake, his park's extended bounds,
Space for his horses, equipage, and hounds;
The robe that wraps his limbs in silken sloth
280    Has robbed the neighboring fields of half their growth;
His seat, where solitary sports are seen,
Indignant spurns the cottage from the green;
Around the world each needful product flies,
For all the luxuries the world supplies:
285    While thus the land adorned for pleasure, all
In barren splendor feebly waits the fall.
        As some fair female unadorned and plain,
Secure to please while youth confirms her reign,
Slights every borrowed charm that dress supplies,
290    Nor shares with art the triumph of her eyes;
But when those charms are past, for charms are frail,
When time advances, and when lovers fail,
She then shines forth, solicitous to bless,
In all the glaring impotence of dress:
295    Thus fares the land, by luxury betrayed;
In nature's simplest charms at first arrayed;
But verging to decline, its splendors rise,
Its vistas strike, its palaces surprise;
While scourged by famine from the smiling land,
300    The mournful peasant leads his humble band;
And while he sinks without one arm to save,
The country blooms—a garden, and a grave.
        Where then, ah where, shall Poverty reside,
To 'scape the pressure of contiguous Pride?
305    If to some common's fenceless limits strayed,
He drives his flock to pick the scanty blade,
Those fenceless fields the sons of wealth divide,
And even the bare-worn common is denied.
        If to the city sped—What waits him there?
310    To see profusion that he must not share;
To see ten thousand baneful arts combined
To pamper luxury, and thin mankind;
To see those joys the sons of pleasure know,
Extorted from his fellow creature's woe.
315    Here, while the courtier glitters in brocade,
There the pale artist[8] plies the sickly trade;

8. Artisan.

Here, while the proud their long-drawn pomps display,
There the black gibbet glooms beside the way.
The dome where Pleasure holds her midnight reign,
Here, richly decked, admits the gorgeous train; 320
Tumultuous grandeur crowds the blazing square,
The rattling chariots clash, the torches glare.
Sure scenes like these no troubles e'er annoy!
Sure these denote one universal joy!
Are these thy serious thoughts?—Ah, turn thine eyes 325
Where the poor houseless shivering female lies.
She once, perhaps, in village plenty blest,
Has wept at tales of innocence distressed;
Her modest looks the cottage might adorn,
Sweet as the primrose peeps beneath the thorn; 330
Now lost to all; her friends, her virtue fled,
Near her betrayer's door she lays her head,
And pinched with cold, and shrinking from the shower,
With heavy heart deplores that luckless hour,
When idly first, ambitious of the town, 335
She left her wheel and robes of country brown.
   Do thine, sweet Auburn, thine, the loveliest train,
Do thy fair tribes participate her pain?
Even now, perhaps, by cold and hunger led,
At proud men's doors they ask a little bread! 340
   Ah, no. To distant climes, a dreary scene,
Where half the convex world intrudes between,
Through torrid tracts with fainting steps they go,
Where wild Altama murmurs to their woe.
Far different there from all that charmed before, 345
The various terrors of that horrid shore;
Those blazing suns that dart a downward ray,
And fiercely shed intolerable day;
Those matted woods where birds forget to sing,
But silent bats in drowsy clusters cling, 350
Those poisonous fields with rank luxuriance crowned,
Where the dark scorpion gathers death around;
Where at each step the stranger fears to wake
The rattling terrors of the vengeful snake;
Where crouching tigers[9] wait their hapless prey, 355
And savage men, more murderous still than they;
While oft in whirls the mad tornado flies,
Mingling the ravaged landscape with the skies.
Far different these from every former scene,
The cooling brook, the grassy-vested green, 360
The breezy covert of the warbling grove,
That only sheltered thefts of harmless love.
   Good Heaven! what sorrows gloomed that parting day,
That called them from their native walks away;

9. Pumas.

365   When the poor exiles, every pleasure past,
Hung round their bowers, and fondly looked their last,
And took a long farewell, and wished in vain
For seats like these beyond the western main;
And shuddering still to face the distant deep,
370   Returned and wept, and still returned to weep.
The good old sire the first prepared to go
To new-found worlds, and wept for other's woe;
But for himself, in conscious virtue brave,
He only wished for worlds beyond the grave.
375   His lovely daughter, lovelier in her tears,
The fond companion of his helpless years,
Silent went next, neglectful of her charms,
And left a lover's for a father's arms.
With louder plaints the mother spoke her woes,
380   And blessed the cot where every pleasure rose;
And kissed her thoughtless babes with many a tear,
And clasped them close in sorrow doubly dear;
Whilst her fond husband strove to lend relief
In all the silent manliness of grief.
385     O luxury! Thou cursed by Heaven's decree,
How ill exchanged are things like these for thee!
How do thy potions, with insidious joy,
Diffuse their pleasures only to destroy!
Kingdoms, by thee, to sickly greatness grown,
390   Boast of a florid vigor not their own.
At every draught more large and large they grow,
A bloated mass of rank unwieldy woe;
Till sapped their strength, and every part unsound,
Down, down they sink, and spread a ruin round.
395     Even now the devastation is begun,
And half the business of destruction done;
Even now, methinks, as pondering here I stand,
I see the rural Virtues leave the land.
Down where yon anchoring vessel spreads the sail,
400   That idly waiting flaps with every gale,
Downward they move, a melancholy band,
Pass from the shore, and darken all the strand.
Contented Toil, and hospitable Care,
And kind connubial Tenderness are there;
405   And Piety, with wishes placed above,
And steady Loyalty, and faithful Love:
And thou, sweet Poetry, thou loveliest maid,
Still first to fly where sensual joys invade;
Unfit in these degenerate times of shame,
410   To catch the heart, or strike for honest fame;
Dear charming Nymph, neglected and decried,
My shame in crowds, my solitary pride;
Thou source of all my bliss, and all my woe,
That found'st me poor at first, and keep'st me so;

Thou guide by which the nobler arts excel,                                      415
Thou nurse of every virtue, fare thee well.
Farewell, and O! where'er thy voice be tried,
On Torno's cliffs, or Pambamarca's side,
Whether where equinoctial fervors glow,
Or winter wraps the polar world in snow,                                        420
Still let thy voice, prevailing over time,
Redress the rigors of the inclement clime;
Aid slighted truth, with thy persuasive strain
Teach erring man to spurn the rage of gain;
Teach him that states of native strength possessed,                             425
Though very poor, may still be very blest;
That Trade's proud empire hastes to swift decay,
As ocean sweeps the labored mole[1] away;
While self-dependent power can time defy,
As rocks resist the billows and the sky.                                        430

                                                                        1770

## QUESTIONS

1. Consider the setting of Auden's "Musée des Beaux Arts" both in the sense of the painting and of its location in the museum. In what different ways do the two settings become important? How does the use of setting relate to the way the speaker is conceived? Define the role played by all of the other characters in the poem, including the people on the ship. Whose attitudes (or perhaps words) are being echoed or parodied in line 20? Describe the poem's structure.
2. Consider the elements of speaker and situation simultaneously when you analyze Herbert's "The Collar."
3. Consider the interrelation of the elements of speaker, words and word order, and stanza form in Dickinson's "My Life had stood—a Loaded Gun—."
4. Consider the interrelationships among speaker, structure, stanza form, and tone in Frost's "Design."
5. Consider the question of word choices in connection with the issues of speaker and setting in Lawrence's "Piano."

## WRITING SUGGESTIONS

1. Find a reproduction of the Brueghel painting on which Auden's poem "Musée des Beaux Arts" is based. "Read" the painting carefully, and notice which details Auden mentions and which he does not. What aspect(s) of the painting does he choose to emphasize? What does he ignore? Write a three-page essay in which you show exactly how Auden *uses* the Brueghel painting in his poem.
2. Consider Frost's "Design" as a sonnet. What features of the sonnet seem especially important to the effects Frost achieves here? Consider the structure, rhyme scheme, and imagery

1. Breakwater.

of the poem. Now look at another Frost poem, "Range-Finding" (page 536), and ask the same questions about this poem. Which poem seems to you to use the sonnet form more effectively? Why?

Write a four- to five-page essay, comparing the two poems and evaluating their use of the sonnet form.

# STUDENT WRITING

Below is a whole-text analysis of Maxine Kumin's "Woodchucks" (page 41). In it, the student addresses the setting, language, tone, structure, rhythm, and, finally, the meaning of the poem.

Tragedy in Five Stanzas: "Woodchucks"

Meaghan E. Parker

Maxine Kumin's poem, "Woodchucks," is not, as the title might suggest, about cute, furry woodchucks, but instead describes how the speaker changes as she tries to kill them, revealing aspects of human attitudes towards killing. The speaker undergoes an internal conflict as she realizes her capacity for murder during her battle with the woodchucks. She is caught up in the age-old struggle of humans against nature, except that this time, it takes place in the modern, technological world. This battle is presented in five dramatic scenes, marked by six-line stanzas; the poem's structure echoes the format of a classical tragedy in five acts. The poem is subtly organized, each stanza rhyming *abcacb*, and more or less employing a pentameter line, mixing iambs with anapests. Although the rhyme and meter remain mostly constant over the course of this highly structured poem, the tone and pacing change with each stanza, as the speaker's attitudes transform during the struggle with the woodchucks. The poet indicates the development of the speaker's internal conflict by employing word choice to change the tone from slightly humorous and relaxed to indignant martial righteousness and finally to a harsh and primitive hunter's voice, and utilizing pacing and meter to build the action to its climax.

The poem is set in small-town North America, where the speaker grows marigolds, broccoli, carrots, roses and chard in her garden. Although the speaker buys the gas bomb from the "Feed and Grain Exchange," she is not a farmer, since she has only a "vegetable patch" (lines 2 and 11). Therefore, her killing of the woodchucks is not an occupational or economic necessity; the woodchucks were merely a nuisance, and the speaker is sort of dabbling in killing. The first line states that the "gassing . . . didn't turn out right," not that it didn't work, emphasizing with this understatement the dilettantish air of the speaker's activities (line 1). The first stanza employs a playful humor: the gas is called a "knockout bomb," like some comic-book weapon, and the speaker makes a pun on the word "airtight" (lines 2-4). The store "featured" the bomb, as if it were displayed and advertised as a consumer desirable, not as a agent of death (line 3). Line 3 utilizes anapestic feet to add to the humorous tone, and most of the lines of stanza 1 are composed of long clauses, creating an even, calm pacing. The speaker and her compatriots ("we") had a made a "case against them," suggesting that the decision to kill the woodchucks was a calm, rational, legal event, yet the woodchucks evade the law by escaping "out of range" underground (lines 4-6). The escalation of the battle is indicated by the military term "range" and the woodchucks' refusal to play by the rules (line 6).

The second stanza is less light-hearted; even though the irrepressible woodchucks "turned up again" "up to scratch," they are now unmistakably opponents to the "we," who attacked them with "cyanide" (lines 7-9). The weapon seems more sinister now; not just gas from a "merciful" "knockout bomb," but murderous cyanide. The last three lines are a litany of the woodchuck's crimes against nature, each one described as increasing in savagery and wanton destruction. First, they merely "brought down the marigolds," but in a "matter of course," thoughtless way, then they "took over" the vegetables, as if they were marauding bandits conquering the speaker's territory (lines 10-11). The speaker is horrified at the "nipping" and "beheading" of the vegetables;

the use of the execution-style word "beheading" to create indignation
at the death of a plant is ironic, probably consciously on the part of
the speaker, since she had tried to execute the woodchuck (line 12).
The litany of crimes is reeled off in quick anapestic feet, subtly
hinting at the irony of the speaker's anger at the woodchucks and the
ridiculousness of the escalating battle.

The action picks up pace in stanza 3, the center of the poem and the
point at which the speaker makes her transformation from silent killer
to murderous hunter. She indignantly implies that the woodchucks would
steal "the food from our mouths": a cliché that is supposed to indicate
what heartless criminals the woodchucks are, even though the poem does
not indicate that the speaker is a subsistence farmer who would starve
without the vegetables (line 13). Even so, she enjoys the feel of the
gun, "righteously thrilling" to have the weapon of her justified revenge
in her hands (line 13). The ".22" and the "bullets' neat noses" feel
right and good, and while the woodchucks are depersonalized into the
enemy, the bullets gain "noses" (line 14). The killer is "righteous,"
"fallen from grace" and "puffed with Darwinian pieties"; these heavy-
handed, Bible-thumping words echo religious and political leaders'
sermons against evil enemies. The pace of the first four lines of this
stanza is heavy and martial, booming with polysyllabic words and
stirring phrases. The meter is the most irregular in this stanza, with
the two stressed syllables and similar sounds of "*lapsed*" and "*paci*fist"
pounding the contrast home between the speaker's current manifestation
as righteous killer and her former beliefs (line 15). Lines 15 and 16
begin with a stress, on "I" and "puffed"; the majority of the other
lines in the poem begin with an unstressed syllable, so this pair of
exceptions stands out, at the exact center of the poem, and present the
turning point of her attitudes towards killing. Now "fallen from
grace," she is "puffed" like a self-righteous windbag, and exchanges
her pacifism for the maxim of survival of the fittest (lines 15–16). Line
17 begins the switch in tone from martial sloganeering to impersonal,
hunting slang, as the speaker "drew a bead" on a woodchuck and kills
him. His death is contrasted with the perennialness of the "everbearing
roses," for whose sake he dies; this phrase indicates an undercurrent
of regret at the killing of the woodchuck (line 18).

The fourth stanza speeds up, using short, harsh clashing words in short simple clauses, instead of the sermonizing phrases of the last stanza. The speaker says she "dropped the mother": "drop" is a crude, impersonal, and unfeeling word for "shot dead," and indicates the speaker's new callous attitude towards the killing of the woodchucks (line 19). Similarly, the description of the woodchuck "flipflopp[ing] in the air" is gratuitous and violent, and the stress on "flip," since the first syllable of the line should be unstressed, emphasizes the visual image of the helpless, blown-away woodchuck (line 20). The speaker immediately moves on: "another baby next" is killed without comment (line 22). In the same line, she counts down "O one-two-three" for the three woodchucks she's killed, and the three strong stresses lead into the climax of the poem, where she announces what she's become: "murderer" and "hawkeye killer" (lines 23-24). The killer comes "on stage forthwith," as the speaker appears fully transformed by her killing, her capability for murderous action arising from her nature to triumph over her professed pacifism. The stage metaphor reinforces the five-act tragic structure that the poem mirrors and line 24 brings the poem to its climax in the fourth stanza.

Throughout the poem, the poet uses the directions down and up to contrast life and death. The woodchucks "turn up" alive (line 7), "up to scratch" (line 9) from their "sub-sub-basement," but then they "brought down the marigolds" (line 10), so they "died down in the . . . roses" (line 18), "flipflopped and fell" after being "dropped" (lines 19-20). The speaker, on the other hand, was "up to scratch" (line 9) but "[fell] from grace" (line 15), so the "murderer inside [her] rose up hard," as her former pacifist self died down and was reborn as a killer (line 23). In the final stanza, the speaker, now living as this new self, describes her continuing struggle with the woodchuck and the tolls this battle is taking on her, as she remains "cocked and ready day after day after day" and her obsession with hunting this elusive prey keeps her awake at night, dreaming of shooting (lines 26-28). The pacing slows, as the action falls from the climax, and an unenumerated amount of time elapses, but still there is not resolution and thus no victory; the speaker realizes she has lost already to the woodchucks; the tragedy is that they have already stolen her former innocence of murder and killing and now she will never have peace. The final two lines echo the beginning of the poem: "gassing" from line 1 and "gassed" from line 30 are each stressed syllables beginning a line, thus neatly bookending the poem. The speaker suggests that if the woodchucks had died from the gas, she would not have directly confronted the woodchucks and their deaths and thus undergone this tragic change into an obsessive hunter. However, this statement contains a telling historical allusion which suggests that the gassing wouldn't have been an easy moral way out either: the speaker wishes they had died "gassed underground the quiet Nazi way" (line 30). The speaker wished the deaths had been quiet, efficient, clean, non-confrontational and unwitnessed by her, so she could deny any complicity to her conscience. However, this indicates an important contradiction: gassing is still murder, as the Nazis made abundantly clear, no matter how "merciful." The poet draws a parallel between what we consider the "mercy killing" of animals and the "murder" of human beings, and thus the poem describes how delusions of righteousness cause people to wield unnecessary power over others, and how this damages and changes their sense of self as they realize and accept the human capability for acts of murder.

# Exploring Contexts

## 9

## THE AUTHOR'S WORK AS CONTEXT: JOHN KEATS

Poems are not all written in the same style, as if they were produced by a corporation or put together in a committee. Even though all poets share the same medium (language) and usually have some common notions of their craft, they put the unique resources of their individual minds and consciousness into what they create. A poet may rely on tradition extensively and use devices that others have developed without surrendering his or her own individuality, just as the integrity and uniqueness of an individual are not compromised by characteristics the individual may share with others—political affiliations, religious beliefs, tastes in clothes and music. Sometimes this uniqueness is hard to define—what exactly is it that defines the singular personality of an individual?—but it is always there, and we recognize and depend upon it in our relationships with other people. And so with poets: most don't make a conscious effort to put an individual stamp on their work; they don't have to. The stamp is there, just in the way they choose subjects, words, configurations. Every individual's consciousness uniquely marks what it records, imagines, and decides to print. The poems of John Keats, for example, are among the most distinctive in the English language. In this chapter, after considering what makes the poems of any poet distinctive, we will look at the features of Keats's poems that stamp them specifically as his own, and in the next chapter (on the poems of Adrienne Rich), we will look at how development and change occur over the course of a poet's career even though the author's character and integrity remain constant.

Experienced readers can often identify a poem as the distinctive work of an individual poet even though they may never have seen the poem before, much as experienced listeners can identify a particular composer, singer, or group after hearing only a few phrases of a piece of new music. Such an ability depends upon a lot of reading of that author or a lot of listening to music, but any reasonably sensitive reader can learn, over time, to do it with great accuracy. Developing this ability, however, is not really an end in itself; rather, it is a by-product of learning to notice the particular, distinctive qualities in the workmanship of any poet. Once you've read several poems by the same poet, you will usually begin to see some features that the poems all have in common, and gradually you may come to think of those features as characteristic. Earlier chapters have included several poems by Howard Nemerov; read them over again, and make a list of the things that strike you as similar in all of them. Then look at another poem by the same poet, "A

Way of Life," on page 563. (The Index of Authors will guide you to additional Nemerov poems as well, and it can also provide you with a list of other poets [Emily Dickinson and John Donne, for example] whose work is represented generously here and on whom you could perform the same experiment.)

In what ways is "A Way of Life" like the other poems you have read by Nemerov? The concern with contemporary life, the tendency to concentrate on modern conveniences and luxuries, and the interest in isolating and defining aspects of the distinctively modern sensibility are all characteristic of Nemerov, as is the tendency to create a short drama, with a speaker who is not altogether admirable. Several of Nemerov's other poems also share an attitude that seems deeply imbedded in this poem, a kind of antiromanticism that emerges when someone tries to sound or feel *too* proud or cheerful and is shown, by events in the poem, to be part of a grimmer reality instead. The concentration upon one or more physical objects is also characteristic, and often (as in "The Vacuum") the main object is a mechanical one that symbolizes modernity and our modern dependency on things rather than our concern with human relationships. Americanness is emphasized here, too, as if the poem were concerned with helping us define our culture and its habits and values. The mood of loneliness is also typical of Nemerov, and so is the poem's witty conversational style. The verbal wit here—

John Keats

although not as prominent as the puns and double entendres of "Boom!" (page 365)—is characteristically informal. Often it seems to derive from the language of commercials and street speech, and the undercutting of this language by the poet—having a paranoid and simpleminded speaker talk about a gangster in "a state of existential despair"—is similar to the strategy of "Boom!" or "The Vacuum." The regular stanzas, rhymed but not in a traditional or regular way and with a number of near-rhymes, are also typical (look, for example, at "The Goose Fish," page 228). Nemerov's thematic interests and ideas, his verbal style, and his cast of mind are all plainly visible in "A Way of Life."

Noticing common features does not mean that every poem by a particular author will be predictable and contain all these features. Most poets like to experiment with new subjects, tones, forms, and various kinds of poetic strategies and devices. But a characteristic way of thinking—the distinct stamp imposed by a unique consciousness—is likely to be visible anyway. The work of any writer will have certain *tendencies* that are identifiable, although not all of them will show up in any one poem.

Of what practical use is it to notice the distinctive voice and mind of a particular poet? One use (not the most important one for the casual reader, but one that nonetheless gives pleasure) is the pleasant surprise that occurs when you recognize something familiar. Reading a new poem by a familiar poet is a bit like meeting an old friend whose face or conversation reminds you of experiences you have had together. Poetic friendships can be treasures just as personal friendships are, even though they are necessarily more distant and somewhat more abstract. Just as novelty—meeting something or someone altogether new to you—is one kind of pleasure, so revisiting or recalling the familiar is another, its equal and opposite. Just *knowing* and *recognizing* often feel good in and of themselves. Many people have favorite poets—just as they may have favorite rock groups—whose sounds and themes and style are attractive, familiar, and identifiable to them.

There are other reasons as well to look at the various works of a single writer. Just as you learn from watching other people—seeing how they react and respond to people and events, observing how they cope with various situations—you also learn from watching poets at work, seeing how they learn and develop, how they change their minds, how they discover the reach and limits of their imaginations and talents, how they find their distinctive voices and come to terms with their own identities. Watching someone at work over a period of years (as you can Adrienne Rich in the next chapter) is a little like watching an autobiography unfold, except that the individual poems continue to exist separately and for themselves at the same time they provide a record of a distinctive but gradually changing and evolving consciousness.

A third reason to study in some detail the work of an individual is a very practical one: the more you know about the poet, the better a reader you are likely to be of any individual poem by that poet. It is not so much that the external facts of a writer's life find their way into whatever he or she writes—be it poem, essay, letter, or autobiography—but that a reader gets used to habits and manners and means of expression, and learns what to expect. Coming to a new poem by a poet you already know is not completely a new experience. You adjust faster, know what to look for, have some specific expectations (although they may be unconscious and unarticulated) of what the poem will be like. The more poems you read by any author, the better a reader you are likely to be of any one poem by him or her.

## *On First Looking into Chapman's Homer*[1]

*Signs of genius*

Much have I traveled in the realms of gold,
And many goodly states and kingdoms seen;
Round many western islands have I been
Which bards in fealty[2] to Apollo hold.
5   Oft of one wide expanse had I been told
That deep-browed Homer ruled as his demesne;
Yet did I never breathe its pure serene[3]
Till I heard Chapman speak out loud and bold:
*Swift* —   Then felt I like some watcher of the skies
10   When a new planet swims into his ken;[4]
Or like stout Cortez[5] when with eagle eyes

1. George Chapman's were among the most famous Renaissance translations; his *Iliad* was completed in 1611, *The Odyssey* in 1616. Keats wrote the sonnet after being led to Chapman by his former teacher and reading *The Iliad* all night long.    2. Literally, the loyalty owed by a vassal to his feudal lord. Apollo was the Greek god of poetry and music.    3. Atmosphere.    4. Range of vision.    5. Actually, Balboa; he first viewed the Pacific from Darien, in Panama.

He stared at the Pacific—and all his men
Looked at each other with a wild surmise—
Silent, upon a peak in Darien.                                    1816


## On the Grasshopper and the Cricket

The poetry of earth is never dead:
When all the birds are faint with the hot sun,
And hide in cooling trees, a voice will run
From hedge to hedge about the new-mown mead;
That is the grasshopper's—he takes the lead                        5
In summer luxury—he has never done
With his delights; for when tired out with fun
He rests at ease beneath some pleasant weed.
The poetry of earth is ceasing never:
On a lone winter evening, when the frost                          10
Has wrought a silence, from the stove there shrills
The cricket's song, in warmth increasing ever,
And seems to one in drowsiness half lost,
The grasshopper's among some grassy hills.

December 30, 1816


## On Seeing the Elgin Marbles[6]

My spirit is too weak—mortality
Weighs heavily on me like unwilling sleep,
And each imagined pinnacle and steep
Of godlike hardship tells me I must die
Like a sick eagle looking at the sky.                              5
Yet 'tis a gentle luxury to weep
That I have not the cloudy winds to keep
Fresh for the opening of the morning's eye.
Such dim-conceived glories of the brain
Bring round the heart an indescribable feud;                      10
So do these wonders a most dizzy pain,
That mingles Grecian grandeur with the rude
Wasting of old Time—with a billowy main—
A sun—a shadow of a magnitude.

1817


6. Figures and friezes from the Athenian Parthenon. They were taken from the site by Lord Elgin, brought
to England in 1806, and then sold to the British Museum, where Keats saw them.

# from *Endymion (Book 1)*[7]

A thing of beauty is a joy for ever:
Its loveliness increases; it will never
Pass into nothingness; but still will keep
A bower quiet for us, and a sleep
Full of sweet dreams, and health, and quiet breathing.
Therefore, on every morrow, are we wreathing
A flowery band to bind us to the earth,
Spite of despondence, of the inhuman dearth
Of noble natures, of the gloomy days,
Of all the unhealthy and o'er-darkened ways
Made for our searching: yes, in spite of all,
Some shape of beauty moves away the pall
From our dark spirits. Such the sun, the moon,
Trees old, and young sprouting a shady boon
For simple sheep; and such are daffodils
With the green world they live in; and clear rills
That for themselves a cooling covert make
'Gainst the hot season; the mid forest brake,[8]
Rich with a sprinkling of fair musk-rose blooms:
And such too is the grandeur of the dooms[9]
We have imagined for the mighty dead;
All lovely tales that we have heard or read:
An endless fountain of immortal drink,
Pouring unto us from the heaven's brink.
    Nor do we merely feel these essences
For one short hour; no, even as the trees
That whisper round a temple become soon
Dear as the temple's self, so does the moon,
The passion poesy, glories infinite,
Haunt us till they become a cheering light
Unto our souls, and bound to us so fast,
That, whether there be shine, or gloom o'ercast,
They always must be with us, or we die.

1817

# *When I Have Fears*

When I have fears that I may cease to be
Before my pen has gleaned my teeming brain,
Before high-piléd books, in charact'ry,
Hold like rich garners the full-ripened grain;

---

7. Keats's long poem about the myth of a mortal (Endymion) loved by the goddess of the moon.
8. Thicket.     9. Judgments.

When I behold, upon the night's starred face,                    5
Huge cloudy symbols of a high romance,
And think that I may never live to trace
Their shadows, with the magic hand of chance;
And when I feel, fair creature of an hour!
That I shall never look upon thee more,                         10
Never have relish in the faery power
Of unreflecting love!—then on the shore
Of the wide world I stand alone, and think
Till Love and Fame to nothingness do sink.

1818

## Ode to a Nightingale

### I

My heart aches, and a drowsy numbness pains
  My sense, as though of hemlock I had drunk,
Or emptied some dull opiate to the drains
  One minute past, and Lethe-wards[1] had sunk:
'Tis not through envy of thy happy lot,                         5
  But being too happy in thine happiness,
    That thou, light-wingéd Dryad[2] of the trees,
      In some melodious plot
  Of beechen green, and shadows numberless,
    Singest of summer in full-throated ease.                10

### II

O, for a draught of vintage! that hath been
  Cooled a long age in the deep-delvéd earth,
Tasting of Flora[3] and the country green,
  Dance, and Provençal song,[4] and sunburnt mirth!
O for a beaker full of the warm South,                          15
  Full of the true, the blushful Hippocrene,[5]
    With beaded bubbles winking at the brim,
      And purple-stainéd mouth;
  That I might drink, and leave the world unseen,
    And with thee fade away into the forest dim:            20

### III

Fade far away, dissolve, and quite forget
  What thou among the leaves hast never known,
The weariness, the fever, and the fret

1. Toward the river of forgetfulness (Lethe) in Hades.    2. Wood nymph.    3. Roman goddess of flowers.    4. The medieval troubadors of Provence were famous for their love songs.    5. The fountain of the Muses on Mt. Helicon, whose waters bring poetic inspiration.

Here, where men sit and hear each other groan;
25  Where palsy shakes a few, sad, last gray hairs,
    Where youth grows pale, and specter-thin, and dies;
        Where but to think is to be full of sorrow
            And leaden-eyed despairs,
    Where Beauty cannot keep her lustrous eyes,
30      Or new Love pine at them beyond tomorrow.


            IV

Away! away! for I will fly to thee,
    Not charioted by Bacchus and his pards,[6]
But on the viewless[7] wings of Poesy,
    Though the dull brain perplexes and retards:
35  Already with thee! tender is the night,
    And haply the Queen-Moon is on her throne,
        Clustered around by all her starry Fays;[8]
            But here there is no light,
    Save what from heaven is with the breezes blown
40      Through verdurous glooms and winding mossy ways.


            V

I cannot see what flowers are at my feet,
    Nor what soft incense hangs upon the boughs,
But, in embalméd[9] darkness, guess each sweet
    Wherewith the seasonable month endows
45  The grass, the thicket, and the fruit-tree wild;
    White hawthorn, and the pastoral eglantine;[1]
        Fast fading violets covered up in leaves;
            And mid-May's eldest child,
    The coming musk-rose, full of dewy wine,
50      The murmurous haunt of flies on summer eves.


            VI

Darkling[2] I listen; and, for many a time
    I have been half in love with easeful Death,
Called him soft names in many a muséd rhyme,
    To take into the air my quiet breath;
55  Now more than ever seems it rich to die,
    To cease upon the midnight with no pain,
        While thou art pouring forth thy soul abroad
            In such an ecstasy!
    Still wouldst thou sing, and I have ears in vain—
60      To thy high requiem become a sod.


6. The Roman god of wine was sometimes portrayed in a chariot drawn by leopards.    7. Invisible.
8. Fairies.    9. Fragrant, aromatic.    1. Sweetbriar or honeysuckle.    2. In the dark.

VII

Thou wast not born for death, immortal Bird!
    No hungry generations tread thee down;
The voice I hear this passing night was heard
    In ancient days by emperor and clown:
Perhaps the selfsame song that found a path                   65
    Through the sad heart of Ruth,³ when, sick for home,
        She stood in tears amid the alien corn;
            The same that ofttimes hath
    Charmed magic casements, opening on the foam
        Of perilous seas, in faery lands forlorn.            70

VIII

Forlorn! the very word is like a bell
    To toll me back from thee to my sole self!
Adieu! the fancy cannot cheat so well
    As she is famed to do, deceiving elf.
Adieu! adieu! thy plaintive anthem fades                     75
    Past the near meadows, over the still stream,
        Up the hillside; and now 'tis buried deep
            In the next valley-glades:
    Was it a vision, or a waking dream?
        Fled is that music:—Do I wake or sleep?              80

May 1819

## *Ode on a Grecian Urn*

I

Thou still unravished bride of quietness,
    Thou foster-child of silence and slow time,
Sylvan⁴ historian, who canst thus express
    A flowery tale more sweetly than our rhyme:
What leaf-fringed legend haunts about thy shape               5
    Of deities or mortals, or of both,
        In Tempe or the dales of Arcady?⁵
What men or gods are these? What maidens loath?
    What mad pursuit? What struggle to escape?
        What pipes and timbrels? What wild ecstasy?          10

3. A virtuous Moabite widow who, according to the Old Testament Book of Ruth, left her own country to accompany her mother-in-law Naomi back to Naomi's native land. She supported herself as a gleaner.    4. Woodland.    5. Arcadia. Tempe is a beautiful valley near Mt. Olympus in Greece, and the valley ("dales") of Arcadia a picturesque section of the Peloponnesus; both came to be associated with the pastoral ideal.

## II

Heard melodies are sweet, but those unheard
    Are sweeter; therefore, ye soft pipes, play on;
Not to the sensual[6] ear, but, more endeared,
    Pipe to the spirit ditties of no tone:
15  Fair youth, beneath the trees, thou canst not leave
    Thy song, nor ever can those trees be bare;
      Bold Lover, never, never canst thou kiss,
Though winning near the goal—yet, do not grieve
    She cannot fade, though thou hast not thy bliss,
20      For ever wilt thou love, and she be fair!

## III

Ah, happy, happy boughs! that cannot shed
    Your leaves, nor ever bid the Spring adieu;
And, happy melodist, unweariéd,
    For ever piping songs for ever new;
25  More happy love! more happy, happy love!
    For ever warm and still to be enjoyed,
      For ever panting, and for ever young;
All breathing human passion far above,
    That leaves a heart high-sorrowful and cloyed,
30      A burning forehead, and a parching tongue.

## IV

Who are these coming to the sacrifice?
    To what green altar, O mysterious priest,
Lead'st thou that heifer lowing at the skies,
    And all her silken flanks with garlands dressed?
35  What little town by river or sea shore,
    Or mountain-built with peaceful citadel,
      Is emptied of this folk, this pious morn?
And, little town, thy streets for evermore
    Will silent be; and not a soul to tell
40      Why thou art desolate, can e'er return.

## V

O Attic shape! Fair attitude! with brede[7]
    Of marble men and maidens overwrought,[8]
With forest branches and the trodden weed;
    Thou, silent form, dost tease us out of thought
45  As doth eternity: Cold Pastoral!
    When old age shall this generation waste,
      Thou shalt remain, in midst of other woe

6. Of the senses, as distinguished from the "ear" of the spirit or imagination.    7. Woven pattern. *Attic:*
Attica was the district of ancient Greece surrounding Athens.    8. Ornamented all over.

Than ours, a friend to man, to whom thou say'st,
　Beauty is truth, truth beauty[9]—that is all
　　Ye know on earth, and all ye need to know.　　　　　50

May 1819

## Ode on Melancholy

### I

No, no, go not to Lethe,[1] neither twist
　Wolfsbane, tight-rooted, for its poisonous wine;[2]
Nor suffer thy pale forehead to be kissed
　By nightshade, ruby grape of Proserpine;
Make not your rosary of yew-berries,[3]　　　　　　5
　Nor let the beetle, nor the death-moth be
　　Your mournful Psyche,[4] nor the downy owl
A partner in your sorrow's mysteries;
　For shade to shade will come too drowsily,
　　And drown the wakeful anguish of the soul.　　　10

### II

But when the melancholy fit shall fall
　Sudden from heaven like a weeping cloud,
That fosters the droop-headed flowers all,
　And hides the green hill in an April shroud;
Then glut thy sorrow on a morning rose,　　　　　15
　Or on the rainbow of the salt sand-wave,
　　Or on the wealth of globéd peonies;
Or if thy mistress some rich anger shows,
　Emprison her soft hand, and let her rave,
　　And feed deep, deep upon her peerless eyes.　　20

### III

She[5] dwells with Beauty—Beauty that must die;
　And Joy, whose hand is ever at his lips
Bidding adieu; and aching Pleasure nigh,
　Turning to poison while the bee-mouth sips:
Ay, in the very temple of Delight　　　　　　25

9. In some texts of the poem "Beauty is truth, truth beauty" is in quotation marks and in some texts it is not, leading to critical disagreements about whether the last line and a half are also inscribed on the urn or spoken by the poet.　　1. The river of forgetfulness in Hades.　　2. Like nightshade (line 4), wolfsbane is a poisonous plant. *Proserpine:* queen of Hades.　　3. Which often grow in cemeteries and which are traditionally associated with death.　　4. *Psyche* means both "soul" and "breath," and sometimes it was anciently represented by a moth leaving the mouth at death. Owls and beetles were also traditionally associated with darkness and death.　　5. The goddess Melancholy, whose chief place of worship ("shrine") is described in lines 25–26.

Veiled Melancholy has her sov'reign shrine,
  Though seen of none save him whose strenuous tongue
Can burst Joy's grape against his palate fine;[6]
  His soul shall taste the sadness of her might,
30      And be among her cloudy trophies hung.[7]

May 1819

## To Autumn

### I

Season of mists and mellow fruitfulness,
  Close bosom-friend of the maturing sun;
Conspiring with him how to load and bless
  With fruit the vines that round the thatch-eves run;
5  To bend with apples the mossed cottage-trees,
  And fill all fruit with ripeness to the core;
    To swell the gourd, and plump the hazel shells
With a sweet kernel; to set budding more,
  And still more, later flowers for the bees,
10  Until they think warm days will never cease,
    For Summer has o'er-brimmed their clammy cells.

### II

Who hath not seen thee oft amid thy store?
  Sometimes whoever seeks abroad may find
Thee sitting careless on a granary floor,
  Thy hair soft-lifted by the winnowing wind;[8]
15  Or on a half-reaped furrow sound asleep,
  Drowsed with the fume of poppies, while thy hook[9]
    Spares the next swath and all its twinéd flowers:
And sometimes like a gleaner thou dost keep
  Steady thy laden head across a brook;
20  Or by a cider-press, with patient look,
    Thou watchest the last oozings hours by hours.

### III

Where are the songs of Spring? Ay, where are they?
  Think not of them, thou hast thy music too—
25  While barréd clouds bloom the soft-dying day,
  And touch the stubble-plains with rosy hue;
Then in a wailful choir the small gnats mourn
  Among the river sallows,[1] borne aloft
    Or sinking as the light wind lives or dies;

6. Sensitive, discriminating.    7. The ancient Greeks and Romans hung trophies in their gods' tem-
ples.    8. Which sifts the grain from the chaff.    9. Scythe or sickle.    1. Willows.

And full-grown lambs loud bleat from hilly bourn;[2]    30
  Hedge-crickets sing; and now with treble soft
  The red-breast whistles from a garden-croft;[3]
  And gathering swallows twitter in the skies.

September 19, 1819

2. Domain.    3. An enclosed garden near a house.

## PASSAGES FROM LETTERS AND THE PREFACE TO *ENDYMION*

## from *Letter to Benjamin Bailey, November 22, 1817*[4]

* * * I am certain of nothing but of the holiness of the Heart's affections and the truth of Imagination—What the imagination seizes as Beauty must be truth—whether it existed before or not—for I have the same Idea of all our Passions as of Love they are all in their sublime, creative of essential Beauty * * * The Imagination may be compared to Adam's dream[5]—he awoke and found it truth. I am the more zealous in this affair, because I have never yet been able to perceive how any thing can be known for truth by consequitive reasoning—and yet it must be—Can it be that even the greatest Philosopher ever ~~when~~ arrived at his goal without putting aside numerous objections—However it may be, O for a Life of Sensations rather than of Thoughts! It is "a Vision in the form of Youth" a Shadow of reality to come—and this consideration has further conv[i]nced me for it has come as auxiliary to another favorite Speculation of mine, that we shall enjoy ourselves here after by having what we called happiness on Earth repeated in a finer tone and so repeated—And yet such a fate can only befall those who delight in sensation rather than hunger as you do after Truth—Adam's dream will do here and seems to be a conviction that Imagination and its empyreal reflection is the same as human Life and its spiritual repetition. But as I was saying—the simple imaginative Mind may have its rewards in the repeti[ti]on of its own silent Working coming continually on the spirit with a fine suddenness—to compare great things with small—have you never by being surprised with an old Melody—in a delicious place—by a delicious voice, fe[l]t over again your very speculations and surmises at the time it first operated on your soul—do you not remember forming to yourself the singer's face more beautiful that [*for* than] it was possible and yet with the elevation of the Moment you did not think so—even then you were mounted on the Wings of Imagination so high—that the Prototype must be here after—that delicious face you will see—What a time! I am continually running away from the subject—sure this cannot be exactly the case with a complex Mind—one that is imaginative and at the same time careful of its fruits—who would exist partly on sensation partly on thought—to whom it is necessary that years should bring the philosophic Mind—such an one I consider your's and therefore it is necessary to your eternal Happiness that you not only ~~have~~ drink this old Wine of Heaven which I shall call the redigestion of our most ethereal Musings on Earth; but also increase in knowledge and know all things. * * *

---

4. Keats's private letters, often carelessly written, are reprinted uncorrected.   5. In *Paradise Lost* VIII.460–90.

# from *Letter to George and Thomas Keats, December 21, 1817*

\* \* \* I spent Friday evening with Wells[6] & went the next morning to see *Death on the Pale horse.*[7] It is a wonderful picture, when West's age is considered; But there is nothing to be intense upon; no women one feels mad to kiss, no face swelling into reality. the excellence of every Art is its intensity, capable of making all disagreeables evaporate, from their being in close relationship with Beauty & Truth— Examine King Lear & you will find this exemplified throughout; but in this picture we have unpleasantness without any momentous depth of speculation excited, in which to bury its repulsiveness—The picture is larger than Christ rejected—I dined with Haydon the sunday after you left, & had a very pleasant day, I dined too (for I have been out too much lately) with Horace

George Keats

Smith & met his two Brothers with Hill & Kingston & one Du Bois,[8] they only served to convince me, how superior humour is to wit in respect to enjoyment— These men say things which make one start, without making one feel, they are all alike; their manners are alike; they all know fashionables; they have a mannerism in their very eating & drinking, in their mere handling a Decanter—They talked of Kean[9] & his low company—Would I were with that company instead of yours said I to myself! I know such like acquaintance will never do for me & yet I am going to Reynolds, on wednesday—Brown & Dilke walked with me & back from the Christmas pantomime. I had not a dispute but a disquisition with Dilke, on various subjects; several things dovetailed in my mind, & at once it struck me, what quality went to form a Man of Achievement especially in Literature & which Shakespeare possessed so enormously—I mean *Negative Capa-*

Thomas Keats

*bility,* that is when man is capable of being in uncertainties, Mysteries, doubts, without any irritable reaching after fact & reason—Coleridge, for instance, would let go by a fine isolated verisimilitude caught from the Penetralium of mystery,

---

6. Charles Wells (1800–1879), an author.    7. By Benjamin West (1738–1820), American painter and president of the Royal Academy; *Christ Rejected* (mentioned below) is also by West.    8. Thomas Hill (1760–1840), a book collector, and Edward duBois (1774–1850), a journalist.    9. Edmund Kean (1789–1833), a famous Shakespearean actor.

from being incapable of remaining content with half knowledge. This pursued through Volumes would perhaps take us no further than this, that with a great poet the sense of Beauty overcomes every other consideration, or rather obliterates all consideration.

## Letter to John Hamilton Reynolds, February 19, 1818

I have an idea that a Man might pass a very pleasant life in this manner—let him on any certain day read a certain Page of full Poesy or distilled Prose and let him

John Hamilton Reynolds

wander with it, and muse upon it, and reflect from it, and bring home to it, and prophesy upon it, and dream upon it—untill it becomes stale—but when will it do so? Never—When Man has arrived at a certain ripeness in intellect anyone grand and spiritual passage serves him as a starting post towards all "the two- and-thirty Pallaces"[1] How happy is such a "voyage of conception," what delicious diligent Indolence! A doze upon a Sofa does not hinder it, and a nap upon Clover engenders ethereal finger-pointings—the prattle of a child gives it wings, and the converse of middle age a strength to beat them—a strain of musick conducts to "an odd angle of the Isle",[2] and when the leaves whisper it puts a girdle round the earth",[3] Nor will this sparing touch of noble Books be any irreverance to their

Writers—for perhaps the honors paid by Man to Man are trifles in comparison to the Benefit done by great Works to the "Spirit and pulse of good" by their mere passive existence. Memory should not be called knowledge—Many have original minds who do not think it—they are led away by Custom—Now it appears to me that almost any Man may like the Spider spin from his own inwards his own airy Citadel—the points of leaves and twigs on which the Spider begins her work are few and she fills the Air with a beautiful circuiting: man should be content with as few points to tip with the fine Webb of his Soul and weave a tapestry empyrean—full of Symbols for his spiritual eye, of softness for his spiritual touch, of space for his wandering of distinctness for his Luxury—But the Minds of Mortals are so different and bent on such diverse Journeys that it may at first appear impossible for any common taste and fellowship to exist ~~bettween~~ between two or three under these suppositions—It is however quite the contrary—Minds would leave each other in contrary directions, traverse each other in Numberless

---

1. "Places of delight" in Buddhism.    2. *The Tempest* I.ii.223.    3. The phrase is from *A Midsummer Night's Dream* II.i.175.

points, and all [*for* at] last greet each other at the Journeys end—An old Man and a child would talk together and the old Man be led on his Path, and the child left thinking—Man should not dispute or assert but whisper results to his neighbor, and thus by every germ of Spirit sucking the Sap from mould ethereal every human might become great, and Humanity instead of being a wide heath of Furse[4] and Briars with here and there a remote Oak or Pine, would become a grand democracy of Forest Trees. It has been an old Comparison for our urging on—the Bee hive—however it seems to me that we should rather be the flower than the Bee—for it is a false notion that more is gained by receiving than giving—no, the receiver and the giver are equal in their benefits—The f[l]ower I doubt not receives a fair guerdon from the Bee—its leaves blush deeper in the next spring—and who shall say between Man and Woman which is the most delighted? Now it is more noble to sit like Jove that [*for* than] to fly like Mercury—let us not therefore go hurrying about and collecting honey bee like, buzzing here and there impatiently from a knowledge of what is to be arrived at; but let us open our leaves like a flower and be passive and receptive—budding patiently under the eye of Apollo and taking hints from every noble insect that favors us with a visit—sap will be given us for Meat and dew for drink—I was led into these thoughts, my dear Reynolds, by the beauty of the morning operating on a sense of Idleness—I have not read any Books—the Morning said I was right—I had no Idea but of the Morning, and the Thrush said I was right—seeming to say—

> O thou whose face hath felt the Winter's wind,
> Whose eye has seen the snow-clouds hung in mist,
> And the black elm tops 'mong the freezing stars,
> To thee the spring will be a harvest-time.
> O thou, whose only book has been the light
> Of supreme darkness which thou feddest on
> Night after night when Phœbus was away,
> To thee the spring shall be a triple morn.
> O fret not after knowledge—I have none,
> And yet my song comes native with the warmth.
> O fret not after knowledge—I have none,
> And yet the Evening listens. He who saddens
> At thought of idleness cannot be idle,
> And he's awake who thinks himself asleep.

Now I am sensible all this is a mere sophistication, however it may neighbor to any truths, to excuse my own indolence—so I will not deceive myself that Man should be equal with jove—but think himself very well off as a sort of scullion-Mercury, or even a humble Bee—It is not [*for* no] matter whether I am right or wrong either one way or another, if there is sufficient to lift a little time from your Shoulders.

---

4. *The Tempest* II.i.68–69.

# from *Letter to John Taylor, February 27, 1818*

\* \* \* It is a sorry thing for me that any one should have to overcome Prejudices in reading my Verses—that affects me more than any hyper-criticism on any particular Passage. In *Endymion* I have most likely but moved into the Go-cart from the leading strings. In Poetry I have a few Axioms, and you will see how far I am from their Centre. 1st I think Poetry should surprise by a fine excess and not by Singularity—it should strike the Reader as a wording of his own highest thoughts, and appear almost a Remembrance—2nd Its touches of Beauty should never be half way therby making the reader breathless instead of content: the rise, the progress, the setting of imagery should like the Sun come natural natural too him—shine over him and set soberly although in magnificence leaving him in the Luxury of twilight—but it is easier to think what Poetry should be than to write it—and this leads me on to another axiom. That if Poetry comes not as naturally as the Leaves to a tree it had better not come at all. However it may be with me I cannot help looking into new countries with "O for a Muse of fire to ascend!"[5]—If Endymion serves me as a Pioneer perhaps I ought to be content. I have great reason to be content, for thank God I can read and perhaps understand Shakspeare to his depths, and I have I am sure many friends, who, if I fail, will attribute any change in my Life and Temper to Humbleness rather than to Pride—to a cowering under the Wings of great Poets rather than to a Bitterness that I am not appreciated. I am anxious to get Endymion printed that I may forget it and proceed. \* \* \*

# from *the Preface to* Endymion, *dated April 10, 1818*

The imagination of a boy is healthy, and the mature imagination of a man is healthy; but there is a space of life between, in which the soul is in a ferment, the character undecided, the way of life uncertain, the ambition thick-sighted: thence proceeds mawkishness, and all the thousand bitters which those men I speak of must necessarily taste in going over the following pages.

I hope I have not in too late a day touched the beautiful mythology of Greece, and dulled its brightness: for I wish to try once more, before I bid it farewell.

## CHRONOLOGY

1795    John Keats born October 31 at Finsbury, just north of London, the eldest child of Thomas and Frances Jennings Keats. Thomas Keats was head ostler at a livery stable.

1797–1803    Birth of three younger brothers and sisters: George in 1797, Thomas in 1799, Frances Mary (Fanny) in 1803.

1803    With George, begins school in Enfield.

---

5. *Henry* V Prologue 1.

1804    Father killed by a fall from his horse, April 15. On June 27 his mother remarries, and the children go to live with their maternal grandparents at Enfield. The grandfather dies a year later, and the children move with their grandmother to Lower Edmonton.

1809    Begins a literary friendship with Charles Cowden Clarke, the son of the headmaster at the Enfield school, and develops a strong interest in reading.

1810    Mother dies of tuberculosis, after a long illness.

1811    Leaves school to become apprenticed to an apothecary-surgeon in Edmonton; completes a prose translation of the *Aeneid,* begun at school.

1814    Earliest known attempts at writing verse. In December his grandmother dies, and the family home is broken up.

1815    In October moves to next stage of his medical training at Guy's Hospital, south of the Thames in London.

1816    On May 5 his first published poem, "O Solitude," appears in Leigh Hunt's *Examiner.* In October writes "On First Looking into Chapman's Homer," published in December. Meets Hunt, Benjamin Haydon, John Hamilton Reynolds, and Shelley. By the spring of 1817, gives up the idea of medical practice.

1817    In March, moves with brothers to Hampstead, sees the Elgin Marbles with Haydon, and publishes his first collection of *Poems.* Composes *Endymion* between April and November. Reads Milton, Shakespeare, and Coleridge and rereads Wordsworth during the year.

1818    *Endymion* published in April, unfavorably reviewed in September, defended by Reynolds in October. During the summer goes on walking tour of the lake country and Scotland, but returns to London in mid-August with a sore throat and severe chills. His brother Tom also seriously ill by late summer, dying on December 1. In September, Keats first meets Fanny Brawne (eighteen years old), with whom he arrives at an "understanding" by Christmas.

1819    Writes *The Eve of St. Agnes* in January, revises it in September. Fanny Brawne and her mother move in April into the other half of the double house in which Keats lives. During April and May writes "La Belle Dame sans Merci" and all the major odes except "To Autumn," written in September. Rental arrangements force separation from Fanny Brawne during the summer (Keats on Isle of Wight from June to August), and in the fall he tries to break his dependence on her, but they become engaged by Christmas. Earlier in December suffers a recurrence of his sore throat.

1820    In February has a severe hemorrhage and in June an attack of blood-spitting. In July his doctor orders him to Italy for the winter; he sails in September and finally arrives in Rome on November 15. In July a volume of poems published, *Lamia, Isabella, The Eve of St. Agnes and Other Poems.* Fanny Brawne nurses him through the late summer.

1821    Dies at 11 P.M., February 23. Buried in the English Cemetery at Rome.

## QUESTIONS

1.  Once you have read at least half a dozen poems by Keats, make a list of the ideas that you have found in more than one poem. Make a list as well of any distinctive stylistic features you have noticed. What kinds of experiences or events does he tend to write about? Do you notice any pattern in his use of speaker? Does he have favorite words that he uses in a particular way? What about metaphors? What are his habits in putting poems together? (You might want to look ahead to some examples of his revisions in Chapter 14.) In which poems do you feel as if you want to know more about the author and his experiences before you can interpret them confidently?

2.  What stanza forms does Keats seem especially fond of? How do you explain his fondness

for repeated rhymes? What kinds of tonal effects are produced by the rhyme-rich sound patterns of the poem? What effect on meaning does the emphasis on rhyme have?

3. What kinds of images dominate Keats's poems? What kinds of settings? Do Keats's poems tend to have a distinctive, describable speaker? What tones are characteristic of Keats?

## WRITING SUGGESTION

Pick out one poem that seems to you "typical" in that it uses many of the strategies found in other poems by Keats and displays themes that seem central to his work. Write a detailed paper (of eight to ten pages) in which you analyze the poem you have chosen, showing in exactly what ways it is typical of Keats's work. Be sure to cite specific passages in other poems (as well as details from the main poem you are writing about) to prove your points.

# THE AUTHOR'S WORK IN CONTEXT: ADRIENNE RICH

The poet featured in this chapter, Adrienne Rich, has had a long and very distinguished career. Many readers and critics regard her as the best poet writing today. And a careful reader of her work will find similarities of interest, strategy, and taste from her earliest poems—published shortly after World War II, in 1951—to her newest ones. There is a distinctive mind and orientation at work in all her poems; one can speak about characteristic features in Rich's poetry just as surely as one does about characteristic features in the work of Keats even though she has already written many more poems over a much longer period of years. Throughout her career of almost fifty years, Rich has, for example, steadfastly remained interested in social and political issues and has often concentrated on themes relating to women's consciousness and the societal roles of women. Furthermore, her poems have always been conceived with a powerful sense of functional structure and cast into lyric modes that reflect sensitively their respective moods and tones. And the voice has always been firm and clear, setting out images vividly and taking a stand in matters of conscience. But over the years the voice has changed quite a lot, too, and Rich's views on a number of issues have modified and developed. Many of the changes in Rich's ideas and attitudes reflect changing concerns among American (and especially women) intellectuals in the second half of the twentieth century, and her poems represent both changed social conditions and sharply altered social, political, and philosophical attitudes. But they also reflect altered personal circumstances and changes in lifestyle and expressions of sexual preference. Rich married in her early twenties and had three children by the time she was thirty; many of her early poems are about heterosexual love, and some of them are quite explicitly about sex (see, for example, "Two Songs," page 173). More recently she has been involved in a long-term lesbian relationship and has written, again quite explicitly, about sex between women (see, for example, "My mouth hovers across your breasts," page 349). In her poems one can trace not only the contours of her evolving personal and political life and commitments, but (even more important for the study of poetry generally) one can see as well how changes *within* the poet and *in her social and cultural*

> *The fear of poetry is an indication that we are cut off from our own reality.*
>
> —MURIEL RUKEYSER

*context* alter the themes and directions of her work and even change the formal nature of what she tries to do.

One way to study Rich as an "author in context" is to read carefully what she has to say about herself and her poems: she is unusually straightforward, explicit, and articu-

Adrienne Rich circa 1970

late, and to read her describing her own development is to be guided carefully through her changing ideas about what is important both to the individual subjective consciousness and to societal attitudes and changing roles. Gathered at the end of this chapter are a series of excerpts from Rich's writing about herself and about poetry more generally, and you can use these self-conscious reflections as a kind of commentary on the poems included here and elsewhere in the book.

Here is a chronological list of the poems and prose commentary included elsewhere in this book. You can deal with the issues of an author in context in one of three ways: (1) read the commentary, then the poems; (2) read the poems, then the commentary; or (3) read the poems and commentary intermixed, in chronological order. Each selection is dated, usually (as throughout this volume) by publication date below the poem on the right, but sometimes (when Rich herself has been insistent about it) by the date of composition listed below the poem on the left.

| | | |
|---|---|---|
| Aunt Jennifer's Tigers | (1951) | p.  41 |
| Two Songs | (1964) | p. 173 |
| Letters in the Family | (1989) | p.  66 |

An even better way to study Adrienne Rich (or any poet) is to go to the library and read all (or as much as you can find) of her writing and consider in detail how the various texts interact. Most poets, even John Keats, who lived only to age twenty-five, change a lot during their careers, and many of the changes correspond to larger social and cultural changes in their own time and nation. The best way to think about the contexts of a poet's life and career is to read as much as possible of her or his own work along with that of relevant contemporaries. Watching a poet develop within various traditions and contexts can lead to a relatively balanced assessment of a particular career and also to a more exact assessment of what poetry is about in a particular time, era, or culture.

Studying Rich's career in context suggests a number of larger literary, cultural, and historical issues—the kinds of issues that will be explored more fully in the next two chapters. You may well want to think about Adrienne Rich again after you have read the poems in the other chapters—especially the poems in the "Constructing Identity, Exploring Gender" section of Chapter 12.

# At a Bach Concert

Coming by evening through the wintry city
We said that art is out of love with life.
Here we approach a love that is not pity.

This antique discipline, tenderly severe,
Renews belief in love yet masters feeling,                                    5
Asking of us a grace in what we bear.

Form is the ultimate gift that love can offer—
The vital union of necessity
With all that we desire, all that we suffer.

A too-compassionate art is half an art.                                       10
Only such proud restraining purity
Restores the else-betrayed, too-human heart.                        1951


# Storm Warnings

The glass has been falling all the afternoon,
And knowing better than the instrument
What winds are walking overhead, what zone
Of gray unrest is moving across the land,
I leave the book upon a pillowed chair                                        5
And walk from window to closed window, watching
Boughs strain against the sky

And think again, as often when the air
Moves inward toward a silent core of waiting,
How with a single purpose time has traveled                                   10
By secret currents of the undiscerned
Into this polar realm. Weather abroad
And weather in the heart alike come on
Regardless of prediction.

Between foreseeing and averting change                                        15
Lies all the mastery of elements
Which clocks and weatherglasses cannot alter.
Time in the hand is not control of time,
Nor shattered fragments of an instrument
A proof against the wind; the wind will rise,                                 20
We can only close the shutters.

I draw the curtains as the sky goes black
And set a match to candles sheathed in glass
Against the keyhole draught, the insistent whine
Of weather through the unsealed aperture.                                     25
This is our sole defense against the season;
These are the things that we have learned to do
Who live in troubled regions.                                        1951

## *Living in Sin*

She had thought the studio would keep itself;
no dust upon the furniture of love.
Half heresy, to wish the taps less vocal,
the panes relieved of grime. A plate of pears,
a piano with a Persian shawl, a cat
stalking the picturesque amusing mouse
had risen at his urging.
Not that at five each separate stair would writhe
under the milkman's tramp; that morning light
so coldly would delineate the scraps
of last night's cheese and three sepulchral bottles;
that on the kitchen shelf among the saucers
a pair of beetle-eyes would fix her own—
envoy from some village in the moldings . . .
Meanwhile, he, with a yawn,
sounded a dozen notes upon the keyboard,
declared it out of tune, shrugged at the mirror,
rubbed at his beard, went out for cigarettes;
while she, jeered by the minor demons,
pulled back the sheets and made the bed and found
a towel to dust the table-top,
and let the coffee-pot boil over on the stove.
By evening she was back in love again,
though not so wholly but throughout the night
she woke sometimes to feel the daylight coming
like a relentless milkman up the stairs.

1955

## *Snapshots of a Daughter-in-Law*

### 1

You, once a belle in Shreveport,
with henna-colored hair, skin like a peachbud,
still have your dresses copied from that time,
and play a Chopin prelude
called by Cortot: *"Delicious recollections*
*float like perfume through the memory."*

Your mind now, mouldering like wedding-cake,
heavy with useless experience, rich
with suspicion, rumor, fantasy,
crumbling to pieces under the knife-edge
of mere fact. In the prime of your life.

Nervy, glowering, your daughter
wipes the teaspoons, grows another way.

### 2

Banging the coffee-pot into the sink
she hears the angels chiding, and looks out                              15
past the raked gardens to the sloppy sky.
Only a week since They said: *Have no patience.*

The next time it was: *Be insatiable.*
Then: *Save yourself; others you cannot save.*[1]
Sometimes she's let the tapstream scald her arm,                         20
a match burn to her thumbnail,

or held her hand above the kettle's snout
right in the woolly steam. They are probably angels,
since nothing hurts her any more, except
each morning's grit blowing into her eyes.                               25


### 3

A thinking woman sleeps with monsters.
The beak that grips her, she becomes. And Nature,
that sprung-lidded, still commodious
steamer-trunk of *tempora* and *mores*[2]
gets stuffed with it all:      the mildewed orange-flowers,              30
the female pills, the terrible breasts
of Boadicea[3] beneath flat foxes' heads and orchids.

Two handsome women, gripped in argument,
each proud, acute, subtle, I hear scream
across the cut glass and majolica                                        35
like Furies[4] cornered from their prey:
The argument *ad feminam,*[5] all the old knives
that have rusted in my back, I drive in yours,
*ma semblable, ma soeur!*[6]


### 4

Knowing themselves too well in one another:                             40
their gifts no pure fruition, but a thorn,
the prick filed sharp against a hint of scorn . . .
Reading while waiting

---

1. According to Matthew 27:42, the chief priests, scribes, and elders mocked the crucified Jesus by saying, "He saved others; himself he cannot save."      2. Times and customs.      3. Queen of the ancient Britons. When her husband died, the Romans seized the territory he ruled and scourged Boadicea; she then led a heroic but ultimately unsuccessful revolt.      4. In Roman mythology, the three sisters were the avenging spirits of retributive justice.      5. "To the woman" (Latin). The *argumentum ad hominem* (literally, argument to the man) is (in logic) an argument aimed at a person's individual prejudices or special interests.      6. "My mirror-image [or 'double'], my sister." Baudelaire, in the prefatory poem to *Les Fleurs du Mal*, addresses (and attacks) his "hypocrite reader" as "mon semblable, mon frère" ("my double, my brother").

for the iron to heat,
writing, *My Life had stood—a Loaded Gun—*[7]
in that Amherst pantry while the jellies boil and scum,
or, more often,
iron-eyed and beaked and purposed as a bird,
dusting everything on the whatnot every day of life.

### 5

*Dulce ridens, dulce loquens,*[8]
she shaves her legs until they gleam
like petrified mammoth-tusk.

### 6

When to her lute Corinna sings[9]
neither words nor music are her own;
only the long hair dipping
over her cheek, only the song
of silk against her knees
and these
adjusted in reflections of an eye.

Poised, trembling and unsatisfied, before
an unlocked door, that cage of cages,
tell us, you bird, you tragical machine—
is this *fertilisante douleur?*[1] Pinned down
by love, for you the only natural action,
are you edged more keen
to prise the secrets of the vault? has Nature shown
her household books to you, daughter-in-law,
that her sons never saw?

### 7

*"To have in this uncertain world some stay
which cannot be undermined, is
of the utmost consequence."*[2]
Thus wrote
a woman, partly brave and partly good,
who fought with what she partly understood.
Few men about her would or could do more,
hence she was labeled harpy, shrew and whore.

---

7. " 'My Life had stood—a Loaded Gun—' [Poem No. 754], Emily Dickinson, *Complete Poems*, ed. T. H. Johnson, 1960, p. 369." (AR)   8. "Sweet [or 'winsome'] laughter, sweet chatter." The phrase (slightly modified here) concludes Horace's *Ode* 1.22, describing the appeal of a mistress.   9. The opening line of a famous Elizabethan lyric (by Thomas Campion) in which Corinna's music is said to control totally the poet's happiness or despair.   1. "Enriching pain" (French).   2. " ' . . . is of the utmost consequence,' from Mary Wollstonecraft, *Thoughts on the Education of Daughters*, London, 1787." (AR)

8

"You all die at fifteen," said Diderot,[3]
and turn part legend, part convention.
Still, eyes inaccurately dream
behind closed windows blankening with steam.
Deliciously, all that we might have been,                    80
all that we were—fire, tears,
wit, taste, martyred ambition—
stirs like the memory of refused adultery
the drained and flagging bosom of our middle years.

9

*Not that it is done well, but*                              85
*that it is done at all?*[4] Yes, think
of the odds! or shrug them off forever.
This luxury of the precocious child,
Time's precious chronic invalid,—
would we, darlings, resign it if we could?                   90
Our blight has been our sinecure:
mere talent was enough for us—
glitter in fragments and rough drafts.

Sigh no more, ladies.
                    Time is male
and in his cups drinks to the fair.                          95
Bemused by gallantry, we hear
our mediocrities over-praised,
indolence read as abnegation,
slattern thought styled intuition,
every lapse forgiven, our crime                              100
only to cast too bold a shadow
or smash the mould straight off.

For that, solitary confinement,
tear gas, attrition shelling.
Few applicants for that honor.

10

                    Well,                                    105
    she's long about her coming, who must be

3. " 'Vous mourez toutes a quinze ans,' from the *Lettres à Sophie Volland*, quoted by Simone de Beauvoir in *Le Deuxième Sexe*, vol. II, pp. 123–4." (AR) Editor of the *Encyclopédie* (the central document of the French Enlightenment), Diderot became disillusioned with the traditional education of women and undertook an experimental education for his own daughter.    4. Samuel Johnson's comment on women preachers: "Sir, a woman's preaching is like a dog's walking on his hinder legs. It is not done well, but you are surprised to find it done at all." (Boswell's *Life of Johnson*, ed. L. F. Powell and G. B. Hill [Oxford: Clarendon, 1934–64], I, 463.)

more merciless to herself than history.[5]
Her mind full to the wind, I see her plunge
breasted and glancing through the currents,
110    taking the light upon her
at least as beautiful as any boy
or helicopter,
                poised, still coming,
her fine blades making the air wince

but her cargo
115    no promise then:
delivered
palpable
ours.

1958–1960

In *When We Dead Awaken,* Rich describes her consciousness during the time she was writing this poem:

Over two years I wrote a 10-part poem called "Snapshots of a Daughter-in-Law," in a longer, looser mode than I've ever trusted myself with before. It was an extraordinary relief to write that poem. It strikes me now as too literary, too dependent on allusion; I hadn't found the courage yet to do without authorities, or even to use the pronoun "I"—the woman in the poem is always "she." One section of it, #2, concerns a woman who thinks she is going mad; she is haunted by voices telling her to resist and rebel, voices which she can hear but not obey.

## Planetarium

(*Thinking of Caroline Herschel, 1750–1848, astronomer, sister of
William; and others*)

A woman in the shape of a monster
a monster in the shape of a woman
the skies are full of them

a woman      "in the snow
5    among the Clocks and instruments
or measuring the ground with poles"

in her 98 years to discover
8 comets

---

5. "Cf. *Le Deuxième Sexe,* vol. II, p. 574: ' . . . elle arrive du fond des ages, de Thèbes, de Minos, de Chichen Itza; et elle est assui le totem planté au coeur de la brousse africaine; c'est un helicoptère et c'est un oiseau; et voilà la plus grande merveille: sous ses cheveux peints le bruissement des feuillages devient une pensée et des paroles s'échappent de ses seins.' " (AR)

she whom the moon ruled
like us                                                                                   10
levitating into the night sky
riding the polished lenses

Galaxies of women, there
doing penance for impetuousness
ribs chilled                                                                              15
in those spaces      of the mind

An eye,
        "virile, precise and absolutely certain"
        from the mad webs of Uranisborg
                                          encountering the NOVA            20

every impulse of light exploding
from the core
as life flies out of us

            Tycho[6] whispering at last
            "Let me not seem to have lived in vain"            25

What we see, we see
and seeing is changing

the light that shrivels a mountain
and leaves a man alive

Heartbeat of the pulsar                                                       30
heart sweating through my body

The radio impulse
pouring in from Taurus
            I am bombarded yet      I stand

I have been standing all my life in the                           35
direct path of a battery of signals
the most accurately transmitted most
untranslatable language in the universe
I am a galactic cloud so deep      so invo-
luted that a light wave could take 15                          40
years to travel through me      And has
taken      I am an instrument in the shape
of a woman trying to translate pulsations
into images      for the relief of the body
and the reconstruction of the mind.                          45

1968

6. Tycho Brahe (1546–1601), Danish astronomer whose cosmology tried to fuse the Ptolemaic and Copernican systems. He discovered and described (*De Nova Stella*, 1573) a new star in what had previously been considered a fixed star-system. Uranisborg (line 19) was Tycho's famous and elaborate palace-laboratory-observatory.

## Dialogue

She sits with one hand poised against her head, the
other turning an old ring to the light
for hours our talk has beaten
like rain against the screens
a sense of August and heat-lightning
I get up, go to make tea, come back
we look at each other
then she says (and this is what I live through
over and over)—she says: *I do not know
if sex is an illusion*

*I do not know
who I was when I did those things
or who I said I was
or whether I willed to feel
what I had read about
or who in fact was there with me
or whether I knew, even then
that there was doubt about these things*                    1972

## Diving into the Wreck

First having read the book of myths,
and loaded the camera,
and checked the edge of the knife-blade,
I put on
the body-armor of black rubber
the absurd flippers
the grave and awkward mask.
I am having to do this
not like Cousteau with his
assiduous team
aboard the sun-flooded schooner
but here alone.

There is a ladder.
The ladder is always there
hanging innocently
close to the side of the schooner.
We know what it is for,
we who have used it.
Otherwise
it's a piece of maritime floss
some sundry equipment.

I go down.
Rung after rung and still

the oxygen immerses me
the blue light                                                          25
the clear atoms
of our human air.
I go down.
My flippers cripple me,
I crawl like an insect down the ladder                                   30
and there is no one
to tell me when the ocean
will begin.

First the air is blue and then
it is bluer and then green and then                                      35
black I am blacking out and yet
my mask is powerful
it pumps my blood with power
the sea is another story
the sea is not a question of power                                       40
I have to learn alone
to turn my body without force
in the deep element.

And now: it is easy to forget
what I came for                                                          45
among so many who have always
lived here
swaying their crenellated fans
between the reefs
and besides                                                              50
you breathe differently down here.

I came to explore the wreck.
The words are purposes.
The words are maps.
I came to see the damage that was done                                   55
and the treasures that prevail.
I stroke the beam of my lamp
slowly along the flank
of something more permanent
than fish or weed                                                        60

the thing I came for:
the wreck and not the story of the wreck
the thing itself and not the myth
the drowned face always staring
toward the sun                                                           65
the evidence of damage
worn by salt and sway into this threadbare beauty
the ribs of the disaster
curving their assertion
among the tentative haunters.                                            70

This is the place.
And I am here, the mermaid whose dark hair
streams black, the merman in his armored body
We circle silently
75      about the wreck
we dive into the hold.
I am she: I am he
whose drowned face sleeps with open eyes
whose breasts still bear the stress
80      whose silver, copper, vermeil cargo lies
obscurely inside barrels
half-wedged and left to rot
we are the half-destroyed instruments
that once held to a course
85      the water-eaten log
the fouled compass

We are, I am, you are
by cowardice or courage
the one who find our way
90      back to this scene
carrying a knife, a camera
a book of myths
in which
our names do not appear.

1972

## Origins and History of Consciousness

I

Night-life. Letters, journals, bourbon
sloshed in the glass. Poems crucified on the wall,
dissected, their bird-wings severed
like trophies. No one lives in this room
5      without living through some kind of crisis.

No one lives in this room
without confronting the whiteness of the wall
behind the poems, planks of books,
photographs of dead heroines.
10     Without contemplating last and late
the true nature of poetry. The drive
to connect. The dream of a common language.

Thinking of lovers, their blind faith, their
experienced crucifixions,
15     my envy is not simple. I have dreamed of going to bed
as walking into clear water ringed by a snowy wood
white as cold sheets, thinking, *I'll freeze in there.*

My bare feet are numbed already by the snow
but the water
is mild, I sink and float                                      20
like a warm amphibious animal
that has broken the net, has run
through fields of snow leaving no print;
this water washes off the scent—
*You are clear now*                                           25
*of the hunter, the trapper*
*the wardens of the mind—*

yet the warm animal dreams on
of another animal
swimming under the snow-flecked surface of the pool,          30
and wakes, and sleeps again.

No one sleeps in this room without
the dream of a common language.

###### II

It was simple to meet you, simple to take your eyes
into mine, saying: these are eyes I have known              35
from the first. . . . It was simple to touch you
against the hacked background, the grain of what we
had been, the choices, years. . . . It was even simple
to take each other's lives in our hands, as bodies.

What is not simple: to wake from drowning                   40
from where the ocean beat inside us like an afterbirth
into this common, acute particularity
these two selves who walked half a lifetime untouching—
to wake to something deceptively simple: a glass
sweated with dew, a ring of the telephone, a scream        45
of someone beaten up far down in the street
causing each of us to listen to her own inward scream

knowing the mind of the mugger and the mugged
as any woman must who stands to survive this city,
this century, this life . . .                               50

each of us having loved the flesh in its clenched or loosened beauty
better than trees or music (yet loving those too
as if they were flesh—and they are—but the flesh
of beings unfathomed as yet in our roughly literal life).

###### III

It's simple to wake from sleep with a stranger,            55
dress, go out, drink coffee,
enter a life again. It isn't simple
to wake from sleep into the neighborhood
of one neither strange nor familiar

60          whom we have chosen to trust. Trusting, untrusting,
                  we lowered ourselves into this, let ourselves
                  downward hand over hand as on a rope that quivered
                  over the unsearched. . . . We did this. Conceived
                  of each other, conceived each other in a darkness
65          which I remember as drenched in light.

                                      I want to call this, life.

                  But I can't call it life until we start to move
                  beyond this secret circle of fire
                  where our bodies are giant shadows flung on a wall
70          where the night becomes our inner darkness, and sleeps
                  like a dumb beast, head on her paws, in the corner.

        1972–74                                            1978

## Power

          Living   in the earth-deposits   of our history

          Today a backhoe divulged   out of a crumbling flank of earth
          one bottle  amber  perfect  a hundred-year-old
          cure for fever  or melancholy  a tonic
5          for living on this earth  in the winters of this climate

          Today I was reading about Marie Curie:
          she must have known she suffered  from radiation sickness
          her body bombarded for years  by the element
          she had purified
10        It seems she denied to the end
          the source of the cataracts on her eyes
          the cracked and suppurating skin  of her finger-ends
          till she could no longer hold  a test-tube or a pencil

          She died  a famous woman  denying
15        her wounds
          denying
          her wounds  came  from the same source as her power            1978

## For the Record

          The clouds and the stars didn't wage this war
          the brooks gave no information
          if the mountain spewed stones of fire into the river
          it was not taking sides
5          the raindrop faintly swaying under the leaf
          had no political opinions

          and if here or there a house
          filled with backed-up raw sewage

or poisoned those who lived there
with slow fumes, over years                                               10
the houses were not at war
nor did the tinned-up buildings

intend to refuse shelter
to homeless old women and roaming children
they had no policy to keep them roaming                                   15
or dying, no, the cities were not the problem
the bridges were non-partisan
the freeways burned, but not with hatred

Even the miles of barbed-wire
stretched around crouching temporary huts                                 20
designed to keep the unwanted
at a safe distance, out of sight
even the boards that had to absorb
year upon year, so many human sounds

so many depths of vomit, tears                                            25
slow-soaking blood
had not offered themselves for this
The trees didn't volunteer to be cut into boards
nor the thorns for tearing flesh
Look around at all of it                                                  30

and ask whose signature
is stamped on the orders, traced
in the corner of the building plans
Ask where the illiterate, big-bellied
women were, the drunks and crazies,                                       35
the ones you fear most of all:   ask where you were.              1983


# [*My mouth hovers across your breasts*] [7]

### 3.

My mouth hovers across your breasts
in the short grey winter afternoon
in this bed     we are delicate
and tough     so hot with joy we amaze ourselves
tough     and delicate     we play rings                                  5
around each other     our daytime candle burns
with its peculiar light     and if the snow
begins to fall outside     filling the branches
and if the night falls     without announcement
these are the pleasures of winter                                         10
sudden, wild and delicate     your fingers

7. This poem is taken from Rich's series "Tracking Poems."

exact     my tongue exact at the same moment
stopping to laugh at a joke
my love     hot on your scent     on the cusp of winter                    1986


## Walking down the Road

On a clear night in Live Oak you can see
the stars glittering low as from the deck
of a frigate.
In Live Oak without pavements you can walk
5    the fronts of old homesteads, past tattered palms,
original rosebushes, thick walnut trees
ghosts of the liveoak groves
the whitemen cleared. On a night like this
the old California thickens and bends
10    the Baja streams out like lava-melt
we are no longer the United States
we're a lost piece of Mexico
maybe dreaming the destruction
of the Indians, reading the headlines,
15    how the gringos marched into Mexico City
forcing California into the hand
of Manifest Destiny, law following greed.
And the pale lies trapped in the flickering boxes
here in Live Oak tonight, they too follow.
20    One thing follows on another, that is time:
Carmel in its death-infested prettiness,
thousands of skeletons stacked in the *campo santo:*[8]
the spring fouled by the pickaxe:
the flag dragged on to the moon:
25    the crystal goblet smashed: grains of the universe
flashing their angry tears, here in Live Oak.                    1989


## Delta

If you have taken this rubble for my past
raking through it for fragments you could sell
know that I long ago moved on
deeper into the heart of the matter

5    If you think you can grasp me, think again:
my story flows in more than one direction
a delta springing from the riverbed
with its five fingers spread                    1989

8. Sacred field, cemetery (Spanish).

# History[9]

Should I simplify my life for you?
Don't ask how I began to love men.
Don't ask how I began to love women.
Remember the forties songs, the slowdance numbers
the small sex-filled gas-rationed Chevrolet?                          5
Remember walking in the snow and who was gay?
Cigarette smoke of the movies, silver-and-gray
profiles, dreaming the dreams of he-and-she
breathing the dissolution of the wisping silver plume?
Dreaming that dream we leaned applying lipstick                      10
by the gravestone's mirror when we found ourselves
playing in the cemetery.   In Current Events she said
the war in Europe is over, the Allies
and she wore no lipstick have won the war
and we raced screaming out of Sixth Period.                          15

Dreaming that dream
we had to maze our ways through a wood
where lips were knives breasts razors and I hid
in the cage of my mind scribbling
*this map stops where it all begins*                                 20
into a red-and-black notebook.
Remember after the war when peace came down
as plenty for some and they said we were saved
in an eternal present and we knew the world could end?
—remember after the war when peace rained down                      25
on the winds from Hiroshima Nagasaki Utah Nevada?[1]
and the socialist queer Christian teacher jumps from the hotel window?
and L.G. saying *I want to sleep with you but not for sex*
and the red-and-black enamelled coffee-pot dripped slow through the
    dark grounds
—appetite terror power tenderness                                    30
the long kiss in the stairwell the switch thrown
on two Jewish Communists[2] married to each other
the definitive crunch of glass at the end of the wedding?
*(When shall we learn, what should be clear as day,*
*We cannot choose what we are free to love?)*                        35

1995

---

9. The fourth poem in a series called "Inscriptions."     1. Sites of atomic-bomb explosions, the first two
in Japan near the end of World War II, the last two test sites in the desert.     2. Julius and Ethel Rosen-
berg, executed by the United States as spies.

## INTERVIEWS AND PERSONAL REFLECTIONS

# from *Talking with Adrienne Rich*[3]

* * * I think of myself as using poetry as a chief means of self-exploration—one of several means, of which maybe another would be dreams, really thinking about, paying attention to dreams, but the poem, like the dream, does this through images and it is in the images of my poems that I feel I am finding out more about my own experience, my sense of things. But I don't think of myself as having a position or a self-description which I'm then going to present in the poem.

When I started writing poetry I was tremendously conscious of, and very much in need of, a formal structure that could be obtained from outside, into which I could pour whatever I had, whatever I thought I had to express. But I think that was a part of a whole thing that I see, now as a teacher, very much with young writers, of using language more as a kind of fac,ade than as either self-revelation or as a probe into one's own consciousness. I think I would attribute a lot of the change in my poetry simply to the fact of growing older, undergoing certain kinds of experiences, realizing that formal metrics were not going to suffice me in dealing with those experiences, realizing that experience itself is much more fragmentary, much more sort of battering, much ruder than these structures would allow, and it had to find its own form.

I have a very strong sense about the existence of poetry in daily life and poetry being part of the world as it is, and that the attempt to reduce poetry to what is indited on a page just limits you terribly. . . . The poem is the poetry of things lodged in the innate shape of the experience. My saying "The moment of change is the only poem" is the kind of extreme statement you feel the need to make at certain times if only to force someone to say, "But I always thought a poem is something written on a piece of paper," you know, and to say: "But look, how did those words get on that piece of paper." There had to be a mind; there had to be an experience; the mind had to go through certain shocks, certain stresses, certain strains, and if you're going to carry the poem back to its real beginnings it's that moment of change. I feel that we are always writing.

When I was in my twenties * * * I was going through a very sort of female thing— of trying to distinguish between the ego that is capable of writing poems, and then this other kind of being that you're asked to be if you're a woman, who is, in a sense, denying that ego. I had great feelings of split about that for many years actually, and there are a lot of poems I couldn't write even, because I didn't want to confess to having that much aggression, that much ego, that much sense of myself. I had always thought of my first book as being a book of very well-tooled

3. A transcript of a conversation recorded March 9, 1971, and printed in the *Ohio Review*, Fall 1971.

poems of a sort of very bright student, which I was at that time, but poems in which the unconscious things never got to the surface. But there's a poem in that book about a woman who sews a tapestry and the tapestry has figures of tigers on it. But the woman is represented as being completely . . . her hand is burdened by the weight of the wedding band, and she's meek, and she's fearful, and the only way in which she can express any other side of her nature is in embroidering these tigers. Well, I thought of that as almost a formal exercise, but when I go back and look at that poem I really think it's saying something about what I was going through. And now that's lessened a great deal for all sorts of reasons . . . that split.

# from *An Interview with Adrienne Rich*[4]

I would have said ten or fifteen years ago that I would not even want to identify myself as a woman poet. That term *has* been used pejoratively; I just don't think it can be at this point. You know, for a woman the act of creation is prototypically to produce children, while the act of creating with language—I'm not saying that women writers haven't been accepted; certainly, more have been accepted than women lawyers or doctors. Still, a woman writer feels, she is going against the grain—or there has been this sense until very recently (if there isn't still). Okay, it's all right to be a young thing and write verse. But a friend of mine was telling me about meeting a noted poet at a cocktail party. She'd sent him a manuscript for a contest he was judging. She went up to him and asked him about it, and he looked at her and said, "Young girls *are* poems; they shouldn't write them." This attitude toward women poets manifests itself so strongly that you are made to feel you are becoming the thing you are not.

If a man is writing, he's gone through all the nonsense and said "Okay, I am a poet and I'm still a man. They don't cancel each other out or, if they do, then I'll opt to be a poet." He's not writing for a hostile sex, a breed of critics who by virtue of their sex are going to look at his language and pass judgment on it. That does happen to a woman. I don't know why the woman poet has been slower than the woman novelist in taking risks though I'm very grateful that this is no longer so. I feel that I dare to think further than I would have dared to think ten years ago—and *that* certainly is going to affect my writing. And I now dare to entertain thoughts and speculations that then would have seemed unthinkable.

Many of the male writers whom I very much admire—Galway Kinnell, James Wright, W. S. Merwin—are writing poetry of such great desolation. They come from different backgrounds, write in different ways, and yet all seem to write out of a sense of doom, as if we were fated to carry on these terribly flawed relationships. I think it's expressive of a feeling that "we, the masters, have created a world that's impossible to live in and that probably may not be livable in, in a very

---

4. By David Kalstone, in the *Saturday Review*, April 22, 1972.

literal sense. What we thought, what we'd been given to think is our privilege, our right, and our sexual prerogative has led to this, to our doom." I guess a lot of women—if not a lot of women poets—are feeling that there has to be some other way, that human life is messed-up but that it doesn't have to be *this* desolate.

Today, much poetry by women is charged with anger and uses voices of rage and anger that I don't think were ever used in poetry before. In poets like Sylvia Plath and Diane Wakoski, say, those voices are so convincing that it is impossible to describe them by using those favorite adjectives of phallic criticism—shrill and hysterical. Well, Sylvia Plath is dead. I always maintained from the first time I read her last poems that her suicide was not necessary, that she could have gone on and written poems that would have given us even more insight into the states of anger and willfulness, even of self-destructiveness, that women experience. She didn't need literally to destroy herself in order to reflect and express those things. Diane Wakoski is a young woman. She's changing a lot and will continue to change. What I admire in her, besides her energy and dynamism and quite a beautiful gift for snatching the image that she wants out of the air, is her honesty. No woman has written before about her face and said she hated it, that it had served her ill, that she wished she could throw acid in it. That's very shocking. But I think all women, even the most beautiful women, at times have felt that in a kind of self-hatred. Because the *face* is supposed to be the *woman*.

A lot of poetry is becoming more oral. Certainly, it's true of women and black poets. Reading black poetry on the printed page gives no sense of the poem, if you're going to look at that poetry the way you look at poems by Richard Wilbur. Yet you can hear these poets read and realize it's the oldest kind of poetry.

I think the energy of language comes somewhat from the pressure and need and unbearableness of what's being done to you. It's not the same energy you find in the blues. The blues are a grief language, a lost language, and a cry of pain, usually in a woman's voice, which is interesting. For a long time you sing the blues, and then you begin to say, "I'm tired of singing the blues. I want something else." And that's what you're hearing now. There seems to be a connection between an oppressed condition and having access to certain kinds of energy, vitality, and subjectivity. For women as well as blacks. Though I don't feel there is a necessary cause-and-effect relationship; what seems to happen is that being on top, being in a powerful position leads to a divorce between one's unruly, chaotic, revolutionary sensitivity and one's reason, sense of order and of maintaining a hold. And, therefore, you have at the bottom of the pile, so to speak, a kind of churning energy that gets lost up there among the administrators.

I don't know how or whether poetry changes anything. But neither do I know how or whether bombing or even community organizing changes anything when we are pitted against a massive patriarchal system armed with supertechnology. I believe in subjectivity—that a lot of male Left leaders have turned into Omnipotent Administrators, because their "masculinity" forced them to deny their subjectivity. I believe in dreams and visions and "the madness of art." And at moments I can conceive of a women's movement that will show the way to humanizing technology and fusing dreams and skills and visions and reason to begin the healing of the human race. But I don't want women to take over the world and run it the way men have, or to take on—yet again!—the burden of carrying the subjectivity of the race. Women are a vanguard now, and I believe will increasingly become so, because we have—Western women, Third World women, all women—known and felt the pain of the human condition most consistently. But in the end it can't be women alone.

## from *When We Dead Awaken: Writing as Re-Vision*[5]

Most, if not all, human lives are full of fantasy—passive daydreaming which need not be acted on. But to write poetry or fiction, or even to think well, is not to fantasize, or to put fantasies on paper. For a poem to coalesce, for a character or an action to take shape, there has to be an imaginative transformation of reality which is in no way passive. And a certain freedom of the mind is needed—free-

dom to press on, to enter the currents of your thought like a glider pilot, knowing that your motion can be sustained, that the buoyancy of your attention will not be suddenly snatched away. Moreover, if the imagination is to transcend and transform experience it has to question, to challenge, to conceive of alternatives, perhaps to the very life you are living at that moment. You have to be free to play around with the notion that day might be night, love might be hate, nothing can be too sacred for the imagination to turn into its opposite or to call experimentally by another name. For writing is re-naming. Now, to be maternally with small children all day in the old way, to be with a man in the old way of marriage, requires a holding-back, a putting-aside of

Rich in the classroom circa 1978

that imaginative activity, and demands instead a kind of conservatism. I want to make it clear that I am *not* saying that in order to write well, or think well, it is necessary to become unavailable to others, or to become a devouring ego. This has been the myth of the masculine artist and thinker; and I do not accept it. But

---

5. First published in *College English* in 1972; this version, slightly revised, is included in *On Lies, Secrets, and Silence: Selected Prose: 1966–1978* (1979).

to be a female human being trying to fulfill traditional female functions in a traditional way *is* in direct conflict with the subversive function of the imagination. The word traditional is important here. There must be ways, and we will be finding out more and more about them, in which the energy of creation and the energy of relation can be united. But in those earlier years I always felt the conflict as a failure of love in myself. I had thought I was choosing a full life: the life available to most men, in which sexuality, work, and parenthood could coexist. But I felt, at twenty-nine, guilt toward the people closest to me, and guilty toward my own being.

I wanted, then, more than anything, the one thing of which there was never enough: time to think, time to write. The fifties and early sixties were years of rapid revelations: the sit-ins and marches in the South, the Bay of Pigs, the early antiwar movement, raised large questions—questions for which the masculine world of the academy around me seemed to have expert and fluent answers. But I needed to think for myself—about pacifism and dissent and violence, about poetry and society, and about my own relationship to all these things. For about ten years I was reading in fierce snatches, scribbling in notebooks, writing poetry in fragments; I was looking desperately for clues, because if there were no clues then I thought I might be insane. I wrote in a notebook about this time:

> Paralyzed by the sense that there exists a mesh of relationships—e.g., between my anger at the children, my sensual life, pacifism, sex (I mean sex in its broadest significance, not merely sexual desire)—an interconnectedness which, if I could see it, make it valid, would give me back myself, make it possible to function lucidly and passionately. Yet I grope in and out among these dark webs.

I think I began at this point to feel that politics was not something "out there" but something "in here" and of the essence of my condition.

In the late fifties I was able to write, for the first time, directly about experiencing myself as a woman. The poem was jotted in fragments during children's naps, brief hours in a library, or at 3 A.M. after rising with a wakeful child. I despaired of doing any continuous work at this time. Yet I began to feel that my fragments and scraps had a common consciousness and a common theme, one which I would have been very unwilling to put on paper at an earlier time because I had been taught that poetry should be "universal," which meant, of course, nonfemale. Until then I had tried very much *not* to identify myself as a female poet.

## *How Does a Poet Put Bread on the Table?*[6]

But how does a poet put bread on the table? Rarely, if ever, by poetry alone. Of the four lesbian poets at the Nuyorican Poets Café about whose lives I know something, one directs an underfunded community arts project, two are untenured college teachers, one an assistant dean of students at a state university. Of

6. From *What Is Found There: Notebooks on Poetry and Politics* (1993).

other poets I know, most teach, often part time, without security but year round; two are on disability; one does clerical work; one cleans houses; one is a paid organizer; one has a paid editing job. Whatever odd money comes in erratically from readings and workshops, grants, permissions fees, royalties, prizes can be very odd money indeed, never to be counted on and almost always small: checks have to be chased down, grants become fewer and more competitive in a worsening political and economic climate. Most poets who teach at universities are untenured, without pension plans or group health insurance, or are employed at public and community colleges with heavy teaching loads and low salaries. Many give unpaid readings and workshops as part of their political "tithe."

Inherited wealth accounts for the careers of some poets: to inherit wealth is to inherit time. Most of the poets I know, hearing of a sum of money, translate it not into possessions, but into time—that precious immaterial necessity of our lives. It's true that a poem can be attempted in brief interstitial moments, pulled out of the pocket and worked on while waiting for a bus or riding a train or while children nap or while waiting for a new batch of clerical work or blood samples to come in. But only certain kinds of poems are amenable to these conditions. Sometimes the very knowledge of coming interruption dampens the flicker. And there is a difference between the ordinary "free" moments stolen from exhausting family strains, from alienating labor, from thought chained by material anxiety, and those other moments that sometimes arrive in a life being lived at its height though under extreme tension; perhaps we are waiting to initiate some act we believe will catalyze change but whose outcome is uncertain; perhaps we are facing personal or communal crisis in which everything unimportant seems to fall away and we are left with our naked lives, the brevity of life itself, and words. At such times we may experience a speeding-up of our imaginative powers, images and voices rush together in a kind of inevitability, what was externally fragmented is internally recognized, and the hand can barely keep pace.

But such moments presuppose other times: when we could simply stare into the wood grain of a door, or the trace of bubbles in a glass of water as long as we wanted to, *almost* secure in the knowledge that there would be no interruption—times of slowness, or purposelessness.

Often such time feels like a luxury, guiltily seized when it can be had, fearfully taken because it does not seem like work, this abeyance, but like "wasting time" in a society where personal importance—even job security—can hinge on acting busy, where the phrase "keeping busy" is a common idiom, where there is, for activists, so much to be done.

Most, if not all, of the names we know in North American poetry are the names of people who have had some access to freedom in time—that privilege of some which is actually a necessity for all. The struggle to limit the working day is a sacred struggle for the worker's freedom in time. To feel herself or himself, for a few hours or a weekend, as a free being with choices—to plant vegetables and later sit on the porch with a cold beer, to write poetry or build a fence or fish or play cards, to walk without a purpose, to make love in the daytime. To sleep late. Ordinary human pleasures, the self's re-creation. Yet every working generation has to reclaim that freedom in time, and many are brutally thwarted in the effort. Capitalism is based on the abridgment of that freedom.

Poets in the United States have either had some kind of private means, or help from people with private means, have held full-time, consuming jobs, or have chosen to work in low-paying, part-time sectors of the economy, saving their creative energies for poetry, keeping their material wants simple. Interstitial living, where the art itself is not expected to bring in much money, where the artist may move from a clerical job to part-time, temporary teaching to subsistence living on the land to waitressing or doing construction or translating, typesetting, or ghostwriting. In the 1990s this kind of interstitial living is more difficult, risky, and wearing than it has ever been, and this is a loss to all the arts—as much as the shrinkage of arts funding, the censorship-by-clique, the censorship by the Right, the censorship by distribution.

## A Communal Poetry [7]

One day in New York in the late 1980s, I had lunch with a poet I'd known for more than twenty years. Many of his poems were—are—embedded in my life. We had read together at the antiwar events of the Vietnam years. Then, for a long time, we hardly met. As a friend, he had seemed to me withheld, defended in a certain way I defined as masculine and with which I was becoming in general impatient; yet often, in their painful beauty, his poems told another story. On this day, he was as I had remembered him: distant, stiff, shy perhaps. The conversation stumbled along as we talked about our experiences with teaching poetry,

Adrienne Rich today.

which seemed a safe ground. I made some remark about how long it was since last we'd talked. Suddenly, his whole manner changed: *You disappeared! You simply disappeared.* I realized he meant not so much from his life as from a landscape of poetry to which he thought we both belonged and were in some sense loyal.

If anything, those intervening years had made me feel more apparent, more visible— to myself and to others—as a poet. The powerful magnet of the women's liberation movement—and the women's poetry movement it released—had drawn me to coffeehouses where women were reading new kinds of poems; to emerging "journals of liberation" that published women's poems, often in a context of political articles and the beginnings of feminist criticism; to bookstores selling chapbooks and

7. From *What Is Found There: Notebooks on Poetry and Politics* (1993).

pamphlets from the new women's presses; to a woman poet's workshops with women in prison; to meetings with other women poets in Chinese restaurants, coffee shops, apartments, where we talked not only of poetry, but of the conditions that make it possible or impossible. It had never occurred to me that I was disappearing—rather, that I was, along with other women poets, beginning to appear. In fact, we were taking part in an immense shift in human consciousness.

My old friend had, I believe, not much awareness of any of this. It was, for him, so off-to-the-edge, so out-of-the-way; perhaps so dangerous, it seemed I had sunk, or dived, into a black hole. Only later, in a less constrained and happier meeting, were we able to speak of the different ways we had perceived that time.

He thought there had been a known, defined poetic landscape and that as poetic contemporaries we simply shared it. But whatever poetic "generation" I belonged to, in the 1950s I was a mother, under thirty, raising three small children. Notwithstanding the prize and the fellowship to Europe that my first book of poems had won me, there was little or no "appearance" I then felt able to claim as a poet, against that other profound and as yet unworded reality.

## CHRONOLOGY

1929   Born in Baltimore, Maryland, May 16. Began writing poetry as a child under the encouragement and supervision of her father, Dr. Arnold Rich, from whose "very Victorian, pre-Raphaelite" library, Rich later recalled, she read Tennyson, Keats, Arnold, Blake, Rossetti, Swinburne, Carlyle, and Pater.

1951   A.B., Radcliffe College. Phi Beta Kappa. *A Change of World* chosen by W. H. Auden for the Young Poets Award and published.

1952–1953   Guggenheim Fellowship; travel in Europe and England. Marriage to Alfred H. Conrad, an economist who taught at Harvard. Residence in Cambridge, Massachusetts, 1953–66.

1955   Birth of David Conrad. Publication of *The Diamond Cutters and Other Poems*, which won the Ridgely Torrence Memorial Award of the Poetry Society of America.

1957   Birth of Paul Conrad.

1959   Birth of Jacob Conrad.

1960   National Institute of Arts and Letters Award for poetry. Phi Beta Kappa poet at William and Mary College.

1961–1962   Guggenheim Fellowship; residence with family in the Netherlands.

1962   Bollingen Foundation grant for translation of Dutch poetry.

1962–1963   Amy Lowell Travelling Fellowship.

1963   *Snapshots of a Daughter-in-Law* published. Bess Hokin Prize of *Poetry* magazine.

1965   Phi Beta Kappa poet at Swarthmore College.

1966   *Necessities of Life* published, nominated for the National Book Award. Phi Beta Kappa poet at Harvard College. Move to New York City, where Alfred Conrad taught at City College of New York. Residence there from 1966 on. Increasingly active politically in protests against the war in Vietnam.

1966–1968   Lecturer at Swarthmore College.

1967–1969   Adjunct Professor of Writing in the Graduate School of the Arts, Columbia University.

1967   *Selected Poems* published in Britain. Litt.D., Wheaton College.

1968   Eunice Tietjens Memorial Prize of *Poetry* magazine. Began teaching in the SEEK and Open Admissions Programs at City College of New York.

1969   *Leaflets* published.

1970   Death of Alfred Conrad.

1971   *The Will to Change* published. Shelley Memorial Award of the Poetry Society of America. Increasingly identifies with the women's movement as a radical feminist.

1972–1973   Fanny Hurst Visiting Professor of Creative Literature at Brandeis University.

1973   *Diving into the Wreck* published.

1973–1974   Ingram Merrill Foundation research grant; began work on a book on the history and myths of motherhood.

1974   National Book Award for *Diving into the Wreck*. Rich rejected the award as an individual, but accepted it, in a statement written with Audre Lorde and Alice Walker, two other nominees, in the name of all women:

> We . . . together accept this award in the name of all the women whose voices have gone and still go unheard in a patriarchal world, and in the name of those who, like us, have been tolerated as token women in this culture, often at great cost and in great pain. . . . We symbolically join here in refusing the terms of patriarchal competition and declaring that we will share this prize among us, to be used as best we can for women. . . . We dedicate this occasion to the struggle for self-determination of all women, of every color, identification or derived class . . . the women who will not understand yet; the silent women whose voices have been denied us, the articulate women who have given us strength to do our work.

Professor of English, City College of New York.

1975   *Poems: Selected and New* published.

1976   Professor of English at Douglass College. *Of Woman Born: Motherhood as Experience and Institution* published. *Twenty-one Love Poems* published.

1978   *The Dream of a Common Language: Poems 1974–1977* published.

1979   *On Lies, Secrets, and Silence: Selected Prose 1966–1978* published. Leaves Douglass College and New York City; moves to Montague, Massachusetts; edits, with Michelle Cliff, the lesbian-feminist journal, *Sinister Wisdom*.

1981   *A Wild Patience Has Taken Me This Far: Poems 1978–1981* published.

1984   *The Fact of a Doorframe: Poems Selected and New 1950–1984* published. Moves to Santa Cruz, California.

1986   *Blood, Bread, and Poetry: Selected Prose 1979–1985* published. Professor of English at Stanford University.

1989   *Time's Power: Poems 1985–1988* published.

1990   Member of the Department of Literature of the American Academy and Institute of Arts and Letters.

1991   *An Atlas of the Difficult World* published.

1992   Wins *Los Angeles Times* Book Prize for *An Atlas of the Difficult World,* the Lenore Marshall / *Nation* Prize for Poetry, and Nicholas Roerich Museum Poet's Prize; is co-winner of the Frost Silver Medal for distinguished lifetime achievement.

1993   *What Is Found There: Notebooks on Poetry and Politics* published.

1994   Awarded MacArthur fellowship.

1996   Awarded the Tanning Prize, given by the Academy of American Poets.

## QUESTION

What significant differences do you notice among the poems by Adrienne Rich that appear throughout this volume? Can you tell quickly an early Rich poem from a later one? What are the differences in subject matter? in style? in situation? in strategies of argument? Try to read all the Rich poems in the book at one sitting, working in poems to be found elsewhere in the text in their appropriate chronological place. Characterize, as fully as you can, the voice of the poems written in the 1950s; in the 1960s; 1970s; 1980s; 1990s. In what ways does the voice seem to change? What similarities do you see in her work from beginning to end?

## WRITING SUGGESTIONS

1. In what sense is "At a Bach Concert" typical of Rich's early poetry? Compare "Storm Warnings" and "Aunt Jennifer's Tigers" in terms of the comments Rich makes about her early work in the passage quoted from *When We Dead Awaken: Writing as Re-Vision* (page 355). What "typical" features do the poems share? Write a detailed analysis (about 1,500 words) of "At a Bach Concert," showing how it is (or is not) typical of Rich's early work.
2. Carefully considering plot, characterization, and structure, write an essay in which you detail the ways "Diving into the Wreck" is and is not typical of Rich's recent work. (Alternate version: Are there other poems that strike you as more typical of later Rich? If so, choose one and show how it is characteristic of Rich's later ideas and strategies.)

# 11

## LITERARY TRADITION AS CONTEXT

The more poetry you read, the better a reader of poetry you are likely to be. This is not just because your skills will improve and develop, but also because you will come to know more about poetic traditions and can thus understand more fully how poets draw upon each other. Poets are conscious of other poets, and often they refer to each other's work or use it as a starting point for their own in ways that may not be immediately obvious to an outsider. Poetry can be thought of as a form of argument: poets agree or disagree over basic matters. Sometimes a quiet (or even noisy) competitiveness is at the bottom of their concern with what other poems have done or can do; at other times, playfulness and a sense of humor about poetic possibilities take over, and the competitiveness dwindles to fun and poetic games. And often poets want to tap the rich mine of artistic expression in order to share in the bounty of our heritage. In any case, a poet's consciousness of what others have done leads to a sense of tradition that is often hard to articulate but nevertheless is very important to the effects of poetry—and this sense of tradition is something of a problem for a relatively new reader of poetry. How can I possibly read this poem intelligently, we are likely to ask sometimes in exasperation, until I've read all the other poems ever written? It's a real problem. Poets don't actually expect that all of their readers have Ph.D.'s in literature, but sometimes it *seems* as if they do. For some poets—John Milton, T. S. Eliot, and Richard Wilbur are examples—it does help if one has read practically everything imaginable.

Why are poets so dependent on each other? What is the point of their relentless consciousness of what has already been done by others? Why do they repeatedly answer, allude to, and echo other poems? Why is tradition so important to them?

A sense of common task, a kind of communality of purpose, accounts for some traditional poetic practice, and the competitive desire of individual poets to achieve a place in the English and American poetic tradition accounts for more. Many poets are anxious to be counted among those who achieve, through their writing, a place in history; and a way of establishing that place is to define for oneself the relationship between one's own work and that of others whose place is already secure. There is, for many poets, an awareness of a serious and abiding cultural tradition that they wish to share and pass on; but also important is a shared sense of playfulness, a kind of poetic gamesmanship. Making words dance on the page or in

> *The truest poetry is the most feigning.*
>
> —WILLIAM SHAKESPEARE

our heads provides in itself a satisfaction and delight for many writers—pride in craft that is like the pride of a painter or potter or tennis player. Often poets set themselves a particular task to see what they can do. One way of doing that is to introduce a standard traditional **motif** (a recurrent device, formula, or situation that deliberately connects a poem with common patterns of existing thought), and then to play variations on it much as a musician might do. Another way is to provide an alternative answer to a question that has repeatedly been asked and answered in a traditional way. Poetic playfulness by no means excludes serious intention—the poems in this chapter often make important statements about their subject, however humorous they may be in their method. Some teasing of the tradition and of other poets is pure fun, a kind of kidding among good friends; some is harsher and represents an attempt to see the world very differently—to define and articulate a very different set of attitudes and values.

The Anglophone poetic tradition is a rich and varied heritage, and individual poets draw upon it in countless ways. You have probably noticed, in the poems you have read so far, a number of allusions, glances at the tradition or at individual expressions of it. The more poems you read, the more you will notice and the more you will yourself become a comfortable member of the audience poets write for. Poets do expect a lot from readers—not always but often enough to make a new reader feel nervous and sometimes inadequate. The other side of that discomfort comes when you begin to notice things that other readers don't. The groups of poems in this chapter illustrate some of the ways that the tradition energizes individual poets and suggest some of the things poets like to do with their heritage.

## ECHO AND ALLUSION

The poems in this group illustrate the familiar poetic strategy of echoing or alluding to other texts as a way of importing meaning into a particular poem, similar to the strategy of "sampling" words in rap music. An **echo** may simply recall a word, phrase, or sound in another text as a way of associating what is going on in *this* poem with something in another, familiar text. The familiarity itself may sometimes be the point: writers often like to associate what they do with what has already been thought or expressed, especially if they can sound like a text that is already much admired. Echoes of Shakespeare (or other much admired writers) often have the function of implying that this new text shares concerns (and, therefore, insight or quality?) with something that has gone before. An **allusion** more insistently connects a particular word, phrase, or section of a poem with some similar formulation in a previous text; it *invokes* a previous text as a kind of gloss on this one—that is, it asks the reader to interpret this text in the light of some previous one, depending explicitly on the reader's recognition of the previous text and asking for interpretation based on the implied similarity.

Strategies of echo and allusion can be very complicated, for the question of just how much of one text can carry over—or be forcibly brought over—into another one cannot be answered categorically.

Often poets quote—or echo with variations—a passage from another text in order to suggest some thematic, ideological, tonal, or other link. Sometimes the purpose is simply to invoke an idea or attitude from another text, another place, or another culture. Thus, in Rich's "Two Songs" (page 173) Chaucer's familiar formulation of the rites of spring (with its description of all things coming to life, their vital juices flowing, as they follow the natural progress of the seasons) is introduced into the text to suggest the way the sap rises and bodies merge in ordinary lusty human beings. The speaker's attraction to a lover is thus put into a larger human perspective, and her sense of herself as a subject and object of lust comes to seem ordinary, part of the natural course of events.

The first poem in "Echo and Allusion" belongs, uncomfortably, in the *carpe diem* ("seize the day") tradition; but unlike ordinary *carpe diem* poems, it is moralistic. It undercuts the speaker by having him allude to familiar biblical passages that imply a condemnation of live-for-today attitudes and ideas. By echoing Satan's tempting addresses to Eve in Genesis, the speaker in Jonson's "Come, My Celia" condemns himself in the eyes of readers and becomes a seducer-tempter instead of a libertine-hero. The other poems here variously recall individual lines, passages, poems, ideas, or traditions in order to establish a particular stance or develop a position or attitude. The meaning of each poem derives primarily from a sorting through of the allusion.

Poems do not necessarily need earlier texts to exist or have meaning, but prior texts may set up what happens in a particular poem or govern how it is to be construed. Allusion is the strategy of using one text to comment on—and influence the interpretation of—another. It is one of the most popular, familiar, and frequent strategies that poets use.

## BEN JONSON

## *Come, My Celia*[1]

Come, my Celia, let us prove,[2]
While we can, the sports of love;
Time will not be ours forever:
He at length our good will sever.
5    Spend not, then, his gifts in vain;
Suns that set may rise again,
But if once we lose this light,
'Tis with us perpetual night.
Why should we defer our joys?
10   Fame and rumor are but toys.
Cannot we delude the eyes
Of a few poor household spies?
Or his easier ears beguile,
Thus removéd by our wile?
15   'Tis no sin love's fruits to steal,
But the sweet thefts to reveal;
To be taken, to be seen,
These have crimes accounted been.                    1606

---

1. A song from *Volpone*, sung by the play's villain and would-be seducer. Part of the poem paraphrases *Catullus* V.      2. Try.

WILLIAM BLAKE

## The Lamb

Little Lamb, who made thee?
Dost thou know who made thee?
Gave thee life, and bid thee feed
By the stream and o'er the mead;
Gave thee clothing of delight,                                      5
Softest clothing woolly bright;
Gave thee such a tender voice,
Making all the vales rejoice?
   Little Lamb, who made thee?
   Dost thou know who made thee?                         10

Little Lamb, I'll tell thee!
Little Lamb, I'll tell thee:
He is callèd by thy name,
For he calls himself a Lamb,
He is meek and he is mild;                                          15
He became a little child.
I a child and thou a lamb,
We are callèd by his name.
   Little Lamb, God bless thee!
   Little Lamb, God bless thee!                          20

1789

HOWARD NEMEROV

## Boom!

### Sees Boom in Religion, too

*Atlantic City, June 23, 1957* (AP).—*President Eisenhower's pastor said tonight that Americans are living in a period of "unprecedented religious activity" caused partially by paid vacations, the eight-hour day and modern conveniences.*

*"These fruits of material progress," said the Rev. Edward L. R. Elson of the National Presbyterian Church, Washington, "have provided the leisure, the energy, and the means for a level of human and spiritual values never before reached."*

Here at the Vespasian-Carlton,[3] it's just one
religious activity after another; the sky

---

3. Vespasian was emperor of Rome 70–79, shortly after the reign of Nero. In French, *vespasienne* means "public toilet."

is constantly being crossed by cruciform
airplanes, in which nobody disbelieves
5  for a second and the tide, the tide
of spiritual progress and prosperity
miraculously keeps rising, to a level
never before attained. The churches are full,
the beaches are full, and the filling-stations
10  are full, God's great ocean is full
of paid vacationers praying an eight-hour day
to the human and spiritual values, the fruits,
the leisure, the energy, and the means, Lord,
the means for the level, the unprecedented level,
15  and the modern conveniences, which also are full.
Never before, O Lord, have the prayers and praises
from belfry and phonebooth, from ballpark and barbecue
the sacrifices, so endlessly ascended.

It was not thus when Job in Palestine
20  sat in the dust and cried, cried bitterly;[4]
when Damien kissed the lepers on their wounds
it was not thus;[5] it was not thus
when Francis worked a fourteen-hour day
strictly for the birds;[6] when Dante took
25  a week's vacation without pay and it rained
part of the time,[7] O Lord, it was not thus.

But now the gears mesh and the tires burn
and the ice chatters in the shaker and the priest
in the pulpit and Thy Name, O Lord,
30  is kept before the public, while the fruits
ripen and religion booms and the level rises
and every modern convenience runneth over,
that it may never be with us as it hath been
with Athens and Karnak and Nagasaki,[8]
35  nor Thy sun for one instant refrain from shining
on the rainbow Buick by the breezeway
or the Chris Craft with the uplift life raft;
that we may continue to be the just folks we are,
plain people with ordinary superliners and

4. According to the Book of Job, he was afflicted with the loss of prosperity, children, and health as a test of his faith. His name means, in Hebrew, "he cries"; see especially Job 2:7–13.    5. "Father Damien" (Joseph Damien de Veuster, 1840–1889), a Roman Catholic missionary from Belgium, was known for his work among lepers in Hawaii; he ultimately contracted leprosy himself and died there.    6. St. Francis of Assisi, thirteenth-century founder of the Franciscan order, was noted for his love of all living things, and one of the most famous stories about him tells of his preaching to the birds. *Strictly for the birds*: a mid-twentieth-century expression for worthless or unfashionable activity.    7. Dante's journey through Hell, Purgatory, and Paradise (in *The Divine Comedy*) takes a week, beginning on Good Friday, 1300. It rains in the third chasm of Hell.    8. Athens, the cultural center of ancient Greek civilization; Karnak, a village on the Nile, built on the site of ancient Thebes; Nagasaki, a large Japanese port city, virtually destroyed by a U.S. atomic bomb in 1945.

disposable diaperliners, people of the stop'n'shop                40
'n'pray as you go, of hotel, motel, boatel,
the humble pilgrims of no deposit no return
and please adjust thy clothing, who will give to Thee,
if Thee will keep us going, our annual
Miss Universe, for Thy Name's Sake, Amen.                         45

1960


MARIANNE MOORE

## Love in America?

Whatever it is, it's a passion—
a benign dementia that should be
engulfing America, fed in a way
   the opposite of the way
in which the Minotaur[9] was fed.                                 5
It's a Midas[1] of tenderness;
   from the heart;
nothing else. From one with ability
to bear being misunderstood—
   take the blame, with "nobility                  10
   that is action,"[2] identifying itself with
· pioneer unperfunctoriness

without brazenness[3] or
bigness of overgrown
undergrown shallowness.                                           15


Whatever it is, let it be without
   affection.

Yes, yes, yes, *yes*.                                             1967


9. "The Minotaur demanded a virgin to devour once a year." (MM)      1. "Midas, who had the golden
touch, was inconvenienced when eating or picking things up." (MM)    2. "Unamuno said that what
we need as a cure for unruly youth is 'nobility that is action.' " (MM)    3. "*without brazenness or bigness*
. . . Winston Churchill: 'Modesty becomes a man.' " (MM)

ROBERT HOLLANDER

# *You Too? Me Too—Why Not? Soda Pop*

                    I am
                    look
                    ing at
                    the Co
5                   caCola
                    bottle
                    which is
                    green wi
                    th ridges
10                  just–like

          c       c       c
          o       o       o
          l       l       l
          u       u       u
15        m       m       m
          n       n       n
          s       s       s
               and on itself it says

                    COCA-COLA
20                  reg.u.s.pat.off.

          exactly  like  an  art  pop
          statue  of  that  kind  of
          bottle  but  not  so  green
          that   the   juice   inside
25        gives other than the co-
          lor it has when I pour
          it  out  in  a  clear  glass
          glass  on  this  table  top
          (It's  making  me  thirsty
30        all   this   winking   and
          beading  of  Hippocrene
          please let me pause drink-
          ing     the     fluid     in)
          ah! it is enticing how each
35        color    is    the    same
          brown  in  green  bottle
          brown  in  uplifted  glass
          making  each  utensil  on
          the  table  laid  a  brown
40        fork  in  a  brown  shade
          making me long to watch
          them harvesting the crop
          which makes the deep-aged
          rich brown wine of America
45        that  is  to  say  which  makes
          soda                    pop                    p. 1968

DANNIE ABSE

## Brueghel in Naples

*About suffering they were never wrong,*
*The Old Masters . . .*

—W. H. AUDEN

Ovid would never have guessed how far
and father's notion about wax melting, bah!
It's ice up there. Freezing.
Soaring and swooping over solitary altitudes
I was breezing along (a record I should think)          5
when my wings began to moult not melt.
These days, workmanship, I ask you.
Appalling.

There's a mountain down there on fire
and I'm falling, falling away from it.                    10
Phew, the sun's on the horizon
or am I upside down?

Great Bacchus, the sea is rearing
up. Will I drown? My white legs
the last to disappear? (I have no trousers on)            15
A little to the left the ploughman,
a little to the right a galleon,
a sailor climbing the rigging,
a fisherman casting his line,
and now I hear a shepherd's dog barking.                  20
I'm that near.

Lest I have no trace
but a few scattered feathers on the water
show me your face, sailor,
look up, fisherman,                                       25
look this way, shepherd,
turn around, ploughman.
Raise the alarm! Launch a boat!

My luck. I'm seen
only by a jackass of an artist                            30
interested in composition, in the green
tinge of the sea, in the aesthetics
of disaster—not in me.

I drown, bubble by bubble,
(Help, Save me!)                                          35
while he stands ruthlessly
before the canvas, busy busy,
intent on becoming an Old Master.                         1991

WILLIAM SHAKESPEARE

# [Not marble, nor the gilded monuments]

Not marble, nor the gilded monuments
Of princes, shall outlive this powerful rhyme;
But you shall shine more bright in these conténts
Than unswept stone, besmeared with sluttish time.
5    When wasteful war shall statues overturn,
And broils root out the work of masonry,
Nor Mars his sword nor war's quick fire shall burn
The living record of your memory.
'Gainst death and all-oblivious enmity
10   Shall you pace forth; your praise shall still find room
Even in the eyes of all posterity
That wear this world out to the ending doom.[4]
So, till the judgment that yourself arise,
You live in this, and dwell in lovers' eyes.

1609

4. Judgment Day.

# POETIC "KINDS"

There are all sorts of poems. By now you have experienced poems on a variety of subjects and with all kinds of tones—short poems, long poems, poems that rhyme and poems that don't. And there are, of course, many other sorts of poems that we haven't looked at. Some poems, for example, are thousands of lines long and differ substantially from the poems that can be included in a book like this.

Poems may be classified in a variety of ways—by subject, topic, or theme; by their length, appearance, and formal features; by the way they are organized; by the level of language they use; by the poet's intention and what kinds of effects the poem tries to generate.

Classification may be, of course, simply an intellectual exercise. Recognizing a poem that is, for example, an elegy (like *Lycidas* [page 558]), a parody, or a satire, may be very much like the satisfaction involved in recognizing a scarlet tanager, a weeping willow, a French phrase, or a 1967 Ford Thunderbird. Just *knowing* what others don't know may give us a sense of importance, accomplishment, and power. But there are also *uses* for classification: we can experience a poem more fully if we understand early on exactly what kind of poem we are dealing with. A fuller response is possible because the poet has consciously chosen to play by certain defined rules, and the **conventions** he or she employs indicate certain standard ways of saying things to achieve certain expected effects. The **tradition** that is involved in a particular poetic kind is thus employed by the poet in order to produce predictable standard responses. For example, much of the humor and fun in the following poem is premised on the assumption that readers will recognize the *kind* of poem they are reading.

## CHRISTOPHER MARLOWE

# *The Passionate Shepherd to His Love*

Come live with me and be my love,
And we will all the pleasures prove[5]
That valleys, groves, hills, and fields,
Woods, or steepy mountain yields.

And we will sit upon the rocks,                    5
Seeing the shepherds feed their flocks,
By shallow rivers to whose falls
Melodious birds sing madrigals.

And I will make thee beds of roses
And a thousand fragrant posies,                    10
A cap of flowers, and a kirtle[6]
Embroidered all with leaves of myrtle;

5. Try.    6. Grown.

A gown made of the finest wool
Which from our pretty lambs we pull;
15  Fair lined slippers for the cold,
With buckles of the purest gold;

A belt of straw and ivy buds,
With coral clasps and amber studs:
And if these pleasures may thee move,
20  Come live with me, and be my love.

The shepherd swains[7] shall dance and sing
For thy delight each May morning:
If these delights thy mind may move,
Then live with me and be my love.                    1600

A beginning reader of poetry might easily protest that a plea such as this one is unrealistic and fanciful, and thus feel unsure of the poem's tone. What could such a reader think of a speaker who constructs his argument in such a dreamlike way? But the traditions behind the poem and the conventions of the poetic kind make its intention and effects clear. "The Passionate Shepherd to His Love" is a **pastoral poem,** a poetic kind that concerns itself with the simple life of country folk and describes that life in stylized, idealized terms. The people in a pastoral poem are usually (as here) shepherds, although they may be fishermen or other rustics who lead an outdoor life and are involved in tending to basic human needs in a simplified society; the world of the poem is one of simplicity, beauty, music, and love. The world always seems timeless in pastoral; people are eternally young, and the season is always spring, usually May. Nature seems endlessly green and the future entirely golden. Difficulty, frustration, disappointment, and obligation do not belong in this world at all; it is blissfully free of problems. Shepherds sing instead of tending sheep, and they make love and play music instead of having to watch out for wolves in the night. If only the shepherd boy and shepherd girl can agree with each other to make love joyously and passionately, they will live happily ever after. The language of pastoral is informal and fairly simple, although always a bit more sophisticated than that of real shepherds with real problems and real sheep.

Unrealistic? Of course. No real shepherd gets to spend even a single day like that, and certainly the world of simple country folk includes ferocities of nature, human falsehood and knavery, disease, bad weather, old age, moments that are not all green and gold. And probably no poet ever thought that shepherds really live that way, but it is an attractive fantasy, and poets who write pastoral simply choose one formulaic way to isolate a series of idealized moments. Fantasies can be personal and private, of course, but there is also a certain pleasure in shared public fantasies, and one central moment is that point in a love relationship when two people are contemplating the joys of ecstatic love. The vision here is self-consciously constructed by poets in order to present a certain tone, attitude, and wholeness; it is a world that is self-existent, self-contained, and self-referential.

It can be lovely to contemplate a world in which the birds sing only for our delight and other shepherds take care of the sheep, a world in which there is no work that does

7. Youths.

not turn into magic and in which the lambs bring themselves to us so that we can transform their wool instantly into a beautiful gown. It is also fun to "answer" such a vision. The next subsection of this chapter contains three poems that directly "answer" Marlowe's poem and thus offer a kind of critique of the pastoral vision. But in a sense no critique is necessary; the pastoral poet builds an awareness of artificiality into the whole idea of the poem. It is conceived in full consciousness that its fantasy avoids implication, and in filtering that implication carefully out of the poem, poets implicitly provide their own criticism of the fantasy world. Satire is, in a sense, the other side of the pastoral world—a city poet who fantasizes about being a shepherd usually knows all about dirt and grime and human failure and urban corruption—and satire and pastoral are often seen as complementary poetic kinds.

Several other poetic kinds are exemplified in this book; each has its own characteristics and conventions that have become established by tradition, repetition, and habit.

| epic | from *Paradise Lost* | p. 162 |
|---|---|---|
| pastoral | "The Passionate Shepherd to His Love" | p. 371 |
| elegy | *Lycidas* | p. 558 |
| lyric | "The Lamb" | p. 365 |
| ballad | "Sir Patrick Spens" | p. 237 |
| protest poem | "Hard Rock Returns . . . " | p. 38 |
| aubade | "The Sun Rising" | p. 111 |
| confessional poem | "Skunk Hour" | p. 553 |
| meditation | "Love Calls Us to the Things of This World" | p. 492 |
| dramatic monologue | "My Last Duchess" | p. 432 |
| soliloquy | "Soliloquy of the Spanish Cloister" | p. 70 |

You will find definitions and brief descriptions of these poetic kinds in the glossary. Each of these established kinds is worthy of detailed discussion and study, and your teacher may want to examine how the conventions of several different kinds work. Here, we have chosen to examine in depth two particular poetic kinds, the **epigram** and the **haiku,** by including several poems that typify these kinds.

## THE EPIGRAM

Following are several epigrams that together add up almost to a definition of that poetic kind. Like most poetic kinds, the epigram has a history that has shaped its form and content. Originally, an epigram was an inscription upon, or an engraving in, some object such as a monument, triumphal arch, tombstone, or gate; hence brevity and conciseness were absolutely necessary. But over a period of time, the term "epigram" came to mean a short, witty poem that tried to attract concentrated attention in the same way that an inscription attracts the eyes of passersby.

As the poems here suggest, epigrams have been popular over a long period of time. The modern tradition of epigrams has two more or less separate ancient sources, one in Greece, one in Rome. In classical Greece, epigrams were composed over a period of two thousand years; the earliest surviving ones date from the eighth century B.C. Apparently there were several anthologies of epigrams in early times, and fragments of these anthologies were later preserved, especially in large collections like the so-called *Greek Anthology,* which dates from the tenth century A.D. Mostly short inscriptions, these epigrams also included some love poems (including many on homosexual love), comments on life and morality, riddles, and so forth. The father of the Roman tradition is generally agreed to be Martial (Marcus Valerius Martialis, A.D. 40?–104?), whose epigrams are witty and satirical. Modern epigrams have more frequently followed Martial's lead, but occasionally the distinctive influence of the older Greek tradition can be seen.

## SAMUEL TAYLOR COLERIDGE

## *What Is an Epigram?*

What is an epigram? a dwarfish whole,
Its body brevity, and wit its soul.

                                                                    p. 1802

## BEN JONSON

## *Epitaph on Elizabeth, L. H.*

Wouldst thou hear what man can say
In a little? Reader, stay.
Underneath this stone doth lie
As much beauty as could die;
5    Which in life did harbor give
To more virtue than doth live.
If at all she had a fault,
Leave it buried in this vault.
One name was Elizabeth;
10    Th' other, let it sleep with death:
Fitter, where it died, to tell,
Than that it lived at all. Farewell.

                                                                    1616

## MARTIAL

## *[You've told me, Maro, whilst you live]*[8]

You've told me, Maro, whilst you live
You'd not a single penny give,
But that whene'er you chanced to die,
You'd leave a handsome legacy;

---

8. Translated from the Latin by F. Lewis.

You must be mad beyond redress,                                                 5
If my next wish you cannot guess.

ca. 100


## DOROTHY PARKER

## *Comment*

Oh, life is a glorious cycle of song,
A medley of extemporanea;
And love is a thing that can never go wrong;
And I am Marie of Rumania.                                                      1926


## JOHN GAY

## *My Own Epitaph*

Life is a jest; and all things show it.
I thought so once; but now I know it.                                           1720


## RICHARD CRASHAW

## *An Epitaph upon a Young Married Couple, Dead and Buried Together*

To these, whom death again did wed,
This grave's their second marriage-bed.
For though the hand of fate could force
'Twixt soul and body a divorce,
It could not sunder man and wife                                                5
'Cause they both livéd but one life.
Peace, good reader. Do not weep.
Peace, the lovers are asleep.
They, sweet turtles,⁹ folded lie
In the last knot love could tie.                                                10
And though they lie as they were dead,

9. Turtledoves.

Their pillow stone, their sheets of lead,
(Pillow hard, and sheets not warm)
Love made the bed; they'll take no harm;
15   Let them sleep, let them sleep on.
Till this stormy night be gone,
Till th' eternal morrow dawn;
Then the curtains will be drawn
And they wake into a light,
20   Whose day shall never die in night.                    1646


X. J. KENNEDY

## Epitaph for a Postal Clerk

Here lies wrapped up tight in sod
Henry Harkins c/o God.
On the day of Resurrection
May be opened for inspection.                               1961


COUNTEE CULLEN

## For a Lady I Know

She even thinks that up in heaven
Her class lies late and snores,
While poor black cherubs rise at seven
To do celestial chores.                                     1925


MARY BARBER

## To Novella, *on her saying deridingly, that a Lady of great Merit, and fine Address, was bred in the* Old Way.

An EPIGRAM:

YOU cry, *She's bred in the Old Way;*
    Then into Laughter fall:
Were she as just to you, she'd say,
    *You are not bred at all.*                              1734

PETER PINDAR

# Epigram

Midas, they say, possessed the art of old
Of turning whatsoe'er he touched to gold;
This modern statesmen can reverse with ease—
Touch *them* with gold, *they'll turn to what you please.*

ca. 1780


EDNA ST. VINCENT MILLAY

# First Fig

My candle burns at both ends;
    It will not last the night;
But ah, my foes, and oh, my friends—
    It gives a lovely light!

1920

## HAIKU

A second poetic kind that, because of its conciseness and brevity, may be readily illustrated by several examples is the *haiku*. Like the epigram, the haiku is an import into the English poetic tradition, and it, too, has a long history in its original-language tradition, Japanese. Originally, the haiku (then called *hokku*) was a short section of a longer poem (called a *renga* or *haikai*) composed by several poets who wrote segments in response to one another in a long, cumulative poetic exercise or game. But early on, at least as early as the seventeenth century, the distinctive subject matter and mode of the haiku, together with the creative discipline required by its formal demands, made it an attractive form in itself, and several major poets built their reputations largely on the basis of their skill in the form.

Traditionally, the Japanese haiku was an unrhymed poem consisting of seventeen sounds—or, rather, characters representing seventeen sounds—and distributed over three lines in a five, seven, five pattern—that is, five distinctive sounds in the first line, seven in the second, and five in the third. "Sounds" in the Japanese language are not exactly the same as "syllables" in English, but there is a rough parallel—close enough so that when English writers began to write haiku about a century ago, they ordinarily translated the sound requirement into syllables. Here, for example, is a haiku (in translation) that conforms in its Japanese original to the standard formal definition:

### CHIYOJO

## [*Whether astringent*][1]

Whether astringent
I do not know. This is my first
Persimmon picking.

The ideal of conciseness and compression is just as important to the haiku as it is to the epigram, but the haiku's aim and effects are quite different. The epigram privileges verbal wit, clear intellectual distinctions, contrasts based on parallels, and pointed judgments that sometimes sting, and it often makes a comic or satirical statement at the expense of someone. An epigram can be quite biting, harsh, or even mean-spirited in achieving a compressed statement of something definite, explicit, and definable. Haiku poems, on the other hand, are suggestive and leave a lot unsaid; they imply connections and relationships but seldom make them explicit. Typically, a haiku describes a natural object—a flower, say, or an animal, or a place—and implies a relationship between a perception of that object and some human feeling or state of mind. Haiku thus depend heavily on emotive language, and they try to be suggestive rather than definitive, to

---

1. Translation by Daniel C. Buchanan (1973). Chiyojo (1703–1775) is probably the most famous Japanese woman haiku poet. Tradition has it that this poem was written at the time of (and about) her engagement.

imply rather than state causes or relationships. Haiku involve not so much conclusions or summaries or closures as openings up; they try to alert the mind to possibility, rather than finding a neat answer: they are suggestive rather than conclusive. Some commentators think of the epigram as a kind of brief summary of Western poetic values (involving reason, certainty, intellection, egotism, closure, and cleverness), and the haiku as embodying Eastern values (openness, emotion, intuition, and associational or extralogical connections), although such generalizations are a bit too neat and easy.

Three other characteristics of haiku are also crucial to its history and to the expectations of readers—perhaps even more important than the formal expectation of a certain number of lines and sounds. One is the so-called "seasonal" requirement—the tradition that each poem associates itself specifically with one of the four seasons of the year so that the poem is "dated" in relation to a sense of predictable, revolving, patterned change. The seasonal association is often quite subtle and indirect, through (for example) a flower or event or condition traditionally associated with a particular season. The second involves natural description—that is, description of nature—more generally; a haiku poem often begins with the observation of a specific natural phenomenon—a plant or animal or aspect of landscape—which is then often connected, explicitly or implicitly, with a human emotion or feeling. The use of nature in haiku develops out of a strong Buddhist sense of nature as orderly and benign but also contingent and transient. Human beings are a part of that unified nature, and thus it is easy to conceive scenes or objects in nature as reflections of (or as associated with) human feelings. Haiku adapted into other languages and cultures cannot, of course, draw on the same religious assumptions or world view, but most haiku strive to retain a sense of the human and natural as being mutually reflective and mutually interdependent. The third characteristic involves the way the connection is made between the "natural" and the human, something that usually involves observation and an imaginative connection that amounts to a larger claim, something almost visionary. Haiku often blur the usual Western distinction between seeing something literally and having some larger sense or "vision" of its end or meaning, though in haiku a specific claim to larger perspective is seldom articulated explicitly.

Some of the traditional "masters" of haiku from the seventeenth to the early twentieth century—Basho⁻, Issa, and Buson, for example—are illustrated (in English translations) in the examples that follow. But haiku has now become an international form, and during the last half century or so there have been conscious, concentrated attempts to create a haiku tradition in a great variety of languages around the world: haiku poems have now been written in at least fifty languages. The habits and traditions of different languages and literatures have necessarily influenced and modified the way haiku poems are written, something that might offend some traditional masters of haiku, just as it would amuse others to see their work so readily but loosely adapted. The seventeen-syllable and three-line requirements, for example, are not always observed by later poets or by translators of even classic verses. As in any other poetic kind, the conventions are both demanding and adaptable to the particular needs of different situations, different languages, and different individual poets. (If you become interested in writing haiku yourself, you may wish to consult some of the guides written for just this purpose—for example, *The Haiku Handbook* by William J. Higginson with Penny Harter [1985].)

BASHŌ

# [A village without bells—][2]

A village without bells—
how do they live?
spring dusk.

# [This road—]

This road—
no one goes down it,
autumn evening.

# [First snow]

First snow
falling
on the half-finished bridge.

# [Another year gone—]

Another year gone—
hat in my hand,
sandals on my feet.

BUSON

# [Coolness—][3]

Coolness—
the sound of the bell
as it leaves the bell.

---

2. Matsuo Bashō (1644–1694) is usually considered the first great master poet of haiku. This and the following Bashō poems are all translations by Robert Hass.   3. Yosa Buson (1716–1783). This and the following Buson poem are translations by Robert Hass.

# [*Listening to the moon*]

Listening to the moon,
gazing at the croaking of frogs
in a field of ripe rice.

ISSA

# [*The moon and the flowers*][4]

The moon and the flowers,
forty-nine years,
walking around, wasting time.

# [*The snail gets up*]

The snail gets up
and goes to bed
with very little fuss.

# [*Insects on a bough*]

Insects on a bough
floating downriver,
still singing.

# [*As I grow older*]

As I grow older,
Even the much longer days
Bring plentiful tears.

4. Kobayashi Issa (1763–1827). This and the two following poems by Issa are translations by Robert Hass. The final Issa poem ("As I grow older") is a translation by Daniel C. Buchanan.

## SEIFŪ

# [The faces of dolls][5]

The faces of dolls.
In unavoidable ways
I must have grown old.

## CHIYOJO

# [Bearing no flowers][6]

Bearing no flowers,
I am free to toss madly
Like the willow tree.

## HASHIN

# [No sky and no earth][7]

No sky and no earth
At all. Only the snowflakes
Fall incessantly.

## ONITSURA

# [Come! Come! Though I call][8]

Come! Come! Though I call
The fireflies are quite heedless
And go flitting by.

5. Seifū (1650–1721) was a nun. Translation by Daniel C. Buchanan.   6. Translation by Daniel C. Buchanan.   7. Hashin (1864–?). Translation by Daniel C. Buchanan.   8. Onitsura (1661–1738) was a monk. Translation by Daniel C. Buchanan.

Perhaps the single most famous haiku poem is by Bashō. Here are six different trans-lations into English of that poem. (For an even greater variety of examples, consult Hiroaki Sato, *One Hundred Frogs* [New York and Tokyo: Weatherhill, 1983], from which these examples are selected.)

### LAFCADIO HEARN

## [*Old pond— . . .* ]

Old pond—frogs jumped in—sound of water.                    1898

### CLARA A. WALSH

## [*An old-time pond, from off whose shadowed depth*]

An old-time pond, from off whose shadowed depth
Is heard the splash where some lithe frog leaps in.          1910

### JOHN THOMAS BRYAN

## [*There is the old pond!*]

There is the old pond!
   Lo, into it jumps a frog:
hark, water's music!                                         1929

### R. H. BLYTH

## [*The old pond*]

The old pond.
   A frog jumps in—
      Plop!                                                  1949

EARL MINER

## [*The still old pond*]

The still old pond
and as a frog leaps in it
the sound of a splash.                                    1979


ALLEN GINSBERG

## [*The old pond— . . .*]

The old pond—a frog jumps in, kerplunk!                  1979


The following haiku poems were all written in English:


BABETTE DEUTSCH

## [*The falling flower*]⁹

The falling flower
I saw drift back to the branch
Was a butterfly.                                          1957


J. W. HACKETT

## [*Up close, at the place*]

Up close, at the place
    where spider's leg lays his line,
        there seems no design.                           1968


9. An adaptation of a sixteenth-century poem by Arakida Moritake (1473–1549).

ETHERIDGE KNIGHT

## [*Eastern guard tower*]

Eastern guard tower
glints in sunset; convicts rest
like lizards on rocks.                                              1960


ALLEN GINSBERG

## [*Looking over my shoulder*]

Looking over my shoulder
my behind was covered
with cherry blossoms.                                              1955


RICHARD WRIGHT

## [*In the falling snow*]

In the falling snow
A laughing boy holds out his palms
Until they are white.                                              1960


Knowing what to do with a poem often is aided by knowing what it is or what it means to be. Many modern poems are not consciously conceived in terms of a traditional kind, and not all older poems are either, but a knowledge of kind can often provide one more way of deciding what to look for in a poem, helping one to find the right questions to ask.

## IMITATING AND ANSWERING

Poems often respond directly—sometimes point by point or even line by line or word by word—to another poem. Often the point is teasing or comic, but often, too, there is a real issue behind the idea of such a facetious answer, a serious criticism perhaps of the poem's point or the tradition it represents, or sometimes an attempt to provide a different way of looking at the issue. Sometimes poems follow their models slavishly in order to emphasize their likeness; sometimes key words or details are substituted so that readers will easily notice the differences in tone or attitude.

Often these poems seem self-conscious—as if the poets are aware of the tradition they share and are each trying to do something a little bit different. However "sincere" these poems may be, their sense of play is equally important. The first three poems playfully pick on Marlowe's "The Passionate Shepherd to His Love" (page 371). In effect, all of them provide "answers" to that poem. It is as if his "love" were telling the shepherd what is the matter with his argument, and the poets are answering Marlowe, too. These poets know full well what Marlowe was doing in the fantasy of his original poem, and they clearly have a lot of fun telling him how people in various circumstances might feel about his fantasy. There is in the end a lot of joy in their "realistic" deflation of his magic and not much hostility. The poems by Koch, Skirrow, Hecht, and Cope poke gentle fun at other famous works, offering a summary or another version of what might have happened in each (see, respectively, Williams's "This Is Just to Say" [page 593], Keats's "Ode on a Grecian Urn" [page 323], Arnold's "Dover Beach" [page 104], and Shakespeare's "Not marble, nor the gilded monuments" [page 370]).

A **parody** is a poem that imitates another poem closely but changes details for a comic or critical effect. Strictly speaking, only two of the poems that follow (those by Koch and Cope) are parodies—that is, they pretend to write in the style of the original poem but comically exaggerate that style and change the content. The others make fun of an original in less direct phraseological ways, but they share a similar objective of answering an original, even though they use very different styles to alter totally the poetic intention of that original. Skirrow's "Ode on a Grecian Urn Summarized" teases Keats as well as the whole notion of poetic summaries; the effects of the summary are not very much like those of the Keats poem. Hecht's "The Dover Bitch," on the other hand, is as its subtitle suggests much more than just a different perspective on the situation presented in Arnold's "Dover Beach"; it uses the tradition to criticize art and life.

All these poems offer a revised version of what reality may be like. Poems like these may have a serious purpose, but their method is comic and usually light. And fun is not always easy to explain intellectually or to demonstrate.

SIR WALTER RALEGH

## *The Nymph's Reply to the Shepherd*

If all the world and love were young,
And truth in every shepherd's tongue,

These pretty pleasures might me move
To live with thee and be thy love.

Time drives the flocks from field to fold,                                    5
When rivers rage, and rocks grow cold,
And Philomel[1] becometh dumb;
The rest complain of cares to come.

The flowers do fade, and wanton fields
To wayward winter reckoning yields:                                          10
A honey tongue, a heart of gall,
Is fancy's spring, but sorrow's fall.

Thy gowns, thy shoes, thy beds of roses,
Thy cap, thy kirtle, and thy posies
Soon break, soon wither, soon forgotten;                                     15
In folly ripe, in reason rotten.

Thy belt of straw and ivy buds,
Thy coral clasps and amber studs,
All these in me no means can move
To come to thee and be thy love.                                             20

But could youth last, and love still breed,
Had joys no date,[2] nor age no need,
Then these delights my mind might move
To live with thee and be thy love.                                         1600

## WILLIAM CARLOS WILLIAMS

# *Raleigh Was Right*

We cannot go to the country
for the country will bring us no peace
What can the small violets tell us
that grow on furry stems in
the long grass among lance shaped leaves?                                     5

Though you praise us
and call to mind the poets
who sung of our loveliness
it was long ago!
long ago! when country people                                                10
would plow and sow with
flowering minds and pockets at ease—
if ever this were true.

1. The nightingale.    2. End.

Not now. Love itself a flower
with roots in a parched ground.
Empty pockets make empty heads.
Cure it if you can but
do not believe that we can live
today in the country
for the country will bring us no peace.

1941

E. E. CUMMINGS

# [(ponder,darling,these busted statues]

(ponder,darling,these busted statues
of yon motheaten forum be aware
notice what hath remained
—the stone cringes
clinging to the stone,how obsolete

lips utter their extant smile. . . .
remark

a few deleted of texture
or meaning monuments and dolls

resist Them Greediest Paws of careful
time all of which is extremely
unimportant)whereas Life

matters if or

when the your-and my-
idle vertical worthless
self unite in a peculiarly
momentary

partnership(to instigate
constructive
                    Horizontal
business. . . . even so,let us make haste
—consider well this ruined aqueduct

lady,
which used to lead something into somewhere)

1926

PETER DE VRIES

## To His Importunate Mistress

Andrew Marvell Updated

Had we but world enough, and time,
My coyness, lady, were a crime,
But at my back I always hear
Time's wingèd chariot, striking fear.
The hour is nigh when creditors                             5
Will prove to be my predators.
As wages of our picaresque,
Bag lunches bolted at my desk
Must stand as fealty to you
For each expensive rendezvous.                             10
Obeisance at your marble feet
Deserves the best-appointed suite,
And would have, lacked I not the pelf
To pleasure also thus myself;
But aptly sumptuous amorous scenes                         15
Rule out the rake of modest means.

Since mistress presupposes wife,
It means a doubly costly life;
For fools by second passion fired
A second income is required,                               20
The earning which consumes the hours
They'd hoped to spend in rented bowers.
To hostelries the worst of fates
That weekly raise their daily rates!
I gather, lady, from your scoffing                         25
A bloke more solvent in the offing.
So revels thus to rivals go
For want of monetary flow.
How vexing that inconstant cash
The constant suitor must abash,                            30
Who with excuses vainly pled
Must rue the undishevelled bed,
And that for paltry reasons given
His conscience may remain unriven.                    p. 1986

C. DAY LEWIS

## Song

Come, live with me and be my love,
And we will all the pleasures prove
Of peace and plenty, bed and board,
That chance employment may afford.

5   I'll handle dainties on the docks
And thou shalt read of summer frocks:
At evening by the sour canals
We'll hope to hear some madrigals.

Care on thy maiden brow shall put
10   A wreath of wrinkles, and thy foot
Be shod with pain: not silken dress
But toil shall tire thy loveliness.

Hunger shall make thy modest zone
And cheat fond death of all but bone—
15   If these delights thy mind may move,
Then live with me and be my love.

1935

ALLEN GINSBERG

## A Further Proposal

Come live with me and be my love,
And we will some old pleasures prove.
Men like me have paid in verse
This costly courtesy, or curse;

5   But I would bargain with my art
(As to the mind, now to the heart),
My symbols, images, and signs
Please me more outside these lines.

For your share and recompense,
10   You will be taught another sense:
The wisdom of the subtle worm
Will turn most perfect in your form.

Not that your soul need tutored be
By intellectual decree,
15   But graces that the mind can share
Will make you, as more wise, more fair,

Till all the world's devoted thought
Find all in you it ever sought,

And even I, of skeptic mind,
A Resurrection of a kind.                                                                    20

This compliment, in my own way,
For what I would receive, I pay;
Thus all the wise have writ thereof,
And all the fair have been their love.

1947

KENNETH KOCH

# Variations on a Theme by William Carlos Williams

### 1

I chopped down the house that you had been saving to live in next
    summer.
I am sorry, but it was morning, and I had nothing to do
and its wooden beams were so inviting.

### 2

We laughed at the hollyhocks together
and then I sprayed them with lye.                                                       5
Forgive me. I simply do not know what I am doing.

### 3

I gave away the money that you had been saving to live on for the
    next ten years.
The man who asked for it was shabby
and the firm March wind on the porch was so juicy and cold.

### 4

Last evening we went dancing and I broke your leg.                         10
Forgive me. I was clumsy, and
I wanted you here in the wards, where I am the doctor!            1962

DESMOND SKIRROW

## Ode on a Grecian Urn Summarized

Gods chase
Round vase.
What say?
What play?
5    Don't know.
Nice, though.

p. 1960

ANTHONY HECHT

## The Dover Bitch

### A Criticism of Life

*for Andrews Wanning*

So there stood Matthew Arnold and this girl
With the cliffs of England crumbling away behind them,
And he said to her, "Try to be true to me,
And I'll do the same for you, for things are bad
5    All over, etc., etc."
Well now, I knew this girl. It's true she had read
Sophocles in a fairly good translation
And caught that bitter allusion to the sea,[3]
But all the time he was talking she had in mind
10   The notion of what his whiskers would feel like
On the back of her neck. She told me later on
That after a while she got to looking out
At the lights across the channel, and really felt sad,
Thinking of all the wine and enormous beds
15   And blandishments in French and the perfumes.
And then she got really angry. To have been brought
All the way down from London, and then be addressed
As a sort of mournful cosmic last resort
Is really tough on a girl, and she was pretty.
20   Anyway, she watched him pace the room
And finger his watch-chain and seem to sweat a bit,
And then she said one or two unprintable things.
But you mustn't judge her by that. What I mean to say is,
She's really all right. I still see her once in a while
25   And she always treats me right. We have a drink

---

3. In Sophocles' *Antigone*, lines 583–91. See "Dover Beach," lines 9–18.

And I give her a good time, and perhaps it's a year
Before I see her again, but there she is,
Running to fat, but dependable as they come.
And sometimes I bring her a bottle of *Nuit d'Amour*.                    1968


WENDY COPE

# [*Not only marble, but the plastic toys*]

Not only marble, but the plastic toys
From cornflake packets will outlive this rhyme:
I can't immortalize you, love—our joys
Will lie unnoticed in the vault of time.
When Mrs Thatcher has been cast in bronze                    5
And her administration is a page
In some O-level text-book,[4] when the dons
Have analysed the story of our age,
When travel firms sell tours of outer space
And aeroplanes take off without a sound                    10
And Tulse Hill has become a trendy place
And Upper Norwood's on the underground[5]
Your beauty and my name will be forgotten—
My love is true, but all my verse is rotten.                    1986

4. A text designed to prepare secondary-school students for the first hurdle in entrance exams for British universities. *Dons*: academics.    5. London subway.

## CULTURAL BELIEF AND TRADITION

The poems in this group draw on a tradition that is larger than just "literary." Mythologies involve whole systems of belief, usually cultural in scope, and the familiar literary formulations of these mythologies are just the surface articulations of a larger view of why the world works the way it does.

Every culture develops stories to explain itself. These stories, about who we are and why we are the way we are, constitute what are often called **myths.** Calling something a myth does not mean that it is false. In fact, it means nearly the opposite, for cultures that subscribe to various myths, or that have ever subscribed to particular myths about culture or history, become infused with and defined by those views. Myth, in the sense in which it is used here, involves explanations of life that are more or less universally believed within a particular culture; it is a frame of reference that people within the culture understand and share. A sharing of this frame of reference does not mean that all people within a culture are carbon copies of each other or that popular stereotypes represent reality accurately, nor does it mean that every individual in the culture *knows* the perceived history and can articulate its events, ideas, and values. But it does mean that a shared history and a shared set of symbols lie behind any particular culture and that the culture is to some extent aware of its distinctiveness from other cultures.

A **culture** may be of many sizes and shapes. Often we think of a nation as a culture (and so speak of American culture, American history, the myth of America, the American dream, the American frame of reference), and it is equally useful to make smaller and larger divisions—as long as there is some commonality of history and some cohesiveness of purpose within the group. One can speak of southern culture, for example, or of urban culture, or of the drug culture, or of the various popular music cultures, or of a culture associated with a particular political belief, economic class, or social group. Most of us belong, willingly or not, to a number of such cultures at one time, and to some extent our identity and destiny are linked with the distinctive features of those cultures and with the ways each culture perceives its identity, values, and history. Some of these cultures we choose to join; some are thrust upon us by birth and circumstances. It is these larger and more persistent forms of culture—not those chosen by an individual—that are illustrated in this chapter.

Poets, aware of their heritage, often like to probe its history and beliefs and plumb its depths, just as they like to articulate and play variations on the poetic tradition they feel a part of. For poetry written in the English language over the last four hundred years or so, both the Judeo-Christian frame of reference and the classical frame of reference (drawing on the civilizations of ancient Greece and Rome) have been quite important. Western culture, a broad culture that includes many nations and many religious and social groups, is largely defined within these two frames of reference—or it has been until quite recently. As religious belief in the West has eroded over the past two or three centuries, and as classical civilization has been less emphasized and less studied, poets have felt increasingly less comfortable in assuming that their audiences share a knowledge of their systems, but they have often continued to use them to isolate and articulate human traits that have cultural continuity and importance. More recently, poets have drawn on other cultural myths—Native American, African, and Asian, for example—to expand our sense of common heritage and give new meaning to the "American" and "Western" experience. The poems that follow draw on details from different myths and do so in a variety of ways and tones.

JOHN HOLLANDER

## Adam's Task

*And Adam gave names to all cattle, and to the fowl of the air, and to*
*every beast of the field . . .*

—Gen. 2:20

Thou, paw-paw-paw; thou, glurd; thou, spotted
   Glurd; thou, whitestap, lurching through
The high-grown brush; thou, pliant-footed,
   Implex; thou, awagabu.

Every burrower, each flier            5
   Came for the name he had to give:
Gay, first work, ever to be prior,
   Not yet sunk to primitive.

Thou, verdle; thou, McFleery's pomma;
   Thou; thou; thou—three types of grawl;       10
Thou, flisket; thou, kabasch; thou, comma-
   Eared mashawk; thou, all; thou, all.

Were, in a fire of becoming,
   Laboring to be burned away,
Then work, half-measuring, half-humming,     15
   Would be as serious as play.

Thou, pambler; thou, rivarn; thou, greater
   Wherret, and thou, lesser one;
Thou, sproal; thou, zant; thou, lily-eater.
   Naming's over. Day is done.        20

1971

SUSAN DONNELLY

## Eve Names the Animals

To me, *lion* was sun on a wing
over the garden. *Dove,*
a burrowing, blind creature.

I swear that man
never knew animals. Words       5
he lined up according to size,

while elephants slipped flat-eyed
through water

and trout
10   hurtled from the underbrush, tusked
and ready for battle.

The name he gave me stuck
me to him. He did it to comfort me,
for not being first.

15   Mornings, while he slept,
I got away. Pickerel
hopped on the branches above me.
Only spider accompanied me,
nosing everywhere,
20   running up to lick my hand.

Poor finch. I suppose I was
woe to him—
the way he'd come looking for me,
not wanting either of us
25   to be ever alone

But to myself I was
palomino
        raven
            fox . . .

30   I strung words
by their stems and wore them
as garlands on my long walks.

The next day
I'd find them withered.

35   I liked change.                                    1985


CHRISTINA ROSSETTI

*Eve*

"While I sit at the door,
Sick to gaze within,
Mine eye weepeth sore
For sorrow and sin:
5    As a tree my sin stands
To darken all lands;
Death is the fruit it bore.

"How have Eden bowers grown
Without Adam to bend them!
10   How have Eden flowers blown,
Squandering their sweet breath,

Without me to tend them!
The Tree of Life was ours,
Tree twelvefold-fruited,[6]
Most lofty tree that flowers,                                    15
Most deeply rooted:
I chose the Tree of Death.[7]

"Hadst thou but said me nay,
    Adam, my brother,
I might have pined away—                                        20
    I, but none other:
God might have let thee stay
Safe in our garden,
By putting me away
Beyond all pardon.                                              25

"I, Eve, sad mother
Of all who must live,
I, not another,
Plucked bitterest fruit to give
My friend, husband, lover.                                      30
O wanton eyes run over!
Who but I should grieve?—
Cain hath slain his brother:[8]
Of all who must die mother,
Miserable Eve!"                                                 35

Thus she sat weeping,
Thus Eve our mother,
Where one lay sleeping
Slain by his brother.
Greatest and least                                             40
Each piteous beast
To hear her voice
Forgot his joys
And set aside his feast.

The mouse paused in his walk                                   45
And dropped his wheaten stalk:
Grave cattle wagged their heads
In rumination;
The eagle gave a cry
From his cloud station:                                        50
Larks on thyme beds
Forbore to mount or sing;
Bees dropped upon the wing;
The raven perched on high

6. The tree of life is so described in Revelation 22:2, 14, but the account there is of the New Jerusalem, not of Eden.    7. The Genesis account distinguishes between the tree of life and the tree of the knowledge of good and evil; the latter is forbidden, and eating of it brings labor, sickness, and death into the world. See Genesis 2:9, 3:1–24.    8. Abel (see Genesis 4:1–15).

55      Forgot his ration;
     The conies[9] in their rock,
     A feeble nation,
     Quaked sympathetical;
     The mocking-bird left off to mock;
60      Huge camels knelt as if
     In deprecation;
     The kind hart's tears were falling;
     Chattered the wistful stork;
     Dove-voices with a dying fall
65      Cooed desolation
     Answering grief by grief.

     Only the serpent in the dust,
     Wriggling and crawling,
     Grinned an evil grin, and thrust
70      His tongue out with its fork.

       1865

## ALFRED, LORD TENNYSON

## *Ulysses*[1]

     It little profits that an idle king,
     By this still hearth, among these barren crags,
     Matched with an agéd wife,[2] I mete and dole
     Unequal laws unto a savage race,
5      That hoard, and sleep, and feed, and know not me.

     I cannot rest from travel; I will drink
     Life to the lees.[3] All times I have enjoyed
     Greatly, have suffered greatly, both with those
     That loved me, and alone; on shore, and when
10      Through scudding drifts the rainy Hyades[4]
     Vexed the dim sea. I am become a name;
     For always roaming with a hungry heart
     Much have I seen and known—cities of men
     And manners, climates, councils, governments,
15      Myself not least, but honored of them all—
     And drunk delight of battle with my peers,

9. A common term for rabbits, but here probably the small pachyderms mentioned in Proverbs 30:26.
1. After the end of the Trojan War, Ulysses (or Odysseus), king of Ithaca and one of the Greek heroes of the war, returned to his island home (line 34). Homer's account of the situation is in *The Odyssey* XI, but Dante's account of Ulysses in *The Inferno* XXVI is the more immediate background of the poem.
2. Penelope.     3. All the way down to the bottom of the cup.     4. A group of stars that were supposed to predict rain when they rose at the same time as the sun.

Far on the ringing plains of windy Troy.
I am a part of all that I have met;
Yet all experience is an arch wherethrough
Gleams that untraveled world, whose margin fades          20
For ever and for ever when I move.
How dull it is to pause, to make an end,
To rust unburnished, not to shine in use!
As though to breathe were life. Life piled on life
Were all too little, and of one to me                     25
Little remains; but every hour is saved
From that eternal silence, something more,
A bringer of new things; and vile it were
For some three suns to store and hoard myself,
And this gray spirit yearning in desire                   30
To follow knowledge like a sinking star,
Beyond the utmost bound of human thought.

   This is my son, mine own Telemachus,
To whom I leave the scepter and the isle—
Well-loved of me, discerning to fulfill                   35
This labor by slow prudence to make mild
A rugged people, and through soft degrees
Subdue them to the useful and the good.
Most blameless is he, centered in the sphere
Of common duties, decent not to fail                      40
In offices of tenderness, and pay
Meet adoration to my household gods,
When I am gone. He works his work, I mine.

   There lies the port; the vessel puffs her sail:
There gloom the dark, broad seas. My mariners,            45
Souls that have toiled, and wrought, and thought with me—
That ever with a frolic welcome took
The thunder and the sunshine, and opposed
Free hearts, free foreheads—you and I are old;
Old age hath yet his honor and his toil.                  50
Death closes all; but something ere the end,
Some work of noble note, may yet be done,
Not unbecoming men that strove with Gods.
The lights begin to twinkle from the rocks;
The long day wanes; the slow moon climbs; the deep        55
Moans round with many voices. Come, my friends.
'Tis not too late to seek a newer world.
Push off, and sitting well in order smite
The sounding furrows; for my purpose holds
To sail beyond the sunset, and the baths                  60
Of all the western stars, until I die.
It may be that the gulfs will wash us down;[5]

5. Beyond the Gulf of Gibraltar was supposed to be a chasm that led to Hades.

It may be we shall touch the Happy Isles,[6]
And see the great Achilles, whom we knew.
65    Though much is taken, much abides; and though
We are not now that strength which in old days
Moved earth and heaven, that which we are, we are:
One equal temper of heroic hearts,
Made weak by time and fate, but strong in will
70    To strive, to seek, to find, and not to yield.

1833

---

MIRIAM WADDINGTON

## *Ulysses Embroidered*

You've come
at last from
all your journeying
to the old blind woman
5    in the tower,
Ulysses.

After all adventurings
through seas and
mountains through
10    giant battles,
storms and death,
from pinnacles
to valleys;

Past sirens
15    naked on rocks
between Charybdis
and Scylla, from
dragons' teeth,
from sleep in
20    stables choking
on red flowers
walking through weeds
and through shipwreck.

And now you are
25    climbing the stairs,
taking shape,
a figure in shining
thread rising from

6. Elysium, the Islands of the Blessed, where heroes like Achilles (line 64) abide after death.

a golden shield:
a medallion                                                             30
emblazoned in
tapestry you grew
from the blind hands
of Penelope.

Her tapestry                                                            35
saw everything,
her stitches
embroidered the
painful colors
of her breath the                                                      40
long sighing touch
of her hands.

She made many
journeys.                                                            1992


## EDNA ST. VINCENT MILLAY

## *An Ancient Gesture*

I thought, as I wiped my eyes on the corner of my apron:
Penelope did this too.
And more than once: you can't keep weaving all day
And undoing it all through the night;
Your arms get tired, and the back of your neck gets tight            5
And along towards morning, when you think it will never be light,
And your husband has been gone, and you don't know where, for years,
Suddenly you burst into tears;
There is simply nothing else to do.
And I thought, as I wiped my eyes on the corner of my apron:         10
This is an ancient gesture, authentic, antique,
In the very best tradition, classic, Greek;
Ulysses did this too.
But only as a gesture,—a gesture which implied
To the assembled throng that he was much too moved to speak.         15
He learned it from Penelope . . .
Penelope, who really cried.                                         1954

LANGSTON HUGHES

## The Negro Speaks of Rivers

I've known rivers:
I've known rivers ancient as the world and older than the flow of
     human blood in human veins.

My soul has grown deep like the rivers.

I bathed in the Euphrates when dawns were young.
5   I built my hut near the Congo and it lulled me to sleep.
I looked upon the Nile and raised the pyramids above it.
I heard the singing of the Mississippi when Abe Lincoln went down to
     New Orleans, and I've seen its muddy bosom turn all golden in the
     sunset.

I've known rivers:
Ancient, dusky rivers.

10  My soul has grown deep like the rivers.                                    1926


JUNE JORDAN

## Something Like a Sonnet for
## Phillis Miracle Wheatley

Girl from the realm of birds florid and fleet
flying full feather in far or near weather
Who fell to a dollar lust coffled like meat
Captured by avarice and hate spit together
5   Trembling asthmatic alone on the slave block
built by a savagery travelling by carriage
viewed like a species of flaw in the livestock
A child without safety of mother or marriage

Chosen by whimsy but born to surprise
10  They taught you to read but you learned how to write
Begging the universe into your eyes:
They dressed you in light but you dreamed with the night.
From Africa singing of justice and grace,
Your early verse sweetens the fame of our Race.                             1989

MAYA ANGELOU

## Africa

Thus she had lain
sugar cane sweet
deserts her hair
golden her feet
mountains her breasts                                              5
two Niles her tears
Thus she has lain
Black through the years.

Over the white seas
rime white and cold                                               10
brigands ungentled
icicle bold
took her young daughters
sold her strong sons
churched her with Jesus                                           15
bled her with guns.
Thus she has lain.

Now she is rising
remember her pain
remember the losses                                               20
her screams loud and vain
remember her riches
her history slain
now she is striding
although she had lain.                                            25

                                                          1975


DEREK WALCOTT

## A Far Cry from Africa

A wind is ruffling the tawny pelt
Of Africa. Kikuyu,[7] quick as flies,
Batten upon the bloodstreams of the veldt.[8]
Corpses are scattered through a paradise.
Only the worm, colonel of carrion, cries:                          5
"Waste no compassion on these separate dead!"
Statistics justify and scholars seize

---

7. An East African tribe whose members, as Mau Mau fighters, conducted an eight-year terrorist campaign against British colonial settlers in Kenya.    8. Open country, neither cultivated nor forest (Afrikaans).

The salients of colonial policy.
What is that to the white child hacked in bed?
To savages, expendable as Jews?

Threshed out by beaters,[9] the long rushes break
In a white dust of ibises whose cries
Have wheeled since civilization's dawn
From the parched river or beast-teeming plain.
The violence of beast on beast is read
As natural law, but upright man
Seeks his divinity by inflicting pain.
Delirious as these worried beasts, his wars
Dance to the tightened carcass of a drum,
While he calls courage still that native dread
Of the white peace contracted by the dead.

Again brutish necessity wipes its hands
Upon the napkin of a dirty cause, again
A waste of our compassion, as with Spain,[1]
The gorilla wrestles with the superman.
I who am poisoned with the blood of both,
Where shall I turn, divided to the vein?
I who have cursed
The drunken officer of British rule, how choose
Between this Africa and the English tongue I love?
Betray them both, or give back what they give?
How can I face such slaughter and be cool?
How can I turn from Africa and live?

1962

---

ISHMAEL REED

## I Am a Cowboy in the Boat of Ra

*The devil must be forced to reveal any such physical evil (potions, charms, fetishes, etc.) still outside the body and these must be burned.*

> —*Rituale Romanum,* published 1947, endorsed by the coat of arms and introduction letter from Francis Cardinal Spellman

I am a cowboy in the boat of Ra,[2]
sidewinders in the saloons of fools
bit my forehead  like        O
the untrustworthiness of Egyptologists

---

9. In big-game hunting, natives are hired to beat the brush, driving birds—such as ibises—and animals into the open.    1. The Spanish Civil War (1936–39), in which the Loyalists were supported by liberals in the West and militarily by Soviet Communists, and the rebels by Nazi Germany and Fascist Italy. 2. Chief of the ancient Egyptian gods, creator and protector of humans and vanquisher of Evil.

Who do not know their trips. Who was that                                    5
dog-faced man?³ they asked, the day I rode
from town.

School marms with halitosis cannot see
the Nefertiti⁴ fake chipped on the run by slick
germans, the hawk behind Sonny Rollins' head or                             10
the ritual beard of his axe,⁵ a longhorn winding
its bells thru the Field of Reeds.

I am a cowboy in the boat of Ra. I bedded
down with Isis,⁶ Lady of the Boogaloo, dove
down deep in her horny, stuck up her Wells-Far-ago                          15
in daring midday get away. "Start grabbing the
blue," i said from top of my double crown.

I am a cowboy in the boat of Ra. Ezzard Charles⁷
of the Chisholm Trail. Took up the bass but they
blew off my thumb. Alchemist in ringmanship but a                          20
sucker for the right cross.

I am a cowboy in the boat of Ra. Vamoosed from
the temple i bide my time. The price on the wanted
poster was a-going down, outlaw alias copped my stance
and moody greenhorns were making me dance; while my mouth's                 25
shooting iron got its chambers jammed.

I am a cowboy in the boat of Ra. Boning-up in
the ol West i bide my time. You should see
me pick off these tin cans whippersnappers. I
write the motown long plays for the comeback of                            30
Osiris.⁸ Make them up when stars stare at sleeping
steer out here near the campfire. Women arrive
on the backs of goats and throw themselves on
my Bowie.⁹

I am a cowboy in the boat of Ra. Lord of the lash,                         35
the Loup Garou¹ Kid. Half breed son of Pisces and
Aquarius. I hold the souls of men in my pot. I do
the dirty boogie with scorpions. I make the bulls
keep still and was the first swinger to grape the taste.

I am a cowboy in his boat. Pope Joan² of the                               40
Ptah Ra. C/mere a minute willya doll?

---

3. The Egyptian god of the dead, Anubis was usually depicted as a man with the head of a dog or
jackal.    4. Fourteenth-century-B.C. Egyptian queen; elsewhere Reed says that German scholars are
responsible for the notion that her dynasty was white.    5. Saxophone. *Sonny Rollins:* jazz player
(b. 1930) who came to prominence in the late 1950s and early 1960s.    6. Principal goddess of ancient
Egypt.    7. World heavyweight boxing champion, 1949–51.    8. Husband of Isis and constant foe of
his brother Set (line 48). Tricked by Set, he died violently but later rose from the dead.    9. Large
hunting knife.    1. French for werewolf; in voodoo, a priest who has run amok or gone mad.
2. Mythical female pope, supposed to have succeeded to the papacy in 855. *Ptah Ra:* chief god of Mem-
phis, capital of ancient Egypt.

Be a good girl and
Bring me my Buffalo horn of black powder
Bring me my headdress of black feathers
45   Bring me my bones of Ju-Ju snake
Go get my eyelids of red paint.
Hand me my shadow
I'm going into town after Set

I am a cowboy in the boat of Ra
50   look out Set      here i come Set
to get Set      to sunset Set
to unseat Set      to Set down Set
             usurper of the Royal couch
             imposter RAdio of Moses' bush[3]
55           party pooper O hater of dance
             vampire outlaw of the milky way                1969

JUDITH ORTIZ COFER

## How to Get a Baby

*To receive the* waiwaia *(spirit children) in the water seems to be the most usual way of becoming pregnant. . . . They come along on large tree trunks, and they may be attached to seascum and dead leaves floating on the surface.*

　　—BRONISLAW MALINOWSKI, *Baloma: The Spirits of the Dead in the Trobriand Islands*

Go to the sea
the morning after a rainstorm,
preferably
fresh from your man's arms—
5   the *waiwaia* are drawn
to love smell.
They are tiny luminous fish
and blind. You must call
the soul of your child
10   in the name of your ancestors:
*Come to me, little fish, come
to Tamala, Tudava, come to me.*
Sit in shallow water
up to your waist until the tide
15   pulls away from you

3. Which, according to Exodus 3:2, burned but was not consumed and from which Moses heard the voice of God telling him to lead the Israelites out of Egypt.

like an exhausted lover.
You will by then
be carrying new life.
Make love that night,
and every night,                                                        20
to let the little one
who chooses you know
she is one with your joy.                                    1993


ALBERTO ALVARO RÍOS

## Advice to a First Cousin

The way the world works is like this:
for the bite of scorpions, she says,
my grandmother to my first cousin,
because I might die and someone must know,
go to the animal jar                                                      5
the one with the soup of green herbs
mixed with the scorpions I have been putting in
still alive. Take one out
put it on the bite. It has had time to think
there with the others—put the lid back tight—          10
and knows that a biting is not the way to win
a finger or a young girl's foot.
It will take back into itself the hurting
the redness and the itching and its marks.

But the world works like this, too:                               15
look out for the next scorpion you see,
she says, and makes a big face to scare me
thereby instructing my cousin, look out!
for one of the scorpion's many
illegitimate and unhappy sons.                                     20
It will be smarter, more of the devil.
It will have lived longer than these dead ones.
It will know from them something more
about the world, in the way mothers know
when something happens to a child, or how       25
I knew from your sadness you had been bitten.
It will learn something stronger than biting.
Look out most for that scorpion, she says,
making a big face to scare me again and it works
I go—crying—she lets me go—they laugh,              30
the way you must look out for men
who have not yet bruised you.                             1985

LOUISE ERDRICH

# *Jacklight*

*The same Chippewa word is used both for flirting and hunting game,*
*while another Chippewa word connotes both using force in intercourse*
*and also killing a bear with one's bare hands.*

—DUNNING 1959

We have come to the edge of the woods,
out of brown grass where we slept, unseen,
out of knotted twigs, out of leaves creaked shut,
out of hiding.

5    At first the light wavered, glancing over us.
Then it clenched to a fist of light that pointed,
searched out, divided us.
Each took the beams like direct blows the heart answers.
Each of us moved forward alone.

10   We have come to the edge of the woods,
drawn out of ourselves by this night sun,
this battery of polarized acids,
that outshines the moon.

We smell them behind it
15   but they are faceless, invisible,
We smell the raw steel of their gun barrels,
mink oil on leather, their tongues of sour barley.
We smell their mother buried chin-deep in wet dirt.

We smell their fathers with scoured knuckles,
20   teeth cracked from hot marrow.
We smell their sisters of crushed dogwood, bruised apples,
of fractured cups and concussions of burnt hooks.

We smell their breath steaming lightly behind the jacklight.
We smell the itch underneath the caked guts on their clothes.
25   We smell their minds like silver hammers
cocked back, held in readiness
for the first of us to step into the open.

We have come to the edge of the woods,
out of brown grass where we slept, unseen,
30   out of leaves creaked shut, out of our hiding.
We have come here too long.

It is their turn now,
their turn to follow us. Listen,
they put down their equipment.
35   It is useless in the tall brush.
And now they take the first steps, not knowing

how deep the woods are and lightless.
How deep the woods are.                                            1984


## QUESTIONS

1. How, specifically, is the speaker undercut in Jonson's "Come, My Celia"? Explain how the strategy of allusion works in this poem.
2. Are Moore's notes to "Love in America?" adequate to explain the allusions in her poem? What other information do you wish to have? After you have unearthed that information in your college library, show in detail how each separate allusion in the poem works. How would you paraphrase the poem? Why is there a question mark in the poem's title?
3. List all the metaphors you can find in Crashaw's "An Epitaph upon a Young Married Couple, Dead and Buried Together." How closely are the metaphors related to each other? Which metaphors seem especially appropriate to an epitaph? to the epigram as a poetic kind?
4. Which epitaph in the chapter seems to you the most likely to end up on a tombstone? Why? What features would prevent most of the "epitaphs" here from actually being used? Which epitaph here seems to you the wittiest? In what, exactly, does the wit consist? Do you like the epigrams better or worse that have a "sting" at the end? Why?
5. Read through a number of the very short poems in this book, and pick out one of no more than eight lines that does not seem to you to qualify as an epigram. What features of the poem make that label inappropriate? On the basis of what you know about poetic kinds, can you assign a label to it?
6. Read the Cummings poem "(ponder,darling,these busted statues" closely in relation to Marvell's "To His Coy Mistress." In what specific ways does it echo Marvell's poem? Which images are specifically derived from Marvell? In what specific ways does the Cummings poem undercut the argument of the Marvell poem? In what ways does it undercut its own argument? to what purpose? In what ways does Ginsberg's "A Further Proposal" differ from the other poems written in imitation of Marvell?
7. Indicate the specific ways in which Ralegh's poem "replies" to Marlowe's. In what points does Williams agree with Ralegh? What, exactly, is "unfair" about Skirrow's summary of Keats? How do you think Keats would justify himself against Skirrow's summary?
8. What attitudes toward Adam and Eve are displayed in the Donnelly, Hollander, and Rossetti poems? Which poems develop the strongest negative attitudes toward their "heroes" or "heroines"? How do Waddington's and Millay's versions differ? What values are associated with Africa in the Hughes, Angelou, and Reed poems? What is the "cowboy" doing in Reed's poem?


## WRITING SUGGESTIONS

1. In what specific ways is Marvell's "To His Coy Mistress" anchored to its historical or cultural context? Can you tell that it is written by a seventeenth-century poet? How? What historical or cultural "allusions" anchor the poem to its specific moment in time? to its philosophical or thematic contexts? In what specific ways does the De Vries poem establish itself as contemporary? Write a short (500–700 word) essay in which you show how De Vries undercuts the assumptions of Marvell. (Alternative: write a short essay in which you show how Cummings undercuts the assumptions of Marvell.)
2. Choose randomly any six of the epigrams in this chapter, and try to decide on the basis of them what a good definition for *epigram* might be. Write down your definition, mentioning any features of epigram that seem to you crucial to the kind. Then choose a seventh poem from the chapter, one that seems to you entirely typical of the epigram kind, and write a brief, three-paragraph analysis of it, showing exactly how it uses (or refuses) features mentioned in your definition.

3. Using one of the poems in this chapter as your model, try your hand at writing an epigram (of no more than four lines) of your own. When you have completed your poem, write a brief paragraph about it, describing how you have used features characteristic of the poetic kind.

4. Using a poetry index (available in the reference section of your college library), find half a dozen poems that use the term "elegy" in their titles, and compare their tones and strategies. Try to decide what features and expectations seem to be central to the poetic kind. Then look back at Jonson's "On My First Son" (page 9), often said to be a typical elegy, and write a brief (two-page) analysis of the poem in which you show how it uses and transforms the expectations associated with the elegy as a poetic kind.

5. In an essay of about three pages, show how the primary effects of Reed's "I Am a Cowboy in the Boat of Ra" relate to its use of cultural myths. (Alternative: apply this same question to Rossetti's "Eve," Tennyson's "Ulysses," or Erdrich's "Jacklight.")

# 12

## HISTORICAL AND CULTURAL CONTEXTS

The more you know, the better a reader of poetry you are likely to be. And that goes for general knowledge as well as knowledge of other poetry and literary traditions. Poems often draw upon a larger fund of human knowledge about all sorts of things, asking us to bring to bear on a poem facts and values we have taken on from earlier reading or from our experiences in the world more generally. The first nine chapters on poetry suggest how practice and the learning of specific skills make interpretation easier and better: the more you read and the more close analysis you do, the better an interpreter you are likely to become. But in this "contextual" section we are concerned with information you need to read richly and fully: information about authors, about events that influenced them or became the inspiration or basis for their writing, and about literary traditions that provide a context for their work. Poets always write in a specific time, under particular circumstances, and with some awareness of the world around them, whether or not they specifically refer to contemporary matters in a particular poem. In this chapter, our concern is with the specifically historical and cultural—events, movements, ideas that directly influence poets or that poets in some way represent in the poems they write.

Very little that you know will ultimately go to waste in your reading of poetry. The best potential reader of poetry is someone who has already developed reading skills to perfection, read everything, thought deeply about all kinds of things, and who is wise beyond belief—wise enough to know exactly how to apply what she or he knows accurately to a given text. But that is the ideal reader we all strive to be, not the one any of us actually is. Although no poet really expects any reader to be all those things, good readers try. Poems can be just as demanding of readers about historical information as about the intricacies of language and form. Poems not only *refer to* people, places, and events—things that exist in time—but they also *are* themselves products of given moments, participating in both the potentialities and the limitations of the times in which they were created.

Things that happen every day frequently find their way into poetry in an easy and yet often forceful manner. Making love in a junkyard, as in Dickey's "Cherrylog Road," is one kind of example; a reader doesn't need to know what particular junkyard was involved—or imaginatively involved—in order to understand the poem, but a reader does need to know what an auto junkyard was like in the mid-twentieth century, with more or less whole car bodies being scattered in various states of disarray over a large

411

plot of ground. But what if, over the next generation or two, junkyards completely disappear as other ways are found to dispose of old cars? Already a lot of old cars are crushed into small metal blocks, especially in large cities. But what if the metal is all melted down, or the junk is orbited into space? If that should happen, readers then will have never seen a junkyard, and they will need a footnote to explain what such junk-yards were like. The history of junkyards will not be lost—there will be pictures, films, records, and someone will write definitive books about the forms and functions of junk-yards, probably even including the fact that lovers occasionally visited them—but the public memory of junkyards will soon disappear. No social customs, nothing that is made, no institutions or sites last forever.

Readers may still be able to experience "Cherrylog Road" when junkyards disappear, but they will need some help, and they may think its particulars a little quaint, much as we regard literature that involves a horse and buggy—or even making love in the back seat of a parked car—as quaint now. Institutions change, habits change, times change, places and settings change—all kinds of particulars change, even when people's wants, needs, and foibles pretty much go on in the same way. Footnotes never provide a precise or adequate substitute for the ease and pleasure that come from already knowing, but they can help us understand and pave the way for feeling and experience. A kind of imaginative historical sympathy can be simulated, and in fact created, for poems from earlier times that refer to specific contemporary details (and that have now become to us, in our own time, *historical* details) often describe human nature and human experiences very much as we still know and experience them. Today's poem may need tomorrow's footnote, but the poem need not be tomorrow's puzzle or only a curiosity or fossil.

The following poem, not many years old, already requires some explanation. Many readers will not know the factual details of its occasion, and (even more important) most readers will not recall the powerful reaction throughout the United States to the event.

JAMES A. EMANUEL

## Emmett Till[1]

I hear a whistling
Through the water.
Little Emmett
Won't be still.
5   He keeps floating
Round the darkness,
Edging through
The silent chill.
Tell me, please,
10  That bedtime story
Of the fairy

1. In 1955, Till, a fourteen-year-old from Chicago, was lynched in Mississippi for allegedly making sexual advances toward a white woman.

River Boy
Who swims forever,
Deep in treasures,
Necklaced in                                                                15
A coral toy.                                                      1968


How do you know what you need to know? The easiest clue is your own puzzlement. When it seems that something is happening in a poem that you don't recognize—and yet the poem makes no apparent effort to clarify it—you have a clue that readers at the time the poem was written must have recognized something that is not now such common knowledge. Once you know you don't know, it only takes a little work to find out: most college libraries contain far more information than you will ever need, and the trick is to search efficiently. Your ability to find the information will depend upon how well you know the written reference materials and computer searches available to you. Practice helps. Knowledge accumulates. Most poems printed in textbooks like this one will be annotated for you with basic facts, but often you may need additional information to interpret the poem's full meaning and resonance. An editor, trying to satisfy the needs of a variety of readers, may not always decide to write the note you in particular may need, so there could be digging to do in the library for any poem you read, certainly for those you come upon in magazines and books of poetry without notes. Few poets like to annotate their own work (they'd rather let you struggle a little to appreciate them), and besides, many things that now need notes didn't when they were written.

The two poems that follow both require from the reader some specific "referential" information, but they differ considerably in their emphasis on the particularities of time and place. The first poem, Hardy's "Channel Firing," reflects and refers to a moment just before the outbreak of World War I when British naval forces were preparing for combat by taking gunnery practice in the English Channel. The second, Gilbert's "Sonnet: The Ladies' Home Journal," reflects a longer cultural moment in which attitudes and assumptions, rather than some specific event, are crucial to understanding the poem.


THOMAS HARDY

## Channel Firing

That night your great guns, unawares,
Shook all our coffins as we lay,
And broke the chancel window squares,[2]
We thought it was the Judgment-day

And sat upright. While drearisome                                          5
Arose the howl of wakened hounds:

2. The windows near the altar in a church.

The mouse let fall the altar-crumb,[3]
The worms drew back into the mounds,

The glebe cow[4] drooled. Till God called, "No;
10   It's gunnery practice out at sea
Just as before you went below;
The world is as it used to be:

"All nations striving strong to make
Red war yet redder. Mad as hatters
15   They do no more for Christés sake
Than you who are helpless in such matters.

"That this is not the judgment-hour
For some of them's a blessed thing,
For if it were they'd have to scour
20   Hell's floor for so much threatening . . .

"Ha, ha. It will be warmer when
I blow the trumpet (if indeed
I ever do; for you are men,
And rest eternal sorely need)."

25   So down we lay again. "I wonder,
Will the world ever saner be,"
Said one, "than when He sent us under
In our indifferent century!"

And many a skeleton shook his head.
30   "Instead of preaching forty year,"
My neighbor Parson Thirdly said,
"I wish I had stuck to pipes and beer."

Again the guns disturbed the hour,
Roaring their readiness to avenge.
35   As far inland as Stourton Tower,
And Camelot, and starlit Stonehenge.[5]

April 1914

3. Breadcrumbs from the sacrament of Communion.     4. Parish cow pastured on the meadow next to the churchyard.     5. Stourton Tower, built in the eighteenth century to commemorate King Alfred's ninth-century victory over the Danes, in Stourhead Park, Wiltshire. Camelot is the legendary site of King Arthur's court, said to have been in Cornwall or Somerset. Stonehenge, a circular formation of upright stones dating from about 1800 B.C., is on Salisbury Plain, Wiltshire; it is thought to have been a ceremonial site for political and religious occasions or an early scientific experiment in astronomy.

SANDRA GILBERT

## Sonnet: The Ladies' Home Journal

The brilliant stills of food, the cozy
glossy, bygone life—mashed potatoes
posing as whipped cream, a neat mom
conjuring shapes from chaos, trimming the flame—
how we ached for all that,                                                5
that dance of love in the living room,
those paneled walls, that kitchen golden
as the inside of a seed: how we leaned
on those shiny columns of advice,
stroking the *thank yous*, the firm thighs, the wise        10
closets full of soap.
                      But even then
we knew it was the lies we loved, the lies
we wore like Dior coats,[6] the clean-cut airtight
lies that laid out our lives in black and white.                    1984

"Channel Firing" is not ultimately *about* World War I, for it presumes that human behavior stays the same from age to age, but it begins from a particular historical vantage point. It would be difficult to make much sense of the poem if the reader were not to recognize the importance of that specific reference, and the poem's situation (with a waking corpse as the main speaker) is difficult enough to sort out even with the clue of the careful dating at the end (the date here is actually a part of the poem, recorded on the manuscript by the author and always printed as part of the text). The firing of the guns has awakened the dead who are buried near the channel, and in their puzzlement they assume it is Judgment Day, time for them to arise, until God enters and tells them what is happening. Much of the poem's effect depends on character portrayal—a God who laughs and sounds cynical, a parson who regrets his selfless life and wishes he had indulged himself more—as well as the sense that nothing ever changes. But particularity of time and place are crucial to this sense of changelessness; even so important a con- temporary moment as the beginning of a world war—a moment viewed by most people at the time as unique and world-changing—fades into a timeless parade of moments that stretches over centuries of history. The geographical particulars cited at the end—as the sound of the guns moves inland to be heard in place after place—make the same point. Great moments in history are all encompassed in the sound of the guns and its message about human behavior. Times, places, and events, however important they seem, all become part of some larger pattern that denies individuality or uniqueness.

The particulars in "Sonnet: The Ladies' Home Journal" work differently—to remind us not of a specific time that readers need to identify but to characterize a way of seeing and thinking. The referentiality here is more cultural than historical; it is based more on ideas and attitudes characteristic of a particular period than on a specific moment or

6. Designer coats by Christian Dior.

location. The pictures in the magazine stand for a whole way of thinking about women that was characteristic of the time—the mid-twentieth century—when the *Ladies' Home Journal* flourished as a popular magazine. The poem implicitly contrasts the "lies" (line 12) of the magazine with the truth of the present—that women's lives and values are not to be seen as some fantasized sense of beautiful food, motherhood, social rituals, and commercial products. Two vastly different cultural attitudes—that of the poem's present, with its skeptical view of traditional women's roles, and that of a past that equated the superficiality of glossy photographs with gender identity—are at the heart of the poem. It is about cultural attitudes and their effects on actual human beings. Readers need to know what the *Ladies' Home Journal* was like in order to understand the poem; we do not need to know the date or contents of a specific issue, only that this popular magazine reflected the attitudes and values of a whole age and culture. The referentiality of this poem involves information about ideas and consciousness more than time and event.

To get at appropriate factual, cultural, and historical information, we need to learn to ask three kinds of questions. One kind is obvious: it is the "Do I understand the reference to . . . ?" kind. When events, places, or people unfamiliar to you come up, you will need to find out what or who they are. The second kind of question is more difficult: How do you know, in a poem that does *not* refer specifically to events, people, or ideas that you do not recognize, that you *need* to know more? When there are no specific references to look up, no people or events to identify, how do you know that there is a specific context? To get at this sort of question, you have to trust two people: the poet and yourself. Usually, good poets will not want to puzzle you more than necessary, so that you can safely assume that something that is not self-explanatory will merit close attention and possibly some digging in the library. (Poets do make mistakes and miscalculations about their readers, but it is a good working procedure at the start to assume they know what they are doing and why they are doing it.) References that are not in themselves clear provide a strong clue that you need more information. And that is why you need to trust yourself: when something doesn't click, when the information given you does not seem enough, you need to trust your puzzlement and try to find the missing facts that will allow the poem to make sense. But how? Often the date of the poem is a help; sometimes the title gives a clue or a point of departure; sometimes you can uncover, by reading about the author, some of the things he or she was interested in or concerned about. There is no single all-purpose way to discover what to look for, but that kind of research—looking for clues, adding up the evidence—can be interesting in itself and very rewarding when it is successful.

> When I came to poetry it was through the struggles of tribal peoples to assert our human rights, to secure our sovereign rights as nations in the early seventies. It was the struggle begun by my grandmothers and grandfathers when they fought the move from our homelands in the Southeast to Indian Territory. This, too, was my personal struggle as a poet. It was in this wave of cultural renaissance for Indian peoples in this country that I heard the poetry that would change me, a poetry that could have been written those mornings of creation from childhood. This poetry named me as it jolted the country into sharp consciousness.
>
> —JOY HARJO

The third question is why? For every factual reference, one needs to ask why. Why does the poem refer to this particular person instead of some other? What function does the reference serve?

Beyond the level of simply understanding that a particular poem is about an event or place or movement is the matter of developing a full sense of historical context, a sense of the larger significance and resonance of the historical occurrence or attitude referred to. Often a poem expects you to bring with you some sense of that significance; just as often it works to continue your education, telling you more, wanting you to understand and appreciate on the level of feeling some further things about this occurrence.

What we need to bring to our reading varies from poem to poem. For example, Owen's "Dulce et Decorum Est" (page 427) needs our knowledge that poison gas was used in World War I; the green tint through which the speaker sees the world in lines 13–14 comes from green glass in the goggles of the gas mask he has just put on. But some broader matters are important as well. Harder to specify but probably even more important is the climate of opinion that surrounded the war. To idealists, it was "the war to end all wars," and many participants—as well as politicians and propagandists— considered it a sacred mission, regarding the threat of Germany's expansionist policy as dangerous to Western civilization. No doubt you will read the poem more intelligently— and with more feeling—the more you know about World War I, and the same is true of poems about any historical occurrence or that refer to things that happen or situations that exist in a temporal or spatial context. But it is also true that your sense of these events will grow as a result of reading sensitively and thoughtfully the poems themselves. Facts are no substitute for skills. Once you have read individually the poems in this section, try taking a breather; and then at one sitting read them all again. Reading poetry can be a form of gaining knowledge as well as an aesthetic experience. One doesn't go to poetry to seek information as such, but poems often give us more than we came for. The ways to wisdom are paved with facts, and although poetry is not primarily a data-conscious art, it often requires us to be aware, sometimes in detail, of its referents in the real world.

## TIMES, PLACES, AND EVENTS

MILLER WILLIAMS

## *Thinking about Bill, Dead of AIDS*

We did not know the first thing about
how blood surrenders to even the smallest threat
when old allergies turn inside out,

5      the body rescinding all its normal orders
to all defenders of flesh, betraying the head,
pulling its guards back from all its borders.

Thinking of friends afraid to shake your hand,
we think of your hand shaking, your mouth set,
your eyes drained of any reprimand.

10    Loving, we kissed you, partly to persuade
both you and us, seeing what eyes had said,
that we were loving and were not afraid.

If we had had more, we would have given more.
As it was we stood next to your bed,
15    stopping, though, to set our smiles at the door.

Not because we were less sure at the last.
Only because, not knowing anything yet,
we didn't know what look would hurt you least.           1989

IRVING LAYTON

## *From Colony to Nation*

A dull people,
but the rivers of this country
are wide and beautiful

A dull people
5    enamoured of childish games,
but food is easily come by
and plentiful

Some with a priest's voice
in their cage of ribs: but

on high mountain-tops and in thunderstorms          10
the chirping is not heard

Deferring to beadle and censor;
not ashamed for this,
but given over to horseplay,
the making of money                                 15

A dull people, without charm or
ideas,
settling into the clean empty look
of a Mountie or dairy farmer
as into a legacy                                    20

One can ignore them
(the silences, the vast distances help)
and suppose them at the bottom
of one of the meaner lakes,
their bones not even picked for souvenirs.          25

1956

MARY JO SALTER

# Welcome to Hiroshima

is what you first see, stepping off the train:
a billboard brought to you in living English
by Toshiba Electric. While a channel
silent in the TV of the brain

projects those flickering re-runs of a cloud          5
that brims its risen columnful like beer
and, spilling over, hangs its foamy head,
you feel a thirst for history: what year

it started to be safe to breathe the air,
and when to drink the blood and scum afloat           10
on the Ohta River. But no, the water's clear,
they pour it for your morning cup of tea

in one of the countless sunny coffee shops
whose plastic dioramas advertise
mutations of cuisine behind the glass:               15
a pancake sandwich; a pizza someone tops

with a maraschino cherry. Passing by
the Peace Park's floral hypocenter (where
how bravely, or with what mistaken cheer,
humanity erased its own erasure),                    20

you enter the memorial museum
and through more glass are served, as on a dish

of blistered grass, three mannequins. Like gloves
a mother clips to coatsleeves, strings of flesh

25  hang from their fingertips; or as if tied
to recall a duty for us, *Reverence*
*the dead whose mourners too shall soon be dead,*
but all commemoration's swallowed up

in questions of bad taste, how re-created
30  horror mocks the grim original,
and thinking at last *They should have left it all*
you stop. This is the wristwatch of a child.

Jammed on the moment's impact, resolute
to communicate some message, although mute,
35  it gestures with its hands at eight-fifteen
and eight-fifteen and eight-fifteen again

while tables of statistics on the wall
update the news by calling on a roll
of tape, death gummed on death, and in the case
40  adjacent, an exhibit under glass

is glass itself: a shard the bomb slammed in
a woman's arm at eight-fifteen, but some
three decades on—as if to make it plain
hope's only as renewable as pain,

45  and as if all the unsung
debasements of the past may one day come
rising to the surface once again—
worked its filthy way out like a tongue.                    1984


DWIGHT OKITA

## Notes for a Poem
## on Being Asian American

As a child, I was a fussy eater
and I would separate the yolk from the egg white
as I now try to sort out what is Asian
in me from what is American—
5  the east from the west, the dreamer from the dream.
But countries are not
like eggs—except in the fragileness
of their shells—and eggs resemble countries
only in that when you crack one open and look inside,
10  you know even less than when you started.

And so I crack open the egg,
and this is what I see:
two moments from my past that strike me
as being uniquely Asian American.

In the first, I'm walking down Michigan Avenue                    15
one day—a man comes up to me out of the blue and says:
"I just wanted to tell you . . . I was on the plane that
bombed Hiroshima. And I just wanted you to know that
what we did was for the good of everyone." And it
seems as if he's asking for my forgiveness. It's 1983,          20
there's a sale on Marimekko sheets at the Crate &
Barrel, it's a beautiful summer day and I'm talking to
a man I've never seen before and will probably never
see again. His statement has no connection to me—
and has every connection in the world. But it's not          25
for me to forgive him. He must forgive himself.
"It must have been a very difficult decision to do what
you did," I say and I mention the sale on Marimekko
sheets across the street, comforters, and how the
pillowcases have the pattern of wheat printed on them,        30
and how some nights if you hold them before an open
window to the breeze, they might seem like flags—
like someone surrendering after a great while, or
celebrating, or simply cooling themselves in the summer
breeze as best they can.                                      35

In the second moment—I'm in a taxi and the Iranian
cabdriver looking into the rearview mirror notices my
Asian eyes, those almond shapes, reflected in the glass
and says, "Can you really tell the difference between
a Chinese and a Japanese?"                                    40

                                                    1992


## HENRY WADSWORTH LONGFELLOW

# *The Jewish Cemetery at Newport*

How strange it seems! These Hebrews in their graves,
    Close by the street of this fair seaport town,
Silent beside the never-silent waves,
    At rest in all this moving up and down!

The trees are white with dust, that o'er their sleep          5
    Wave their broad curtains in the southwind's breath,
While underneath these leafy tents they keep
    The long, mysterious Exodus of Death.

And these sepulchral stones, so old and brown,
    That pave with level flags their burial-place,
Seem like the tablets of the Law, thrown down
    And broken by Moses at the mountain's base.

The very names recorded here are strange,
    Of foreign accent, and of different climes;
Alvares and Rivera interchange
    With Abraham and Jacob of old times.

"Blessed be God! for he created Death!"
    The mourners said, "and Death is rest and peace";
Then added, in the certainty of faith,
    "And giveth Life that nevermore shall cease."

Closed are the portals of their Synagogue,
    No Psalms of David now the silence break,
No Rabbi reads the ancient Decalogue
    In the grand dialect the Prophets spake.

Gone are the living, but the dead remain,
    And not neglected; for a hand unseen,
Scattering its bounty, like a summer rain,
    Still keeps their graves and their remembrance green.

How came they here? What burst of Christian hate,
    What persecution, merciless and blind,
Drove o'er the sea—the desert desolate—
    These Ishmaels and Hagars of mankind?

They lived in narrow streets and lanes obscure,
    Ghetto and Judenstrass,[7] in mirk and mire;
Taught in the school of patience to endure
    The life of anguish and the death of fire.

All their lives long, with the unleavened bread
    And bitter herbs of exile and its fears,
The wasting famine of the heart they fed,
    And slaked its thirst with marah[8] of their tears.

Anathema maranatha![9] was the cry
    That rang from town to town, from street to street;
At every gate the accursed Mordecai[1]
    Was mocked and jeered, and spurned by Christian feet.

Pride and humiliation hand in hand
    Walked with them through the world wher'er they went;

10

15

20

25

30

35

40

45

---

7. German for "Street of Jews."    8. The Hebrew word for "bitter" or "bitterness"; salt water (symboliz-ing tears), unleavened bread, and bitter herbs are all part of the Passover meal.    9. A Greek-Aramaic phrase signifying a terrible curse, applied specifically to the Jews.    1. A Jew whose foster daughter, Esther, became the queen of Ahasuerus (Xerxes), king of Persia. When Haman, Ahasuerus' favored advi-sor, sought to destroy Mordecai and the Jews, Mordecai stood at the king's gate crying out against the persecution.

Trampled and beaten were they as the sand,
   And yet unshaken as the continent.

For in the background figures vague and vast
   Of patriarchs and of prophets rose sublime,        50
And all the great traditions of the Past
   They saw reflected in the coming time.

And thus forever with reverted look
   The mystic volume of the world they read,
Spelling it backward, like a Hebrew book,        55
   Till life became a Legend of the Dead.

But ah! what once has been shall be no more!
   The growing earth in travail and in pain
Brings forth its races, but does not restore,
   And the dead nations never rise again.        60

1852

DONALD JUSTICE

## Children Walking Home from School through Good Neighborhood

They are like figures held in some glass ball,
One of those in which, when shaken, snowstorms occur;
But this one is not yet shaken.
     And they go unaccompanied still,
Out along this walkway between two worlds,        5
This almost swaying bridge.
     October sunlight checkers their path;
It frets their cheeks and bare arms now with shadow
Almost too pure to signify itself.
And they progress slowly, somewhat lingeringly,        10
Independent, yet moving all together,
Like polyphonic voices that crisscross
In short-lived harmonies.

     Today, a few stragglers.
One, a girl, stands there with hands spaced out, so—        15
A gesture in a story. Someone's school notebook spills,
And they bend down to gather up the loose pages.
(Bright sweaters knotted at the waist; solemn expressions.)
Not that they would shrink or hold back from what may come,
For now they all at once run to meet it, a little swirl of colors,        20
Like the leaves already blazing and falling farther north.        1987

CLAUDE McKAY

# America

Although she feeds me bread of bitterness,
And sinks into my throat her tiger's tooth,
Stealing my breath of life, I will confess
I love this cultured hell that tests my youth!
5   Her vigor flows like tides into my blood,
Giving me strength erect against her hate.
Her bigness sweeps my being like a flood.
Yet as a rebel fronts a king in state,
I stand within her walls with not a shred
10   Of terror, malice, not a word of jeer.
Darkly I gaze into the days ahead,
And see her might and granite wonders there,
Beneath the touch of Time's unerring hand,
Like priceless treasures sinking in the sand.

1922

LANGSTON HUGHES

# Harlem (A Dream Deferred)

What happens to a dream deferred?

Does it dry up
like a raisin in the sun?
Or fester like a sore—
And then run?
5   Does it stink like rotten meat?
Or crust and sugar over—
like a syrupy sweet?

Maybe it just sags
like a heavy load.
10

*Or does it explode?*

1951

ROBERT HAYDEN

## Frederick Douglass[2]

When it is finally ours, this freedom, this liberty, this beautiful
and terrible thing, needful to man as air,
usable as earth; when it belongs at last to all,
when it is truly instinct, brain matter, diastole, systole,
reflex action; when it is finally won; when it is more                    5
than the gaudy mumbo jumbo of politicians:
this man, this Douglass, this former slave, this Negro
beaten to his knees, exiled, visioning a world
where none is lonely, none hunted, alien,
this man, superb in love and logic, this man                              10
shall be remembered. Oh, not with statues' rhetoric,
not with legends and poems and wreaths of bronze alone,
but with the lives grown out of his life, the lives
fleshing his dream of the beautiful, needful thing.                       1966


MBUYISENI OSWALD MTSHALI

## Boy on a Swing

Slowly he moves
to and fro, to and fro,
then faster and faster
he swishes up and down.

His blue shirt                                                            5
billows in the breeze
like a tattered kite.

The world whirls by:
east becomes west,
north turns to south;                                                    10
the four cardinal points
meet in his head.

    Mother!
Where did I come from?
When will I wear long trousers?                                          15
Why was my father jailed?                                                1982

---

2. Frederick Douglass (1817–1895), escaped slave. Douglass was involved in the Underground Railroad
and became the publisher of the famous abolitionist newspaper the *North Star*, in Rochester, New York.

THOMAS HARDY

## The Convergence of the Twain

Lines on the Loss of the "Titanic"[3]

### I

In a solitude of the sea
Deep from human vanity,
And the Pride of Life that planned her, stilly couches she.

### II

Steel chambers, late the pyres
Of her salamandrine[4] fires,
Cold currents thrid,[5] and turn to rhythmic tidal lyres.

### III

Over the mirrors meant
To glass the opulent
The sea-worm crawls—grotesque, slimed, dumb, indifferent.

### IV

Jewels in joy designed
To ravish the sensuous mind
Lie lightless, all their sparkles bleared and black and blind.

### V

Dim moon-eyed fishes near
Gaze at the gilded gear
And query: "What does this vaingloriousness down here?" . . .

### VI

Well: while was fashioning
This creature of cleaving wing,
The Immanent Will that stirs and urges everything

### VII

Prepared a sinister mate
For her—so gaily great—
A Shape of Ice, for the time far and dissociate.

5

10

15

20

3. On the night of April 14, 1912, the *Titanic*, the largest ship afloat and on her maiden voyage to New York from Southampton, collided with an iceberg in the North Atlantic and sank in less than three hours; 1,500 of 2,206 passengers were lost.     4. Bright red; the salamander was supposed to be able to live in fire.     5. Thread.

VIII

And as the smart ship grew
In stature, grace, and hue,
In shadowy silent distance grew the Iceberg too.


IX

Alien they seemed to be:                                          25
No mortal eye could see
The intimate welding of their later history,


X

Or sign that they were bent
By paths coincident
On being anon twin halves of one august event,                   30


XI

Till the Spinner of the Years
Said "Now!" And each one hears,
And consummation comes, and jars two hemispheres.        1914


WILFRED OWEN

## Dulce et Decorum Est[6]

Bent double, like old beggars under sacks,
Knock-kneed, coughing like hags, we cursed through sludge,
Till on the haunting flares we turned our backs
And towards our distant rest began to trudge.
Men marched asleep. Many had lost their boots                    5
But limped on, blood-shod. All went lame; all blind;
Drunk with fatigue; deaf even to the hoots
Of disappointed shells that dropped behind.

Gas! Gas! Quick, boys!—An ecstasy of fumbling,
Fitting the clumsy helmets just in time;                          10
But someone still was yelling out and stumbling
And floundering like a man in fire or lime.—

6. Part of a phrase from Horace, quoted in full in the last lines: "It is sweet and proper to die for one's country."

Dim, through the misty panes and thick green light
As under a green sea, I saw him drowning.

15  In all my dreams, before my helpless sight,
He plunges at me, guttering, choking, drowning.

If in some smothering dreams you too could pace
Behind the wagon that we flung him in,
And watch the white eyes writhing in his face,
20  His hanging face, like a devil's sick of sin;
If you could hear, at every jolt, the blood
Come gargling from the froth-corrupted lungs,
Obscene as cancer, bitter as the cud
Of vile, incurable sores on innocent tongues,—
25  My friend, you would not tell with such high zest
To children ardent for some desperate glory,
The old Lie: Dulce et decorum est
Pro patria mori.

1917

## RICHARD EBERHART

# *The Fury of Aerial Bombardment*

You would think the fury of aerial bombardment
Would rouse God to relent; the infinite spaces
Are still silent. He looks on shock-pried faces.
History, even, does not know what is meant.

5  You would feel that after so many centuries
God would give man to repent; yet he can kill
As Cain could, but with multitudinous will,
No farther advanced than in his ancient furies.

Was man made stupid to see his own stupidity?
10  Is God by definition indifferent, beyond us all?
Is the eternal truth man's fighting soul
Wherein the Beast ravens in its own avidity?

Of Van Wettering I speak, and Averill,
Names on a list, whose faces I do not recall
15  But they are gone to early death, who late in school
Distinguished the belt feed lever from the belt holding pawl.[7]        1947

7. Machine-gun parts.

WILLIAM STAFFORD

## At the Bomb Testing Site

At noon in the desert a panting lizard
waited for history, its elbows tense,
watching the curve of a particular road
as if something might happen.

It was looking at something farther off                                5
than people could see, an important scene
acted in stone for little selves
at the flute end of consequences.

There was just a continent without much on it
under a sky that never cared less.                                    10
Ready for a change, the elbows waited.
The hands gripped hard on the desert.                    1966


DUDLEY RANDALL

## Ballad of Birmingham

*(On the bombing of a church in Birmingham, Alabama, 1963)*

"Mother dear, may I go downtown
Instead of out to play,
And march the streets of Birmingham
In a Freedom March today?"

"No, baby, no, you may not go,                                        5
For the dogs are fierce and wild,
And clubs and hoses, guns and jails
Aren't good for a little child."

"But, mother, I won't be alone.
Other children will go with me,                                       10
And march the streets of Birmingham
To make our country free."

"No, baby, no, you may not go,
For I fear those guns will fire.
But you may go to church instead                                      15
And sing in the children's choir."

She has combed and brushed her night-dark hair,
And bathed rose petal sweet,
And drawn white gloves on her small brown hands,
And white shoes on her feet.                                          20

The mother smiled to know her child
Was in the sacred place,
But that smile was the last smile
To come upon her face.

25   For when she heard the explosion,
Her eyes grew wet and wild.
She raced through the streets of Birmingham
Calling for her child.

She clawed through bits of glass and brick,
30   Then lifted out a shoe.
"Oh, here's the shoe my baby wore,
But, baby, where are you?"                                    1969

AI

# Riot Act, April 29, 1992

I'm going out and get something.
I don't know what.
I don't care.
Whatever's out there, I'm going to get it.
5   Look in those shop windows at boxes
and boxes of Reeboks and Nikes
to make me fly through the air
like Michael Jordan
like Magic.
10   While I'm up there, I see Spike Lee.
Looks like he's flying too
straight through the glass
that separates me
from the virtual reality
15   I watch everyday on TV.
I know the difference between
what it is and what it isn't.
Just because I can't touch it
doesn't mean it isn't real.
20   All I have to do is smash the screen,
reach in and take what I want.
Break out of prison.
South Central homey's newly risen
from the night of living dead,
25   but this time he lives,
he gets to give the zombies
a taste of their own medicine.
Open wide and let me in,
or else I'll set your world on fire,

but you pretend that you don't hear.                                    30
You haven't heard the word is coming down
like the hammer of the gun
of this black son, locked out of the big house,
while massa looks out the window and sees only smoke.
Massa doesn't see anything else,                                        35
not because he can't,
but because he won't.
He'd rather hear me talking about mo' money,
mo' honeys and gold chains
and see me carrying my favorite things                                  40
from looted stores
than admit that underneath my Raiders' cap,
the aftermath is staring back
unblinking through the camera's lens,
courtesy of CNN,                                                        45
my arms loaded with boxes of shoes
that I will sell at the swap meet
to make a few cents on the declining dollar.
And if I destroy myself
and my neighborhood                                                     50
"ain't nobody's business, if I do,"
but the police are knocking hard
at my door
and before I can open it,
they break it down                                                      55
and drag me in the yard.
They take me in to be processed and charged,
to await trial,
while Americans forget
the day the wealth finally trickled down                                60
to the rest of us.                                             1993

# CONSTRUCTING IDENTITY, EXPLORING GENDER

## ROBERT BROWNING

### *My Last Duchess*

Ferrara[8]

That's my last Duchess painted on the wall,
Looking as if she were alive. I call
That piece a wonder, now: Frà Pandolf's hands[9]
Worked busily a day, and there she stands.
5    Will't please you sit and look at her? I said
"Frà Pandolf" by design, for never read
Strangers like you that pictured countenance,
The depth and passion of its earnest glance,
But to myself they turned (since none puts by
10   The curtain I have drawn for you, but I)
And seemed as they would ask me, if they durst,
How such a glance came there; so, not the first
Are you to turn and ask thus. Sir, 'twas not
Her husband's presence only, called that spot
15   Of joy into the Duchess' cheek: perhaps
Frà Pandolf chanced to say "Her mantle laps
Over my lady's wrist too much," or "Paint
Must never hope to reproduce the faint
Half-flush that dies along her throat": such stuff
20   Was courtesy, she thought, and cause enough
For calling up that spot of joy. She had
A heart—how shall I say?—too soon made glad,
Too easily impressed; she liked whate'er
She looked on, and her looks went everywhere.
25   Sir, 'twas all one! My favor at her breast,
The dropping of the daylight in the West,
The bough of cherries some officious fool
Broke in the orchard for her, the white mule
She rode with round the terrace—all and each
30   Would draw from her alike the approving speech,
Or blush, at least. She thanked men,—good! but thanked
Somehow—I know not how—as if she ranked

---

8. Alfonso II, duke of Ferrara in Italy in the mid-sixteenth century, is the presumed speaker of the poem, which is loosely based on historical events. The duke's first wife—whom he had married when she was fourteen—died under suspicious circumstances at seventeen, and he then negotiated through an agent (to whom the poem is spoken) for the hand of the niece of the count of Tyrol in Austria.    9. Frà Pandolf is, like Claus (line 56), fictitious.

My gift of a nine-hundred-years-old name
With anybody's gift. Who'd stoop to blame
This sort of trifling? Even had you skill                                    35
In speech—which I have not—to make your will
Quite clear to such an one, and say, "Just this
Or that in you disgusts me; here you miss,
Or there exceed the mark"—and if she let
Herself be lessoned so, nor plainly set                                      40
Her wits to yours, forsooth, and made excuse,
—E'en then would be some stooping; and I choose
Never to stoop. Oh sir, she smiled, no doubt,
Whene'er I passed her; but who passed without
Much the same smile? This grew; I gave commands;                             45
Then all smiles stopped together. There she stands
As if alive. Will't please you rise? We'll meet
The company below, then. I repeat,
The Count your master's known munificence
Is ample warrant that no just pretense                                       50
Of mine for dowry will be disallowed;
Though his fair daughter's self, as I avowed
At starting, is my object. Nay, we'll go
Together down, sir. Notice Neptune, though,
Taming a sea-horse, thought a rarity,                                        55
Which Claus of Innsbruck cast in bronze for me!                    1842


## RICHARD LOVELACE

## *Song: To Lucasta, Going to the Wars*

Tell me not, sweet, I am unkind,
    That from the nunnery
Of thy chaste breast and quiet mind
    To war and arms I fly.

True: a new mistress now I chase,                                             5
    The first foe in the field;
And with a stronger faith embrace
    A sword, a horse, a shield.

Yet this inconstancy is such
    As you too shall adore;                                                   10
I could not love thee, dear, so much,
    Loved I not honor more.                                          1649

ISAAC ROSENBERG

## *Break of Day in the Trenches*

The darkness crumbles away—
It is the same old druid[1] Time as ever.
Only a live thing leaps my hand—
A queer sardonic rat—
As I pull the parapet's poppy[2]
To stick behind my ear.
Droll rat, they would shoot you if they knew
Your cosmopolitan sympathies.
Now you have touched this English hand
You will do the same to a German—
Soon, no doubt, if it be your pleasure
To cross the sleeping green between.
It seems you inwardly grin as you pass
Strong eyes, fine limbs, haughty athletes
Less chanced than you for life,
Bonds to the whims of murder,
Sprawled in the bowels of the earth,
The torn fields of France.
What do you see in our eyes
At the shrieking iron and flame
Hurled through still heavens?
What quaver—what heart aghast?
Poppies whose roots are in man's veins
Drop, and are ever dropping;
But mine in my ear is safe,
Just a little white with the dust.

ca. 1917

EDGAR A. GUEST

## *The Things That Make a Soldier Great*

The things that make a soldier great and send him out to die,
To face the flaming cannon's mouth, nor ever question why,
Are lilacs by a little porch, the row of tulips red,
The peonies and pansies, too, the old petunia bed,

1. Magician or priest.   2. Flower growing on the earthwork built to shield soldiers from enemy fire. The poppy became a standard symbol for the war dead because a large burial field in Flanders was covered with poppies.

The grass plot where his children play, the roses on the wall:    5
'Tis these that make a soldier great. He's fighting for them all.

'Tis not the pomp and pride of kings that make a soldier brave;
'Tis not allegiance to the flag that over him may wave;
For soldiers never fight so well on land or on the foam
As when behind the cause they see the little place called home.    10
Endanger but that humble street whereon his children run—
You make a soldier of the man who never bore a gun.

What is it through the battle smoke the valiant soldier sees?
The little garden far away, the budding apple trees,
The little patch of ground back there, the children at their play,    15
Perhaps a tiny mound behind the simple church of gray.
The golden thread of courage isn't linked to castle dome
But to the spot, where'er it be—the humble spot called home.

And now the lilacs bud again and all is lovely there,
And homesick soldiers far away know spring is in the air;    20
The tulips come to bloom again, the grass once more is green,
And every man can see the spot where all his joys have been.
He sees his children smile at him, he hears the bugle call,
And only death can stop him now—he's fighting for them all.

1918

WILFRED OWEN

## Disabled

He sat in a wheeled chair, waiting for dark,
And shivered in his ghastly suit of grey,
Legless, sewn short at elbow. Through the park
Voices of boys rang saddening like a hymn,
Voices of play and pleasure after day,    5
Till gathering sleep had mothered them from him.

About this time Town used to swing so gay
When glow-lamps budded in the light blue trees,
And girls glanced lovelier as the air grew dim,—
In the old times, before he threw away his knees.    10
Now he will never feel again how slim
Girls' waists are, or how warm their subtle hands;
All of them touch him like some queer disease.

There was an artist silly for his face,
For it was younger than his youth, last year.    15
Now, he is old; his back will never brace;
He's lost his color very far from here,
Poured it down shell-holes till the veins ran dry,

And half his lifetime lapsed in the hot race,
20    And leap of purple spurted from his thigh.

One time he liked a blood-smear down his leg,
After the matches,[3] carried shoulder-high
It was after football, when he'd drunk a peg,[4]
He thought he'd better join.—He wonders why.
25    Someone had said he'd look a god in kilts,
That's why; and may be, too, to please his Meg;
Aye, that was it, to please the giddy jilts
He asked to join. He didn't have to beg;
Smiling they wrote his lie; aged nineteen years.

30    Germans he scarcely thought of; all their guilt,
And Austria's, did not move him. And no fears
Of Fear came yet. He thought of jeweled hilts
For daggers in plaid socks; of smart salutes;
And care of arms; and leave; and pay arrears;
35    *Esprit de corps;* and hints for young recruits.
And soon, he was drafted out with drums and cheers.

Some cheered him home, but not as crowds cheer Goal.[5]
Only a solemn man who brought him fruits
*Thanked* him; and then inquired about his soul.
40    Now, he will spend a few sick years in Institutes,
And do what things the rules consider wise,
And take whatever pity they may dole.
Tonight he noticed how the women's eyes
Passed from him to the strong men that were whole.
45    How cold and late it is! Why don't they come
And put him into bed? Why don't they come?                    1917


PAULETTE JILES

## *Paper Matches*

My aunts washed dishes while the uncles
squirted each other on the lawn with
    garden hoses. Why are we in here,
I said, and they are out there.
5        That's the way it is,
        said Aunt Hetty, the shrivelled-up one.
    I have the rages that small animals have,
being small, being animal.
        Written on me was a message,

---

3. Soccer games.     4. A drink, usually brandy and soda.     5. In soccer.

"At Your Service" like a book of                                    10
paper matches. One by one we were
taken out and struck.
   We come bearing supper.
our heads on fire.                                              1973


## MARGE PIERCY

# *What's That Smell in the Kitchen?*

All over America women are burning dinners.
It's lambchops in Peoria; it's haddock
in Providence; it's steak in Chicago;
tofu delight in Big Sur; red
rice and beans in Dallas.                                           5
All over America women are burning
food they're supposed to bring with calico
smile on platters glittering like wax.
Anger sputters in her brainpan, confined
but spewing out missiles of hot fat.                                10
Carbonized despair presses like a clinker
from a barbecue against the back of her eyes.
If she wants to grill anything, it's
her husband spitted over a slow fire.
If she wants to serve him anything                                  15
it's a dead rat with a bomb in its belly
ticking like the heart of an insomniac.
Her life is cooked and digested,
nothing but leftovers in Tupperware.
Look, she says, once I was roast duck                               20
on your platter with parsley but now I am Spam.
Burning dinner is not incompetence but war.              1983


## DOROTHY PARKER

# *Indian Summer*

In youth, it was a way I had
   To do my best to please,
And change, with every passing lad,
   To suit his theories.

But now I know the things I know,                                   5
   And do the things I do;

And if you do not like me so,
    To hell, my love, with you!

1937

ELIZABETH[6]

# When I Was Fair and Young

When I was fair and young, and favor graced me,
    Of many was I sought, their mistress for to be;
But I did scorn them all, and answered them therefore,
    "Go, go, go, seek some otherwhere,
5        Importune me no more!"

How many weeping eyes I made to pine with woe,
    How many sighing hearts, I have no skill to show;
Yet I the prouder grew, and answered them therefore,
    "Go, go, go, seek some otherwhere,
10        Importune me no more!"

Then spake fair Venus' son, that proud victorious boy,[7]
    And said: "Fine dame, since that you be so coy,
I will so pluck your plumes that you shall say no more,
    'Go, go, go, seek some otherwhere,
15        Importune me no more!' "

When he had spake these words, such change grew in my breast
    That neither night nor day since that, I could take any rest.
Then lo! I did repent that I had said before,
    "Go, go, go, seek some otherwhere,
20        Importune me no more!"

ca. 1585?

THEODORE ROETHKE

# I Knew a Woman

I knew a woman, lovely in her bones,
When small birds sighed, she would sigh back at them;
Ah, when she moved, she moved more ways than one:
The shapes a bright container can contain!
5    Of her choice virtues only gods should speak;

6. The attribution of this poem to Queen Elizabeth I of England (1533–1603) is likely but not certain.
7. Cupid.

Or English poets who grew up on Greek
(I'd have them sing in chorus, cheek to cheek).

How well her wishes went! She stroked my chin,
She taught me Turn, and Counter-turn, and Stand;[8]
She taught me Touch, that undulant white skin;            10
I nibbled meekly from her proffered hand;
She was the sickle; I, poor I, the rake,
Coming behind her for her pretty sake
(But what prodigious mowing we did make).

Love likes a gander, and adores a goose:              15
Her full lips pursed, the errant note to seize;
She played it quick, she played it light and loose;
My eyes, they dazzled at her flowing knees;
Her several parts could keep a pure repose,
Or one hip quiver with a mobile nose              20
(She moved in circles, and those circles moved).

Let seed be grass, and grass turn into hay:
I'm martyr to a motion not my own;
What's freedom for? To know eternity.
I swear she cast a shadow white as stone.              25
But who would count eternity in days?
These old bones live to learn her wanton ways:
(I measure time by how a body sways).              1958

## RUTH STONE

## Second-Hand Coat

I feel
in her pockets; she wore nice cotton gloves,
kept a handkerchief box, washed her undies,
ate at the Holiday Inn, had a basement freezer,
belonged to a bridge club.              5
I think when I wake in the morning
that I have turned into her.
She hangs in the hall downstairs,
a shadow with pulled threads.
I slip her over my arms, skin of a matron.              10
Where are you? I say to myself, to the orphaned body,
and her coat says,
Get your purse, have you got your keys?              1987

8. Literary terms for the parts of a Pindaric ode.

## RICHARD WILBUR

### *She*

What was her beauty in our first estate
When Adam's will was whole,[9] and the least thing
Appeared the gift and creature of his king,
How should we guess? Resemblance had to wait

5    For separation, and in such a place
She so partook of water, light, and trees
As not to look like any one of these.
He woke and gazed into her naked face.

But then she changed, and coming down amid
10   The flocks of Abel and the fields of Cain,
Clothed in their wish, her Eden graces hid,
A shape of plenty with a mop of grain,

She broke upon the world, in time took on
The look of every labor and its fruits.
15   Columnar in a robe of pleated lawn
She cupped her patient hand for attributes,

Was radiant captive of the farthest tower
And shed her honor on the fields of war,
Walked in her garden at the evening hour,
20   Her shadow like a dark ogival[1] door,

Breasted the seas for all the westward ships
And, come to virgin country, changed again—
A moonlike being truest in eclipse,
And subject goddess of the dreams of men.

25   Tree, temple, valley, prow, gazelle, machine,
More named and nameless than the morning star,
Lovely in every shape, in all unseen,
We dare not wish to find you as you are,

Whose apparition, biding time until
30   Desire decay and bring the latter age,
Shall flourish in the ruins of our will
And deck[2] the broken stones like saxifrage.[3]

1961

9. Before the Fall.    1. In the form of a pointed (Gothic) arch.    2. Adorn.    3. A tufted plant with
bright flowers, often rooted in the clefts of rocks.

DOROTHY LIVESAY

## The Taming

Be woman. You did say me, be
woman.      I did not know
the measure of the words

> until a black man
> as I prepared him chicken                                    5
> made me listen:
> —No, dammit.
> Not so much salt.
> Do what I say, woman:
> just that                                                    10
> and nothing more.

Be woman. I did not know
the measure of the words
until that night
when you denied me darkness,                                   15
even the right
to turn in my own light.

Do as I say, I heard you faintly
over me fainting:
be woman.                                                      20

1967


KATHERINE PHILIPS

## L'amitié: To Mrs. M. Awbrey

Soul of my soul, my Joy, my crown, my friend!
A name which all the rest doth comprehend;
How happy are we now, whose souls are grown,
By an incomparable mixture, One:
Whose well acquainted minds are now as near                    5
As Love, or vows, or secrets can endear.
I have no thought but what's to thee reveal'd,
Nor thou desire that is from me conceal'd.
Thy heart locks up my secrets richly set,
And my breast is thy private cabinet.                          10
Thou shedst no tear but what my moisture lent,
And if I sigh, it is thy breath is spent.
United thus, what horror can appear

Worthy our sorrow, anger, or our fear?
15   Let the dull world alone to talk and fight,
And with their vast ambitions nature fright;
Let them despise so innocent a flame,
While Envy, Pride, and Faction play their game:
But we by Love sublim'd so high shall rise,
20   To pity Kings, and Conquerors despise,
Since we that sacred union have engrossed,
Which they and all the sullen world have lost.                    1667


KAY SMITH

## Annunciation

*for Kathy*


In all the old paintings
The Virgin is reading—
No one knows what,
When she is disturbed
5    By an angel with a higher mission,
Beyond books.

She looks up reluctantly,
Still marking the place with her finger.
The angel is impressive,
10   With red shoes and just
A hint of wing and shine everywhere.
Listening to the measured message
The Virgin bows her head,
Her eyes aslant
15   Between the angel and the book.

At the Uffizi[4]
We stood
Before a particularly beautiful angel
And a hesitant Sienese Virgin,
20   We two sometimes women.
Believing we could ignore
All messages,
Unobliged to wings or words,
We laughed in the vibrant space
25   Between the two,
Somewhere in the angled focus
Of the Virgin's eye.

---

4. The richest art gallery in Italy, located in Florence. Its collection includes a painting of the Annunciation by the fourteenth-century Sienese painter Simone Martini.

Now, in the harder times,
I do not laugh so often;
Still the cheap postcard in my room                          30
Glints with the angel's robe.
I look with envy
At the angel and the book,
Wishing I had chosen
One or the other,                                           35
Anything but the space between.                      1986


EDNA ST. VINCENT MILLAY

## [*Women have loved before as I love now*]

Women have loved before as I love now;
At least, in lively chronicles of the past—
Of Irish waters by a Cornish prow
Or Trojan waters by a Spartan mast
Much to their cost invaded—here and there,            5
Hunting the amorous line, skimming the rest,
I find some woman bearing as I bear
Love like a burning city in the breast.
I think however that of all alive
I only in such utter, ancient way                     10
Do suffer love; in me alone survive
The unregenerate passions of a day
When treacherous queens, with death upon the tread,
Heedless and wilful, took their knights to bed.        1931


APHRA BEHN

## *To the Fair Clarinda, Who Made Love to Me, Imagined More Than Woman*

Fair lovely maid, or if that title be
Too weak, too feminine for nobler thee,
Permit a name that more approaches truth,
And let me call thee, lovely charming youth.
This last will justify my soft complaint,              5
While that may serve to lessen my constraint;
And without blushes I the youth pursue,

When so much beauteous woman is in view.
Against thy charms we struggle but in vain
10   With thy deluding form thou giv'st us pain,
While the bright nymph betrays us to the swain.
In pity to our sex sure thou wert sent,
That we might love, and yet be innocent:
For sure no crime with thee we can commit;
15   Or if we should—thy form excuses it.
For who, that gathers fairest flowers believes
A snake lies hid beneath the fragrant leaves.

    Thou beauteous wonder of a different kind,
Soft Cloris with the dear Alexis joined;
20   When e'er the manly part of thee, would plead
Thou tempts us with the image of the maid,
While we the noblest passions do extend
The love to Hermes, Aphrodite[5] the friend.

1685

## ROBERT BROWNING

# *Women and Roses*

### 1

I dream of a red-rose tree.
And which of its roses three
Is the dearest rose to me?

### 2

Round and round, like a dance of snow
5   In a dazzling drift, as its guardians, go
Floating the women faded for ages,
Sculptured in stone, on the poet's pages.
Then follow women fresh and gay,
Living and loving and loved today.
10   Last, in the rear, flee the multitude of maidens,
Beauties yet unborn. And all, to one cadence,
They circle their rose on my rose tree.

### 3

Dear rose, thy term is reached,
Thy leaf hangs loose and bleached:
15   Bees pass it unimpeached.

---

5. The Greek messenger god (Hermes) and the Greek goddess of love (Aphrodite); their offspring, Hermaphroditus, had both male and female characteristics.

### 4

Stay then, stoop, since I cannot climb,
You, great shapes of the antique time!
How shall I fix you, fire you, freeze you,
Break my heart at your feet to please you?
Oh, to possess and be possessed!                           20
Hearts that beat 'neath each pallid breast!
Once but of love, the poesy, the passion,
Drink but once and die!—In vain, the same fashion,
They circle their rose on my rose tree.

### 5

Dear rose, thy joy's undimmed,                             25
Thy cup is ruby-rimmed,
Thy cup's heart nectar-brimmed.

### 6

Deep, as drops from a statue's plinth[6]
The bee sucked in by the hyacinth,
So will I bury me while burning,                           30
Quench like him at a plunge my yearning,
Eyes in your eyes, lips on your lips!
Fold me fast where the cincture[7] slips,
Prison all my soul in eternities of pleasure,
Girdle me for once! But no—the old measure,               35
They circle their rose on my rose tree.

### 7

Dear rose without a thorn,
Thy bud's the babe unborn:
First streak of a new morn.

### 8

Wings, lend wings for the cold, the clear!                 40
What is far conquers what is near.
Roses will bloom nor want beholders,
Sprung from the dust where our flesh molders.
What should arrive with the cycle's change?
A novel grace and a beauty strange.                        45
I will make an Eve, be the artist that began her,
Shaped her to his mind!—Alas! in like manner
They circle their rose on my rose tree.

1852                                                       1855

6. Base.    7. Belt.

LIZ ROSENBERG

## The Silence of Women

Old men, as time goes on, grow softer, sweeter,
while their wives get angrier.
You see them hauling the men across the mall
or pushing them down on chairs,
"Sit there! and don't you move!"
A lifetime of *yes* has left them
hissing bent as snakes.
It seems even their bones will turn
against them, once the fruitful years are gone.
Something snaps off the houselights,
and the cells go dim;
the chicken hatching back into the egg.

Oh lifetime of silence!
words scattered like a sybil's leaves.
Voice thrown into a baritone storm—
whose shrilling is a soulful wind
blown through an instrument
that cannot beat time

but must make music
any way it can.

1994

ANNE SEXTON

## The Farmer's Wife

From the hodge porridge
of their country lust,
their local life in Illinois,
where all their acres look
like a sprouting broom factory,
they name just ten years now
that she has been his habit;
as again tonight he'll say
honey bunch let's go
and she will not say how there
must be more to living
than this brief bright bridge
of the raucous bed or even
the slow braille touch of him
like a heavy god grown light,

that old pantomime of love
that she wants although
it leaves her still alone,
built back again at last,
mind's apart from him, living                    20
her own self in her own words
and hating the sweat of the house
they keep when they finally lie
each in separate dreams
and then how she watches him,                    25
still strong in the blowzy bag
of his usual sleep while
her young years bungle past
their same marriage bed
and she wishes him cripple, or poet,             30
or even lonely, or sometimes,
better, my lover, dead.                     1960


SHARON OLDS

## The Elder Sister

When I look at my elder sister now
I think how she had to go first, down through the
birth canal, to force her way
head-first through the tiny channel,
the pressure of Mother's muscles on her brain,        5
the tight walls scraping her skin.
Her face is still narrow from it, the long
hollow cheeks of a Crusader on a tomb,
and her inky eyes have the look of someone who has
been in prison a long time and                       10
knows they can send her back. I look at her
body and think how her breasts were the first to
rise, slowly, like swans on a pond.
By the time mine came along, they were just
two more birds in the flock, and when the hair       15
rose on the white mound of her flesh, like
threads of water out of the ground, it was the
first time, but when mine came
they knew about it. I used to think
only in terms of her harshness, sitting and          20
pissing on me in bed, but now I
see I had her before me always
like a shield. I look at her wrinkles, her clenched
jaws, her frown-lines—I see they are
the dents on my shield, the blows that did not reach me.   25
She protected me, not as a mother

protects a child, with love, but as a
hostage protects the one who makes her
escape as I made my escape, with my sister's
30    body held in front of me.                                          1984


DORIANNE LAUX

## *The Laundromat*

My clothes somersault in the dryer. At thirty
I float in and out of a new kind of horniness,
the kind where you get off on words and gestures;
long talks about art are foreplay, the climax
5    is watching a man eat a Napoleon while he drives.
Across from me a fifty year old matron folds clothes,
her eyes focused on the nipples of a young man in
silk jogging shorts. He looks up, catching her.
She giggles and blurts out, "Hot, isn't it?"
10   A man on my right eyes the line of my shorts, waiting
for me to bend over. I do. An act of animal kindness.
A long black jogger swings in off the street to
splash his face in the sink and I watch the room
become a sweet humid jungle. We crowd around
15   the Amazon at the watering hole, twitching our noses
like wildebeests or buffalo, snorting, rooting out
mates in the heat. I want to hump every moving thing
in this place. I want to lie down in the dry dung
and dust and twist to scratch my back. I want to
20   stretch and prowl and grow lazy in the shade. I want
to have a slew of cubs. "Do you have change for
a quarter?" he asks, scratching the inside of his thigh.
Back in the laundromat my socks are sticking to my
sheets. Caught in the crackle of static electricity,
25   I fold my underwear. I notice the honey-colored
stains in each silk crotch. Odd-shaped, like dreams,
I make my panties into neat squares and drop them,
smiling, into the wicker basket.                                      1990


ELIZABETH BISHOP

## *Exchanging Hats*

Unfunny uncles who insist
in trying on a lady's hat,

—oh, even if the joke falls flat,
we share your slight transvestite twist

in spite of our embarrassment.                                                    5
Costume and custom are complex.
The headgear of the other sex
inspires us to experiment.

Anandrous aunts, who, at the beach
with paper plates upon your laps,                                                10
keep putting on the yachtsmen's caps
with exhibitionistic screech,

the visors hanging o'er the ear
so that the golden anchors drag,
—the tides of fashion never lag.                                                 15
Such caps may not be worn next year.

Or you who don the paper plate
itself, and put some grapes upon it,
or sport the Indian's feather bonnet,
—perversities may aggravate                                                      20

the natural madness of the hatter.
And if the opera hats collapse
and crowns grow draughty, then, perhaps,
he thinks what might a miter matter?

Unfunny uncle, you who wore a                                                    25
hat too big, or one too many,
tell us, can't you, are there any
stars inside your black fedora?

Aunt exemplary and slim,
with avernal eyes, we wonder                                                     30
what slow changes they see under
their vast, shady, turned-down brim.                                  1956


JUDITH ORTIZ COFER

## The Changeling

                        As a young girl
vying for my father's attention,
I invented a game that made him look up
from his reading and shake his head
as if both baffled and amused.                                                    5

In my brother's closet, I'd change
into his dungarees—the rough material
molding me into boy shape; hide
my long hair under an army helmet

10   he'd been given by Father, and emerge
transformed into the legendary Ché[8]
of grown-up talk.

Strutting around the room,
I'd tell of life in the mountains,
15   of carnage and rivers of blood,
and of manly feasts with rum and music
to celebrate victories *para la libertad.*[9]
He would listen with a smile
to my tales of battles and brotherhood
20   until Mother called us to dinner.

She was not amused
by my transformations, sternly forbidding me
from sitting down with them as a man.
She'd order me back to the dark cubicle
25   that smelled of adventure, to shed
my costume, to braid my hair furiously
with blind hands, and to return invisible,
as myself,
to the real world of her kitchen.                                    1993

ALLEN GINSBERG

## *Personals Ad*

*"I will send a picture too
if you will send me one of you"*
                    —R. CREELEY

Poet professor in autumn years
seeks helpmate companion protector friend
young lover w/ empty compassionate soul
exuberant spirit, straightforward handsome
5   athletic physique & boundless mind, courageous
warrior who may also like women & girls, no problem,
to share bed meditation apartment Lower East Side,
help inspire mankind conquer world anger & guilt,
empowered by Whitman Blake Rimbaud Ma Rainey & Vivaldi,
10   familiar respecting Art's primordial majesty, priapic carefree
playful harmless slave or master, mortally tender passing swift time,
photographer, musician, painter, poet, yuppie or scholar—
Find me here in New York alone with the Alone
going to lady psychiatrist who says Make time in your life

8. Ché Guevara (1928–1967): revolutionary leader, martyred companion of Fidel Castro.   9. "For free-dom" (Spanish).

for someone you can call darling, honey, who holds you dear          15
can get excited & lay his head on your heart in peace.

*October 8, 1987*                                                   1994


AMY LOWELL

## *The Lonely Wife*[1]

The mist is thick. On the wide river, the water-plants float smoothly.
No letters come; none go.
There is only the moon, shining through the clouds of a hard, jade-
    green sky,
Looking down at us so far divided, so anxiously apart.
All day, going about my affairs, I suffer and grieve, and press the
    thought of you closely to my heart.                              5
My eyebrows are locked in sorrow, I cannot separate them.
Nightly, nightly, I keep ready half the quilt,
And wait for the return of that divine dream which is my Lord.

Beneath the quilt of the Fire-Bird, on the bed of the Silver-Crested Love-
    Pheasant,
Nightly, nightly, I drowse alone.                                   10
The red candles in the silver candlesticks melt, and the wax runs from
    them,
As the tears of your so Unworthy One escape and continue constantly to
    flow.
A flower face endures but a short season,
Yet still he drifts along the river Hsiao and the river Hsiang.
As I toss on my pillow, I hear the cold, nostalgic sound of the water-
    clock:                                                          15
Shêng! Shêng! it drips, cutting my heart in two.

I rise at dawn. In the Hall of Pictures
They come and tell me that the snow-flowers are falling.
The reed-blind is rolled high, and I gaze at the beautiful, glittering, pri-
    meval snow,
Whitening the distance, confusing the stone steps and the courtyard.  20
The air is filled with its shining, it blows far out like the smoke of a
    furnace.
The grass-blades are cold and white, like jade girdle pendants.
Surely the Immortals in Heaven must be crazy with wine to cause such
    disorder,
Seizing the white clouds, crumpling them up, destroying them.

                                                                    1921

---

1. A translation/adaptation of a poem by the Chinese poet Li Po.

ELIZABETH SPIRES

## *The Bodies*

Here, in the half-dark of the sauna,
       the bodies of the women glisten . . .

Naked, disproportionate, lush,
hung and burdened with flesh, they open slowly,
like orchids blooming out of season.

Sweat beads my forehead.
Heat rings my breasts, like circlets,
and I *am* my body, all shimmering flesh.

Secrets are whispered here. Stories told.
The bodies, alabaster, abalone,
relax, give up their pose, to ask,
How shall we be joined?
How shall we know each other?
By doors, by chains and linkages
through which we shall be
       entered, touched, possessed.

I see them, row upon row, the rank and file
of generations moving without pause:
—the bodies of the young girls, the willows,
complete unto themselves, androgynous;
—the great bodies of the mothers,
circled by their little moons, adoring;
—the mothers of the mothers,
the old wise ones, ponderous and slow.
And in another room, not far from this one,
the restless bodies of men, searching
without knowing what it is they search for.

Body of the world! Body of flesh!
Leaving this room, I leave the orbit of women.
I dress and walk into the snowy night,
into the great body of the world,
cold, still, and expectant.
Bodying forth, I am taken by the dark.

What am I? Asked, shall I say:
    *Struck by a spark, I quickened*
    *and was born to flashing*
    *days and nights, a small significance*
    *of one. I did not wish to change,*
    *but changed, feeling desire and fear*
    *and love, failing many times.*
    *My meaning made, I died,*
    *the windows darkening for the last time.*

We move, we love, we cry out,
we hold or cannot hold to what we are
and finally wake to find ourselves                                    45
changed beyond all imagining.
Was it enough to have lived?
In that moment of still approach,
will it be given to us to know?                                    1995


MARILYN HACKER

## [*Who would divorce her lover . . .*]

Who would divorce her lover with a phone
call? You did. Like that, it's finished, done—
or is for you. I'm left with closets of
grief (you moved out your things next day). I love
you. I want to make the phone call this                            5
time, say, pack your axe, cab uptown, kiss
me, lots. I'll run a bubble bath; we'll sing
in the tub. We worked for love, loved it. Don't sling
that out with Friday's beer cans, or file-card it
in a drawer of anecdotes: "My Last                                 10
Six Girlfriends: How a Girl Acquires a Past."
I've got "What Becomes of the Broken-Hearted"
run on a loop, unwanted leitmotif.
Lust, light, love, life all tumbled into grief.
You closed us off like a parenthesis                               15
and left me knowing just enough to miss.            1986


HA JIN

## The Past

I have supposed my past is a part of myself.
As my shadow appears whenever I'm in the sun
the past cannot be thrown off and its weight
must be borne, or I will become another man.

But I saw someone wall his past into a garden             5
whose produce is always in fashion.
If you enter his property without permission
he will welcome you with a watchdog or a gun.

I saw someone set up his past as a harbor.
Wherever it sails, his boat is safe—                              10

if a storm comes, he can always head for home.
His voyage is the adventure of a kite.

I saw someone drop his past like trash.
He buried it and shed it altogether.
15    He has shown me that without the past
one can also move ahead and get somewhere.

Like a shroud my past surrounds me,
but I will cut it and stitch it,
to make good shoes with it,
20    shoes that fit my feet.                     1996

DIANE WAKOSKI

## *The Ring of Irony*

What do you say to the mother
of a homosexual man
whom you once were married to,
when she asks you to return your wedding ring
5    because it's a family heirloom?
        "I want to keep it on my key ring
        where I carry it now,
        to remind me of loss?"
or perhaps, in spite,
10        "It was the only thing
        I ever got out of the marriage.
        No. I won't give it back."
Do you say that you love irony
and have imagined your whole life
15    governed by understatement
and paradox?
Yet, the obvious dominates and
I ask myself,
"Why do you want to keep it?
20    Surely the woman deserves some comfort/
if a small piece of gold can do it,
who can object?"
Wallowing again, in the obvious,
I wonder at my meanness,
25    my own petty anger
at men who love other men,
alas, some of them are/have been
my best friends. Irony?
No. The obvious.
30    Why do you want that circle of gold
lying in your purse with keys

and checkbooks? I nudge myself.
Why don't you purchase an ounce of gold
and carry it in a velvet bag instead. Your
own.                                                                        35
Worth so much more.
Of course. The obvious.
Because the other was given,
not bought, and you
have never asked the return of your gifts, but                              40
you know, Diane, why
you anguish over putting the ring in the box and
mailing it off to
Corona, California.
So obvious.                                                                 45
Because you believe in the gifts
freely given
to appease destiny.
You too would sacrifice
Iphigenia or Isaac²                                                         50
for the cap of darkness,
having given your children
for poetry,
having given your sexuality
for beautiful men,                                                          55
having relinquished honor
for music.
The circle of gold,
that ring, symbolizes
the pact.                                                                   60
To give it back says the giving was meaningless.
Fate does not honor your bargain,
Ms. Wakoski. Not irony,
the obvious:
you have no husband,                                                        65
          no house,
          no children,
          no country.
You have no fame,
          fortune,                                                          70
only remaindered books,
and innocent students who
stab you
with their lack of understanding,
asking, no not ironically,                                                  75
"Did you give a lot of readings
when you were young?"

---

2. Agamemnon, in Greek mythology, planned to sacrifice his daughter Iphigenia; Abraham (in the Judeo-Christian tradition) was about to sacrifice his son Isaac when God intervened.

Finally, the understatement, the irony, when I say,
"yes," and the past swallows up everything,
80    leaving the obvious,
and now that handsome woman in California
wants to take the ring.

Soap opera of the middle-aged
mid-Western
85    schoolteacher?
What do you say when irony deserts you
for the maudlin obvious?
"I am mailing you the ring.
Your claim is greater than mine."

90    Irony? No, the obvious.                                        1986


EDNA ST. VINCENT MILLAY

# [*I, being born a woman and distressed*]

I, being born a woman and distressed
By all the needs and notions of my kind,
Am urged by your propinquity to find
Your person fair, and feel a certain zest
5    To bear your body's weight upon my breast:
So subtly is the fume of life designed,
To clarify the pulse and cloud the mind,
And leave me once again undone, possessed.
Think not for this, however, the poor treason
10    Of my stout blood against my staggering brain,
I shall remember you with love, or season
My scorn with pity,—let me make it plain:
I find this frenzy insufficient reason
For conversation when we meet again.                              1923


JORIE GRAHAM

## Short History of the West

Tap tap.
   A blue sky. A sun and moon in it.
Peel it back.
   The angels in ranks, the *about*.
5    Peel it back.

Tap tap the underneath.
Blood where the sky has opened.
   And numbers in there—god how they sing—tap tap—

and the little hammer underneath
   and a hand holding the lid true.                         10
What are you building little man?

   What's it like, what's it for?
We're going now, you stay in there.
   Deep in, nail at a time.
We're putting this back down, down over you, you stay in there,     15
   and then the storyline which starts where the gold doors

fold over the grassy curtain, click,
   and then the *and so*—hair falling
down all over—and the sky on now and the red sun on and the sunbeam,
   and the thing at the end of its reach—the girl            20
in the room down there, at her kitchen table,
   the last pool of light on her plate,

and how you must think of her now—tired, or free,
   or full of *feeling*—and the light she should rise
to switch on now,                                     25
   and how she will not rise.                        1991

## QUESTIONS

1. What additional information would you like to have about the events referred to in Hayden's "Frederick Douglass" and Randall's "Ballad of Birmingham"? What details in these poems seem to require additional information about the events on which each is based? What details about the life and writings of Frederick Douglass, and about his character, would help your reading of the poem named for him? What do you make of the mention of "dogs," "clubs," and "hoses" in "Ballad of Birmingham"? What did "Freedom March" mean in 1969? Given the poem's structure and its portrayal of children's voices and attitudes, what difference might it make to your reading of the poem if you had factual information about the actual casualties of the bombing? If you were editing this poem, what other footnotes would you provide? Reread "Sir Patrick Spens" (page 237). In what ways does Randall's poem allude to it? why?
2. What details about the physical suffering from poison gas are specifically suggested in Owen's "Dulce et Decorum Est"? what details about the physical effects of atomic explosions in Salter's "Welcome to Hiroshima"? How accurate are these representations? Using the reference resources in your college library, look up news accounts of gassings in World War I and the atomic bombing of Hiroshima, and compare the journalistic details with those given in the poems. How careful does each poet seem to have been in representing historical events? What evidence do you find of distortion or "poetic license"? Which details are specifically chosen for powerful rhetorical effects in each poem?
3. Compare the images of fire and burning in Piercy's "What's That Smell in the Kitchen?," Rosenberg's "Married Love" (page 23) and Jiles's "Paper Matches." How are the images used differently in each poem? What common thread of meaning informs the images in these poems? On what kind of cultural assumptions about women and their roles do these images seem to be based? In what ways are these images like other images of passion in

other poems you have read? In what ways are the images like other images of destruction?

4. Which poems in the "Constructing Identity, Exploring Gender" group are especially concerned to suggest the importance of physical space? In what ways do they portray its absence? In what ways do they represent the male sense of a woman's "place"?

5. What images of passivity, deferentiality, and compliance can you find about women in the poems in this group? How is each image treated in the individual poem? In what ways do images of assertion and resistance compete with these images? What differences in imagery do you notice between men's portrayal of women and women's portrayal of women?

## WRITING SUGGESTIONS

1. Using reference materials available in your college's library, construct a short but detailed narrative (of about 500 to 700 words) of the Birmingham bombing. Then "read" the poem in the context of the full story, showing how the poem uses specific details of the incident to create its effects.

2. Compare the way Wakoski (in "The Ring of Irony") and Levertov (in "Wedding-Ring," page 7) conceive and describe the central object in their poems. How important is the appearance of the ring in each case? In what ways is it symbolic to the speaker in each case? Write an essay of about 1,000 words comparing the speakers' values in the two poems, giving special attention to the ways each speaker describes the ring itself.

3. Which poem in the "Constructing Identity, Exploring Gender" group seems to you most effective in describing how men construct their gender and identity? Which is most successful in describing how women do? In a brief essay of about 500 words, show what devices one of the two poems you have chosen uses to accomplish its task.

# CRITICAL CONTEXTS:
# A POETRY CASEBOOK

As the previous context chapters have suggested, poems draw on all kinds of earlier texts, experiences, and events. But they also produce new contexts of discussion and interpretation, a kind of ongoing conversation about the poem itself. Because readers reading poems see different things in them, and because readers bring different interests to their readings, differences and disagreements develop about how poems are to be experienced and interpreted. Just as what you say about a poem differs from what your classmates say, and just as the paper you write about a poem differs from—and often disagrees with—what other students will write, various observations and comments develop around any poem that is read repeatedly by various readers. Many of those interpretations are published in specialized journals and books (the selections that follow are all reprinted from published sources), and a kind of dialogue develops among readers, producing a body of interpretations and commentaries about the poem. Professional interpreters of texts are often called **literary critics,** and the textual analysis they provide is called **criticism**—not because their work is necessarily negative or corrective, but because they ask hard, analytical, "critical" questions and try to provide interpretations based on the application of a wide variety of literary, historical, biographical, psychological, aesthetic, moral, political, or social issues.

Your own interpretive work may seem to you more private and far removed from such "professional" writing about poems. But once you engage in class discussion with your teacher or even talk informally with a fellow student about a poem, you are in effect practicing your own literary criticism—offering comments, interpreting, judging, putting the poem into some kind of perspective that makes it more knowable and understandable to yourself or to other readers. You are, in effect, joining the ongoing conversation about the poem. The accumulated criticism of any particular poem is, in fact, basically just public conversation and discussion—give and take, competing interpretations, accumulation of relevant facts and information—on the topic of how that poem is to be read, interpreted, and evaluated. And when you *write* about the poem, you may often engage specifically the opinions of others—your teacher, fellow students, or published "criticism." You may not have the experience or specific expertise of professional critics, but you can modify or answer the work of others and use them in your own work.

There are many different ways to engage literary criticism and put it to work for you. The most common is to draw on published work for specific information about the poem: glossings of particular terms; explanations of references or situations you don't recognize; accounts of how, when, and under what circumstances the poem was written. Another common use of criticism in writing a paper is as a springboard for your own interpretation, either building upon what someone else has said or using it as a point of departure to disagree and launch a different view. In either case, your own paper may readily develop out of your reading or out of a class lecture or class discussion that you may drawn on just like written accounts. When you use the work of others, be sure to give full credit, carefully detailing the source not only of direct quotations, but all individual points and ideas. Your reader should always be told exactly how to find the material you are quoting or summarizing. Usually, this means careful notes and a list of citations (or bibliography) at the end of your paper. Your instructor will guide you to appropriate handbooks—for example, the *MLA Handbook* or *The Chicago Manual of Style*—that show you how to cite each item according to the habits and practices current in your school.

It can seem intimidating to become involved in critical dialogue, especially with those who are "authorities" or "experts" whose work has been published and widely read. But your own reading experience gives you a legitimate perspective, too, and often it is good interpretive practice to argue out your views against those with extensive interpretive experiences. Besides, as you will quickly discover when you read several critical pieces on a particular poem, the experts often disagree; your participation in the conversation will draw on the reading and interpreting skills you have been developing, and often you will have evidence to add from the analysis you have done *before* you get involved with reading criticism.

Procedurally, it is usually best to do your own extensive analysis of a poem *before* consulting what other critics have said and then to use other people's ideas to supplement, refine, extend, or challenge your own tentative conclusions. That way, you will have a clear base from which to begin, and you can confront other views (and any new facts they may present) from a firm position of your own. It is important to take in new information and to challenge both your own first impressions and considered analyses, but don't be too quick to adopt somebody else's ideas. The best way to test the views of others is to compare them critically to your own conclusions. Usually, that means proceeding just as you have been proceeding—asking the questions you have learned to ask, sorting out the evidence you have noticed, and moving toward an integrated interpretation of the poem.

This chapter provides examples of criticism written about Sylvia Plath's powerful poem "Daddy." Read the poem itself carefully—not just once, but several times—before you look at what the critics who are reprinted here have to say. Ask all of the analytical questions you have found useful in other cases: Who is speaking? To whom? When? Under what conditions? What is the full dramatic situation behind the poem? What kind of language does the poem use? To what effect? How does the poem use metaphor? allusion? historical reference? What kinds of strategy of rhythm and sound does the poem use? To what effect? What is the poem's tone? In what ways is this poem like other poems or other texts on similar topics? When was the poem written? What do you know about the person who wrote the poem? In what ways is this poem like others you have read by this poet or by this poet's contemporaries? How do the poem's issues and attitudes reflect the culture and times in which it was written?

SYLVIA PLATH

# *Daddy*

You do not do, you do not do
Any more, black shoe
In which I have lived like a foot
For thirty years, poor and white,
Barely daring to breathe or Achoo.                              5

Daddy, I have had to kill you.
You died before I had time—
Marble-heavy, a bag full of God,
Ghastly statue with one gray toe
Big as a Frisco seal                                            10

And a head in the freakish Atlantic
Where it pours bean green over blue
In the waters off beautiful Nauset.[1]
I used to pray to recover you.
Ach, du.[2]                                                     15

In the German tongue, in the Polish town
Scraped flat by the roller
Of wars, wars, wars.
But the name of the town is common.
My Polack friend                                                20

Says there are a dozen or two.
So I never could tell where you
Put your foot, your root,
I never could talk to you.
The tongue stuck in my jaw.                                     25

It stuck in a barb wire snare.
Ich, ich, ich, ich,
I could hardly speak.
I thought every German was you.
And the language obscene                                        30

An engine, an engine
Chuffing me off like a Jew.
A Jew to Dachau, Auschwitz, Belsen.[3]
I began to talk like a Jew.
I think I may well be a Jew.                                    35

The snows of the Tyrol,[4] the clear beer of Vienna
Are not very pure or true.
With my gypsy-ancestress and my weird luck

1. An inlet on Cape Cod.     2. "Oh, you" in German. Plath often portrays herself as Jewish and her oppressors as German. *Ich* (below): German for "I."     3. Sites of World War II German death camps.
4. An Alpine region in Austria and northern Italy. The snow there is, legendarily, as pure as the beer is clear in Vienna.

And my Taroc[5] pack and my Taroc pack
40    I may be a bit of a Jew.

I have always been scared of *you,*
With your Luftwaffe,[6] your gobbledygoo.
And your neat moustache
And your Aryan eye, bright blue.
45    Panzer-man, panzer-man, O You—

Not God but a swastika
So black no sky could squeak through.
Every woman adores a Fascist,
The boot in the face, the brute
50    Brute heart of a brute like you.

You stand at the blackboard, daddy,
In the picture I have of you,
A cleft in your chin instead of your foot
But no less a devil for that, no not
55    Any less the black man who

Bit my pretty red heart in two.
I was ten when they buried you.
At twenty I tried to die
And get back, back, back to you.
60    I thought even the bones would do

But they pulled me out of the sack,
And they stuck me together with glue.
And then I knew what to do.
I made a model of you,
65    A man in black with a Meinkampf[7] look

And a love of the rack and the screw.
And I said I do, I do.
So daddy, I'm finally through.
The black telephone's off at the root,
70    The voices just can't worm through.

If I've killed one man, I've killed two—
The vampire who said he was you
And drank my blood for a year,
Seven years, if you want to know.
75    Daddy, you can lie back now.

There's a stake in your fat black heart
And the villagers never liked you.
They are dancing and stamping on you.
They always *knew* it was you.
80    Daddy, daddy, you bastard, I'm through.

1966

---

5. Tarot, playing cards used mainly for fortune-telling.    6. The German air force.    7. The title of
Adolf Hitler's autobiography and manifesto (1925–27); German for "my struggle."

Once you have a "reading" of your own and have made extensive notes about your conclusions, look at the selections that follow. You can read them in a variety of ways:

- skim them all quickly, and look for things that surprise you or that provide you with specific challenges; or
- read each critical piece carefully one by one, and keep close track of all the things with which you agree and (even more important) of those things with which you disagree; or
- look specifically for facts or apparently crucial information new to you, examine and question the information carefully, and see how it affects the interpretation you have previously decided on; or
- look for points of disagreement in the different interpretations, make a list of the most important issues raised, and look for the crucial parts of the poem where the basis for these disagreements occurs.

You will also find your own ways to respond to and use the various critical views you come upon here. Working the views of others into your own arguments and your own writing is complicated; it is difficult to do well so as to be at once fair to what others say and helpful to your own conclusions. But learning to use the facts, opinions, and interpretations of others will clarify your own thoughts and will often hone or add to your own analytical skills and complicate your views. And participating in the larger conversation about a specific poem—or about poetry in general—can contribute mightily to helping you learn to read, respond, and write more effectively.

Sylvia Plath

Sylvia Plath's father, Otto Plath

GEORGE STEINER

## *Dying Is an Art**

\* \* \*

\* \* \* [N]o group of poems since Dylan Thomas' *Deaths and Entrances* has had as vivid and disturbing an impact on English critics and readers as has *Ariel*. Sylvia Plath's last poems have already passed into legend as both representative of our present tone of emotional life and unique in their implacable, harsh brilliance. Those among the young who read new poetry will know "Daddy," "Lady Lazarus," and "Death & Co." almost by heart, and reference to Sylvia Plath is constant where poetry and the conditions of its present existence are discussed.

The spell does not lie wholly in the poems themselves. The suicide of Sylvia Plath at the age of thirty-one in 1963, and the personality of this young woman who had come from Massachusetts to study and live in England (where she married Ted Hughes, himself a gifted poet), are vital parts of it. To those who knew her and to the greatly enlarged circle who were electrified by her last poems and sudden death, she had come to signify the specific honesties and risks of the poet's condition. Her personal style, and the price in private harrowing she so obviously paid to achieve the intensity and candor of her principal poems, have taken on their own dramatic authority.

All this makes it difficult to judge the poems. I mean that the vehemence and intimacy of the verse is such as to constitute a very powerful rhetoric of sincerity. The poems play on our nerves with their own proud nakedness, making claims so immediate and sharply urged that the reader flinches, embarrassed by the routine discretions and evasions of his own sensibility. Yet if these poems are to take life among us, if they are to be more than exhibits in the history of modern psychological stress, they must be read with all the intelligence and scruple we can muster. They are too honest, they have cost too much, to be yielded to myth.

\* \* \*

\* \* \* It requires no biographical impertinence to realize that Sylvia Plath's life was harried by bouts of physical pain, that she sometimes looked on the accumulated exactions of her own nerve and body as "a trash / To annihilate each decade." She was haunted by the piecemeal, strung-together mechanics of the flesh, by what could be so easily broken and then mended with such searing ingenuity. The hospital ward was her exemplary ground:

> My patent leather overnight case like a black pillbox,
> My husband and child smiling out of the family photo;
> Their smiles catch onto my skin, little smiling hooks.

*From George Steiner, *Language and Silence: Essays on Language, Literature, and the Inhuman* (1967; New York: Atheneum, 1974), pp. 295–302.

This brokenness, so sharply feminine and contemporary, is, I think, her principal realization. It is by the graphic expression she gave to it that she will be judged and remembered. Sylvia Plath carries forward, in an intensely womanly and aggravated note, from Robert Lowell's *Life Studies,* a book that obviously had a great impact on her. This new frankness of women about the specific hurts and tangles of their nervous-physiological makeup is as vital to the poetry of Sylvia Plath as it is to the tracts of Simone de Beauvoir or to the novels of Edna O'Brien and Brigid Brophy. Women speak out as never before:

> The womb
> Rattles its pod, the moon
> Discharges itself from the tree with nowhere to go.
>
> ("Childless Woman")

> They have swabbed me clear of my loving associations.
> Scared and bare on the green plastic-pillowed trolley. . . .
>
> ("Tulips")

It is difficult to think of a precedent to the fearful close of "Medusa" (the whole poem is extraordinary):

> I shall take no bite of your body,
> Bottle in which I live,

> Ghastly Vatican.
> I am sick to death of hot salt.
> Green as eunuchs, your wishes
> Hiss at my sin.
> Off, off, eely tentacle!

> There is nothing between us.

The ambiguity and dual flash of insight in this final line are of a richness and obviousness that only a very great poem can carry off.

The progress registered between the early and the mature poems is one of concretion. The general Gothic means with which Sylvia Plath was so fluently equipped become singular to herself and therefore fiercely honest. What had been style passes into need. It is the need of a superbly intelligent, highly literate young woman to cry out about her especial being, about the tyrannies of blood and gland, of nervous spasm and sweating skin, the rankness of sex and childbirth in which a woman is still compelled to be wholly of her organic condition. Where Emily Dickinson could—indeed was obliged to—shut the door on the riot and humiliations of the flesh, thus achieving her particular dry lightness, Sylvia Plath "fully assumed her own condition." This alone would assure her of a place in modern literature. But she took one step further, assuming a burden that was not naturally or necessarily hers.

Born in Boston in 1932 of German and Austrian parents, Sylvia Plath had no personal, immediate contact with the world of the concentration camps. I may be mistaken, but so far as I know there was nothing Jewish in her background. But

her last, greatest poems culminate in an act of identification, of total communion
with those tortured and massacred. The poet sees herself on

> An engine, an engine
> Chuffing me off like a Jew.
> A Jew to Dachau, Auschwitz, Belsen.
> I began to talk like a Jew.
> I think I may well be a Jew.
>
> The snows of the Tyrol, the clear beer of Vienna
> Are not very pure or true.
> With my gypsy ancestress and my weird luck
>
> And my Tarot pack and my Tarot pack
> I may be a bit of a Jew.

Distance is no help; nor the fact that one is "guilty of nothing." The dead men cry
out of the yew hedges. The poet becomes the loud cry of their choked silence:

> Herr God, Herr Lucifer
> Beware
> Beware.
> Out of the ash
> I rise with my red hair
> And I eat men like air.

Here the almost surrealistic wildness of the gesture is kept in place by the insistent
obviousness of the language and beat; a kind of Hieronymus Bosch[1] nursery
rhyme.

Sylvia Plath is only one of a number of young contemporary poets, novelists,
and playwrights, themselves in no way implicated in the actual holocaust, who
have done most to counter the general inclination to forget the death camps.
Perhaps it is only those who had no part in the events who *can* focus on them
rationally and imaginatively; to those who experienced the thing, it has lost the
hard edges of possibility, it has stepped outside the real.

Committing the whole of her poetic and formal authority to the metaphor, to
the mask of language, Sylvia Plath *became* a woman being transported to Ausch-
witz on the death trains. The notorious shards of massacre seemed to enter into
her own being:

> A cake of soap,
> A wedding ring,
> A gold filling.

In "Daddy" she wrote one of the very few poems I know of in any language to
come near the last horror. It achieves the classic act of generalization, translat-

---

1. A fifteenth-century Netherlandish artist whose nightmarish paintings are filled with obscure symbol-
ism.

ing a private, obviously intolerable hurt into a code of plain statement, of instantaneously public images which concern us all. It is the "Guernica"[2] of modern poetry. And it is both histrionic and, in some ways, "arty," as is Picasso's outcry.

Are these final poems entirely legitimate? In what sense does anyone, himself uninvolved and long after the event, commit a subtle larceny when he invokes the echoes and trappings of Auschwitz and appropriates an enormity of ready emotion to his own private design? Was there latent in Sylvia Plath's sensibility, as in that of many of us who remember only by fiat of imagination, a fearful envy, a dim resentment at not having been there, of having missed the rendezvous with hell? In "Lady Lazarus" and "Daddy" the realization seems to me so complete, the sheer rawness and control so great, that only irresistible need could have brought it off. These poems take tremendous risks, extending Sylvia Plath's essentially austere manner to the very limit. They are a bitter triumph, proof of the capacity of poetry to give to reality the greater permanence of the imagined. She could not return from them.

* * *

IRVING HOWE

## *The Plath Celebration: A Partial Dissent\**

* * *

Sylvia Plath's most famous poem, adored by many sons and daughters, is "Daddy." It is a poem with an affecting theme, the feelings of the speaker as she regathers the pain of her father's premature death and her persuasion that he has betrayed her by dying:

> I was ten when they buried you.
> At twenty I tried to die
> And get back, back, back to you.

In the poem Sylvia Plath identifies the father (we recall his German birth) with the Nazis ("Panzer-man, panzer-man, O You") and flares out with assaults for which nothing in the poem (nor, so far as we know, in Sylvia Plath's own life) offers any warrant: "A cleft in your chin instead of your foot / But no less a devil for that. . . ." Nor does anything in the poem offer warrant, other than the free-flowing hysteria of the speaker, for the assault of such lines as, "There's a stake in

2. Picasso's famous painting (1937) depicting the brutalities of war.

*From Irving Howe, *The Critical Point of Literature and Culture* (1973; New York: Horizon Press, 1977), pp. 231–33.

your fat black heart / And the villagers never liked you." Or for the snappy violence of

> Every woman adores a Fascist,
> The boot in the face, the brute
> Brute heart of a brute like you.

What we have here is a revenge fantasy, feeding upon filial love-hatred, and thereby mostly of clinical interest. But seemingly aware that the merely clinical can't provide the materials for a satisfying poem, Sylvia Plath tries to enlarge upon the personal plight, give meaning to the personal outcry, by fancying the girl as victim of a Nazi father:

> An engine, an engine
> Chuffing me off like a Jew.
> A Jew to Dachau, Auschwitz, Belsen.
> I began to talk like a Jew,
> I think I may well be a Jew.

The more sophisticated admirers of this poem may say that I fail to see it as a dramatic presentation, a monologue spoken by a disturbed girl not necessarily to be identified with Sylvia Plath, despite the similarities of detail between the events of the poem and the events of her life. I cannot accept this view. The personal-confessional element, strident and undisciplined, is simply too obtrusive to suppose the poem no more than a dramatic picture of a certain style of disturbance. If, however, we did accept such a reading of "Daddy," we would fatally narrow its claims to emotional or moral significance, for we would be confining it to a mere vivid imagining of pathological state. That, surely, is not how its admirers really take the poem.

It is clearly not how the critic George Steiner takes the poem when he calls it "the 'Guernica' of modern poetry." But then, in an astonishing turn, he asks: "In what sense does anyone, himself uninvolved and long after the event, commit a subtle larceny when he invokes the echoes and trappings of Auschwitz and appropriates an enormity of ready emotion to his own private design?" The question is devastating to his early comparison with "Guernica." Picasso's painting objectifies the horrors of Guernica, through the distancing of art; no one can suppose that he shares or participates in them. Plath's poem aggrandizes on the "enormity of ready emotion" invoked by references to the concentration camps, in behalf of an ill-controlled if occasionally brilliant outburst. There is something monstrous, utterly disproportionate, when tangled emotions about one's father are deliberately compared with the historical fate of the European Jews; something sad, if the comparison is made spontaneously. "Daddy" persuades once again, through the force of negative example, of how accurate T. S. Eliot was in saying, "The more perfect the artist, the more completely separate in him will be the man who suffers and the mind which creates."

A. ALVAREZ

## *Sylvia Plath**

\* \* \* The reasons for Sylvia Plath's images are always there, though sometimes you have to work hard to find them. She is, in short, always in intelligent control of her feelings. Her work bears out her theories:

> I think my poems come immediately out of the sensuous and emotional experiences I have, but I must say I cannot sympathise with these cries from the heart that are informed by nothing except a needle or a knife or whatever it is. I believe that one should be able to control and manipulate experiences, even the most terrifying—like madness, being tortured, this kind of experience—and one should be able to manipulate these experiences with an informed and intelligent mind. I think that personal experience shouldn't be a kind of shut box and mirror-looking narcissistic experience. I believe it should be generally relevant, to such things as Hiroshima and Dachau, and so on.

It seems to me that it was only by her determination both to face her most inward and terrifying experiences and to use her intelligence in doing so—so as not to be overwhelmed by them—that she managed to write these extraordinary last poems, which are at once deeply autobiographical and yet detached, generally relevant.

'Lady Lazarus' is a stage further on from 'Fever 103°'; its subject is the total purification of achieved death. It is also far more intimately concerned with the drift of Sylvia Plath's life. The deaths of Lady Lazarus correspond to her own crises: the first just after her father died, the second when she had her nervous breakdown, the third perhaps a presentiment of the death that was shortly to come. Maybe this closeness of the subject helped make the poem so direct. The details don't clog each other: they are swept forward by the current of immediate feeling, marshalled by it and ordered. But what is remarkable about the poem is the objectivity with which she handles such personal material. She is not just talking about her own private suffering. Instead, it is the very closeness of her pain which gives it a general meaning; through it she assumes the suffering of all the modern victims. Above all, she becomes an imaginary Jew. I think this is a vitally important element in her work. For two reasons. First, because anyone whose subject is suffering has a ready-made modern example of hell on earth in the concentration camps. And what matters in them is not so much the physical torture—since sadism is general and perennial—but the way modern, as it were industrial, techniques can be used to destroy utterly the human identity. Individual suffering can be heroic provided it leaves the person who suffers a sense of his own individuality—provided, that is, there is an illusion of choice remaining to him. But when

*From A. Alvarez, "Sylvia Plath" (1963), in *The Art of Sylvia Plath*, ed. Charles Newman (Bloomington and London: Indiana University Press, 1970), pp. 64–66.

suffering is mass-produced, men and women become as equal and identity-less as objects on an assembly line, and nothing remains—certainly no values, no humanity. This anonymity of pain, which makes all dignity impossible, was Sylvia Plath's subject. Second, she seemed convinced, in these last poems, that the root of her suffering was the death of her father, whom she loved, who abandoned her, and who dragged her after him into death. And in her fantasies her father was pure German, pure Aryan, pure anti-semite.

It all comes together in the most powerful of her last poems, 'Daddy' * * *, about which she wrote the following bleak note:

> The poem is spoken by a girl with an Electra complex. Her father died while she thought he was God. Her case is complicated by the fact that her father was also a Nazi and her mother very possibly part Jewish. In the daughter the two strains marry and paralyse each other—she has to act out the awful little allegory once over before she is free of it.[1]

* * * What comes through most powerfully, I think, is the terrible *unforgiving-ness* of her verse, the continual sense not so much of violence—although there is a good deal of that—as of violent resentment that this should have been done to *her*. What she does in the poem is, with a weird detachment, to turn the violence against herself so as to show that she can equal her oppressors with her self-inflicted oppression. And this is the strategy of the concentration camps. When suffering is there whatever you do, by inflicting it upon yourself you achieve your identity, you set yourself free.

Yet the tone of the poem, like its psychological mechanisms, is not single or simple, and she uses a great deal of skill to keep it complex. Basically, her trick is to tell this horror story in a verse form as insistently jaunty and ritualistic as a nursery rhyme. And this helps her to maintain towards all the protagonists—her father, her husband and herself—a note of hard and sardonic anger, as though she were almost amused that her own suffering should be so extreme, so grotesque. The technical psychoanalytic term for this kind of insistent gaiety to protect you from what, if faced nakedly, would be insufferable, is 'manic defence'. But what, in a neurotic, is a means of avoiding reality can become, for an artist, a source of creative strength, a way of handling the unhandleable, and presenting the situation in all its fullness. When she first read me the poem a few days after she wrote it, she called it a piece of 'light verse'. It obviously isn't, yet equally obviously it also isn't the racking personal confession that a mere description or précis of it might make it sound.

Yet neither is it unchangingly vindictive or angry. The whole poem works on one single, returning note and rhyme, echoing from start to finish:

> You do not do, you do not do . . .
> . . . I used to pray to recover you.
> Ach, du . . .

There is a kind of cooing tenderness in this which complicates the other, more savage note of resentment. It brings in an element of pity, less for herself and her own suffering than for the person who made her suffer. Despite everything, 'Daddy' is a love poem.

\* \* \*

JUDITH KROLL

## Rituals of Exorcism: "Daddy"*

Poems explicitly about the protagonist's father, read in order of composition, show that the attitude toward him evolves from nostalgic mournfulness, regret, and guilt, to resentment and a bitter resolve to break his hold on her. * * *

The recital of the myth in "Daddy" ends in a ritual intended to cancel the earlier "sacred marriage" which has suffocated her:

> You do not do, you do not do
> Any more, black shoe
> In which I have lived like a foot
> For thirty years, poor and white,
> Barely daring to breathe or Achoo.[1]

In this image of passive and victimized domesticity, the speaker implicitly compares her past self to the 'old woman who lived in a shoe' who 'didn't know what to do'; now, however, she makes it clear that she does know what to do.

As a preamble to the exorcism, she recounts the development of her father's image, beginning with his earlier status as a "bag full of God, / Ghastly statue" (that is, a godlike colossus—mentioning the ghastliness, the ghostly, deathlike, pallid nature of the statue, anticipates the inversions to come) and then introduces the revised images: "panzer-man," "swastika," "Fascist," "brute," "devil," "bastard." Daddy must be cast in this new light, transformed from god to devil, if he is to be successfully expelled, but there must also be some real basis for it. To be effectively exposed, he must first appear as godly. But the speaker soon shows that she now attributes his godliness in part to his authoritarianism and personal inaccessibility—qualities which became intensified through his death, and which later became transferred to "a model of you"—her husband. Both men are really variations on a familiar type, even a stereotype: the "god" who, like Marco the

*From Judith Kroll, *Chapters in a Mythology: The Poetry of Sylvia Plath* (New York: Harper & Row, 1976), pp. 122–26.    1. When Plath introduced "Daddy" as being about "a girl with an Electra complex" (with, in effect, the female version of an Oedipus complex), she gave a clue to what may be a play on words in the poem. "Oedipus" means "swell-foot," and therefore the speaker's identification of herself as a "foot" may be a private way of saying "I am Oedipus" and incorporating into the poem an allusion to the Electra complex. (JK) "woman-hater" in *The Bell Jar,* is "chock-full of power" * * * over women precisely because of his deadness, or ultimate inaccessibility, to them. Loving a man literally or metaphorically dead ("The face that lived in this mirror is the face of a dead man" ["The Courage of Shutting-Up"]) becomes a kind of persecution or punishment; and so, by the end of the incantation, Daddy deserves to be cast out. The "black telephone . . . off at the root," conveys the finality of the intended exorcism.

The 'venomousness,' ambiguous from the beginning, is not the whole story. "Daddy" is not primarily a poem of "father-hatred" or abuse as Robert Lowell, Elizabeth Hardwick, and others have contended. The need for exorcising her father's ghost lies, after all, in the extremity of her attachment to him. Alvarez very justly remarks that

> The whole poem works on one single, returning note and rhyme, echoing from start to finish:
>
>> You do not do, you do not do . . .
>> . . . [I] used to pray to recover you.
>> Ach, du . . .
>
> There is a kind of cooing tenderness in this which complicates the other, more savage note of resentment. It brings in an element of pity, less for herself and her own suffering than for the person who made her suffer. Despite everything, 'Daddy' is a love poem.[2]

The love is not merely conveyed by the rhythm and sound of the poem, it is a necessary part of the poem's meaning, a part of the logic of its act.

The exorcism serves another purpose because through it she attempts to reject the pattern of being abandoned and made to suffer by a god, a man who is "chock-full of power": she creates "a model of you"—an image of her father—and marries this proxy. Then she kills both father and husband at once, magically using each as the other's representative.[3] Each death entails that of the other: the stake in her father's heart also kills the "vampire who said he was you"; and the killing of her marriage (for which she now claims to take responsibility, as she does for having allowed her marriage to perpetuate, by proxy, her relationship to her father) finally permits Daddy to "lie back." Formerly an acquiescent victim, she now vengefully cancels that role. The marriage to and killing of her father by proxy are acts of what Frazer[4] calls "sympathetic magic," in which "things act on each other at a distance through a secret sympathy" * * *. Such magic, which assumes that human beings can either directly influence the course of nature or can induce gods to influence nature in the desired way, nearly always constitutes the logic of the rituals Frazer discusses. The ritual marriage of a Whitsun bride and bridegroom, for example, aims at assuring abundant crops by sympathetically encouraging a marriage between the powers of fertility. Likewise, diseases may be either

2. Alvarez, "Sylvia Plath," p. 66. (JK)    3. The biographical basis for this identification is evident in *Letters Home.* * * * (JK)    4. Sir James George Frazer (1854–1941), Scottish anthropologist whose book *The Golden Bough* analyzes early religious and magical practices. (Editor)

inflicted or drawn off by sympathetic magic on the principle that "as the image suffers, so does the man" * * *.

Plath was familiar with and used such ideas; for example, she transcribed, from *The Golden Bough,* Frazer's remark about the fertility or barrenness of a man's wife affecting his garden; and she echoes Frazer again in a line, excised from her poem "The Other," in which opening doors and windows is connected with the facilitation of childbirth. (Also, being "lame in the memory" and self, associated with the lameness and death of her father, is at once a homeopathic wound and a sympathetic attachment to him.) The notion that "as the image suffers, so does the man"—affecting the real subject through a proxy—nicely describes marriage to a model of Daddy, and explains why "If I've killed one man, I've killed two." The earlier attempt of the speaker in "Daddy" to recover her father also involved sympathetic magic; she had tried to rejoin him by dying and becoming like him:

> At twenty I tried to die
> And get back, back, back to you.

She finally exorcises her father as if he were a scapegoat invested with the evils of her spoiled history. Frazer's discussion of rituals in which the dying god is also a scapegoat is germane here. He conjectures that two originally separate rituals merged to form this combination, and the father in "Daddy" may well be described as such a divine scapegoat figure.[5]

Sometimes it is a place from which a devil must be cast out, but usually it is a person who is possessed. In Plath's mythology the speaker is not possessed by her father in this sense, but by the false self who is in his thrall. That is why the true self is released (as in "Purdah" and "Lady Lazarus") when the oppressor is made hateful, and thereby overthrown. Rituals of exorcism in Plath's poetry therefore inherently involve the idea of rebirth. When exorcism, or attempted exorcism, of father or proxy occurs, it is preliminary to a rebirth which will entail expulsion of the false self and spoiled history. And even when a ritual of rebirth does not involve an explicit exorcism, one is usually implied.

The logic of sympathetic magic, which appears widely in Plath's late poetry, might well be called one of the physical laws of her poems. * * * Such a logic seems poetically appropriate for a mythology: that the Moon-muse (or one of her agents, such as "The Rival") governs and affects her by a "secret sympathy" seems natural to a mythic drama.

The motifs 'released'—or triggered—in her late poems contain the potential for a sympathetic association of those details which express the same motif. Because the details are not incidental, called forth as they are by her mythology,

---

5. Frazer says: "If we ask why a dying god should be chosen to take upon himself and carry away the sins and sorrows of the people, it may be suggested that in the practice of using the divinity as a scapegoat we have a combination of two customs . . . the result would be the employment of the dying god as a scapegoat. He was killed, not originally to take away sin, but to save the divine life from the degeneracy of old age; but, since he had to be killed at any rate, people may have thought that they might as well seize the opportunity to lay upon him the burden of their sufferings and sins, in order that he might bear it away with him to the unknown world beyond the grave." [Pp. 667–68] (JK) * * *

the sympathy is in a sense guaranteed. The images of blood, violent death, and red poppies, all of which release the death and rebirth motif, have the potential for sympathetically affecting one another through their family resemblance. "Tulips" contains an example of the secret sympathy which operates through such resemblance (that is, through expressing the same motif):

> The tulips are too red in the first place, they hurt me.
>
> . . .
>
> Their redness talks to my wound, it corresponds.[6]

The word "corresponds" refers both to the communication between tulips and wound and to their underlying likeness. The tulips stand in the same relation to the incipient health or normalcy of the speaker that the poppies in later poems do to her suppressed true self, to (or with) which the poppies correspond. In a sense, this correspondence, and the contrast between it and the speaker's death-in-life existence, *is* the underlying motif in these poems.

It has already been suggested that the Moon-muse has a "sympathetic"—even though not entirely welcome—relation with the speaker[7] (as mother, totem, familiar, emblem) which can be activated without her consent, just as in "Tulips" she cannot prevent her wound from corresponding with the red flowers. Similarly, the coldness and sterility of the Moon-muse may infect the speaker, causing and not merely representing her state of being. The Moon therefore functions as both "emblem" and "real agent."

MARY LYNN BROE

# from *Protean Poetic**

Among the other poems that display the performing self, "Daddy" and "Lady Lazarus" are two of the most often quoted, but most frequently misunderstood, poems in the Plath canon. The speaker in "Daddy" performs a mock poetic exorcism of an event that has already happened—the death of her father who she feels

---

6. By the time "Tulips" was written, she had clearly developed much of the technique, imagery, and themes (such as the logic of sympathetic magic) of the late poems. (JK)     7. The belief Frazer mentions, that "a barren wife infects her husband's garden with her own sterility" is the sort of contagion that occurs in *Three Women*, in which the Secretary has been infected by the Moon's sterility and by that of the men with whom she works. Men, who cannot bear children, have the disease of "flatness," for they create only negations of and abstractions about life rather than life itself. This disease can (through the mediumship of the Moon) be caught from men, and it is therefore also an inversion or parody of conception. Referring to her miscarriage, the Secretary says: "I watched the men walk about me in the office. They were so flat!/There was something about them like cardboard, and now I had caught it, . . . " (JK)

*From Mary Lynn Broe, *Protean Poetic: The Poetry of Sylvia Plath* (Columbia and London: University of Missouri Press, 1980), pp. 172–75.

withdrew his love from her by dying prematurely: "Daddy, I have had to kill you. /You died before I had time—."

The speaker attempts to exorcise not just the memory of her father but her own *Mein Kampf* model of him as well as her inherited behavioral traits that lead her graveward under the Freudian banner of death instinct or Thanatos's libido. But her ritual reenactment simply does not take. The event comically backfires as pure self-parody: the metaphorical murder of the father dwindles into Hollywood spectacle, while the poet is lost in the clutter of the collective unconscious.

Early in the poem, the ritual gets off on the wrong foot both literally and figuratively. A sudden rhythmic break midway through the first stanza interrupts the insistent and mesmeric chant of the poet's own freedom:

> You do not do, you do not do
> Any more, black shoe
> In which I have lived like a foot
> For thirty years, poor and white,
> Barely daring to breathe or Achoo.

The break suggests, on the one hand, that the nursery-rhyme world of contained terror is here abandoned; on the other, that the poet-exorcist's mesmeric control is superficial, founded in a shaky faith and an unsure heart—the worst possible state for the strong, disciplined exorcist.

At first she kills her father succinctly with her own words, demythologizing him to a ludicrous piece of statuary that is hardly a Poseidon or the Colossus of Rhodes:[1]

> Marble-heavy, a bag full of God,
> Ghastly statue with one grey toe
> Big as a Frisco seal
>
> And a head in the freakish Atlantic
> Where it pours bean green over blue
> In the waters off beautiful Nauset.
> I used to pray to recover you.
> Ach, du.

Then as she tries to patch together the narrative of him, his tribal myth (the "common" town, the "German tongue," the war-scraped culture), she begins to lose her own powers of description to a senseless Germanic prattle ("The tongue stuck in my jaw. / It stuck in a barb wire snare. / Ich, ich, ich, ich"). The individual man is absorbed by his inhuman archetype, the "panzer man," "an engine / Chuffing me off like a Jew." Losing the exorcist's power that binds the spirit and then casts out the demon, she is the classic helpless victim of the swastika man. As she

---

1. One of the seven wonders of the ancient world, a gigantic statue of the Greek sun god, Helios; *Poseidon:* the chief sea god in the Greek pantheon.

culls up her own picture of him as a devil, he refuses to adopt this stereotype. Instead he jumbles his trademark:

> A cleft in your chin instead of your foot
> But no less a devil for that, no not
> Any less the black man who
>
> Bit my pretty red heart in two.

The overt Nazi-Jew allegory throughout the poem suggests that, by a simple inversion of power, father and daughter grow more alike. But when she tries to imitate his action of dying, making all the appropriate grand gestures, she once again fails: "but they pulled me out of the sack, / And they stuck me together with glue." She retreats to a safe world of icons and replicas, but even the doll image she constructs turns out to be "the vampire who said he was you." At last, she abandons her father to the collective unconscious where it is *he* who is finally recognized ("they always *knew* it was you"). *She* is lost, impersonally absorbed by his irate persecutors, bereft of both her power and her conjuror's discipline, and possessed by the incensed villagers. The exorcist's ritual, one of purifying, cleansing, commanding silence and then ordering the evil spirit's departure, has dwindled to a comic picture from the heart of darkness. Mad villagers stamp on the devil-vampire creation.

In the course of performing the imaginative "killing," the speaker moves through a variety of emotions, from viciousness ("a stake in your fat black heart"), to vengefulness ("You bastard, I'm through"), finally to silence ("the black telephone's off at the root"). It would seem that the real victim is the poet-performer who, despite her straining toward identification with the public events of holocaust and destruction of World War II, becomes more murderously persecuting than the "panzer-man" who smothered her, and who abandoned her with a paradoxical love, guilt, and fear. Unlike him, she kills three times: the original subject, the model to whom she said "I do, I do," and herself, the imitating victim. But each of these killings is comically inverted. Each backfires. Instead of successfully binding the spirits, commanding them to remain silent and cease doing harm, and then ordering them to an appointed place, the speaker herself is stricken dumb.

The failure of the exorcism and the emotional ambivalence are echoed in the curious rhythm. The incantatory safety of the nursery-rhyme thump (seemingly one of controlled, familiar terrors) also suggests some sinister brooding by its repetition. The poem opens with a suspiciously emphatic protest, a kind of psychological whistling-in-the-dark. As it proceeds, "Daddy's" continuous life-rhythms—the assonance, consonance, and especially the sustained *oo* sounds—triumph over either the personal or the cultural-historical imagery. The sheer sense of organic life in the interwoven sounds carries the verse forward in boisterous spirit and communicates an underlying feeling of comedy that is also echoed in the repeated failure of the speaker to perform her exorcism.

Ultimately, "Daddy" is like an emotional, psychological, and historical autopsy, a final report. There is no real progress. The poet is in the same place in the beginning as in the end. She begins the poem as a hesitant but familiar fairy-tale daughter who parodies her attempt to reconstruct the myth of her father. Suffocating in her shoe house, she is unable to do much with that "bag full of God." She ends as a murderous member of a mythical community enacting the ritual or vampire killing, but only for a surrogate vampire, not the real thing ("the vampire who said he was you"). Although it seems that the speaker has moved from identification with the persecuted to identity as persecutor, Jew to vampire-killer, powerless to powerful, she has simply enacted a performance that allows her to live with what is unchangeable. She has used her art to stave off suffocation, and performs her self-contempt with a degree of bravado.[2]

MARGARET HOMANS

# from *A Feminine Tradition**

To place an exclusive valuation on the literal, expecially to identify the self as literal, is simply to ratify women's age-old and disadvantageous position as the other and the object. Contemporary poetry by women that takes up this self-defeating strategy risks encounters with death that are destructive both poetically and actually. The current belief in a literal "I" present in poetry is responsible for the popular superstition that Sylvia Plath's death was the purposeful completion of her poetry's project, the assumption being that if the speaker is precisely the same as the biographical Plath, the poetry's self-destructive violence is directed toward Plath herself, not toward an imagined speaker. This reading of Plath is unfair to the woman and, by calling it merely unmediated self-expression, obscures her poetry's real power. In poem after poem depicting or wishing for physical violence, the imagery of violence is part of a symmetrical figurative system, and death is figured as a way of achieving rebirth or some other transcendence.[1] Plath's project may not thus be very different from that of Dickinson, who speaks quite often from beyond the grave, reimagining and repossessing death as her own in order to dispel the terrors of literal death. However, within that figurative system the poet embraces a self-destructive program that must soon have been poetically terminal, even if it did not bring about the actual death.

Several of Plath's late poems come to terms with a father figure (who may include the poetic fathers she acknowledges in *The Colossus*), whose crime, no

---

2. What remains the most thorough and enlightening account of the poem is A. R. Jones, "On 'Daddy,' " *The Art of Sylvia Plath*, [ed. Newman], pp. 230–36. (MLB)

*From Margaret Homans, *Women Writers and Poetic Identity: Dorothy Wordsworth, Emily Brontë, and Emily Dickinson* (Princeton: Princeton University Press, 1982), pp. 218–21.   1. I am indebted here, for their persuasively positive readings of Plath, to Judith Kroll, *Chapters in a Mythology: The Poetry of Sylvia Plath* (New York: Harper & Row, 1976), and to Stacy Pies, "Coming Clear of the Shadow: The Poetry of Sylvia Plath," unpublished essay (Yale University, 1979). (MH).

different from that identified by nineteenth-century women, is of attempting to transform the feminine self into objects. "Lady Lazarus" borrows the most appalling of Nazi imagery to accuse a generalized figure of male power of the ultimate reification. Not only is the dead victim of "Herr Doktor" and "Herr Enemy" an object in being dead, but she is also reduced to the actual physical objects from which the Nazis profited by destroying human bodies: "a Nazi lamp-shade,"

> A cake of soap,
> A wedding ring,
> A gold filling.

The poem combines the tradition of woman as medium of exchange with that of woman as object to produce a desperately concise picture of literalization.

> I am your opus,
> I am your valuable,
> The pure gold baby
>
> That melts to a shriek.

Though the poet is here objecting to literalization, not embracing it, the poetic myth of suicide through which the oppression may be lifted amounts to the same thing: the speaker must submit to this literalization in order to transcend it.

> Out of the ash
> I rise with my red hair
> And I eat men like air.

Their death costs her death, and powerful though the poem is, this is an extraordinarily high price for retribution. And as always, it is the process of objectification that makes up the poem, not the final, scarcely articulable transcendence.

"Daddy" uses Nazi imagery to make the same accusation about objectification brought against men as oppressors in "Lady Lazarus" and makes the corollary accusation against the father (and the husband modelled after him) that objectification has silenced her:

> I never could talk to you.
> The tongue stuck in my jaw.
>
> It stuck in a barb wire snare.
> Ich, ich, ich, ich,
> I could hardly speak.

In this context defiance and retribution take the form of her speaking, but again this counterattack is counterproductive. Punning on the expression "being through" to mean both establishing a telephone connection and being finished, she at once makes and conclusively severs communication:

> So daddy, I'm finally through.
> The black telephone's off at the root,
> The voices just can't worm through.

The poem concludes, "Daddy, daddy, you bastard, I'm through." Suppressing the power of the one who silenced her, she simultaneously returns herself to the silence that the poem came into being to protest.

PAMELA J. ANNAS

# from *A Disturbance in Mirrors**

* * * [T]he particular sexual metaphor in "Daddy" is sado-masochism, which stands for the authority structure of a partriarchal and war-making society. * * * "Daddy" is an analysis of the structure of the society in which the individual is enmeshed. Intertwined with the image of sadist and masochist in "Daddy" is a parallel image of vampire and victim. In "Daddy," father, husband, and a larger patriarchal and competitive authority structure, which the speaker of the poem sees as having been responsible for the various imperialisms of the twentieth century, all melt together and become demonic, finally a gigantic vampire figure. In the modulation from one image to another to form an accumulated image that is characteristic of many of Plath's late poems, the male figure at the center of "Daddy" takes four major forms: the statue, the Gestapo officer, the professor, and the vampire. The poem begins, however, with an image of a black shoe, an image which, like the black shoe in "The Munich Mannequins" and like the black suit in "The Applicant," can be seen to stand for corporate man. The second stanza of the poem refers back to the title poem of *The Colossus,* where the speaker's father, representative of a gigantic male other, so dominated her world that her horizon was bounded by his scattered pieces. In "Daddy," she describes him as:

> Marble-heavy, a bag full of God,
> Ghastly statue with one grey toe
> Big as a Frisco seal
>
> And a head in the freakish Atlantic
> Where it pours bean green over blue
> In the waters off beautiful Nauset.

Between "The Colossus" and "Daddy" there has been a movement from a mythic and natural landscape to one with social and political boundaries. Here the image of her father, grown larger than the earlier Colossus of Rhodes, stretches across and subsumes the whole of the United States, from the Pacific to the Atlantic ocean.

The next seven stanzas of "Daddy" construct the image of the Gestapo officer, using her family background—her parents were both of German origin—to mediate between her personal sense of suffocation and the social history of the Nazi

*From Pamela J. Annas, *A Disturbance in Mirrors: The Poetry of Sylvia Plath*, Contributions in Women's Studies no. 89 (New York, Westport, and London: Greenwood Press, 1988), pp. 139–43.

invasions. The black shoe of the first stanza in which she says she has been wedged like a foot "barely daring to breathe" becomes in stanza ten, at the end of the Nazi section, a larger social image of suffocation: "Not God but a swastika / So black no sky could squeak through." The Gestapo figure recurs briefly three stanzas later as the speaker of the poem transfers the image from father to husband and incidentally suggests that the victim has some control in a brutalized association—at least to the extent she chooses to be there.[1]

> I made a model of you,
> A man in black with a Meinkampf look
>
> And a love of the rack and the screw.
> And I said I do, I do.

The Gestapo figure becomes "Herr Professor" in stanza eleven, an actual image of Plath's father, and also an image of what has for centuries been seen as the prototypical and even ideal relationship between a man and a woman.[2] The professor, who is a man, talks and is active; the woman, who is a student, listens and is passive. A patriarchal social structure is at its purest and, superficially, at its most benign in the stereotyped relationship of male teacher and female student and is a stock romantic fantasy even in women's literature—Emma and Mr. Knightley, Lucy Snowe and the professor in *Villette*.[3] But Plath places this image between the images of Nazi / Jew and vampire / victim so that it becomes the center of a series. Indeed, the image of daddy as teacher turns almost immediately into a devil / demon / vampire:

> A cleft in your chin instead of your foot
> But no less a devil for that, no not
> Any less the black man who
>
> Bit my pretty red heart in two.

The last two stanzas of "Daddy" are like the conclusion of "Lady Lazarus" in their assertion that the speaker of the poem is breaking out of the cycle and that,

1. See Wilhelm Reich's *The Mass Psychology of Fascism* (New York: Simon and Schuster, 1969), particularly his chapter on "The Authoritarian Personality," for an analysis of how an oppressed class can contribute to its own oppression. Judith Lewis Herman, in *Father-Daughter Incest* (Cambridge, Mass.: Harvard University Press, 1981), discusses the history of the suppression of incest beginning with Freud and continuing into contemporary psychological literature, the attribution of reports of incest to hysterical female oedipal fantasizing or, when the fact of incest is impossible to deny, assigning blame to the victim: what Herman calls the Seductive Daughter and/or the Collusive Mother (Chapter 1, "A Common Occurrence"). Writing in the early 1960s and familiar with some of these attitudes, it is not surprising that Plath assigns some culpability to the victim. Herman goes on to say, "Even when the girl does give up her erotic attachment to her father, she is encouraged to persist in the fantasy that some other man, like her father, will some day take possession of her, raising her above the common lot of woman-kind" (p. 57).
   I am not of course suggesting that Plath literally had an incestuous relationship with her father—there is no evidence one way or the other—but she does make recurrent use of father/daughter incest as a symbol for male/female relations in a patriarchal society. * * * (PJA)   2. This photograph of Otto Plath is reproduced on page 17 of *Letters Home*. (PJA)   3. [Mary] Ellmann, *Thinking About Women* [New York: Harcourt Brace Jovanovich, 1968], pp. 119–23. (PJA)

in order to do so, she must turn on and kill Herr God, Herr Lucifer in the one poem, and Daddy in his final metamorphosis as vampire in the other poem. Plath explained this in Freudian terms in an introductory note to the poem for a BBC Third Programme reading:

> The poem is spoken by a girl with an Electra complex. The father died while she thought he was God. Her case is complicated by the fact that her father was also a Nazi and her mother very possibly part Jewish. In the daughter the two strains marry and paralyze each other—she has to act out the awful little allegory once over before she is free of it.[4]

This reenacting of the allegory becomes at the end of "Daddy" a frenzied communal ritual of exorcism.

> Daddy, you can lie back now.
>
> There's a stake in your fat black heart
> And the villagers never liked you.
> They are dancing and stamping on you.
> They always *knew* it was you.
> Daddy, daddy, you bastard, I'm through.

This cycle of victim/vampire is, left alone, a closed and repetitive cycle, like the repeated suicides of "Lady Lazarus." According to the legends and the Hollywood film versions of these legends we all grew up on, once consumed by a vampire, one dies and is reborn a vampire and preys upon others, who in their turn die and become vampires. The vampire imagery in Sylvia Plath's poetry intersects on one level with her World War II imagery and its exploitation and victimization and on another level intersects with her images of a bureaucratic, fragmented, and dead—in the sense of numbed and unaware—society. The connections are sometimes confused, but certainly World War II is often imaged in her poetry as a kind of grisly, vampiric feast. * * *

The whole of "Daddy" is an exorcism to banish the demon, put a stake through the vampire's heart, and thus break the cycle of vampire→victim. It is crucial to the poem that the exorcism is accomplished through communal action by the "villagers." The rhythm of the poem is powerfully and deliberately primitive: a child's chant, a formal curse. The hard sounds, short lines, and repeated rhymes of "do," "you," "Jew," and "through" give a hard pounding quality to the poem that is close to the sound of a heart beat. "Daddy," as well as "Lady Lazarus" and, to a lesser extent, "Fever 103°," is structured as a magical formula or incantation. In *The Colossus* poems, Plath also used poetry as a ritual incantation, but in those early poems it was most often directed toward transformation of self. By 1961, she is less often attempting to transform self into some other, but rather attempting to rid herself and her world of demons. That is, rebirth cannot occur until after the demons have been exorcised. In all three of these poems, the possibilities of the individual are very much tied to those of her society.

4. Quoted in [M. L.] Rosenthal, *The New Poets* [New York: Oxford University Press, 1967], p. 82. (PJA)

Purity, which is what exorcism aims at, is for Plath an ambiguous concept. On the one hand it means integrity of self, wholeness rather than fragmentation, as unspoiled state of being, rest, perfection, aesthetic beauty, and loss of self through transformation into some reborn other. On the other hand, it also means absence, isolation, blindness, a kind of autism which shuts out the world, stasis and death, and a loss of self through dispersal into some other. In "Lady Lazarus" and "Fever 103°" the emphasis is on exorcising the poet's previous selves, though within a social context that makes that unlikely. "Daddy," however, is a purification of the world; in "Daddy" it is the various avatars of the other—the male figure who represents the patriarchal society she lives in—that are being exorcised. In all three cases, the exorcism is violent and, perhaps, provisional. Does she believe, in any of these cases, that a rebirth under such conditions is really possible, that an exorcism is truly taking place, that once the allegory is reenacted, she will be rid of it? The more the speaker of the poems defines her situation as desperate, the more violent and vengeful becomes the agent of purification and transformation. All three of these poems are retaliatory fantasies: in "Lady Lazarus" she swallows men, in "Fever 103°" she leaves them behind, in "Daddy" she kills them. * * *

STEVEN GOULD AXELROD

## *Jealous Gods* *

* * * [Although "Daddy"] has traditionally been read as "personal" (Aird 78)[1] or "confessional" (M. L. Rosenthal 82),[2] Margaret Homans has more recently suggested that it concerns a woman's dislocated relations to speech (*Women Writers* 220–21).[3] Plath herself introduced it on the BBC as the opposite of confession, as a constructed fiction: "Here is a poem spoken by a girl with an Electra complex. Her father died while she thought he was God. Her case is complicated by the fact that her father was also a Nazi and her mother very possibly part Jewish. In the daughter the two strains marry and paralyze each other—she has to act out the awful little allegory once over before she is free of it" (*CP* 293).[4] We might interpret this preface as an accurate retelling of the poem; or we might regard it as a case of an author's estrangement from her text, on the order of Coleridge's preface to "Kubla Khan" in which he claims to be unable to finish the poem, having forgotten what it was about. However we interpret Plath's preface, we must agree that "Daddy" is dramatic and allegorical, since its details depart freely from the facts of her biography. In this poem she again figures her unresolved conflicts with paternal authority as a textual issue. Significantly, her father was a published

*From Steven Gould Axelrod, *Sylvia Plath: The Wound and the Cure of Words* (Baltimore and London: Johns Hopkins University Press, 1990), pp. 51–70, 237.    1. Eileen Aird, *Sylvia Plath: Her Life and Work* (New York: Harper & Row, 1973).    2. M. L. Rosenthal, *The New Poets: American and British Poetry since World War II* (London: Oxford University Press, 1967).    3. Margaret Homans, *Women Writers and Poetic Identity: Dorothy Wordsworth, Emily Brontë, and Emily Dickinson* (Princeton: Princeton University Press, 1980).    4. *CP* = *The Collected Poems*.

writer, and his successor, her husband, was also a writer. Her preface asserts that the poem concerns a young woman's paralyzing self-division, which she can defeat only through allegorical representation. Recalling that paralysis was one of Plath's main tropes for literary incapacity, we begin to see that the poem evokes the female poet's anxiety of authorship and specifically Plath's strategy of delivering herself from that anxiety by making it the topic of her discourse. Viewed from this perspective, "Daddy" enacts the woman poet's struggle with "daddy-poetry." It represents her effort to eject the "buried male muse" from her invention process and the "jealous gods" from her audience (*J* 223;[5] *CP* 179).

Plath wrote "Daddy" several months after Hughes left her, on the day she learned that he had agreed to a divorce (October 12, 1962). George Brown and Tirril Harris have shown that early loss makes one especially vulnerable to subsequent loss (Bowlby 250–59),[6] and Plath seems to have defended against depression by almost literally throwing herself into her poetry. She followed "Daddy" with a host of poems that she considered her greatest achievement to date: "Medusa," "The Jailer," "Lady Lazarus," "Ariel," the bee sequence, and others. The letters she wrote to her mother and brother on the day of "Daddy," and then again four days later, brim with a sense of artistic self-discovery: "Writing like mad. . . . Terrific stuff, as if domesticity had choked me" (*LH* 466).[7] Composing at the "still blue, almost eternal hour before the baby's cry, before the glassy music of the milkman, settling his bottles" (quoted in Alvarez, *Savage God* 21),[8] she experienced an "enormous" surge in creative energy (*LH* 467). Yet she also expressed feelings of misery: "The half year ahead seems like a lifetime, and the half behind an endless hell" (*LH* 468). She was again contemplating things German: a trip to the Austrian Alps, a renewed effort to learn the language. If "German" was Randall Jarrell's "favorite country," it was not hers, yet it returned to her discourse like clock work at times of psychic distress. Clearly Plath was attempting to find and to evoke in her art what she could not find or communicate in her life. She wished to compensate for her fragmenting social existence by investing herself in her texts: "Hope, when free, to write myself out of this hole" (*LH* 466). Desperately eager to sacrifice her "flesh," which was "wasted," to her "mind and spirit," which were "fine" (*LH* 470), she wrote "Daddy" to demonstrate the existence of her voice, which had been silent or subservient for so long. She wrote it to prove her "genius" (*LH* 468).

Plath projected her struggle for textual identity onto the figure of a partly Jewish young woman who learns to express her anger at the patriarch and at his language of male mastery, which is as foreign to her as German, as "obscene" as murder (st. 6), and as meaningless as "gobbledygoo" (st. 9). The patriarch's death "off beautiful Nauset" (st. 3) recalls Plath's journal entry in which she associated the "green seaweeded water" at "Nauset Light" with "the deadness of a being . . . who no longer creates" (*J* 164). Daddy's deadness—suggesting Plath's unwillingness to let her father, her education, her library, or her husband inhibit her any

5. *J* = The Journals.   6. John Bowlby, *Attachment and Loss*, III: *Loss: Sadness and Depression* (London Hogarth, 1980).   7. *LH* = Letters Home.   8. A. Alvarez, *The Savage God: A Study of Suicide* (1971; New York, Bantam, 1973).

longer—inspires the poem's speaker to her moment of illumination. At a basic level, "Daddy" concerns its own violent, transgressive birth as a text, its origin in a culture that regards it as illegitimate—a judgment the speaker hurls back on the patriarch himself when she labels *him* a bastard (st. 16). Plath's unaccommodating worldview, which was validated by much in her childhood and adult experience, led her to understand literary tradition not as an expanding universe of beneficial influence (as depicted in Eliot's "Tradition and the Individual Talent") but as a closed universe in which every addition required a corresponding subtraction—a Spencerian agon in which only the fittest survived. If Plath's speaker was to be born as a poet, a patriarch must die.

As in "The Colossus," the father here appears as a force or an object rather than as a person. Initially he takes the form of an immense "black shoe," capable of stamping on his victim (st. 1). Immediately thereafter he becomes a marble "statue" (st. 2), cousin to the monolith of the earlier poem. He then transforms into Nazi Germany (st. 6–7, 9–10), the archetypal totalitarian state. When the protagonist mentions Daddy's "boot in the face" (st. 10), she may be alluding to Orwell's comment in *1984*, "If you want a picture of the future, imagine a boot stomping on a human face—forever" (3.3). Eventually the father declines in stature from God (st. 2) to a devil (st. 11) to a dying vampire (st. 15). Perhaps he shrinks under the force of his victim's denunciation, which de-creates him as a power as it creates him as figure. But whatever his size, he never assumes human dimensions, aspirations, and relations—except when posing as a teacher in a photograph (st. 11). Like the colossus, he remains figurative and symbolic, not individual.

Nevertheless, the male figure of "Daddy" does differ significantly from that of "The Colossus." In the earlier poem, which emphasizes his lips, mouth, throat, tongue, and voice, the colossus allegorically represents the power of speech, however fragmented and resistant to the protagonist's ministrations. In the later poem Daddy remains silent, apart from the gobbledygoo attributed to him once (st. 9). He uses his mouth primarily for biting and for drinking blood. The poem emphasizes his feet and, implicitly, his phallus. He is a "black shoe" (st. 1), a statue with "one gray toe" (st. 2), a "boot" (st. 10). The speaker, estranged from him by fear, could never tell where he put his "foot," his "root" (st. 5). Furthermore, she is herself silenced by his shoe: "I never could talk to you" (st. 5). Daddy is no "male muse" (*J* 223), not even one in ruins, but frankly a male censor. His boot in the face of "every woman" is presumably lodged in her mouth (st. 10). He stands for all the elements in the literary situation and in the female ephebe's internalization of it, that prevent her from producing any words at all, even copied or subservient ones. Appropriately, Daddy can be killed only by being stamped on: he lives and dies by force, not language. If "The Colossus" tells a tale of the patriarch's speech, his grunts and brays, "Daddy" tells a tale of the daughter's effort to speak.

Thus we are led to another important difference between the two poems. The "I" of "The Colossus" acquires her identity only through serving her "father," whereas the "I" of "Daddy" actuates her gift only through opposition to him. The latter poem precisely inscribes the plot of Plath's dream novel of 1958: "a girl's search for her dead father—for an outside authority which must be developed, instead, from the inside" (*J* 258). As the child of a Nazi, the girl could "hardly speak" (st. 6), but as a Jew she begins "to talk" and to acquire an identity (st. 7). In Plath's allegory, the outsider Jew corresponds to "the rebel, the artist, the odd" (*JP* 55),[9] and particularly to the woman artist. Otto Rank's *Beyond Psychology*,[1] which had a lasting influence on her, explicitly compares women to Jews, since "woman . . . has suffered from the very beginning a fate similar to that of the Jew, namely, suppression, slavery, confinement, and subsequent persecution" (287–88). Rank, whose discourse I would consider tainted by anti-Semitism, argues that Jews speak a language of pessimistic "self-hatred" that differs essentially from the language of the majority cultures in which they find themselves (191, 281–84). He analogously, though more sympathetically, argues that woman speaks in a language different from man's, and that as a result of man's denial of woman's world, "woman's 'native tongue' has hitherto been unknown or at least unheard" (248). Although Rank's essentializing of woman's "nature" lapses into the sexist clichés of his time ("intuitive," "irrational" [249]), his idea of linguistic difference based on gender and his analogy between Jewish and female speech seem to have embedded themselves in the substructure of "Daddy" (and in many of Plath's other texts as well). For Plath, as later for Adrienne Rich, the Holocaust and the patriarchy's silencing of women were linked outcomes of the masculinist interpretation of the world. Political insurrection and female self-assertion also interlaced symbolically. In "Daddy," Plath's speaker finds her voice and motive by identifying herself as antithetical to her Fascist father. Rather than getting the colossus "glued" and properly jointed, she wishes to stick herself "together with glue" (st. 13), an act that seems to require her father's dismemberment. Previously devoted to the patriarch—both in "The Colossus" and in memories evoked in "Daddy" of trying to "get back" to him (st. 12)—she now seeks only to escape from him and to see him destroyed.

Plath has unleashed the anger, normal in mourning as well as in revolt, that she suppressed in the earlier poem. But she has done so at a cost. Let us consider her childlike speaking voice. The language of "Daddy," beginning with its title, is often regressive. The "I" articulates herself by moving backward in time, using the language of nursery rhymes and fairy tales (the little old woman who lived in a shoe, the black man of the forest). Such language accords with a child's conception of the world, not an adult's. Plath's assault on the language of "daddy-poetry" has turned inward, on the language of her own poem, which teeters precariously on the edge of a preverbal abyss—represented by the eerie, keening "oo" sound with which a majority of the verses end. And then let us consider the play on "through" at the poem's conclusion. Although that last line allows for multiple readings, one interpretation is that the "I" has unconsciously carried out her father's wish: her discourse, by transforming itself into cathartic oversimplifications, has undone itself.

Yet the poem does contain its verbal violence by means more productive than

9. *JP = Johnny Panic and the Bible of Dreams.*   1. Otto Rank, *Beyond Psychology* (Baltimore: Johns Hopkins University Press, 1990).

silence. In a letter to her brother, Plath referred to "Daddy" as "gruesome" (*LH* 472), while on almost the same day she described it to A. Alvarez as a piece of "light verse" (Alvarez, *Beyond* 56).[2] She later read it on the BBC in a highly ironic tone of voice. The poem's unique spell derives from its rhetorical complexity: its variegated and perhaps bizarre fusion of the horrendous and the comic. As Uroff has remarked, it both shares and remains detached from the fixation of its protagonist (159).[3] The protagonist herself seems detached from her own fixation. She is "split in the most complex fashion," as Plath wrote of Ivan Karamazov[4] in her Smith College honors thesis. Plath's speaker uses potentially self-mocking melodramatic terms to describe both her opponent ("so black no sky could squeak through" [st. 10]) and herself ("poor and white" [st. 1]). While this aboriginal speaker quite literally expresses black-and-white thinking, her civilized double possesses a sensibility sophisticated enough to subject such thinking to irony. Thus the poem expresses feelings that it simultaneously parodies—it may be parodying the very idea of feeling. The tension between erudition and simplicity in the speaker's voice appears in her pairings that juxtapose adult with childlike diction: "breathe or Achoo," "your Luftewaffe, your gobbledygoo" (st. 1, 9). She can expound such adult topics as Taroc packs, Viennese beer, and Tyrolean snowfall; can specify death camps by name; and can employ an adult vocabulary of "recover," "ancestress," "Aryan," "*Meinkampf*," "obscene," and "bastard." Yet she also has recourse to a more primitive lexicon that includes "chuffing," "your fat black heart," and "my pretty red heart." She proves herself capable of careful intellectual discriminations ("so I never could tell" [st. 5]), conventionalized description ("beautiful Nauset" [st. 3]), and moral analogy ("if I've killed one man, I've killed two" [st. 15], while also exhibiting regressive fantasies (vampires), repetitions ("wars, wars, wars" [st. 4]), and inarticulateness ("panzer-man, panzer-man, O You—" [st. 9]). She oscillates between calm reflection ("You stand at the blackboard, daddy,/In the picture I have of you" [st. 11]) and mad incoherence ("Ich, ich, ich, ich" [st. 6]). Her sophisticated language puts her wild language in an ironic perspective, removing the discourse from the control of the archaic self who understands experience only in extreme terms.

The ironies in "Daddy" proliferate in unexpected ways, however. When the speaker proclaims categorically that "every woman adores a Fascist" (st. 10), she is subjecting her victimization to irony by suggesting that sufferers choose, or at least accommodate themselves to, their suffering. But she is also subjecting her authority to irony, since her claim about "every woman" is transparently false. It simply parodies patriarchal commonplaces, such as those advanced by Helene Deutsch concerning "feminine masochism" (192–99, 245–85).[5] The adult, sophisticated self seems to be speaking here: Who else would have the confidence to make a sociological generalization? Yet the content of the assertion, if taken straightforwardly, returns us to the regressive self who is dominated by extrava-

2. A. Alvarez, *Beyond All This Fiddle* (London: Allen Lane-Penguin, 1968).    3. Margaret Dickie Uroff, *Sylvia Plath and Ted Hughes* (Urbana: University of Illinois Press, 1979).    4. A character in Fyodor Dostoyevsky's novel *The Brothers Karamazov*, who suffers debilitating guilt for having wished for his father's death.    5. Helen Deutsch, *The Psychology of Women*, I: *Girlhood* (1944; repr. New York: Bantam, 1973).

gant emotions she cannot begin to understand. Plath's mother wished that Plath would write about "decent, courageous people" (*LH* 477), and she herself heard an inner voice demanding that she be a perfect "paragon" in her language and feeling (*J* 176). But in the speaker of "Daddy," she inscribed the opposite of such a paragon: a divided self whose veneer of civilization is breached and infected by unhealthy instincts.

Plath's irony cuts both ways. At the same time that the speaker's sophisticated voice undercuts her childish voice, reducing its melodrama to comedy, the childish or maddened voice undercuts the pretensions of the sophisticated voice, revealing the extremity of suffering masked by its ironies. While demonstrating the inadequacy of thinking and feeling in opposites, the poem implies that such a mode can locate truths denied more complex cognitive and affective systems. The very moderation of the normal adult intelligence, its tolerance of ambiguity, its defenses against the primal energies of the id, results in falsification. Reflecting Schiller's idea that the creative artist experiences a "momentary and passing madness" (quoted by Freud in a passage of *The Interpretation of Dreams* [193][6] that Plath underscored), "Daddy" gives voice to that madness. Yet the poem's sophisticated awareness, its comic vision, probably wins out in the end, since the poem concludes by curtailing the power of its extreme discourse * * *. Furthermore, Plath distanced herself from the poem's aboriginal voice by introducing her text as "a poem spoken by a girl with an Electra complex"—that is, as a study of the *girl's* pathology rather than her father's—and as an allegory that will "free" her from that pathology. She also distanced herself by reading the poem in a tone that emphasized its irony. And finally, she distanced herself by laying the poem's wild voice permanently to rest after October. The aboriginal vision was indeed purged. "Daddy" represents not Dickinson's madness that is divinest sense, but rather an entry into a style of discourse and a mastery of it. The poem realizes the trope of suffering by means of an inherent irony that both questions and validates the trope in the same gestures, and that finally allows the speaker to conclude the discourse and to remove herself from the trope with a sense of completion rather than wrenching, since the irony was present from the very beginning.

Plath's poetic revolt in "Daddy" liberated her pent-up creativity, but the momentary success sustained her little more than self-sacrifice had done. "Daddy" became another stage in her development, an unrepeatable experiment, a vocal opening that closed itself at once. The poem is not only an elegy for the power of "daddy-poetry" but for the powers of speech Plath discovered in composing it.

When we consider "Daddy" generically, a further range of implications presents itself. Although we could profitably consider the poem as the dramatic monologue Plath called it in her BBC broadcast, let us regard it instead as the kind of poem most readers have taken it to be: a domestic poem. I have chosen this term, rather than M. L. Rosenthal's better-known "confessional poem" or the more neutral "autobiographical poem," because "confessional poem" implies a

---

6. Sigmund Freud, *The Interpretation of Dreams*, ed. James Strachey, Standard Edition, IV (1900; New York: Norton, 1976).

confession rather than a making (though Steven Hoffman[7] and Lawrence Kramer[8] have recently indicated the mode's conventions) and because "autobiographical poem" is too general for our purpose. I shall define the domestic poem as one that represents and comments on a protagonist's relationship to one or more family members, usually a parent, child, or spouse. To focus our discussion even further, I shall emphasize poetry that specifically concerns a father.

* * *

* * * In the 1950s the "domestic poem" proper appeared on the scene, with its own conventions and expectations, and with its own complex cultural and literary reasons for being. Perhaps the precursive poems made the genre's eventual flowering inevitable, while its precise timing depended on a reaction against modernism's aesthetic of impersonality. Theodore Roethke wrote several early poems that initiated the genre: "My Papa's Waltz" (1948), "The Lost Son" (1948), and "Where Knock Is Open Wide" (1951). Lowell's "Life Studies" sequence (1959) was, and is, the genre's most prominent landmark. Other poems in the genre include John Berryman's *The Dream Songs* (1969); Frank Bidart's "Golden State" (1973) and "Confessional" (1983); Robert Duncan's "My Mother Would Be a Falconress" (1968); Allen Ginsberg's *Kaddish* (1960); Randall Jarrell's "The Lost World" (1965); Maxine Kumin's "The Thirties Revisited" (1975), "My Father's Neckties" (1978), and "Marianne, My Mother, and Me" (1989); Stanley Kunitz's "Father and Son" (1958) and "The Testing Tree" (1971); Lowell's "To Mother" (1977), "Robert T. S. Lowell" (1977), and "Unwanted" (1977); James Merrill's "Scenes of Childhood" (1962); Adrienne Rich's "After Dark" (1966); Anne Sexton's "Division of the Parts" (1960) and "The Death of the Fathers" (1972); W. D. Snodgrass' "Heart's Needle" (1959); Diane Wakoski's "The Father of My Country" (1968); and of course Sylvia Plath's "Daddy" (1962). In all these poems, the parent-child relationship serves as a locus for psychological investigation. In many of them it also serves as a means of representing the acquisition of poetic identity and of exploring the bounds of textuality itself. Because later writers were conscious of the Roethke-Lowell domestic poem as at least a genre in embryo, they chose to use its features, or perhaps the power of the genre was such that the features chose them. The "domestic poem" became a system of signs in which each individual text's adherence to the system and deviations within the system produced its particular literary meaning.

* * *

In 1959 Plath did not consciously attempt to write in the domestic poem genre, perhaps because she was not yet ready to assume her majority. Her journal entries of that period bristle with an impatience at herself that may derive from this reluctance. She may have feared asserting her "I am I am I am," which seemed to

7. Steven Hoffman, "Impersonal Personalism: The Making of a Confessional Poetic," *English Literary History* 45 (Winter 1978): 687–709.     8. Lawrence Kramer, "Freud and the Skunks: Genre and Language in *Life Studies*," in *Robert Lowell: Essays on the Poetry*, ed. Steven Gould Axelrod and Helen Deese (New York: Cambridge University Press, 1986).

carry with it a countervailing impulse of self-retribution. But by fall 1962, when she had already lost so much, she was ready to chance tackling poetic tradition, and specifically her chief male instructors, Roethke and Lowell. In "Daddy" she achieved her victory in two ways. First, as we have seen, she symbolically assaults a father figure who is identified with male control of language. All her anxiety of influence comes to the fore in the poem: her sense of belatedness, her awareness of constraint, her fears of inadequacy, her furious need to overcome her dependency, her guilt at her own aggressivity. Since the precursors "do not do/Any more" (st. 1), she wishes to escape their paralyzing influence and to empty the "bag full of God" that has kept her tongue stuck in her jaw for so long (st. 2, 5). The father whose power she attacks is not simply Roethke or Lowell, or even Hughes or Otto Plath, but a literary character who includes reference to all of them as categories of masculine authority. Although the Daddy of poetry has already "died" (st. 2)—the fate of all published texts in Plath's postromantic perspective—the speaker must symbolically "kill" him from her own discourse. The poem ironically depicts poetry as both an aggression and a suicide. The female ephebe herself becomes a "brute" in the act of voicing (st. 10), just as have her teachers before her. But the aggression of her speech yields to the self-annihilation of language. By the end of the poem she too, like her male precursors, is "through." The speaker's textual life will be misread on innumerable occasions in innumerable ways, whereas her own misreading and miswriting of the precursors is finished. In its conclusion, the poem acknowledges its alienation from itself, confessing the transitoriness of its unbounded power.

In addition to killing the father in its fictional plot, the poem seeks to discredit the forefathers through its status as poetic act. Taking a genre established by Roethke and Lowell, "Daddy" fundamentally alters it through antithesis and parody. Like all strong poems, it transforms its genre and therefore the way we perceive the precursive examples, making them seem not fulfillments but anticipations. Thus the later work projects its anxiety retrospectively back through its predecessors. Haunted by fears of inadequacy and redundancy, it seeks to make the earlier poems seem incompetent by comparison—a kind of juvenilia in the career of the genre, to represent the final possible stroke, or at the very least to inaugurate some new and important genre, of which the whole domestic genre was but a foreshadowing.

This point comes clearer if we compare "Daddy" with two analogues, Roethke's "The Lost Son" (1948) and Lowell's "Commander Lowell" (1959). In the Freudian drama of "The Lost Son," the protagonist subjectively relives his childhood fears and fantasies. Like the speaker of the companion piece, "My Papa's Waltz," he is still enmeshed in the family romance, remembering the father ambivalently as powerful, protective, and threatening. After locating himself at his father's grave, where he feels both grief and estrangement (in a scene that adumbrates "Electra on Azalea Path"), he descends into his unconscious, seeking, as Roethke later explained, "some clue to existence" (*Poet* 38).[9] He encounters his death wish, his

---

9. *On the Poet and His Craft: Selected Prose of Theodore Roethke,* ed. Ralph J. Mills, Jr. (Seattle and London: University of Washington Press, 1965).

memory of his father as "Father Fear," his sexual anxieties, and finally the "dark swirl" of a blackout, after which a childhood memory of his "Papa" shouting "order" in German returns him to consciousness. Although the figure of "Papa" blends earthly and heavenly father (*Poet* 39), he also symbolizes the superego, restoring order to a psyche and a poem that had fallen into chaos. At the poem's conclusion, as the "lost son" waits for his "understandable spirit" to revive, he appears to be purged, though not cured, of the conflicts that incapacitated him.

The speaker of "Commander Lowell," in contrast, is objective, precise, and witty. His discourse reflects a detached perspective on the past rather than a psychic reimmersion in it. He portrays his father as one who threatened him only through weakness. This father "was nothing to shout/about to the summer colony at 'Matt' "; took "four shots with his putter to sink his putt"; sang "Anchors Aweigh" in the bathtub; was fired from his job; and squandered his inheritance. Whereas Roethke's poem represents a cathartic experience, Lowell's converts chaotic feelings into intellectual irony. Whereas Roethke's poem can be read as an allegory of man's relationship to God or as a model of the Freudian psyche, Lowell's remains a realistic narrative, though it does suggest the cultural and financial decline of a social class.

Plath's poem combines features of both of these precursors: Roethke's evocation of a German-speaking authoritarian with Lowell's sarcastic deflation of a man without qualities; Roethke's subjective anguish with Lowell's social comedy. Like Roethke's Papa, Plath's title character is an intimidating patriarch; like Lowell's Father, he is a buffoon ("big as a Frisco seal"). Finally, Plath's poem, like those of her predecessors, has little to do with psychological cure: the speaker's defenses remain in place. But in a deeper sense, "Daddy" swerves sharply from its precursors, curtailing their power. It turns the psychological depth of Roethke's poem and the ironically detached surface of Lowell's poem into a fury of denunciation, an extravagance of emotion, an exaggeration of acts and effects, perhaps revealing the subtexts of both precursors. If in a sense the texts by Roethke and Lowell constitute what Ned Lukacher[1] might term the primal scene of "Daddy," the latter poem's raw intensity succeeds in reversing the relationship, making itself resemble *their* primal scene. It unmasks Roethke's implicitly oppressive father figure as a monster and Lowell's sophisticated comedy as slapstick. It transforms the domestic genre alternately into a horror show, encapsulating every political, cultural, and familial atrocity of the age, and a theater of cruelty, evoking nervous laughter. "Daddy" takes the genre as far as it can go—and then further.

---

1. Ned Lukacher, *Primal Scenes: Literature, Philosophy, Psychoanalysis* (Ithaca and London: Cornell University Press, 1986).

# 14

## THE PROCESS OF CREATION

Poems do not write themselves. Even if the idea for a poem comes in a flash (as it sometimes does), poets often struggle to get the final effect just right. For some poems that means draft after draft, and sometimes poets write more than one version of a poem and allow the different versions to compete as rival authorized texts, or poets develop a text that seems to be complete and set but then later alter it in some crucial way. Often a study of the manuscript or of the several drafts suggests the various kinds of decisions a poet may make as a poem moves toward its final form. In this chapter you will find examples of several poems as they take shape—or take different forms—in the poet's mind.

> *I find laundry a great help to the conception of angels, and I suppose one thing I'm saying in that poem ["Love Calls Us to the Things of This World"] is that I don't really want to have much truck with angels who aren't in the laundry, who aren't involved in the everyday world. It's a poem against dissociated and abstracted spirituality.*
>
> —RICHARD WILBUR

The first example involves early drafts of the first stanza of Richard Wilbur's "Love Calls Us to the Things of This World," which in its finished form is printed right after the drafts. Wilbur is one of the most careful craftsmen writing today, and in the early drafts of the first stanza we can see him moving toward the brilliant and surprising effects he achieves in the "final" version, that is, the version he decided to publish. Someone is just awaking, and through a window sees laundry on a clothesline blowing in the breeze. But he is not quite awake and not quite sure what he sees: his body and soul, the poet says playfully in lines 26 and 27, are not yet quite reunited, and he seems for a moment still suspended in a world of spirit and dream; the blowing clothes look like disembodied angels. Ultimately, the poem captures that sense of suspension between worlds, the uncertainty of where one is and what is happening in that first half-conscious moment when normal physical laws don't seem to apply. It is a delicate moment to catch, and in the six successive drafts printed below we can see the poet moving toward the more precise effect of the completed poem.

In the first three drafts the speaker seems to speak about himself—not quite right because that device makes him too conscious, and part of the basic effect of the finished poem involves a lack of consciousness and control. By the fourth draft "My eyes came open" has become "The eyes open," and the effect of being a little lost and unsure of identity is becoming clearer. Another major change in the early drafts is that the sound of the laundry pulley changes from "squeak" to "shriek" to "cry": the first two words capture the shrill sound of a moving pulley faithfully, but "cry" makes it seem personal and human, and now it is as if the pulleys were in fact calling the speaker from sleep. The image changes, too: in the first draft the world of sleep is a brothel, but those connotations are eliminated in later drafts, and instead by the sixth draft the "spirit" has become "soul" and is bodiless. Every new draft changes the conception just a little, and in the drafts printed here we can see effects gradually getting clearer in the poet's mind and falling into place. Notice how rhyme appears in draft and then disappears again, notice how the poet tries out and rejects words that don't have quite the right connotation: "wallow" (draft c), "frothing" (draft d), "rout" (draft f). In a detailed set of drafts like this one, we can see the poet weighing different visual and verbal possibilities, choosing every single word with care.

The other poems and passages similarly give us a chance to compare the effects of more than one version of a poem or passage. In several cases, a poem is "finished" in more than one version, and the poets invite us to choose among the competing versions instead of choosing one themselves. In each selection a few crucial words create significant differences in the text.

1. Early drafts of the first stanza of "Love Calls Us to the Things of This World," reprinted by permission of the author:

(a) My eyes came open to the squeak of pulleys
    My spirit, shocked from the brothel of itself

(b) My eyes came open to the shriek of pulleys,
    And the soul, spirited from its proper wallow,
    Hung in the air as bodiless and hollow

(c) My eyes came open to the pulleys' cry.
    The soul, spirited from its proper wallow,
    Hung in the air as bodiless and hollow
    As light that frothed upon the wall opposing;
    But what most caught my eyes at their unclosing
    Was two gray ropes that yanked across the sky.
    One after one into the window frame
    . . . the hosts of laundry came

(d)    The eyes open to a cry of pulleys,
    And the soul, so suddenly spirited from sleep,
    As morning sunlight frothing on the floor,
        While just outside the window
    The air is solid with a dance of angels.

(e)    The eyes open to a cry of pulleys,
    And spirited from sleep, the astounded soul
    Hangs for a moment bodiless and simple
    As dawn light in the moment of its breaking:
        Outside the open window
    The air is crowded with a

(f)     The eyes open to a cry of pulleys,
        And spirited from sleep, the astounded soul
        Hangs for a moment bodiless and simple
        As false dawn
            Outside the open window,
        Their air is leaping with a rout of angels.
            Some are in bedsheets, some are in dresses,
            it does not seem to matter

Final version, 1956:


        The eyes open to a cry of pulleys,
    And spirited from sleep, the astounded soul
    Hangs for a moment bodiless and simple
    As false dawn.
                Outside the open window
        The morning air is all awash with angels.                    5

        Some are in bed-sheets, some are in blouses,
    Some are in smocks: but truly there they are.
    Now they are rising together in calm swells
    Of halcyon[1] feeling, filling whatever they wear
    With the deep joy of their impersonal breathing;               10
        Now they are flying in place,[2] conveying
    The terrible speed of their omnipresence, moving
    And staying like white water; and now of a sudden
    They swoon down into so rapt a quiet
    That nobody seems to be there.
                        The soul shrinks                            15

        From all that it is about to remember,
    From the punctual rape of every blesséd day,
    And cries,
            "Oh, let there be nothing on earth but laundry,
    Nothing but rosy hands in the rising steam
    And clear dances done in the sight of heaven."                 20

        Yet, as the sun acknowledges
    With a warm look the world's hunks and colors,
    The soul descends once more in bitter love
    To accept the waking body, saying now
    In a changed voice as the man yawns and rises,                 25

        "Bring them down from their ruddy gallows;
    Let there be clean linen for the backs of thieves;
    Let lovers go fresh and sweet to be undone,
    And the heaviest nuns walk in a pure floating
    Of dark habits,
                keeping their difficult balance."                  30

1. Serene.     2. Like planes in a formation.

2. Two versions of Keats's "Bright star! would I were stedfast as thou art!"

Original version, 1819:

> Bright star! would I were stedfast as thou art!
> Not in lone splendor hung amid the night;
> Not watching, with eternal lids apart,
> Like Nature's devout sleepless Eremite,
> 5  The morning waters at their priestlike task
> Of pure ablution round earth's human shores;
> Or, gazing on the new soft fallen mask
> Of snow upon the mountains and moors:—
> No;—yet still stedfast, still unchangeable.
> 10  Cheek-pillow'd on my Love's white ripening breast,
> To touch, for ever, its warm sink and swell,
> Awake, for ever, in a sweet unrest;
> To hear, to feel her tender taken breath,
> Half-passionless, and so swoon on to death.

Revised version, 1820:

> Bright star! would I were steadfast as thou art—
>   Not in lone splendor hung aloft the night
> And watching, with eternal lids apart,
>   Like nature's patient, sleepless Eremite,
> 5  The moving waters at their priestlike task
>   Of pure ablution round earth's human shores,
> Or gazing on the new soft fallen mask
>   Of snow upon the mountains and the moors—
> No—yet still steadfast, still unchangeable,
> 10  Pillowed upon my fair love's ripening breast,
> To feel for ever its soft fall and swell,
>   Awake for ever in a sweet unrest,
> Still, still to hear her tender-taken breath,
> And so live ever—or else swoon to death.

3.  Manuscript and transcription of Keats's "To Autumn."

Manuscript:

Season of Mists and mellow fruitfulness,
Close bosom friend of the maturing sun;
Conspiring with him how to load and bless
The Vines with fruit that round the thatch eves run;
To bend with apples the mossd Cottage trees
And fill all fruits with ripeness to the core
To swell the gourd, and plump the hazle shells
With a white kernel; to set budding more
And still more, later flowers for the bees,
Until they think warm days will never cease
For Summer has o'erbrimmd their clammy cells.

Who hath not seen thee? for thy haunts are many
Sometimes whoever seeks abroad may find
Thee sitting careless on a granary floor
Thy hair soft lifted by the winnowing wind
While bright the sun slants through the barn
or on a half reapd furrow sound asleep
Dosed with red poppies; while thy reeping hook
Spares from some slumberous minutes the next swath
Or on a half reapd furrow sound asleep
Dosd with the fume of poppies, while thy hook
Spares the next swath, and all its twined flowers
And sometimes like a gleaner thou dost keep
Steady thy laden head across the brook;
Or by a Cyder-press with patient look
Thou watchest the last oozing hours by hours

> Season of Mists and mellow fruitfulness
>> Close bosom friend of the naturring sun;
> Conspiring with him how to load and bless
>> The Vines with fruit that round the thatch eves run
>>> To bend with apples the moss'd Cottage trees
>>> And fill all furuits with sweeness to the core
>>>> To swell the gourd, and plump the hazle shells
>> With a white kernel; to set budding more
>> And still more later flowers for the bees
>>> Until they think wam days with never cease
>>>> For Summer has o'erbrimm'd their clammy cells—

5

10

>>> oft amid thy stores?
> Who hath not seen thee? ~~for thy haunts are many~~
>>> abroad
> Sometimes whoeever seeks ~~for thee~~ may find
> Thee sitting careless on a granary floorr
>> Thy hair soft lifted by the winnowing wind

15

>>>>> husky
>> ~~While bright the Sun slants through the~~ barn;
>>> orr on a half reap d furrow sound asleep
>> ~~Or sound asleep in a half reaped old~~
>>> ~~Dose d with read poppies; while thy reeping hook~~
>> ~~Spares form Some slumbrous~~
>>>> ~~minutes while wam slumpers creep~~
>> Or on a half reap'd furrow sound asleep
>>> Dos'd with the fume of poppies, while thy hook
>>> Spares the next swath and all its twined ouers
> ~~Spares for some slumbrous minutes the next swath;~~
>> And sometimes like a gleans thost dost keep
>>> Steady thy laden head across the brook;
>>> Or by a Cyder-press with patent look
> Thou watchest the last oozing hours by hours

20

25

4.  Three versions of Alexander Pope's "Ode on Solitude."

1709 manuscript version:

> Happy the man, who free from care,
> The business and the noise of towns,
> Contented breathes his native air,
>> In his own grounds.

> Whose herds with milk, whose fields with bread,
> Whose flocks supply him with attire,
> Whose trees in summer yield him shade,
>> In winter fire.

5

> Blest! who can unconcern'dly find
> His years slide silently away,

10

In health of body, peace of mind,
    Quiet by day,

Repose at night; study and ease
Together mix'd; sweet recreation,
And innocence, which most does please,          15
    With meditation.

Thus let me live, unseen, unknown;
Thus unlamented let me die;
Steal from the world, and not a stone
    Tell where I lie.          20

First printed version, 1717:

How happy he, who free from care,
The rage of courts, and noise of towns;
Contented breathes his native air,
    In his own grounds.
Whose herds with milk, whose fields with bread,     5
Whose flocks supply him with attire.
Whose trees in summer yield him shade,
    In winter fire.
Blest! who can unconcern'dly find
Hours, days, and years slide swift away,     10
In health of body, peace of mind,
    Quiet by day,
Sound sleep by night; study and ease
Together mix'd; sweet recreation,
And innocence, which most does please,     15
    With meditation.
Thus let me live, unheard, unknown;
Thus unlamented let me die;
Steal from the world, and not a stone
    Tell where I lie.     20

Final version, 1736:

Happy the man, whose wish and care
A few paternal acres bound,
Content to breathe his native air,
    In his own ground.
Whose herds with milk, whose fields with bread,     5
Whose flocks supply him with attire,
Whose trees in summer yield him shade,
    In winter fire.
Blest! who can unconcern'dly find
Hours, days, and years slide soft away,     10
In health of body, peace of mind,
    Quiet by day,
Sound sleep by night; study and ease
Together mix'd; sweet recreation,

15    And innocence, which most does please,
                With meditation.
      Thus let me live, unseen, unknown;
      Thus unlamented let me die;
      Steal from the world, and not a stone
20                Tell where I lie.

  5. This famous folk ballad was sung and recited in many variations; here are two written versions. Neither version can be dated precisely.

      "O where ha' you been, Lord Randal, my son?
      And where ha' you been, my handsome young man?"
      "I ha' been at the greenwood; mother, mak my bed soon,
      For I'm wearied wi' huntin', and fain wad[3] lie down."

5     "And wha met ye there, Lord Randal, my son?
      And wha met you there, my handsome young man?"
      "O I met wi' my true-love; mother, mak my bed soon,
      For I'm wearied wi' huntin', and fain wad lie down."

      "And what did she give you, Lord Randal, my son?
10    And what did she give you, my handsome young man?"
      "Eels fried in a pan; mother, mak my bed soon,
      For I'm wearied wi' huntin', and fain wad lie down."

      "And wha gat your leavin's, Lord Randal, my son?
      And wha gat your leavin's, my handsome young man?"
15    "My hawks and my hounds; mother, mak my bed soon,
      For I'm wearied wi' huntin', and fain wad lie down."

      "And what becam of them, Lord Randal, my son?
      And what becam of them, my handsome young man?"
      "They stretched their legs out and died; mother, mak my bed soon,
20    For I'm wearied wi' huntin', and fain wad lie down."

      "O I fear you are poisoned, Lord Randal, my son!
      I fear you are poisoned, my handsome young man!"
      "O yes, I am poisoned; mother, mak my bed soon,
      For I'm sick at the heart, and I fain wad lie down."

25    "What d'ye leave to your mother, Lord Randal, my son?
      What d'ye leave to your mother, my handsome young man?"
      "Four and twenty milk kye;[4] mother, mak my bed soon,
      For I'm sick at the heart, and I fain wad lie down."

      "What d'ye leave to your sister, Lord Randal, my son?
30    What d'ye leave to your sister, my handsome young man?"
      "My gold and my silver; mother, mak my bed soon,
      For I'm sick at the heart, and I fain wad lie down."

      "What d'ye leave to your brother, Lord Randal, my son?
      What d'ye leave to your brother, my handsome young man?"

---

3. Would like to.    4. Cows.

"My houses and my lands; mother, mak my bed soon,
For I'm sick at the heart, and I fain wad lie down."                    35

"What d'ye leave to your true-love, Lord Randal, my son?
What d'ye leave to your true-love, my handsome young man?"
"I leave her hell and fire; mother, mak my bed soon,
For I'm sick at the heart, and I fain wad lie down."                    40

Shorter version:

"O where hae ye been, Lord Randal, my son?
O where hae ye been, my handsome young man?"
"I hae been to the wild wood; mother, make my bed soon,
For I'm weary wi' hunting, and fain wald lie down."

"Where gat ye your dinner, Lord Randal, my son?                          5
Where gat ye your dinner, my handsome young man?"
"I dined wi' my true-love; mother, make my bed soon,
For I'm weary wi' hunting, and fain wald lie down."

"What gat ye to your dinner, Lord Randal, my son?
What gat ye to your dinner, my handsome young man?"                     10
"I gat eels boiled in broo; mother, make my bed soon,
For I'm weary wi' hunting, and fain wald lie down."

"What became of your bloodhounds, Lord Randal, my son?
What became of your bloodhounds, my handsome young man?"
"O they swelled and they died; mother, make my bed soon,                15
For I'm weary wi' hunting, and fain wald lie down."

"O I fear ye are poisoned, Lord Randal, my son!
O I fear ye are poisoned, my handsome young man!"
"O yes! I am poisoned; mother, make my bed soon,
For I'm sick at the heart, and I fain wald lie down."                   20

6. "Poetry," by Marianne Moore, appears on page 272 in a version that was origi-
nally published in 1921. Here are two later versions.

The 1925 version:

I too, dislike it:
there are things that are important beyond all this fiddle.
The bat, upside down; the elephant pushing,
the tireless wolf under a tree,
the base-ball fan, the statistician—                                    5
"business documents and schoolbooks"—
these phenomena are pleasing,
but when they have been fashioned
into that which is unknowable,
we are not entertained.                                                 10
It may be said of all of us
that we do not admire what we cannot understand;
enigmas are not poetry.

The version Moore chose to print in her *Complete Poems* in 1967:

> I, too, dislike it.
>     Reading it, however, with a perfect contempt for it, one discovers in
> it after all, a place for the genuine.

7.  Two versions of Emily Dickinson's "Safe in their Alabaster Chambers—":

1859 version:

> Safe in their Alabaster Chambers—
> Untouched by Morning
> And untouched by Noon—
> Sleep the meek members of the Resurrection—
> Rafter of satin,
> And Roof of stone.
>
> Light laughs the breeze
> In her Castle above them—
> Babbles the Bee in a stolid Ear,
> Pipe the Sweet Birds in ignorant cadence—
> Ah, what sagacity perished here!

1861 version:

> Safe in their Alabaster Chambers—
> Untouched by Morning—
> And untouched by Noon—
> Lie the meek members of the Resurrection—
> Rafter of Satin—and Roof of Stone!
>
> Grand go the Years—in the Crescent—above them—
> Worlds scoop their Arcs—
> And Firmaments—row—
> Diadems—drop—and Doges—surrender—
> Soundless as dots—on a Disc of Snow—

8. Drafts of "The Tyger" by William Blake. The final version, published in 1790, can be found on page 502.

First draft:[5]

### The Tyger

1        Tyger Tyger burning bright
         In the forests of the night

---

5. These drafts have been taken from a notebook used by William Blake called the Rossetti MS because it was once owned by Dante Gabriel Rossetti, the Victorian poet and painter; David V. Erdman's edition of *The Notebook of William Blake* (1973) contains a photographic facsimile. This stanza numbers were written by Blake in the manuscript.

What immortal hand or eye

<sup>Dare</sup> ~~Could~~ frame thy fearful symmetry

<sup>Burnt in</sup>
2    ~~In what~~ distant deeps or skies

~~The cruel~~ ~~Burnt the~~ fire of thine eyes

On what wings dare he aspire

What the hand dare sieze the fire

3    And what shoulder & what art

Could twist the sinews of thy heart

And when thy heart began to beat

What dread hand & what dread feet

~~Could fetch it from the furnace deep~~

~~And in thy horrid ribs dare steep~~

~~In the well of sanguine woe~~

~~In what clay & what mould~~

Were thy eyes of fury rolld

<sup>Where</sup>                       <sup>where</sup>
4    ~~What~~ the hammer ~~what~~ the chain

In what furnace was thy brain

                                                    <sup>dread grasp</sup>
What the anvil what ~~the arm~~ arm ~~grasp~~ ~~clasp~~

<sup>Dare</sup> ~~Could~~ its deadly terrors ~~clasp~~ ~~grasp~~ clasp

6    Tyger Tyger burning bright

In the forests of the night

What immortal hand & eye

<sup>frame</sup>
Dare ~~form~~ thy fearful symmetry

Trial stanzas:

Burnt in distant deeps or skies

The cruel fire of thine eye,

Could heart descend or wings aspire

What the hand dare sieze the fire

                  <sup>dare he ~~smile laugh~~</sup>
5 ♪    And ~~did he laugh~~ his work to see

                  <sup>ankle</sup>
What the ~~shoulder~~ what the ~~knee~~

           <sup>Dare</sup>
4    ~~Did~~ he who made the lamb make thee

1    When the stars threw down their spears

2    And waterd heaven with their tears

Second full draft:

Tyger Tyger burning bright

In the forests of the night

What Immortal hand & eye
Dare frame thy fearful symmetry

And what shoulder & what art
Could twist the sinews of thy heart
And when thy heart began to beat
What dread hand & what dread feet

When the stars threw down their spears
And waterd heaven with their tears
Did he smile his work to see
Did he who made the lamb make thee

Tyger Tyger burning bright
In the forests of the night
What immortal hand & eye
Dare frame thy fearful symmetry

Final version:

Tyger! Tyger! burning bright
In the forests of the night,
What immortal hand or eye
Could fame thy fearful symmetry?

5    In what distant deeps or skies
Burnt the fire of thine eyes?
On what wings dare he aspire?
What the hand dare seize the fire?

And what shoulder, & what art,
10    Could twist the sinews of thy heart?
And when they heart began to beat,
What dread hand? & what dread feet?

What the hammer? what the chain?
In what furance was thy brain?
15    What the anvil? what dread grasp
Dare its deadly terrors clasp?

When the stars threw down their spears
And water'd heaven with their tears,
Did he smile his work to see?
Did he who made the Lamb make thee?
20
Tyger! Tyger! burning bright
In the forests of the night,
What immortal hand or eye
Dare frame they fearful symmetry?

# *Evaluating Poetry*

How do you know a good poem when you see one? This is not an easy question to answer—partly because deciding about the *value* of poems is a complex, difficult, and often lengthy process, and partly because there is no single and absolute criterion that will measure texts and neatly divide the good from the not so good. People who long for a nice, infallible sorter—some test that will automatically pick out the best poems and distinguish variations of quality much as a litmus test separates acids from bases—often are frustrated at what they perceive to be the "relativity" of judgment in evaluating poems. But because an issue is complex does not mean it is impossible, and even if there is no easy and absolute standard to be discovered, there are nevertheless distinctions to be made. Some poems are better—that is, more consistently effective with talented and experienced readers—than others. Even if we cannot sensibly rate poems on a 1-to-10 scale or universally agree on the excellence of a single poem, it is possible to set out some criteria that are helpful to readers who may not yet have developed confidence in their own judgments. It isn't necessary, of course, to spend all of our time asking about quality and being judgmental about poetry. But because life isn't long enough to read everything, it is often useful to separate those poems that are likely to be worth your time from those that aren't. Besides, the process of sorting—in which you begin to articulate your own judgments and poetic values—can be a very useful strategy in making yourself a better reader and a more informed, better-educated, and wiser person. Evaluating poems can

> *Poetry is a language that tells us, through a more or less emotional reaction, something that cannot be said.*
>
> —EDWIN ARLINGTON ROBINSON

be, among other things, a way to learn more about yourself, for what you like in poetry has a lot to say about where your own values really lie.

"I like it." That simple, unreflective statement about a poem is often a way to begin the articulation of standards—as long as your next move is to ask yourself why. Answers to *why* are often, at first, quite simple, even for experienced and sophisticated readers. "I like the way it sounds" or "I like its rhythm and pace" might be good, if partial, reasons for liking a poem. The popularity of nursery rhymes and simple childish ditties, or even the haunting, predictable, and repeated sounds and phrases of a poem like "The Raven" owe a lot (if not necessarily everything) to the use of sound. Another frequent answer might be: "because it is true" or "because I agree with what it says." All of us are apt to like sentiments or ideas that resemble our own more than those that challenge or disturb us, though bad formulations of some idea we treasure, like bad behavior in someone we love, can sometimes be more embarrassing than comforting. But the longer we struggle with our reasons for liking a poem, the more complex and revealing our answers are likely to be: "I like the *way* it expresses something I had thought but had never quite been able to articulate." "I like the way its sounds and rhythms imitate the sounds of what is being described." "I like the way it presents conflicting emotions, balancing negative and positive feelings that seem to exist at the same time in about equal intensity." "I like its precision in describing just how something like that affects a person." Such statements as "I like . . ." begin quietly to cross the border into the area of "I admire," and to include a second clause, beginning with "because" and offering complex reasons for that admiration, is to begin to move into the process of critical evaluation.

What kinds of reasons might we expect different readers to agree on? *Groups* of readers might well agree on certain ideas—questions of politics or economics or religion, for example—but not readers across the board. More likely to generate consensus are technical criteria, questions of craft. How precise are the word choices at crucial moments in the poem? How rich, suggestive, and resonant are the words that open up the poem to larger statements and claims? How appropriate are the metaphors and other figures of speech? How original and imaginative? How carefully is the poem's situation set up? How clearly? How full and appropriate is the characterization of the speaker? How well matched are the speaker, situation, and setting with the poem's sentiments and ideas? How consistent is the poem's tone? How appropriate to its themes? How carefully worked out is the poem's structure? How appropriate to the desired effects are the line breaks, the stanza breaks, and the pattern of rhythms and sounds?

One way of seeing how good a poem is in its various aspects is to look at what it is not—to consider the choices *not* made by the poet. Often it is possible to consider what a poem would be like if a different artistic choice had been made, as a way of seeing the importance of the choice actually made. What if, for example, Sylvia Plath had described a black *crow* in rainy weather instead of a rook? What if William Carlos Williams had described a *white* wheelbarrow? Sometimes we have the benefit, if we have a working manuscript or an autobiographical account of composition, of actually watching the process of selection. Look again, for example, at the several drafts of the first stanza of Richard Wilbur's "Love Calls Us to the Things of This World":

(a)  My eyes came open to the squeak of pulleys
     My spirit, shocked from the brothel of itself

(b)  My eyes came open to the shriek of pulleys,
     And the soul, spirited from its proper wallow,
     Hung in the air as bodiless and hollow

(c)  My eyes came open to the pulleys' cry.
     The soul, spirited from its proper wallow,
     Hung in the air as bodiless and hollow
     As light that frothed upon the wall opposing;
     But what most caught my eyes at their unclosing
     Was two gray ropes that yanked across the sky.
     One after one into the window frame
     . . . the hosts of laundry came       ·

(d)    The eyes open to a cry of pulleys,
     And the soul, so suddenly spirited from sleep,
     As morning sunlight frothing on the floor,
         While just outside the window
     The air is solid with a dance of angels.

(e)    The eyes open to a cry of pulleys,
       And spirited from sleep, the astounded soul
       Hangs for a moment bodiless and simple
       As dawn light in the moment of its breaking:
          Outside the open window
       The air is crowded with a

(f)    The eyes open to a cry of pulleys,
       And spirited from sleep, the astounded soul
       Hangs for a moment bodiless and simple
       As false dawn
          Outside the open window,
       Their air is leaping with a rout of angels.
          Some are in bedsheets, some are in dresses,
          it does not seem to matter

 

Notice how much more appropriate to the total poem is the choice of "cry" over "shriek" or "squeak" to describe the sound of pulleys or how much more effective than the metaphor of a spirit's "brothel" is the image of the soul hanging "bodiless." Notice the things Wilbur excised from the early drafts as well as the things he added when the poem became more clear and more of a piece in his mind. Read some of the other revised versions of poems or passages printed in Chapter 14. Do you think all the revisions improve on the originals? in what specific way? What are your criteria for deciding? Do any of the revisions seem pointless to you—or (worse) make the poem less than it was? On what basis did you make the evaluation?

Let's look again at one of the first poems we discussed, Adrienne Rich's "Aunt Jennifer's Tigers" (page 41). Some of the power of this poem comes from the poet's clear and sympathetic engagement with Aunt Jennifer's situation, but the effects are carefully generated through a series of specific technical choices. Rich herself may or may not have made all these choices consciously; her later comments on the poem suggest that her creative instincts, as well as her then-repressed sense of gender, may have governed some decisions more fully than her own deliberate calculations. But however conscious, the choices of speaker, situation, metaphor, and connotative words work brilliantly together to create a strong feminist statement, almost a manifesto on the subject of mastery and compliance, even while (at the same time) making powerful assertions about the power of art to overcome human circumstances.

In a sense there is no speaker in this poem, no specified personality—only a faceless niece who observes the central character—but the effacing of this speaker in the light of the vivid Jennifer amounts to a brilliant artistic decision. Jennifer, powerless to articulate and possibly even to understand her own plight, nevertheless is allowed almost to speak for herself, primarily through her hands. The seeming refusal of the narrator to do more than simply describe Jennifer's hands and their product gives Jennifer the crucial central role; she is the center of attention throughout, and the poem emphasizes only what one sees, with little apparent "editorial" comment (though the speaker does make three evaluative statements, saying that Jennifer was "mastered" by her ordeals [line 10], and noting that her hands are "terrified" [line 9] and that the wedding band "sits heavily" [line 9] on one of them). The tigers are ultimately more eloquent than the speaker seems to be: they "prance" (lines 1 and 12) and "pace" (line 4), and they are "proud" (line 12) and unafraid of men (lines 3 and 12), embodying the guarded message Jennifer sends to the world even though she herself is "mastered" and "ringed" (line 10). The brightly conceived colors in the tapestry, the expressive description of Jennifer's fingers and hands (note especially the excitement implied in "fluttering" [line 5]), and the action of the panel itself combine with the characterization of Jennifer to present a strong statement of generational repression—and boldness. The image of knitting as art, suggestive of the way the classical Fates determine the future and the nature of things, also hints at what is involved in Rich's art. The quality of the poem lies in the care, precision, and imaginativeness of Rich's craftsmanship. In later years, Rich has become clearer and more vocal about her values, but the direction and intensity of her vision are already apparent in this excellent poem taken from her first book, published nearly half a century ago.

Here is another celebrated poem that similarly accomplishes a great deal in a short space:

## WILLIAM SHAKESPEARE

## [Th' expense of spirit in a waste of shame]

Th' expense[1] of spirit in a waste[2] of shame
Is lust in action; and, till action, lust
Is perjured, murderous, bloody, full of blame,
Savage, extreme, rude, cruel, not to trust;
5    Enjoyed no sooner but despiséd straight:
Past reason hunted; and no sooner had,
Past reason hated, as a swallowed bait,
On purpose laid to make the taker mad:
Mad in pursuit, and in possession so;
10    Had, having, and in quest to have, extreme;
A bliss in proof;[3] and proved, a very woe;
Before, a joy proposed; behind, a dream.
All this the world well knows; yet none knows well
To shun the heaven that leads men to this hell.

1609

Here the speaker *is* fully characterized, and the economical skill with which the characterization is achieved is one of the most striking aspects of the poem. The poem sets up its situation carefully and, at first, not altogether clearly. But the delay in clarity is functional: we do not know for a while just what disturbs the speaker so much, except that it has to do with "lust in action" (line 2). What we do know quickly is how powerful his feeling is. The two explosive *p*'s in the first half of the first line get the poem off to a fast and powerful start, and by the fourth line the speaker has listed nine separate unpleasant human characteristics driven by lust. He virtually spits them out. Here is one angry speaker, and it swiftly becomes clear that he is speaking from (undescribed) personal experience.

But the poem is not only angry and negative about lust. It also admits that there are

1. Expending.    2. Using up; also, desert.    3. In the act.

definite, and powerful, pleasures in lust: it is "enjoyed" (line 5) at the time ("a bliss in proof," line 11), and anticipated with pleasure ("a joy proposed," line 12). Such inconsistencies (or at least complexities) in the speaker's opinion are characteristic of the poem. Everything about his views, and according to him about lust itself, is "extreme" (line 10). There are no easy conclusions about lust in the first twelve lines of the poem, just a confusing movement back and forth between positives and negatives. The powerful condemnation of lust in the beginning—detailed in terms of how it makes people feel about themselves and how it affects their actions—quickly shifts into admissions of pleasure and joy, but then shifts back again. No opinion sticks for long. The only consistent thing about the speaker's feelings is his certainty of lust's power—to drive individuals to behavior that they may love or hate. Only at the end is there any kind of reasoned conclusion, and the "moral" is hardly comforting: everybody knows what I've been saying, the speaker says, and yet nobody knows how to avoid lust and its consequences because its pleasures are so sensational, both in prospect and in actual experience ("the heaven that leads men to this hell").

The vacillation of the speaker's opinions and moods is not the only confusing thing about the poem's organization. His account of lust repeatedly skips around in time. Are we talking here about lust at the time it is being satisfied ("lust in action")? Or are we talking about desire and anticipation? Or are we talking about what happens afterward? The answer is all three, and the discussion is hardly systematic. The first line and a half describe the present, and the meter of the first line even imitates the rhythms and force of male ejaculation: note how the basic iambic-pentameter strategy of the poem does not regularize until near the end of the second line. But soon we are talking about what happens before lust in action ("till action," line 2), and by line 5, after. Lines 6 and 7 contrast before and after, and line 9

> *Poems may or may not follow classical patterns—they explode out of everyday experience.*
>
> —DOROTHY LIVESAY

compares before and during. Line 10 describes all three positions in time ("Had, having, and in quest to have"). Line 11 compares during and after, line 12 before and after. The poem, or rather the speaker, does not seem able to decide exactly what he wants to talk about and what he thinks of his subject.

All this shifting around in focus and in feelings could easily be regarded as a serious flaw. Don't we expect a short poem, and especially a sonnet, to be very carefully organized and carefully focused toward a single end? Shouldn't the poet make up his mind about what he thinks and what the poem is about? It would be easy to construct an argument, on the basis of consistency or clarity of purpose, that this is not a very good poem, that perhaps the greatest poet in the English language was not, here, at the top of his form. But doing so would ignore the power of the poem's effects and underrate another principle of consistency—that of character. If we regard the poem as representative of a mind wrestling with the complex feelings brought about by lust—someone out of control because of lust, conscious enough to see his plight but unable to do anything about it—we can see a higher consistency here that helps explain the poem's powerful effect on many readers. Here is an account of a human mind grappling with an often-repeated human experience, the subject of many much longer works of literature. Lust is beautiful but terrifying, certainly to be avoided but impossible to avoid. Shakespeare has managed, in the unlikely space of fourteen lines and in a form in which we expect tight organization and intense focus, to portray succinctly the human recognition of confusion and powerlessness in the face of a passion larger than our ability to control it.

Here is another poem that is something of a challenge to evaluate:

## JOHN DONNE

### *Song*

Go, and catch a falling star,
   Get with child a mandrake root,[4]
Tell me, where all past years are,
   Or who cleft the devil's foot,
5   Teach me to hear mermaids singing
Or to keep off envy's stinging,
     And find
     What wind
Serves to advance an honest mind.

10  If thou beest born to strange sights,[5]
   Things invisible to see,
Ride ten thousand days and nights,
   Till age snow white hairs on thee;
Thou, when thou return'st, wilt tell me
15 All strange wonders that befell thee,
    And swear
    No where
Lives a woman true, and fair.

If thou find'st one, let me know:
20   Such a pilgrimage were sweet.
Yet do not, I would not go,
   Though at next door we might meet:
Though she were true when you met her,
And last till you write your letter,
25    Yet she
    Will be
False, ere I come, to two, or three.        1633

One immediate problem to confront here is the irregular, jerky rhythm. In a poem called "Song," we are likely to expect music, harmony, something pleasant and (within limits) predictable in its rhythm and movement. But this "song" is nothing like that. At first its message sounds lyrical and romantic: to go and catch a falling star is, if impossible, a romantic thing to propose, a motif that often comes up (and has for centuries) in love poems and popular songs; and lines 3 and 5 propose similar traditional romantic activities that evoke wonder and pleasure in contemplation. But the activities suggested in the alternate lines (2, 4, and 6) contrast sharply; they are just as bold in their unromantic or antiromantic sentiments. Making a mandrake root pregnant does not sound like an especially pleasant male activity, however much such a root may look like a female body, and knowledge of the devil's cleft foot or envy's stinging are not usually the stuff

4. The forked mandrake root looks vaguely human.    5. That is, if you have supernatural powers.

of romantic poems or songs. Besides, the strange interruptions of easy rhythm (indicated by commas) in otherwise pleasant lines like 1 and 3 suggest that something less than lyrical is going on there, too.

By the time we get to the last stanza, what is going on is a lot clearer. We have here a portrait of an angry and disillusioned man who is obsessed with the infidelity of women. He is talking to another man, apparently someone who has far more positive, perhaps even romantic, notions of women, and the poem is a kind of argument, except that the disillusioned speaker does all the talking. He pretends to take into account some traditional romantic rhetoric but turns it all on its head, intermixing the traditional impossible quests of lovers with a quest of his own—to find a "woman true, and fair" (line 18). But he knows cynically—he would probably say from experience, though he offers no evidence of his experience and no account of why he feels the way he does—that all these quests are impossible. The speaker is a bitter man, and the song he sings wants nothing to do with love or romance.

If we were to evaluate this "song" on the basis of harmonic and romantic expectations, looking for evenness of rhythms, pleasant sounds, and an attractive series of images consonant with romantic attitudes, we would certainly find it wanting. But again (as with the Shakespeare poem above) a larger question of appropriateness begs to be applied. Do the sounds, tone, images, and organization of the poem "work" in terms of the speaker portrayed here and the kind of artistic project this poem represents? The displeasure we feel in the speaker's words, images, feelings, and attitudes ultimately needs to be directed toward the speaker; the poet has done a good job of portraying a character whose bitterness, however generated, is unpleasant and off-putting. The poem "works" on its own terms. We may or may not like to hear attitudes like this expressed in a poem; we may or may not approve of using a pretended "song" to mouth such sentiments. But whether or not we "like" the poem in terms of what it says, we can evaluate, through close analysis of its several different elements (much as we have been doing analytically in earlier chapters), how *well* it does what it does. There are, of course, still larger questions of whether what it tries to do is worth doing, and readers of different philosophical or political persuasions may differ widely in their opinions and evaluations of that matter.

Different people do admire different things, and when we talk about criteria for evaluating poetry, we are talking about, at best, elements that a fairly large number of people have, over a long period of time, agreed on as important. There may be substantial agreement about political or social values in a particular group, and a consensus may exist within a group of, say, misogynists or feminists about the value of such a poem as Donne's "Song." But more general agreements that bridge social and ideological divisions are more likely to involve the kinds of matters that have come up for analysis in earlier chapters, matters involving how well a poem *works*, how well it uses the resources it has within its conceptual limits. For some readers, ideology is everything, and there is no such thing as quality beyond political views or moral conclusions. But for others, different, more pluralistic evaluations can be made about accomplishment and quality. You need to decide on your own criteria.

Consistency. Appropriateness. Coherence. Effectiveness. Such terms are likely to be key ones for most readers in making their evaluations—as they have been in this discussion. But individual critics or readers will often have their own emphases, their own highly personal preferences, their own axes to grind. For some critics in past generations, *organic unity* was the key to all evaluation, whether a poem achieved, like something grown in nature, a wholeness of conception and effect. For others, the key term may be *tension* or *ambiguity* or *complexity* or *simplicity* or *authenticity* or *cultural truth* or *representation* or *psychological accuracy*. With experience, you will develop your own set of criteria that may or may not involve a single ruling concept or term. But wherever (and whenever) you come out, you will learn something about yourself and your values in the process of articulating exactly what you like and admire—and why.

IRVING LAYTON

## Street Funeral

Tired of chewing
the flesh
of other animals;
Tired of subreption and conceit;
5    of the child's
bewildered conscience
fretting the sly man;
Tired of holding down
a job; of giving insults,
10   taking insults;
Of excited fornication,
failing heart valves,
septic kidneys . . .

This frosty morning,
15   the coffin wood bursting
into brilliant flowers,
Is he glad
that after all the lecheries,
betrayals, subserviency,
20   After all the lusts,
false starts, evasions
he can begin
the unobstructed change
into clean grass
25   Done forever
with the insult
of birth,
the long adultery
with illusion?                                                                 1956

GEOFFREY HILL

## In Memory of Jane Fraser

When snow like sheep lay in the fold
And winds went begging at each door

And the far hills were blue with cold
And a cold shroud lay on the moor

She kept the siege. And every day                                    5
We watched her brooding over death
Like a strong bird above its prey.
The room filled with the kettle's breath.

Damp curtains glued against the pane
Sealed time away. Her body froze                                    10
As if to freeze us all and chain
Creation to a stunned repose.

She died before the world could stir.
In March the ice unloosed the brook
And water ruffled the sun's hair.                                   15
Dead cones upon the alder shook.                          1959


## GALWAY KINNELL

### Blackberry Eating

I love to go out in late September
among the fat, overripe, icy, black blackberries
to eat blackberries for breakfast,
the stalks very prickly, a penalty
they earn for knowing the black art                                5
of blackberry-making; and as I stand among them
lifting the stalks to my mouth, the ripest berries
fall almost unbidden to my tongue,
as words sometimes do, certain peculiar words
like *strengths* or *squinched,*                                   10
many-lettered, one-syllabled lumps,
which I squeeze, squinch open, and splurge well
in the silent, startled, icy, black language
of blackberry-eating in late September.                   1980


## EMILY DICKINSON

### [The Brain—is wider than the Sky—]

The Brain—is wider than the Sky—
For—put them side by side—
The one the other will contain
With ease—and You—beside—

The Brain is deeper than the sea—                                  5
For—hold them—Blue to Blue—

The one the other will absorb—
As Sponges—Buckets—do—

The Brain is just the weight of God—
10    For—Heft them—Pound for Pound—
And they will differ—if they do—
As Syllable from Sound—

ca. 1862

## CHIDIOCK TICHBORNE

## *Elegy*

My prime of youth is but a frost of cares,
  My feast of joy is but a dish of pain,
My crop of corn is but a field of tares,
  And all my good is but vain hope of gain;
5      The day is past, and yet I saw no sun,
      And now I live, and now my life is done.

My tale was heard and yet it was not told,
  My fruit is fallen and yet my leaves are green,
My youth is spent and yet I am not old,
10   I saw the world and yet I was not seen;
      My thread is cut and yet it is not spun,
      And now I live, and now my life is done.

I sought my death and found it in my womb,
  I looked for life and saw it was a shade,
15  I trod the earth and knew it was my tomb,
    And now I die, and now I was but made;
      My glass[6] is full, and now my glass is run,
      And now I live, and now my life is done.

1586

## WALLACE STEVENS

## *Anecdote of the Jar*

I placed a jar in Tennessee,
And round it was, upon a hill.
It made the slovenly wilderness
Surround that hill.

---

6. Hourglass.

The wilderness rose up to it,                                                                5
And sprawled around, no longer wild.
The jar was round upon the ground
And tall and of a port in air.

It took dominion everywhere.
The jar was gray and bare.                                                                  10
It did not give of bird or bush,
Like nothing else in Tennessee.                                              1923


ELIZABETH BISHOP

## *The Armadillo*

for Robert Lowell


This is the time of year
when almost every night
the frail, illegal fire balloons appear.
Climbing the mountain height,

rising toward a saint                                                                        5
still honored in these parts,
the paper chambers flush and fill with light
that comes and goes, like hearts.

Once up against the sky it's hard
to tell them from the stars—                                                                10
planets, that is—the tinted ones:
Venus going down, or Mars,

or the pale green one. With a wind,
they flare and falter, wobble and toss;
but if it's still they steer between                                                         15
the kite sticks of the Southern Cross,

receding, dwindling, solemnly
and steadily forsaking us,
or, in the downdraft from a peak,
suddenly turning dangerous.                                                                  20

Last night another big one fell.
It splattered like an egg of fire
against the cliff behind the house.
The flame ran down. We saw the pair

of owls who nest there flying up                                                             25
and up, their whirling black-and-white
stained bright pink underneath, until
they shrieked up out of sight.

The ancient owls' nest must have burned.
30    Hastily, all alone,
      a glistening armadillo left the scene,
      rose-flecked, head down, tail down,

      and then a baby rabbit jumped out,
      *short*-eared, to our surprise.
35    So soft!—a handful of intangible ash
      with fixed, ignited eyes.

      *Too pretty, dreamlike mimicry!*
      *O falling fire and piercing cry*
      *and panic, and a weak mailed fist*
40    *clenched ignorant against the sky!*                    1965


JOHN CROWE RANSOM

## *Bells for John Whiteside's Daughter*

There was such speed in her little body,
And such lightness in her footfall,
It is no wonder her brown study[7]
Astonishes us all.

5     Her wars were bruited in our high window.
      We looked among orchard trees and beyond
      Where she took arms against her shadow,
      Or harried unto the pond

      The lazy geese, like a snow cloud
10    Dripping their snow on the green grass,
      Tricking and stopping, sleepy and proud,
      Who cried in goose, Alas,

      For the tireless heart within the little
      Lady with rod that made them rise
15    From their noon apple-dreams and scuttle
      Goose-fashion under the skies!

      But now go the bells, and we are ready,
      In one house we are sternly stopped
      To say we are vexed at her brown study,
20    Lying so primly propped.                               1924


7. Stillness, as if in meditation or deep thought.

ALICE WALKER

## Revolutionary Petunias

Sammy Lou of Rue
sent to his reward
the exact creature who
murdered her husband,
using a cultivator's hoe                              5
with verve and skill;
and laughed fit to kill
in disbelief
at the angry, militant
pictures of herself                                   10
the Sonneteers quickly drew:
not any of them people that
she knew.
A backwoods woman
her house was papered with                            15
funeral home calendars and
faces appropriate for a Mississippi
Sunday School. She raised a George,
a Martha, a Jackie and a Kennedy. Also
a John Wesley Junior                                  20
"Always respect the word of God,"
she said on her way to she didn't
know where, except it would be by
electric chair, and she continued
"Don't yall forgit to *water*                         25
my purple petunias."                          1973

QUESTIONS

1. What seems to you the most important single factor in whether you like or dislike a poem? Read back over the poems that you have liked most; what do they have in common?
2. How adaptable do you think you are in adjusting to a poem's emphases? Which poems have you liked though you didn't especially like the conclusions they came to?
3. How important to you is the *precision* of words in a poem? Do you tend to like poems better if they are definite and explicit in what they say? if they are ambiguous, uncertain, or complex?
4. Which issues and concepts in Chapters 1 through 8 have you found most useful? most surprising? Which chapters did you enjoy most? From which did you learn the most about yourself and your tastes and values?
5. What do you value most in poetry generally? Do you read poems that are not assigned? How did you choose which ones? Do you read poems outside this textbook or outside the course? If so, what kinds of poems do you tend to seek out? Do specific titles draw you in? particular subjects, topics, or themes?
6. How important to you is the *tone* of a poem? Do you tend to like funny poems more than

serious ones? tragic situations more than comic ones? unusual treatments of standard or predictable subjects and themes?

7.  Which poem in this chapter did you most enjoy reading? Which one did you like best after reading the commentary about it? Are there any poems you have read this term that you have violently disliked? What about them particularly irritated you? Have you changed your mind about some poems after you have reread or discussed them? How did your criteria change?

8.  Are certain subjects or themes always appealing to you? always unappealing? What variable seems to you most important in determining whether you will like or dislike a poem?

## WRITING SUGGESTIONS

1.  Choose one poem that you especially admire and one that you do not. Write a two-or three-page essay about each in which you try to show what specific accomplishments (or lack of them) led you to your evaluative conclusions. Treat each poem in detail, and suggest fully not only how but *why* things "work"—or don't work. Try to construct your argument as "objectively" as possible so that you are not simply pitting your personal judgment against someone else's. (Alternative: find two poems that are very much alike in subject matter, theme, or situation, but that seem to you to succeed to different degrees. Write one *comparative* essay in which you account for the difference in quality by showing in detail the difference between what works and what does not.)

2.  Discuss with classmates a variety of poems you have read this term, and choose one poem about which a number of you disagree. Discuss among yourselves the different perspectives you have on the poem, and try to sort out in the discussion exactly what issues are at stake. Take notes on the discussion, trying to be clear about how your position differs from that of other students. Once you believe that you have the issues sorted out and can be clear about your own position, write a two-or three-page personal letter to your instructor in which you outline a position contrary to your own and then answer it point by point. Be sure to make clear in your letter the *grounds* for your evaluative position, positive or negative—that is, the principles or values on which you base your evaluation. (Hint: in the conversation with classmates, try to steer the discussion to a clear disagreement on no more than two or three points, and in your letter focus carefully on these points. State the arguments of your classmates as effectively and forcefully as you can so that your own argument will be as probing and sophisticated as you can make it.)

3.  Choose a poem you have read this term that you admire but really don't like very much. In thinking over the poem again, try to account for the conflict between your feelings and your intellectual judgment: what questions of content or form, social or political assumption, personal style, or manner of argument in the poem seem to make it less attractive to you? In a personal letter to a friend who is not in the class and who thus has not heard the class discussions of the issues, describe your dilemma, being careful to first outline why you think the poem is admirable. Say frankly what your personal reservations about the poem are, and at the end use the discussion of the poem to talk about your own values, as they pertain to poetry in general.

# *Reading More Poetry*

## *Cutting the Cake*

Gowned and veiled for tribal ritual
in a maze of tulle and satin
with her eyes rimmed round in cat fur
and the stylish men about her
kissing kin and carefree suitors                                   5

long she looked unseeing past him
to her picture in the papers
print and photoflash embalming
the demise of the familiar
and he trembled as her fingers                                     10

took the dagger laid before them
for the ceremonial cutting
of the mounting tiers of sweetness
crowned with manikin and maiden
and her chop was so triumphant                                     15

that the groomlike little figure
from his lover at the apex
toppled over in the frosting
where a flower girl retrieved him
sucked him dry and bit his head off.                               20

1996

## *Peeling an Orange*

Between you and a bowl of oranges I lie nude
Reading *The World's Illusion* through my tears.
You reach across me hungry for global fruit,
Your bare arm hard, furry and warm on my belly.

<sup>5</sup>
Your fingers pry the skin of a navel orange
Releasing tiny explosions of spicy oil.
You place peeled disks of gold in a bizarre pattern
On my white body. Rearranging, you bend and bite
The disks to release further their eager scent.
<sup>10</sup>
I say "Stop, you're tickling," my eyes still on the page.
Aromas of groves arise. Through green leaves
Glow the lofty snows. Through red lips
Your white teeth close on a translucent segment.
Your face over my face eclipses *The World's Illusion.*
<sup>15</sup>
Pulp and juice pass into my mouth from your mouth.
We laugh against each other's lips. I hold my book
Behind your head, still reading, still weeping a little.
You say "Read on, I'm just an illusion," rolling
Over upon me soothingly, gently moving,
<sup>20</sup>
Smiling greenly through long lashes. And soon
I say "Don't stop. Don't disillusion me."
Snows melt. The mountain silvers into many a stream.
The oranges are golden worlds in a dark dream.                    1996


W. H. AUDEN

## *In Memory of W. B. Yeats*

### *(d. January, 1939)*

I

He disappeared in the dead of winter:
The brooks were frozen, the airports almost deserted,
And snow disfigured the public statues;
The mercury sank in the mouth of the dying day.
<sup>5</sup>
What instruments we have agree
The day of his death was a dark cold day.

Far from his illness
The wolves ran on through the evergreen forests,
The peasant river was untempted by the fashionable quays;
<sup>10</sup>
By mourning tongues
The death of the poet was kept from his poems.

But for him it was his last afternoon as himself,
An afternoon of nurses and rumors;
The provinces of his body revolted,
<sup>15</sup>
The squares of his mind were empty,
Silence invaded the suburbs,
The current of his feeling failed; he became his admirers.

Now he is scattered among a hundred cities
And wholly given over to unfamiliar affections,

To find his happiness in another kind of wood                                           20
And be punished under a foreign code of conscience.
The words of a dead man
Are modified in the guts of the living.

But in the importance and noise of tomorrow
When the brokers are roaring like beasts on the floor of the Bourse,[1]        25
And the poor have the sufferings to which they are fairly accustomed,
And each in the cell of himself is almost convinced of his freedom,
A few thousand will think of this day
As one thinks of a day when one did something slightly unusual.
What instruments we have agree                                                          30
The day of his death was a dark cold day.


        II

You were silly like us; your gift survived it all:
The parish of rich women, physical decay,
Yourself. Mad Ireland hurt you into poetry.
Now Ireland has her madness and her weather still,                                      35
For poetry makes nothing happen: it survives
In the valley of its making where executives
Would never want to tamper, flows on south
From ranches of isolation and the busy griefs,
Raw towns that we believe and die in; it survives,                                      40
A way of happening, a mouth.


        III

Earth, receive an honored guest:
William Yeats is laid to rest.
Let the Irish vessel lie
Emptied of its poetry.                                                                  45

In the nightmare of the dark
All the dogs of Europe bark,
And the living nations wait,
Each sequestered in its hate;

Intellectual disgrace                                                                   50
Stares from every human face,
And the seas of pity lie
Locked and frozen in each eye.

Follow, poet, follow right
To the bottom of the night,                                                             55
With your unconstraining voice
Still persuade us to rejoice;

With the farming of a verse
Make a vineyard of the curse,

1. The Paris stock exchange.

60    Sing of human unsuccess
      In a rapture of distress;

      In the deserts of the heart
      Let the healing fountain start,
      In the prison of his days
65    Teach the free man how to praise.

      1939

### GWENDOLYN BROOKS

## To the Diaspora

*you did not know you were Afrika*

When you set out for Afrika
you did not know you were going.
Because
you did not know you were Afrika.
5    You did not know the Black continent
that had to be reached
was you.

I could not have told you then that some sun
would come,
10    somewhere over the road,
would come evoking the diamonds
of you, the Black continent—
somewhere over the road.
You would not have believed my mouth.

15    When I told you, meeting you somewhere close
to the heat and youth of the road,
liking my loyalty, liking belief,
you smiled and you thanked me but very little believed me.

Here is some sun. Some.
20    Now off into the places rough to reach.
Though dry, though drowsy, all unwillingly a-wobble,
into the dissonant and dangerous crescendo.
Your work, that was done, to be done to be done to be done.        1981

## The Coora Flower

Today I learned the *coora* flower
grows high in the mountains of Itty-go-luba Bésa.

Province Meechee.
Pop. 39.

Now I am coming home.                                                              5
This, at least, is Real, and what I know.

It was restful, learning nothing necessary.
School is tiny vacation. At least you can sleep.
At least you can think of love or feeling your boy friend against you
(which is not free from grief).                                                    10

But now it's Real Business.
I am Coming Home.

My mother will be screaming in an almost dirty dress.
The crack is gone. So a Man will be in the house.

I must watch myself.                                                               15
I must not dare to sleep.                                            1991


SAMUEL TAYLOR COLERIDGE
_____

## *Kubla Khan: or, a Vision in a Dream*[2]

In Xanadu did Kubla Khan
    A stately pleasure-dome decree:
Where Alph, the sacred river, ran
Through caverns measureless to man
    Down to a sunless sea.                                                         5
So twice five miles of fertile ground
With walls and towers were girdled round:
And here were gardens bright with sinuous rills
Where blossomed many an incense-bearing tree;
And here were forests ancient as the hills,                                        10
Enfolding sunny spots of greenery.
But oh! that deep romantic chasm which slanted
Down the green hill athwart a cedarn cover![3]
A savage place! as holy and enchanted
As e'er beneath a waning moon was haunted                                          15
By woman wailing for her demon-lover![4]
And from this chasm, with ceaseless turmoil seething,
As if this earth in fast thick pants were breathing,
A mighty fountain momently was forced,
Amid whose swift half-intermitted burst                                            20

2. Coleridge said he wrote this fragment immediately after waking from an opium dream and that after he was interrupted by a caller he was unable to finish the poem.      3. From side to side of a cover of cedar trees.      4. In a famous and often-imitated German ballad, the lady Lenore is carried off on horseback by the specter of her lover and married to him at his grave.

Huge fragments vaulted like rebounding hail,
Or chaffy grain beneath the thresher's flail:
And 'mid these dancing rocks at once and ever
It flung up momently the sacred river.
Five miles meandering with a mazy motion
Through wood and dale the sacred river ran,
Then reached the caverns measureless to man,
And sank in tumult to a lifeless ocean:
And 'mid this tumult Kubla heard from far
Ancestral voices prophesying war!

    The shadow of the dome of pleasure
    Floated midway on the waves;
    Where was heard the mingled measure
    From the fountain and the caves.
It was a miracle of rare device,
A sunny pleasure-dome with caves of ice!
    A damsel with a dulcimer
    In a vision once I saw:
    It was an Abyssinian maid,
    And on her dulcimer she played,
    Singing of Mount Abora.
    Could I revive within me
    Her symphony and song,
    To such a deep delight 'twould win me,
That with music loud and long,
I would build that dome in air,
That sunny dome! those caves of ice!
And all who heard should see them there,
And all should cry, Beware! Beware!
His flashing eyes, his floating hair!
Weave a circle round him thrice,
And close your eyes with holy dread,
For he on honey-dew hath fed,
And drunk the milk of Paradise.

Line numbers: 25, 30, 35, 40, 45, 50

1798

---

HART CRANE

## *To Emily Dickinson*

You who desired so much—in vain to ask—
Yet fed your hunger like an endless task,
Dared dignify the labor, bless the quest—
Achieved that stillness ultimately best,

Being, of all, least sought for: Emily, hear!
O sweet, dead Silencer, most suddenly clear

Line number: 5

When singing that Eternity possessed
And plundered momently in every breast;

—Truly no flower yet withers in your hand.
The harvest you descried and understand                    10
Needs more than wit to gather, love to bind.
Some reconcilement of remotest mind—

Leaves Ormus rubyless, and Ophir[5] chill.
Else tears heap all within one clay-cold hill.             1933

## Exile

### (after the Chinese)

My hands have not touched pleasure since your hands,—
No,—nor my lips freed laughter since 'farewell',
And with the day, distance again expands
Voiceless between us, as an uncoiled shell.

Yet love endures, though starving and alone.               5
A dove's wings cling about my heart each night
With surging gentleness, and the blue stone
Set in the tryst-ring has but worn more bright.        p. 1918

COUNTEE CULLEN

## Yet Do I Marvel

I doubt not God is good, well-meaning, kind,
And did He stoop to quibble could tell why
The little buried mole continues blind,
Why flesh that mirrors Him must some day die,
Make plain the reason tortured Tantalus[6]                 5
Is baited by the fickle fruit, declare
If merely brute caprice dooms Sisyphus
To struggle up a never-ending stair.
Inscrutable His ways are, and immune
To catechism by a mind too strewn                          10
With petty cares to slightly understand
What awful brain compels His awful hand.
Yet do I marvel at this curious thing:
To make a poet black, and bid him sing!                    1925

5. An ancient country from which Solomon secured gold and precious stones. *Ormus*: presumably Ormuz, an ancient city on the Persian Gulf.    6. In Greek myth, he was condemned to stand thirsty in water up to his neck.

E. E. CUMMINGS

# [anyone lived in a pretty how town]

anyone lived in a pretty how town
(with up so floating many bells down)
spring summer autumn winter
he sang his didn't he danced his did.

5      Women and men(both little and small)
cared for anyone not at all
they sowed their isn't they reaped their same
sun moon stars rain

children guessed(but only a few
10     and down they forgot as up they grew
autumn winter spring summer)
that noone loved him more by more

when by now and tree by leaf
she laughed his joy she cried his grief
15     bird by snow and stir by still
anyone's any was all to her

someones married their everyones
laughed their cryings and did their dance
(sleep wake hope and then)they
20     said their nevers they slept their dream

stars rain sun moon
(and only the snow can begin to explain
how children are apt to forget to remember
with up so floating many bells down)

25     one day anyone died i guess
(and noone stooped to kiss his face)
busy folk buried them side by side
little by little and was by was

all by all and deep by deep
30     and more by more they dream their sleep
noone and anyone earth by april
wish by spirit and if by yes.

Women and men(both dong and ding)
summer autumn winter spring
35     reaped their sowing and went their came
sun moon stars rain                                              1940

## H.D. (HILDA DOOLITTLE)

# *Sea Rose*

Rose, harsh rose,
marred and with stint of petals,
meagre flower, thin,
sparse of leaf,

more precious                                                                5
than a wet rose
single on a stem—
you are caught in the drift.

Stunted, with small leaf,
you are flung on the sand,                                                   10
you are lifted
in the crisp sand
that drives in the wind.
Can the spice-rose
drip such acrid fragrance                                                    15
hardened in a leaf?                                                    1916

# *Garden*

### I

You are clear
O rose, cut in rock,
hard as the descent of hail.

I could scrape the color
from the petals                                                              5
like split dye from a rock.

If I could break you
I could break a tree.
If I could stir
I could break a tree—                                                       10
I could break you.

### II

O wind, rend open the heat,
cut apart the heat,
rend it to tatters.

Fruit cannot drop                                                           15
through this thick air—
fruit cannot fall into heat
that presses up and blunts

the points of pears
20      and rounds the grapes.

Cut the heat—
plough through it,
turning it on either side
of your path.                                                      1916


## Helen

All Greece[7] hates
the still eyes in the white face,
the luster as of olives
where she stands,
5        and the white hands.

All Greece reviles
the wan face when she smiles,
hating it deeper still
when it grows wan and white,
10      remembering past enchantments
and past ills.

Greece sees unmoved
God's daughter, born of love,[8]
the beauty of cool feet
15      and slenderest of knees,
could love indeed the maid,
only if she were laid,
white ash amid funereal cypresses.                                  1924


EMILY DICKINSON

## [Because I could not stop for Death—]

Because I could not stop for Death—
He kindly stopped for me—
The Carriage held but just Ourselves—
And Immortality.

5        We slowly drove—He knew no haste
And I had put away

7. Helen's husband, Menelaus, was king of Sparta; the Greeks attacked Troy to get her back from Paris,
son of the Trojan king.    8. Helen was the daughter of Zeus, king of the gods, and Leda, a mortal.

My labor and my leisure too,
For His Civility—

We passed the School, where Children strove
At Recess—in the Ring—                                          10
We passed the Fields of Gazing Grain—
We passed the Setting Sun—

Or rather—He passed Us—
The Dews drew quivering and chill—
For only Gossamer,⁹ my Gown—                                    15
My Tippet—only Tulle¹—

We paused before a House that seemed
A Swelling of the Ground—
The Roof was scarcely visible—
The Cornice—in the Ground—                                      20

Since then—'tis Centuries—and yet
Feels shorter than the Day
I first surmised the Horses' Heads
Were toward Eternity—

ca. 1863

# [*I reckon—when I count at all—*]

I reckon—when I count at all—
First—Poets—Then the Sun—
Then Summer—Then the Heaven of God—
And then—the List is done—

But, looking back—the First so seems                            5
To Comprehend the Whole—
The Others look a needless Show—
So I write—Poets—All—

Their Summer—lasts a Solid Year—
They can afford a Sun                                           10
The East—would deem extravagant—
And if the Further Heaven—

Be Beautiful as they prepare
For Those who worship Them—
It is too difficult a Grace—                                    15
To justify the Dream—

ca. 1862

9. A soft, sheer fabric.   1. A fine net fabric. *Tippet*: scarf.

## [*My life closed twice before its close—*]

My life closed twice before its close—
It yet remains to see
If Immortality unveil
A third event to me

5   So huge, so hopeless to conceive
As these that twice befell.
Parting is all we know of heaven,
And all we need of hell.                                    1896

## [*We do not play on Graves—*]

We do not play on Graves—
Because there isn't Room—
Besides—it isn't even—it slants
And People come—

5   And put a Flower on it—
And hang their faces so—
We're fearing that their Hearts will drop—
And crush our pretty play—

And so we move as far
10   As Enemies—away—
Just looking round to see how far
It is—Occasionally—

  ca. 1862

## [*She dealt her pretty words like Blades—*]

She dealt her pretty words like Blades—
How glittering they shone—
And every One unbared a Nerve
Or wantoned with a Bone—

5   She never deemed—she hurt—
That—is not Steel's Affair—
A vulgar grimace in the Flesh—
How ill the Creatures bear—

To Ache is human—not polite—
10   The Film upon the eye
Mortality's old Custom—
Just locking up—to Die.

  1862

JOHN DONNE

## The Canonization

For God's sake hold your tongue and let me love!
   Or chide my palsy or my gout,
My five gray hairs or ruined fortune flout;
With wealth your state, your mind with arts improve,
   Take you a course, get you a place,          5
   Observe his Honor or his Grace,
Or the king's real or his stampéd face[2]
   Contemplate; what you will, approve,
      So you will let me love.

Alas, alas, who's injured by my love?          10
   What merchant's ships have my sighs drowned?
Who says my tears have overflowed his ground?
When did my colds a forward spring remove?
   When did the heats which my veins fill
   Add one man to the plaguy bill?[3]          15
Soldiers find wars, and lawyers find out still
   Litigious men which quarrels move,
      Though she and I do love.

Call us what you will, we are made such by love.
   Call her one, me another fly,          20
We're tapers[4] too, and at our own cost die;
And we in us find th' eagle and the dove.[5]
   The phoenix riddle[6] hath more wit[7]
   By us; we two, being one, are it.
So to one neutral thing both sexes fit,          25
   We die and rise the same, and prove
      Mysterious by this love.

We can die by it, if not live by love;
   And if unfit for tombs and hearse
Our legend be, it will be fit for verse;[8]          30
And if no piece of chronicle we prove,
   We'll build in sonnets[9] pretty rooms
   (As well a well-wrought urn becomes[1]
The greatest ashes, as half-acre tombs),

---

2. On coins.   3. List of plague victims.   4. Which consume themselves. To "die" is Renaissance slang for consummating the sexual act, which was popularly believed to shorten life by one day. *Fly*: a traditional symbol of transitory life.   5. Traditional symbols of strength and purity.   6. According to tradition, only one phoenix existed at a time, dying in a funeral pyre of its own making and being reborn from its own ashes. The bird's existence was thus a riddle akin to a religious mystery (line 27), and a symbol sometimes fused with Christian representations of immortality.   7. Meaning.   8. That is, if we don't turn out to be an authenticated piece of historical narrative.   9. Love poems. In Italian, *stanza* means room.   1. Befits.

35      And by these hymns all shall approve
            Us canonized for love.

    And thus invoke us: "You whom reverent love
        Made one another's hermitage,
    You to whom love was peace, that now is rage,
40      Who did the whole world's soul extract, and drove[2]
            Into the glasses of your eyes
            (So made such mirrors and such spies
        That they did all to you epitomize)
            Countries, towns, courts; beg from above
45          A pattern of your love!"                                    1633


# [Death be not proud, though some have callèd thee]

    Death be not proud, though some have callèd thee
    Mighty and dreadful, for thou art not so;
    For those whom thou think'st thou dost overthrow
    Die not, poor Death, nor yet canst thou kill me.
5   From rest and sleep, which but thy pictures[3] be,
    Much pleasure; then from thee much more must flow,
    And soonest[4] our best men with thee do go,
    Rest of their bones, and soul's delivery.[5]
    Thou art slave to Fate, Chance, kings, and desperate men,
10  And dost with Poison, War, and Sickness dwell;
    And poppy or charms can make us sleep as well,
    And better than thy stroke; why swell'st[6] thou then?
    One short sleep past, we wake eternally
    And death shall be no more; Death, thou shalt die.              1633


# A Valediction: Forbidding Mourning

    As virtuous men pass mildly away,
        And whisper to their souls to go,
    Whilst some of their sad friends do say,
        "The breath goes now," and some say, "No,"

5   So let us melt, and make no noise,
        No tear-floods, nor sigh-tempests move;
    'Twere profanation of our joys
        To tell the laity our love.

    Moving of the earth[7] brings harms and fears,
10      Men reckon what it did and meant;

---

2. Compressed.    3. Likenesses.    4. Most willingly.    5. Deliverance.    6. Puff with pride.    7. Earth-
quakes.

But trepidation of the spheres,[8]
    Though greater far, is innocent.

Dull sublunary[9] lovers' love
    (Whose soul is sense) cannot admit
Absence, because it doth remove                    15
    Those things which elemented[1] it.

But we, by a love so much refined
    That our selves know not what it is,
Inter-assured of the mind,
    Care less, eyes, lips, and hands to miss.          20

Our two souls therefore, which are one,
    Though I must go, endure not yet
A breach, but an expansion,
    Like gold to airy thinness beat.

If they be two, they are two so                   25
    As stiff twin compasses are two:
Thy soul, the fixed foot, makes no show
    To move, but doth, if the other do;

And though it in the center sit,
    Yet when the other far doth roam,           30
It leans, and hearkens after it,
    And grows erect, as that comes home.

Such wilt thou be to me, who must,
    Like the other foot, obliquely run;
Thy firmness makes my circle[2] just,          35
    And makes me end where I begun.

1611?

## PAUL LAURENCE DUNBAR

# *Sympathy*

I know what the caged bird feels, alas!
    When the sun is bright on the upland slopes;
When the wind stirs soft through the springing grass,
And the river flows like a stream of glass;
    When the first bird sings and the first bud opens,     5

8. The Renaissance hypothesis that the celestial spheres trembled and thus caused unexpected variations in their orbits. Such movements are "innocent" because earthlings do not observe or fret about them.    9. Below the moon—that is, changeable. According to the traditional cosmology that Donne invokes here, the moon was considered the dividing line between the immutable celestial world and the earthly mortal one.    1. Comprised.    2. A traditional symbol of perfection.

And the faint perfume from its chalice steals—
I know what the caged bird feels!

I know why the caged bird beats his wing
    Till its blood is red on the cruel bars;
10  For he must fly back to his perch and cling
When he fain would be on the bough a-swing;
    And a pain still throbs in the old, old scars
And they pulse again with a keener sting—
I know why he beats his wing!

15  I know why the caged bird sings, ah me,
    When his wing is bruised and his bosom sore,—
When he beats his bars and he would be free;
It is not a carol of joy or glee,
    But a prayer that he sends from his heart's deep core,
20  But a plea, that upward to Heaven he flings—
I know why the caged bird sings!                    1893


## We Wear the Mask

We wear the mask that grins and lies,
It hides our cheeks and shades our eyes,—
This debt we pay to human guile;
With torn and bleeding hearts we smile,
5  And mouth with myriad subtleties.

Why should the world be over-wise,
In counting all our tears and sighs?
Nay, let them only see us, while
    We wear the mask.

10  We smile, but, O great Christ, our cries
To thee from tortured souls arise.
We sing, but oh the clay is vile
Beneath our feet, and long the mile;
But let the world dream otherwise,
15      We wear the mask!                    1896


T. S. ELIOT

## The Love Song of J. Alfred Prufrock

*S'io credesse che mia risposta fosse*
*A persona che mai tornasse al mondo,*
*Questa fiamma staria senza piu scosse.*

*Ma perciocche giammai di questo fondo*
*Non torno vivo alcun, s'i'odo il vero,*
*Senza tema d'infamia ti rispondo.*[3]

Let us go then, you and I,
When the evening is spread out against the sky
Like a patient etherized upon a table;
Let us go, through certain half-deserted streets,
The muttering retreats                                          5
Of restless nights in one-night cheap hotels
And sawdust restaurants with oyster-shells:
Streets that follow like a tedious argument
Of insidious intent
To lead you to an overwhelming question . . .                  10
Oh, do not ask, "What is it?"
Let us go and make our visit.

  In the room the women come and go
Talking of Michelangelo.

  The yellow fog that rubs its back upon the window-panes,      15
The yellow smoke that rubs its muzzle on the window-panes
Licked its tongue into the corners of the evening,
Lingered upon the pools that stand in drains,
Let fall upon its back the soot that falls from chimneys,
Slipped by the terrace, made a sudden leap,                    20
And seeing that it was a soft October night,
Curled once about the house, and fell asleep.

  And indeed there will be time[4]
For the yellow smoke that slides along the street,
Rubbing its back upon the window-panes;                        25
There will be time, there will be time
To prepare a face to meet the faces that you meet;
There will be time to murder and create,
And time for all the works and days[5] of hands
That lift and drop a question on your plate;                   30
Time for you and time for me,
And time yet for a hundred indecisions,

---

3. Dante's *Inferno* XXVII.61–66. In the Eighth Chasm, Dante and Virgil meet Count Guido de Montefel-
trano, one of the False Counselors. The spirits there are in the form of flames, and Guido speaks from the
trembling tip of the flame, responding to Dante's request that he tell his life story: "If I thought that my
answer were to someone who would ever go back to Earth, this flame would be still, without any more
movement. But because no one has ever gone back alive from this chasm (if what I hear is true) I answer
you without fear of infamy."    4. See Ecclesiastes 3:1 ff.: "To everything there is a season, and a time to
every purpose under the heaven: A time to be born, and a time to die; a time to plant, and a time to pluck
up that which is planted; A time to kill, and a time to heal. . . ." Also see Marvell's "To His Coy Mistress":
"Had we but world enough and time. . . ."    5. Hesiod's ancient Greek didactic poem *Works and Days*
prescribed in practical detail how to conduct one's life.

And for a hundred visions and revisions,
Before the taking of a toast and tea.

35          In the room the women come and go
Talking of Michelangelo.

          And indeed there will be time
To wonder, "Do I dare?" and, "Do I dare?"
Time to turn back and descend the stair,
40    With a bald spot in the middle of my hair—
(They will say: "How his hair is growing thin!")
My morning coat, my collar mounting firmly to the chin,
My necktie rich and modest, but asserted by a simple pin—
(They will say: "But how his arms and legs are thin!")
45    Do I dare
Disturb the universe?

In a minute there is time
For decisions and revisions which a minute will reverse.

          For I have known them all already, known them all:—
50    Have known the evenings, mornings, afternoons,
I have measured out my life with coffee spoons;
I know the voices dying with a dying fall
Beneath the music from a farther room.
          So how should I presume?

55          And I have known the eyes already, known them all—
The eyes that fix you in a formulated phrase,
And when I am formulated, sprawling on a pin,
When I am pinned and wriggling on the wall,
Then how should I begin
60    To spit out all the butt-ends of my days and ways?
          And how should I presume?

          And I have known the arms already, known them all—
Arms that are braceleted and white and bare
(But in the lamplight, downed with light brown hair!)
65    Is it perfume from a dress
That makes me so digress?
Arms that lie along a table, or wrap about a shawl.
          And should I then presume?
          And how should I begin?

                    · · · · ·

70    Shall I say, I have gone at dusk through narrow streets
And watched the smoke that rises from the pipes
Of lonely men in shirt-sleeves, leaning out of windows? . . .

          I should have been a pair of ragged claws
Scuttling across the floors of silent seas

                    · · · · ·

And the afternoon, the evening, sleeps so peacefully!                           75
Smoothed by long fingers,
Asleep . . . tired . . . or it malingers,
Stretched on the floor, here beside you and me.
Should I, after tea and cakes and ices,
Have the strength to force the moment to its crisis?                            80
But though I have wept and fasted, wept and prayed,
Though I have seen my head (grown slightly bald) brought in upon a
    platter,[6]
I am no prophet—and here's no great matter;
I have seen the moment of my greatness flicker,
And I have seen the eternal Footman hold my coat, and snicker,                  85
And in short, I was afraid.

    And would it have been worth it, after all,
After the cups, the marmalade, the tea,
Among the porcelain, among some talk of you and me,
Would it have been worth while,                                                 90
To have bitten off the matter with a smile,
To have squeezed the universe into a ball[7]
To roll it toward some overwhelming question,
To say: "I am Lazarus,[8] come from the dead,
Come back to tell you all, I shall tell you all"—                              95
If one, settling a pillow by her head,
    Should say: "That is not what I meant at all.
    That is not it, at all."

    And would it have been worth it, after all,
Would it have been worth while,                                                100
After the sunsets and the dooryards and the sprinkled streets,
After the novels, after the teacups, after the skirts that trail along the
    floor—
And this, and so much more?—
It is impossible to say just what I mean!
But as if a magic lantern[9] threw the nerves in patterns on a screen:          105
Would it have been worth while
If one, settling a pillow or throwing off a shawl,
And turning toward the window, should say:
    "That is not it at all,
    That is not what I meant, at all."                         110

     . . . . .

---

6. See Matthew 14:1–12 and Mark 6:17–29: John the Baptist was decapitated, upon Salome's request and at Herod's command, and his head delivered on a platter.   7. See Marvell's "To His Coy Mistress," lines 41–42: "Let us roll all our strength and all / our sweetness up into one ball. . . ."   8. One Lazarus was raised from the dead by Jesus (see John 1:1–2:2), and another (in the parable of the rich man Dives) is discussed in terms of returning from the dead to warn the living (Luke 16:19–31).   9. A nonelectric projector used as early as the seventeenth century.

No! I am not Prince Hamlet, nor was meant to be;
Am an attendant lord,[1] one that will do
To swell a progress,[2] start a scene or two,
Advise the prince; no doubt, an easy tool,
115 Deferential, glad to be of use,
Politic, cautious, and meticulous;
Full of high sentence, but a bit obtuse;
At times, indeed, almost ridiculous—
Almost, at times, the Fool.

120    I grow old . . . I grow old . . .
I shall wear the bottoms of my trousers rolled.

    Shall I part my hair behind? Do I dare to eat a peach?
I shall wear white flannel trousers, and walk upon the beach.
I have heard the mermaids singing, each to each.

125    I do not think that they will sing to me.

    I have seen them riding seaward on the waves
Combing the white hair of the waves blown back.
When the wind blows the water white and black.

    We have lingered in the chambers of the sea
130 By sea-girls wreathed with seaweed red and brown
Till human voices wake us, and we drown.                    1917


ROBERT FROST

## *Range-Finding*

The battle rent a cobweb diamond-strung
And cut a flower beside a groundbird's nest
Before it stained a single human breast.
The stricken flower bent double and so hung.
5 And still the bird revisited her young.
A butterfly its fall had dispossessed,
A moment sought in air his flower of rest,
Then lightly stooped to it and fluttering clung.
On the bare upland pasture there had spread
10 O'ernight 'twixt mullein[3] stalks a wheel of thread
And straining cables wet with silver dew.
A sudden passing bullet shook it dry.
The indwelling spider ran to greet the fly,
But finding nothing, sullenly withdrew.                    1916

---

1. Like Polonius in *Hamlet,* who is full of maxims ("high sentence," line 117).   2. Procession of state.   3. Weed.

## The Road Not Taken

Two roads diverged in a yellow wood,
And sorry I could not travel both
And be one traveler, long I stood
And looked down one as far as I could
To where it bent in the undergrowth;                                5

Then took the other, as just as fair,
And having perhaps the better claim,
Because it was grassy and wanted wear;
Though as for that the passing there
Had worn them really about the same,                               10

And both that morning equally lay
In leaves no step had trodden black.
Oh, I kept the first for another day!
Yet knowing how way leads on to way,
I doubted if I should ever come back.                              15

I shall be telling this with a sigh
Somewhere ages and ages hence:
Two roads diverged in a wood, and I—
I took the one less traveled by,
And that has made all the difference.                              20

                                                              1916


## Stopping by Woods on a Snowy Evening

Whose woods these are I think I know.
His house is in the village, though;
He will not see me stopping here
To watch his woods fill up with snow.

My little horse must think it queer                                5
To stop without a farmhouse near
Between the woods and frozen lake
The darkest evening of the year.

He gives his harness bells a shake
To ask if there is some mistake.                                   10
The only other sound's the sweep
Of easy wind and downy flake.

The woods are lovely, dark, and deep,
But I have promises to keep,
And miles to go before I sleep,                                    15
And miles to go before I sleep.
                                                              1923

ALLEN GINSBERG

## *A Supermarket in California*

What thoughts I have of you tonight, Walt Whitman,[4] for I walked down the sidestreets under the trees with a headache self-conscious looking at the full moon.

In my hungry fatigue, and shopping for images, I went into the neon fruit supermarket, dreaming of your enumerations![5]

What peaches and what penumbras! Whole families shopping at night! Aisles full of husbands! Wives in the avocados, babies in the tomatoes!—and you, Garcia Lorca,[6] what were you doing down by the watermelons?

I saw you, Walt Whitman, childless, lonely old grubber, poking among the meats in the refrigerator and eyeing the grocery boys.

I heard you asking questions of each: Who killed the pork chops? What price bananas? Are you my Angel?

I wandered in and out of the brilliant stacks of cans following you, and followed in my imagination by the store detective.

We strode down the open corridors together in our solitary fancy tasting artichokes, possessing every frozen delicacy, and never passing the cashier.

Where are we going, Walt Whitman? The doors close in an hour. Which way does your beard point tonight?

(I touch your book and dream of our odyssey in the supermarket and feel absurd.)

Will we walk all night through solitary streets? The trees add shade to shade, lights out in the houses, we'll both be lonely.

Will we stroll dreaming of the lost America of love past blue automobiles in driveways, home to our silent cottage?

Ah, dear father, graybeard, lonely old courage-teacher, what America did you have when Charon quit poling his ferry and you got out on a smoking bank and stood watching the boat disappear on the black waters of Lethe?[7]

Berkeley 1955

---

4. Whitman's free verse, strong individualism, and passionate concern with America as an idea have led many modern poets to consider him the father of a new poetry.    5. Whitman's highly rhetorical poetry often contains long lists or parallel constructions piled up for cumulative effect.    6. Early-twentieth-century Spanish poet and playwright, author of *Blood Wedding*. Murdered in 1936, at the beginning of the Spanish Civil War, his works were banned by the Franco government.    7. The River of Forgetfulness in Hades. Charon is the boatman who, according to classical myth, ferries souls to Hades.

# From *Howl*

*For Carl Solomon*

1

I saw the best minds of my generation destroyed by madness, starving
hysterical naked,

dragging themselves through the negro streets at dawn looking for an
angry fix,

angelheaded hipsters burning for the ancient heavenly connection to the
starry dynamo in the machinery of night,

who poverty and tatters and hollow-eyed and high sat up smoking in the
supernatural darkness of cold-water flats floating across the tops of cit-
ies contemplating jazz,

who bared their brains to Heaven under the El and saw Mohammedan
angels staggering on tenement roofs illuminated                              5

who passed through universities with radiant cool eyes hallucinating
Arkansas and Blake-light tragedy among the scholars of war,

who were expelled from the academies for crazy & publishing obscene
odes on the windows of the skull,

who cowered in unshaven rooms in underwear, burning their money in
wastebaskets and listening to the Terror through the wall,

who got busted in their pubic beards returning through Laredo with a
belt of marijuana for New York.

who ate fire in paint hotels or drank turpentine in Paradise Alley, death,
or purgatoried their torsos night after night                               10

with dreams, with drugs, with waking nightmares, alcohol and cock and
endless balls,

incomparable blind streets of shuddering cloud and lightning in the
mind leaping toward poles of Canada & Paterson, illuminating all the
motionless world of Time between,

Peyote solidities of halls, backyard green tree cemetery dawns, wine
drunkenness over the rooftops, storefront boroughs of teahead joyride
neon blinking traffic light, sun and moon and tree vibrations in the
roaring winter dusks of Brooklyn, ashcan rantings and kind king light
of mind,

who chained themselves to subways for the endless ride from Battery to
holy Bronx on benzedrine until the noise of wheels and children
brought them down shuddering mouth-wracked and battered bleak of
brain all drained of brilliance in the drear light of Zoo,

who sank, all night in submarine light of Bickford's floated out and sat
through the stale beer afternoon in desolate Fugazzi's, listening to the
crack of doom on the hydrogen jukebox,                                      15

who talked continuously seventy hours from park to pad to bar to Belle-
vue to museum to the Brooklyn Bridge,

a lost battalion of platonic conversationalists jumping down the stoops
off fire escapes off windowsills off Empire State out of the moon,

yacketayakking screaming vomiting whispering facts and memories and
anecdotes and eyeball kicks and shocks of hospitals and jails and wars,

whole intellects disgorged in total recall for seven days and nights with
    brilliant eyes, meat for the Synagogue cast on the pavement,

who vanished into nowhere Zen New Jersey leaving a trail of ambiguous
20    picture postcards of Atlantic City Hall,

suffering Eastern sweats and Tangerian bone-grindings and migraines of
    China under junk-withdrawal in Newark's bleak furnished room,

who wandered around and around at midnight in the railroad yard won-
    dering where to go, and went, leaving no broken hearts,

who lit cigarettes in boxcars boxcars boxcars racketing through snow
    toward lonesome farms in grandfather night,

who studied Plotinus Poe St. John of the Cross telepathy and bop
    kaballa because the cosmos instinctively vibrated at their feet in Kan-
    sas,

who loned it through the streets of Idaho seeking visionary indian angels
25    who were visionary indian angels,

who thought they were only mad when Baltimore gleamed in supernat-
    ural ecstasy,

who jumped in limousines with the Chinaman of Oklahoma on the
    impulse of winter midnight streetlight smalltown rain,

who lounged hungry and lonesome through Houston seeking jazz or sex
    or soup, and followed the brilliant Spaniard to converse about America
    and Eternity, a hopeless task, and so took ship to Africa,

who disappeared into the volcanoes of Mexico leaving behind nothing
    but the shadow of dungarees and the lava and ash of poetry scattered
    in fireplace Chicago,

who reappeared on the West Coast investigating the F.B.I. in beards and
    shorts with big pacifist eyes sexy in their dark skin passing out incom-
30    prehensible leaflets,

who burned cigarette holes in their arms protesting the narcotic tobacco
    haze of Capitalism,

who distributed Supercommunist pamphlets in Union Square weeping
    and undressing while the sirens of Los Alamos wailed them down, and
    wailed down Wall, and the Staten Island ferry also wailed,

who broke down crying in white gymnasiums naked and trembling
    before the machinery of other skeletons,

who bit detectives in the neck and shrieked with delight in policecars for
    committing no crime but their own wild cooking pederasty and intox-
    ication,

who howled on their knees in the subway and were dragged off the roof
35    waving genitals and manuscripts,

who let themselves be fucked in the ass by saintly motorcyclists, and
    screamed with joy,

who blew and were blown by those human seraphim, the sailors, caresses
    of Atlantic and Caribbean love,

who balled in the morning in the evenings in rosegardens and the grass
    of public parks and cemeteries scattering their semen freely to whom-
    ever come who may,

who hiccupped endlessly trying to giggle but wound up with a sob
    behind a partition in a Turkish Bath when the blonde & naked angel
    came to pierce them with a sword,

who lost their loveboys to the three old shrews of fate the one eyed shrew
of the heterosexual dollar the one eyed shrew that winks out of the
womb and the one eyed shrew that does nothing but sit on her ass and
snip the intellectual golden threads of the craftsman's loom,                    40

who copulated ecstatic and insatiate with a bottle of beer a sweetheart a
package of cigarettes a candle and fell off the bed, and continued along
the floor and down the hall and ended fainting on the wall with a
vision of ultimate cunt and come eluding the last gyzym of conscious-
ness,

who sweetened the snatches of a million girls trembling in the sunset,
and were red eyed in the morning but prepared to sweeten the snatch
of the sunrise, flashing buttocks under barns and naked in the lake,

who went out whoring through Colorado in myriad stolen night-cars,
N.C., secret hero of these poems, cocksman and Adonis of Denver—
joy to the memory of his innumerable lays of girls in empty lots &
diner backyards, moviehouses' rickety rows, on mountaintops in caves
or with gaunt waitresses in familiar roadside lonely petticoat upliftings
& especially secret gas-station solipsisms of johns, & hometown alleys
too,

who faded out in vast sordid movies, were shifted in dreams, woke on a
sudden Manhattan, and picked themselves up out of basements hung-
over with heartless Tokay and horrors of Third Avenue iron dreams &
stumbled to unemployment offices,

who walked all night with their shoes full of blood on the snowbank
docks waiting for a door in the East River to open to a room full of
steam-heat and opium,                    45

who created great suicidal dramas on the apartment cliff-banks of the
Hudson under the wartime blue floodlight of the moon & their heads
shall be crowned with laurel in oblivion,

who ate the lamb stew of the imagination or digested the crab at the
muddy bottom of the rivers of Bowery,

who wept at the romance of the streets with their pushcarts full of onions
and bad music,

who sat in boxes breathing in the darkness under the bridge, and rose up
to build harpsichords in their lofts,

who coughed on the sixth floor of Harlem crowned with flame under the
tubercular sky surrounded by orange crates of theology,                    50

who scribbled all night rocking and rolling over lofty incantations which
in the yellow morning were stanzas of gibberish,

who cooked rotten animals lung heart feet tail borsht & tortillas dream-
ing of the pure vegetable kingdom,

who plunged themselves under meat trucks looking for an egg,

who threw their watches off the roof to cast their ballot for Eternity
outside of Time, & alarm clocks fell on their heads every day for the
next decade,

who cut their wrists three times successively unsuccessfully, gave up and
were forced to open antique stores where they thought they were grow-
ing old and cried,                    55

who were burned alive in their innocent flannel suits on Madison Ave-
nue amid blasts of leaden verse & the tanked-up clatter of the iron

regiments of fashion & the nitroglycerine shrieks of the fairies of adver-
tising & the mustard gas of sinister intelligent editors, or were run
down by the drunken taxicabs of Absolute Reality,
who jumped off the Brooklyn Bridge this actually happened and walked
away unknown and forgotten into the ghostly daze of Chinatown soup
alleyways & firetrucks, not even one free beer,
who sang out of their windows in despair, fell out of the subway window,
jumped in the filthy Passaic, leaped on negroes, cried all over the street,
danced on broken wineglasses barefoot smashed phonograph records
of nostalgic European 1930's German jazz finished the whiskey and
threw up groaning into the bloody toilet, moans in their ears and the
blast of colossal steamwhistles,
who barreled down the highways of the past journeying to each other's
hotrod-Golgotha jail-solitude watch or Birmingham jazz incarnation,
who drove crosscountry seventytwo hours to find out if I had a vision or
you had a vision or he had a vision to find out Eternity,
who journeyed to Denver, who died in Denver, who came back to Denver
& waited in vain, who watched over Denver & brooded & loned in
Denver and finally went away to find out the Time, & now Denver is
lonesome for her heroes,
who fell in hopeless cathedrals praying for each other's salvation and
light and breasts, until the soul illuminated its hair for a second,
who crashed through their minds in jail waiting for impossible criminals
with golden heads and the charm of reality in their hearts who sang
sweet blues to Alcatraz,
who retired to Mexico to cultivate a habit, or Rocky Mount to tender
Buddha or Tangiers to boys or Southern Pacific to the black locomotive
or Harvard to Narcissus to Woodlawn to the daisychain or grave,
who demanded sanity trials accusing the radio of hypnotism & were left
with their insanity & their hands & a hung jury,
who threw potato salad at CCNY lecturers on Dadaism and subsequently
presented themselves on the granite steps of the madhouse with
shaven heads and harlequin speech of suicide, demanding instantane-
ous lobotomy,
and who were given instead the concrete void of insulin metrasol elec-
tricity hydrotherapy psychotherapy occupational therapy pingpong &
amnesia,
who in humorless protest overturned only one symbolic pingpong table,
resting briefly in catatonia,
returning years later truly bald except for a wig of blood, and tears and
fingers, to the visible madman doom of the wards of the madtowns of
the East,
Pilgrim State's Rockland's and Greystone's foetid halls, bickering with
the echoes of the soul, rocking and rolling in the midnight solitude-
bench dolmen-realms of love, dream of life a nightmare, bodies turned
to stone as heavy as the moon,
with mother finally ******, and the last fantastic book flung out of the
tenement window, and the last door closed at 4 AM and the last tele-
phone slammed at the wall in reply and the last furnished room emp-

tied down to the last piece of mental furniture, a yellow paper rose
   twisted on a wire hanger in the closet, and even that imaginary, noth-
   ing but a hopeful little bit of hallucination—
ah, Carl, while you are not safe I am not safe, and now you're really in
   the total animal soup of time—
and who therefore ran through the icy streets obsessed with a sudden
   flash of the alchemy of the use of the ellipse the catalog the meter &
   the vibrating plane,
who dreamt and made incarnate gaps in Time & Space through images
   juxtaposed, and trapped the archangel of the soul between 2 visual
   images and joined the elemental verbs and set the noun and dash of
   consciousness together jumping with sensation of Pater Omnipotens
   Aeterna Deus
to recreate the syntax and measure of poor human prose and stand before
   you speechless and intelligent and shaking with shame, rejected yet
   confessing out the soul to conform to the rhythm of thought in his
   naked and endless head,                                                   75
the madman bum and angel beat in Time, unknown, yet putting down
   here what might be left to say in time come after death,
and rose reincarnate in the ghostly clothes of jazz in the goldhorn
   shadow of the band and blew the suffering of America's naked mind
⤶ for love into an eli eli lamma lamma sabacthani saxophone cry that
   shivered the cities down to the last radio
with the absolute heart of the poem of life butchered out of their own
   bodies good to eat a thousand years.

San Francisco 1955                                            1956


## Velocity of Money

*For Lee Berton*

I'm delighted by the velocity of money as it whistles through windows
   of Lower East Side
Delighted skyscrapers rise grungy apartments fall on 84th Street's pave-
   ment
Delighted this year inflation drives me out on the street
with double digit interest rates in Capitalist worlds
I always was a communist, now we'll win                                      5
as usury makes walls thinner, books thicker & dumber
Usury makes my poetry more valuable
Manuscripts worth their weight in useless gold—
The velocity's what counts as the National Debt gets trillions higher
Everybody running after the rising dollar                                    10
Crowds of joggers down Broadway past City Hall on the way to the Fed
Nobody reads Dostoyevsky books anymore so they'll have to give pass-
   ing ear
to my fragmented ravings in between President's speeches

15    Nothing's happening but the collapse of the Economy
      so I can go back to sleep till the landlord wins his eviction suit in court

February 18, 1986, 10:00 A.M.

THOMAS HARDY

## *The Darkling Thrush*

I leant upon a coppice gate
    When Frost was specter gray,
And Winter's dregs made desolate
    The weakening eye of day.
5   The tangled bine-stems scored the sky
    Like strings of broken lyres,
And all mankind that haunted nigh
    Had sought their household fires.

The land's sharp features seemed to be
10      The Century's corpse outleant,
His crypt the cloudy canopy,
    The wind his death-lament.
The ancient pulse of germ and birth
    Was shrunken hard and dry,
15  And every spirit upon earth
    Seemed fervorless as I.

At once a voice arose among
    The bleak twigs overhead
In a full-hearted evensong
20      Of joy illimited;
An aged thrush, frail, gaunt, and small,
    In blast-beruffled plume,
Had chosen thus to fling his soul
    Upon the growing gloom.

25  So little cause for carolings
    Of such ecstatic sound
Was written on terrestrial things
    Afar or nigh around,
That I could think there trembled through
30      His happy good-night air
Some blessed Hope, whereof he knew
    And I was unaware.

December 31, 1900

# During Wind and Rain

They sing their dearest songs—
He, she, all of them—yea,
Treble and tenor and bass,
   And one to play;
With the candles mooning each face. . . .        5
   Ah, no; the years O!
How the sick leaves reel down in throngs!

They clear the creeping moss—
Elders and juniors—aye,
Making the pathway neat        10
   And the garden gay;
And they build a shady seat. . . .
   Ah, no; the years, the years;
See, the white stormbirds wing across!

They are blithely breakfasting all—        15
Men and maidens—yea,
Under the summer tree,
   With a glimpse of the bay,
While pet fowl come to the knee. . . .
   Ah, no; the years O!        20
And the rotten rose is ripped from the wall.

They change to a high new house,
He, she, all of them—aye,
Clocks and carpets, and chairs
   On the lawn all day,        25
And brightest things that are theirs. . . .
   Ah, no; the years, the years;
Down their carved names the rain drop ploughs.        1917

SEAMUS HEANEY

# The Summer of Lost Rachel

Potato crops are flowering,
   Hard green plums appear
On damson trees at your back door
   And every berried briar

Is glittering and dripping        5
   Whenever showers plout down
On flooded hay and flooding drills.
   There's a ring around the moon.

The whole summer was waterlogged
    Yet everyone is loath
10    To trust the rain's soft-soaping ways
    And sentiments of growth

Because all confidence in summer's
    Unstinting largesse
15    Broke down last May when we laid you out
    In white, your whited face

Gashed from the accident, but still,
    So absolutely still,
And the setting sun set merciless
20    And every merciful

Register inside us yearned
    To run the film back,
For you to step into the road
    Wheeling your bright-rimmed bike,

25 Safe and sound as usual,
    Across, then down the lane,
The twisted spokes all straightened out,
    The awful skid-marks gone.

But no. So let the downpours flood
30    Our memory's riverbed
Until, in thick-webbed currents,
    The life you might have led

Wavers and tugs dreamily
    As soft-plumed waterweed
35 Which tempts our gaze and quietens it
    And recollects our need.

        1987

---

GERARD MANLEY HOPKINS

## God's Grandeur

The world is charged with the grandeur of God.
    It will flame out, like shining from shook foil;[8]
    It gathers to a greatness, like the ooze of oil
Crushed. Why do men then now not reck his rod?[9]
5 Generations have trod, have trod, have trod;
    And all is seared with trade; bleared, smeared with toil;

8. "I mean foil in its sense of leaf or tinsel. . . . Shaken goldfoil gives off broad glares like sheet lightning and also, and this is true of nothing else, owing to its zig-zag dints and creasings and network of small many cornered facets, a sort of fork lightning too." *Letters of Gerard Manley Hopkins to Robert Bridges*, ed. C. C. Abbott (1955), p. 169.   9. Heed his authority.

And wears man's smudge and shares man's smell: the soil
Is bare now, nor can foot feel, being shod.

And for all this, nature is never spent;
   There lives the dearest freshness deep down things;          10
And though the last lights off the black West went
   Oh, morning, at the brown brink eastward, springs—
Because the Holy Ghost over the bent
   World broods with warm breast and with ah! bright wings.     1918

## The Windhover[1]

*to Christ our Lord*

I caught this morning morning's minion,[2] king-
   dom of daylight's dauphin,[3] dapple-dawn-drawn Falcon, in his
                              riding
   Of the rolling level underneath him steady air, and striding
High there, how he rung upon the rein of a wimpling[4] wing
In his ecstasy! then off, off forth on swing,              5
   As a skate's heel sweeps smooth on a bow-bend: the hurl and
                             gliding
   Rebuffed the big wind. My heart in hiding
Stirred for a bird,—the achieve of, the mastery of the thing!

Brute beauty and valor and act, oh, air, pride, plume, here
   Buckle![5] AND the fire that breaks from thee then, a billion    10
Times told lovelier, more dangerous, O my chevalier![6]

   No wonder of it: sheér plód makes plow down sillion[7]
Shine, and blue-bleak embers, ah my dear,
   Fall, gall themselves, and gash gold-vermilion.

1877

LANGSTON HUGHES

## Theme for English B

The instructor said,

   *Go home and write*
   *a page tonight.*

---

1. A small hawk, the kestrel, which habitually hovers in the air, headed into the wind.    2. Favorite, beloved.   3. Heir to regal splendor.   4. Rippling.   5. Several meanings may apply: to join closely, to prepare for battle, to grapple with, to collapse.   6. Horseman, knight.   7. The narrow strip of land between furrows in an open field divided for separate cultivation.

> *And let that page come out of you—*
> *Then, it will be true.*

I wonder if it's that simple?
I am twenty-two, colored, born in Winston-Salem.
I went to school there, then Durham,[8] then here
to this college[9] on the hill above Harlem.
I am the only colored student in my class.
The steps from the hill lead down into Harlem,
through a park, then I cross St. Nicholas,[1]
Eighth Avenue, Seventh, and I come to the Y,
the Harlem Branch Y, where I take the elevator
up to my room, sit down, and write this page:

It's not easy to know what is true for you or me
at twenty-two, my age. But I guess I'm what
I feel and see and hear, Harlem, I hear you:
hear you, hear me—we two—you, me, talk on this page.
(I hear New York, too.) Me—who?

Well, I like to eat, sleep, drink, and be in love.
I like to work, read, learn, and understand life.
I like a pipe for a Christmas present,
or records—Bessie,[2] bop, or Bach.
I guess being colored doesn't make me *not* like
the same things other folks like who are other races.
So will my page be colored that I write?

Being me, it will not be white.
But it will be
a part of you, instructor.
You are white—
yet a part of me, as I am a part of you.
That's American.
Sometimes perhaps you don't want to be a part of me.
Nor do I often want to be a part of you.
But we are, that's true!
As I learn from you,
I guess you learn from me—
although you're older—and white—
and somewhat more free.

This is my page for English B.                                    1959

---

8. Winston-Salem and Durham are cities in North Carolina.    9. Columbia University.    1. An ave-
nue east of Columbia University.    2. Bessie Smith (1898?–1937), famous blues singer.

BEN JONSON

## To Penshurst³

Thou art not, Penshurst, built to envious show,
Of touch⁴ or marble; nor canst boast a row
Of polished pillars, or a roof of gold;
Thou hast no lantern⁵ whereof tales are told,
Or stair, or courts; but stand'st an ancient pile,     5
And, these grudged at,⁶ art reverenced the while.
Thou joy'st in better marks, of soil, of air,
Of wood, of water; therein thou art fair.
Thou hast thy walks for health, as well as sport;
Thy mount, to which the dryads do resort,     10
Where Pan and Bacchus⁷ their high feasts have made
Beneath the broad beech and the chestnut shade,
That taller tree, which of a nut was set
At his great birth⁸ where all the Muses met.
There in the writhéd bark are cut the names     15
Of many a sylvan, taken with his flames;⁹
And thence the ruddy satyrs oft provoke
The lighter fauns to reach thy Lady's Oak.¹
Thy copse too, named of Gamage,² thou hast there,
That never fails to serve thee seasoned deer     20
When thou wouldst feast, or exercise, thy friends.
The lower land, that to the river bends,
Thy sheep, thy bullocks, kine, and calves do feed;
The middle grounds thy mares and horses breed.
Each bank doth yield thee conies;³ and the tops,     25
Fertile of wood, Ashore and Sidney's copse,
To crown thy open table, doth provide
The purpled pheasant with the speckled side;
The painted partridge lies in every field,
And for thy mess is willing to be killed.     30
And if the high-swollen Medway⁴ fail thy dish,
Thou hast thy ponds that pay thee tribute fish,
Fat agéd carps that run into thy net,
And pikes, now weary their own kind to eat,

3. The country seat (in Kent) of the Sidney family, owned by Sir Robert, brother of the poet, Sir Philip. Jonson's celebration of the estate is one of the earliest "house" poems and a prominent example of topographical or didactic-descriptive poetry.      4. Touchstone: basanite, a smooth dark stone similar to black marble.      5. A glassed or open tower or dome atop the roof.      6. I.e., although these (more pretentious structures) are envied. *The while*: anyway.      7. Ancient gods of nature and wine, both associated with spectacular feasting and celebration.      8. Sir Philip Sidney's, on November 30, 1554; the tree stood for nearly 150 years.      9. Inspired by Sidney's love poetry.      1. Where, according to legend, a former lady of the house (Lady Leicester) began labor pains. *Satyrs*: half-men, half-goats who participated in the rites of Bacchus.      2. The maiden name of the owner's wife. *Copse*: thicket.      3. Rabbits.      4. A river bordering the estate.

35       As loath the second draught[5] or cast to stay,
      Officiously[6] at first themselves betray;
      Bright eels that emulate them, and leap on land
      Before the fisher, or into his hand.
      Then hath thy orchard fruit, thy garden flowers,
40       Fresh as the air, and new as are the hours.
      The early cherry, with the later plum,
      Fig, grape, and quince, each in his time doth come:
      The blushing apricot and woolly peach
      Hang on thy walls, that every child may reach.
45       And though thy walls be of the country stone,
      They're reared with no man's ruin, no man's groan;
      There's none that dwell about them wish them down,
      But all come in, the farmer and the clown,[7]
      And no one empty-handed, to salute
50       Thy lord and lady, though they have no suit.[8]
      Some bring a capon, some a rural cake,
      Some nuts, some apples; some that think they make
      The better cheeses bring 'em, or else send
      By their ripe daughters, whom they would commend
55       This way to husbands, and whose baskets bear
      An emblem of themselves in plum or pear.
      But what can this (more than express their love)
      Add to thy free[9] provisions, far above
      The need of such? whose liberal board doth flow
60       With all that hospitality doth know;
      Where comes no guest but is allowed to eat,
      Without his fear, and of thy lord's own meat;
      Where the same beer and bread, and selfsame wine,
      That is his lordship's shall be also mine.
65       And I not fain[1] to sit (as some this day
      At great men's tables), and yet dine away.[2]
      Here no man tells[3] my cups; nor, standing by,
      A waiter doth my gluttony envý,
      But gives me what I call, and lets me eat;
70       He knows below he shall find plenty of meat.
      Thy tables hoard not up for the next day;
      Nor, when I take my lodging, need I pray
      For fire, or lights, or livery;[4] all is there,
      As if thou then wert mine, or I reigned here:
75       There's nothing I can wish, for which I stay.
      That found King James when hunting late this way
      With his brave son, the prince,[5] they saw thy fires

---

5. Of a net. *Stay*: await.    6. Obligingly.    7. Rustic, peasant.    8. Request for favors.    9. Generous.    1. Obliged.    2. Possibly, "elsewhere," because they do not get enough to eat; or "away" in the sense of far from the party of honor.    3. Counts.    4. Provisions (or, possibly, servants). 5. Prince Henry, who died in 1612.

Shine bright on every hearth, as the desires
Of thy Penates had been set on flame
To entertain them; or the country came                                  80
With all their zeal to warm their welcome here.
What (great I will not say, but) sudden cheer
Didst thou then make 'em! and what praise was heaped
On thy good lady then! who therein reaped
The just reward of her high housewifery;[6]                             85
To have her linen, plate, and all things nigh,
When she was far; and not a room but dressed
As if it had expected such a guest!
These, Penshurst, are thy praise, and yet not all.
Thy lady's noble, fruitful, chaste withal.                             90
His children thy great lord may call his own,
A fortune in this age but rarely known.
They are, and have been, taught religion; thence
Their gentler spirits have sucked innocence.
Each morn and even they are taught to pray,                            95
With the whole household, and may, every day,
Read in their virtuous parents' noble parts
The mysteries of manners, arms, and arts.
Now, Penshurst, they that will proportion[7] thee
With other edifices, when they see                                    100
Those proud, ambitious heaps, and nothing else,
May say, their lords have built, but thy lord dwells.          1616

A. M. KLEIN

## Heirloom

My father bequeathed me no wide estates;
No keys and ledgers were my heritage;
Only some holy books with *yahrzeit*[8] dates
Writ mournfully upon a blank front page—

Books of the Baal Shem Tov,[9] and of his wonders;            5
Pamphlets upon the devil and his crew;
Prayers against road demons, witches, thunders;
And sundry other tomes for a good Jew.

Beautiful: though no pictures on them, save
The scorpion crawling on a printed track;                    10

6. Domestic economy.    7. Compare.    8. Anniversary of the death of a parent or near rela-
tive.    9. A title given to someone who possesses the secret knowledge of Jewish holy men and who,
therefore, could work miracles.

The Virgin floating on a scriptural wave,
Square letters twinkling in the Zodiac.

The snuff left on this page, now brown and old,
The tallow stains of midnight liturgy—
15    These are my coat of arms, and these unfold
My noble lineage, my proud ancestry!

And my tears, too, have stained this heirloomed ground,
When reading in these treatises some weird
Miracle, I turned a leaf and found
20    A white hair fallen from my father's beard.                    1940

RICHARD LOVELACE

## To Amarantha, That She Would Dishevel Her Hair

Amarantha sweet and fair,
Ah, braid no more that shining hair!
    As my curious hand or eye
Hovering round thee, let it fly.

5        Let it fly as unconfined
As its calm ravisher, the wind,
    Who hath left his darling, th' East,
To wanton o'er that spicy nest.

    Every tress must be confessed
10    But neatly tangled at the best,
    Like a clue[1] of golden thread,
Most excellently raveléd.

    Do not then wind up that light
In ribands, and o'ercloud in night;
15        Like the sun in's early ray,
But shake your head and scatter day.

    See, 'tis broke! Within this grove,
The bower and the walks of love,
    Weary lie we down and rest
20    And fan each other's panting breast.

    Here we'll strip and cool our fire
In cream below, in milk-baths higher;

1. Ball.

And when all wells are drawn dry,
I'll drink a tear out of thine eye.

Which our very joys shall leave,                                    25
That sorrows thus we can deceive;
    Or our very sorrows weep,
That joys so ripe so little keep.                                   1649

ROBERT LOWELL

## Skunk Hour

*for Elizabeth Bishop*

Nautilus Island's hermit
heiress still lives through winter in her Spartan cottage;
her sheep still graze above the sea.
Her son's a bishop. Her farmer
is first selectman² in our village,                                 5
she's in her dotage.

Thirsting for
the hierarchic privacy
of Queen Victoria's century,
she buys up all                                                     10
the eyesores facing her shore,
and lets them fall.

The season's ill—
we've lost our summer millionaire,
who seemed to leap from an L. L. Bean³                              15
catalogue. His nine-knot yawl
was auctioned off to lobstermen.
A red fox stain covers Blue Hill.

And now our fairy
decorator brightens his shop for fall,                              20
his fishnet's filled with orange cork,
orange, his cobbler's bench and awl,
there is no money in his work,
he'd rather marry.

One dark night,                                                     25
my Tudor Ford climbed the hill's skull,
I watched for love-cars. Lights turned down,
they lay together, hull to hull,

2. An elected New England town official.      3. Famous old Maine sporting goods firm.

where the graveyard shelves on the town. . . .
My mind's not right.

A car radio bleats,
"Love, O careless Love. . . ."[4] I hear
my ill-spirit sob in each blood cell,
as if my hand were at its throat. . . .
I myself am hell;
nobody's here—

only skunks, that search
in the moonlight for a bite to eat.
They march on their soles up Main Street:
white stripes, moonstruck eyes' red fire
under the chalk-dry and spar spire
of the Trinitarian Church.

I stand on top
of our back steps and breathe the rich air—
a mother skunk with her column of kittens swills the garbage pail.
She jabs her wedge head in a cup
of sour cream, drops her ostrich tail,
and will not scare.                                        1959


ANDREW MARVELL

## The Garden

How vainly men themselves amaze[5]
To win the palm, the oak, or bays,[6]
And their incessant labors see
Crowned from some single herb, or tree,
Whose short and narrow-vergèd[7] shade
Does prudently their toils upbraid;
While all flowers and all trees do close[8]
To weave the garlands of repose!

Fair Quiet, have I found thee here,
And Innocence, thy sister dear?
Mistaken long, I sought you then
In busy companies of men.
Your sacred plants,[9] if here below,
Only among the plants will grow;
Society is all but rude[1]
To[2] this delicious solitude.

4. A popular song.    5. Become frenzied.    6. Awards for athletic, civic, and literary achieve-
ments.    7. Narrowly cropped.    8. Unite.    9. Cuttings.    1. Barbarous.    2. Compared to.

No white nor red was ever seen
So am'rous as this lovely green.
Fond lovers, cruel as their flame,
Cut in these trees their mistress' name:                    20
Little, alas, they know, or heed
How far these beauties hers exceed!
Fair trees, wheresoe'er your barks I wound,
No name shall but your own be found.

When we have run our passion's heat,                        25
Love hither makes his best retreat.
The gods, that mortal beauty chase,
Still in a tree did end their race:
Apollo hunted Daphne so,
Only that she might laurel grow;                            30
And Pan did after Syrinx speed,
Not as a nymph, but for a reed.[3]

What wondrous life is this I lead!
Ripe apples drop about my head;
The luscious clusters of the vine                           35
Upon my mouth do crush their wine;
The nectarine and curious[4] peach
Into my hands themselves do reach;
Stumbling on melons, as I pass,
Insnared with flowers, I fall on grass.                     40

Meanwhile the mind, from pleasure less,
Withdraws into its happiness;[5]
The mind, that ocean where each kind
Does straight its own resemblance find;[6]
Yet it creates, transcending these,                         45
Far other worlds and other seas,
Annihilating[7] all that's made
To a green thought in a green shade.

Here at the fountain's sliding foot,
Or at some fruit tree's mossy root,                         50
Casting the body's vest[8] aside,
My soul into the boughs does glide:
There, like a bird, it sits and sings,
Then whets[9] and combs its silver wings,
And, till prepared for longer flight,                       55
Waves in its plumes the various[1] light.

3. In Ovid's *Metamorphoses*, Daphne, pursued by Apollo, is turned into a laurel, and Syrinx, pursued by Pan, into a reed that Pan makes into a flute.    4. Exquisite.    5. That is, the mind withdraws from lesser-sense pleasure into contemplation.    6. All land creatures were supposed to have corresponding sea creatures.    7. Reducing to nothing by comparison.    8. Vestment, clothing; the flesh is being considered as simply clothing for the soul.    9. Preens.    1. Many-colored.

Such was that happy garden-state,
While man there walked without a mate:
After a place so pure, and sweet,
60    What other help could yet be meet!²
But 'twas beyond a mortal's share
To wander solitary there:
Two paradises 'twere in one
To live in paradise alone.

65    How well the skillful gardener drew
Of flowers and herbs this dial³ new,
Where, from above, the milder sun
Does through a fragrant zodiac run;
And as it works, th' industrious bee
70    Computes its time as well as we!
How could such sweet and wholesome hours
Be reckoned but with herbs and flowers?                    1681


# The Mower, against Gardens

Luxurious⁴ man, to bring his vice in use,
    Did after him the world seduce,
And from the fields the flowers and plants allure,
    When nature was most plain and pure.
5    He first enclosed within the garden's square
    A dead and standing pool of air,
And a more luscious earth for them did knead,
    Which stupefied them while it fed.
The pink⁵ grew then as double as his mind;
10    The nutriment did change the kind.
With strange perfumes he did the roses taint;
    And flowers themselves were taught to paint.⁶
The tulip, white, did for complexion seek,
    And learned to interline its cheek;
15    Its onion root⁷ they then so high did hold
    That one was for a meadow sold.⁸
Another world was searched, through oceans new,
    To find the Marvel of Peru.⁹
And yet these rarities might be allowed
20    To man, that sov'reign thing and proud,
Had he not dealt¹ between the bark and tree,
    Forbidden mixtures there to see.

---

2. Appropriate.    3. A garden planted in the shape of a sundial, complete with zodiac.    4. Self-indulgent.    5. A dianthus flower; figuratively, the embodiment of perfection.    6. Use artificial coloring.    7. Bulb.    8. In the seventeenth century tulips were held in extremely high regard, so much so that some countries were said to have tulipomania.    9. The "four-o'clock" plant.    1. Artificially placed.

No plant now knew the stock from which it came;
   He grafts upon the wild the tame,
That the uncertain and adult'rate fruit                         25
   Might put the palate in dispute.
His green seraglio has its eunuchs too,
   Lest any tyrant him outdo;
And in the cherry he does nature vex,
   To procreate without a sex.                                  30
'Tis all enforced;[2] the fountain and the grot,
   While the sweet fields do lie forgot,
Where willing nature does to all dispense
   A wild and fragrant innocence;
And fauns and fairies do the meadows till                      35
   More by their presence than their skill.
Their statues, polished by some ancient hand,
   May to adorn the gardens stand;
But, howsoe'er the figures do excel,
   The gods themselves with us do dwell.                    40

                                             1681

# On a Drop of Dew

See how the orient[3] dew
Shed from the bosom of the morn
   Into the blowing roses,
Yet careless of its mansion new
For[4] the clear region where 'twas born                   5
   Round in itself incloses,
   And in its little globe's extent
Frames as it can its native element;
   How it the purple flow'r does slight,
   Scarce touching where it lies,                         10
But gazing back upon the skies,
   Shines with a mournful light
      Like its own tear,
Because so long divded from the sphere.[5]
   Restless it rolls and unsecure,                      15
      Trembling lest it grow impure,

   Till the warm sun pity its pain,
And to the skies exhale it back again.
      So the soul, that drop, that ray
Of the clear fountain of eternal day,                    20
Could it within the human flower be seen,
   Rememb'ring still its former height,

2. Imposed.    3. Shining.    4. By reason of.    5. Of heaven.

Shuns the sweet leaves and blossoms green;
And, recollecting its own light,
25  Does, in its pure and circling thoughts, express
The greater Heaven in an Heaven less.
        In how coy[6] a figure wound,
        Every way it turns away;
        So the world excluding round,
30      Yet receiving in the day:
        Dark beneath, but bright above,
        Here disdaining, there in love.

How loose and easy hence to go,
How girt and ready to ascend;
35  Moving but on a point below,
It all about does upwards bend.
Such did the manna's sacred dew distill,
White and entire, though congealed and chill;[7]
Congealed on earth, but does, dissolving, run
40  Into the glories of th' almighty sun.                    1681


JOHN MILTON

# *Lycidas*[8]

In this monody the author bewails a learned friend, unfortunately
drowned in his passage from Chester on the Irish Seas, 1637.[9] And
by occasion foretells the ruin of our corrupted clergy then in their
height.


Yet once more, O ye laurels, and once more
Ye myrtles brown, with ivy never sere,[1]
I come to pluck your berries harsh and crude,[2]
And with forced fingers rude,
5   Shatter your leaves before the mellowing year.
Bitter constraint, and sad occasion dear,[3]
Compels me to disturb your season due:
For Lycidas is dead, dead ere his prime,
Young Lycidas, and hath not left his peer.

---

6. Reserved, withdrawn, modest.    7. In the wilderness, the Israelites fed upon manna from heaven
(distilled from the dew; see Exodus 16:10–21); manna became a traditional symbol for divine
grace.    8. The name of a shepherd in Virgil's *Eclogue* III. Milton's elegy works from the convention of
treating the dead man as if he were a shepherd and also transforms other details to a pastoral setting and
situation.    9. Edward King, a student with Milton at Cambridge, and at the time of his death a young
clergyman. *Monody*: a song sung by a single voice.    1. Withered. The laurel, myrtle, and ivy were all
materials used to construct traditional evergreen garlands signifying poetic accomplishment. *Brown*:
dusky, dark.    2. Unripe.    3. Dire.

Who would not sing for Lycidas? He knew 10
Himself to sing, and build the lofty rhyme.
He must not float upon his wat'ry bier
Unwept, and welter[4] to the parching wind,
Without the meed[5] of some melodious tear.
    Begin then, sisters of the sacred well,[6] 15
That from beneath the seat of Jove doth spring,
Begin, and somewhat loudly sweep the string.
Hence with denial vain and coy excuse;
So may some gentle muse[7]
With lucky words favor my destined urn, 20
And as he passes turn,
And bid fair peace be to my sable shroud.
For we were nursed upon the self-same hill,
Fed the same flock, by fountain, shade, and rill.
    Together both, ere the high lawns[8] appeared 25
Under the opening eyelids of the morn,
We drove afield, and both together heard
What time the gray-fly winds[9] her sultry horn,
Batt'ning[1] our flocks with the fresh dews of night,
Oft till the star that rose, at ev'ning, bright, 30
Towards Heav'n's descent had sloped his westering wheel.
Meanwhile the rural ditties were not mute,
Tempered to the oaten flute;[2]
Rough satyrs danced, and fauns with clov'n heel,
From the glad sound would not be absent long, 35
And old Damaetas[3] loved to hear our song.
    But O the heavy change, now thou art gone,
Now thou art gone, and never must return!
Thee, shepherd, thee the woods and desert caves,
With wild thyme and the gadding[4] vine o'ergrown, 40
And all their echoes mourn.
The willows and the hazel copses[5] green
Shall now no more be seen,
Fanning their joyous leaves to thy soft lays.
As killing as the canker[6] to the rose, 45
Or taint-worm to the weanling herds that graze,
Or frost to flowers, that their gay wardrobe wear,
When first the white-thorn blows:[7]
Such, Lycidas, thy loss to shepherd's ear.
    Where were ye, nymphs,[8] when the remorseless deep 50
Closed o'er the head of your loved Lycidas?
For neither were ye playing on the steep,

---

4. Tumble about.　　5. Tribute.　　6. The muses, who lived on Mt. Helicon. At the foot of the mountain were two fountains, or wells, where the muses danced around Jove's altar.　　7. Poet.　　8. Grasslands, pastures.　　9. Blows; that is, the insect hum of midday.　　1. Fattening.　　2. Shepherds' pipes. 3. A traditional pastoral name, possibly referring here to a Cambridge tutor.　　4. Wandering. 5. Thickets.　　6. Cankerworm.　　7. Blossoms.　　8. Nature deities.

Where your old Bards, the famous Druids, lie,
Nor on the shaggy top of Mona high,
55    Nor yet where Deva spreads her wizard stream:[9]
Ay me, I fondly[1] dream!
Had ye been there—for what could that have done?
What could the Muse[2] herself that Orpheus bore,
The Muse herself, for her enchanting[3] son
60    Whom universal nature did lament,
When by the rout that made the hideous roar,
His gory visage down the stream was sent,
Down the swift Hebrus to the Lesbian shore?
    Alas! What boots[4] it with uncessant care
65    To tend the homely slighted shepherd's trade,
And strictly meditate the thankless Muse?
Were it not better done, as others use[5]
To sport with Amaryllis in the shade,
Or with the tangles of Neaera's hair?
70    Fame is the spur that the clear spirit doth raise
(That last infirmity of noble mind)
To scorn delights, and live laborious days;
But the fair guerdon[6] when we hope to find,
And think to burst out into sudden blaze,
75    Comes the blind Fury[7] with th' abhorréd shears,
And slits the thin-spun life. "But not the praise,"
Phoebus[8] replied, and touched my trembling ears:
"Fame is no plant that grows on mortal soil,
Nor in the glistering foil[9]
80    Set off to th' world, nor in broad rumor lies,
But lives and spreads aloft by those pure eyes
And perfect witness of all-judging Jove;
As he pronounces lastly on each deed,
Of so much fame in Heav'n expect thy meed."
85        O fountain Arethuse,[1] and thou honored flood,
Smooth-sliding Mincius, crowned with vocal reeds,
That strain I heard was of a higher mood.
But now my oat[2] poceeds,

9. The River Dee, reputed to have prophetic powers. *Mona*: the Isle of Anglesey. The steep (line 52) may be a burial ground, in northern Wales, for Druids, ancient priests and magicians; all three locations are near the place where King drowned.    1. Foolishly.    2. Calliope, the muse of epic poetry, whose son Orpheus was torn limb from limb by frenzied orgiasts. His head, thrown into the Hebrus (lines 62–63), floated into the sea and finally to Lesbos, where it was buried.    3. Orpheus was reputed to be able to charm even inanimate things with his music; he once persuaded Pluto to release his dead wife, Eurydice, from the infernal regions.    4. Profits.    5. Customarily do. Amaryllis (line 68) and Neaera (line 69) are stock names of women celebrated in pastoral love poetry.    6. Reward.    7. Atropos, the Fate who cuts the threads of human life after they are spun and measured by her two sisters.    8. Apollo, god of poetic inspiration. In Roman tradition, touching the ears of one's hearers meant asking them to remember what they heard.    9. Flashy setting, used to make inferior gems glitter.    1. A Sicilian fountain, associated with the pastoral poetry of Theocritus. The River Mincius (line 86) is associated with Vergil's pastorals.    2. Oaten pipe: pastoral song.

And listens to the herald of the sea,[3]
That came in Neptune's plea.                                         90
He asked the waves and asked the felon-winds,
What hard mishap hath doomed this gentle swain,[4]
And questioned every gust of rugged wings
That blows from off each beakéd promontory.
They knew not of his story,                                          95
And sage Hippotades[5] their answer brings:
That not a blast was from his dungeon strayed;
The air was calm, and on the level brine,
Sleek Panopë[6] with all her sisters played.
It was that fatal and perfidious bark                                100
Built in th' eclipse, and rigged with curses dark,
That sunk so low that sacred head of thine,
    Next Camus,[7] reverend sire, went footing slow,
His mantle hairy, and his bonnet sedge,
Inwrought with figures dim, and on the edge                          105
Like to that sanguine flower inscribed with woe.[8]
"Ah! who hath reft," quoth he, "my dearest pledge?"
Last came, and last did go,
The pilot of the Galilean Lake;[9]
Two massy keys he bore of metals twain                               110
(The golden opes, the iron shuts amain).
He shook his mitered locks, and stern bespake:
"How well could I have spared for thee, young swain,
Enow[1] of such as for their bellies' sake
Creep and intrude, and climb into the fold![2]                       115
Of other care they little reck'ning make,
Than how to scramble at the shearers' feast,
And shove away the worthy bidden guest.
Blind mouths! that scarce themselves know how to hold
A sheep-hook,[3] or have learned aught else the least                120
That to the faithful herdman's art belongs!
What recks it[4] them? What need they? They are sped,[5]
And when they list,[6] their lean and flashy songs
Grate on their scrannel[7] pipes of wretched straw.
The hungry sheep look up and are not fed,                            125
But swoln with wind, and the rank mist they draw,

---

3. Triton, who maintains the innocence of Neptune, the Roman god of the sea, in the death of Lyci-
das.    4. Youth, shepherd, poet.    5. Aeolus, god of the winds and son of Hippotas.    6. According
to Vergil, the greatest of the Nereids (sea nymphs).    7. God of the river Cam, which flows through
Cambridge.    8. The hyacinth, which was supposed to bear marks that meant "alas" because the flower
was created by Phoebus from the blood of a youth he had killed accidentally.    9. St. Peter, a fisherman
before he became a disciple. According to Matthew 16:19, Christ promised him "the keys of the kingdom
of heaven"; he was traditionally regarded as the first head of the Church, hence the bishop's miter in line
112.    1. The old plural of "enough."    2. According to John 10:1, "He that entereth not by the door
into the sheepfold, but climbeth up some other way . . . is a thief and a robber."    3. A bishop's staff
was shaped like a sheephook to suggest his role as "pastor" (shepherd) of the flock of saints.    4. Does it
matter to.    5. Have attained their purpose—but also, destroyed.    6. Desire.    7. Feeble.

Rot inwardly, and foul contagion spread,
Besides what the grim wolf with privy paw[8]
Daily devours apace, and nothing said;
130    But that two-handed engine[9] at the door
Stands ready to smite once, and smite no more."
    Return, Alpheus,[1] the dread voice is past,
That shrunk thy streams; return, Sicilian Muse,
And call the vales, and bid them hither cast
135    Their bells and flowrets of a thousand hues.
Ye valleys low, where the mild whispers use,[2]
Of shades and wanton winds and gushing brooks,
On whose fresh lap the swart star[3] sparely looks,
Throw hither all your quaint enameled eyes,
140    That on the green turf suck the honeyed showers,
And purple all the ground with vernal flowers.
Bring the rathe[4] primrose that forsaken dies,
The tufted crow-toe, and pale jessamine,
The white pink, and the pansy freaked[5] with jet,
145    The glowing violet,
The musk-rose, and the well-attired woodbine,
With cowslips wan that hang the pensive head,
And every flower that sad embroidery wears.
Bid amaranthus[6] all his beauty shed,
150    And daffodillies fill their cups with tears,
To strew the laureate hearse[7] where Lycid lies.
For so to interpose a little ease,
Let our frail thoughts dally with false surmise.
Ay me! Whilst thee the shores and sounding seas
155    Wash far away, where'er thy bones are hurled,
Whether beyond the stormy Hebrides,[8]
Where thou perhaps under the whelming tide
Visit'st the bottom of the monstrous world;[9]
Or whether thou to our moist vows denied,
160    Sleep'st by the fable of Bellerus old,[1]
Where the great vision of the guarded mount
Look toward Namancos and Bayona's hold;
Look homeward, Angel, now, and melt with ruth.[2]

8. The Roman Catholic Church.       9. Not identified. Guesses include the two-handed sword of the arch-
angel Michael, the two houses of Parliament, and St. Peter's keys.       1. A river god who, according to
Ovid, fell in love with Arethusa. She fled in the form of an underground stream and became a fountain
in Sicily, but Alpheus dived under the sea and at last his waters mingled with hers. See above, line 85.
*Sicilian Muse*: the muse of Theocritus.       2. Frequent.       3. Sirius, the Dog Star, which supposedly with-
ers plants in late summer.       4. Early.       5. Flecked.       6. A legendary flower that cannot fade.
7. Bier.       8. Islands off Scotland, the northern edge of the sea where King drowned.       9. World where
monsters live.       1. A legendary giant, supposedly buried at Land's End in Cornwall. At the tip of Land's
End is St. Michael's Mount (line 161), from which the archangel is pictured looking south across the
Atlantic toward Spanish (Catholic) strongholds (Namancos and Bayona, line 162).       2. Pity.

And, O ye dolphins,[3] waft the hapless youth.
   Weep no more, woeful shepherds, weep no more,     165
For Lycidas your sorrow is not dead,
Sunk though he be beneath the wat'ry floor,
So sinks the day-star[4] in the ocean bed,
And yet anon repairs his drooping head,
And tricks[5] his beams, and with new-spangled ore     170
Flames in the forehead of the morning sky:
So Lycidas sunk low, but mounted high,
Through the dear might of him that walked the waves,[6]
Where, other groves and other streams along,
With nectar pure his oozy locks he laves,     175
And hears the unexpressive nuptial song,[7]
In the blest kingdoms meek of joy and love.
There entertain him all the saints above,
In solemn troops and sweet societies
That sing, and singing in their glory move,     180
And wipe the tears forever from his eyes.
Now, Lycidas, the shepherds weep no more;
Henceforth thou art the genius[8] of the shore,
In thy large recompense, and shalt be good
To all that wander in that perilous flood.     185
   Thus sang the uncouth swain[9] to th' oaks and rills,
While the still morn went out with sandals gray;
He touched the tender stops of various quills,[1]
With eager thought warbling his Doric[2] lay.
And now the sun had stretched out all the hills,     190
And now was dropped into the western bay.
At last he rose, and twitched his mantle blue:
Tomorrow to fresh woods, and pastures new.     1637

## HOWARD NEMEROV

## *A Way of Life*

It's been going on a long time.
For instance, these two guys, not saying much, who slog
Through sun and sand, fleeing the scene of their crime,
Till one turns, without a word, and smacks
His buddy flat with the flat of an axe,     5
Which cuts down on the dialogue

3. According to Roman legend, dolphins brought the body of a drowned youth, Melicertes, to land, where a temple was erected to him as the protector of sailors.    4. The sun.    5. Dresses.    6. Christ. See Matthew 14:25–26.    7. Sung at the "marriage of the Lamb," according to Revelation 19; *unexpressive*: inexpressible.    8. Protecting deity.    9. Unlettered shepherd: that is, Milton.    1. Reeds in the shepherd's pipes.    2. The Greek dialect of Theocritus, Bion, and Moschus, the first writers of pastoral.

Some, but is viewed rather as normal than sad
By me, as I wait for the next ad.

It seems to me it's been quite a while
Since the last vision of blonde loveliness
Vanished, her shampoo and shower and general style
Replaced by this lean young lunk-
head parading along with a gun in his back to confess
How yestereve, being drunk
And in a state of existential despair,
He beat up his grandma and pawned her invalid chair.

But here at last is a pale beauty
Smoking a filter beside a mountain stream,
Brief interlude, before the conflict of love and duty
Gets moving again, as sheriff and posse expound,
Between jail and saloon, the American Dream
Where Justice, after considerable horsing around,
Turns out to be Mercy; when the villain is knocked off,
A kindly uncle offers syrup for my cough.

And now these clean-cut athletic types
In global hats are having a nervous debate
As they stand between their individual rocket ships
Which have landed, appropriately, on some rocks
Somewhere in Space, in an atmosphere of hate
Where one tells the other to pull up his socks
And get going, he doesn't say where; they fade,
And an angel food cake flutters in the void.

I used to leave now and again;
No more. A lot of violence in American life
These days, mobsters and cops all over the scene.
But there's a lot of love, too, mixed with the strife,
And kitchen-kindness, like a bedtime story
With rich food and a more kissable depilatory.
Still, I keep my weapons handy, sitting here
Smoking and shaving and drinking the dry beer.                    1967


MICHAEL ONDAATJE

## King Kong Meets Wallace Stevens

Take two photographs—
Wallace Stevens and King Kong
(Is it significant that I eat bananas as I write this?)

Stevens is portly, benign, a white brush cut
striped tie. Businessman but

for the dark thick hands, the naked brain
the thought in him.

Kong is staggering
lost in New York streets again
a spawn of annoyed cars at his toes.                              10
The mind is nowhere.
Fingers are plastic, electric under the skin.
He's at the call of Metro-Goldwyn-Mayer.

Meanwhile W. S. in his suit
is thinking chaos is thinking fences.                             15
In his head—the seeds of fresh pain
his exorcising,
the bellow of locked blood.

The hands drain from his jacket,
pose in the murderer's shadow.                                    20

1979

SYLVIA PLATH

## Black Rook in Rainy Weather

On the stiff twig up there
Hunches a wet black rook
Arranging and rearranging its feathers in the rain.
I do not expect a miracle
Or an accident                                                    5

To set the sight on fire
In my eye, nor seek
Any more in the desultory weather some design,
But let spotted leaves fall as they fall,
Without ceremony, or portent                                      10

Although, I admit, I desire,
Occasionally, some backtalk
From the mute sky, I can't honestly complain:
A certain minor light may still
Leap incandescent                                                 15

Out of kitchen table or chair
As if a celestial burning took
Possession of the most obtuse objects now and then—
Thus hallowing an interval
Otherwise inconsequent                                            20

By bestowing largesse, honor,
One might say love. At any rate, I now walk

Wary (for it could happen
Even in this dull, ruinous landscape); skeptical,
25    Yet politic; ignorant

Of whatever angel may choose to flare
Suddenly at my elbow. I only know that a rook
Ordering its black feathers can so shine
As to seize my senses, haul
30    My eyelids up, and grant

A brief respite from fear
Of total neutrality. With luck,
Trekking stubborn through this season
Of fatigue, I shall
35    Patch together a content

Of sorts. Miracles occur,
If you care to call those spasmodic
Tricks of radiance miracles. The wait's begun again,
The long wait for the angel,
40    For that rare, random descent.[3]                            1960


## Lady Lazarus

I have done it again.
One year in every ten
I manage it—

A sort of walking miracle, my skin
5    Bright as a Nazi lampshade,
My right foot

A paperweight,
My face a featureless, fine
Jew linen.[4]

10    Peel off the napkin
O my enemy.
Do I terrify?—

The nose, the eye pits, the full set of teeth?
The sour breath
15    Will vanish in a day.

Soon, soon the flesh
The grave cave ate will be
At home on me

3. According to Acts 2, the Holy Ghost at Pentecost descended like a tongue of fire upon Jesus' disciples.    4. During World War II, in some Nazi camps, prisoners were gassed to death, their body parts then turned into home furnishings like lampshades and paperweights.

And I a smiling woman.
I am only thirty.
And like the cat I have nine times to die.                                    20

This is Number Three.
What a trash
To annihilate each decade.

What a million filaments.                                                      25
The peanut-crunching crowd
Shoves in to see

Them unwrap me hand and foot—
The big strip tease.
Gentlemen, ladies                                                              30

These are my hands
My knees.
I may be skin and bone,

Nevertheless, I am the same, identical woman.
The first time it happened I was ten.                                          35
It was an accident.

The second time I meant
To last it out and not come back at all.
I rocked shut

As a seashell.                                                                 40
They had to call and call
And pick the worms off me like sticky pearls.

Dying
Is an art, like everything else.
I do it exceptionally well.                                                    45

I do it so it feels like hell.
I do it so it feels real.
I guess you could say I've a call.

It's easy enough to do it in a cell.
It's easy enough to do it and stay put.                                        50
It's the theatrical

Comeback in broad day
To the same place, the same face, the same brute
Amused shout:

"A miracle!"                                                                   55
That knocks me out.
There is a charge

For the eyeing of my scars, there is a charge
For the hearing of my heart—
It really goes.                                                                60

And there is a charge, a very large charge
For a word or a touch
Or a bit of blood

Or a piece of my hair or my clothes.
65    So, so Herr Doktor.
So, Herr Enemy.

I am your opus,
I am your valuable,
The pure gold baby

70    That melts to a shriek.
I turn and burn.
Do not think I underestimate your great concern

Ash, ash—
You poke and stir.
75    Flesh, bone, there is nothing there—

A cake of soap,
A wedding ring,
A gold filling.

Herr God, Herr Lucifer
80    Beware
Beware.

Out of the ash
I rise with my red hair
And I eat men like air.

1965


## EZRA POUND

## *The Garden*

*En robe de parade.*
—SAMAIN[5]


Like a skein of loose silk blown against a wall
She walks by the railing of a path in Kensington Gardens,[6]
And she is dying piece-meal
        of a sort of emotional anæmia.

5. Albert Samain, late-nineteenth-century French poet. The phrase is from the first line of the prefatory poem in his first book of poems, *Au Jardin de l'Infante*: "Mon âme est une infante en robe de parade" ("My soul is an Infanta in ceremonial dress"). An "Infanta" is a daughter of the Spanish royal family, which, long inbred, had for many years been afflicted with a rare blood disease, hemophilia.    6. A fashionable park near the center of London.

And round about there is a rabble                                                    5
Of the filthy, sturdy, unkillable infants of the very poor.
They shall inherit the earth.

In her is the end of breeding.
Her boredom is exquisite and excessive.
She would like some one to speak to her,                                      10
And is almost afraid that I
       will commit that indiscretion.                                    1916


## In a Station of the Metro[7]

The apparition of these faces in the crowd;
Petals on a wet, black bough.                                                      p. 1913


## A Virginal

No, no! Go from me. I have left her lately.
I will not spoil my sheath with lesser brightness,
For my surrounding air hath a new lightness;
Slight are her arms, yet they have bound me straitly
And left me cloaked as with a gauze of aether;                             5
As with sweet leaves; as with a subtle clearness.
Oh, I have picked up magic in her nearness
To sheathe me half in half the things that sheathe her.
No, no! Go from me, I have still the flavor,
Soft as spring wind that's come from birchen bowers.                  10
Green come the shoots, aye April in the branches,
As winter's wound with her sleight hand she staunches,
Hath of the trees a likeness of the savor:
As white their bark, so white this lady's hours.                            1912


THEODORE ROETHKE
_____

## Elegy for Jane

(MY STUDENT, THROWN BY A HORSE)

I remember the neckcurls, limp and damp as tendrils;
And her quick look, a sidelong pickerel smile;

7. The Paris subway.

And how, once startled into talk, the light syllables leaped for her,
And she balanced in the delight of her thought,
A wren, happy, tail into the wind,
Her song trembling the twigs and small branches.
The shade sang with her;
The leaves, their whispers turned to kissing;
And the mould sang in the bleached valleys under the rose.

Oh, when she was sad, she cast herself down into such a pure depth,
Even a father could not find her:
Scraping her cheek against straw;
Stirring the clearest water.

My sparrow, you are not here,
Waiting like a fern, making a spiney shadow.
The sides of wet stones cannot console me,
Nor the moss, wound with the last light.

If only I could nudge you from this sleep,
My maimed darling, my skittery pigeon.
Over this damp grave I speak the words of my love:
I, with no rights in this matter,
Neither father nor lover.                                    1953

## The Dream

### 1

I met her as a blossom on a stem
Before she ever breathed, and in that dream
The mind remembers from a deeper sleep:
Eye learned from eye, cold lip from sensual lip.
My dream divided on a point of fire;
Light hardened on the water where we were;
A bird sang low; the moonlight sifted in;
The water rippled, and she rippled on.

### 2

She came toward me in the flowing air,
A shape of change, encircled by its fire.
I watched her there, between me and the moon;
The bushes and the stones danced on and on;
I touched her shadow when the light delayed;
I turned my face away, and yet she stayed.
A bird sang from the center of a tree;
She loved the wind because the wind loved me.

### 3

Love is not love until love's vulnerable.
She slowed to sigh, in that long interval.

A small bird flew in circles where we stood;
The deer came down, out of the dappled wood.                    20
All who remember, doubt. Who calls that strange?
I tossed a stone, and listened to its plunge.
She knew the grammar of least motion, she
Lent me one virtue, and I live thereby.

                4

She held her body steady in the wind;                           25
Our shadows met, and slowly swung around;
She turned the field into a glittering sea;
I played in flame and water like a boy
And I swayed out beyond the white seafoam;
Like a wet log, I sang within a flame.                          30
In that last while, eternity's confine,
I came to love, I came into my own.                             1958

## The Waking

I wake to sleep, and take my waking slow.
I feel my fate in what I cannot fear.
I learn by going where I have to go.

We think by feeling. What is there to know?
I hear my being dance from ear to ear.                          5
I wake to sleep, and take my waking slow.

Of those so close beside me, which are you?
God bless the Ground! I shall walk softly there,
And learn by going where I have to go.

Light takes the Tree; but who can tell us how?                  10
The lowly worm climbs up a winding stair;
I wake to sleep, and take my waking slow.

Great Nature has another thing to do
To you and me; so take the lively air,
And, lovely, learn by going where to go.                        15

This shaking keeps me steady. I should know.
What falls away is always. And is near.
I wake to sleep, and take my waking slow.
I learn by going where I have to go.                            1953

MURIEL RUKEYSER

## Reading Time  :  1 Minute 26 Seconds

The fear of poetry is the
fear  :  mystery and fury of a midnight street
of windows whose low voluptuous voice
issues, and after that there is no peace.

5  That round waiting moment in the
theatre  :  curtain rises, dies into the ceiling
and here is played the scene with the mother
bandaging a revealed son's head.   The bandage is torn off.
Curtain goes down.   And here is the moment of proof.

10  That climax when the brain acknowledges the world,
all values extended into the blood awake.
Moment of proof.   And as they say Brancusi did,
building his bird to extend through soaring air,
as Kafka planned stories that draw to eternity
15  through time extended.   And the climax strikes.

Love touches so, that months after the look of
blue stare of love, the footbeat on the heart
is translated into the pure cry of birds
following air-cries, or poems, the new scene.
20  Moment of proof.   That strikes long after act.

They fear it.   They turn away, hand up palm out
fending off moment of proof, the straight look, poem.
The prolonged wound-consciousness after the bullet's shot.
The prolonged love after the look is dead,
25  the yellow joy after the song of the sun.                           1939


## Myth

Long afterward, Oedipus, old and blinded, walked the
roads.      He smelled a familiar smell.      It was
the Sphinx.      Oedipus said, "I want to ask one question.
Why didn't I recognize my mother?"      "You gave the
5  wrong answer," said the Sphinx.      "But that was what
made everything possible," said Oedipus.      "No," she said.
"When I asked, What walks on four legs in the morning,
two at noon, and three in the evening, you answered,
Man.      You didn't say anything about woman."
10  "When you say Man," said Oedipus, "you include women
too. Everyone knows that."      She said, "That's what
you think."                                                     1973

WILLIAM SHAKESPEARE

## [*Hark, hark! the lark at heaven's gate sings*][8]

Hark, hark! the lark at heaven's gate sings,
   And Phoebus'[9] gins arise,
His steeds to water at those springs
   On chaliced[1] flowers that lies;
And winking Mary-buds[2] begin            5
   To ope their golden eyes:
With every thing that pretty is,
   My lady sweet, arise!
   Arise, arise!

ca. 1610

## [*Two loves I have of comfort and despair*]

Two loves I have of comfort and despair,
Which like two spirits do suggest[3] me still:
The better angel is a man right fair,
The worser spirit a woman, color'd ill.[4]
To win me soon to hell, my female evil         5
Tempteth my better angel from my side,
And would corrupt my saint to be a devil,
Wooing his purity with her foul pride.
And whether that my angel be turn'd fiend
Suspect I may, but not directly tell         10
But being both from me,[5] both to each friend,
I guess one angel in another's hell:
   Yet this shall I ne'er know, but live in doubt,
   Till my bad angel fire[6] my good one out.        1609

## [*They that have power to hurt and will do none*]

They that have power to hurt and will do none,
That do not do the thing they most do show,
Who, moving others, are themselves as stone,
Unmovèd, cold, and to temptation slow;
They rightly do inherit heaven's graces         5

---

8. From *Cymbeline* II.iii.   9. Apollo, the sun god.   1. Cup-shaped.   2. Buds of marigolds.
3. Tempt. *Still*: constantly.   4. Badly.   5. Away from me. *Both to each friend*: friends to each
other.   6. Drive out with fire ("fire" was Elizabethan slang for venereal disease).

And husband nature's riches from expense;
They are the lords and owners of their faces,
Others but stewards of their excellence.
The summer's flower is to the summer sweet,
Though to itself it only live and die;
But if that flower with base infection meet,
The basest weed outbraves his dignity:
 For sweetest things turn sourest by their deeds;
 Lilies that fester smell far worse than weeds.

1609

WALLACE STEVENS

## The Idea of Order at Key West

She sang beyond the genius of the sea.
The water never formed to mind or voice,
Like a body wholly body, fluttering
Its empty sleeves; and yet its mimic motion
Made constant cry, caused constantly a cry,
That was not ours although we understood,
Inhuman, of the veritable ocean.

The sea was not a mask. No more was she.
The song and water were not medleyed sound
Even if what she sang was what she heard,
Since what she sang was uttered word by word.
It may be that in all her phrases stirred
The grinding water and the gasping wind;
But it was she and not the sea we heard.

For she was the maker of the song she sang.
The ever-hooded, tragic-gestured sea
Was merely a place by which she walked to sing.
Whose spirit is this? we said, because we knew
It was the spirit that we sought and knew
That we should ask this often as she sang.

If it was only the dark voice of the sea
That rose, or even colored by many waves;
If it was only the outer voice of sky
And cloud, of the sunken coral water-walled,
However clear, it would have been deep air,
The heaving speech of air, a summer sound
Repeated in a summer without end
And sound alone. But it was more than that,
More even than her voice, and ours, among
The meaningless plungings of water and the wind,

Theatrical distances, bronze shadows heaped
On high horizons, mountainous atmospheres
Of sky and sea.
              It was her voice that made
The sky acutest at its vanishing.
She measured to the hour its solitude. 35
She was the single artificer of the world
In which she sang. And when she sang, the sea,
Whatever self it had, became the self
That was her song, for she was the maker. Then we,
As we beheld her striding there alone, 40
Knew that there never was a world for her
Except the one she sang and, singing, made.

Ramon Fernandez,[7] tell me, if you know,
Why, when the singing ended and we turned
Toward the town, tell why the glassy lights, 45
The lights in the fishing boats at anchor there,
As the night descended, tilting in the air,
Mastered the night and portioned out the sea,
Fixing emblazoned zones and fiery poles,
Arranging, deepening, enchanting night. 50

Oh! Blessed rage for order, pale Ramon,
The maker's rage to order words of the sea,
Words of the fragrant portals, dimly-starred,
And of ourselves and of our origins,
In ghostlier demarcations, keener sounds. 55

1935

## The Emperor of Ice-Cream

Call the roller of big cigars,
The muscular one, and bid him whip
In kitchen cups concupiscent curds.[8]
Let the wenches dawdle in such dress
As they are used to wear, and let the boys 5
Bring flowers in last month's newspapers.

7. French classicist and critic, 1894–1944, who emphasized the ordering role of a writer's consciousness upon the materials he used. Stevens denied that he had Fernandez in mind, saying that he combined a Spanish first name and surname at random: "I knew of Ramon Fernandez, the critic, and had read some of his criticisms, but I did not have him in mind." (*Letters* [New York: Knopf, 1960], p. 798) Later, Stevens wrote to another correspondent that he did not have the critic "consciously" in mind. (*Letters*, p. 823)    8. "The words 'concupiscent curds' have no genealogy; they are merely expressive: at least, I hope they are expressive. They express the concupiscence of life, but, by contrast with the things in relation in the poem, they express or accentuate life's destitution, and it is this that gives them something more than a cheap lustre." (Wallace Stevens, *Letters* [New York: Knopf, 1966], p. 500)

Let be be finale of seem.[9]
The only emperor is the emperor of ice-cream.

Take from the dresser of deal,
10   Lacking the three glass knobs, that sheet
On which she embroidered fantails[1] once
And spread it so as to cover her face.
If her horny feet protrude, they come
To show how cold she is, and dumb.
15   Let the lamp affix its beam.
The only emperor is the emperor of ice-cream.                    1923

## Sunday Morning

### I

Complacencies of the peignoir, and late
Coffee and oranges in a sunny chair,
And the green freedom of a cockatoo
Upon a rug mingle to dissipate
5   The holy hush of ancient sacrifice.
She dreams a little, and she feels the dark
Encroachment of that old catastrophe,[2]
As a calm darkens among water-lights.
The pungent oranges and bright, green wings
10   Seem things in some procession of the dead,
Winding across wide water, without sound,
The day is like wide water, without sound,
Stilled for the passing of her dreaming feet
Over the seas, to silent Palestine,
15   Dominion of the blood and sepulchre.

### II

Why should she give her bounty to the dead?
What is divinity if it can come
Only in silent shadows and in dreams?
Shall she not find in comforts of the sun,
20   In pungent fruit and bright, green wings, or else
In any balm or beauty of the earth,
Things to be cherished like the thought of heaven.
Divinity must live within herself:
Passions of rain, or moods in falling snow;
25   Grievings in loneliness, or unsubdued
Elations when the forest blooms; gusty

9. " . . . the true sense of Let be be the finale of seem is let being become the conclusion of denouement of appearing to be: in short, ice cream is an absolute good. The poem is obviously not about ice cream, but about being as distinguished from seeming to be." (Stevens, *Letters*, p. 341)    1. Fantail pigeons.    2. The Crucifixion.

Emotions on wet roads on autumn nights;
All pleasures and all pains, remembering
The bough of summer and the winter branch.
These are the measures destined for her soul.                    30

### III

Jove in the clouds has his inhuman birth.
No mother suckled him, no sweet land gave
Large-mannered motions to his mythy mind
He moved among us, as a muttering king,
Magnificent, would move among his hinds,[3]                      35
Until our blood, commingling, virginal,
With heaven, brought such requital to desire
The very hinds discerned it, in a star.[4]
Shall our blood fail? Or shall it come to be
The blood of paradise? And shall the earth                       40
Seem all of paradise that we shall know?
The sky will be much friendlier then than now,
A part of labor and a part of pain,
And next in glory to enduring love,
Not this dividing and indifferent blue.                          45

### IV

She says, "I am content when wakened birds,
Before they fly, test the reality
Of misty fields, by their sweet questionings;
But when the birds are gone, and their warm fields
Return no more, where, then, is paradise?"                       50
There is not any haunt of prophecy,
Nor any old chimera of the grave,
Neither the golden underground, nor isle
Melodious, where spirits gat[5] them home,
Nor visionary south, nor cloudy palm                             55
Remote on heaven's hill, that has endured
As April's green endures, or will endure
Like her remembrance of awakened birds,
Or her desire for June and evening, tipped
By the consummation of the swallow's wings.                      60

### V

She says, "But in contentment I still feel
The need of some imperishable bliss."
Death is the mother of beauty; hence from her,
Alone, shall come fulfillment to our dreams
And our desires. Although she strews the leaves                  65
Of sure obliteration on our paths,

---

3. Lowliest rural subjects.     4. The star of Bethlehem.     5. Got.

The path sick sorrow took, the many paths
Where triumph rang its brassy phrase, or love
Whispered a little out of tenderness,
70  She makes the willow shiver in the sun
For maidens who were wont to sit and gaze
Upon the grass, relinquished to their feet.
She causes boys to pile new plums and pears
On disregarded plate.[6] The maidens taste
75  And stray impassioned in the littering leaves.

### VI

Is there no change of death in paradise?
Does ripe fruit never fall? Or do the boughs
Hang always heavy in that perfect sky,
Unchanging, yet so like our perishing earth,
80  With rivers like our own that seek for seas
They never find, the same receding shores
That never touch with inarticulate pang?
Why set the pear upon those river-banks
Or spice the shores with odors of the plum?
85  Alas, that they should wear our colors there,
The silken weavings of our afternoons,
And pick the strings of our insipid lutes!
Death is the mother of beauty, mystical,
Within whose burning bosom we devise
90  Our earthly mothers awaiting, sleeplessly.

### VII

Supple and turbulent, a ring of men
Shall chant in orgy[7] on a summer morn
Their boisterous devotion to the sun,
Not as a god, but as a god might be,
95  Naked among them, like a savage source.
Their chant shall be a chant of paradise,
Out of their blood, returning to the sky;
And in their chant shall enter, voice by voice,
The windy lake wherein their lord delights,
100  The trees, like serafin,[8] and echoing hills,
That choir among themselves long afterward.
They shall know well the heavenly fellowship
Of men that perish and of summer morn.
And whence they came and whither they shall go
105  The dew upon their feet shall manifest.

6. "Plate is used in the sense of so-called family plate. Disregarded refers to the disuse into which things fall that have been possessed for a long time. I mean, therefore, that death releases and renews. What the old have come to disregard, the young inherit and make use of." (Stevens, *Letters*, pp. 183–84).    7. Ceremonial revelry.    8. Seraphim, the highest of the nine orders of angels.

VIII

She hears, upon that water without sound,
A voice that cries, "The tomb in Palestine
Is not the porch of spirits lingering.
It is the grave of Jesus, where he lay."
We live in an old chaos of the sun,                                        110
Or old dependency of day and night,
Or island solitude, unsponsored, free,
Of that wide water, inescapable.
Deer walk upon our mountains, and the quail
Whistle about us their spontaneous cries;                                   115
Sweet berries ripen in the wilderness;
And, in the isolation of the sky,
At evening, casual flocks of pigeons make
Ambiguous undulations as they sink,
Downward to darkness, on extended wings.                                    120

1915

ALFRED, LORD TENNYSON

## *Tears, Idle Tears*[9]

    Tears, idle tears, I know not what they mean,
Tears from the depth of some divine despair
Rise in the heart, and gather to the eyes,
In looking on the happy autumn-fields,
And thinking of the days that are no more.                                  5

    Fresh as the first beam glittering on a sail,
That brings our friends up from the underworld,
Sad as the last which reddens over one
That sinks with all we love below the verge;
So sad, so fresh, the days that are no more.                                10

    Ah, sad and strange as in dark summer dawns
The earliest pipe of half-awakened birds
To dying ears, when unto dying eyes
The casement slowly grows a glimmering square;
So sad, so strange, the days that are no more.                             15

    Dear as remembered kisses after death,
And sweet as those by hopeless fancy feigned
On lips that are for others; deep as love,

9. A song from *The Princess*, a long narrative poem about what the mid-nineteenth century called the "new woman."

Deep as first love, and wild with all regret;
20       O Death in Life, the days that are no more!

1847


## *Tithonus*[1]

The woods decay, the woods decay and fall,
The vapors weep their burthen to the ground,
Man comes and tills the field and lies beneath,
And after many a summer dies the swan.
5   Me only cruel immortality
Consumes; I wither slowly in thine arms,
Here at the quiet limit of the world,
A white-haired shadow roaming like a dream
The ever-silent spaces of the East,
10   Far-folded mists, and gleaming halls of morn.
       Alas! for this gray shadow, once a man—
So glorious in his beauty and thy choice,
Who madest him thy chosen, that he seemed
To his great heart none other than a God!
15   I asked thee, "Give me immortality."
Then didst thou grant mine asking with a smile,
Like wealthy men who care not how they give.
But thy strong Hours indignant worked their wills,
And beat me down and marred and wasted me,
20   And though they could not end me, left me maimed
To dwell in presence of immortal youth,
Immortal age beside immortal youth,
And all I was in ashes. Can thy love,
Thy beauty, make amends, though even now,
25   Close over us, the silver star, thy guide,
Shines in those tremulous eyes that fill with tears
To hear me? Let me go; take back thy gift.
Why should a man desire in any way
To vary from the kindly race of men,
30   Or pass beyond the goal of ordinance
Where all should pause, as is most meet for all?
       A soft air fans the cloud apart; there comes
A glimpse of that dark world where I was born.
Once more the old mysterious glimmer steals
35   From thy pure brows, and from thy shoulders pure
And bosom beating with a heart renewed.
Thy cheek begins to redden through the gloom,
Thy sweet eyes brighten slowly close to mine,

1. Prince of Troy. He is loved by Aurora, goddess of the dawn, to whom he speaks the poem. Aurora obtained for him the gift of eternal life but forgot to ask for eternal youth.

Ere yet they blind the stars, and the wild team
Which love thee, yearning for thy yoke, arise,                    40
And shake the darkness from their loosened manes,
And beat the twilight into flakes of fire.
    Lo! ever thus thou growest beautiful
In silence, then before thine answer given
Departest, and thy tears are on my cheek.                        45
    Why wilt thou ever scare me with thy tears,
And make me tremble lest a saying learnt,
In days far-off, on that dark earth, be true?
"The Gods themselves cannot recall their gifts."
    Ay me! ay me! with what another heart          50
In days far-off, and with what other eyes
I used to watch—if I be he that watched—
The lucid outline forming round thee; saw
The dim curls kindle into sunny rings;
Changed with thy mystic change, and felt my blood               55
Glow with the glow that slowly crimsoned all
Thy presence and thy portals, while I lay,
Mouth, forehead, eyelids, growing dewy-warm
With kisses balmier than half-opening buds
Of April, and could hear the lips that kissed                   60
Whispering I knew not what of wild and sweet,
Like that strange song I heard Apollo sing,
While Ilion like a mist rose into towers.
    Yet hold me not forever in thine East;
How can my nature longer mix with thine?                        65
Coldly thy rosy shadows bathe me, cold
Are all thy lights, and cold my wrinkled feet
Upon thy glimmering thresholds, when the steam
Floats up from those dim fields about the homes
Of happy men that have the power to die,                        70
And grassy barrows of the happier dead.
Release me, and restore me to the ground.
Thou seest all things, thou wilt see my grave;
Thou wilt renew thy beauty morn by morn,
I earth in earth forget these empty courts,                     75
And thee returning on thy silver wheels.                   1860

## DYLAN THOMAS

## *Fern Hill*

Now as I was young and easy under the apple boughs
  About the lilting house and happy as the grass was green,
    The night above the dingle starry,
      Time let me hail and climb

<sub>5</sub>                Golden in the heydays of his eyes,
        And honored among wagons I was prince of the apple towns
        And once below a time I lordly had the trees and leaves
                    Trail with daisies and barley
                Down the rivers of the windfall light.

<sub>10</sub>        And as I was green and carefree, famous among the barns
        About the happy yard and singing as the farm was home,
                In the sun that is young once only,
                    Time let me play and be
                Golden in the mercy of his means,
<sub>15</sub>        And green and golden I was huntsman and herdsman, the calves
        Sang to my horn, the foxes on the hills barked clear and cold,
                    And the sabbath rang slowly
                In the pebbles of the holy streams.

        All the sun long it was running, it was lovely, the hay
<sub>20</sub>        Fields high as the house, the tunes from the chimneys, it was air
                And playing, lovely and watery
                    And fire green as grass.
                And nightly under the simple stars
        As I rode to sleep the owls were bearing the farm away,
<sub>25</sub>        All the moon long I heard, blessed among stables, the nightjars[2]
                Flying with the ricks,[3] and the horses
                    Flashing into the dark.

        And then to awake, and the farm, like a wanderer white
        With the dew, come back, the cock on his shoulder: it was all
<sub>30</sub>                Shining, it was Adam and maiden,
                    The sky gathered again
                And the sun grew round that very day.
        So it must have been after the birth of the simple light
        In the first, spinning place, the spellbound horses walking warm
<sub>35</sub>                Out of the whinnying green stable
                    On to the fields of praise.

        And honored among foxes and pheasants by the gay house
        Under the new made clouds and happy as the heart was long,
                In the sun born over and over,
<sub>40</sub>                    I ran my heedless ways,
                My wishes raced through the house-high hay
        And nothing I cared, at my sky-blue trades, that time allows
        In all his tuneful turning so few and such morning songs
                Before the children green and golden
<sub>45</sub>                Follow him out of grace,

        Nothing I cared, in the lamb white days, that time would take me
        Up to the swallow-thronged loft by the shadow of my hand,
                In the moon that is always rising,

2. Birds.    3. Haystacks.

Nor that riding to sleep
    I should hear him fly with the high fields
And wake to the farm forever fled from the childless land.    50
Oh as I was young and easy in the mercy of his means,
    Time held me green and dying
    Though I sang in my chains like the sea.    1946

## In My Craft or Sullen Art

In my craft or sullen art
Exercised in the still night
When only the moon rages
And the lovers lie abed
With all their griefs in their arms,    5
I labor by singing light
Not for ambition or bread
Or the strut and trade of charms
On the ivory stages
But for the common wages    10
Of their most secret heart.

Not for the proud man apart
From the raging moon I write
On these spindrift[4] pages
Nor for the towering dead    15
With their nightingales and psalms
But for the lovers, their arms
Round the griefs of the ages,
Who pay no praise or wages
Nor heed my craft or art.    20

    1946

JEAN TOOMER

## Song of the Son[5]

Pour O pour that parting soul in song,
O pour it in the sawdust glow of night,
Into the velvet pine-smoke air tonight,
And let the valley carry it along.
And let the valley carry it along.    5

4. Literally, wind-driven sea spray.    5. From the novel *Cane*.

O land and soil, red soil and sweet-gum tree,
So scant of grass, so profligate of pines,
Now just before an epoch's sun declines
Thy son, in time, I have returned to thee,
10   Thy son, I have in time returned to thee.

In time, for though the sun is setting on
A song-lit race of slaves, it has not set;
Though late, O soil, it is not too late yet
To catch thy plaintive soul, leaving, soon gone,
15   Leaving, to catch thy plaintive soul soon gone.

O Negro slaves, dark purple ripened plums,
Squeezed, and bursting in the pine-wood air,
Passing, before they strip the old tree bare
One plum was saved for me, one seed becomes

20   An everlasting song, a singing tree,
Caroling softly souls of slavery,
What they were, and what they are to me,
Caroling softly souls of slavery.                              1923


WALT WHITMAN

## *Facing West from California's Shores*

Facing west, from California's shores,
Inquiring, tireless, seeking what is yet unfound,
I, a child, very old, over waves, towards the house of maternity,[6] the
    land of migrations, look afar,
Look off the shores of my Western sea, the circle almost circled:
5   For starting westward from Hindustan, from the vales of Kashmere,
From Asia, from the north, from the God, the sage, and the hero,
From the south, from the flowery peninsulas and the spice islands,
Long having wandered since, round the earth having wandered,
Now I face home again, very pleased and joyous;
10   (But where is what I started for, so long ago?
And why is it yet unfound?)                                    1860


## *I Hear America Singing*

I hear America singing, the varied carols I hear,
Those of mechanics, each one singing his as it should be blithe and
    strong,
The carpenter singing his as he measures his plank or beam,

---

6. Asia, as the supposed birthplace of the human race.

The mason singing his as he makes ready for work, or leaves off work,
The boatman singing what belongs to him in his boat, the deckhand
    singing on the steamboat deck,                                            5
The shoemaker singing as he sits on his bench, the hatter singing as he
    stands,
The wood-cutter's song, the ploughboy's on his way in the morning, or
    at noon intermission or at sundown,
The delicious singing of the mother, or of the young wife at work, or of
    the girl sewing or washing,
Each singing what belongs to him or her and to none else,
The day what belongs to the day—at night the party of young fellows,
    robust, friendly,                                                         10
Singing with open mouths their strong melodious songs.

                                                                          1860

## A Noiseless Patient Spider

A noiseless patient spider,
I marked where on a little promontory it stood isolated,
Marked how to explore the vacant vast surrounding,
It launched forth filament, filament, filament, out of itself,
Ever unreeling them, ever tirelessly speeding them.                          5

And you O my soul where you stand,
Surrounded, detached, in measureless oceans of space,
Ceaselessly musing, venturing, throwing, seeking the spheres to connect
    them,
Till the bridge you will need be formed, till the ductile anchor hold,
Till the gossamer thread you fling catch somewhere, O my soul.              10

                                                                          1881

## When Lilacs Last in the Dooryard Bloomed[7]

### 1

When lilacs last in the dooryard bloomed,
And the great star early drooped in the western sky in the night,
I mourned, and yet shall mourn with ever-returning spring.

Ever-returning spring, trinity sure to me you bring,
Lilac blooming perennial and drooping star in the west,                      5
And thought of him I love.

### 2

O powerful western fallen star!
O shades of night—O moody, tearful night!

7. The "occasion" of the poem is the assassination of Abraham Lincoln.

O great star disappeared—O the black murk that hides the star!
O cruel hands that hold me powerless—O helpless soul of me!
O harsh surrounding cloud that will not free my soul.

### 3

In the dooryard fronting an old farm-house near the white-washed pal-
        ings,
Stands the lilac-bush tall-growing with heart-shaped leaves of rich green,
With many a pointed blossom rising delicate, with the perfume strong I
        love,
With every leaf a miracle—and from this bush in the dooryard,
With delicate-colored blossoms and heart-shaped leaves of rich green,
A sprig with its flower I break.

### 4

In the swamp in secluded recesses,
A shy and hidden bird is warbling a song.

Solitary the thrush,
The hermit withdrawn to himself, avoiding the settlements,
Sings by himself a song.

Song of the bleeding throat,
Death's outlet song of life (for well dear brother I know,
If thou wast not granted to sing thou would'st surely die).

### 5

Over the breast of the spring, the land, amid cities,
Amid lanes and through old woods, where lately the violets peeped from
        the ground, spotting the gray debris,
Amid the grass in the fields each side of the lanes, passing the endless
        grass,
Passing the yellow-speared wheat, every grain from its shroud in the
        dark-brown fields uprisen,
Passing the apple-tree blows of white and pink in the orchards,
Carrying a corpse to where it shall rest in the grave,
Night and day journeys a coffin.

### 6

Coffin that passes through lanes and streets,[8]
Through day and night with the great cloud darkening the land,
With the pomp of the inlooped flags with the cities draped in black,
With the show of the States themselves as of crepe-veiled women stand-
        ing,

8. The funeral cortege stopped at many towns between Washington and Springfield, Illinois, where Lin-
coln was buried.

With processions long and winding and the flambeaus of the night,
With the countless torches lit, with the silent sea of faces and the unbared
   heads,
With the waiting depot, the arriving coffin, and the somber faces,
With dirges through the night, with the thousand voices rising strong
   and solemn,                                                                        40
With all the mournful voices of the dirges poured around the coffin,
The dim-lit churches and the shuddering organs—where amid these you
   journey,
With the tolling tolling bells' perpetual clang,
Here, coffin that slowly passes,
I give you my sprig of lilac.                                                         45


                7

(Nor for you, for one alone,
Blossoms and branches green to coffins all I bring,
For fresh as the morning, thus would I chant a song for you O sane and
   sacred death.

All over bouquets of roses,
O death, I cover you over with roses and early lilies,                                50
But mostly and now the lilac that blooms the first,
Copious I break, I break the sprigs from the bushes,
With loaded arms I come, pouring for you,
For you and the coffins all of you O death.)


                8

O western orb sailing the heaven,                                                     55
Now I know what you must have meant as a month since I walked,
As I walked in silence the transparent shadowy night,
As I saw you had something to tell as you bent to me night after night,
As you drooped from the sky low down as if to my side (while the other
   stars all looked on),
As we wandered together the solemn night (for something I know not
   what kept me from sleep),                                                          60
As the night advanced, and I saw on the rim of the west how full you
   were of woe,
As I stood on the rising ground in the breeze in the cool transparent
   night,
As I watched where you passed and was lost in the netherward black of
   the night,
As my soul in its trouble dissatisfied sank, as where you sad orb,
Concluded, dropped in the night, and was gone.                                        65


                9

Sing on there in the swamp,
O singer bashful and tender, I hear your notes, I hear your call,
I hear, I come presently, I understand you,

But a moment I linger, for the lustrous star has detained me,
70    The star my departing comrade holds and detains me.

### 10

O how shall I warble myself for the dead one there I loved?
And how shall I deck my song for the large sweet soul that has gone?
And what shall my perfume be for the grave of him I love?

Sea-winds blown from east and west,
Blown from the Eastern sea and blown from the Western sea, till there
75        the prairies meeting,
These and with these and the breath of my chant,
I'll perfume the grave of him I love.

### 11

O what shall I hang on the chamber walls?
And what shall the pictures be that I hang on the walls,
80    To adorn the burial-house of him I love?

Pictures of growing spring and farms and homes,
With the Fourth-month eve at sundown, and the gray smoke lucid and
        bright,
With floods of the yellow gold of the gorgeous, indolent, sinking sun,
        burning, expanding the air,
With the fresh sweet herbage under foot, and the pale green leaves of the
        trees prolific,
In the distance the flowing glaze, the breast of the river, with a wind-
85        dapple here and there,
With ranging hills on the banks, with many a line against the sky, and
        shadows,
And the city at hand with dwellings so dense, and stacks of chimneys,
And all the scenes of life and the workshops, and the workmen home-
        ward returning.

### 12

Lo, body and soul—this land,
My own Manhattan with spires, and the sparkling and hurrying tides,
90        and the ships,
The varied and ample land, the South and the North in the light, Ohio's
        shores and flashing Missouri,
And ever the far-spreading prairies covered with grass and corn.

Lo, the most excellent sun so calm and haughty,
The violet and purple morn with just-felt breezes,
95    The gentle soft-born measureless light,
The miracle spreading bathing all, the fulfilled noon,
The coming eve delicious, the welcome night and the stars,
Over my cities shining all, enveloping man and land.

### 13

Sing on, sing on you gray-brown bird,
Sing from the swamps, the recesses, pour your chant from the bushes,   100
Limitless out of the dusk, out of the cedars and pines.

Sing on dearest brother, warble your reedy song,
Loud human song, with voice of uttermost woe.

O liquid and free and tender!
O wild and loose to my soul—O wondrous singer!   105
You only I hear—yet the star holds me (but will soon depart),
Yet the lilac with mastering odor holds me.

### 14

Now while I sat in the day and looked forth,
In the close of the day with its light and the fields of spring, and the
    farmers preparing their crops,
In the large unconscious scenery of my land with its lakes and forests,   110
In the heavenly aerial beauty (after the perturbed winds and the storms),
Under the arching heavens of the afternoon swift passing, and the
    voices of children and women.
The many-moving sea-tides, and I saw the ships how they sailed,
And the summer approaching with richness, and the fields all busy with
    labor,
And the infinite separate houses, how they all went on, each with its
    meals and minutia of daily usages,   115
And the streets how their throbbings throbbed, and the cities pent—lo,
    then and there,
Falling upon them all and among them all, enveloping me with the rest,
Appeared the cloud, appeared the long black trail,
And I knew death, its thought, and the sacred knowledge of death.

Then with the knowledge of death as walking one side of me,   120
And the thought of death close-walking the other side of me,
And I in the middle as with companions, and as holding the hands of
    companions,
I fled forth to the hiding receiving night that talks not,
Down to the shores of the water, the path by the swamp in the dimness,
To the solemn shadowy cedars and ghostly pines so still.   125

And the singer so shy to the rest received me,
The gray-brown bird I know received us comrades three,
And he sang the carol of death, and a verse for him I love.

From deep secluded recesses,
From the fragrant cedars and the ghostly pines so still,   130
Came the carol of the bird.

And the charm of the carol rapt me,
As I held as if by their hands my comrades in the night,
And the voice of my spirit tallied the song of the bird.

135  *Come lovely and soothing death,*
     *Undulate round the world, serenely arriving, arriving,*
     *In the day, in the night, to all, to each,*
     *Sooner or later delicate death.*

     *Praised be the fathomless universe,*
140  *For life and joy, and for objects and knowledge curious,*
     *And for love, sweet love—but praise! praise! praise!*
     *For the sure-enwinding arms of cool-enfolding death.*

     *Dark mother always gliding near with soft feet,*
     *Have none chanted for thee a chant of fullest welcome?*
145  *Then I chant it for thee, I glorify thee above all,*
     *I bring thee a song that when thou must indeed come, come unfalteringly.*

     *Approach strong deliveress,*
     *When it is so, when thou hast taken them I joyously sing the dead,*
     *Lost in the loving floating ocean of thee,*
150  *Laved in the flood of thy bliss O death.*

     *From me to thee glad serenades,*
     *Dances for thee I propose saluting thee, adornments and feastings for thee,*
     *And the sights of the open landscape and the high-spread sky are fitting,*
     *And life and the fields, and the huge and thoughtful night.*

155  *The night in silence under many a star,*
     *The ocean shore and the husky whispering wave whose voice I know,*
     *And the soul turning to thee O vast and well-veiled death,*
     *And the body gratefully nestling close to thee.*

     *Over the tree-tops I float thee a song,*
160  *Over the rising and sinking waves, over the myriad fields and the prairies wide,*
     *Over the dense-packed cities all and the teeming wharves and ways,*
     *I float this carol with joy, with joy to thee O death.*

## 15

     To the tally of my soul,
     Loud and strong kept up the gray-brown bird,
165  With pure deliberate notes spreading filling the night.

     Loud in the pines and cedars dim,
     Clear in the freshness moist and the swamp-perfume,
     And I with my comrades there in the night.

     While my sight that was bound in my eyes unclosed,
170  As to long panoramas of visions.

     And I saw askant[9] the armies,
     I saw as in noiseless dreams hundreds of battle-flags,
     Borne through the smoke of the battles and pierced with missiles I saw
          them,

---

9. Askance: sideways.

And carried hither and yon through the smoke, and torn and bloody,
And at last but a few shreds left on the staffs (and all in silence),                  175
And the staffs all splintered and broken.

I saw battle-corpses, myriads of them,
And the white skeletons of young men, I saw them,
I saw the debris and debris of all the slain soldiers of the war,
But I saw they were not as was thought,                  180
They themselves were fully at rest, they suffered not,
The living remained and suffered, the mother suffered,
And the wife and the child and the musing comrade suffered,
And the armies that remained suffered.

      16

Passing the visions, passing the night,                  185
Passing, unloosing the hold of my comrades' hands,
Passing the song of the hermit bird and the tallying song of my soul,
Victorious song, death's outlet song, yet varying ever-altering song,
As low and wailing, yet clear the notes, rising and falling, flooding the
    night,
Sadly sinking and fainting, as warning and warning, and yet again burst-
    ing with joy,                  190
Covering the earth and filling the spread of the heaven,
As that powerful psalm in the night I heard from recesses,
Passing, I leave thee lilac with heart-shaped leaves,
I leave thee there in the door-yard, blooming, returning with spring.

I cease from my song for thee,                  195
From my gaze on thee in the west, fronting the west, communing with
    thee,
O comrade lustrous with silver face in the night.

Yet each to keep and all, retrievements out of the night,
The song, the wondrous chant of the gray-brown bird,
And the tallying chant, the echo aroused in my soul,                  200
With the lustrous and drooping star with the countenance full of woe,
With the holders holding my hand nearing the call of the bird,
Comrades mine and I in the midst, and their memory ever to keep, for
    the dead I loved so well,
For the sweetest, wisest soul of all my days and lands—and this for his
    dear sake,
Lilac and star and bird twined with the chant of my soul,                  205
There in the fragrant pines and the cedars dusk and dim.

                                    1865–1866

RICHARD WILBUR

## The Beautiful Changes

One wading a Fall meadow finds on all sides
The Queen Anne's Lace[1] lying like lilies
On water; it glides
So from the walker, it turns
5    Dry grass to a lake, as the slightest shade of you
Valleys my mind in fabulous blue Lucernes.[2]

The beautiful changes as a forest is changed
By a chameleon's tuning his skin to it;
As a mantis, arranged
10    On a green leaf, grows
Into it, makes the leaf leafier, and proves
Any greenness is deeper than anyone knows.

Your hands hold roses always in a way that says
They are not only yours; the beautiful changes
15    In such kind ways,
Wishing ever to sunder
Things and things' selves for a second finding, to lose
For a moment all that it touches back to wonder.                    1947

## Museum Piece

The good gray guardians of art
Patrol the halls on spongy shoes,
Impartially protective, though
Perhaps suspicious of Toulouse.[3]

5    Here dozes one against the wall,
Disposed upon a funeral chair.
A Degas[4] dancer pirouettes
Upon the parting of his hair.

See how she spins! The grace is there,
10    But strain as well is plain to see.

---

1. A delicate-looking plant, with finely divided leaves and flat clusters of small white flowers, sometimes called "wild carrot."    2. Alfalfa, a plant resembling clover, with small purple flowers. Lake Lucerne is famed for deep blue color and its picturesque Swiss setting amid limestone mountains.    3. Toulouse-Lautrec, nineteenth-century French painter famous for his posters, drawings, and paintings of singers, dancers, and actresses.    4. Degas, a nineteenth-century French impressionist, usually considered the master of the human figure in movement.

Degas loved the two together:
Beauty joined to energy.

Edgar Degas purchased once
A fine El Greco,[5] which he kept
Against the wall beside his bed                                    15
To hang his pants on while he slept.                         1950


## Transit

A woman I have never seen before
Steps from the darkness of her town-house door
At just that crux of time when she is made
So beautiful that she or time must fade.

What use to claim that as she tugs her gloves           5
A phantom heraldry of all the loves
Blares from the lintel? That the staggered sun
Forgets, in his confusion, how to run?

Still, nothing changes as her perfect feet
Click down the walk that issues in the street,           10
Leaving the stations of her body there
As a whip maps the countries of the air.                   1987

## This Is Just to Say

I have eaten
the plums
that were in
the icebox

and which                                                                 5
you were probably
saving
for breakfast

Forgive me
they were delicious                                                   10
so sweet
and so cold                                                              1934

5. El Greco, a sixteenth-century Spanish painter, known for the mannered disproportion of his figures.

WILLIAM WORDSWORTH

## Lines Composed a Few Miles above Tintern Abbey on Revisiting the Banks of the Wye during a Tour, July 13, 1798[6]

Five years have passed; five summers, with the length
Of five long winters! and again I hear
These waters, rolling from their mountain-springs
With a soft inland murmur. Once again
5    Do I behold these steep and lofty cliffs,
That on a wild secluded scene impress
Thoughts of more deep seclusion; and connect
The landscape with the quiet of the sky.
The day is come when I again repose
10   Here, under this dark sycamore, and view
These plots of cottage-ground, these orchard tufts,
Which at this season, with their unripe fruits,
Are clad in one green hue, and lose themselves
'Mid groves and copses.[7] Once again I see
15   These hedge-rows, hardly hedge-rows, little lines
Of sportive wood run wild: these pastoral farms,
Green to the very door; and wreaths of smoke
Sent up, in silence, from among the trees!
With some uncertain notice, as might seem
20   Of vagrant dwellers in the houseless woods,
Or of some hermit's cave, where by his fire
The hermit sits alone.
                 These beauteous forms,
Through a long absence, have not been to me
As is a landscape to a blind man's eye;
25   But oft, in lonely rooms, and 'mid the din
Of towns and cities, I have owed to them,
In hours of weariness, sensations sweet,
Felt in the blood, and felt along the heart;
And passing even into my purer mind,
30   With tranquil restoration—feelings too
Of unremembered pleasure: such, perhaps,
As have no slight or trivial influence
On that best portion of a good man's life,
His little, nameless, unremembered acts
35   Of kindness and of love. Nor less, I trust,
To them I may have owed another gift,

---

6. Wordsworth had first visited the Wye valley and the ruins of the medieval abbey there in 1793, while on a solitary walking tour. He was twenty-three then, twenty-eight when he wrote this poem.
7. Thickets.

Of aspect more sublime; that blessèd mood,
In which the burthen[8] of the mystery,
In which the heavy and the weary weight
Of all this unintelligible world,                                    40
Is lightened—that serene and blessèd mood,
In which the affections gently lead us on—
Until, the breath of this corporeal frame
And even the motion of our human blood
Almost suspended, we are laid asleep                                 45
In body, and become a living soul;
While with an eye made quiet by the power
Of harmony, and the deep power of joy,
We see into the life of things.
                                   If this
Be but a vain belief, yet, oh! how oft—                              50
In darkness and amid the many shapes
Of joyless daylight; when the fretful stir
Unprofitable, and the fever of the world,
Have hung upon the beatings of my heart—
How oft, in spirit, have I turned to thee,                           55
O sylvan Wye! thou wanderer through the woods,
How often has my spirit turned to thee!

    And now, with gleams of half-extinguished thought,
With many recognitions dim and faint,
And somewhat of a sad perplexity,                                    60
The picture of the mind revives again;
While here I stand, not only with the sense
Of present pleasure, but with pleasing thoughts
That in this moment there is life and food
For future years. And so I dare to hope,                             65
Though changed, no doubt, from what I was when first
I came among these hills; when like a roe
I bounded o'er the mountains, by the sides
Of the deep rivers, and the lonely streams,
Wherever nature led: more like a man                                 70
Flying from something that he dreads than one
Who sought the thing he loved. For nature then
(The coarser[9] pleasures of my boyish days,
And their glad animal movements all gone by)
To me was all in all—I cannot paint                                  75
What then I was. The sounding cataract
Haunted me like a passion; the tall rock,
The mountain, and the deep and gloomy wood,
Their colors and their forms, were then to me
An appetite; a feeling and a love,                                   80
That had no need of a remoter charm.

8. Burden.    9. Physical.

By thought supplied, nor any interest
Unborrowed from the eye. That time is past,
And all its aching joys are now no more,
And all its dizzy raptures. Not for this
Faint I,[1] nor mourn nor murmur; other gifts
Have followed; for such loss, I would believe,
Abundant recompense. For I have learned
To look on nature, not as in the hour
Of thoughtless youth; but hearing oftentimes
The still, sad music of humanity,
Nor harsh nor grating, though of ample power
To chasten and subdue. And I have felt
A presence that disturbs me with the joy
Of elevated thoughts, a sense sublime
Of something far more deeply interfused,
Whose dwelling is the light of setting suns,
And the round ocean and the living air,
And the blue sky, and in the mind of man:
A motion and a spirit, that impels
All thinking things, all objects of all thought,
And rolls through all things. Therefore am I still
A lover of the meadows and the woods
And mountains; and of all that we behold
From this green earth; of all the mighty world
Of eye, and ear—both what they half create,
And what perceive; well pleased to recognize
In nature and the language of the sense
The anchor of my purest thoughts, the nurse,
The guide, the guardian of my heart, and soul
Of all my moral being.
                                 Nor perchance,
If I were not thus taught, should I the more
Suffer my genial spirits[2] to decay:
For thou art with me here upon the banks
Of this fair river; thou my dearest Friend,[3]
My dear, dear Friend; and in thy voice I catch
The language of my former heart, and read
My former pleasures in the shooting lights
Of thy wild eyes. Oh! yet a little while
May I behold in thee what I was once,
My dear, dear Sister! and this prayer I make,
Knowing that Nature never did betray
The heart that loved her; 'tis her privilege,
Through all the years of this our life, to lead
From joy to joy: for she can so inform

85
90
95
100
105
110
115
120
125

---

1. Am I discouraged.    2. Natural disposition; that is, the spirits that are part of his individual genius.
3. His sister Dorothy.

The mind that is within us, so impress
With quietness and beauty, and so feed
With lofty thoughts, that neither evil tongues,
Rash judgments, nor the sneers of selfish men,
Nor greetings where no kindness is, nor all                    130
The dreary intercourse of daily life,
Shall e'er prevail against us, or disturb
Our cheerful faith that all which we behold
Is full of blessings. Therefore let the moon
Shine on thee in thy solitary walk;                            135
And let the misty mountain-winds be free
To blow against thee: and, in after years,
When these wild ecstasies shall be matured
Into a sober pleasure; when thy mind
Shall be a mansion for all lovely forms,                       140
Thy memory be as a dwelling-place
For all sweet sounds and harmonies; oh! then,
If solitude, or fear, or pain, or grief,
Should be thy portion, with what healing thoughts
Of tender joy wilt thou remember me,                           145
And these my exhortations! No, perchance—
If I should be where I no more can hear
Thy voice, nor catch from thy wild eyes these gleams
Of past existence—wilt thou then forget
That on the banks of this delightful stream                    150
We stood together; and that I, so long
A worshiper of Nature, hither came
Unwearied in that service; rather say
With warmer love—oh! with far deeper zeal
Of holier love. Nor wilt thou then forget,                     155
That after many wanderings, many years
Of absence, these steep woods and lofty cliffs,
And this green pastoral landscape, were to me
More dear, both for themselves and for thy sake!          1798

W. B. YEATS

## Easter 1916[4]

I have met them at close of day
Coming with vivid faces

4. On Easter Monday 1916, an Irish Republic was proclaimed by nationalist leaders, who launched an unsuccessful revolt against the British government. After a week of street fighting, the Easter Rebellion was put down. A number of prominent nationalists were executed, including the four leaders mentioned in lines 75–76, all of whom Yeats knew personally.

From counter or desk among gray
Eighteenth-century houses.
5      I have passed with a nod of the head
Or polite meaningless words,
Or have lingered awhile and said
Polite meaningless words,
And thought before I had done
10     Of a mocking tale or a gibe
To please a companion
Around the fire at the club,
Being certain that they and I
But lived where motley is worn:
15     All changed, changed utterly:
A terrible beauty is born.

That woman's[5] days were spent
In ignorant good-will,
Her nights in argument
20     Until her voice grew shrill.
What voice more sweet than hers
When, young and beautiful,
She rode to harriers?
This man[6] had kept a school
25     And rode our wingéd horse;[7]
This other[8] his helper and friend
Was coming into his force;
He might have won fame in the end,
So sensitive his nature seemed,
30     So daring and sweet his thought.
This other man[9] I had dreamed
A drunken, vainglorious lout.
He had done most bitter wrong
To some who are near my heart,
35     Yet I number him in the song;
He, too, has resigned his part
In the casual comedy;
He, too, has been changed in his turn,
Transformed utterly:
40     A terrible beauty is born.

Hearts with one purpose alone
Through summer and winter seem

---

5. Countess Constance Georgina Markiewicz, a beautiful and well-born young woman from County Sligo who became a vigorous and bitter nationalist. At first condemned to death, she later had her sentence commuted to life imprisonment, and she gained amnesty in 1917.    6. Patrick Pearse, who led the assault on the Dublin Post Office, from which the proclamation of a republic was issued. A schoolmaster by profession, he had vigorously supported the restoration of the Gaelic language in Ireland and was an active political writer and poet.    7. Pegasus, a traditional symbol of poetic inspiration.    8. Thomas MacDonagh, also a writer and teacher.    9. Major John MacBride, who had married Yeats's beloved Maud Gonne in 1903 but separated from her two years later.

Enchanted to a stone
To trouble the living stream.
The horse that comes from the road,                45
The rider, the birds that range
From cloud to tumbling cloud,
Minute by minute they change;
A shadow of cloud on the stream
Changes minute by minute;                          50
A horse-hoof slides on the brim,
And a horse plashes within it;
The long-legged moor-hens dive,
And hens to moor-cocks call;
Minute by minute they live:                        55
The stone's in the midst of all.

Too long a sacrifice
Can make a stone of the heart.
O when may it suffice?
That is Heaven's part, our part                    60
To murmur name upon name,
As a mother names her child
When sleep at last has come
On limbs that had run wild.
What is it but nightfall?                          65
No, no, not night but death;
Was it needless death after all?
For England may keep faith[1]
For all that is done and said.
We know their dream; enough                        70
To know they dreamed and are dead;
And what if excess of love
Bewildered them till they died?
I write it out in a verse—
MacDonagh and MacBride                             75
And Connolly[2] and Pearse
Now and in time to be,
Wherever green is worn,
Are changed, changed utterly;
A terrible beauty is born.                         80

1916

---

1. Before the uprising the English had promised eventual home rule to Ireland.    2. James Connolly, the leader of the Easter uprising.

# The Second Coming[3]

Turning and turning in the widening gyre[4]
The falcon cannot hear the falconer;
Things fall apart; the center cannot hold;
Mere anarchy is loosed upon the world,
5    The blood-dimmed tide is loosed, and everywhere
The ceremony of innocence is drowned;
The best lack all conviction, while the worst
Are full of passionate intensity.
Surely some revelation is at hand;
10    Surely the Second Coming is at hand.
The Second Coming! Hardly are those words out
When a vast image out of *Spiritus Mundi*[5]
Troubles my sight: somewhere in sands of the desert
A shape with lion body and the head of a man,
15    A gaze blank and pitiless as the sun,
Is moving its slow thighs, while all about it
Reel shadows of the indignant desert birds.[6]
The darkness drops again; but now I know
That twenty centuries of stony sleep
20    Were vexed to nightmare by a rocking cradle,
And what rough beast, its hour come round at last,
Slouches towards Bethlehem to be born?                    p. 1920

# Leda and the Swan[7]

A sudden blow: the great wings beating still
Above the staggering girl, her thighs caressed
By the dark webs, her nape caught in his bill,
He holds her helpless breast upon his breast.

3. The Second Coming of Christ, according to Matthew 24:29–44, will come after a time of "tribulation." Disillusioned by Ireland's continued civil strife, Yeats saw his time as the end of another historical cycle. In *A Vision* (1937) Yeats describes his view of history as dependent on cycles of about 2,000 years: the birth of Christ had ended the cycle of Greco-Roman civilization, and now the Christian cycle seemed near an end, to be followed by an antithetical cycle, ominous in its portents.     4. Literally, the widening spiral of a falcon's flight. "Gyre" is Yeats's term for a cycle of history, which he diagrammed in terms of a series of interpenetrating cones.     5. Or *Anima Mundi*, the spirit or soul of the world. Yeats considered this universal consciousness or memory a fund from which poets drew their images and symbols.     6. Yeats later wrote of the "brazen winged beast . . . described in my poem *The Second Coming*" as "associated with laughing, ecstatic destruction." "Our civilization was about to reverse itself, or some new civilization about to be born from all that our age had rejected . . . ; because we had worshiped a single god it would worship many."     7. According to Greek myth, Zeus took the form of a swan to seduce Leda, who became the mother of Helen of Troy and also of Clytemnestra, Agamemnon's wife and murderer. Helen's abduction from her husband, Menelaus, brother of Agamemnon, began the Trojan War (line 10). Yeats described the visit of Zeus to Leda as an annunciation like that to Mary (see Luke 1: 26–38): "I imagine the annunciation that founded Greece as made to Leda. . . ." (*A Vision*).

How can those terrified vague fingers push                                          5
The feathered glory from her loosening thighs?
And how can body, laid in that white rush,
But feel the strange heart beating where it lies?

A shudder in the loins engenders there
The broken wall, the burning roof and tower                                        10
And Agamemnon dead.
                                Being so caught up,
So mastered by the brute blood of the air,
Did she put on his knowledge with his power
Before the indifferent beak could let her drop?

1923

## *Sailing to Byzantium*[8]

### I

That[9] is no country for old men. The young
In one another's arms, birds in the trees
—Those dying generations—at their song,
The salmon-falls, the mackerel-crowded seas
Fish, flesh, or fowl, commend all summer long                                       5
Whatever is begotten, born, and dies.
Caught in that sensual music all neglect
Monuments of unaging intellect.

### II

An aged man is but a paltry thing,
A tattered coat upon a stick, unless                                               10
Soul clap its hands and sing, and louder sing
For every tatter in its mortal dress,
Nor is there singing school but studying
Monuments of its own magnificence;
And therefore I have sailed the seas and come                                      15
To the holy city of Byzantium.

### III

O sages standing in God's holy fire
As in the gold mosaic of a wall,

---

8. The ancient name of Istanbul, the capital and holy city of Eastern Christendom from the late fourth century until 1453. It was famous for its stylized and formal mosaics, its symbolic, nonnaturalistic art, and its highly developed intellectual life. Yeats repeatedly uses it to symbolize a world of artifice and timelessness, free from the decay and death of the natural and sensual world.      9. Ireland, as an instance of the natural, temporal world.

Come from the holy fire, perne in a gyre,[1]
20    And be the singing-masters of my soul.
Consume my heart away; sick with desire
And fastened to a dying animal
It knows not what it is; and gather me
Into the artifice of eternity.

IV

25    Once out of nature I shall never take
My bodily form from any natural thing,
But such a form as Grecian goldsmiths make
Of hammered gold and gold enameling
To keep a drowsy Emperor awake;[2]
30    Or set upon a golden bough[3] to sing
To lords and ladies of Byzantium
Of what is past, or passing, or to come.

1927

## Among School Children

I

I walk through the long schoolroom questioning;
A kind old nun in a white hood replies;
The children learn to cipher and to sing,
To study reading-books and history,
5    To cut and sew, be neat in everything
In the best modern way—the children's eyes
In momentary wonder stare upon
A sixty-year-old smiling public man.[4]

II

I dream of a Ledaean body,[5] bent
10    Above a sinking fire, a tale that she
Told of a harsh reproof, or trivial event
That changed some childish day to tragedy—
Told, and it seemed that our two natures blent
Into a sphere from youthful sympathy,

---

1. That is, whirl in a coiling motion, so that his soul may merge with its motion as the timeless world invades the cycles of history and nature. "Perne" is Yeats's coinage (from the noun "pirn"): to spin around in the kind of spiral pattern that thread makes as it comes off a bobbin or spool.    2. "I have read somewhere that in the Emperor's palace at Byzantium was a tree made of gold and silver, and artificial birds that sang." (WBY)    3. In Book VI of *The Aeneid*, the sybil tells Aeneas that he must pluck a golden bough from a nearby tree in order to descend to Hades. There is only one such branch there, and when it is plucked an identical one takes its place.    4. At sixty (in 1925) Yeats had been a senator of the Irish Free State.    5. Like that of Helen of Troy, daughter of Leda. The memory dream is of Maud Gonne (see also lines 29–30), with whom Yeats had long been hopelessly in love.

Or else, to alter Plato's parable,                                          15
Into the yolk and white of the one shell.[6]

### III

And thinking of that fit of grief or rage
I look upon one child or t'other there
And wonder if she stood so at that age—
For even daughters of the swan can share                                    20
Something of every paddler's heritage—
And had that color upon cheek or hair,
And thereupon my heart is driven wild:
She stands before me as a living child.

### IV

Her present image floats into the mind—                                      25
Did Quattrocento finger[7] fashion it
Hollow of cheek as though it drank the wind
And took a mess of shadows for its meat?
And I though never of Ledaean kind
Had pretty plumage once—enough of that,                                     30
Better to smile on all that smile, and show
There is a comfortable kind of old scarecrow.

### V

What youthful mother, a shape upon her lap
Honey of generation[8] had betrayed,
And that must sleep, shriek, struggle to escape                             35
As recollection or the drug decide,
Would think her son, did she but see that shape
With sixty or more winters on its head,
A compensation for the pang of his birth,
Or the uncertainty of his setting forth?                                    40
### VI

Plato thought nature but a spume that plays
Upon a ghostly paradigm of things;[9]
Solider Aristotle played the taws

---

6. In Plato's *Symposium*, the origin of human love is explained by parable: Human beings were once spheres, but Zeus was fearful of their power and cut them in half; now each half longs to be reunited with its missing half. Helen and Pollux were hatched from one of two eggs born to Leda after her union with Zeus in the form of a swan; the other contained Castor and Clytemnestra. According to Yeats in *A Vision*, "from one of [Leda's] eggs came Love and from the other War."    7. The hand of a fifteenth-century artist. Yeats especially admired Botticelli, and in *A Vision* praises his "deliberate strangeness everywhere [that] gives one an emotion of mystery which is new to painting."    8. Porphyry, a third-century Greek scholar and Neoplatonic philosopher, says "honey of generation" means the "pleasure arising from copulation" that draws souls "downward" to generation.    9. Plato considered the world of nature an imperfect and illusory copy of the ideal world.

Upon the bottom of a king of kings;[1]
World-famous golden-thighed Pythagoras[2]
Fingered upon a fiddle-stick or strings       .
What a star sang and careless Muses heard:
Old clothes upon old sticks to scare a bird.

### VII

Both nuns and mothers worship images,
But those the candles light are not as those
That animate a mother's reveries
But keep a marble or a bronze repose.
And yet they too break hearts—O Presences
That passion, piety or affection knows,
And that all heavenly glory symbolize—
O self-born mockers of man's enterprise;

### VIII

Labor is blossoming or dancing where
The body is not bruised to pleasure soul,
Nor beauty born out of its own despair,
Nor blear-eyed wisdom out of midnight oil.
O chestnut-tree, great-rooted blossomer,
Are you the leaf, the blossom or the bole?
O body swayed to music, O brightening glance,
How can we know the dancer from the dance?                    1927

## Byzantium

The unpurged images of day recede;
The Emperor's drunken soldiery are abed;
Night resonance recedes, night-walkers' song
After great cathedral gong;
A starlit or a moonlit dome[3] disdains
All that man is,
All mere complexities,
The fury and the mire of human veins.

Before me floats an image, man or shade,
Shade more than man, more image than a shade;
For Hades' bobbin bound in mummy-cloth
May unwind the winding path;

---

1. Aristotle, the teacher of Alexander the Great, disciplined him with a strap ("taw," line 43). His philosophy, insisting on the interdependence of form and matter, took the world of nature far more seriously than did Plato's.    2. Pythagoras (580?–500? B.C.), the Greek mathematician and philosopher, was highly revered, and one legend describes his godlike golden thighs.    3. According to Yeats's philosophy, the full moon ("moonlit") represents the mind "completely absorbed in being."

A mouth that has no moisture and no breath
Breathless mouths may summon;
I hail the superhuman;                                                    15
I call it death-in-life and life-in-death.

Miracle, bird or golden handiwork,
More miracle than bird or handiwork,
Planted on the star-lit golden bough
Can like the cocks of Hades crow,[4]                                      20
Or, by the moon embittered, scorn aloud
In glory of changeless metal
Common bird or petal
And all complexities of mire or blood.

At midnight on the Emperor's pavement flit                                25
Flames that no faggot feeds, nor steel has lit,
Nor storm disturbs, flames begotten of flame,
Where blood-begotten spirits come
And all complexities of fury leave,
Dying into a dance,                                                       30
An agony of trance,
An agony of flame that cannot singe a sleeve.

Astraddle on the dolphin's mire and blood,[5]
Spirit after spirit! The smithies break the flood,
The golden smithies of the Emperor!                                       35
Marbles of the dancing floor
Break bitter furies of complexity,
Those images that yet
Fresh images beget,
That dolphin-torn, that gong-tormented sea.                               40

                                                    1932


# The Circus Animals' Desertion

### 1

I sought a theme and sought for it in vain,
I sought it daily for six weeks or so,
Maybe at last, being but a broken man,
I must be satisfied with my heart, although
Winter and summer till old age began                                      5
My circus animals were all on show,
Those stilted boys, that burnished chariot,
Lion and woman and the Lord knows what.

---

4. As the bird of dawn, the cock has from antiquity been a symbol of rebirth and resurrection.    5. In ancient art, dolphins symbolize the soul moving from one state to another, and sometimes they provide a vehicle for the dead. Palaemon, for example, in Greek tradition is often mounted on a dolphin.

2

What can I but enumerate old themes?
First that sea-rider Oisin led by the nose
Through three enchanted islands, allegorical dreams,
Vain gaiety, vain battle, vain repose,
Themes of the embittered heart, or so it seems,
That might adorn old songs or courtly shows;
But what cared I that set him on to ride,
I, starved for the bosom of his faery bride?

And then a counter-truth filled out its play,
*The Countess Cathleen* was the name I gave it;
She, pity-crazed, had given her soul away,
But masterful Heaven had intervened to save it.
I thought my dear must her own soul destroy,
So did fanaticism and hate enslave it,
And this brought forth a dream and soon enough
This dream itself had all my thought and love.

And when the Fool and Blind Man stole the bread
Cuchulain fought the ungovernable sea;
Heart-mysteries there, and yet when all is said
It was the dream itself enchanted me:
Character isolated by a deed
To engross the present and dominate memory.
Players and painted stage took all my love,
And not those things that they were emblems of.

3

Those masterful images because complete
Grew in pure mind, but out of what began?
A mound of refuse or the sweeping of a street,
Old kettles, old bottles, and a broken can,
Old iron, old bones, old rags, that raving slut
Who keeps the till. Now that my ladder's gone,
I must lie down where all the ladders start,
In the foul rag-and-bone shop of the heart.                    1939

# Appendices

# Writing about Poetry

# INTRODUCTION

Writing about literature ought to be easier than writing about anything else. When you write about painting, for example, you have to translate shapes and colors and textures into words. When you write about music, you have to translate various aspects and combinations of sounds into words. When you write about that complex, mysterious, fleeting thing called "reality" or "life," you have an even more difficult task. Worst of all, perhaps, is trying to put into words all that is going on at any given moment inside your particular and unique self. So you ought to be relieved to know that you are going to write about literature—that is, use words to write about words.

But writing about poetry will not be easy if you haven't learned to *read* poetry, for in order to write about anything you have to know that something rather well. Helping you to learn to read poetry is what the earlier chapters of this book are about; this chapter is about the writing. (But, as you will see, you cannot fully separate the writing from the reading.)

Another thing keeps writing about poetry from being easy: writing itself is not easy. Writing well requires a variety of language skills—a good working vocabulary, for example—and a sense of how to order your ideas, of how to link one idea or statement to another, of what to put in and what to leave out. Worse, writing is not a finite or definite skill or art; you never really "know how to write," you just learn how to write a little better about a little more. These very words you are reading have been written and revised several times, even though the author has had many years of practice.

# REPRESENTING THE LITERARY TEXT

## COPYING

If writing about poetry is using words about words, what words should you use? Since most writers work very hard to get each word exactly right and in exactly the right order, there are no better words to use in discussing what the literature is about than those of the literary work itself. Faced with writing about a poem, then, you could just write the poem over again, word for word:

> Once upon a midnight dreary, while I pondered weak and weary,
> Over many a quaint and curious volume of forgotten lore . . .

and so on until the end. Copying texts was useful in medieval monasteries, but in our electronic age, with printing, word processors, and fax machines available to us, it would not seem to be very useful. Besides, if you try to copy a text, you will probably find that spelling or punctuation errors, reversed word order, and missing or added or just different words seem mysteriously to appear. Still, it's a good exercise for teaching yourself accuracy and attention to detail, and you will probably discover things about the text you are copying that you would be unlikely to notice otherwise. Early in a poetry course, particularly, copying can be a useful step in learning how to read and write about poetry; later, being able to copy a passage accurately will help when you want to quote a passage to illustrate or prove a point you are making. But copying is not, in itself, writing *about* poetry.

Reading aloud, a variation of copying, may be a more original and interpretive exercise than copying itself, since by tone, emphasis, and pace you are clarifying the text or indicating the way you understand the text. But it, too, is not *writing* about poetry, and you will not long be satisfied with merely repeating someone else's words. You will have perceptions, responses, and ideas that you will want to express for yourself about what you are reading. And having something to say and wanting to say or write it is the first and most significant step in learning to write about poetry.

## PARAPHRASE

If you look away from the text for a while and then write the same material but in your own words, you are writing a paraphrase.

But what good is that? First of all, it enables us to test whether we really understand what we are reading. Second, certain elements of the text become clearer: to paraphrase accurately, you will need to take into account the way the words are said, their tone. Third, we can check our paraphrase with those of others—our classmates' versions, for example—to compare our understanding of the passage with theirs. Finally, we have learned how dependent literature is upon words. A paraphrase, no matter how precise, can render only an approximate equivalent of the meaning of a text—a paraphrase is usually flat compared to the original.

Paraphrasing, like copying, is not in itself an entirely satisfactory way of writing about literature, but, like copying, it can be a useful tool when you write about literature in other ways. In trying to explain or clarify a literary text for someone, to illustrate a point you are making about that text, or to remind your readers of or to acquaint them with a text or passage, you will at times want to paraphrase. Unlike an exact copy, a paraphrase, being in your own words, adds something of yours to the text or passage—your emphasis, your perspective, your understanding.

## SUMMARY

Paraphrase follows faithfully the outlines of the text. But if you stand back far enough from the text so as not to see its specific words or smaller details and put down briefly in your own words what you believe the work is about, you will have a summary. How briefly? Well, you could summarize the one hundred eight lines of Poe's "The Raven" in about one hundred eighty words or so like this, for example:

> The speaker of Poe's "The Raven" is sitting in his room late at night reading in order to forget the death of his beloved Lenore. There's a tap at the door; after some hesitation he opens it and calls Lenore's name, but there is only an echo. When he goes back into his room he hears the rapping again, this time at his window, and when he opens it a raven enters. He asks the raven its name, and it answers very clearly, "Nevermore." When the speaker says that the bird, like his friends, will leave, the raven again says, "Nevermore." As the speaker's thoughts run back to Lenore, he realizes the aptness of the raven's word: she shall sit there nevermore. But, he says, sooner or later he will forget her and the grief will lessen. "Nevermore," the raven says again, too aptly. Now the speaker wants the bird to leave, but "Nevermore," the raven says once again. At the end, the speaker knows he'll never escape the raven or its dark message.

To summarize means to select and emphasize and so to interpret: that is, not to replicate the text in miniature, as a reduced photograph might replicate the original, but while reducing it to change the angle of vision and even the filter, to represent the essentials as the reader or summarizer sees them. When you write a summary you should try to be as objective as possible; nevertheless, your summary will reflect not only the literary text but also your own understanding and attitudes. There's nothing wrong with your fingerprints or "mindprints" appearing on the summary, so long as you recognize that in summarizing you are doing more than copying, paraphrasing, or merely reflecting the literary text. You might learn something about both literature and yourself by comparing your summaries of, say, three or four short poems with summaries of the same works by several of your classmates. As you read their summaries, try to understand how each viewed the text differently from you. You might then write a composite summary that would include all that any one reader felt important. You might try the same exercise again on different texts. Has the practice made you more careful? More inclusive? Is there a greater degree of uniformity or inclusiveness in your summaries?

A good summary can be a form of literary criticism. Though you will seldom be called upon merely to summarize a work, a good deal of writing about poetry requires that at some point or other you do summarize—a whole work, a particular incident or aspect, a stanza or line. But beware: a mere summary, no matter how accurate, will seldom fulfill an assignment for a critical essay.

# REPLYING TO THE TEXT

## IMITATION AND PARODY

While paraphrase is something like translation—a faithful following of the original text but in different words—and summary is the faithful, but inevitably interpretive, reduction of the text, there is another kind of writing about poetry that faithfully follows the manner or matter or both of a literary text, but that does so for different ends. It's called imitation.

For many generations, students were taught to write by "writing from models"—imitating good writing. Many serious works are, in one way or another, imitations: *The Aeneid,* for example, may be said to be an imitation of *The Odyssey,* and, in a very different way, so might James Joyce's *Ulysses.* You, too, may be able to learn a good deal about writing—and reading—by trying your hand at an imitation.

To write an imitation, first analyze the original—that is, break it down into its characteristics or qualities—and decide just what you want to preserve in your version. Sometimes you can poke fun at a work by imitating it but at the same time exaggerating its style or prominent characteristics, or placing it in an inappropriate context; that kind of imitation, a kind that is still popular, is called a parody. The list of qualities and the model might be much the same for a serious imitation and for a parody, only in a parody you can exaggerate a little—or a lot.

To parody Poe's "The Raven," we may decide to stick closely to Poe's rhythms, his use of repetitive mood words or of several words that mean almost the same thing, and his frequent use of alliteration (words that begin with the same sound). We might want to exaggerate the characteristic stylistic devices as C. L. Edson does in his parody; it begins,

Once upon a midnight dreary, eerie, scary,
I was wary, I was weary, full of worry, thinking of my lost Lenore,
Of my cheery, airy, faerie, fierie Dearie—(Nothing more).

We may choose another kind of parody, keeping the form as close as possible to the original but applying it to a ludicrously unsuitable subject, as Pope does in his mock epic "The Rape of the Lock," where he uses pretentious epic machinery in a poem about cutting off a lock of a woman's hair. In writing such a parody of "The Raven," we will keep the rhythm closer to Poe's and the subject matter less close. How about this?

> Once upon a midday murky, crunching on a Christmas turkey,
> And guzzling giant Jereboams of gin . . .

And maybe we could use the "Nevermore" refrain as if it were an antacid commercial.

You will have noticed that in order to write a good imitation or parody you must read and reread the original very carefully, examine it, and identify just those elements and qualities that make it a unique and recognizable text. Since you admire works you wish to imitate, such close study should be a pleasure. You may or may not greatly admire a work you wish to parody, but parody itself is fun to do and fun to read. In either case, you are having fun while gaining a deeper, more intimate knowledge of the nature and details of a work of literature. Moreover, such close attention to how a professional piece of writing is put together and how its parts function together along with your effort to reproduce the effects in your own imitation or parody are sure to help you understand the process of writing and so help you improve your own ability to write about literature knowledgeably.

## RE-CREATION AND REPLY

Sometimes a poem will seem so partial, biased, or unrealistic that it will stimulate a response that is neither an imitation nor a parody, but a retort. While Christopher Marlowe's "shepherd" in "The Passionate Shepherd to His Love" paints an idyllic scene of love in the country for his beloved and pleads, "Come live with me and be my love," Sir Walter Ralegh apparently feels obliged to reply in the name of the beloved "nymph": it won't always be spring, she says in "The Nymph's Reply to the Shepherd"; we won't always be young, and, besides, I can scarcely trust myself to someone who offers me such a phony view of reality.

Ralegh's nymph confronts the invitation and the words of Marlowe's shepherd directly and almost detail for detail. You may have noticed that while retorts can often be witty, they are also serious. Usually they say not merely, "That's not how the story went," but "That's not what life is really like." Try to read literature initially with the aim of understanding it and taking it at its highest value (rather than reducing it and quibbling). Try to "hear" what it is saying; avoid imposing your own notions of reality prematurely upon a work. Open your mind to learning from the work, and let it broaden your views. Finally, read it critically as well, asking, "Is this the way things *really* are?" or, more generously, "If I were standing over there, where the poem (poet, speaker) is, would things really look that way?"

# EXPLAINING THE TEXT

## DESCRIPTION

To give an account of the form of a work or passage rather than merely a brief version of its content or plot (and a plot summary, even of a poem, is usually what we mean by "summary") you may wish to write a description. We have given a summary of Poe's "The Raven" earlier, concentrating there, as summaries tend to do, on subject and plot. A description, on the other hand, may concentrate on the form of the stanzas, the lines, the rhyme scheme, perhaps like this:

> Poe's "The Raven" is a poem of one hundred eight lines divided into eighteen six-line stanzas. If in describing the rhyme scheme you were to look just at the ends of the lines, you would notice only one or two unusual features: not only is there only one rhyme sound per stanza, lines 2, 4, 5, and 6 rhyming, but one rhyme sound is the same in all eighteen stanzas, so that there are seventy-two lines ending with the sound "ore"; in addition, the fourth and fifth lines of each stanza end with the identical word, and in six of the stanzas that word is "door" and in four others "Lenore." There is even more repetition: the last line of six of the first seven stanzas ends with the words "nothing more," and the last eleven stanzas end with the word "Nevermore." The rhyming lines—other than the last, which is very short—in each stanza are fifteen syllables long, the unrhymed lines sixteen. The longer lines give the effect of shorter ones, however, and add still further to the frequency of repeated sounds, for the first half of each opening line rhymes with the second half of the line, and so do the halves of line 3. There is still more: the first half of line 4 rhymes with the halves of line 3 (in the first stanza the rhymes are "dreary"/"weary" and "napping"/"tapping"/"rapping"). So at least nine words in each eight-line stanza are involved in the regular rhyme scheme, and in many stanzas there are added instances of rhyme or repetition. As if this were not enough, all the half-line rhymes are rich feminine rhymes, where both the accented and the following unaccented syllables rhyme— "drēarÿ"/"wēarÿ."

This is a detailed and complicated description of a complex and unusual pattern of rhymes. Though there are many other elements of the poem we could describe—images and symbols, for example—the unusual and dominant element in this poem is clearly the intricate and insistent pattern of rhyme and repetition. Moreover, this paragraph shows how you can describe at length, in depth, and with considerable complexity certain aspects of a work without mentioning the content at all.

# ANALYSIS

Like copying, paraphrase, and summary, a description of a work or passage rarely stands alone as a piece of writing about literature. It is, instead, a tool, a means of supporting a point or opinion. Even the description we have given above borders on analysis. To analyze is to break something down into its parts to discover what they are and, usually, how they function in and relate to the whole. The description of the rhyme scheme of "The Raven" tells you what that scheme or pattern is but says nothing about how it functions in the poem. If you were to add such an account to the description, then, you would have analyzed one aspect of the poem. In order to do so, however, you would first have to decide what, in general, the poem is about: what its *theme* is. If you defined the theme of "The Raven" as "inconsolable grief," you could then write an analytical paper suggesting how the rhyme scheme reinforces that theme. You might begin like this:

Obsessive Rhyme in "The Raven"

We all know that gloomy poem with that gloomy bird, Edgar Allan Poe's "The Raven." The time is midnight, the room is dark, the bird is black, and the poem is full of words like "dreary," "sad," "mystery," and "ghastly." We all know, too, it has a rather singsong rhythm and repeated rhymes, but we do not often stop to think how the rhymes contribute to the mood or meaning. Before we do so here, perhaps it would be a good idea to describe in detail just what that rhyme scheme is.

Then follow with the description of the rhyme scheme, and go on like this:

Of course, the most obvious way in which the rhyme scheme reinforces the theme of inconsolable loss is through the emphatic repetition of "Nevermore." Since this refrain comes at the very end of each of the last stanzas it is even more powerful in its effect.

What is not so obvious as the effect of repeating "Nevermore" is the purpose of the overall abundance and richness of rhyme. Some might say it is not abundant and rich, but excessive and cloying. These harsh critics cynically add that in a way the rhymes and repetitions are appropriate to this poem because the whole poem is excessive and cloying: grief over loss, even intense grief, does, human experience tells us, pass away. This criticism is just, however, only if we have accurately defined the theme of the poem as "inconsolable sorrow." The very insistence of the rhyme and repetition, however, suggests that we may need to adjust slightly our definition of that theme. Perhaps the poem is not about "inconsolable sorrow" in so neutral a way; maybe it would be better to say it is about obsessive grief. Then the insistent, pounding rhyme and repetition make sense (just as the closed-in dark chamber does). Obsessive repetition of words and sounds thus helps to create the meaning of the poem almost as much as the words themselves do.

# INTERPRETATION

## PRINCIPLES AND PROCEDURES

If you have been reading carefully, you may have noticed what looks like a catch: to turn description into analysis, you must relate what you are describing to the theme, the overall effect, and meaning of the text. But how do you know what the theme is? If analysis relates the part to the whole, how can you know the "whole" before you have analyzed each part? But, then, how can you analyze each part—relating it to the whole— if you don't know what that whole is?

Interpretation, or the expression of your understanding of a literary work and its meaning, involves an initial general impression that is then supported and often modified by analysis of the particulars. It involves looking at the whole, the part, the whole, the part, the whole, the part in a series of approximations and adjustments. (Note, in particular, the need to keep your mind open for modifications or changes, rather than forcing your analysis to confirm your first impressions.)

This procedure should, in turn, suggest something of the nature and even the form of the critical essay, or essay of interpretation. The essay should present the overall theme and support that generalization with close analyses of the major elements of the text (or, in some essays, an analysis of one significant element)—showing how one or more such elements as rhyme or speaker, plot or setting reinforce, define, or modify the theme of the poem. Often the conclusion of such an essay will be a fuller, more refined statement of the theme.

Both the definition of and the procedures for interpreting a work suggest that a literary text is unified, probably around a theme, a meaning, and an effect. In interpreting, you therefore keep asking of each element or detail, "How does it fit? How does it contribute to *the* theme or whole?" In most instances, especially when you are writing on shorter works, if you dig hard and deep enough, you will find a satisfactory interpretation or central theme. Even after you have done your best, however, you must hold your "reading" or interpretation as a hypothesis rather than a final truth. Your experience of reading criticism has probably already shown you that more than one reading of a literary work is possible and that no reading exhausts the meaning and totality of a work. Nonetheless, you will want to begin reading a literary text as if it were going to make a central statement and create a single effect, no matter how complex. Try as conscientiously as you can to make sense of the work, to analyze it, to show how its elements work together. In analyzing elements, you kept your initial sense of the whole as hypothesis and did not try to force evidence to fit your first impression. Here, too, you will want to hold your interpretation as a hypothesis even in its final stages, even at the end. It is, you must be sure, the fullest and best "reading" of the text you are capable of at this time, with the evidence and knowledge you have at this moment—but only that. In other words, an interpretation is "only an opinion." But just as your political and other opinions are not lightly held but are what you really feel and believe based on all you know and have experienced and all you have thought and felt, so your opinion or interpretation of a literary work should be as responsible as you can make it. Your opinions are a measure of your knowledge, intelligence, and sensibility. They should not be lightly changed, but neither should they be obstinately and inflexibly held.

## READING AND THEME MAKING

Because you need a sense of the whole text before you can analyze it, analysis and interpretation would seem to be possible only after repeated readings. Though obvious, logical, and partially true, this may not be *entirely* true. In reading, we actually anticipate theme or meaning much as we anticipate what will happen next. Often this anticipation or expectation of theme or effect begins with our first opening a book—or even before, in reading the title. A title may provide clues to give you some idea of what a poem is about. "The Raven" does not immediately imply a poem about inconsolable loss, but it introduces the main vehicle for the poem's statement, and titles such as "To His Coy Mistress," "The Passionate Shepherd to His Love," or "My Papa's Waltz" suggest situation, plot, and something of tone. Titles may of course be ironic—or misleading—and thus set the reader up for a surprise, but they almost always set our expectations in motion, providing at least some hint of the contours of possibility.

Just as we have more than one expectation of what may happen next as we read a poem, so we may have more than one expectation of what it is going to be "about" in the more general sense: as we read along we have expectations or hypotheses of meaning, and so we consciously or unconsciously try to fit together the pieces of elements of what we are reading into a pattern of significance. By the end of our first reading we should have a fairly well-defined sense of what the poem is "about," what it means, even how some of the elements have worked together to produce that meaning and effect. Indeed, isn't this the way we read when we are not reading for a class or performance? Don't most people read most poems only once? And don't we usually think we have understood what we have read? Shouldn't we be able to read a very short poem in class just once and immediately write an interpretive paper based on that first reading?

This is not to say that we cannot understand more about a work by repeated readings or that there is some virtue or purity of response in the naive first reading that is lost in closer study. Our first "reading"—"reading" in the sense of both "casting our eye over" and "interpretation"—is almost certain to be modified or refined by rereading: if nothing else, we know from the beginning what the speaker's situation is and why he is so prone to interpret a raven's song as significant, or what kind of coyness in his mistress the speaker is trying to overcome. The next time, then, we can concentrate on the speaker's state of mind, or the "logic" of the seduction argument, or how the language of the poem relates to the situation and theme. The theme or meaning is likely to be modulated by later readings, the way the elements function in defining or embodying meaning is likely to be clearer; the effect of the second reading is certain to be different from that of the first. It may be instructive to reread several times the short work we interpreted in class after a single reading, write a new interpretive essay, and see how our understanding has been changed and enriched by subsequent readings.

## OPINIONS, RIGHT AND WRONG

Just as each of our separate readings is different, so naturally one reader's fullest and "final" reading, interpretation, or opinion will differ somewhat from another's. Seldom will readers agree entirely with any full statement of the theme of a literary text. Nor is one of these interpretations entirely "right" and all the others necessarily "wrong." For no thematic summary, no analysis or interpretation, no matter how full, can exhaust the affective or intellectual significance of a major literary text. There are various approximate readings of diverse degrees of acceptability, various competent or "good" readings, not just one single "right" reading.

Anyone who has heard two accomplished musicians faithfully perform the same work, playing all the same notes, or anyone who has seen two performances of *Hamlet* will recognize how "interpretations" can be both correct and different. You might try to get hold of several recordings of one or more of Hamlet's soliloquies—by John Barrymore, Sir John Gielgud, Richard Burton, Sir Laurence Olivier, or Mel Gibson, for example—and notice how each of these actors lends to identical passages his own emphasis, pacing, tone, color, effect, and so, ultimately, his own meaning. These actors reading the identical words are, in effect, "copying." They are not paraphrasing or putting Shakespeare's Elizabethan poetry into modern American prose, not "interpreting" as we have defined it, or putting his play into their own words. If merely performing or reading the words aloud generates significant differences in interpretation, it is no wonder that when you write an interpretive essay about literature, when you give your conception of the meaning and effect of the literary text in your own words, your interpretation will differ from other interpretations, even when each of the different interpretations is competent and "correct."

Any communication, even a work of literature, is refracted—that is, interpreted and modified—by the recipient. In one sense, it is not complete until it is received, just as, in a sense, a musical score is not "music" until it is played. Philip Roth reported, not long ago, how perturbed he was by what the critics and other readers said of his first novel— that was not at all what he intended, what the novel really was, he thought at first. But then he realized that once he had had his say in the novel, it was "out there," and each reader had to understand it within the limits and range of his or her own perspectives and literary and life experiences. His novel, once in print, was no longer merely "his," and rightly so.

That different interpretations may be "correct" is not to say, with Alice's Humpty-Dumpty, that a word or a work "means just what I choose it to mean." Though there may not be one "right" reading, some readings are more appropriate and convincing than others and some readings are demonstrably wrong.

## READER AND TEXT

If it is difficult to say exactly what a piece of literature *says,* it is usually not because it is vague or meaning*less* but because it is too specific and meaning*ful* to paraphrase satis-factorily in any language other than its own. Since no two human beings are identical and no two people can inhabit the same space at the same time, no two people can see exactly the same reality from the same angle and vantage point. Most of us get around this awkward truth by saying that we see what we are "supposed" to see, a generalized, commonsense approximation of reality. We are all, in effect, like Polonius in the third act of *Hamlet,* who sees in a cloud, a camel, a weasel, a whale—whatever Hamlet tells him he sees.

Some individuals struggle to see things as fully and clearly as possible from their unique vantage point and to communicate to others their particular—even peculiar— vision. But here, too, we are individuated, for though we speak of our "common language," we each speak a unique language, made up of "dialects" that are not only regional and ethnic but also conditioned by our age group, our profession, our education, travel, reading—all our experiences. Yet if we want to express our unique vision to others who have different visions and different "languages," we have to find some medium that is both true to ourselves and understandable to others.

There is for these individuals—these writers of literature—a constant tug-of-war between the uniqueness of their individual visions and the generalizing nature of language. The battle does not always result in sheer loss, however. Often, in the very struggle to get their own perceptions into language, writers sharpen those perceptions or discover what they themselves did not know when they began to write. You have probably made similar discoveries in the process of writing a letter or an assigned paper. But writers also find that what they have written does not perfectly embody what they meant it to, just as you perhaps have found that your finished papers have been not quite as brilliant as your original idea.

"Understanding" is not a passive reception of a text, but an active reaching out from our own experiences toward the text. At least at first we need to do so by meeting the author on the ground of a common or general language and set of conventions—things that everybody "knows." The first task of the reader, therefore, is to get not to the author's intention, but to the general statement that the work itself makes—that is, its theme or thesis. After a few readings we can usually make a stab at articulating the theme of a text. What a work says in the way of a general theme, however, is not necessarily its full or ultimate meaning; otherwise we would read theme summaries and not stories. The theme is the meaning accessible to all through close reading of the text and common to all, but a literary text is not all statement. There are often cloudy areas in the text where we cannot be sure what is implication, the suggestion of the text, and what is our inference, or interpretation, of the text. What is the speaker of "The Raven" doing, for example, in the opening lines of that poem? He is reading, or, rather, pondering over "many a quaint and curious volume of forgotten lore." Now why should a man so stricken by the death of a loved one be reading? The poem does not say, but we might infer from our own experience that he is trying to forget, to distract his attention from his loss, and indeed the final "message" of the raven is that he shall nevermore be able to escape his grief. But why is he reading quaint old educational or instructional books instead of entertaining ones, if he is merely seeking to distract himself? No wonder he's weary. Words like "quaint," "curious," "forgotten," and "lore" in the context of his obsessive grief may suggest to you, especially if other macabre works of Poe's are part of your past reading experience, that he has been studying black magic, some way of raising or communicating with the dead Lenore. The black carrion-eating bird enters then to tell him there is no way, not even by magic; he will see Lenore nevermore. Poe's poem does not *say* what the volumes are about. Many readers, however, will find this inference convincing. If accepted, this changes the theme of the poem to some degree. Still, it need not be accepted; the poem does not, will never, say what those volumes contain. The meaning of the poem for the reader who is convinced will differ from the meaning for the reader who is not convinced.

The full meaning of a work for you is not only in its stated theme, one that everyone can agree on, but in the meaning you derive by bringing together that generalized theme, the precise language of the text, and your own response and experiences—including reading experience—and imagination. That "meaning" is not the total meaning of the work, not what the author originally perceived and "meant to say"; it is the vision of the author as embodied in the work *and re-viewed from your own angle of vision.*

Your role in producing a meaning from the text does not free you from paying very close attention to the precise language of the text, the words and their meanings, their order, the syntax of the sentences, and even such mundane details as punctuation. You cannot impose a meaning on the text, no matter how sincerely and intensely you feel it, in defiance of the rules of grammar and the nature of the language.

Still, the reader has to be an artist too, trying to experience the reality of the work as the author experienced reality, and with the same reverence and sense of responsibility for the original. To write about literature you need to embody your reading experience—or interpretation—of the work in language. Alas, writing about literature, using words about words, is not as easy as it sounds at first. But it is more exciting, giving you a chance to see with another's eyes, to explore another's perceptions or experiences, and to explore and more fully understand your own in the process, thus expanding the horizon of your experience, perception, consciousness.

When some rich works of literature, like *Hamlet,* seem to have more than one meaning or no entirely satisfactory meaning or universally agreed-upon single theme, it is not that they are not saying something, and saying something very specific, but that what they are saying is too specific and complex and profound (and true, perhaps) to be generalized or paraphrased in a few dozen words. The literary work is meaning*ful*—that is, full of meaning or meanings; but it is the reader who produces each particular meaning from the work, using the work itself, the language of the community and of the work, and his or her own language, experience, and imagination.

As a reader trying to understand the unique perception and language of the author, you should try to translate the text as best you can into terms you can understand. Do your best to approach the text with an open, receptive mind.

An interpretation, then, is not a clarification of what the writer "was trying to say"; it is a process that itself says, in effect, "The way I am trying to understand this work is. . . ."

# CRITICAL APPROACHES

The way you read and talk about a literary text depends on your assumptions, usually unconscious or unarticulated, about what a work of literature is, what it is supposed to do, and what makes it good. Literary critics, however, often define their assumptions about literature and the proper way to go about reading it and writing about it. The results are critical theories or critical approaches. Looking at a few of these, you may recognize some of your own assumptions, see new and exciting ways of looking at literature, or, at the very least, become aware of your own critical premises and prejudices.

## OBJECTIVISM

We might begin by asking just what, literally, a work of literature is. There are critics who think of it as a fixed and freestanding object made up of words on a page. It is "freestanding" in that it has no connection, on the one hand, with the author or his or her intention or life or, on the other hand, with the historical or cultural context of the author or the reader. These we might call objectivist critics; they believe that a text is an independent object, free from the subjectivity of author and reader.

### FORMALISM

Among the objectivist critics are the formalists. One common formalist conception is that a work is autotelic, that is, complete in itself, written for its own sake, and unified by its form—that which makes it a work of art. Content is less important than form. Literature involves a special kind of language that sets it apart from merely utilitarian writing; the formal strategies that organize and animate that language elevate literature and give it a special, almost religious character.

NEW CRITICISM One group of formalists, the New Critics, dominated literary criticism in the middle of the twentieth century, and New Criticism remains an important influence today. Their critical practice is to demonstrate formal unity by showing how every part of a work—every word, every image, every element—contributes to a central unifying theme. Because the details of the work relate to a theme or idea, they are generally treated as *symbolic,* as figurative or allegorical, representations of that central, unifying idea. The kind of unity thus demonstrated, in which every part is related to the whole and the whole is reflected in each part, is called organic unity. The New Critics differentiate organic unity from (and much prefer it to) mechanical unity, the external, preconceived structure or rules that do not arise from the individuality of the work, but from the type or genre. New Critical analysis, or explication of the text, is especially effective in the critical reading of lyric poetry. It has become so universally accepted as *at least the first step* in the understanding of literature that it is almost everywhere the critical approach taught in introductory literature courses, even in those that do not share its fundamental autotelic assumption. It is, indeed, the basic approach of the "Understanding the Text" sections in *The Norton Introduction to Poetry.*

The New Critics' focus on theme or meaning as well as form signifies that for them literature is referential: it points to something outside itself, things in the real, external world or in human experience—a tree, a sound wave, love. The New Critics, in general, do not question the reality of the phenomenal world or the ability of language to represent it.

## STRUCTURALISM

For many formalists, however, literature is not referential. The words in a story, poem, or play no longer point outward to the things, people, or world they are supposed to denote, as they might do in ordinary, "nonliterary" discourse, but point inward to each other and to the formal system they create. The critic still focuses on interrelatedness but is less concerned with "meaning"; words are treated not as referential symbols, but as natural numbers; poetry is likened to mathematics or music.

Structuralism focuses on the text as an independent aesthetic object and also tends to detach literature from history and social and political implications, but (much more than New Criticism) structuralism emphasizes systematic analysis, aspiring to make literary criticism a branch of scientific inquiry. It sees every literary work as a separate "system" and seeks to discover the principles or general laws that govern the interaction of parts within the system. Structuralism has its roots in modern linguistic theory; it looks especially to the work of Ferdinand de Saussure (1857–1913), who founded structural linguistics early in the twentieth century. Structuralism in criticism did not, however, flourish internationally until the early 1960s, when a combination of space-age preoccupation with science and cold-war fear of implication led to a view of literature as intellectually challenging yet socially and politically noncontroversial.

Although based on linguistic theory, structuralism tries to extend newly discovered principles about language to other aspects of literature. Drawing on the semiotic principle that a vast and intricate system of signs enables human beings to communicate through language, structuralism asks readers to consider the way that other kinds of sign systems within a work—structures all—combine to produce meaning. Language and its characteristic habits are important to structuralists, but it is not enough to consider any single part of a work or any single kind of sign—linguistic or otherwise—within it. Structuralism aspires to elucidate the meaning of a work of literature by seeing the way all of its parts work together toward some wholeness of structure and meaning. Like formalism, it shows little interest in the creative process as such and has virtually no interest in authors, their intentions, or the circumstances or contexts of creation. It takes texts to represent interactions of words and ideas apart from individual human identities or sociopolitical commitments, and concentrates its analytical attention on what can be said about how different elements or processes in a text operate in relation to one another. Structuralists are less likely than formalists to concentrate their attention on some single all-explaining characteristic of literature (such as Cleanth Brooks's "tension" or William Empson's "ambiguity"), and its practitioners are less likely to privilege a particular text for its revelation or authority. Structuralism may be seen as a sort of secular equivalent of formalism; it is less mysterious and authoritarian, and it has both the advantage and disadvantage of seeming to be less arbitrary and more "objectively" reliable. But in some ways it seems to promise too much for method and "objectivity," and by the 1970s its insights into the ways of language were already beginning to be used against it to attack the certitudes it appeared to promise and to emphasize instead the uncertainties and indeterminateness of texts.

## POST-STRUCTURALISM

Post-Structuralism is the broad term used to designate the several directions of literary criticism that, while depending crucially on the insights of science-based theory, attack the very idea that any kind of certitude can exist about the meaning, understandability, or sharability of texts. Post-structuralists, disturbed at the optimism of positivist philosophy in suggesting that the world is knowable and explainable, ultimately doubt the possibility of certainties of any kind, and they see language as especially elusive and unfaithful. Much of post-structuralism involves undoing; the best-known variety of post-structuralism, deconstruction, suggests as much in its very name.

DECONSTRUCTION  Deconstruction takes the observations of structuralism to their logical conclusion, arguing that the elaborate web of semiotic differentiations created by the principle of difference in language means that no text can ultimately have any stable, definite, or discoverable meaning.

For the deconstructionist, language consists just in black marks on a page that repeat or differ from each other and the reader is the only author, one who can find whatever can be found in, or be made to appear in, those detached, isolated marks. The deconstructionist conception of literature is thus very broad—almost any writing will do. While this may seem "subjective" in that the critical reader has great freedom, it is the object—the black marks on the blank page—that is the sole subject/object of intention/attention.

As practiced by its most famous proponent, the French philosopher Jacques Derrida (b. 1930), deconstruction endeavors to trace the way texts challenge or cancel their explicit meanings and wrestle themselves into stasis or neutrality. Many deconstructionists have strong radical political commitments (it is possible to argue that the radical counterculture of the 1960s and especially the political events in Paris of 1968 are the crucial context for understanding the origins of deconstructionism), but the retreat from meaning and denial of clear signification that characterize deconstruction also have affinities with formalism and structuralism, particularly as deconstruction is practiced by American critics. Rather than emphasizing form over content, however, deconstruction tries to deny the possibility of content and places value instead on verbal play as a characteristic outlet of a fertile, adroit, and supple human mind. Like structuralism, it lives almost completely in a self-referential verbal world rather than a world in which texts represent some larger or other reality, but unlike structuralism it denies that the verbal world adds up to anything coherent, consistent, or meaningful in itself. Deconstruction also influences other varieties of post-structuralism with different kinds of interests in history and ideology. Michel Foucault (1926–1984), Julia Kristeva (b. 1941), and Jacques Lacan (1901–1981), though their disciplinary interests are in social history, feminist philosophy, and psychoanalysis, respectively, all come out of deconstructionist assumptions and carry the indeterminacies of post-structuralism (and of post-modernism more generally) into kinds of literary criticism with interests fundamentally different from those of structuralism.

# SUBJECTIVISM

Opposed to objectivism is what might be called subjectivism. This loose term can be used to embrace many forms of psychological and self-, subject-, or reader-centered criticism.

## PSYCHOLOGICAL CRITICISM

The assumption is that literature is the expression of the author's psyche, often his or her unconscious, and, like dreams, needs to be interpreted.

FREUDIAN CRITICISM The dominant school is the Freudian, based on the work of Sigmund Freud (1856–1939). Many of its practitioners assert that the meaning of a literary work does not lie on its surface but in the psyche (some would even claim, in the neuroses) of the author. The value of the work, then, lies in how powerfully and convincingly it expresses the author's unconscious and how universal the psychological elements are. A well-known Freudian reading of *Hamlet,* for example, insists that Hamlet is upset because he is jealous of his uncle, for Hamlet, *like all male children,* unconsciously wants to go to bed with his mother. The ghost may then be a manifestation of Hamlet's unconscious desire; his madness is not just acting, but is the result of this frustrated desire; his cruelly gross mistreatment of Ophelia is a deflection of his disgust at his mother's being "lecherous," "unfaithful" in her love for him. A Freudian critic may assume then that Hamlet is suffering from an Oedipus complex, a Freudian term for the desire of the son for his mother, its name derived from the Greek myth that is the basis of Sophocles' play *Oedipus the King.*

Some Freudian critics stress the author's psyche and find *Hamlet* the expression of Shakespeare's own Oedipus complex. Others stress the effect on the reader, the work having a purgative or cleansing effect by expressing in socially and morally acceptable ways unconscious desires that would be unacceptable if expressed directly.

LACANIAN CRITICISM As it absorbs the indeterminacies of post-structuralism under the influence of thinkers such as Jacques Lacan, psychological criticism has become increasingly complex. Accepting the Oedipal paradigm and the unconscious as the realm of repressed desire, Lacanian psychology (and the critical theory that comes from that psychology) conflates these concepts with the deconstructionist emphasis on language as expressing absence—you use a word to represent an absent object but you cannot make it present. The word, then, like the unconscious desire, is something that cannot be fulfilled. Language, reaching out with one word after the other, striving for but never reaching its object, is the arena of desire.

JUNGIAN CRITICISM Just as a Freudian assumes that human psyches have similar histories and structures, the Jungian critic assumes that we all share a universal or collective unconscious (as well as having a racial and individual unconscious). According to Carl Gustav Jung (1875–1961) and his followers, in the collective and in our individual unconscious are universal images, patterns, and forms of human experiences, or arche-types. These archetypes can never be known directly, but they surface in art in an imperfect, shadowy way, taking the form of archetypal images—the snake with its tail in its mouth, rebirth, mother, the double, the descent into Hell. To get a sense of the archetype beneath the archetypal images or shadows in the characters, plot, language, and images of a work, to bring these together in an archetypal interpretation, is the function of the Jungian critic. Just as, for the Freudian literary critic, the "family romance," out of which the Oedipus story comes, is central, so the Jungian assumes there is a monomyth that underlies the archetypal images and gives a clue as to how they can be related to suggest the archetypes themselves. The myth is that of the quest. In that all-encompassing myth the hero struggles to free himself (the gender of the pro-noun is specific and significant) from the Great Mother, to become a separate, self-sufficient being who is then rewarded by union with his ideal other, the feminine anima.

## PHENOMENOLOGICAL CRITICISM

Another kind of subjectivist criticism is phenomenology, especially as it is practiced by critics of consciousness. They consider all the writings of an author—shopping lists and letters as well as lyrics—as the expression of his or her mind-set or way of looking at reality. Such a critic looks for repeated or obsessive use of certain key words, incidents, patterns, and angles of vision, and, using these, maps out thereby the inner world of the writer.

## READER-RESPONSE CRITICISM

The formalists focus on the text. Though the psychological critics focus most frequently on the author, their assumptions about the similarity or universality of the human mind make them consider as well the role of the reader. There is another approach that, though not psychological in the usual sense of the word, also focuses on the reception of the text, on reader response. The conventional notion of reading is that a writer or speaker has an "idea," encodes it—that is, turns it into words—and the reader or listener decodes it, deriving, when successful, the writer/speaker's "idea." What the reader-response critic assumes, however, is that such equivalency between sender and receiver is impossible. The literary work, therefore, does *not* exist on the page; that is only the text. The text becomes a work only when it is read, just as a score becomes music only when it is played. And just as every musical performance, even of exactly the same notes, is somewhat different, a different "interpretation," so no two readers read or perform exactly the same work from identical texts. Besides the individual differences of readers, space is made for different readings or interpretations by gaps in a text itself. Some of these are temporary—such as the withholding of the name of the murderer until the end—and are closed by the text sooner or later, though each reader will in the meantime fill them differently. But others are permanent and can never be filled with certainty; the result is a degree of uncertainty or indeterminacy in the text.

The reader-response critic's focus on the reading process is especially useful in the study of long works such as novels. The critic follows the text sequentially, observing what expectations are being aroused, how they are being satisfied or modified, how the reader recapitulates "evidence" from the portion of the text he has read to project for-ward a configuration, a tentative assumption of what the work as a whole will be and mean once it is done. The expectations are in part built by the text and in part by the repertoire of the reader—that is, the reader's reading experience plus his or her social and cultural knowledge.

# HISTORICAL CRITICISM

## DIALOGISM

Another critical approach that gives a significant role to the reader and is particularly useful for long fiction is dialogism, largely identified with the work of Mikhail Bakhtin (1895–1975). The dialogic critic bases the study of language and literature on the individual utterance, taking into account the specific time, the place, the speaker, and the listener or reader. Such critics thus see language as a continuous dialogue, each utterance being a reply to what has gone before. Even thought, which they define as inner speech, is a dialogue between utterances that you have taken in. Even your own language (and thus thought) is itself dialogic, for it is made up of the dialogue in which you are engaged, that which you have heard from parents and peers, teachers and television, all kinds of social and professional discourse and reading. Indeed, you speak many "languages"—those of your ethnic, social, economic, national, professional, gender, and other identities. Your individual language consists in the combination of those languages. The literary form in which the dialogic is most interesting, complex, and significant is the novel, for there you have the languages not only of the characters (as you do in drama), but also that of a mediator or narrator and passages of description or analysis or information that seem to come from other voices—newspapers, whaling manuals, legal cases, and so on. Because the world is growing more interrelated and we have multiple voices rather than one dominant voice or language, the novel has become the most appropriate form for the representation of that world.

Because the dialogic sees utterances, including literary utterances or works, as specific to a time and place, one of its dimensions, unlike formalist, structuralist, or psychological criticism, is *historical*. Nineteenth-century historical criticism took the obvious fact that a work is created in a specific historical and cultural context and that the author is a part of that context in order to treat literature as a product of the culture. Formalists and others emphasizing the aesthetic value of literature saw this as reducing the literary work to the status of a mere historical document and the abandonment of literary study to history. The dialogic critic sees the work in relation to its host context, a part of the dialogue of the culture. The work in turn helps to create the context for other utterances, literary and otherwise. Some consider dialogic criticism a form of sociological criticism.

## SOCIOLOGICAL CRITICISM

More recently, as scientists from psychology to physics recognized the role of the perceiver in perception, historians realized that they were not only discovering and looking at facts, but were finding what they were looking for, selecting facts to fit preconceived views or interpretations. Literary historians or historical critics began to see literature not as a mere passive product of "history," but a contributor and even creator of history. An early form of this kind of historicism was sociological criticism, in which literature is seen as one aspect of the larger processes of history, especially those processes involving people acting in social groups or as members of social institutions or movements. Much sociological criticism uses literary texts to illustrate social attitudes and tendencies—and, therefore, has been strongly resisted by formalists, structuralists, and other "objectivist" critics as not being properly literary—but sociological criticism also attempts to relate what happens in texts to social events and patterns, and is as concerned about the effects of texts on human events as about the effects of historical events on texts. Sociological criticism assumes that the most significant aspects of human beings are social and that the most important functions of literature thus involve the way that literature both portrays and influences human interactions. Much sociological criticism centers its attention on contemporary life and texts, seeking to affect both societal directions and literary ones in the present, but some sociological criticism is historical, concerned with differences in different times and places, and anxious to interpret directions of literature in terms of historical emphases and patterns.

## MARXIST CRITICISM

The most insistent and vigorous historicism through most of the twentieth century has been Marxism, based on the work of Karl Marx (1818–1883). Marxist criticism, like other historical critical methods in the nineteenth century, treated literature as a passive product of the culture, specifically of the economic aspect, and, therefore, of class warfare. Economics, the underlying cause of history, was thus the *base,* and culture, including literature and the other arts, the *superstructure.* Viewed from the Marxist perspective, the literary works of a period would, then, reveal the state of the struggle between classes in the historical place and moment.

Marxist critics, however, early on recognized the role of perception. They insisted that all use of language, including literary and critical language, is ideological—that is, that it derives from and expresses preconceived ideas, particularly economic or class values. Criticism is thus not just the product of the culture but part of the discourse or "conversation" that we call history. Formalism and even the extreme apolitical position of aestheticism, "art for art's sake," by placing art in a realm above the grubbiness of everyday life—above such mundane things as politics and money—removes art from having any importance in that life. According to Marxists, this "bourgeois mystification of art" tends to support the class in power. Marxism has traditionally been sensitive to and articulate about power politics in both life and literature, and both its social and literary analyses have often been based on an explicit or implicit political agenda, though many Marxist critics are motivated more by theoretical than practical aims. In recent years, especially in the wake of post-structuralism and the psychoanalytical criticism of the 1970s and 1980s, Marxist criticism has become increasingly theoretical and less doctrinaire politically. Critics such as Raymond Williams, Fredric Jameson, Terry Eagleton, Pierre Macherey, Walter Benjamin, and Louis Althusser have gained wide audiences among readers with a variety of political and literary commitments. Over the course of the century, it has been Marxism that has most often and most consistently raised referential and historical issues about literature, and those readers who have been interested in the interactive relationship between literature and life have most often turned for their guidance on such issues to Marxist analysts, whether or not they share their philosophical or political assumptions. In the past decade, however, two other critical schools with strong commitments to historical and cultural issues have become very powerful intellectually and have attracted many practitioners and adherents. These two, feminism and new historicism, have (along with Marxism and, in its way, dialogism) turned critical attention powerfully toward historical and representational issues, and since the mid-1980s they have set the dominant directions in literary criticism.

## FEMINIST CRITICISM

Like Marxist criticism, feminist criticism derives from firm political and ideological commitments and insists that literature both reflects and influences human behavior in the larger world. Feminist criticism often, too, has practical and political aims. Strongly conscious that most of recorded history has given grossly disproportionate attention to the interests, thoughts, and actions of men, feminist thought endeavors both to extend contemporary attention to distinctively female concerns, ideas, and accomplishments and to recover the largely unrecorded and unknown history of women in earlier times. Not all directions of feminist criticism are historical; feminism has, in fact, taken many different directions and forms in recent years, and it has many different concerns. French feminist criticism, for example, has been deeply influenced by psychoanalysis, especially Lacanian psychoanalysis, and by French post-structuralist emphasis on language. Beyond their common aim of explicating and furthering specifically female interests, feminist critics may differ substantially in their assumptions and emphases. Like Marxism, feminism draws creatively on various other approaches and theories for its several methodologies. The most common historical directions of American feminism in particular involve the recovery of neglected or forgotten texts written by women in earlier times, the redrawing of literary values to include forms of writing (letters and autobiography, for example) that women were able to create when more public and accepted forms were denied to them, the discovery of the roles (positive and negative) that reading played in the lives and consciousnesses of women when they were unable to pursue more "active" and "public" courses, and the sorting out of cultural values implicit in the way women are represented in the texts of particular times and places.

## NEW HISTORICISM

New historicism has less obvious ideological commitments than Marxism or feminism, but it shares their interest in the investigation of how power is distributed and used in different cultures. Drawing on the insights of modern anthropology (and especially on the work of Clifford Geertz), new historicism wishes to isolate the fundamental values in texts and cultures, and it regards texts both as evidence of basic cultural patterns and as forces in cultural and social change. Many of the most influential practitioners of the new historicism come out of the ranks of Marxism and feminism, and new historicists are usually knowledgeable about most varieties of literary theory. Like Marxists and feminists, they are anxious to uncover the ideological commitments in texts, and they care deeply about historical and cultural difference and the way texts represent it. But personal commitments and specific political agendas usually are less important—at least explicitly—to new historicists, and one of the main contentions between feminists and new historicists—or between Marxists and new historicists—involves disagreement about the role that one's own politics should play in the practice of criticism. Many observers regard new historicism as politically to the left in its analysis of traditional cultural values; but critics on the left are suspicious of new historicism, especially of its reluctance to state its premises openly, and they generally regard its assumptions as conservative. Whatever its fundamental political commitments, however (or whether its commitments can be fairly described as having a consistent and specifiable bias), new historicism is far more interested than any other literary approach in social groups generally ignored by literary historians, and it refuses to privilege "literature" over other printed, oral, or material texts. "Popular literature" often gets major attention in the work of new historicists, who see all texts in a culture as somehow expressive of its values and directions, and thus as equally useful in determining the larger intellectual, epistemological, and ethical system of which any text is a part. Texts here are thus seen as less specifically individual and distinctive than in most objectivist criticisms, and although new historicists are sometimes interested in the psychology of authors or readers their main concern is with the prevailing tendencies shared across a culture and thus shared across all kinds of texts, whatever their class status, literary value, or political aim.

# PLURALISM

These classifications are not pigeonholes, and you will notice that many of the approaches overlap: many feminists, especially French feminist critics, are Lacanian or post-structuralist as well, while British feminists often lean toward sociological, especially Marxist, criticism; dialogic critics accept many of the starting points and methods of reader-response and sociological critics, and so on. These crossovers or combinations are generally enriching; they cause problems only when the critic seems to be operating out of contradictory assumptions.

There is a lively debate among critics and theorists at present involving the question of whether readers should bring together the insights and methods of different schools (practitioners of the mixing of methods are usually called pluralists) or whether they should commit themselves wholeheartedly to a single system. Pluralists contend that they make use of promising insights or methods wherever they find them and argue that putting together the values of different approaches leads to a fairer and more balanced view of texts and their uses. Opponents—those who insist on a consistency of ideological commitment—argue that pluralists are simply unwilling to state or admit their real commitments, and that any mixing of methods leads to confusion, uncertainty, and inconsistency rather than fairness. Readers, conscious or not of their assumptions and their methods, make this basic choice—to follow one lead or many—and the kind of reading they do and the conclusions they come to depend not only on this basic choice, but many others suggested by the dominant strands of recent criticism that have been described here. Not all critics are aware of their assumptions, methodologies, or values, and some would even deny that they begin with any particular assumptions or biases. But for readers newly learning to practice literary criticism, it is often useful for them to sort out their own beliefs carefully and see exactly what kind of difference it makes in the way they read literature and ask questions of it.

# FURTHER READING ON CRITICAL APPROACHES

For good introductions to the issues discussed here, see the following books from which we have drawn in our discussion and definitions:

Robert Alter, *The Pleasures of Reading: Thinking about Literature in an Ideological Age,* New York, 1989
Jonathan Culler, *The Pursuit of Signs,* London, 1981
Jonathan Culler, *On Deconstruction,* London, 1983
Robert Con Davis and Ronald Schleifer, *Contemporary Literary Criticism,* 2d ed., New York, 1989
Mary Eagleton (ed.), *Feminist Literary Theory: A Reader,* Oxford, 1986
Terry Eagleton, *Literary Theory: An Introduction,* Minneapolis, 1983
Michael Grodon and Martin Kreiswirth, *The Johns-Hopkins Guide to Literary Theory and Criticism,* Baltimore, 1994
Nannerl Keohane, Michelle Z. Rosaldo, and Barbara C. Gelpi (eds.), *Feminist Theory: A Critique of Ideology,* Chicago, 1982
Dominick LaCapra, *History and Criticism,* Ithaca, New York, 1985
Vincent B. Leitch, *American Literary Criticism from the 30s to the 80s,* New York, 1988
Frank Lentricchia, *After the New Criticism,* Chicago, 1980

Frank Lentricchia and Thomas McLaughlin (eds.), *Critical Terms for Literary Study*, Chicago, 1990

Richard Macksey and Eugenio Donato (eds.), *The Structuralist Controversy: The Languages of Criticism and the Sciences of Man*, Baltimore, 1972

Toril Moi, *Sexual-Textual Politics*, New York, 1985

Jean Piaget (translated by Chanihan Maschler), *Structuralism*, New York, 1970

Raman Selden and Peter Widdowson, *A Reader's Guide to Contemporary Literary Theory*, Lexington, Kentucky, 1993

Tzvetan Todorov, *Mikhail Bakhtin: The Dialogic Principle*, Minneapolis, 1984

# DECIDING WHAT TO WRITE ABOUT

## HAVING SOMETHING TO SAY

Deciding what to write about—what approach to use, which questions to ask—seems like the first step in the process of writing a paper about a work of poetry. It isn't. Before that, you have to have confidence that you have something to say. If you are a beginner at this kind of writing, you are likely to have deep doubts about that. Developing confidence is not, at first, easy. You may feel as if you can *never* begin and want to put off the paper forever, or you may want to plunge in fast and get it over with. Either of these approaches, though common and tempting, is a mistake: the best way is to begin preparing for the paper as soon as possible—the moment you know you have one to write—but not to hurry into the writing itself.

The first step is to get close enough to the work to feel comfortable with it. Before you can tell anyone else about what you have read—and writing about poetry is just another form of talking about poetry, although a more formal and organized one—you need to "know" the work, to have a sure sense of what the work itself is like, how its parts function, what ideas it expresses, how it creates particular effects, and what your responses are. And the only way you will get to know the work is to spend time with it, reading it carefully and thoughtfully and turning it over in your mind. There is no substitute for reading, several times and with care, the work you are going to write about *before* you pick up a pen or sit at the keyboard. And let your reading be of the *work itself,* not of something *about* that work, at least at first; later, your instructor may steer you to background materials or to critical readings about the work, but at first you should encounter the work alone and become aware of your own responses to it.

Begin, then, by reading, several times, the work you are going to write about. The first time, read it straight through at one sitting: read slowly, pausing at its natural divisions—sections, stanzas, sentences, even at each line break—to consider how you are responding to the work. Later, when your knowledge of the work is more nearly complete and when you have the "feel" of the whole, you can compare your early responses with your more considered thoughts, in effect "correcting" your first impressions in whatever way seems necessary on the basis of new and better knowledge. But if you are noncommittal at first, refusing to notice what you think and feel, you will have nothing to correct, and you may cut yourself off from the most direct routes of response. Feelings are not always reliable—about literature any more than about people—but they are always the first point of contact with a literary work: you feel before you think. Try to start with your mind open, as if it were a blank sheet of paper ready to receive an impression from what you read.

When you have finished a first reading, think about your first impressions. Think about how the work began, how it gained your interest, how it generated expectations, how its conflicts and issues were resolved, how it ended, how it made you feel from beginning to end. Write down any phrases or events that you remember especially vividly, anything you are afraid you might forget. Look back at any parts that puzzled you at first. Write down in one sentence what you think the poem is about. Then read it again, this time much more slowly, making notes as you go on any passages that seem especially significant and pausing over any features or passages that puzzle you. Then write a longer statement—three or four sentences—summarizing the work and suggesting more fully what it seems to be about. Try to write the kind of summary described above on pages A7–A8. If you get stuck, try brainstorming all of your ideas about the work for fifteen minutes, and then write the summary.

Stop. Do something else for a while, something as different as possible—see a movie, do math problems, ride a bicycle, listen to music, have a meal, take a nap. Do NOT do some other reading you have been meaning to do. When you go back to the work and finish reading it for the third time—rapidly and straight through—write down in a sentence the most important thing you would want to tell someone else who was about to read it for the first time: not just whether you liked it or not, but what exactly you liked, how the whole thing seems to have worked.

*Now* you are ready to choose a topic.

## CHOOSING A TOPIC

Once you are ready to choose a topic, the chances are that you have already—quietly and unconsciously—chosen one. The clue is in the last statement you wrote. The desire to tell someone about a work of literature is a wonderful place to begin. Good papers almost always grow out of a desire to communicate. But desire is not enough—the substance (and most of the work, sentence by sentence) is still ahead of you; but desire will get you started. Chances are that what you wrote down as the one thing you most wanted to say is close to the heart of the central issue in the work you are going to write about. Your statement will become, perhaps, in somewhat revised form, your thesis.

The next step is to convert your personal feelings and desire to communicate into a sentence or two that states your purpose—into an "objective" statement about the work, a statement that will mean something to someone else. This will be your thesis. Again, you may already be further along than you realize. Look at the "summary" you wrote after your second reading. The summary will probably sound factual, objective, and general about the work; the personal statement you wrote after the third reading will be more emotional, subjective, and particular about some aspect of the work. Combining the two successfully is the key to a good paper: what you need to do is to write persuasively an elaboration and explanation of the last statement so that your reader comes to share the "objective" view of the whole work that your summary expresses. The summary you have written will, in short, be implicit in the whole essay; your total essay will suggest to your reader the wholeness of the work you are writing about, but it will do so by focusing its attention on some particular aspect of the work—on a part that leads to, or suggests, or represents the whole. What you want to do is build an essay on the basis

. statement, taking a firm hold on the handle you have found. The summary is
.t and guide: it reminds you of where you will come out. Any good topic ulti-
y leads back to the crucial perceptions involved in a summary. Ultimately, any
.d writing about literature leads to a full and resonant sense of the central thrust of the
work, but the most effective way to find that center is by discovering a pathway that
particularly interests you. The best writing about literature presents a clear, well-argued
thesis about a work or works and presents it from the perspective of personal, individual
perception. But the thesis should clarify the central thrust of the work, helping it to open
itself up to readers more completely and more satisfyingly.

Topics often suggest themselves after a second or third reading simply because one
feature or problem stands out so prominently that it almost demands to be talked about.
Sometimes you may be lucky: your instructor may *assign* a topic instead of asking you
to choose your own. At first glance, that may not seem like a good break: it often feels
confining to follow specific directions or to have to operate within limits and rules
prescribed by someone else. The advantage is that it may save a lot of time and prevent
floundering around. If your instructor assigns a topic, it is almost certain to be one that
will work, one that has a payoff if you approach it creatively and without resentment at
being directed so closely and precisely. It is time-consuming, even when you have
tentatively picked a topic, to think through its implications and be sure it works. And an
instructor's directions, especially if they are detailed and call attention to particular
questions or passages, may aid greatly in helping you focus on particular issues or in
leading you to evidence crucial to the topic.

If your instructor does *not* give you a topic and if no topic suggests itself to you after
you have read a particular work three or four times, you may sometimes have to settle
for the kind of topic that will—more or less—be safe for any literary work. Some topics
are almost all-purpose. You can almost always write an adequate paper analyzing
rhythm, or verse form, or imagery, or the connotations of key words. Such "fall-back"
topics are, however, best used only as last resorts, when your instincts have failed you
in a particular instance. When choice is free, a more lively and committed paper is likely
to begin from a particular insight or question, something that grabs you and makes you
want to say something, or solve a problem, or formulate a thesis. The best papers are
usually very personal in origin; even when a topic is set by the assignment, the best
papers come from a sense of having personally found an answer to a significant question.
To turn a promising idea into a good paper, however, personal responses usually need
to be supported by a considerable mass of evidence; the process often resembles the
testing of "evidence" in a laboratory or the formulation of hypotheses and arguments in
a law case. You may need to narrow your topic so that your thesis is focused and can be
supported by examples from throughout the text. If your topic is too broad, your paper
will likely become long, unwieldy, and overly general.

Here are some sample paper topics that have worked for other students. Most are
particular to individual poems, suggesting features or strategies that are unique to a
single work. But some are adaptable, or at least suggestive about how considering ele-
ments of a poem leads to a better appreciation of the whole.

1. Scene, Sequence, and Time in "Sir Patrick Spens"
2. Attitudes toward Authority in "Sir Patrick Spens"
3. Sir Patrick Spens as a Tragic Hero
4. Birth and Death Imagery in "The Death of the Ball Turret Gunner"
5. Varieties of Violence in Frost's "Range-Finding"
6. The Characterization of God in "Channel Firing"

7. The Idea of Flight in "Ode to a Nightingale"
8. Attitudes toward the Past in "Mr. Flood's Party" and "They Flee from Me"
9. Satire of Distinctive American Traits in "Boom," "Dirge," and "What the Motorcycle Said"
10. Male and Female in "Diving into the Wreck"
11. Following the Argument in "The Canonization"
12. Bestial *versus* Human in "Burning the Cat"
13. Syntax as Strategy in "[anyone lived in a pretty how town]"
14. The Power of Complex Words in Blake's "London" (or Yeats's "Byzantium")

Most poems have key words and images. All poems contain attitudes, opinions, and stances. Many take surprising turns, leading readers where they did not necessarily mean to go. The starting question for most topics is "how," and the ultimate question is "why." If you can find a topic that addresses the basic things you find interesting in a particular poem—and that takes *your* reader to a central understanding of the poem itself—you are on your way to a successful paper.

# CONSIDERING YOUR AUDIENCE

Thinking of your paper as an argument or an explanation will also help with one of the most sensitive issues in writing about literature. The issue: For whom are you writing? who is your audience? The obvious answer is, your instructor, but in an important sense, that is the wrong answer. It is wrong because, although it could literally be true that your instructor will be the only person (besides you) who will ever read your paper, your object in writing about literature is to learn to write for an audience of peers, people a lot like yourself who are sensible, educated, and need to have something (in this case a literary work) explained to them so that they will be able to understand it more fully. Picture your ideal reader as someone about your own age and with about the same educational background. Assume that the person is intelligent and has some idea of what literature is like and how it works, but that he or she has just read this particular literary work for the first time and has not yet had a chance to think about it carefully. Don't be insulting and explain the obvious, but don't assume either that your reader has noticed and considered every detail. The object is to inform and convince your reader, not to impress.

Should you, then, altogether ignore the obvious fact that it is an instructor—probably one with a master's degree or Ph.D. in literature—who is your actual reader? Not altogether: you don't want to get so carried away with speaking to people of your own age and interests that you slip into slang, or feel the need to explain what a stanza is, or leave an allusion to a rock star unexplained, and you do want to learn from the kind of advice your instructor has given in class, or from comments he or she may have made on other papers you have written. But don't become preoccupied with the idea that you are writing for someone in "authority" or someone you need to please. Most of all, don't think of yourself as writing for a captive audience, for a reader who *has* to read what you write. It is not always easy to know exactly who your audience is or how interested your readers may be, so you have to make the most of every single word. It is your job to get the reader's attention. And you will have to do it subtly, making conscious assumptions about what your reader already knows and what he or she can readily understand. The tone of your paper should be serious and straightforward and its attitude respectful toward the reader as well as toward the literary work. But its approach and vocabulary, while formal enough for academic writing, should be readily understandable by someone with your own background and reading experience. And it should be lively enough to interest someone like you. Try to imagine, as your ideal reader, the person in your class whom you most respect. Write to get, and hold, that person's serious attention. Try to communicate, try to teach.

# FROM TOPIC TO ROUGH DRAFT

Writing about poetry is very much like talking about poetry. But there is one important difference. When we talk, we organize as we go—trying to get a handle, experimenting, working toward an understanding. And the early stages of preparing a paper—the notetaking, the outlining, the rough drafts—are much like that. A "finished" paper, however, has the uncertainties and tentativeness worked out and presents an argument that moves carefully and compellingly toward a conclusion. How does one get from here to there?

Once you have decided on a topic, the process of planning is fairly straightforward, but it can be time-consuming and (often) frustrating. There are three basic steps in the planning process: first you gather the evidence, then you sort it into order, and finally you develop it into a convincing argument. The easiest way is to take these steps one by one.

## GATHERING EVIDENCE

The first step involves accumulating evidence that supports the statement you have decided to make about your topic (that is, your thesis) and that takes you back to the text. But before you read the text again, look over the notes you have already made in the margin of that text or on separate pieces of paper. Which of them have something to do with the topic you have now defined? Which of them say something about your main point? Which ones can you now set aside as irrelevant to your topic?

Reading over the notes you have already made is a good preparation for re-reading the work again, for this time as you read it you will be looking at it in a new and specific way, searching for all the things in it that relate to the topic you have decided on. This time you will, in effect, be flagging everything—words, phrases, structural devices, changes of tone, and so forth—that bears upon your topic. As you read—very slowly and single-mindedly, with your topic always in mind—keep your pen constantly poised to mark useful points. Be ready to say something about the points as you come upon them; it's a good idea to write down immediately any sentences that occur to you as you reread this time. Some of these sentences will turn out to be useful when you actually begin to write your paper. Some will be incorporated in your paper; but some will not:

you will find that a lot of the notes you take, like a lot of the footage shot in making a film, will end up on the cutting-room floor.

No one can tell you exactly how to take notes, but there are some general guidelines that may be useful. The notes you will need to take and how you take them will depend on the particulars of the paper you are about to write. Here are five hints toward successful notetaking.

1. Keep your topic and your thesis about your topic constantly in mind as you reread and take notes. Mark all passages in the text that bear on your topic, and for each one write on a note card a single sentence that describes how the passage relates to your topic and thesis. Add a "key" word that identifies the note at the top of the card to help you to organize the cards into clusters later in the process. Then indicate, for each passage, the specific location in the text—by line or stanza number. If you are taking notes on a computer, put page breaks between each one, so that when you print them out, there will be one note per page.

2. Keep rereading and taking notes until one of five things happens:
   a. You get too tired and lose your concentration. (If that happens, stop and then start again later, preferably the next day.)
   b. You stop finding relevant passages or perceive a noticeable drying up of your ideas. (Again, time to pause; give the work at least one more reading later when your mind is fresh and see whether the juices start anew. If they don't, you may be ready to outline and write.)
   c. You begin to find yourself annotating every single sentence or line, and the evidence all begins to run together into a single blob. (If this happens, your thesis is probably too broad. Simplify and narrow it so that you don't try to include everything. Then go back to your notetaking and discriminate more carefully between what actually is important to your thesis and what only relates at some distance.)
   d. You become impatient with your notetaking and can't wait to get started writing. (Start writing. Be prepared to go back to systematic notetaking if your ideas or your energy fades. The chances are that the prose passages you write this way will find a place in your paper, but they may not belong exactly where you think they do when you first write them down.)
   e. You find that there is insufficient evidence for your thesis, that the evidence points in another direction, or that the evidence contradicts your thesis. (Revise your topic to reflect the evidence, and begin re-reading once more.)

3. When you think you have finished your notetaking, read all your note cards over slowly, one by one, and jot down any further ideas as they occur to you, each one on a separate note card. Computer users can either read the file on screen and add notes as they wish or print out all of the notes and read through them on paper. (Sometimes it will seem as if note cards beget note cards. Too much is better than too little at the notetaking stage: you can always discard them before the final draft. Don't worry if you seem to have too many notes and too much material. But later, when you boil down to essentials, you will have to be ruthless and omit some of your favorite ideas.)

4. Transfer all of your notes to pieces of paper—or note cards—that are all the same size, one note on each. It is easier to sort them this way when you get ready to organize and outline. If you like to write notes in the margin of your text (or on the backs of envelopes, or on dinner napkins, or on shirtsleeves), systematically transfer every note to uniform sheets of paper or cards before you begin to outline. Having everything easily recorded on sortable cards that can be moved from one pile to another makes organizing

easier later, especially when you change your mind (as you will) and decide to move a point from one part of your paper to another. Index cards—either 3" × 5", if you write small and make economical notes, or 4" × 6", if you need more space—are ideal for notetaking and sorting.

5. When you think you are done taking notes (because you are out of ideas, or out of time, or getting beyond a manageable number of pieces of evidence), read through the whole pile one more time, again letting any new ideas—or ideas that take on a fresh look because you combine them in a new way—spawn new sentences.

How many times should you read a poem before you stop taking notes? There is no right answer. If you have read the work three times before settling on a topic, two more readings may do. But it could take several more. Common sense, endurance, and deadlines will all have an effect on how many rereadings you do. Let your conscience, your judgment, and your clock be your guides.

## ORGANIZING YOUR NOTES

The notes you have taken will become, in the next few hours, almost the whole content of your paper. The task remaining is to give that content the form and shape that will make it appealing and persuasive. It is not an easy task: the best content in the world isn't worth much if it isn't effectively presented. The key to the task is getting all your ideas into the right order—that is, into a sequence that will allow them to argue your thesis most persuasively.

In order to put your notes into a proper order, you will need (ironically) to get a little distance from your notes. (The key to good planning and writing—and to many other pursuits—is in knowing when to back away and get some perspective.) Set your notes aside, but not too far away. On a fresh sheet of paper or in a separate document on your computer, write all the major points you want to be sure to make. Write them randomly, as they occur to you. Now read quickly through your pack of notes and add to your list any important points you have left out. Then decide which ideas should go first, which should go second, and so on.

Putting your points in order is something of a guess at this point. You may well want to reorder them before you begin to write—or later when you are writing a first (or even later) draft. But make your best guess. The easiest way to try out an order is to take your random list and put a "1" in front of the point you will probably begin with, a "2" before the probable second point, and so on. Then copy the list, in numerical order, revising (if you need to) as you go. Do not be surprised if later you have to revise your list further. Your next task is to match up your notes (and the examples they contain) with the points on your outline. If you've added "key" words to the top of each card or file, you can make a "rough cut" according to these words.

Putting things in a particular order is a spatial problem, and by having your notes on cards or pieces of paper of a uniform size you can do much of your organizing physically. Do your sorting on a large table, or sit in the middle of the floor. Prepare a title card for each point in your outline, writing on it the point and its probable place in your paper, then line them up on the table or floor in order before you begin writing. If you're using your computer, you can use the search function to find each instance of a key word, phrase, or name, and arrange your electronic "cards" under the headings on your list by blocking and moving your "cards" to new parts of the document.

Two-thirds of this exercise is quite easy: most examples and ideas you have written down will match quite easily with a particular point. But some cards will resist classification. Some cards will seem to belong in two or more places; others will not seem to belong at all. If a card seems to belong to more than one point, put it in the pile with the lowest number (but write on it the number or numbers of other possible locations). If, for example, a card might belong in point 2 but could also belong in point 6 or 9, put it in the pile of 2's and add the phrase "maybe 6 or 9" to the card; if you don't use it in writing about point 2, move it to pile 6; if you don't use it in 6, move it to 9. Remember that you will work your way through the piles in numerical order, so that you have a safety system for notes that don't seem to belong where you first thought but that still belong somewhere in your paper. Move them to a possible later point, or put them in a special file (marked "?" or "use in revised draft") and, once you have completed a first draft on your paper, go through this file, carefully looking for places in your paper where these ideas may belong. Almost never will everything fit neatly into your first draft. If everything does seem to fit exactly as you had originally planned, you have either done an incredible job of planning and guessing about the organization of your paper, or you are forcing things into inappropriate places.

Don't be surprised if you have a large number of leftover notes—that is, ideas you haven't yet used—after you have written your first draft. You will probably find places for many of these ideas later, but some just won't fit and won't be needed for the paper you ultimately write, no matter how good the ideas are. No paper will do everything it could do. Writing a paper is a *human* project; it has limits.

Before you actually start writing, you may want to develop a more elaborate outline, incorporating your examples and including topic sentences for each paragraph, or you may wish to work from your sketchy outline and the accompanying packs of cards. Do the more detailed outline if it seems right to you, but don't delay the writing too long. You are probably ready right now, and any exercises you invent to delay writing are probably just excuses.

## DEVELOPING AN ARGUMENT

Once you have decided on your major points and assembled your evidence, you have to decide how you are going to present your argument and how you are going to present *yourself.* What you say is, of course, more important than how you say it, but your manner of presentation can make a world of difference. Putting your evidence together effectively—in a coherent and logical order so that your readers' curiosity and questions are answered systematically and fully—is half the task in developing a persuasive argument. The other half involves your choice of a voice and tone that will make readers want to read on—and make them favorably disposed toward what you say.

The tone of your paper is the basis of your relationship with your reader. "I will be just *me,*" you may say, "and write naturally." But writing is not a "natural" act, any more than swinging a tennis racket, carrying a football, or executing a pirouette. The "me" you choose to present is only one of several possible me's; you will project a certain mood, a certain attitude toward your subject, a certain confidence. How do you want your readers to feel about you and your argument? Being too positive can make your audience feel stupid and inadequate, and can turn them into defensive, resistant readers who will rebel at your every point. Friendship with your reader is better than an adversary relationship. Sounding like a nice person who is talking reasonably and sensibly is not enough if in fact you don't make sense or have nothing to say, but the purpose of the tone you choose is to make your reader receptive to your content, not hostile. The rest of the job depends on the argument itself.

It has been said that all good papers should be organized in the same way:

1. Tell 'em what you're going to tell 'em.
2. Tell 'em.
3. Tell 'em what you told 'em.

That description fits—in pretty general terms—the most common kind of organization, which includes an introduction, a body of argument, and a conclusion, but if it is followed too simplistically it can lead to a paper that sounds simple-minded. The beginning does need to introduce the subject, sort out the essential issues, and suggest what your perspective will be, and the conclusion does need to sum up what you have said in the main part of your paper, but the first paragraph shouldn't give *everything* away, nor should the final one simply repeat what is already clear. Lead into your subject clearly but with a little subtlety; arrange your main points in the most effective manner you can think of, building a logical argument and supporting your general points with clear textual evidence, concisely phrased and presented, and at the end *show how* your argument has added up—don't just *say* that it did.

There are, of course, other ways to organize than the basic Tell-3 method, but the imagination and originality that can be exercised in a straightforward Tell-3 paper are practically unlimited.

## WRITING THE FIRST DRAFT

It is now time to set pen to paper or fingers to keyboard. No one will be able to help you much for a while. The main thing is to get started right, with a clear first sentence that expresses your sense of direction and arrests the attention of your readers. (If you can't think of a good first sentence, don't pause over it too long. Write down a paraphrase of what you want it to say—something like the statement you wrote down after your third reading—and then start writing about your main points. Your "first" sentence may sometimes be the last one you will write.) And then you inch along, word by word and sentence by sentence, as you follow your outline from one paragraph to another. Keep at it. Struggle. Stare into space. Bite your pen when you feel like it. Get up and stride about the room. Scratch your head. Sharpen a pencil. Run your fingers through your hair. Groan. Snap your fingers. But keep writing.

It is often frustrating as you search for the right word or struggle to decide how the next sentence begins, but it is satisfying when you get it right. If you get stuck, try working out your ideas on a separate piece of paper or freewriting for a while inside your computer document. Sometimes, working out an idea, away from your draft, can be helpful. Stay with your draft until you're reasonably satisfied with it. Breathe a sigh of relief, and put it away until tomorrow.

# FROM ROUGH DRAFT TO COMPLETED PAPER

## REVISING

This final stage of the process is the most important of all, and it is the easiest one to mismanage. There is a world of difference between a bunch of ideas that present a decent interpretation of a work of literature and a cogent, coherent, persuasive essay that will stir your readers to a nod of agreement and shared pleasure in a moment of insight. If you haven't done good literary analysis and sorted out your insights earlier, nothing you do at this stage will help much; but if what you have done so far is satisfactory, this is the stage that can turn your paper into something special.

The important thing is not to allow yourself to be too easily satisfied. If you have struggled with earlier stages, it may be tempting to think you are finished when you have put a period to the last sentence in your first draft. It will often feel as if you are done: you may feel drained, tired of the subject, anxious to get on to other things, such as sleep or food or friends or another project. And it *is* a good idea to take a break once you've finished a draft and let what you have done settle for a few hours, preferably overnight. (The Roman poet and critic Horace suggested putting a draft aside for nine years, but most instructors won't wait that long.) Rereading it "cold" may be discouraging, though: all those sentences that felt so good when you wrote them often seem flat and stale, or even worthless, when a little time has elapsed. The biggest struggle in moving from a first draft to a second one is to keep from throwing what you have written into a wastebasket. You've spent a lot of time on this already, and with some more work you'll have a paper you can be proud of.

It may take *several* more drafts to produce your best work. Often it is tempting to cut corners—to smooth out a troublesome paragraph by obscuring the issue or by omitting the difficult point altogether instead of confronting it, or to ask a roommate or friend for help in figuring out what is wrong with a particular passage. But you will learn more in the long run—and probably do better in the short run as well—if you make yourself struggle a bit. When a particular word or phrase you have used turns out to be imprecise or misleading or ambiguous, search until you find the *right* word or phrase. (At the least put a big X in the margin so that you will come back and fix it later.) If a paragraph is incomplete or poorly organized, fill it in or reorganize it. If a transition from one point to another does not work, look again at your outline and see if another way of ordering your points would help. *Never* decide that the problem can best be solved by hoping that your reader will not notice. The satisfaction of finally solving the problem will build your confidence and sooner or later make your writing easier and better.

## REVIEWING YOUR WORK AND REVISING AGAIN

Precisely how you move from one draft to another is up to you and will depend on the ways you work best; the key is to find all the things that bother you (and that *should* bother you) and then gradually to correct them, moving toward a better paper with each succeeding draft. Here are some things to watch for.

*Thesis and central thrust:* Is it clear what your main point is? Do you state it clearly, effectively, and early? Do you make clear what the work is about? Are you fair to the spirit and emphasis of the work? Do you make clear the relationship between your thesis and the central thrust of the work? Do you explain *how* the work creates its effect rather than just asserting it?

*Organization:* Does your paper move logically from beginning to end? Does your first paragraph set up the main issue you are going to discuss and suggest the direction of your discussion? Do your paragraphs follow each other in a coherent and logical order? Does the first sentence of each paragraph accurately suggest what that paragraph will contain? Does your final paragraph draw a conclusion that follows from the body of your paper? Do you resolve the issues you say you resolve?

*Use of evidence:* Do you use enough examples? Too many? Does each example prove what you say it does? Do you explain each example fully enough? Are the examples sufficiently varied? Are any of them labored, or overexplained, or made to bear more weight than they can stand? Have you left out any examples useful to your thesis? Do you include any gratuitous ones just because you like them? Have you achieved a good balance between examples and generalizations?

*Tone:* How does your voice sound in the paper? Confident? Does it show off too much? Is it too timid or self-effacing? Do you ever sound smug? Too tentative? Too dogmatic? Would a neutral reader be put off by any of your assertions? By your way of arguing? By your choice of examples? By the language you use?

*Sentences:* Does each sentence read clearly and crisply? Have you rethought and rewritten any sentences you can't explain? Is the first sentence of your paper a strong, clear one likely to gain the interest of a neutral reader? Is the first sentence of each paragraph an especially vigorous one? Are your sentences varied enough? Do you avoid the passive voice and "there is/there are" sentences?

*Word choice:* Have you used any words whose meaning you are not sure of? In any cases in which you were not sure of what word to use, did you stay with the problem until you found the exact word? Do your metaphors and figures of speech make literal sense? Are all the idioms used correctly? Is your terminology correct? Are your key words always used to mean *exactly* the same thing? Have you avoided sounding repetitive by varying your sentences rather than using several different terms to mean precisely the same thing?

*Conciseness:* Have you eliminated all the padding you put in when you didn't think your paper would be long enough? Have you gone through your paper, sentence by sentence, to eliminate all the unnecessary words and phrases? Have you looked for sentences (or even paragraphs) that essentially repeat what you have already said, and eliminated all repetition? Have you checked for multiple examples and pared down to the best and most vivid ones? Have you gotten rid of all inflated phrasing calculated to impress readers? Have you eliminated all roundabout phrases and rewritten long, complicated, or confusing sentences into shorter, clearer ones? Are you convinced that you have trimmed every possible bit of excess and that you cannot say what you have to say any more economically?

*Punctuation and mechanics:* Have you checked the syntax in each *separate* sentence? Have you checked the spelling of any words that you are not sure of or that look funny? Have you examined each sentence separately for punctuation? Have you checked every quotation word by word against the original? Have you given proper credit for all material—written or oral—that you have borrowed from others? Have you followed the directions your instructor gave you for citations, notes, and form?

As you begin to revise, it's a good idea to look first at the larger issues (your thesis, organization, and supporting evidence) to make sure you find and solve any major problems early on. Then you're in a better position to work on your tone, sentences, choice of words, and punctuation and mechanics. In the final stages, the most effective way to revise is to read through your paper looking for one problem at a time—that is, to go through it once looking at paragraphing, another time looking at individual sentences, still another for word choice or problems of grammar. It is almost impossible to check too many things too often—although you can get so absorbed with little things that you overlook larger matters. With practice, you will learn to watch carefully for the kinds of mistakes you are most prone to. Everyone has individual weaknesses and flaws. Here are some of the most common stumbling blocks for beginning writers:

1. Haste. (Don't start too late, or finish too soon after you begin.)
2. Pretentiousness. (Don't use words you don't understand, tackle problems that are too big for you, or write sentences you can't explain; it is more important to make sense than to make a big, empty impression.)
3. Boredom. (The quickest way to bore others is to be bored yourself. If you think your paper will be a drag, you are probably right. It is hard to fake interest in something you can't get excited about; keep at it until you find a spark.)
4. Randomness. (Don't try to string together half a dozen unrelated ideas or insights and con yourself into thinking that you have written a paper.)
5. Imprecision. (Don't settle for approximation, either in words or ideas; something that is 50 percent right is also 50 percent wrong.)
6. Universalism. (Don't try to be a philosopher and make grand statements about life; stick to what is in the work you are writing about.)
7. Vagueness. (Don't settle for a general "sense" of the work you are talking about; get it detailed, get it right.)
8. Wandering. (Don't lose track of your subject or the work that you are talking about.)
9. Sloppiness. (Don't sabotage all your hard work on analysis and writing by failing to notice misspelled words, grammatical mistakes, misquotations, incorrect citations or references, or typographical errors. Little oversights make readers suspicious.)
10. Impatience. (Don't be too anxious to get done. Enjoy the experience; savor the process. Have fun watching yourself learn.)

Being flexible—being willing to rethink your ideas and reorder your argument as you go—is crucial to success in writing, especially in writing about poetry. You will find different (and better) ways to express your ideas and feelings as you struggle with revisions, and you will also find that—in the course of analyzing the work, preparing to write, writing, and rewriting—your response to the work itself will have grown and shifted somewhat. Part of the reason is that you will have become more knowledgeable as a result of the time and effort you have spent, and you will have a more subtle understanding of the work. But part of the reason will also be that the work itself will not be the same. Just as a work is a little different for every reader, it is also a little different with every successive reading by the *same* reader, and what you will be capturing in your words is some of the subtlety of the work, its capacity to produce effects that are alive and that are, therefore, always changing just slightly. Thus, you need not feel that you must say the final word about the work you are writing about, but you do want to say whatever word you have to say in the best possible way.

You can turn all this into a full-time job, of course, but you needn't. It is hard work, and at first the learning seems slow and the payoff questionable. A basketball novice watching the magic of Michael Jordan may find it hard to see the point of practicing layups, but even creative geniuses have to go through those awful moments of sitting down and putting pen to paper (and then crossing out and rewriting again and again). But that's the way you learn to make it seem easy. Art is mostly craft, and craft means methodical work.

It *will* come more easily with practice. But you needn't aspire to professional writing to take pleasure in what you accomplish. Learning to write well about literature will help you with all sorts of tasks, some of them having little to do with writing. Writing trains the mind, creates habits, teaches you procedures that will have all kinds of long-range effects that you may not immediately recognize or be able to predict. And ultimately it is very satisfying, even if it is not easy, to be able to stand back and say, "That is mine. Those are my words. I know what I'm talking about. I understand, and I can make someone else understand."

One final bit of advice: do not follow, too rigidly or too closely, anyone's advice, including ours. We have suggested some general strategies and listed some common pitfalls. But writing is a very personal experience, and you will have talents (and faults) that are a little different from anyone else's. Learn to play to your own strengths and avoid the weaknesses that you are especially prone to. Pay attention to your instructor's comments; learn from your own mistakes.

## SECONDARY SOURCES

It is always preferable to form your own opinion about a poem before consulting the opinions of others. However there are times when it is appropriate, sometimes even necessary, for you to read and then quote from commentary written by professional critics. These critiques and scholarly studies, called *secondary sources,* can very often enlarge and complement your sense and appreciation of a work, and can provide you with valuable evidence that confirms or modifies your thesis.

It is not a good idea to begin consulting secondary sources, however, until you've completed the first stage of your writing (described on page A47, "Stage One"). Once you've written the one-paragraph "promise" of what your paper is going to argue and you've taken notes from the text in support of that argument, then you are prepared to read the critical materials selectively, analytically, and intelligently.

The steps involved in writing a literary research paper are nearly identical to those involved in writing a paper based on your personal response to a work, for writing a research paper involves the same careful and deliberate process of reading and rereading, taking notes, ordering your thoughts, writing an outline, drafting, revising, and proofreading that is involved in writing a personal response. But because a research paper uses other materials in addition to the primary text (that is, the poem), you need to be even more precise and diligent in your notetaking, and you must take on the additional responsibility of fairly and accurately citing your sources.

## FINDING SOURCES

Before you can begin reading secondary sources, you must find them. The best place to find them is, of course, the library. But where do you begin? Two types of resources in particular are especially useful: the library catalog and scholarly bibliographies.

ON-LINE AND CARD CATALOGS    The library catalog will guide you to books about the author and the work, but very often the titles of potentially useful books will be too general for you to determine whether or not the book covers the topic you're writing about. If your library's catalog is on-line, use "keyword searches" to limit the number and range of books that the computer finds. For example, if you're writing about Edgar Allan Poe's "The Raven," first try a search that is limited to items that include "Poe" AND "The Raven." If there are no matches or too few, then you can broaden your search to include all books that are about Edgar Allan Poe.

Most likely, the books that you find through a catalog search will lead you to a section of the library where other books on the subject are filed. Even if you find the books you were looking for right away, you should take a moment to browse the shelves nearby. The books on either side of your source probably cover the same topic, and they may prove even more useful than the ones you sought out.

BIBLIOGRAPHIES    Scholarly bibliographies, most of which appear annually, provide comprehensive lists of scholarly books and articles published during the preceding year. In most libraries, these guides are found in the reference area (that is, they're not available for checkout), but often they are also on-line. Two bibliographies in particular—*The MLA International Bibliography* and the *Reader's Guide to Periodical Literature*—are especially useful to students of literature and the humanities. The best strategy for consulting bibliographies is to start with the most recent year and work your way backward. You will find references not only to relevant books, but also to articles published in scholarly journals. The titles of most journal articles are very specific, so you'll be able to see quickly which are most useful to you. Make sure to give yourself enough time in the library to consult journal articles; unlike books, periodicals may not be checked out on most campuses. If you don't have enough time to read these in the library, photocopy them. As you read the books and articles, check the footnotes for sources that your author, title, and word searches did not find.

USING THE INTERNET    With its innumerable links and pathways, the Internet seems at first to be the perfect resource for research work. And in fact, there are some very good resources available for students of literature. One in particular, called "The Voice of the Shuttle" (http://humanitas.ucsb.edu/), is a great starting point for students and scholars alike. The "Voice of the Shuttle" site provides links to hundreds of other sites that offer valuable and interesting information on authors, genres, specific works, contextual information, literary periods, and critical approaches. If you don't find an appropriate link in the "Voice of the Shuttle" site, you will probably want to conduct a search using one of the commonly available "search engines"—for example, Yahoo (http://www.yahoo.com/) or AltaVista (http://www.altavista.digital.com/). Using keywords such as "Poe" or "poetry" in your Internet searches will lead you to hundreds of possible matches, however, so you should try to limit your search by creating search strings that are longer than one word. As you do so, read the on-screen directions carefully to make sure that your search engine is treating the search string as a unit and not finding every mention of each individual word.

Despite the obvious benefits of the Internet, you should be cautious in your use of on-line sources for research for two reasons. First, although there are many sites that provide solid information, there are many more that provide misinformation or unsubstantiated opinion. Unlike journal articles and books, which are systematically reviewed and critiqued by other scholars and experts before being published, many Internet sources are posted without any sort of review process.[1]

Second, because the Internet and World Wide Web allow you to jump from one site to another with the click of a button and to copy whole pages of text merely by "cutting and pasting," there is a chance that you will lose your place and be unable to provide your reader with a precise citation of your source. Make sure, therefore, to carefully note the specific address of the site that you're quoting; and if the text that you're using has been taken from a printed source such as a book or magazine, note all of the particulars about that original source as well. The point of all of this is to ensure that your reader can retrace your steps and check your sources. The guide to MLA citation formats that follows (page A00) includes some examples of citations from electronic sources.

## TAKING NOTES FROM SOURCES

Taking notes from secondary sources begins with creating a "Works Cited" entry for each source you consult either in a word-processing file (one page per citation) or on an index card (a sample citation is shown below). You'll find guidelines for citing just about any research source in *The MLA Handbook for Writers of Research Papers,* but examples of some of the most common sources can be found later in this guide, starting on page A44.

Read an article all the way through before taking notes from it. During this reading, you should be evaluating the article's relevance to your chosen topic. If an article doesn't apply directly to your topic but nonetheless interests you, create a brief citation of the publication information, and write a one-sentence summary of the article's main argument. This will be useful if you find yourself altering your topic to include some of what's covered in this source.

Once you have read your potential sources and chosen a short list of those that you'll want to use in your paper, you can begin the serious work of taking notes. Taking notes from sources involves three tasks:

(1) noting publication information for your "Works Cited" page (see above); (2) creating a summary or outline (sometimes called a précis) of the critic's argument; and (3) directly quoting or summarizing a passage in your source. Creating a summary of the author's argument ensures that you've understood your source and can accurately convey its sense to your reader. Once you're confident of that, you can use quotations either to support your argument or to take issue with the author's interpretation if it challenges your own.

If you're using a computer to take notes, you will be able to mingle your summary of the author's argument with direct quotations. This works especially well if you've for-

---

1. Though you can usually rely on refereed journals for information, it's important to remember that not everything in print is "true." Cross-checking and confirming sources, as good newspaper reporters do, is always a good idea.

matted your summary in outline form: simply type the quotation along with its page reference under the appropriate heading within the outline. If you're taking notes on cards, you'll want to keep your outline separate from your quotations, and you should use only one card for each quotation. This gives you the freedom to arrange and rearrange the quotations as necessary. Make sure, however, to bind quotations from the same source together with a paper clip or rubber band and to note the author's last name somewhere on each quotation card.

Beaty, Jerome, and William H. Matchett. Poetry: From Statement to Meaning. New York: Oxford UP, 1965.

## USING SOURCES IN YOUR PAPER

Using sources in your paper means using them to provide evidence in support of your thesis or as examples of an interpretation with which you don't completely agree. Either way, you should bear in mind that as you write your paper, the sources shouldn't dominate; they are there to flesh out and verify your thesis, and they should be used as a supplement to, not a replacement for, your own interpretation. Remember, evidence without interpretation, just as in a court of law, is not convincing in itself. Unlike the practice in law, however, merely citing "authorities" or precedents is also not sufficient.

## CITING SOURCES

As you use secondary sources, either through direct quotation or summary of a critic's argument, you must signal to your reader the specific source in each case. Your instructor may have guidelines for citing sources within the body of your paper, but if not, you should follow the guidelines found in the *The MLA Handbook for Writers of Research Papers*. The following is a brief summary of the MLA's guidelines:

### IN-TEXT CITATION

- If you use the author's name to introduce the material, give only the page number in parentheses.

    *Example:*

    As Judith Fetterley says, "Emily, like Georgiana, is a man-made object . . ." (35).

- If you don't use the author's name to introduce the source, put the name and page number(s) in parentheses.

*Example:*

One critic points out that "Emily, like Georgiana, is a man-made

object . . ." (Fetterley 35).

- If you are citing another work by the same author elsewhere in the paper, use a title word before the page number(s).

*Example:*

As Judith Fetterley says, "Emily, like Georgiana, is a man-made

object . . ." (Resisting 35).

- If you don't use the author's name to introduce your source and you are citing another work by the same author, use both name and title with the page number(s).

*Example:*

One critic points out that "Emily, like Georgiana, is a man-made

object . . . " (Fetterley, Resisting 35).

THE "WORKS CITED" PAGE   In addition, every literary research paper must include a "Works Cited" page that lists all secondary sources that you have used in your paper. This list should be in alphabetical order by the author's last name. Here is a brief guide to the proper format for some of the most common sources:

*A book by one author or editor:*

Fetterley, Judith. The Resisting Reader: A Feminist Approach to American

Fiction. Bloomington: Indiana UP, 1978.

*A book by two or three authors or editors:*

Wellek, René, and Austin Warren. Theory of Literature. 3rd ed. Orlando:

Harcourt, Brace and Company, 1956.

*A book by more than three authors or editors:*

Mack, Maynard, et al., eds. The Norton Anthology of World Masterpieces. 6th

ed. Vol. 1. New York: Norton, 1992.

*Editor's Introduction to a book:*

O'Prey, Paul. Introduction. Heart of Darkness. By Joseph Conrad. New York:

Viking, 1983. 7–24.

*A translated book:*

Boccaccio, Giovanni. The Decameron. Trans. G. H. McWilliam. London: Penguin,

1972.

*Essay or any other short work in a book:*

Hass, Robert. "Listening and Making." Twentieth Century Pleasures: Prose on
        Poetry. Hopewell: Ecco, 1984. 107-33.

*Article in a reference book:*

Wihl, Gary. "Marxist Theory and Criticism." The Johns Hopkins Guide to
        Literary Theory and Criticism. Ed. Michael Groden and Martin
        Kreiswirth. Baltimore: Johns Hopkins UP, 1994.

*Article in a newspaper:*

Perlez, Jane. "Winning Literary Acclaim, a Voice of Central Europe." New
        York Times 9 Sept. 1997: C9.

*Article in a magazine:*

Fenton, James. "Becoming Marianne Moore." New York Review of Books 24 Apr.
        1997: 40-45.

*Article in a scholarly journal with continuous pagination:*

(Each *volume* of a journal includes a full year of *issues.* The page numbers of some
journals begin with "1" in the first issue and run continuously through subsequent
issues—that is, issue 1 runs from page 1 to page 323, issue 2 runs from 324 to 656,
and so forth.)

Dickey, Stephen. "Shakespeare's Mastiff Comedy." Shakespeare Quarterly 42
        (1991): 255-75.

*Article in a scholarly journal with separate pagination for each issue:*

Sosnoski, James. "The Theory Junkyard." Minnesota Review 96.41 (1996): 80-
        94.

INTERNET SOURCES   The Modern Language Association is still developing guide-
lines for the citation of sources found on the Internet. The following recommendations,
adapted from MLA guidelines, are taken from *Writing Research Papers: A Norton Guide,*
by Melissa Walker.

*World Wide Web site:*

Murphy, Brenda. "The Man Who Had All the Luck: Miller's Answer to The Master
        Builder." American Drama 6.1 (1996). http://blues.fdl.uc.edu/www/
        amdrama/ (Retrieved 9 Sept. 1997).

*Gopher site:*

Goodwin, John E. "Elements of E-Text Style." 9 Aug. 1993. Internet. gopher://
        wiretap.spies.com/Library/estyle.txt (Retrieved 15 Sept. 1997).

# A SUMMARY OF THE PROCESS

Here, briefly, is a summary, step by step, of the stages that we have suggested you move through in preparing a paper about literature.

*Stage One:* Deciding what to write about

- Read the work straight through, thoughtfully. Make notes at the end on any points that caught your attention.
- Read the work again more slowly, pausing to think through all the parts you don't understand. When you finish, write a three-or four-sentence summary.
- Read the work again, carefully but quickly. Decide what you feel most strongly about in the work, and write down the one thing you would most want to explain to a friend about how the poem works, or (if the work still puzzles you) the one question you would most like to be able to answer.
- Decide how the statement you made at the end of your third reading relates to the summary you wrote down after the second reading.
- Write a one-paragraph "promise" of what your paper is going to argue.

*Stage Two:* Planning and drafting your paper

- Read the work at least twice more, and make notes on anything that relates to your thesis.
- Read through all your notes so far, and for each write a sentence articulating how it relates to your thesis.
- Transfer all your notes to note cards of uniform size.
- Read through all your notes again, and record any new observations or ideas on additional note cards.
- Set aside your note cards for the moment, and make a brief outline of the major points you intend to make.
- Sort the note cards into piles corresponding to the major points in your outline. Sort the cards in each separate pile into the most likely order of their use in the paper.
- Make a more detailed outline (including the most significant examples) from your pile of note cards on each point.

- Reconsider your order of presentation, and make any necessary adjustments.
- Write a first draft.

*Stage Three:* Rewriting

- Go over your writing, word by word, sentence by sentence, and paragraph by paragraph, in draft after draft until your paper expresses your ideas clearly and concisely.

*Stage Four:* Final preparation

- If you have not been working on a computer, type or word-process your paper.
- Proofread carefully for errors of all kinds—spelling, typing, and so forth.
- Proofread again. Find your mistakes before someone else does.
- Congratulate yourself on a job well done.

# Glossary

Within definitions, words that are set **boldface** are themselves defined in the glossary.

**action:** an imagined event or series of events; an event may be verbal as well as physical, so that saying something or telling a story within the story may be an event.

**allegory:** as in **metaphor,** one thing (usually nonrational, abstract, religious) is implicitly spoken of in terms of something concrete, usually sensuous, but in an allegory the comparison is extended to include an entire work or large portion of a work.

**alliteration:** the repetition of initial consonant sounds through a sequence of words—for example, "While I nodded, nearly napping, . . . " from Edgar Allan Poe's "The Raven."

**allusion:** a reference—whether explicit or implicit, to history, the Bible, myth, literature, painting, music, and so on—that suggests the meaning or generalized implication of details in the poem.

**ambiguity:** the use of a word or expression to mean more than one thing.

**analogy:** a comparison based on certain resemblances between things that are otherwise unlike.

**anapestic:** a metrical form in which each foot consists of two unstressed syllables followed by a stressed one.

**archetype:** a **plot** or **character** element that recurs in cultural or cross-cultural **myths** such as "the quest" or "descent into the underworld" or "scapegoat."

**assonance:** the repetition of vowel sounds in a sequence of words with different endings—for example, "The death of the poet was kept from his poems," from W. H. Auden's "In Memory of W. B. Yeats."

**aubade:** a morning song in which the coming of dawn is either celebrated or denounced as a nuisance.

**auditor:** someone other than the reader—a **character** within the work—to whom the story or "speech" is addressed.

**authorial time:** distinct from **plot time** and **reader time,** authorial time denotes the influence that the time in which the author was writing had upon the **conception** and **style** of the text.

**ballad:** a narrative poem that is, or originally was, meant to be sung. Characterized by repetition and often by a repeated refrain (recurrent phrase or series of phrases), ballads were originally a folk creation, transmitted orally from person to person and age to age.

**ballad stanza:** a common **stanza** form, consisting of a quatrain that alternates four-beat and three-beat lines; lines 1 and 3 are unrhymed iambic tetrameter (four beats), and lines 2 and 4 are rhymed iambic trimeter (three beats).

**blank verse:** the verse form most like everyday human speech, blank verse consists of unrhymed lines in iambic pentameter. Many of Shakespeare's plays are in blank verse.

**canon:** when applied to an individual author, *canon* means the sum total of works verifiably written by that author. When used generally, it means the range of works that a consensus of scholars, teachers, and readers of a particular time and culture consider "great" or "major." This second sense of the word is a matter of much debate since the literary canon in Europe and America has long been dominated by the works of white heterosexual men. During the last thirty years, the canon in the United States has expanded considerably to include more women and writers from various ethnic and racial backgrounds.

**character:** (1) a fictional personage who acts, appears, or is referred to in a work; (2) a combination of a person's qualities, especially moral qualities, so that such terms as "good" and "bad," "strong" and "weak," often apply. *See* **nature** and **personality.**

**characterization:** the fictional or artistic presentation of a fictional personage. A term like "a good character" can, then, be ambiguous—it may mean that the personage is virtuous or that he or she is well presented regardless of his or her characteristics or moral qualities.

**colloquial diction:** a level of language in a work that approximates the speech of ordinary people.

**concrete poetry:** poetry that is shaped to look like an object. John Hollander's "A State of Nature," for example, is arranged to look like New York State. Also called **shaped verse.**

**confessional poem:** a relatively new (or recently defined) **kind** in which the speaker describes a confused, chaotic state of mind, which becomes a **metaphor** for the larger world.

**conflict:** a struggle between opposing forces, such as between two people, between a person and something in nature or society, or even between two drives, impulses, or parts of the self.

**connotation:** what is suggested by a word, apart from what it explicitly describes. *See* **denotation.**

**controlling metaphors: metaphors** that dominate or organize an entire poem. In Linda Pastan's "Marks," for example, the controlling metaphor is of marks (grades) as a way of talking about the speaker's performance of roles within her family.

**conventions:** standard or traditional ways of saying things in literary works, employed to achieve certain expected effects.

**cosmic irony:** implies that a god or fate controls and toys with human actions, feelings, lives, outcomes.

**criticism:** the evaluative or interpretive work written by professional interpreters of texts. It is "criticism" not because it is negative or corrective, but rather because those who write criticism ask hard, analytical, crucial or "critical" questions about the works they read.

**culture:** a broad and relatively indistinct term that implies a commonality of history and some cohesiveness of purpose within a group. One can speak of southern culture, for example, or urban culture, or American culture, or rock culture; at any one time, each of us belongs to a number of these cultures.

**dactylic:** the metrical pattern in which each foot consists of a stressed syllable followed by two unstressed ones.

**denotation:** a direct and specific meaning. *See* **connotation.**

**descriptive structure:** a textual organization determined by the requirements of describing someone or something.

**diction:** an author's choice of words.

**discursive structure:** a textual organization based on the form of a treatise, argument, or essay.

**dramatic irony:** a **plot** device in which a **character** holds a position or has an expectation that is reversed or fulfilled in a way that the character did not expect but that we, as readers or as audience members, have anticipated because our knowledge of events or individuals is more complete than the character's.

**dramatic monologue:** a monologue set in a specific situation and spoken to an imaginary audience.

**dramatic structure:** a textual organization based on a series of scenes, each of which is presented vividly and in detail.

**echo:** a verbal reference that recalls a word, phrase, or sound in another text.

**elegy:** in classical times, any poem on any subject written in "elegiac" **meter;** since the Renaissance, usually a formal lament on the death of a particular person.

**English sonnet:** also called a **Shakespearean sonnet;** a **sonnet** form that divides the poem into three units of four lines each and a final unit of two lines (4+4+4+2 structure). Its classic rhyme scheme is *abab cdcd efef gg,* but there are variations.

**epic:** a poem that celebrates, in a continuous narrative, the achievements of mighty **heroes** and **heroines,** usually in founding a nation or developing a **culture,** and uses elevated language and a grand, high style.

**epigram:** originally any poem carved in stone (on tombstones, buildings, gates, and so forth), but in modern usage a very short, usually witty verse with a quick turn at the end.

**extended metaphor:** a detailed and complex **metaphor** that extends over a long section of a work.

**figurative:** usually applied to language that uses **figures of speech.** Figurative language heightens meaning by implicitly or explicitly representing something in terms of some other thing, the assumption being that the "other thing" will be more familiar to the reader.

**figures of speech:** comparisons in which something is pictured or figured in other, more familiar terms.

**formal diction:** language that is lofty, dignified, and impersonal. *See* **colloquial diction** and **informal diction.**

**free verse:** poetry that is characterized by varying line lengths, lack of traditional **meter,** and nonrhyming lines.

**genre:** the largest category for classifying literature—fiction, poetry, drama. *See* **kind** and **subgenre.**

**haiku:** an unrhymed poetic form, Japanese in origin, that contains seventeen syllables arranged in three lines of five, seven, and five syllables, respectively.

**heroic couplet:** rhymed pairs of lines in iambic pentameter.

**history:** the imaginary people, places, chronologically arranged events that we assume exist in the world of the author's imagination, a world from which he or she chooses and arranges or rearranges the story elements.

**hyperbole:** overstatement characterized by exaggerated language.

**iambic:** a metrical form in which each foot consists of an unstressed syllable followed by a stressed one.

**imagery:** broadly defined, any sensory detail or evocation in a work; more narrowly, the use of **figurative** language to evoke a feeling, to call to mind an idea, or to describe an object.

**imitative structure:** a textual organization that mirrors as exactly as possible the structure of something that already exists as an object and can be seen.

**informal diction:** language that is not as lofty or impersonal as **formal diction;** similar to everyday speech. *See* **colloquial diction,** which is one variety of informal diction.

**irony:** a situation or statement characterized by a significant difference between what is expected or understood and what actually happens or is meant. *See* **cosmic irony** and **dramatic irony.**

**Italian sonnet:** a **sonnet** form that divides the poem into one section of eight lines and a second section of six lines, usually following the *abbaabba cdecde* rhyme scheme.

**kind:** a species or subcategory within a **subgenre; Italian sonnet** is a subcategory of the subgenre *sonnet.*

**literary critics:** professional "interpreters" (and often implicitly or explicitly evaluators) of literary texts.

**litotes:** a figure of speech that emphasizes its subject by conscious understatement. An example from common speech is to say "Not bad" as a form of high praise.

**lyric:** originally, poems meant to be sung to the accompaniment of a lyre; now, any short poem in which the **speaker** expresses intense personal emotion rather than describing a narrative or dramatic situation.

**meditation:** a contemplation of some physical object as a way of reflecting upon some larger truth, often (but not necessarily) a spiritual one.

**memory devices:** also called **mnemonic devices;** these devices—including rhyme, repetitive phrasing, and **meter**—when part of the structure of a longer work, make that work easier to memorize.

**metaphor:** (1) one thing pictured as if it were something else, suggesting a likeness or **analogy** between them; (2) an implicit comparison or identification of one thing with another unlike itself without the use of a verbal signal. Sometimes used as a general term for **figure of speech.**

**meter:** the more or less regular pattern of stressed and unstressed syllables in a line of poetry. This is determined by the kind of "foot" (**iambic** and **dactylic,** for example) and by the number of feet per line (five feet=pentameter, six feet=hexameter, for example).

**mode:** style, manner, way of proceeding, as in "tragic mode"; often used synonymously with **genre, kind,** and **subgenre.**

**motif:** a recurrent device, formula, or situation that deliberately connects a poem with common patterns of existing thought.

**myth:** like **allegory,** myth usually is symbolic and extensive, including an entire work. Though it no longer is necessarily specific to or pervasive in a single **culture**—individual authors may now be said to create myths—there is still a sense that myth is communal or cultural, while the symbolic can often be private or personal myths.

**occasional poem:** a poem written about or for a specific occasion, public or private.

**onomatopoeia:** a word capturing or approximating the sound of what it describes; *buzz* is a good example.

**overstatement:** exaggerated language; also called **hyperbole.**

**oxymoron:** a **figure of speech** that combines two apparently contradictory elements, as in "wise fool" ("sophomore").

**paradox:** a statement that seems contradictory but may actually be true, as in "That I may rise and stand, o'erthrow me," from Donne's "Batter My Heart, three-personed God."

**parody:** a work that imitates another work for comic effect by exaggerating the style and changing the content of the original.

**pastoral:** a poem (also called an eclogue, a bucolic, or an idyll) that describes the

simple life of country folk, usually shepherds who live a timeless, painless (and sheep-
less) life in a world that is full of beauty, music, and love.

**personification** (or *prosopopeia*): treating an abstraction as if it were a person by en-
dowing it with humanlike qualities.

**Petrarchan sonnet:** also called **Italian sonnet;** a **sonnet** form that divides the poem
into one section of eight lines and a second section of six lines, usually following the
*abbaabba cdecde* rhyme scheme or, more loosely, an *abbacddc* pattern.

**precision:** exactness, accuracy of language or description.

**protest poem:** a poetic attack, usually quite direct, on allegedly unjust institutions or
social injustices.

**reader time:** the actual time it takes a reader to read a work.

**realism:** the practice in literature of attempting to describe nature and life without
idealization and with attention to detail.

**red herring:** a false lead, something that misdirects expectations.

**referential:** when used to describe a poem, *referential* means making textual use of a
specific historical moment or event or, more broadly, making use of external, "natu-
ral," or "actual" detail.

**reflective/meditative structure:** a textual organization based on the pondering of
a **subject, theme,** or event, and letting the mind play with it, skipping from one sound
to another, or to related thoughts or objects as the mind receives them.

**rhetorical trope:** traditional **figure of speech,** used for specific persuasive effects.

**rhythm:** the modulation of weak and strong (or stressed and unstressed) elements in
the flow of speech. In most poetry written before the twentieth century, rhythm was
often expressed in regular, metrical forms; in prose and in **free verse,** rhythm is
present but in a much less predictable and regular manner.

**sarcasm:** a form of **verbal irony** in which apparent praise is actually harshly or bitterly
critical.

**satire:** a literary work that holds up human failings to ridicule and censure.

**sestina:** an elaborate verse **structure** written in **blank verse** that consists of six **stanzas**
of six lines each followed by a three-line stanza. The final words of each line in the
first stanza appear in variable order in the next five stanzas, and are repeated in the
middle and at the end of the three lines in the final stanza, as in Elizabeth Bishop's
"Sestina."

**setting:** the time and place of the **action** in a poem.

**Shakespearean sonnet:** also called an **English sonnet;** a **sonnet** form that divides the
poem into three units of four lines each and a final unit of two lines (4+4+4+2 struc-
ture). Its classic rhyme scheme is *abab cdcd efef gg,* but there are other variations.

**shaped verse:** another name for **concrete poetry;** poetry that is shaped to look like an
object.

**simile:** a direct, explicit comparison of one thing to another, usually using the words
*like* or *as* to draw the connection. *See* **metaphor.**

**situation:** the context of the literary work's **action,** what is happening when the poem
begins.

**sonnet:** a fixed verse form consisting of fourteen lines usually in iambic pentameter.
*See* **Italian sonnet** and **Shakespearean sonnet.**

**spatial setting:** the place of a poem.

**speaker:** the person, not necessarily the author, who is the voice of a poem.

**Spenserian stanza:** a **stanza** that consists of eight lines of iambic pentameter (five feet)
followed by a ninth line of iambic hexameter (six feet). The rhyme scheme is
*ababbcbcc.*

**stanza:** a section of a poem demarcated by extra line spacing. Some distinguish between a stanza, a division marked by a single pattern of **meter** or rhyme, and a verse paragraph, a division marked by thought rather than pattern.

**stereotype:** a **characterization** based on conscious or unconscious assumptions that some one aspect, such as gender, age, ethnic or national identity, religion, occupation, marital status, and so on are predictably accompanied by certain **character** traits, actions, even values.

**structure:** the organization or arrangement of the various elements in a work.

**style:** a distinctive manner of expression; each author's style is expressed through his/her **diction, rhythm, imagery,** and so on.

**subgenre:** division within the category of a **genre;** *epic, sonnet,* and *pastoral* are subgenres of the genre *poetry.*

**subject:** the general or specific area of concern of a poem; also called **topic.**

**suspense:** the expectation of and doubt about what is going to happen next.

**syllabic verse:** a form in which the poet establishes a precise number of syllables to a line and repeats it in subsequent **stanzas.**

**symbol:** a person, place, thing, event, or pattern in a literary work that designates itself and at the same time figuratively represents or "stands for" something else. Often the thing or idea represented is more abstract, general, non-or superrational, the symbol more concrete and particular.

**symbolic poem:** a poem in which the use of **symbols** is so pervasive and internally consistent that the larger referential world is distanced, if not forgotten.

**syntax:** the way words are put together to form phrases, clauses, and sentences.

**technopaegnia:** the art of "shaped" poems in which the visual force is supposed to work spiritually or magically.

**temporal setting:** the time of a poem.

**terza rima:** a verse form consisting of three-line **stanzas** in which the second line of each rhymes with the first and third of the next.

**theme:** (1) a generalized, abstract paraphrase of the inferred central or dominant idea or concern of a work; (2) the statement a poem makes about its subject.

**tone:** the attitude a literary work takes toward its **subject** and **theme.**

**topic:** the general or specific area of concern of a poem. Also called **subject.**

**tradition:** an inherited, established, or customary practice.

**traditional symbols: symbols** that, through years of usage, have acquired an agreed-upon significance, an accepted meaning. *See* **archetype.**

**trochaic:** a metrical form in which each foot consists of a stressed syllable followed by an unstressed one.

**verbal irony:** a statement in which the literal meaning differs from the implicit meaning. *See* **dramatic irony.**

**verse paragraph:** *see* stanza.

**villanelle:** a verse form consisting of nineteen lines divided into six **stanzas**—five tercets (three-line stanzas) and one quatrain (four-line stanza). The first and third lines of the first tercet rhyme, and this rhyme is repeated through each of the next four tercets and in the last two lines of the concluding quatrain. The villanelle is also known for its repetition of select lines. A good example of a twentieth-century villanelle is Dylan Thomas's "Do Not Go Gentle into That Good Night."

**word order:** the positioning of words in relation to one another.

# Biographical Sketches[1]

## Ai (b. 1947)

Born to parents of Asian, African, and Native American heritage, Ai earned a B.A. in Oriental Studies from the University of Arizona and an M.F.A. from the University of California at Irvine. Her first collection of poetry, *Cruelty*, appeared in 1973. Notable for its dramatic monologues, Ai's subsequent collection, *Killing Floor* (1979), received the Lamont Poetry Prize. Her narrative poetry, most recently *Fate* (1991) and *Greed* (1993), invokes graphic images and defiant characters.

## Agha Shahid Ali (b. 1949)

Born in New Delhi, India, and a graduate of the University of Kashmir, Srinagar, Ali has written poetry in English since the age of ten. He returned to New Delhi, where he received an M.A. from the University of Delhi in 1970 before leaving India to pursue advanced degrees in the United States, including an M.F.A. from the University of Arizona, Tucson (1985), and a Ph.D. from Pennsylvania State University (1984). The recipient of Guggenheim and Ingram-Merrill fellowships, he has taught at Hamilton College and is currently the director of the M.F.A. program in creative writing at the University of Massachusetts, Amherst. Ali is the author of scholarly works, such as *T. S. Eliot as Editor* (1986), in addition to his volumes of poetry, which include *A Walk through the Yellow Pages* (1986), *The Half-Inch Himalayas* (1987), *A Nostalgist's Map of America* (1991), and *The Country without a Post Office* (1997).

## Margaret Atwood (b. 1939)

Atwood spent her first eleven years in sparsely populated areas of northern Ontario and Quebec, where her father worked as an entomologist. After her education at the University of Toronto and Harvard, she held various jobs in Canada, America, England, and Italy. Atwood published her first poem when she was just nineteen, and she has won numerous prizes for her poetry as well as her fiction, which has become increasingly political over the years. Her novels include *The Edible Woman* (1969), *Surfacing* (1972), *Lady Oracle* (1976), *Life before Man* (1979), *Bodily Harm* (1982), *The Handmaid's Tale* (1985), *Cat's Eye* (1988), *Robber Bride* (1993), and *Alias Grace* (1996). Many of her stories have been collected in *Dancing Girls and Other Stories* (1978), *Murder in the Dark* (1983), *Bluebeard's Egg* (1983), and *Wilderness Tips* (1991).

1. Biographical sketches are included for all poets represented by two or more poems.

## W. H. Auden (1907–1973)

A prolific writer of poems, plays, essays, and criticism, Wystan Hugh Auden was born in York, England, to a medical officer and a nurse. Auden studied at Oxford and taught at various universities in the United States, where he became a naturalized citizen in 1946. He won the Pulitzer Prize in 1948 for his collection of poems, *Age of Anxiety,* and is regarded as a poet of political and intellectual conscience. His long-term relationship with poet Chester Kallman has been the subject of several recent biographies.

## Bashō (1644–1694)

Born Matsuo Munefusa, the second son of a low-ranking provincial samurai, the haiku poet who came to be known as Bashō showed little interest in writing until he entered into service with the local ruling military house. There, through a friendship with his employer, he began to develop a taste for the popular new form of poetry and saw his first two poems published in an anthology in 1664. Following the premature death of his poetry companion and protector, Bashō left for Edo (now Tokyo), the military capital of the shogun's new government, in order to pursue a career as a professional poet. He supported himself as a teacher and corrector of other people's poetry but ultimately earned a following and a sizable group of students. A seasoned traveler, Bashō sought to maintain an austere existence on the road as well as at home, casting himself in travel narratives such as *Oku no hosomichi* (*The Narrow Road to the Interior,* 1694) as a pilgrim devoted to nature and the naturalist Zen philosophy.

## Aphra Behn (1640?–1689)

Believed to be the first woman in England to earn her living by writing, Behn was admired for her work as much as she was criticized for the frank and unconventional treatment of eroticism and romance in her plays, poems, and novels. While little is known about where, when, and to whom she was born, most historians agree that she spent part of her childhood in Surinam, West Indies, returned to England when the island was handed over to the Dutch, and was briefly married to a merchant. Following her husband's death in 1666, Behn moved to Antwerp, Belgium, to serve as a spy for King Charles II of England before returning to England, where she was held in debtor's prison for a short time. Upon being released from prison, Behn began to support herself by writing, and although accused of plagiarism and lewdness, she was both a successful and a prolific playwright. Her first play, *The Forc'd Marriage,* was produced in 1671, and she subsequently wrote seventeen plays, including popular works such as *The Rover* (1677, 1681), *The City Heiress* (1682), and *The Lucky Chance* (1686). Her first novel, *Oroonoko; or, The Royal Slave* (1688), tells the story of an African prince sold into slavery in Surinam.

## Earle Birney (1904–1991)

Born in a log cabin on the banks of the Bow River in Calgary, Alberta, when the province was still part of the Northwest Territories, and raised on a farm in Erickson, British Columbia, Birney passed through a variety of careers on his way to becoming a writer. After working as a bank clerk, a farm laborer, and a park ranger, he enrolled at the University of British Columbia intent upon a degree in chemical engineering, but instead graduated in 1926 with a degree in English. Birney went on to study at the University of Toronto and the University of California at Berkeley, receiving a Ph.D. in Old and Middle English. He taught at the Universities of Utah, Toronto, and British Columbia before joining the Canadian Army during World War II. Returning to the

University of British Columbia following the war, he successfully lobbied for the first creative-writing course, which grew into the first department of creative writing in Canada. Birney was the recipient of two Governor General's Awards for literature, the Lorne Pierce Medal for Literature, and several Canada Council's Awards. In addition to his verse collections, which include *David and Other Poems* (1942), *The Strait of Anian* (1948), and *Near False Creek Mouth* (1964), he published the novel *Turvey* (1949), the semiautobiographical *Down the Log Table* (1955), radio plays, stage plays, and literary essays.

## Elizabeth Bishop (1911–1979)

Born in Worcester, Massachusetts, Bishop endured the death of her father before she was a year old and the institutionalization of her mother when she was five. Bishop was raised by her maternal grandmother in Nova Scotia, then by her paternal grand-parents back in Worcester. Bishop attended Vassar College and met the poet Marianne Moore, who encouraged her to give up plans for medical school to pursue the life of a poet. Bishop traveled through Canada, Europe, and South America, finally settling in Rio de Janeiro, where she lived for nearly twenty years. Bishop produced only four volumes of poetry: *North and South* (1946); *A Cold Spring* (1955), which won the Pulitzer Prize; *Questions of Travel* (1965); and *Geography III* (1976), which won the National Book Critics' Circle Award.

## William Blake (1757–1828)

In defense of his unorthodox and original work, Blake once said: "That which can be made Explicit to the Idiot . . . is not worth my care." The son of a London haberdasher, he studied drawing at ten and at fourteen was apprenticed to an engraver for seven years. After a first book of poems, *Poetical Sketches* (1783), he began experimenting with what he called "illuminated printing"—the words and pictures of each page were engraved in relief on copper and the printed sheets partly colored by hand—a laborious and time-consuming process that resulted in books of singular beauty, no two of which were exactly alike. His great *Songs of Innocence* (1789) and *Songs of Experience* (1794) were printed in this manner, as were his increasingly mythic and prophetic books, which include *The Marriage of Heaven and Hell* (1793), *The Four Zoas* (1803), *Milton* (1804), and *Jerusalem* (1809). Blake devoted his later life to pictorial art, illustrating *The Canterbury Tales,* the Book of Job, and *The Divine Comedy,* on which he was hard at work when he died.

## Roo Borson (b. 1952)

While considered a Canadian poet, Ruth Elizabeth Borson was born in Berkeley, California. She later attended the University of California at Santa Barbara and earned her B.A. in 1973 from Gordon College. Four years later, she published her first collection of poetry, *Landfall,* in addition to receiving her M.F.A. from the University of British Columbia, where she was awarded the Macmillan Prize for Poetry. Borson's poetry suggests what she calls the "intricacy of the physical world" as it recognizes the powers of sensuality and memory. She has published a number of collections, including *The Whole Night Coming Home* (1984) and *Intent, or the Weight of the World* (1989).

## Gwendolyn Brooks (b. 1917)

Brooks was born in Topeka, Kansas, and was raised in Chicago, where she began writing poetry at the age of seven. Her formal training began at the Southside Community

Art Center, and she produced her first book of poems, *A Street in Bronzeville,* shortly after, in 1945. Her second book of poems, *Annie Allen* (1949), won Brooks the distinction of being the first African American to win the Pulitzer Prize for Poetry. Brooks's early poetry concentrated on what Langston Hughes called the "ordinary aspects of black life," but her work was transformed in the 1960s and Brooks became a passionate advocate for African American consciousness and activism.

Robert Browning (1812–1889)

Born in London, Browning was an aspiring but unknown poet and playwright when he met the already-famous poet Elizabeth Barrett. After their elopement in 1846, the Brownings moved to Italy, where Elizabeth Barrett Browning authored the chronicle of their love, *Sonnets from the Portuguese* (1850). Browning wrote most of his great poems during this period, and after his wife's death in 1861 he returned to England and began to establish his own literary reputation for his fine dramatic monologues.

Buson (1716–1783)

Although born into a wealthy family in Kemu, Settsu province, Japan, Taniguchi Buson renounced a life of privilege in order to pursue a career in the arts. After spending several years traveling and studying under masters of haiku in northeastern Japan, he settled in Kyoto in 1751, where he established himself as a professional painter. Known in later life as Yosa Buson, or simply Buson, he was responsible for a revival of the work of his prominent predecessor, Bashō. In his own work, Buson was particularly attentive to visual detail and pioneered an experimental form of verse based upon and incorporating Chinese poetry.

John Clare (1793–1864)

Born into poverty in the small Northamptonshire village of Helpston, and forced to work as a herder at age seven, John Clare was nonetheless a poetic prodigy. Although he obtained only enough schooling to read and write, he displayed exceptional poetic talent at an early age. His first book, *Poems Descriptive of Rural Life and Scenery,* published in 1820, brought him a certain amount of fame within London literary circles that were then fascinated by "natural" poets, but his subsequent books were critical and financial failures. Faced with these disappointments, Clare sank into mental illness and spent the final twenty-three years of his life at St. Andrew's Asylum in Northampton.

Judith Ortiz Cofer (b. 1952)

Born in 1952 in Hormigueros, Puerto Rico, Cofer spent her childhood in both Puerto Rico and Patterson, New Jersey, where her father's family lived. This bicultural childhood is a common theme in both her poems and fiction. Cofer attended Augusta College in Georgia and received her M.A. in English from Florida Atlantic University. She received a fellowship to study at Oxford and subsequent scholarships to the Bread Loaf Writers' Conference, where she taught for a number of years. Her first collection of poetry, *Peregrina* (1985), won the Riverstone International Poetry Competition, and in 1989 Cofer was a National Endowment for the Arts Fellow in Poetry. Her novel, *The Line of the Sun,* was published in 1989, and her most recent work, a collection of poetry and essays, is entitled *The Latin Deli* (1993).

## Samuel Taylor Coleridge (1772–1834)

Born in the small town of Ottery St. Mary in rural Devonshire, England, Coleridge was one of the greatest and most original of the nineteenth-century Romantic poets. He wrote three of the most haunting poems in the English tradition—*The Rime of the Ancient Mariner* (1798), *Christabel* (1816), and *Kubla Khan* (1816)—as well as immensely influential literary criticism and a revolutionary treatise on biology, *Hints towards the Formation of a More Comprehensive Theory of Life*. In 1795, in the midst of a failed experiment to establish a "Pantisocracy" (his form of ideal community), he met William Wordsworth, and in 1798 they published together their *Lyrical Ballads,* which was to influence the course of English Romanticism for decades to come. Coleridge's physical ailments, addiction to opium, and profound sense of despair have to this day shaped our sense of the poet suffering for the sake of art.

## Wendy Cope (b. 1945)

Born in Kent, England, Cope studied history and learned to play the guitar at Oxford University. While working as a primary-school teacher, she began writing poetry. Her first volume, *Making Cocoa for Kingsley Amis,* was published in 1986, and the following year she received a Cholmondeley Award for Poetry. Her most recent collection, *Serious Concerns* (1992), includes her trademark optimistic and witty verses. Cope has also published a children's book and a narrative poem, *The River Girl* (1991), commissioned for performance.

## Hart Crane (1899–1932)

Crane's vision of modernist poetry refused the popular pessimism of T. S. Eliot's *The Waste Land* and called for "a more positive, or . . . ecstatic goal." Born in Garretsville, Ohio, Harold Hart Crane spent his childhood in Cleveland, and after adolescent visits to Cuba, Paris, and New York, he opted to leave high school and move to Greenwich Village. In spite of the artistic intensity of the Village, Crane was unable to support himself financially and moved back to Cleveland to work for his father. While back in Ohio, Crane published a number of poems, and in 1923 he again moved to New York City, where he wrote extensively and published his first collection, *White Buildings,* in 1926. At the same time, he was working on his epic poem, *The Bridge,* which received *Poetry* magazine's annual award. Crane was awarded a Guggenheim Fellowship in 1931, but a year later he took his own life.

## Countee Cullen (1903–1946)

A prominent figure in the Harlem Renaissance, Cullen received the most critical acclaim for his race-conscious poems despite his wish to be known "as a poet and not as a Negro poet." He was born in Louisville, Kentucky, and soon moved to New York City, where he was eventually adopted at the age of fifteen by an Episcopal minister and his wife. He graduated from New York University in 1925 and began work on a master's degree at Harvard University. Cullen's first collection of poetry, *Color,* appeared that same year, followed by *Copper Sun* in 1927 and the lauded volume *The Ballad of the Brown Girl: An Old Ballad Retold* in 1928. After working as an assistant editor at *Opportunity* magazine, a periodical of the Harlem Renaissance, from 1926 to 1928, Cullen received a Guggenheim Fellowship to spend a year in Paris. Although he garnered many honors early in his career, including the John Reed Memorial Prize from *Poetry* magazine (1925) and the Harmon Foundation Literary Award for his anthology of African American poetry entitled *Caroling Dusk* (1927), Cullen's later work in poetry, prose, and drama was met with disappointment. From 1934 until his death in 1946, he supported himself by teaching English and French in New York public schools.

## E. E. Cummings (1894–1962)

Cummings's variety of modernism was distinguished by its playful sense of humor, its formal experimentation, its lyrical directness, and above all its celebration of the individual against mass society. Born in Cambridge, Massachusetts, the son of a Congregationalist minister, Edward Estlin Cummings attended Harvard University, where he wrote poetry in the Pre-Raphaelite and Metaphysical traditions. He joined the ambulance corps in France the day after the United States entered World War I and was imprisoned by his own side for his outspoken letters and disdain for bureaucracy; he transmuted the experience into his first literary success, *The Enormous Room* (1922). After the war, Cummings established himself as a poet and artist in Greenwich Village, made frequent trips to France and New Hampshire, and showed little interest in wealth or his growing celebrity.

## James Dickey (1923–1997)

Dickey did not become seriously interested in poetry until he joined the Air Force in 1942. When he returned from World War II, he earned a B.A. and an M.A. at Vanderbilt University, publishing his first poem in *Sewanee Review* in his senior year. Since the publication of his first book of poems, *Into the Stone* (1960), Dickey, while primarily a poet, engaged in diverse careers ranging from advertising writer and novelist to poetry teacher at various universities. His 1965 collection, *Buckdancer's Choice,* received the National Book Award, and from 1967 to 1969 Dickey was Consultant in Poetry to the Library of Congress. He is more popularly known for his best-selling novel, *Deliverance* (1970), which he later adapted for Hollywood. Most recently, he published *The Whole Motion: Collected Poems 1949–1992* (1992) and a novel, *To the White Sea* (1993).

## Emily Dickinson (1830–1886)

From childhood on, Dickinson's life was sequestered and obscure. Yet her verse had a power and influence that has traveled far beyond the cultured yet relatively circumscribed environment in which she lived her life: her room, her father's house, her family, a few close friends, and the small town of Amherst, Massachusetts. Indeed, along with Walt Whitman, her far more public contemporary, she all but invented American poetry. Born in Amherst, the daughter of a respected lawyer and revered father ("His heart was pure and terrible," she once wrote), Dickinson studied for less than a year at the Mount Holyoke Female Seminary, returning permanently to Amherst. In later life she became more and more of a recluse, dressing in white, seeing no visitors, yet working without stint at her poems—nearly eighteen hundred in all, only a few of which were published during her lifetime.

## John Donne (1572–1631)

The first and greatest of what came to be known as the "Metaphysical" school of poets, Donne wrote in a style, revolutionary at the time, that combined highly intellectual conceits with complex, compressed phrasing. Born into an old Roman Catholic family at a time when Catholics were subject to constant harassment, Donne quietly abandoned his religion and had a brilliant early career until a politically disastrous marriage ruined his worldly hopes and forced him to struggle for years to support a large and growing family; impoverished and despairing, he even wrote a treatise (*Biathanatos*) on the lawfulness of suicide. King James (who had ambitions for him as a preacher) eventually forced Donne to take Anglican orders in 1615, and indeed he became one of the great sermonizers of his day, rising to dean of St. Paul's Cathedral in 1621. Donne's private devotions were published in 1624, and he continued to write sacred poetry until a few years before his death.

Rita Dove (b. 1952)

When Dove won the 1987 Pulitzer Prize for Poetry for *Thomas and Beulah* (1986), she became the second African American poet (after Gwendolyn Brooks in 1950) to receive such high recognition. A native of Akron, Ohio, Dove attended Miami University in Ohio, studied for a year in West Germany as a Fulbright scholar, and received an M.F.A. in creative writing from the University of Iowa. She taught creative writing at Arizona State University and is now a professor of English at the University of Virginia as well as an associate editor of *Callaloo*, the journal of African American and African arts and letters. Dove's books include *The Yellow House on the Corner* (1980), *Museum* (1983), *Grace Notes* (1989), and *Mother Love* (1995). In 1993, Dove was appointed Poet Laureate of the United States by the Library of Congress.

John Dryden (1631–1700)

Called "the father of English criticism" by Samuel Johnson, Dryden was a prolific poet and dramatist. He attended Trinity College, Cambridge, where he took his A.B. in 1654, and for most of his career, Dryden wrote nondramatic, occasional, and public poems, celebrating historical moments. In 1667, he wrote "Annus Mirabilis," which marked England's "year of wonders." During his middle years, Dryden focused mostly on creating popular drama and literary criticism. In 1677, he adapted Shakespeare's *Antony and Cleopatra* into a play called *All for Love*, and in "An Essay of Dramatic Poesy" (1668), he outlined new theoretical principles for drama. That same year he was named England's Poet Laureate. Later in his career, Dryden became known for his political satires, like the scathing mock-heroic "Mac Flecknoe" (1678) and "Absalom and Achitophel" (1681).

Paul Laurence Dunbar (1872–1906)

Hailed as "the Poet Laureate of the Negro race" by Booker T. Washington, Dunbar was born the son of former slaves in Dayton, Ohio. He attended a white high school, where he showed an early talent for writing and was elected class president, but was employed as an elevator operator after being unable to fund further education. Writing poems and newspaper articles when he could find the time, Dunbar took out a loan to subsidize the printing of his first book, *Oak and Ivy* (1893). With the subsequent publication of *Majors and Minors* (1895) and *Lyrics of Lowly Life* (1896), his reputation as a poet grew, and he was able to support himself by writing and lecturing in the United States and England. Acclaimed during his lifetime for his lyrical use of black dialect and his tributes to the experiences of rural blacks in volumes such as *Candle-Lightin' Time* (1902) and *Lyrics of Sunshine and Shadow* (1905), Dunbar was later criticized for adopting white literary conventions and frequently pandering to racist images of slaves and ex-slaves. The author of four novels and four books of short stories in addition to collections of poetry, Dunbar began to write frankly about racial injustice in works such as *The Sport of the Gods* (1903) and *The Fourth of July and Race Outrages,* published in the *New York Times* in 1903, shortly before his early death from tuberculosis.

### Richard Eberhart (b. 1904)

Eberhart was born in Austin, Minnesota, the son of a wealthy businessman. He attended the University of Minnesota and received his B.A. from Dartmouth in 1926. After holding a variety of jobs he landed in England and took a second B.A. from St. John's College in Cambridge in 1929. He published his first book of poems the following year. During World War II he was an aerial gunner, and afterward he returned to Dartmouth as a teacher and poet-in-residence. Since 1970 he has held various visiting professorships, and he has received many prizes and honorary degrees. His recent books include *Maine Poems* (1988) and *Richard Eberhart, New and Selected Poems 1930–1990* (1990).

### T. S. Eliot (1888–1965)

Thomas Stearns Eliot—from his formally experimental and oblique writings to his brilliant arguments in defense of "orthodoxy" and "tradition"—dominated the world of English poetry between the world wars. Born in St. Louis, Missouri, of New England stock, Eliot studied literature and philosophy at Harvard and later in France and Germany. He came to England in 1914, read Greek philosophy at Oxford, and published his first major poem, "The Love Song of J. Alfred Prufrock," the next year. In 1922, with the help of his great supporter and adviser, Ezra Pound, Eliot published his long poem, *The Waste Land* (1922), which would profoundly influence a whole generation of poets. In his later work, particularly the *Four Quartets* (completed in 1945), Eliot explored religious questions in a quieter, more controlled idiom. He was awarded the Nobel Prize for Literature in 1948.

### Carolyn Forché (b. 1950)

Born in Detroit, Michigan, Forché studied creative writing and international relations at Michigan State University and did graduate work at Bowling Green State University. Her first book of poetry, *Gathering the Tribes* (1976), won the Yale Series of Younger Poets Award. Forché was a journalist for Amnesty International in El Salvador and Beirut correspondent for National Public Radio's *All Things Considered*. She has taught at many universities and has published several volumes of poetry, including *The Country between Us* (1981) and *The Angel of History* (1994).

### Robert Frost (1874–1963)

Though his poetry forever identifies Frost with rural New England, he was born and lived to the age of eleven in San Francisco. Coming to New England after his father's death, Frost studied classics in high school, entered and dropped out of both Dartmouth and Harvard, and spent difficult years as an unrecognized poet before his first book, *A Boy's Will* (1913), was accepted and published in England. Frost's character was full of contradiction—he held "that we get forward as much by hating as by loving"—yet by the end of his long life he was one of the most honored poets of his time. In 1961, two years before his death, he was invited to read a poem at John F. Kennedy's presidential inauguration ceremony.

John Gay (1685–1732)

After attending school in Devon, Gay moved to London to work as an apprentice; within five years he was involved in contemporary literary circles as well as the publishing world. Known for both his playfulness and his serious social commentary, Gay, with Pope, Swift, and Arbuthnot, founded the Scriblerus Club, which became famous for its literary satires and practical jokes. In addition to poems like "The Shepherd's Week" (1714) and "Trivia, or the Art of Walking the Streets of London" (1716), Gay wrote *The Beggar's Opera* (1728), a ballad-opera that satirized contemporary political corruption.

Allen Ginsberg (1926–1997)

After a childhood in Paterson, New Jersey, overshadowed by his mother's severe mental illness, Ginsberg enrolled at Columbia University, intent upon following his father's advice and becoming a labor lawyer. He soon became friends with fellow students Lucien Carr and Jack Kerouac, as well as locals William S. Burroughs and Neal Cassady, and with them he began experimenting with drugs, taking cross-country treks, and developing a new poetic vision. Eventually graduating from Columbia in 1948, Ginsberg briefly entertained a more conservative lifestyle before embracing the young poetry movement in San Francisco. In 1956 Ginsberg published *Howl and Other Poems* with an introduction by his mentor William Carlos Williams. The title poem, which condemned bourgeois culture and celebrated the emerging counterculture, became a manifesto for the Beat movement and catapulted Ginsberg to fame. Deeply involved in radical politics and Eastern spiritualism, Ginsberg wrote such prose works as *Declaration of Independence for Dr. Timothy Leary* (1971) in addition to numerous volumes of poetry, including *Kaddish and Other Poems* (1961), *For the Soul of the Planet Is Wakening . . .* (1970), and *Mostly Sitting Haiku* (1978).

Jorie Graham (b. 1951)

Born in Italy to religious historian Curtis Graham and sculptor Beverly Pepper, Graham was raised in Italy and France and educated at the Sorbonne, Columbia University, and the University of Iowa, where she has taught in the Iowa Writer's Workshop since 1983. Linked variously to Blake, Dickinson, and Wallace Stevens, Graham explores philosophical and metaphysical questions in a tough-minded yet lyrical style. Her collection *The Dream of the Unified Field: Selected Poems 1974–1994* won the 1996 Pulitzer Prize for poetry.

Thomas Hardy (1840–1928)

In a preface dated 1901, Hardy called his poems "unadjusted impressions," which nevertheless might, by "humbly recording diverse readings of phenomena as they are forced upon us by chance and change," lead to a philosophy. Indeed, though he was essentially retrospective in his outlook, Hardy anticipated the concerns of modern poetry by treating the craft as an awkward, often skeptical means of penetrating the facade of language. Born at Upper Bockhampton in Dorset, England, the son of a master mason, Hardy began to write while in the midst of an architectural career. After a long and successful career as a novelist, he turned exclusively to poetry; he died while preparing his last book, *Winter Words* (1929), for publication.

Robert Hayden (1913–1980)

Hayden was born in Detroit, Michigan, and studied at Wayne State University and the University of Michigan. He taught at Fisk University for over twenty years and at the University of Michigan for more than ten. Although Hayden produced ten volumes of poetry, he did not receive acclaim until late in life. In the 1960s, Hayden resisted pressure to express the militancy some African Americans wanted and thus alienated himself from a growing African American literary tradition.

H.D. (Hilda Doolittle) (1886–1961)

The only surviving daughter in a prominent family that included five sons, Hilda Doolittle grew up in Pennsylvania. She moved to London in 1911, in the footsteps of her friend and one-time fiancé Ezra Pound, who helped her begin her poetic career. Her first book of poems, *Sea Garden,* was published in 1916, followed by *Hymen* (1921), *Heliodora and Other Poems* (1924), *Collected Poems* (1925), and *Red Roses for Bronze* (1931), among others. After surviving the bombings of London in World War II, she wrote two major epics about war, *Trilogy* (1944–1946) and *Helen in Egypt* (1961). In 1960, she was given the Award of Merit Medal for Poetry from the American Academy of Arts and Letters.

Seamus Heaney (b. 1939)

Heaney, whose poems explore themes of rural life, memory, and history, was born on a farm in Mossbawn, County Derry (Castledawson, Londonderry), Northern Ireland. Educated at Queen's University in Belfast, he began to publish work in university magazines under the pseudonym "Incertus" while serving as a lecturer in English. He produced his first volume, *Eleven Poems,* in 1965, and has continued to write while holding teaching positions at the University of California at Berkeley, Carysfort College in Dublin, and Oxford University. Currently on the faculty at Harvard University, Heaney has received numerous awards for his work, including the 1995 Nobel Prize for Literature. Deemed by Robert Lowell "the most important Irish poet since Yeats," he is the author of multiple collections of poems, including *Death of a Naturalist* (1966), *Wintering Out* (1972), *The Haw Lantern* (1987), *Seeing Things* (1991), and *The Spirit Level* (1996), and prose works such as *The Government of the Tongue* (1988) and *The Place of Writing* (1989).

Anthony Hecht (b. 1923)

Hecht was born in New York City. After graduating from Bard College, he joined the army and was stationed in Europe and Japan. He has taught at, among other schools, Kenyon College (where he first met and studied informally with fellow faculty member John Crowe Ransom), the University of Rochester, and Georgetown University. In addition to his poetry, Hecht has published three books of criticism and several translations, most notably of the Greek tragedian Aeschylus. In addition to his resonant philosophical poetry, Hecht is known for the "double dactyl" verse form that he and John Hollander co-invented.

George Herbert (1593–1633)

After the early death of his Welsh father, Herbert was raised by his mother, a literary patron of John Donne. Herbert graduated with honors from Cambridge and was subsequently elected public orator at the university. He twice served as a member of Parliament in the 1620s, but his political career never flourished. Instead, he began to work for the church in 1626, married, and took holy orders in 1630. While living in Bemerton, he became known as "Holy Mr. Herbert" for his diligent care of the members of his ministry. He died of consumption in 1633, and his most famous poetry collection, *The Temple,* was published posthumously by a friend.

Robert Herrick (1591–1674)

The son of a London goldsmith, Herrick would have liked nothing better than to live a life of leisured study, discussing literature and drinking sack with his hero, Ben Jonson. For a number of reasons, though, he decided to take religious orders and moved to a parish in Devonshire. Herrick eventually made himself at home there, inventing dozens of imaginary mistresses with exotic names (his housekeeper was prosaically named Prudence) and practicing, half-seriously, his own peculiar form of paganism. When the Puritans came to power, Herrick was driven from his post to London, where, in 1648, he published a volume of over fourteen hundred poems with two titles, *Hesperides* for the secular poems and *Noble Numbers* for those with sacred subjects. Though they did not survive the harsh atmosphere of Puritanism and were virtually forgotten until the nineteenth century, Herrick was eventually restored to his post in Devonshire, where he lived out his last years quietly.

John Hollander (b. 1929)

Known for his originality, wit, and keen perception of language, Hollander plays with words and shapes in his poetry. Hollander was born in New York City and later attended Columbia University, earning a B.A. in 1950 and an M.A. in 1952. He received his Ph.D. from Indiana University after serving as a Junior Fellow in the Society of Fellows at Harvard and teaching there. He now teaches at Yale. While he is most widely known as a poet, he has also written extensive criticism and created several children's books. His first book, *A Crackling of Thorns* (1958), was introduced by W. H. Auden as the 1958 volume in the Yale Series of Younger Poets. Hollander received the Bollingen Prize for Poetry in 1963, and his subsequent collections include *Types of Shape* (1969) and *Powers of Thirteen* (1983). In 1990, Hollander was made a Fellow of the MacArthur Foundation. He has two recent volumes, *Tessarae and Other Poems* and *Selected Poetry;* both were published in 1993.

Gerard Manley Hopkins (1844–1889)

Hopkins's verse, in all its superbly controlled tension, strong rhythm, and sheer exuberance, has been championed by a number of modern poets—yet he made few attempts to publish what many of his contemporaries found nearly incomprehensible, and he was all but unknown until long after his death. Born the eldest of eight children of a marine-insurance adjuster (shipwrecks later figured in his poetry, particularly *The Wreck of the Deutschland*), Hopkins attended Oxford, where his ambition was to become a painter—until he was converted to Catholicism. He taught for a time, decided to become a Jesuit, burnt all his early poetry as too worldly, and was ordained in 1877. Near the end of his life, Hopkins was appointed professor of Greek at University College, Dublin. Out of place and miserable, he died there of typhoid at the age of forty-four.

## Langston Hughes (1902–1967)

Hughes, born in Joplin, Missouri, was a major figure of the intellectual and literary movement called the Harlem Renaissance. A graduate of Lincoln University in 1929, Hughes traveled through the world as a correspondent and columnist. He also founded theaters and produced plays, as well as writing poems and novels. His works include *The Weary Blues* (1926), *Montage of a Dream Deferred* (1951), and *The Panther and the Lash: Poems of Our Time* (1961). Hughes has recently been incorporated into the gay literary canon and has been the subject of the film *Looking for Langston*.

## Ben Jonson (1572?–1637)

Poet, playwright, actor, scholar, critic, translator, and leader, for the first time in English, of a literary "school" (the "Cavalier" poets), Jonson was born the posthumous son of a clergyman and stepson to a master bricklayer of Westminster. He had an eventful early career, going to war against the Spanish, working as an actor and killing an associate in a duel, and converting to Catholicism (which made him an object of deep suspicion after the Gunpowder Plot of Guy Fawkes in 1605). Jonson wrote a number of plays in the midst of all this, including *Every Man in His Humor* (in which Shakespeare acted a leading role), *Volpone* (1606), and *The Alchemist* (1610). He spent the latter part of his life at the center of a vast literary circle. When in 1616 he published his collected works, *The Works of Benjamin Jonson*, it was the first time an English author had been so presumptuous as to consider writing a profession.

## Donald Justice (b. 1925)

A consummate craftsman, Justice is best known for his "well-wrought" poems that explore the pain of loss and desperation. Born and raised in Miami, Justice earned his B.A. from the University of Miami, his M.A. from the University of North Carolina, and his Ph.D. in English from The University of Iowa. His *Selected Poems*, published in 1979, won the Pulitzer Prize for poetry in 1980.

## X. J. Kennedy (b. 1929)

Kennedy's *Nude Descending a Staircase* (1961) is a tour de force performance, one of the most remarkable first volumes of poetry written in this century. Its range, from elegy to lyric to song to light verse, encompasses a great variety of tones and poetic kinds. Born Joseph Charles Kennedy in Dover, New Jersey, he was educated at Seton Hall College in New Jersey, Columbia University, and the Sorbonne in Paris. After serving in the U.S. Navy, he taught at several colleges and universities, was poetry editor of *Paris Review*, and edited anthologies of poetry, fiction, and essays. At present he works as a free-lance writer. His most recent volume, with Dorothy M. Kennedy, is *Talking Like the Rain: A First Book of Poems* (1992).

## Galway Kinnell (b. 1927)

Born in Providence, Rhode Island, Kinnell writes poetry that calls attention to humanity's deep connection with nature. After earning a B.A. from Princeton in 1948 and an M.A. from the University of Rochester, he was a journalist, a civil-rights field worker, and a teacher at numerous colleges and universities. With a keen sense of combining personal and national historical events, Kinnell's 1969 collection, *Body Rags,* calls upon the civil-rights movement, and, more recently, *The Past* (1985) speculates on the Hiroshima and Nagasaki bombings. His early poetry, collected in *What a Kingdom It Was*

(1960) and *First Poems 1946–1954* (1970), is highly formal; his more recent work, however, invokes a more colloquial style. His *Selected Poems* (1982) received both a Pulitzer Prize and the American Book Award. Currently teaching creative writing at New York University, Kinnell has recently published a compilation of earlier work, *Three Books: Body Rags, Mortal Acts, Mortal Words, The Past* (1993), and a collection of new poems, *Imperfect Thirst* (1994).

Etheridge Knight (1931–1991)

A native of Corinth, Mississippi, Knight spent much of his adolescence carousing in pool halls, bars, and juke joints, developing a skillful oratorical style in a black male environment that prized verbal agility. During this time he also became addicted to narcotics, and his predilections to drugs and to the deft manipulation of words shaped much of the rest of his life. After serving in the U.S. Army from 1947 to 1951, Knight was arrested on charges of robbery in 1960 and sentenced to eight years in prison. It was at the Indiana State Prison in Michigan City that he began to write poetry, and by 1968, thanks to acclaim and support from such established African American artists as Dudley Randall and Gwendolyn Brooks, his first collection, *Poems from Prison,* was published. After his release, Knight joined the Black Arts movement and taught at several universities around the country, all the while championing the crucial role of oral artistry in maintaining the functional and communal aspects of poetry. He is the author of *Black Voices from Prison* (1970, originally published in Italian as *Voce negre dal carcere* two years earlier), *Belly Song and Other Poems* (1973), and *Born of a Woman* (1980).

Archibald Lampman (1861–1899)

Born in Ontario to German parents, Lampman, as the son of a clergyman, was headed for the Anglican ministry. After graduating from the University of Toronto in 1882 with honors in languages, however, he went into the civil service, where he worked as a clerk until the end of his life. Along with Duncan Campbell Scott and William Wilfred Campbell, Lampman was a member of the Confederation group, a number of Canadian nature poets who have been praised for their efforts to articulate a Canadian national literature. Inspired by music, Lampman wrote poetry as a peaceful mode of self-expression, and he published his first volume, *Among the Millet,* in 1888. Two subsequent collections appeared after his death, *Lyrics of Earth: Sonnets and Ballads* (1925) and *At the Long Sault and Other New Poems* (1943).

Irving Layton (b. 1912)

Considered Canada's most prolific poet, Layton was born to Jewish parents in Romania in 1912. One year later, his family emigrated to Canada. After a series of unrelated jobs, Layton earned a degree in agriculture before embarking on a career writing poetry. He was critical of both literary tradition and the most representative modernist poetry like that of T. S. Eliot. Pivotal in rethinking the boundaries of poetic conventions, Layton has served on the editorial boards of a number of literary magazines, most prominently the *Black Mountain Review.* His irreverent career is collected in numerous volumes of poetry, including *A Wild Peculiar Joy: Selected Poems 1945–89* (1989).

Denise Levertov (1923–1997)

Poetry and life, Levertov once explained, "fade, wilt, shrink, when they are divorced." Born in England, the daughter of a Jewish Russian immigrant who had become an

Anglican clergyman, Levertov was educated at home. By the time she arrived in New York City with her American husband in 1948, she had already published her first book of poetry, *The Double Image* (1946). In 1957 her second book, *Here and Now,* appeared, and she subsequently published numerous collections, including *With Eyes at the Back of Our Heads* (1960), *The Sorrow Dance* (1967), *To Stay Alive* (1971), *Candles in Babylon* (1982), and *Evening Train* (1992). While her earlier work produced in the United States shows the influence of William Carlos Williams, beginning in the 1960s Levertov's poetry developed a particularly political flavor, reflecting the author's increased social activism. Levertov was the recipient of a multitude of awards and honors, and taught at the University of California at Berkeley, the Massachusetts Institute of Technology, Tufts University, and Stanford University, among others.

### Dorothy Livesay (b. 1909)

One of Canada's most celebrated poets, Livesay was twice honored with the Governor General's Award in poetry and in 1947 was awarded Canada's greatest literary honor, the Lorne Pierce Medal. Equally skilled in writing within boldly political and intensely personal contexts, Livesay was influenced early in her career by imagism, but her experience as a social worker in Montreal during the Depression intensified her interest in more politically engaged verse. Her *Collected Poems* was published in 1972.

### Audre Lorde (1934–1992)

Born in New York City, Lorde grew up in Harlem and attended Hunter College and Columbia University. She later returned to Hunter College in 1980 as a professor of English. Lorde raised a son and a daughter in an interracial lesbian relationship and helped to start Kitchen Table: Women of Color Press. Her poetry publications include *The First Cities* (1968), *The Black Unicorn* (1987), and *Undersong: Chosen Poems Old and New* (1993). Lorde has also published two volumes of essays, *Sister Outsider* (1983) and *Burst of Light* (1988), as well as an autobiograhical novel, *Zami* (1980).

### Richard Lovelace (1618–1657)

Born to a wealthy family in Kent, England, Lovelace attended the Charterhouse School and Gloucester Hall, Oxford, before joining the Scottish military expeditions of 1639–1640. Jailed by Parliament in 1642 for presenting a Royalist petition and again in 1648 for fighting on the side of the French against the Spanish, he is best known for poems and lyrics written during his imprisonment, including "To Althea, from Prison." Considered a leading member of the group of Royalist writers called "Cavalier" poets, Lovelace spent his final years in poverty and published only one volume of poems during his lifetime. The title of the work, *Lucasta* (1649) from *Lux casta* (Latin for "pure light"), probably refers to Lucy Sacheverell, Lovelace's fiancée, who married another man after receiving false news of Lovelace's death.

### Amy Lowell (1874–1925)

The leading proponent of the modernist movement in poetry in the United States, Lowell's status among her poet contemporaries derived as much from her cigars and controversial wit as from her verse. Born into a prominent family in Brookline, Massachusetts, and mainly self-taught, Lowell did not begin to write poetry until 1902, and her first, rather conventional poem wasn't published until eight years later. After reading several poems by H.D., Lowell traveled to England in 1913 to meet with the imagist circle. When Ezra Pound left imagism for vorticism, Lowell succeeded him as the leading figure of imagism, to which Pound later referred derisively as "Amy-gism." Under her eccentric influence, the imagists began to experiment with free verse and mystical expression. Credited with popularizing "polyphonic prose," which employed poetic methods of rhyme and alliteration, Lowell produced collections of her own poetry, including *Sword Blades and Poppy Seed* (1914), *Men, Women, and Ghosts* (1916), *Can Grande's Castle* (1918), and *What's O'Clock* (1925) as well as several critical and biographical works.

Claude McKay (1890–1948)

Born in Sunny Ville, Jamaica, McKay became one of the most prominent figures of the Harlem Renaissance—the oldest as well as the first to publish. Always politically active, he was attracted to Communism and in 1922 met Lenin and Trotsky in Moscow, though he later repudiated this commitment with his 1942 conversion to Catholicism. "[To] have a religion," he wrote, "is very much like falling in love with a woman. You love her for her . . . beauty, which cannot be defined." McKay's conception of black experience, infused with social reform and a consciousness of ethnic vitality, made him a catalytic poet for his generation. His works include *If We Must Die* (1919), *Home to Harlem* (1928), and *A Long Way from Home* (1937).

Andrew Marvell (1621–1678)

Marvell was born in Yorkshire, England, and educated at Cambridge. He was a supporter of the Puritans and a member of the British Parliament. Marvell was known in his day for his satires in prose and verse, but today is better known for his less public poems.

Edna St. Vincent Millay (1892–1950)

Winner of the 1923 Pulitzer Prize for Poetry, Millay was born in Maine and educated at Vassar. After college, with her reputation as a poet already established, Millay moved to Greenwich Village in New York and became notorious for her bohemian life and passionate love affairs. *Selected Poems/the Centenary Edition* (1992) provides a generous sampling of Millay's work.

John Milton (1608–1674)

Born in London, the elder son of a self-made businessman, Milton exhibited unusual literary and scholarly gifts at an early age; before entering Cambridge University, he was already adept at Latin and Greek and was well on his way to mastering Hebrew and most of the European languages. After graduation, he spent six more years reading, day and night, just about everything of importance written in English, Italian, Latin, and Greek—after which his father sent him abroad for another year of travel and study. Returning to England, Milton immediately embroiled himself in political controversy, writing pamphlets defending everything from free speech to the execution of Charles I by Cromwell and his followers. In the midst of this feverish activity, the monarchy was restored, and Milton was imprisoned and his property confiscated—but, worst of all, he lost his sight. Blind, impoverished, and isolated, he set about writing the great works of his later years: *Paradise Lost* (1667), *Paradise Regained* (1671), and *Samson Agonistes* (1671).

## Marianne Moore (1887–1972)

Of poetry, Moore self-consciously wrote, "I, too, dislike it"; the phrase captures her fascinating character. Born in Kirkwood, Missouri, near St. Louis, Moore's family moved to Pennsylvania, where she earned a degree from Bryn Mawr College in 1909. In 1918, she and her mother moved to Brooklyn, New York, where Moore became an avid Brooklyn Dodgers fan. While she began to write and publish poetry in college, she did not immediately devote herself to it full time. Instead, she studied business science, taught stenography, and eventually worked as branch librarian at the New York Public Library from 1921 to 1925. In addition to writing poetry, Moore was a prolific critic and served as the editor of the *Dial* from 1926 to 1929. Her *Collected Poems* (1951) was honored with the Bollingen, Pulitzer, and National Book awards. Her *Complete Poems* (1967), while hardly complete, reveals a poet whose constant revisions showed her changing relationship to both nature and language.

## Pat Mora (b. 1942)

Born to Mexican American parents in El Paso, Texas, Mora earned both her B.A. and M.A. from the University of Texas, El Paso. Her first two collections of poetry, *Chants* (1985) and *Borders* (1986), won Southwest Book awards. Along with these books, her most recent volumes of poetry, *Communion* (1991) and *Agua Santa: Holy Water* (1995), reflect and address her Chicana and southwestern background. She has recently compiled a collection of essays called *Nepantla: Essays from the Land in the Middle* (1993).

## Edwin Morgan (b. 1920)

Best known for his experimental and "concrete" poetry, Morgan is nonetheless a flexible and diverse writer, working in comedic, dialogic, narrative, parodic, satiric, and surrealistic modes and drawing his themes both from life and from the world of fantasy. Born in Glasgow, Scotland, Morgan was educated at the University of Glasgow and returned to the university in 1947 as a lecturer after a brief stint in the Royal Army Medical Corps. His *Collected Poems* was published in 1990.

## Susan Musgrave (b. 1951)

Born in Santa Cruz, California, Musgrave now resides in Canada. *Songs of the Sea-Witch* (1970), her first collection, invokes nightmares and darkness where the speakers live on the border of madness. She was the writer-in-residence at the University of Waterloo in Ontario from 1983 until 1985, when she published *Cocktails at the Mausoleum*. Her work, most recently *The Embalmer's Art* (1991), includes many personal moments, and their explicitness invites confrontation. Musgrave has also written plays, novels, and poetry for children.

## Ogden Nash (1902–1971)

A native of Rye, New York, Nash attended Harvard University for one year, taught French, sold bonds, and wrote copy for streetcar advertisements before embarking on a literary career peppered with word plays and sly limericks. After working for Doubleday and Rinehart Press, he joined the staff at the fledgling *New Yorker* magazine. In addition to producing volumes of humorous and unorthodox poetry such as *Hard Lines* (1931), *The Primrose Path* (1935), *Good Intentions* (1942), *Musical Zoo* (1947), and *You*

*Can't Get There from Here* (1957), Nash wrote children's books, collaborated on several musicals, and lectured across the country.

## Howard Nemerov (1920–1991)

Nemerov once called his poems "bad jokes, and even terrible jokes, emerging from the nature of things as well as from my propensity for coming at things a touch subversively, and from the blind side, or the dark side, the side everyone concerned with 'values' would just as soon forget." The resonance of his poetry may lie in his ability to balance this subversive, wayward imagination with lucid, precise language and traditional verse forms. Born in New York City, Nemerov graduated from Harvard University, served in the air force during World War II, and returned to New York to complete his first book, *The Image and the Law* (1948). He taught at a number of colleges and universities, and published books of poetry, plays, short stories, novels, and essays. His *Collected Poems* won the Pulitzer Prize and the National Book Award in 1978. In addition, he served as Poet Laureate of the United States from 1988 to 1990. *Trying Conclusions: New and Selected Poems 1961–1991* was published in 1991.

## Sharon Olds (b. 1942)

Olds's poems might well be compared with those of the "confessional" poets (particularly Plath and Sexton) in their intense focus on and preoccupation with sexual and family relationships. Born in San Francisco, Olds studied at Stanford and Columbia universities, settling afterward in New York City, where she teaches creative writing at New York University and the Goldwater Hospital (a public facility for the severely physically disabled). Olds's books include *Satan Says* (1980), *The Dead and the Living* (1983; National Book Critics Circle Award), *The Gold Cell* (1987), *The Father* (1992), and *The Wellspring* (1997). She has received a National Endowment for the Arts Grant and a Guggenheim Fellowship.

## Mary Oliver (b. 1935)

Born in Maple Heights, Ohio, Oliver graduated from Vassar College before settling in Provincetown, Massachusetts, where she is the chair of the Writing Department at the Fine Arts Center. Her deep appreciation for the New England landscape and attention to the inhabitants of the natural world have influenced her writing since her first collection, *No Voyage and Other Poems,* was published in 1963. The recipient of a Pulitzer Prize for her *American Primitive* (1983) and a National Book Award in 1992 for *New and Selected Poems,* Oliver is also the author of *The Night Traveler* (1978), *Sleeping in the Forest* (1978), *Twelve Moons* (1979), *Dream Work* (1986), and *House of Light* (1990).

## Simon J. Ortiz (b. 1941)

Asked why he writes, Ortiz once replied, "Because Indians always tell a story. . . . The only way to continue is to tell a story and there is no other way. Your children will not survive unless you tell something about them—how they were born, how they came to this certain place, how they continued." Born and raised in the Acoma Pueblo community in Albuquerque, New Mexico, Ortiz attended the University of New Mexico and later received an M.F.A. from the University of Iowa. He has since taught at San Diego State University and the University of New Mexico, and currently edits the Navajo publication *Rough Rock News*. The recipient of a humanitarian award for literary achievement from the New Mexico Humanities Council in 1989, he also won the Pushcart Prize in 1982 for his *From Sand Creek*. Among his books are *A Good Journey* (1984), *Going for the Rain* (1976), *Fight Back: For the Sake of the People, for the Sake of the Land* (1980), *Woven Stone* (1991), a volume of poetry and prose, and *After and Before the Lightning* (1994).

### Wilfred Owen (1893–1918)

Born in Oswestry, Shropshire, England, Owen was the eldest of four children. He left school in 1911, having failed to win a scholarship to London University, and served as assistant to a vicar in Oxfordshire until 1913, when he went to France to teach English at a Berlitz school in Bordeaux. In 1915, he returned to England to enlist in the army and was sent to the front in France. Suffering from shell shock two years later, Owen was evacuated to Craiglockhart War Hospital, where he met the poets Siegfried Sassoon and Robert Graves. Five of Owen's poems were published in 1918, the year he returned to combat only to be killed one week before the signing of the armistice. Owen's poems, technically refined and poignant, portray the horror of trench warfare and satirize the unthinking patriotism of those who cheered the war from their armchairs. The most authoritative collection of Owen's poetry is the two-volume *Complete Poems and Fragments* (1983).

### Dorothy Parker (1893–1967)

Parker satirized the literary, social, and sexual pieties of her time with a sharp eye and sardonic exuberance. If "Brevity is the soul of Lingerie," as she announced in a *Vogue* advertisement, it is also the heart of her wit. There are a number of "Parkerisms"— brief, witty aphorisms—still in circulation. Parker was born in New York City and was friendly with several other prominent writers and humorists of the 1920s and 1930s, including Harold Ross, founder of the *New Yorker*. Author of poetry, criticism, screenplays, and short stories, she published a number of collections, including *Enough Rope* (1926), *Sunset Gun* (1928), *Death and Taxes* (1931), and *Not So Deep As a Well* (1936).

### Linda Pastan (b. 1932)

Author of more than half a dozen volumes of poetry, Pastan was born in New York City and attended Radcliffe College and Brandeis University before settling in suburban Washington, D.C. Her books include *A Perfect Circle of Sun* (1971), *The Five Stages of Grief* (1978), *A Fraction of Darkness* (1985), and *The Imperfect Paradise* (1988). *PM/AM: New and Selected Poems* (1982) was nominated for the American Book Award. Her latest collection, *An Early Afterlife,* was published in 1995.

### Marge Piercy (b. 1936)

Piercy's earlier poetry examined the complex interplay between personal relationships and political forces, at the same time voicing the rage of women who have for so long been dominated and overwhelmed by men ("I imagine that I speak for a constituency, living and dead," she writes). Her later work, particularly the poems in *Stone, Paper, Knife* (1983), expresses also a sense of inclusiveness, of interconnection with all living things. Born in Detroit, Piercy studied at the University of Michigan and Northwestern University, and taught for some time before the success of her novels allowed her to live a semirural life on Cape Cod. Her books of poetry include *Living in the Open* (1976), *The Moon Is Always Female* (1980), and *Available Light* (1988). In 1990 Piercy received the Golden Rose Award. Her most recent book of poetry, *What Are Big Girls Made Of?*, was published in 1997.

## Sylvia Plath (1932–1963)

Plath has attained the status of a cult figure as much for the splendid and beautiful agony of her poems as for her "martyrdom" to art. Her life, in all its outer banality and inner tragedy, might be seen as a confirmation that poetry is a dangerous vocation. Born the daughter of a Polish immigrant who died in 1940, Plath's early years were a vision of conventional success, including poetry prizes, scholarships at Smith College, and a summa cum laude graduation. She won a Fulbright Scholarship to Cambridge University, where she met and married the English poet Ted Hughes, with whom she had two children. Yet beneath it all was a woman whose acute perceptions and intolerable pain led her to produce a novel, *The Bell Jar* (1963), and three volumes of poetry— and to commit suicide at the age of thirty.

## Alexander Pope (1688–1744)

Born near London, Pope was delicate as a child and deformed early on by tuberculosis of the spine. He nevertheless was encouraged to read widely and exhibited a precocious talent for poetry; his first successes were the *Essay on Criticism* (1711) and *The Rape of the Lock* (1712 and 1714). Pope's Catholicism, which precluded him from attending a university, voting, holding public office, or receiving the sort of patronage commonly bestowed on writers of his generation, led him to embark on translations of Homer's *Iliad* and *Odyssey* in 1713, the success of which would eventually make him the only important writer of his generation to make his living solely by his craft. Pope's extraordinary career resulted in works as diverse as the *Dunciad* (1728 and 1743), his great verse satire, and the *Essay on Man* (1733–1734), his exploration of ethics and philosophy.

## Ezra Pound (1885–1972)

Pound's tremendous ambition—to succeed in his own work and to influence the development of poetry and Western culture in general—led him to found the Imagist school of poetry, to advise and assist a galaxy of great writers (Eliot, Joyce, Williams, Frost, and Hemingway, to name a few), and to write a number of highly influential critical works. It also led him to a charge of treason (Pound served as a propagandist for Mussolini during World War II), a diagnosis of insanity, and twelve years at St. Elizabeth's, an institution for the criminally insane. Born in Hailey, Idaho, Ezra Loomis Pound studied at the University of Pennsylvania and Hamilton College before traveling to Europe in 1908. He remained there, living in Ireland, England, France, and Italy, for much of his life. Pound's verse is collected in *Personae: The Collected Poems* (1949) and *The Cantos* (1976).

## Sir Walter Ralegh (1552–1618)

Clearly a man of immense versatility, Ralegh undertook a variety of adventures in his tumultuous life. Born in Devonshire, England, he briefly attended Oxford but withdrew to fight in the army. He is credited with bringing the potato to Ireland and tobacco to Europe, and through his many explorations, he became an investor in the North American colonies. He was knighted and named a member of Parliament, but after offending the queen, Ralegh was imprisoned in the Tower of London. After his release in 1595, he charted a failed expedition to Guiana, and in 1603 he was again imprisoned on trumped-up treason charges. In prison, he began his unfinished *History of the World*. After another unsuccessful trip to Guiana, he was again imprisoned and executed on the orders of James I. His writings include the popular "The Nymph's Reply to the Shepherd," a response to Marlowe's "Passionate Shepherd," and some extensive writings on his findings in Guiana.

Jarold Ramsey (b. 1937)

Ramsey grew up on a ranch in central Oregon, and his work reflects his ongoing interest in the mythology and culture of Native Americans of the Northwest. He taught for many years at the University of Rochester. His recent books include *Hand Shadows* (1989) and an edited collection, *The Stories We Tell: A Collection of Oregon Folk Literature* (1994).

Ishmael Reed (b. 1938)

Born in Chattanooga, Tennessee, Reed attended the University of Buffalo. Considered a writer of the 1960s and 1970s counterculture, Reed, through his novels, essays, plays, songs, and poems, calls attention to the marginalization of nonwhite cultures and traditions in mainstream America. While he is probably best known for his satirical novel *Mumbo Jumbo* (1972), Reed is a prolific poet. His first volume, *Catechism of D NeoAmerican Hoodoo Church,* was published in 1970. His most recent work is a novel, *Japanese by Spring* (1993). Reed has taught at a variety of colleges and universities; he currently teaches at the University of California, Berkeley.

Alberto Alvaro Ríos (b. 1952)

Ríos was born in Nogales, Arizona, to a British mother and a Mexican father. He graduated from the University of Arizona and teaches at Arizona State University. He has received an NEA Fellowship and the 1981 Academy of American Poets Walt Whitman's Award for his collection of poems entitled *Whispering to Fool the Wind*. His other publications include three books of poetry—*Five Indiscretions* (1985), *The Lime Orchard Woman* (1988), and *Teodoro Luna's Two Kisses* (1990)—as well as two collections of short stories—*The Iguana Killer: Twelve Stories of the Heart* (1984), and *Pig Cookies and Other Stories* (1995).

Theodore Roethke (1908–1963)

Born in Saginaw, Michigan, Roethke grew up around his father's twenty-five-acre greenhouse complex—its associations with nurture and growth became an important subject in his later poetry. He worked for a time at Lafayette College, where he was professor of English and tennis coach, and later at the University of Washington, which appointed him poet-in-residence one year before he died. Roethke was an unhappy man, suffering from periodic mental breakdowns, yet the best of his poetry, with its reverence for and fear of the physical world, its quest for an ecstatic union with nature, seems destined to last. Roethke's books include *Open House* (1942), *Praise to the End!* (1951), and *The Far Field* (1964), which received a posthumous National Book Award.

Liz Rosenberg (b. 1956)

A native of Long Island, New York, Rosenberg received a B.A. from Bennington College in 1976 before earning a master's degree from Johns Hopkins University in 1978. The author of several books of poetry, including *The Angel Poems* (1984), *The Fire Music* (1985), and *Children of Paradise* (1994), she has also written numerous children's books. Currently on the faculty at the State University of New York in Binghamton, Rosenberg has also taught at Colgate University and reviews poetry for the *Boston Globe,* the *New York Times,* and the *Chicago Tribune,* among others.

## Muriel Rukeyser (1913–1980)

Born in New York City, Rukeyser later attended Vassar College and Columbia University. Uncomfortable with her family's wealth, Rukeyser associated herself with more radical issues—namely, the labor movement of the 1920s and 1930s. Her first collection of poetry, *Theory of Flight* (1935), was apparently inspired by her attendance at the Roosevelt Aviation School. In the 1940s Rukeyser wrote poetry highlighting the destruction of World War II. She later protested against U.S. involvement in Korea and Vietnam, and in the 1970s, she addressed feminist issues in her art. *The Collected Poems of Muriel Rukeyser* was published in 1978.

## Anne Sexton (1928–1974)

Born in Newton, Massachusetts, Anne (Harvey) Sexton interrupted her attendance at Garland Junior College to marry. She wrote poetry as a child, abandoned it, and, on the advice of her doctors, began writing again after suffering a nervous breakdown. Sexton attended Boston University with fellow student Sylvia Plath, and she studied poetry with Robert Lowell. Published in 1960, her first book of poems, *To Bedlam and Part Way Back,* recounted her mental collapse and subsequent recovery period. A "confessional" poet, Sexton received many awards, most notably the Pulitzer Prize for *Live or Die* (1966). She committed suicide in 1974. That same year, she had published *Death Notebooks;* a posthumous volume, *The Awful Rowing toward God,* appeared in 1975.

## William Shakespeare (1554–1616)

Considering the great and deserved fame of his work, surprisingly little is known of Shakespeare's life. We do know that between 1585 and 1592 he left his birthplace of Stratford for London to begin a career as playwright and actor. No dates of his professional career are recorded, however, nor can we be certain of the order in which he composed his plays and poetry. By 1594 he had established himself as a poet with two long works—*Venus and Adonis* and *The Rape of Lucrece*—but it was in the theater that he made his strongest reputation. Shakespeare produced perhaps 35 plays in twenty-five years, proving himself a master of many genres in works such as *Macbeth, King Lear, Othello,* and *Antony and Cleopatra* (tragedy); *Richard III* and *Henry IV* (historical drama); *Twelfth Night* and *As You Like It* (comedy); and *The Tempest* (romance). His more than 150 sonnets are supreme expressions of the form.

## Percy Bysshe Shelley (1792–1822)

Born in Sussex to a wealthy member of Parliament, Shelley attended Eton and Oxford. An unconventional young man, Shelley was expelled from Oxford during his first year for collaborating with a friend, Thomas Jefferson Hogg, on a pamphlet entitled "The Necessity of Atheism" (1811). That same year, Shelley eloped with Harriet Westbrook, but within three years, he left her to be with Mary Wollstonecraft Godwin. After Harriet's suicide, Shelley married Mary, and the couple and their children moved permanently to Italy. The death of their two children, coupled with financial difficulties, left Shelley in despair, and it was at this time (1819) that he wrote his most memorable poetry—namely, "Prometheus Unbound" and "Ode to the West Wind." Shelley's important critical essay, "A Defence of Poetry," was published posthumously in 1840.

### Stevie Smith (1902–1971)

Because of her small size, Florence Margaret Smith earned her nickname from a famous jockey, Steve Donoghue. At a young age, her family moved to a London suburb, and later Smith worked as a secretary at a publishing company and as a writer and broadcaster for the BBC. In the 1930s, she began publishing fiction and poetry, which she often illustrated. Her first novel, *Novel on Yellow Paper*, appeared in 1936, followed by her first collection of poetry, *A Good Time Was Had by All* (1937). Her fascination with death was collected in verse in a volume called *Not Waving but Drowning* (1957), in which she maintains her consistently witty voice. In 1966 she was given the Cholmondely Award, and in 1969 she received the Queen's Gold Medal for Poetry. Both her *Collected Poems* (1976) and *Me Again: The Uncollected Writings* (1981) were published after her death.

### Wallace Stevens (1879–1955)

"I believe that with a bucket of sand and a wishing lamp I could create a world in half a second that would make this one look like a hunk of mud," Stevens once remarked to his wife. One of the great imaginative forces of this century, he was nevertheless an extraordinarily self-effacing public man, working for much of his adult life as an executive of the Hartford Accident and Indemnity Company while re-creating the world at night in the "supreme fiction" of poetry. Born in Reading, Pennsylvania, Stevens attended Harvard University and New York Law School; his first book of poems, *Harmonium*, appeared in 1923. Stevens's poetry and prose can be found in *The Palm at the End of the Mind* (1971) and *The Necessary Angel: Essays on Reality and Imagination* (1951).

### Jonathan Swift (1667–1745)

Born to English parents in Dublin, Ireland, Swift later attended Trinity College. In 1689, he moved to England in the service of Sir William Temple. Swift later received an M.A. from Oxford, and in 1695 he took orders to become an Anglican clergyman. He became known for his scathing religious and political satires, and after writing "A Tale of a Tub" and "The Battle of the Books," he returned to Ireland and was named dean of Saint Patrick's Cathedral in Dublin. In his later years, Swift suffered from senility and was removed from his post. He is most popularly known for his 1726 book, *Gulliver's Travels*. His poetry, too, is masterfully satiric.

### Alfred, Lord Tennyson (1809–1892)

Perhaps the most important and certainly the most popular of the Victorian poets, Tennyson demonstrated his talents at an early age; he published his first volume in 1827. Encouraged to devote his life to poetry by a group of undergraduates at Cambridge University known as the "Apostles," Tennyson was particularly close to Arthur Hallam, whose sudden death in 1833 inspired the long elegy *In Memoriam* (1850). With that poem he achieved lasting fame and recognition; he was appointed Poet Laureate the year of its publication. Whatever the popularity of his "journalistic" poetry—"The Charge of the Light Brigade" (1854) is perhaps his best known—Tennyson's great theme was always the past, both personal (*In the Valley of Cauteretz*, 1864) and national (*Idylls of the King*, 1869).

Dylan Thomas (1914–1953)

In a note to his *Collected Poems* (1952), Thomas wrote: "These poems, with all their crudities, doubts, and confusions, are written for the love of Man and in praise of God, and I'd be a damn fool if they weren't." Given their somber undertones and often wrenching awareness of death, his poems are also rich verbal and visual celebrations of life and its sweetness. Born in Swansea, Wales, into what he called "the smug darkness of a provincial town," Thomas published his first book, *18 Poems* (1934), at the age of twenty. Thereafter he had a successful, though turbulent, career publishing poetry, short stories, and plays, including the highly successful *Under Milk Wood* (1954). In his last years he supported himself with lecture tours and poetry readings in the United States, but his extravagant drinking caught up with him and he died in New York City of chronic alcoholism.

Jean Toomer (1894–1967)

Born in Washington, D.C., Toomer later briefly attended a number of colleges and universities. He published poetry and fiction in a variety of small magazines, in addition to African American publications like *Crisis* and *Opportunity*. A crucial text of the Harlem Renaissance, Toomer's landmark, *Cane*, was published in 1923. *Cane* combines a variety of genres, and Toomer's juxtapositions of poetry, drama, and prose foreground his comparisons between rural and urban life for African Americans. After *Cane*, Toomer was unable to publish his work, and he primarily wrote for himself. In 1980, his previously unpublished works appeared in a volume called *The Wayward and the Seeking*.

Walt Whitman (1819–1892)

Born on a farm in West Hills, Long Island, to a British father and a Dutch mother, Whitman eventually worked as a journalist throughout New York for many years. After teaching for a while, he founded his own newspaper, *The Long Islander,* in 1838, but he left journalism to work on *Leaves of Grass,* which was originally intended as a poetic treatise on American democratic idealism. Published privately in multiple editions from 1855 to 1874, the book originally failed to reach a mass audience. In 1881 Boston's Osgood and Company published another edition of *Leaves of Grass,* which sold well until the district attorney called it "obscene literature" and stipulated that Whitman remove certain poems and phrases. He refused, and many years later his works were published in Philadelphia. Whitman's poetry creates tension between the self-conscious and political, the romantic and realistic, the mundane and mystical, and the collective and individual.

Richard Wilbur (b. 1921)

A native of New York City, Wilbur grew up in New Jersey and attended Amherst College. He started to write while serving as an army cryptographer during World War II in an attempt to create a degree of order during the chaos of military campaigns throughout southern Europe and northern Africa. The publication after the war of *The Beautiful Changes and Other Poems* (1947) and *Ceremony and Other Poems* (1950) established his reputation as a significant new poet. After earning an M.A. at Harvard University, Wilbur devoted himself to teaching and has worked at Harvard, Wellesley College, Wesleyan University, and Smith College, among others. He received the Pulitzer Prize for his volume *Things of This World* (1956) and was the second U.S. poet laureate consultant in poetry in 1987–1988. In addition to volumes of poetry such as *Walking to Sleep* (1969) and *The Mind Reader: New Poems* (1976), Wilbur is the author of children's books, critical essays, and numerous translations of classic French works, including Molière's *Tartuffe* (1963) and *The Misanthrope* (1955).

### William Carlos Williams (1883–1963)

Williams influenced a generation of American poets—many of them still living—by bringing to poetry the sense that "life is above all things else at any moment subversive of life as it was the moment before—always new, irregular." Born in Rutherford, New Jersey, Williams attended school in Switzerland and New York, and studied medicine at the University of Pennsylvania, where he met Hilda Doolittle (H.D.) and Ezra Pound. Thereafter he spent most of his life in Rutherford, practicing medicine and crafting a poetry of palpable immediacy, written in vital, local language. His long poem, *Paterson* (completed in 1963), vividly expresses what lies at the heart of his work: "No ideas but in things."

### William Wordsworth (1770–1850)

Born in Cockermouth in the sparsely populated English Lake District (which Coleridge and he would immortalize), Wordsworth spent his early years "drinking in" (to use a favorite metaphor) a rural environment that would provide material for much of his later poetry. After study at Cambridge University, he spent a year in France, hoping to witness firsthand the French Revolution's "glorious renovation." Remarkably, he was able to establish "a saving intercourse with my true self"—and to write some of his finest poetry—after a love affair with a French woman whose sympathies were Royalist, his own disillusionment at the Revolution, a forced return to England, and near emotional collapse. Perhaps because he was, above all, a poet of remembrance (of "emotion recollected in tranquility"), and his own early experience was not an inexhaustible resource, Wordsworth had written most of his great work—including his masterpiece, *The Prelude*—by the time he was forty.

### William Butler Yeats (1865–1939)

Perhaps the greatest twentieth-century poet in English, Yeats was born in Dublin, attended art school for a time, and left to devote himself to poetry (at the start of his career, a self-consciously romantic poetry, dreamy and ethereal). Yeats's reading of Nietzsche, his involvement with the Nationalist cause, and his desperate love for the actress (and Nationalist) Maud Gonne led to a tighter, more actively passionate verse and a number of innovative dramatic works. Bitter and disillusioned at the results of revolution and the rise of the Irish middle class, Yeats later withdrew from contemporary events to "Thoor Ballylee," his Norman Tower in the country, there to construct an elaborate mythology and to write poetry, at once realist, symbolist, and metaphysical, which explored what were, for Yeats, fundamental questions of history and identity. Of the progress of his life, Yeats once said: "Man can embody truth but cannot know it."

# Acknowledgments

DANNIE ABSE: "Brueghel in Naples." Reprinted by permission of The Peters Fraser and Dunlop Group.

DIANE ACKERMAN: "Sweep Me Through Your Many-Chambered Heart" from *Jaguar of Sweet Laughter* by Diane Ackerman. Copyright © 1991 by Diane Ackerman. Reprinted by permission of Random House, Inc.

VIRGINIA HAMILTON ADAIR: "Cutting the Cake" and "Peeling an Orange" from *Ants on the Melon* by Virginia Hamilton Adair. Copyright © 1996 by Virginia Hamilton Adair. Reprinted by permission of Random House, Inc.

AI: "Riot Act April 29, 1992" from *Greed* by Ai. Copyright © 1993 by Ai. Reprinted by permission of W. W. Norton & Company, Inc. "Twenty-Year Marriage" from *Cruelty* by Ai. Reprinted by permission of the author.

ELIZABETH ALEXANDER: "West Indian Primer" from *The Venus Hottentot* by Elizabeth Alexander. Copyright © 1990. Reprinted by permission of the University Press of Virginia.

AGHA SHAHID ALI: "The Dacca Gauzes" and "Postcard from Kashmir" from *The Half-Inch Himalayas* by Agha Shahid Ali. Copyright ©1987 by Wesleyan University Press. Reprinted by permission of University Press of New England.

A. ALVAREZ: "Sylvia Plath" from *The Savage God*. Copyright © 1974. Reprinted by permission of Weidenfeld & Nicolson.

A. R. AMMONS: "Needs" from *Collected Poems 1951–1971* by A. R. Ammons. Copyright © 1968 by A. R. Ammons. Reprinted by permission of W. W. Norton & Company, Inc.

MAYA ANGELOU: "Africa" from *Oh Pray My Wings Are Gonna Fit Me Well* by Maya Angelou. Copyright © 1975 by Maya Angelou. Reprinted by permission of Random House, Inc.

PAMELA J. ANNAS: excerpt from *A Disturbance in Mirrors: The Poetry of Sylvia Plath,* by Pamela J. Annas. Copyright © 1988 by Pamela J. Annas. Reproduced with permission of Greenwood Publishing Group, Inc. (Westport, CT).

RICHARD ARMOUR: "Hiding Place." Copyright © 1954 by Richard Armour. Reprinted by permission of John Hawkins & Associates, Inc.

JOHN ASHBERY: "City Afternoon," copyright © 1974 by John Ashbery, from *Self-Portrait in a Convex Mirror* by John Ashbery. Used by permission of Viking Penguin, a division of Penguin Putnam Inc.

MARGARET ATWOOD: "Death of a Young Son by Drowning" from *Selected Poems 1966–1984* by Margaret Atwood. Copyright © Margaret Atwood, 1990. Reprinted by permission of Oxford University Press. "Siren Song" from *You Are Happy, Selected Poems 1965–1975* and *Selected Poems 1966–1984* by Margaret Atwood. Copyright © 1976 by Margaret Atwood. Reprinted by permission of Houghton Mifflin Co. and Oxford University Press Canada. All rights reserved.

W. H. AUDEN: "As I Walked Out One Evening," "In Memory of W. B. Yeats," and "Stop all the clocks" from *W. H. Auden: Collected Poems* by W. H. Auden, edited by Edward Mendelson. Copyright © 1940 and renewed 1968 by W. H. Auden. Reprinted by permission of Random House, Inc. "Musée des Beaux Arts," from *W. H. Auden: Collected Poems* by W. H. Auden, edited by Edward Mendelson. Copyright © 1940 and renewed 1968 by W. H. Auden. Reprinted by permission of Random House, Inc and Faber & Faber Ltd.

STEVEN GOULD AXELROD: "Jealous Gods" [excerpt from *Sylvia Plath: The Wound and the Cure of Words*] by Steven Gould Axelrod (pp 51–59, 62–63, 67–70). Copyright © 1980 by the Johns Hopkins University Press. Reprinted by permission.

JIMMY SANTIAGO BACA: "Green Chile" from *Black Mesa Poems*. Copyright © 1989 by Jimmy Santiago Baca. Reprinted by permission of the New Directions Publishing Corp.

CAROL JANE BANGS: "Touching Each Other's Surfaces" from *The Bones of the Earth*. Copyright © 1983 by Carol Jane Bangs. Reprinted by permission of New Directions Publishing Corp.

REGINA BARRECA: "Nighttime Fires." First appeared in *The Minnesota Review* 27 (1987). Reprinted by permission.

BASHŌ: "First snow," "This road," "A village without bells," and "Another year gone" from *The Essential Haiku,* edited and with verse translations by Robert Hass. Copyright © 1994 by Robert Hass. Reprinted by permission of the Ecco Press.

APRIL BERNARD: "Praise Psalm of the City-Dweller" from *Psalms* by April Bernard. Copyright © 1993 by April Bernard. Reprinted by permission of W. W. Norton & Company, Inc.

CHARLES BERNSTEIN: "Of Time and the Line" from *Rough Trade* by Charles Bernstein. Reprinted by permission of the author.

JOHN BETJEMAN: "In Westminster Abbey" from *Collected Poems* by John Betjeman. Reprinted by permission of John Murray (Publishers) Ltd.

EARLE BIRNEY: "Anglosaxon Street" and "Irupuato" from *Selected Poems* by Earle Birney. Used by permission of McClelland & Stewart, Inc., Toronto, The Canadian Publishers.

ELIZABETH BISHOP: "The Armadillo," "Casabianca," "Exchanging Hats," and "Sestina" from *The Collected Poems 1927–1979* by Elizabeth Bishop. Copyright © 1979, 1980 by Alice Helen Methfessel. Reprinted by permission of Farrar, Straus & Giroux.

R. H. BLYTH: "The old pond" from *Zen in English Literature and Oriental Classics* (Tokyo: Hokuseido Press). Copyright © 1942 by R. H. Blyth.

LOUISE BOGAN: "Evening in the Sanitarium" and "Single Sonnet" from *Blue Estuaries* Copyright © 1968 by Louise Bogan. Copyright renewed © 1996 by Ruth Limmer. Reprinted by permission of Farrar, Straus & Giroux, Inc.

ROO BORSON: "After a Death" and "Save Us From" from *Intent, or The Weight of the World,* by Roo Borson. Used by permission of McClelland & Stewart, Inc., Toronto, The Canadian Publishers.

MARY LYNN BROE: excerpt from *Protean Poetic: The Poetry of Sylvia Plath* by Mary Lynn Broe. Copyright © 1980 by the Curators of the University of Missouri Press. Reprinted by permission of the publisher.

GWENDOLYN BROOKS: "First Fight, Then Fiddle" and "We Real Cool" from *Blacks* by Gwendolyn Brooks. "To the Diaspora" and "The Coora Flower" from *Children Coming Home* by Gwendolyn Brooks. Copyright © 1991 by Gwendolyn Brooks. Reprinted by permission of the author.

JOHN THOMAS BRYAN: "There is the old pond!" from *The Literature of Japan* by John Thomas Bryan. Copyright © 1929 by John Thomas Bryan. Reprinted by permission of Henry Holt and Company, Inc.

BUSON: "Coolness" and "Listening to the Moon" from *The Essential Haiku,* edited and with verse translations by Robert Hass. Copyright © 1994 by Robert Hass. Reprinted by permission of the Ecco Press.

KAREN CHASE: "Venison." Originally published in *The New Yorker.* Copyright © 1995 by Karen Chase. Reprinted by permission of Harold Matson Co., Inc.

HELEN CHASIN: "Joy Sonnet in a Random Universe" and "The Word Plum" from *Coming Close and Other Poems* by Helen Chasin. Copyright © 1968 by Helen Chasin. Reprinted by permission of Yale University Press.

MARILYN CHIN: "We Are Americans Now, We Live in the Tundra" from *Dwarf Bamboo* by Marilyn Chin. Copyright © 1987. Reprinted by permission of The Greenfield Review Press.

CHIYOJO: "Bearing no flowers" and "Whether astringent I do not know" from *One Hundred Famous Haiku,* selected and translated by Daniel Buchanan. Reprinted by permission of Japan Publications, Inc.

AMY CLAMPITT: "Meridian" from *The Kingfisher* by Amy Clampitt. Copyright © 1983 by Amy Clampitt. Reprinted by permission of Alfred A. Knopf, Inc.

SARAH N. CLEGHORN: ["the golf links lie so near the mill"] from *Portraits and Protests* by Sarah N. Cleghorn, © 1917 by Henry Holt and Company.

JUDITH ORTIZ COFER: "The Changeling" from *Prairie Schooner* by Judith Ortiz Cofer. Copyright © 1992 by the University of Nebraska Press. Reprinted by permission of the publisher. "How to Get a Baby" from *The Latin Deli: Prose & Poetry* by Judith Ortiz Cofer. Reprinted by permission of The University of Georgia Press.

WENDY COPE: "Emily Dickinson" and "From Strugnell's Sonnets IV, 'Not only marble, but the plastic toys' " from *Making Cocoa for Kingsley Amis* by Wendy Cope. Reprinted by permission of Faber & Faber Ltd.

FRANCES CORNFORD: "The New-Born Baby's Song" from *Collected Poems* (Cresset Press, 1954). Reprinted by permission of Hutchinson.

HART CRANE: "To Emily Dickinson," from *Complete Poems of Hart Crane* edited by Marc Simon. Copyright 1933, © 1958, 1966 by Liveright Publishing Corporation. Copyright © 1986 by Marc Simon. Reprinted by permission of Liveright Publishing Corporation.

COUNTEE CULLEN: "For a Lady I Know" and "Yet Do I Marvel" from *Color* by Countee Cullen. Copyright © 1925 by Harper & Brothers, copyright renewed 1953 by Ida M. Cullen. Reprinted by permission of GRM Associates, agents for the Estate of Ida M. Cullen.

E. E. CUMMINGS: "anyone lived in a pretty how town," "l(a," and "(ponder, darling, these busted statues" from *Complete Poems: 1904–1962* by e. e. cummings, edited by George J. Firmage. "anyone lived in a pretty how town," copyright 1940, © 1968, 1991 by the Trustees for the E. E. Cummings Trust. "l(a," copyright © 1958, 1986, 1991 by the Trustees for the E. E. Cummings Trust. "(ponder, darling, these busted statues," copyright © 1926, 1954, © 1991 by the Trustees for the E. E. Cummings Trust. Copyright © 1985 by George James Firmage. "Buffalo Bill's" and "in Just-" from *Complete Poems: 1904–1962* by e. e. cummings, edited by George J. Firmage. Copyright © 1923, 1951, © 1991 by the Trustees for the E. E. Cummings Trust. Copyright © 1976 by George James Firmage. Reprinted by permission of Liveright Publishing Corporation.

WALTER DE LA MARE: "Slim Cunning Hands" from *The Complete Poems of Walter de la Mare*. Reprinted by permission of the Literary Trustees of Walter de la Mare and the Society of Authors as their representative.

BABETTE DEUTSCH: "The Falling Flower . . ." from *Poetry Handbook: A Dictionary of Terms* by Babette Deutsch. Copyright © 1974, 1969, 1962, 1957 by Babette Deutsch. Reprinted by permission of HarperCollins Publishers, Inc.

PETER DE VRIES: "To His Importunate Mistress" Originally published in *The New Yorker*. Reprinted by permission of Jan De Vries and the Watkins/Loomis Agency.

GREG DELANTY: "Leavetaking" by Greg Delanty, in *Southward*, Copyright © 1992 by Greg Delanty. Used with permission of Louisiana State University Press.

JAMES DICKEY: "Cherrylog Road" and "The Leap" from *Poems, 1957–1967*. Copyright © 1964 and 1967 by Wesleyan University Press. Reprinted by permission of University Press of New England.

EMILY DICKINSON: #341 [After great pain, a formal feeling comes—], #479 [She dealt her pretty words like Blades], #657 [I dwell in Possibility], #569 [I Reckon—when I count at all—], and #754 [My Life had stood—a Loaded Gun] from *The Poems of Emily Dickinson* edited by Thomas H. Johnson (Cambridge, Mass.: The Belknap Press of Harvard University Press). Copyright © 1951, 1955, 1979, 1983 by the President and Fellows of Harvard College. Copyright © 1929, 1935 by Martha Dickinson Bianchi; copyright © renewed 1957, 1963 by Mary L. Hampson. Reprinted by permission of the publishers and the Trustees of Amherst College and Little, Brown & Company. #467 [We do not play on Graves—], #632 [The Brain is Wider than the Sky] and #824 [The Wind begun to knead the Grass—] from *The Poems of Emily Dickinson* edited by Thomas H. Johnson (Cambridge, Mass.: The Belknap Press of Harvard University Press). Copyright © 1951, 1955, 1979, 1983 by the President and Fellows of Harvard College. Reprinted by permission of the publishers and the Trustees of Amherst College.

CHITRA BANERJEE DIVAKARUNI: "Indian Movie, New Jersey" from *Leaving Yuba City* by Chitra Banerjee Divakaruni. Copyright © 1997 by Chitra Banerjee Divakaruni. Used by permission of Doubleday, a division of Bantam Doubleday Dell Publishing Group, Inc.

SUSAN DONNELLY: "Eve Names the Animals" from *Eve Names the Animals* by Susan Donnelly. Copyright © 1985 by Susan Donnelly. Reprinted by permission of Northeastern University Press.

HILDA DOOLITTLE: "To Helen," "Garden," and "Sea Rose" from *Collected Poems 1912–1944* by Hilda Doolittle. Copyright © 1982 by the Estate of Hilda Doolittle. Reprinted by permission of New Directions Publishing Corp.

RITA DOVE: "Fifth Grade Autobiography" from *Grace Notes* by Rita Dove. Copyright © 1989 by Rita Dove. Reprinted by permission of W. W. Norton & Company, Inc. "Parsley" from *Museum* by Rita Dove (Carnegie-Mellon University Press, 1983), and "Daystar" from *Thomas and Beulah* by Rita Dove (Carnegie-Mellon University Press, 1986). Copyright © 1983 and © 1986 by Rita Dove. Reprinted by permission of the author.

ALAN DUGAN: "Elegy" from *New and Collected Poems 1961–1983* by Alan Dugan. Copyright © 1961–62, 1968, 1972–74, 1983 by Alan Dugan. Reprinted by permission of Ecco Press.

STEPHEN DUNN: "Dancing With God" from *Between Angels* by Stephen Dunn. Copyright © 1989 by Stephen Dunn. Reprinted by permission of W. W. Norton & Company, Inc.

RICHARD EBERHART: "Fury of Aerial Bombardment" and "The Groundhog" from *Collected Poems 1930–1976* by Richard Eberhart. Copyright © 1976 by Richard Eberhart. Used by permission of Oxford University Press, Inc.

T. S. ELIOT: "Journey of the Magi" and "Morning at the Window" from *Collected Poems 1909–1962* by T. S. Eliot. Copyright © 1936 by Harcourt Brace & Company, copyright © 1964, 1963 by T. S. Eliot. Reprinted by permission of Harcourt Brace & Company and Faber & Faber Ltd. "The Love Song of J. Alfred Prufrock" from *Collected Poems 1909 to 1962* by T. S. Eliot. Reprinted by permission of Faber & Faber Ltd.

JAMES A. EMANUEL: "Emmett Till" from *Whole Grain: Collected Poems,* 1958–1989 by James A. Emanuel. Reprinted by permission of the author.

LOUISE ERDRICH: "Jacklight" from *Jacklight* by Louise Erdrich. Copyright © 1984 by Louise Erdrich. Reprinted by permission of Henry Holt & Co., Inc.

MARTIN ESPADA: "The Sign in My Father's Hands" from *Imagine the Angels of Bread* by Martin Espada. Copyright © 1996 by Martin Espada. Reprinted by permission of W. W. Norton & Company, Inc.

KENNETH FEARING: "Dirge" from *New and Selected Poems* by Kenneth Fearing. Reprinted by permission of Indiana University Press.

CAROLYN FORCHÉ: "Reunion" (all lines) from *The Country Between Us* by Carolyn Forché. Copyright © 1978 by Carolyn Forché. Reprinted by permission of HarperCollins Publishers, Inc. "Taking Off My Clothes" from *Gathering the Tribes* by Carolyn Forché. Copyright © 1976. Reprinted by permission of Yale University Press.

ROBERT FRANCIS: "Hogwash" from *Robert Francis: Collected Poems, 1936–1976* by Robert Francis (Amherst: University of Massachusetts Press, 1976). Copyright © 1976 by Robert Francis. Reprinted by permission of the publisher.

ROBERT FROST: "Design," "Once by the Pacific," "The Rose Family," "Range—Finding," "Stopping by the Woods on a Snowy Evening," and "The Road Not Taken" from *The Poetry of Robert Frost,* edited by Edward Connery Lathem. Copyright © 1916, © 1936, © 1956 by Robert Frost, © 1964 by Lesley Frost Ballantine, Copyright © 1916, 1923, © 1928, © 1969 by Henry Holt & Co., Inc.

TESS GALLAGHER: "Sudden Journey" from *Amplitude: New and Selected Poems* by Tess Gallagher. Copyright © 1984, 1987 by Tess Gallagher. Reprinted with the permission of Graywolf Press (Saint Paul, Minnesota).

SANDRA GILBERT: "Sonnet: The Ladies' Home Journal" from *Emily's Bread* by Sandra M. Gilbert. Copyright © 1984 by Sandra M. Gilbert. Reprinted by permission of W. W. Norton & Company, Inc.

ALLEN GINSBERG: "A Further Proposal" (all lines), copyright © 1984 by Allen Ginsberg; "Howl" (all lines), Copyright © 1955 by Allen Ginsberg; [Looking over my shoulder] (all lines), copyright © 1984 by Allen Ginsberg; "A Supermarket in California" (all lines), copyright © 1955 by Allen Ginsberg; from *Collected Poems 1947–1980* by Allen Ginsberg. "Personals Ad" Copyright © 1994 by Allen Ginsberg, and "Velocity of Money" from *Cosmopolitan Greetings, Poems 1986–1992* by Allen Ginsberg. Reprinted by permission of HarperCollins Publishers, Inc.

SUSAN GLICKMAN: "Beauty" from *Henry Moore's Sheep*, a Signal Edition of Ve'hicule Press. Reprinted by permission.

LOUISE GLÜCK: "Labor Day" from *Firstborn* by Louise Glück. Copyright © 1968 by Louise Glück. Reprinted by permission of Ecco Press.

JORIE GRAHAM: "The Geese" from *Hybrids of Plants and Ghosts*. Copyright © 1980 by Princeton University Press. Reprinted by permission of Princeton University Press. "Short History of the West" from *Regions of Unlikeness* by Jorie Graham. Copyright © 1991 by Jorie Graham. Reprinted by permission of The Ecco Press.

ROBERT GRAVES: "The Naked and the Nude" from *The Collected Poems of Robert Graves* by Robert Graves. Used by permission of Oxford University Press, Inc.

EAMON GRENNAN: "Pause" from *So It Goes* by Eamon Grennan. Copyright © 1995 by Eamon Grennan. Reprinted with the permission of Graywolf Press (Saint Paul, Minnesota).

EDGAR A. GUEST: "The Things That Make a Soldier Great." Reprinted from *The Collected Verse of Edgar A. Guest* © 1984. Used with permission by NTC/CONTEMPORARY PUBLISHING GROUP.

MARILYN HACKER: [Who would divorce her lover . . .] from *Love, Death, and the Changing of the Seasons* by Marilyn Hacker. Copyright © 1986 by Marilyn Hacker. Reprinted by permission of Frances Collin, Literary Agent.

JAMES W. HACKETT: "Up close at the place" from *The Zen Haiku and Other Zen Poems of J. W. Hackett* (Tokyo: Japan Publications, Inc., 1983). Distributed in the USA by Zen View Distributors (P.O. Box 313, La Honda, CA 94020–0313).

MICHAEL S. HARPER: "Dear John, Dear Coltrane" from *Dear John, Dear Coltrane* by Michael S. Harper. Copyright © 1970 by Michael S. Harper. Reprinted by permission of the author.

GWEN HARWOOD: "In the Park" from *Selected Poems* by Gwen Harwood. (ETT Imprint, Watsons Bay 1997). Reprinted by permission of the publisher.

HASHIN: "No sky and no earth" from *One Hundred Famous Haiku,* selected and translated by Daniel Buchanan. Reprinted by permission of Japan Publications, Inc.

ROBERT HAYDEN: "Frederick Douglas" and "Those Winter Sundays," from *Collected Poems of Robert Hayden* edited by Frederick Glaysher. Copyright © 1966 by Robert Hayden. Reprinted by permission of Liveright Publishing Corporation.

SEAMUS HEANEY: "Mid-Term Break" from *Poems 1965–1975* by Seamus Heaney. Copyright © 1980 by Seamus Heaney. Reprinted by permission of Farrar, Straus & Giroux, Inc. and Faber & Faber. Ltd. "The Outlaw" from *Door Into the Dark* by Seamus Heaney. Reprinted by permission of Faber and Faber Ltd.
"The Summer of Lost Rachel" from *The Haw Lantern* by Seamus Heaney. Copyright © 1987 by Seamus Heaney. Reprinted by permission of Farrar, Straus & Giroux and Faber & Faber Ltd.

ANTHONY HECHT: "The Dover Bitch" and "A Hill" from *Collected Earlier Poems* by Anthony Hecht. Copyright © 1990 by Anthony E. Hecht. Reprinted by permission of Alfred A. Knopf, Inc.

GEOFFREY HILL: "In Memory of Jane Fraser" from *New and Collected Poems 1952–1992* by Geoffrey Hill. Copyright © 1994 by Geoffrey Hill. Previously published in *Somewhere Is Such a Kingdom* (1975). Reprinted by permission of Houghton Mifflin Company. All rights reserved.

JOHN HOLLANDER: "Adam's Task" from *Selected Poetry* by John Hollander. Copyright © 1993 by John Hollander. Reprinted by permission of Alfred A. Knopf, Inc. "A State of Nature" from *Types of Shape* by John Hollander. Copyright © 1967 by John Hollander. Reprinted by permission of Yale University Press.

ROBERT HOLLANDER: "You Too? Me Too—Why Not? Soda Pop" from *The Massachusetts Review*. Copyright © 1968 by The Massachusetts Review, Inc. Reprinted by permission of the publisher.

MARGARET HOMANS: "A Feminine Tradition" [excerpt from *Women Writers and Poetic Identity*] by Margaret Homans. Copyright © 1980 by Princeton University Press. Reprinted by permission of Princeton University Press.

IRVING HOWE: "The Plath Celebration: A Partial Dissent" from *The Critical Point of Literature and Culture* by Irving Howe (Horizon Press, 1973). Reprinted by permission of the Literary Estate of Irving Howe.

LANGSTON HUGHES: "Harlem (A Dream Deferred)" from *The Panther and the Lash* by Langston Hughes. Copyright 1951 by Langston Hughes. Reprinted by permission of Alfred A. Knopf, Inc. "The Negro Speaks of Rivers" from *Selected Poems* by Langston Hughes. Copyright 1926 by Alfred A. Knopf, Inc. and renewed 1954 by Langston Hughes. Reprinted by permission of the publisher.

LI-YOUNG LEE: "Persimmons" from *Rose* by Li-Young Lee. Copyright © 1986 by Li-Young Lee. Reprinted by permission of BOA Editions, Ltd. (92 Park Avenue, Brockport, NY 14420).

DENISE LEVERTOV: "Wedding Ring" and "Love Poem" from *Life in the Forest* by Denise Levertov. Copyright © 1978 by Denise Levertov. "What Were They Like" by Denise Levertov, from *Poems 1960–1967.* Copyright © 1966 by Denise Levertov. Reprinted by permission of New Directions Publishing Corp.

C. DAY LEWIS: "Song" from *The Complete Poems* by C. Day Lewis, published by Sinclair–Stevenson (1992). Copyright © 1992 in this edition. The Estate of C. Day Lewis. Reprinted by permission.

AUDRE LORDE: "Hanging Fire" and "Recreation" from *The Black Unicorn* by Audre Lorde. Copyright © 1978 by Audre Lorde. Reprinted by permission of W. W. Norton & Company, Inc.

ROBERT LOWELL: "Skunk Hour" from *Life Studies* by Robert Lowell. Copyright © 1956, 1959 by Robert Lowell. Copyright renewed © 1987 by Harriet Lowell, Sheridan Lowell, and Caroline Lowell. Reprinted by permission of Farrar, Straus & Giroux, Inc.

HEATHER MCHUGH: "Two St. Petersburgs" from *Hinge & Sign* by Heather McHugh. Copyright © 1994 by Wesleyan University Press. By permission of The University Press of New England.

CLAUDE MCKAY: "The White House." Used by permission of The Archives of Claude McKay, Carl Cowl, Administrator.

ARCHIBALD MACLEISH: "Ars Poetica," from *Collected Poems 1917–1982* by Archibald MacLeish. Copyright © 1985 by The Estate of Archibald MacLeish. Reprinted by permission of Houghton Mifflin Company. All rights reserved.

LOUIS MACNEICE: "Sunday Morning" from *Collected Poems.* Reprinted by permission of David Higham Associates.

JAMES MERRILL: "Watching the Dance" from *Nights and Days* by James Merrill. Copyright 1966, 1992 by James Merrill. Reprinted by permission of The Estate of James Merrill.

W. S. MERWIN: "Burning the Cat" from *Green With Beasts.* Copyright © 1955, 1956 by W. S. Merwin. Reprinted by permission of Georges Borchardt, Inc.

RICHARD MICHELSON: "Undressing Aunt Frieda." Reprinted by permission of the author.

EDNA ST. VINCENT MILLAY: "An Ancient Gesture" "I, being born a woman and distressed," and "What lips my lips have kissed" by Edna St. Vincent Millay. From *Collected Poems,* HarperCollins. Copyright © 1923, 1951, 1954, 1982 by Edna St. Vincent Millay and Norma Millay Ellis. "Sonnet XXVI [Women have loved before as I love now]" from *Fatal Interview* by Edna St. Vincent Millay. From *Collected Poems,* HarperCollins. Copyright © 1922, 1931, 1950, 1958 by Edna St, Vincent Millay and Norma Millay Ellis. All rights reserved. Reprinted by permission of Elizabeth Barnett, literary executor.

EARL MINER: "The still old pond" from *Japanese Linked Poetry* by Earl Miner. Copyright © 1979 by Earl Miner. Reprinted by permission of the author.

JAMES MASAO MITSUI: "Because of My Father's Job" from *After the Long Train* by James Masao Mitsui (California: The Bieler Press, 1986). Reprinted by permission of the publisher.

MARIANNE MOORE: "Love in America?" from *The Complete Poems of Marianne Moore* by Marianne Moore. Copyright © 1981 by Clive E. Driver, Literary Executor of the Estate of Marianne Moore. Used by permission of Viking Penguin, a division of Penguin Books USA Inc. "Poetry" from *The Complete Poems of Marianne Moore.* Copyright © 1935 by Marianne Moore; copyright renewed © 1963 by Marianne Moore and T.S. Eliot. Reprinted with the permission of Simon & Schuster.

PAT MORA: "Elena" from *Chants* by Pat Mora. Copyright © 1985 by Arte Publico Press-University of Houston. "Gentle Communion" from *Communion* (Houston: Arte Publico Press-University of Houston, 1991) by Pat Mora. "La Migra" from *Agua Santa: Holy Water* by Pat Mora. Copyright © 1995 by Pat Mora. Reprinted by permission of Beacon Press, Boston. "Sonrisas" from *Borders* by Pat Mora (Houston: Arte Publico Press-University of Houston, 1986). Reprinted with permission from the publisher.

EDWIN MORGAN: "Opening the Cage" and "Message Clear" ["I Am the Resurrection and the Life"] from *Collected Poems* by Edwin Morgan. Reprinted by permission of Carcanet Press Limited.

ERIN MOURE: "Thirteen Years" from *Furious* by Erin Mouré. Reprinted by permission of the author and Stoddart Publishing Co. Limited (Don Mills, Ontario).

MBUYISENI OSWALD MTSHALI: "Boy on a Swing" from *Sounds of a Cowhide Drum* by Oswald Mbuyisenl Mtshali. Copyright © 1972 by Third Press–Joseph Okpaku Pub. Co. By permission of Okpaku Communications, 22 Forest Avenue, New Rochelle, N.Y. 10804.

SUSAN MUSGRAVE: "I Am Not a Conspiracy" from *Cocktails at the Mausoleum* by Susan Musgrave. "Hidden Meaning" and "You Didn't Fit" from *Embalmer's Art* by Susan Musgrave. Copyright © 1991 and 1985 by Susan Musgrave. Reprinted by permission of the author.

OGDEN NASH: "Here, Usually, Comes the Bride," copyright © 1945 by Odgen Nash; first appeared in *Cosmopolitan* and "Reflection on Ice-Breaking," Copyright © 1930 by Odgen Nash Renewed; first appeared in *The New Yorker* from *Verses From 1929 On* by Odgen Nash. Reprinted by permission of Little, Brown and Company and Curtis Brown, Ltd.

HOWARD NEMEROV: "Boom!," "The Goose Fish," "The Town Dump," "The Vacuum," and "A Way of Life" from *The Collected Poems of Howard Nemerov*. Copyright © 1977 by Howard Nemerov. Reprinted by permission of Margaret Nemerov.

DWIGHT OKITA: "Notes for a Poem on Being Asian American" from *Crossing with the Light* by Dwight Okita (Tia Chucha Press, 1992). Copyright © 1992 by Dwight Okita. Reprinted by permission of the author.

SHARON OLDS: "The Glass" and "The Lifting" from *The Father* by Sharon Olds. Copyright © 1992 by Sharon Olds. "I Go Back to May 1937" from *The Gold Cell* by Sharon Olds. Copyright © 1987 by Sharon Olds. "Sex Without Love," "The Elder Sister," and "The Victims" from *The Dead and the Living* by Sharon Olds. Copyright © 1983 by Sharon Olds. Reprinted by permission of Alfred A. Knopf, Inc. "Leningrad Cemetary, Winter of 1941" from *The New Yorker*, December 31, 1979. Copyright © 1979 by The New Yorker Magazine, Inc. Reprinted by permission of the publisher.

MARY OLIVER: "Goldenrod" and "Morning" from *House of Light* by Mary Oliver. Copyright © 1990 by Mary Oliver. "Roses, Late Summer" and "Singapore" from *New and Selected Poems* by Mary Oliver. Copyright © 1992 by Mary Oliver. Reprinted by permission of Beacon Press, Boston.

MICHAEL ONDAATJE: "King Kong Meets Wallace Stevens" from *The Cinammon Peeler* by Michael Ondaatje. Copyright © 1979 by Michael Ondaatje. Reprinted by permission of Michael Ondaatje.

ONITSONA: "Come! Come! Though I call" from *One Hundred Famous Haiku,* selected and translated by Daniel Buchanan. Reprinted by permission of Japan Publications, Inc.

SIMON J. ORTIZ: "My Father's Song" and "Speaking." Permission granted by the author.

DOROTHY PARKER: "A Certain Lady," copyright 1928, © renewed 1956 by Dorothy Parker; "Comment," copyright 1926, © renewed 1954 by Dorothy Parker; "Indian Summer," copyright 1926, © renewed 1954 by Dorothy Parker; "One Perfect Rose," copyright 1929, © 1957 by Dorothy Parker from *The Portable Dorothy Parker* by Dorothy Parker (Introduction by Brendan Gill). Used by permission of Viking Penguin, a division of Penguin Books USA Inc.

LINDA PASTAN: "Erosion," "love poem," and "To a Daughter Leaving Home" from *The Imperfect Paradise* by Linda Pastan. Copyright © 1988 by Linda Pastan. "Marks" from *PM/AM: New and Selected Poems* by Linda Pastan. Copyright © 1978 by Linda Pastan. Reprinted by permission of W. W. Norton & Company, Inc.

MARGE PIERCY: "To Have Without Holding" from *The Moon is Always Female* by Marge Piercy. Copyright © 1980 by Marge Piercy. "Barbie Doll" and "What's That Smell in the Kitchen?" from *Circles on the Water* by Marge Piercy. Copyright © 1982 by Marge Piercy. Reprinted by permission of Alfred A. Knopf, Inc.

SYLVIA PLATH: "Point Shirley" from *The Colossus and Other Poems* by Sylvia Plath. Copyright © 1959 by Sylvia Plath. Reprinted by permission of Alfred A. Knopf, Inc. "Mirror" (all lines) from *Crossing the Water* by Sylvia Plath. Originally appeared in *The New Yorker*. Copyright © 1963 by Ted Hughes. "Black Rook in Rainy Weather" (all lines) from *Crossing the Water* by Sylvia Plath. Copyright © 1960 by Ted Hughes. "Morning Song" (all lines), copyright © 1961 by Ted Hughes, copyright renewed; "Daddy" (all lines) copyright © 1963 by Ted Hughes; and "Lady Lazarus" (all lines) copyright © 1963 by Ted Hughes from *Ariel* by Sylvia Plath. Copyright © 1963 by Ted Hughes, copyright renewed. Reprinted by permission of HarperCollins Publishers, Inc and Faber & Faber Ltd.

KATHA POLLITT: "Two Fish" from *Antarctic Traveler* by Katha Pollitt. Copyright © 1981 by Katha Pollitt. Reprinted by permission of Alfred A. Knopf, Inc.

EZRA POUND: "The Garden," "In a Station of the Metro," "The River-Merchant's Wife: A Letter," and "A Virginal" from *Personae* by Ezra Pound. Copyright © 1926 by Ezra Pound. Reprinted by permission of New Directions Publishing Corp.

JAROLD RAMSEY: "Hunting Arrowheads" and "The Tally Stick." Reprinted by permission of the author.

DUDLEY RANDALL: "Ballad of Birmingham" from *Poem Counter Poem* by Dudley Randall (Michigan: Broadside Press, 1969). Reprinted by permission of the publisher.

JOHN CROWE RANSOM: "Bells for John Whiteside's Daughter" from *Selected Poems* by John Crowe Ransom. Copyright © 1924 by Alfred A. Knopf, Inc. and renewed 1952 by John Crowe Ransom. Reprinted by permission of the publisher.

HENRY REED: "Lessons of the War: Judging Distances" from *Collected Poems* by Henry Reed, edited by Jon Stallworthy. Copyright © 1991 The Executor of Henry Reed's Estate. Reprinted by permission of Oxford University Press.

ISHMAEL REED: "beware: do not read this poem" and "I Am a Cowboy in the Boat of Ra". Copyright © 1972 by Ishmael Reed. Reprinted by permission of Ishmael Reed.

ADRIENNE RICH: "At a Bach Concert," "Aunt Jennifer's Tigers," "Dialogue," "Diving into the Wreck," "For the Record," "Living in Sin," "Planetarium," "Power," "Snapshots of a Daughter-in-Law," "Storm Warnings," and "Two Songs" from *The Fact of a Doorframe, Poems Selected and New 1950–1984* by Adrienne Rich. Copyright © 1984 by Adrienne Rich. Copyright © 1975, 1978 by W. W. Norton & Company, Inc. Copyright © 1981 by Adrienne Rich. "Origins and History of Consciousness" from *The Dream of a Common Language: Poems 1974–1977* by Adrienne Rich. Copyright © 1978 by W. W. Norton & Company, Inc. "Delta," "Letters in the Family," and "Walking Down the Road" from *Time's Power: Poems 1985–1988* by Adrienne Rich. Copyright © 1989 by Adrienne Rich. [my mouth hovers across your breasts] Poem 3 of "Contradictions: Tracking Poems" from *Your Native Land, Your Life: Poems* by Adrienne Rich. Copyright © 1986 by Adrienne Rich. "Four: history" from "Inscriptions" from *Dark Fields of the Republic: Poems 1991–1995* by Adrienne Rich. Copyright © 1995 by Adrienne Rich. Excerpt from "A communal poetry" and "How does a poet put bread on the table?" from *What is Found There: Notebooks on Poetry and Politics* by Adrienne Rich. Copyright © 1993 by Adrienne Rich. Excerpt from "When We Dead Awaken: Writing as Revision," from *On Lies, Secrets, and Silence: Selected Prose 1966–1978* by Adrienne Rich. Copyright © 1979 by W. W. Norton & Company, Inc. All reprinted by permission of the author and W. W. Norton & Company, Inc. "Talking with Adrienne Rich," an interview with Wayne Dodd and Stanley Plumy, *The Ohio Review,* no.1. Reprinted by permission of *The Ohio Review.* "An Interview with Adrienne Rich" by David Kalstone. *The Saturday Review:* The Arts, IV, (April 22, 1972), pp 56–59. Reprinted by permission of Charles Kalstone, M.D.

ALBERTO ALVERO RÍOS: "Advice to a First Cousin" and "Mi Abuelo." Copyright © 1985 and © 1987 by Albert Ríos. Reprinted by permission of the author.

THEODORE ROETHKE: "The Dream," copyright © 1955 by Theodore Roethke; "Elegy for Jane," copyright © 1950 by Theodore Roethke; "I Knew a Woman," copyright © 1954 by Theodore Roethke; "My Papa's Waltz," copyright © 1942 by Hearst Magazines, Inc.; "She," copyright © 1956 by Theodore Roethke; and "The Waking," copyright © 1953 by Theodore Roethke from *The Collected Poems of Theodore Roethke* by Theodore Roethke. Used by permission of Bantam Doubleday Dell Publishing Group, Inc.

LIZ ROSENBERG: "Married Love" from *The Fire Music* by Liz Rosenberg. Copyright © 1986. "A Lesson in Anatomy" and "The Silence of Women" from *Children of Paradise* by Liz Rosenberg. Copyright © 1994. Reprinted by permission of the University of Pittsburgh Press.

MURIEL RUKEYSER: "Myth" and "Reading Time: 1 Minute 26 Seconds" from *A Muriel Rukeyser Reader* (New York: W.W. Norton, 1994). Copyright © 1994 by William L. Rukeyser. Reprinted by permission.

MARY JO SALTER: "Welcome to Hiroshima" from *Henry Purcell in Japan* by Mary Jo Salter. Copyright © 1984 by Mary Jo Salter. Reprinted by permission of Alfred A. Knopf, Inc.

YVONNE SAPIA: "Grandmother, A Caribbean Indian, Described by My Father" from *Valentino's Hair, Poems* by Yvonne Sapia. Copyright © 1987 by Yvonne Sapia. Reprinted with the permission of Northeastern University Press, Boston.

SEIFŪ: "The faces of dolls" from *One Hundred Famous Haiku*, selected and translated by Daniel Buchanan. Reprinted by permission of Japan Publications, Inc.

ANNE SEXTON: "The Fury of Overshoes" from *The Death Notebooks*. Copyright © 1974 by Anne Sexton. "The Farmer's Wife" from *To Bedlam and Part Way Back* by Anne Sexton. Copyright © 1960 by Anne Sexton, renewed ©1988 by Linda G. Sexton. "With Mercy for the Greedy" from *All My Pretty Ones* by Anne Sexton. Copyright © 1962 by Anne Sexton, © renewed 1990 by Linda G. Sexton. Reprinted by permission of Houghton Mifflin Company. All rights reserved.

ALAN SHAPIRO: "Ex-Wife: Infatuation" from *Mixed Company*. Reprinted by permission of the author.

KARL SHAPIRO: "Auto Wreck" Copyright © 1941, 1987 by Karl Shapiro. Reprinted by arrangement with Wieser & Wieser, Inc., New York.

TOM SLEIGH: "Some Larger Motion" from *The Chain* by Tom Sleigh (University of Chicago, 1996). All rights reserved. Reprinted by permission of the author.

KAY SMITH: "Annunciations". Reprinted by permission of Kay Holston Smith.

STEVIE SMITH: "I Remember," "Our Bog is Dood" and "The Jungle Husband" from *Collected Poems of Stevie Smith* by Stevie Smith. Copyright © 1972 by Stevie Smith. Reprinted by permission of the New Directions Publishing Corp.

W. D. SNODGRASS: "Leaving the Motel." Reprinted by permission of the author.

RICHARD SNYDER: "A Mongoloid Child Handling Shells on the Beach" from *Practicing Our Sighs: The Collected Poems of Richard Snyder* by Richard Snyder, edited by Mary Snyder and Robert McGovern. Reprinted by permission of The Ashland Poetry Press (Asland University).

MARY ELLEN SOLT: "Lilac." Copyright © 1968 by Mary Ellen Solt. Reprinted by permission of the author.

CATHY SONG: "Heaven" from *Frameless Windows, Squares of Light:* Poems by Cathy Song. Copyright © 1988 by Cathy Song. Reprinted by permission of W. W. Norton & Company, Inc.

STEPHEN SPENDER: "The Express" from *Collected Poems 1928–1953* by Stephen Spender. Copyright 1934, 1942, 1946 and renewed 1962, 1970, 1974 by Stephen Spender. Reprinted by permission of Random House, Inc.

ELIZABETH SPIRES: "Bodies" from *Worldling* by Elizabeth Spires. Copyright © 1995 by Elizabeth Spires. Reprinted by permission of the author and W. W. Norton & Company, Inc.

WILLIAM STAFFORD: "At the Bomb Testing Site" from *Rescued Year* (Harper and Row). Copyright © 1966 by William Stafford. Reprinted by permission of The Estate of William Stafford.

GEORGE STEINER: "Dying Is An Art" from *Language and Silence* by George Steiner (New York: Atheneum, 1967). Copyright © 1958, 1960, 1961, 1962, 1963, 1964, 1965, 1966, 1967 by George Steiner. Reprinted by permission of Georges Borchardt, Inc.

WALLACE STEVENS: "Anecdote of the Jar," "The Emperor of Ice-Cream," and "Sunday Morning" from *Collected Poems* by Wallace Stevens. Copyright © 1923 and renewed 1951 by Wallace Stevens. "The Idea of Order at Key West" from *Collected Poems* by Wallace Stevens. Copyright © 1936 by Wallace Stevens and renewed 1964 by Holly Stevens. Reprinted by permission of Alfred A. Knopf, Inc.

RUTH STONE: "Second-Hand Coat." Reprinted by permission of the author.

DYLAN THOMAS: "Do Not Go Gentle into That Good Night," "Fern Hill," and "In My Craft or Sullen Art" from *The Poems of Dylan Thomas* by Dylan Thomas. Copyright © 1945 by The Trustees for the Copyrights of Dylan Thomas. Reprinted by permission of David Higham Associates and New Directions Publishing Corp.

JEAN TOOMER: "Reapers" and "Song of the Sun" from *Cane* by Jean Toomer. Copyright © 1923 by Boni & Liveright, renewed 1951 by Jean Toomer. Reprinted by permission of Liveright Publishing Corporation.

MONA VAN DUYN: "What the Motorcycle Said" from *If It Be Not I* by Mona Van Duyn. Copyright © 1973 by Mona Van Duyn. Reprinted by permission of Alfred A. Knopf, Inc.

KAREN VOLKMAN: "Evening" from *Crash's Law* by Karen Volkman. Copyright © 1996 by Karen Volkman. Reprinted by permission of W. W. Norton & Company, Inc.

MIRIAM WADDINGTON: "Ulysses Embroidered" from *The Last Landscape* by Miriam Waddington. Copyright © 1992 by Miriam Waddington. Reprinted by permission of Oxford University Press Canada.

DAVID WAGONER: "My Father's Garden" from *Through the Forest.* Copyright © 1987 by David Wagoner. Reprinted by permission of the author.

DIANE WAKOSKI: "The Ring of Irony" from *The Rings of Saturn* by Diane Wakoski. Copyright © 1986 by Diane Wakoski. Reprinted with the permission of Black Sparrow Press.

DEREK WALCOTT: "A Far Cry from Africa" from *Collected Poems 1948–1984* by Derek Walcott. Copyright © 1986 by Derek Walcott. Reprinted by permission of Farrar, Straus & Giroux, Inc.

ALICE WALKER: "Revolutionary Petunias" from *Revolutionary Petunias & Other Poems* by Alice Walker. Copyright © 1972 by Alice Walker. Reprinted by permission of Harcourt Brace & Company.

TOM WAYMAN: "Wayman in Love." Reprinted by permission of Harbour Publishing Co. Ltd.

RICHARD WILBUR: "The Beautiful Changes" from *The Beautiful Changes and Other Poems* by Richard Wilbur. Copyright © 1947 and renewed 1975 by Richard Wilbur. "Love Calls Us To The Things Of This World" from *Things Of This World* by Richard Wilbur. Copyright © 1956 and renewed 1984 by Richard Wilbur. "Museum Piece" and "The Pardon" from *Ceremony And Other Poems* by Richard Wilbur. Copyright © 1950 and renewed 1978 by Richard Wilbur. "She" from *Advice To A Prophet And Other Poems* by Richard Wilbur. Copyright ©1958 and renewed 1986 by Richard Wilbur. "Transit" from *New And Collected Poems* by Richard Wilbur. Copyright ©1979 by Richard Wilbur. Originally published in *The New Yorker.* Reprinted by permission of Harcourt Brace & Company,

MILLER WILLIAMS: "Thinking about Bill, Dead of AIDS" from *Living on the Surface: New and Selected Poems* by Miller Williams. Copyright © 1989 by Miller Williams. Reprinted by permission of Louisiana State University Press.

WILLIAM CARLOS WILLIAMS: "The Red Wheelbarrow" and "This is Just to Say" from *Collected Poems 1909–1939, Volume I.* Copyright © 1938 by New Directions Publishing Corp. "Raleigh Was Right," "The Dance," and "Poem" from *Collected Poems 1939–1962, Volume II.* Copyright © 1944, 1953 by William Carlos Williams. Reprinted by permission of New Directions Publishing Corp.

YVOR WINTERS: "At the San Francisco Airport" from *The Collected Poems of Yvor Winters* (1980). Reprinted with the permission of Ohio University Press/Swallow Press, Athens.

JAMES WRIGHT: "Arrangements with Earth for Three Dead Friends" reprinted from *Collected Poems* by James Wright. Copyright © 1957 by Wesleyan University Press. Reprinted by permission of University Press of New England.

JUDITH WRIGHT: "Dove-Love" from *Collected Poems* by Judith Wright. Reprinted by permission of HarperCollins Publishers, Austrailia.

RICHARD WRIGHT: "In the falling snow" from *The Richard Wright Reader.* Copyright 1978 by Richard Wright. Reprinted by permission of John Hawkins & Associates, Inc.

W. B. YEATS: "Among School Children" "Leda and the Swan," and "Sailing to byzantium" from *The Collected Works of W.B. Yeats, Volume 1: The Poems.* Revised and edited by Richard J. Finneran. Copyright © 1928 by Macmillan Publishing Company; copyright renewed © 1956 by Georgie Yeats. Reprinted with the permission of Simon & Schuster and A.P. Watt Ltd. on the behalf of Michael Yeats. "Byzantium" from *The Collected Works of W.B. Yeats, Volume 1: The Poems.* Revised and edited by Richard J. Finneran. Copyright © 1933 by Macmillan Publishing Company; copyright renewed © 1961 by Bertha Georgie Yeats. Reprinted with the permission of Simon & Schuster and A.P. Watt Ltd. on the behalf of Anne and Michael Yeats. "A Last Confession" from *The Collected Works of W.B. Yeats, Volume 1: The Poems.* Revised and edited by Richard J. Finneran. Copyright © 1933 by Macmillan Publishing Company; copyright renewed © 1961 by Bertha Georgie Yeats. Reprinted with the permission of Simon & Schuster. "The Circus Animals' Desertion" from *The Collected Works Of W.B. Yeats, Volume 1: The Poems.* Revised and edited by Richard J. Finneran. Copyright © 1940 by Georgie Yeats; copyright renewed © 1968 by Bertha Georgie Yeats, Michael Butler Yeats, and Anne Yeats. Reprinted with the permission of Simon & Schuster and A.P. Watt Ltd. on the behalf of Anne and Michael Yeats.

CYNTHIA ZARIN: "Song" from *Fire Lyric* by Cynthia Zarin. Copyright © 1993 by Cynthia Zarin. Reprinted by the permission of Alfred A. Knopf, Inc.

## ART ACKNOWLEDGMENTS

*John Keats.* Portrait by Joseph Severn. Reprinted by courtesy of the National Portrait Gallery, London.

*George Keats.* Sketch by Joseph Severn. Photographed by Chris Warde Jones. Reprinted with the kind permission of the Keats-Shelley Memorial House, Rome.

*Tom Keats.* Sketch by Joseph Severn. Reprinted with the kind permission of the Keats-Shelley Memorial House, Rome.

*John Hamilton Reynolds.* Miniature by Joseph Severn. Reprinted by permission of The Corporation of London from the Collections at Keats House, Hampstead.

Adrienne Rich, circa 1970. Photograph by Sissy Krook. Reprinted by permission of the photographer.

Adrienne Rich in the classroom, circa 1978. Photograph by Linda Koolish, Ph.D. Reprinted by permission of the photographer.

Adrienne Rich today. Copyright by Jason Langer, photographer. Reprinted by permission.

Sylvia Plath. Courtesy of the Sylvia Plath Collection, Mortimer Rare Book Room, Smith College.

Sylvia Plath's father, Otto Plath. Courtesy of the Sylvia Plath Collection, Mortimer Rare Book Room, Smith College.

Facsimile of Keats's "To Autumn." Autograph Manuscript draft (MS Keats 2.27). Courtesy of the Houghton Library. Reprinted by permission of the Houghton Library, Harvard University, and Harvard University Press.

# Index of Authors

# Index of Titles and First Lines